CHARLIE

CHAPLIN

AND HIS TIMES

BOOKS BY KENNETH S. LYNN

The Dream of Success

Mark Twain and Southwestern Humor

William Dean Howells: An American Life

Visions of America

A Divided People

The Air-Line to Seattle

Hemingway

KENNETH S. LYNN

CHARLIE CHAPLIN

AND HIS TIMES

AURUM PRESS

First published in Great Britain
1998 by Aurum Press Ltd
25 Bedford Avenue, London WC1B 3AT

Designed by Karolina Harris

A catalogue record for this book is available from the British Library.

ISBN 1 85410 555 8

1 3 5 7 9 10 8 6 4 2
1998   2000   2002   2001   1999

Printed and bound in Great Britain by
MPG Books Ltd, Bodmin, Cornwall

To Oscar Handlin

CONTENTS

PREFACE

On the morning of March 2, 1978, nine weeks after Charlie Chaplin's funeral in Vevey, Switzerland, the superintendent of the village cemetery discovered fresh mounds of dirt, wet with rain from the night before, around the great man's burial plot and a yawning hole in the middle. The casket had vanished. Could it be that even in death the most famous comedian in the world was still capable of the tricky moves that had inspired so much laughter? The disappearance of his body was, after all, no less bizarre, no less unexpected, than the comic inventions of his films—or the events of his long and colorful life. To me, the image of his empty gravesite came to symbolize his historic elusiveness, as a person no less than as a performer, and the difficulties he presents to the biographer of pinning him down.

I am accustomed as a historian to dealing with writers. Chaplin composed movie scripts, to be sure, but he was above all an actor—who made most of his movies, moreover, before the advent of the talkies. Did I dare to devote a book-length study—I asked myself six years ago—to a master of wordless communication, with all of its attendant ambiguities?

My answer was, finally, yes, in part because of the endlessly tempting invitations to the imagination that his silent performances extend. The quickly sketched mask of heavily penciled eyebrows and brush mustache that he adopted almost immediately has appealed to me from the earliest days of my moviegoing life, as have the marionettelike body movements, the bawdy daring, and the slapstick rough stuff that characterize the crude pictures he made for Keystone in 1914, and the ache of loneliness and the comic transpositions that he introduced into his work for Essanay in 1915. The more artful psychology and dramatic inventiveness of *The Pawnshop*, *The Pilgrim*, and other Chaplin shorts of ensuing years continue to put me in mind, as they did years ago, of the cunning of Mark Twain. As for the five feature-length Tramp pictures that he released between 1921 and 1936—*The Kid, The Gold Rush, The Circus, City Lights,* and *Modern Times*—I still marvel at the range of their humorous situations and still find only a limited amount of sense in the frequently voiced disparagements of their pathos. For Chaplin's portrayals of basic human insecurities have always been an integral part of his half-realistic, half-absurd poetry.

One of my goals, then, in writing this book was to pay homage to a pantomimic achievement consisting of more than seventy pictures. In spite of many flaws and a number of outright failures, they constitute one of the glories of popular American culture. My homage also embraces certain sequences in *The Great Dictator, Monsieur Verdoux,* and *Limelight* that remain as vivid in my mind as any their maker ever filmed. By and large, however, these pictures do not measure up to their predecessors, for reasons that begin with one that was common to them all: with the straightforward use of sound-recorded speech, which Chaplin had stubbornly and ingeniously resisted as long as he could, the dreamlike qualities of the fantasies he spun were diminished.

Inasmuch as Chaplin wrote, directed, and starred in his movies (and soon enough began to finance them as well), they were clearly expressions of himself—and this, too, drew me to the idea of writing about him. For I have always been fascinated by the detective work of connecting the lives of artists to their art. I soon discovered, however, that in Chaplin's case, this task was made exceptionally difficult by the problem of separating fact from fiction in the accounts of his childhood. By common consent, those years were of decisive importance in shaping his cinematic vision. But what were they really like? His scanty personal correspondence is of no help at all in answering that question. On the other hand, his assertions about a number of matters in his autobiographical writings and in confessional talks with friends proved to be quite illuminating. It is no less true, however, that blurrings of the truth and outright falsehoods mark a lot of the recollections that he chose to share with the public, some of which newspaper reporters, film magazine writers, bio-film producers, and previous biographers have been especially fond of repeating and amplifying. Not until I had penetrated the layers of obfuscation and prevarication was I at last able to appreciate how profoundly autobiographical a filmmaker Chaplin was. Through what he chose to reveal directly about his past and what to transpose or conceal, he charged his pictures with enormous emotional energy.

In striking through the encrustations of myth, I was aided by late-Victorian record-keepers and data-gatherers whose findings made it possible to judge the accuracy of Chaplin's descriptions of his early years. Because of the schooling that the music halls he was familiar with offered to Chaplin's raw talent, the stunning variety of their entertainments also receives attention here, along with the particular contributions of Dan Leno, Fred Karno, and other legendary figures. And no understanding of the provenance of Chaplin's art would be complete without mention of the movie comedies Max Linder made in France before World War I, or of the techniques of cinematic storytelling developed by D. W. Griffith, or of the sex-and-violence sense of humor of the slapstick king, Mack Sennett, who became the mentor Chaplin learned from—and learned to resist.

Figuring in my story, too, is the emergence of southern California as the center of the movie industry, as well as the careers of such early stars as Mabel Normand, Fatty Arbuckle, Douglas Fairbanks, and Mary Pickford. The cultural puzzle of why the young Chaplin received such a terrific boost in his box-office appeal once he assumed the identity of a tramp inspired me to explore the rather complicated attitudes toward tramps that Americans held at the time. And my further attempts to explain his fantastically quick rise to fame include a discussion of the sexual-identity joking in the early comedies against a backdrop of the huge success of female-impersonation vaudeville in the second decade of the twentieth century and the destabilization of traditional relations between the sexes in "advanced" societies that Walter Lippmann, for one, took note of in *Drift and Mastery* (1914). Also essential to an understanding of Chaplin's art were the repeated efforts of reformers to place moral controls on the industry, culminating in the formation of the Legion of Decency in the early 1930s and the establishment of the Breen office.

A good many of the famous people who appear in these pages had highly contradictory personalities, Adolf Hitler and Franklin D. Roosevelt being but two examples. Even so, the radical disjunctions in

Chaplin's life and career stand out as remarkable. The charmer who beguiled the glitterati of movieland, the intellectuals of Greenwich Village, and the hostesses of Mayfair versus the loner who grew bored with company after an hour or so and often shunned it completely. The son who was haunted by memories of his mother's madness and deeply feared that her fate foretold his own versus the humorist who created such incandescently funny scenes of madness in his movies as the chicken hallucinations of famished Big Jim in *The Gold Rush*. The creator of screen situations involving a persona who worshipped women even though they made him suffer versus an off-camera Svengali who was capable of treating them with a sickening contempt. The young man on the make who got rich by playing a bizarrely dressed tramp. The multimillionaire tyrant who spouted the peace messages of the Communist line. The Casanova who became a devoted husband and sternly Victorian paterfamilias. The loyal studio boss who kept the same employees with him decade after decade, and then left the names of most of them out of his autobiography. The self-proclaimed Cold War martyr who railed against the Department of Justice for revoking his reentry permit when he and his young wife and their children left the United States for a visit to Europe in 1952, but who may secretly have been planning all along to quit the country and settle in Switzerland.

Here, then, is Charlie Chaplin, who, in the opinion of the actress Louise Brooks, was the most bafflingly complex man who ever lived.

I

A WOMAN OF SORROWS

Charlie Chaplin in 1915.

ALL eyes were on him. The Essanay Company, housed in a Chicago building that is now an officially designated landmark, was a so-called film factory, in which inexorable production schedules kept everyone on the run. One morning in January 1915, however, the prevailing work pattern gave way to spectator sport, as virtually the entire staff, including the company's best-known leading man, Francis X. Bushman, and, probably, its chief scenario writer, Louella Parsons, gathered around the set where Charlie Chaplin was about to start filming his first picture for Essanay—self-referentially entitled *His New Job*.

On quitting California and the Keystone Company in early December, Chaplin had been forced to leave his costumes behind, so upon arriving in Chicago he purchased a wardrobe. Finding old shoes that were grotesquely too big for him briefly proved to be a problem, but otherwise he had no difficulty picking up what he needed. Thus when the young actor-director-scenario writer walked on to the shooting floor at Essanay with a derby perched atop his flying black hair and nervously twirling a cane, he looked altogether familiar to his fellow cast members and to the onlookers as well who were lined up against the studio wall and clustered on either side of the camera. In the center of the floor, he stopped short, pulled three of his fingers out of joint, bent forward into a professional dancer's pose, and executed a clog dance. The performance continued for five minutes, to the wonderment of his new colleagues. An observer noted that "they didn't know whether he was crazy or doing it just for their amusement." Some laughed; the rest were overcome with amazement. Frank Bushman, however, was not only amazed but annoyed that this upstart who had been acting in movies for only a year had stepped into the limelight at the studio where he was accustomed to being the center of attention. In a testy voice he inquired about the meaning of Chaplin's antics. "Got to limber up," the little comedian softly replied in a Cockney accent. "A little pep, everybody; a little pep. Come on, boys. Shoot your set. I'm ready." His last sentence, startlingly enough, was shouted. One of modern history's most powerful engines of laughter generation and icon creation was revved up and ready to roll.[1]

Within the space of the next few months, America went mad about him. Lines formed in front of movie houses whenever his name appeared in lobby ads or on the marquee, even if the picture being shown was a year-old one-reeler. To howls of delight from Broadway audiences, long-stemmed Ziegfeld Follies lovelies sashayed onstage wearing mustaches, derby hats, big shoes, and baggy trousers, singing a song called "Those Charlie Chaplin Feet." A comparable show-stopper in the revue *Watch Your Step* was Lupino Lane's belted-out, acted-out ode to "That Charlie Chaplin Walk." And to these numbers, Tin Pan Alley tunesmiths, banging out the rhythms on overworked pianos, quickly added

"The Chaplin Waddle," "The Charlie Strut," "The Chaplin Wiggle," "The Charlie Chaplin Glide," and "The Charlie Chaplin—March Grotesque." As if by magic, Charlie Chaplin lapel pins, hats, socks, ties, squirt rings, Christmas decorations, playing cards, and dolls of various sizes materialized on the counters of department stores and five-and-dimes. On June 9 the *Cleveland Plain Dealer* reported that "Cleveland has been getting so full of imitations of Charlie Chaplin that the management of Luna Park [recently] decided to offer a prize to the best imitator and out they flocked." (The winner was an English-born twelve-year-old with a ski-jump nose, a smart-alecky sense of humor, and a budding talent for song and dance who still answered to the name of Leslie T. Hope. With his prize money the famous comedian of years to come bought his mother a new stove.)

Toward the end of July, *Moving Picture World* noted that Chaplin had "imitators aplenty among screen actors and vaudeville and cabaret entertainers," and it singled out for special attention the imitation-Chaplin movies of Minerva Courtney. Miss Courtney was a clever mimic, the magazine conceded; she could walk like Chaplin, she could skid around corners on one foot with one hand on her hat, and she could give a fair imitation of the little fellow's facial expressions. Her failing, however, was that she had not caught "the elusive humor that is a part of Chaplin's personality." The same judgment applied to an indefatigable comedian named Billy West, who carbon-copied Chaplin in dozens of movies, and to the animators who were busily handcrafting Charlie Chaplin cartoons. Recognizable representations of the trademark mannerisms were within their capability, but the ambiguities of Chaplin's spirit eluded them.[2]

2

His name had not appeared, either above or below the title, in his initial comedies. To fill in the blank, the moviegoers of 1914 started watching for press notices that identified him. Once they learned his name, they wanted to know more about him, and this was true not only in the United States but in other countries where his work was a hit— Britain, for instance, which received its first Chaplin shorts two months before the outbreak of war. But it was not until the onrush of America's

Chaplin madness in early 1915 that a veritable avalanche of questions from an avidly curious public sent newspaper and magazine editors scrambling for answers. "From New York to San Francisco, from Maine to California," a writer for *Motion Picture Magazine* would recall, "came the staccato tapping of the telegraph key. 'Who is this man Chaplin? What are his ambitions? What's his theory of humor? Is he married or single? How does he like American life? Does he eat eggs for breakfast? Is he conceited?' The newspapers wanted to know; the country had risen and demanded information."[3]

"Chaplinitis," as the writer dubbed the nation's fever, further heightened the awareness of silent filmmakers in all of the centers of production, from New York City and Fort Lee, New Jersey, to Philadelphia, Chicago, and southern California, that their industry's position in American life was infinitely more powerful—and at the same time more vulnerable—than the theater's. The power inhered in the mass appeal of movies. At one end of the scale, they were now becoming fashionable among intellectually sophisticated young people at socially privileged colleges and universities; at the other, they continued to serve as the prime source of entertainment for underprivileged and uneducated immigrants; and in between lay the great heart of the moviegoing public, the millions of middle-class adults and children of varying levels of education from all regions of the country and a wide range of backgrounds—rural, small-town, and urban. But precisely because of the indiscriminate seductiveness of the "house of dreams," as Jane Addams called the local movie theater,[4] many religious leaders and lay reformers fervently believed that movies should be held to a higher moral standard than other forms of entertainment, and that the private lives of the stars who loomed so large in the public's imagination should likewise be above reproach.

In response to the second of those moral expectations, the moguls of movieland began by recognizing that if current gossip about the Babylonian conduct of some of their top performers was not checked, legions of fans might be induced to boycott their pictures. It was no accident that the publicists whom the moguls had been buying away from Broadway at once set about to fashion appealingly respectable images for the men and women who had vaulted into prominence in the emergent star system. Neither was the cooperation that the publicists received from the staff writers and art directors of such industry-dependent publications as *Motion Picture* and *Photoplay*.

The underlying premise of the new publicity was that the rootless world in which stage actors lived was rife with moral temptation, whereas movie actors belonged to the morally stable world of the good citizens they entertained. As a writer for *Motion Picture* put it in February 1915:

> Stage life, with its night work, its daytime sleep, its irregular meals, its travelling and close contact, does not make for a natural existence and throws a so-called glamor over many people. Contrast its possibilities with those of the picture studio. In the latter place work is done in regular office hours—daylight work; no glamor of night, of orchestra, of artificial light. A player is located in one neighborhood and is recognized as a permanent and respectable citizen. Evenings can be spent at home, and the normal healthiness of one's own fireside is an atmosphere conducive to refining influences. Healthy outdoor work and a permanent circle of friends make for a sane and non-precarious existence. The restlessness and loneliness of a life of travel is . . . eliminated.

Photo layouts of Mabel Normand's lovely house or of Blanche Sweet at the wheel of her custom-built Italian car typified the magazines' ready acknowledgment that the stars lived on a luxurious scale. Nevertheless, they still valued the down-to-earth pleasures of ordinary family life, their image-makers emphasized. A *Photoplay* front view of the palatial residence of Norma Talmadge and her producer husband, Joe Schenck (who in a later and more candid era would be deservedly described as the embodiment of "just about every cliché of Hollywood decadence and debauchery"), caught the fair Norma playing football on the lawn, and the accompanying caption was as cute as it could be: "Where Norma Talmadge and her husband 'keep house'—as well as get their recreation."

Most of the movieland scandals of the late teens and early 1920s would derive a major share of their shock power from the sudden exposure of pathological habits that image-making had kept hidden. The career of leading man Wallace Reid was a stunning example. By 1917, Reid's chiseled features, magnificent athleticism, and engaging manner had made him a hero to countless numbers of moviegoers. In the same year, a fan magazine was moved to affirm that "there is a strong verification in the life of Wallace Reid . . . which condemns the oft-repeated aspersions against the members of the Hollywood film colony." But "behind that flashing façade of health and comeliness," Laurence Stallings would write in retrospect, "there was a shocking secret. Our hero was in the habit of dosing himself with morphine sulfate, just as much of the junk as he deemed necessary to keep him going." In January 1923, the habit killed him.[5]

3

Hiding addictions to sex or drugs or booze was not the only form of deceit to which movieland performers were given. Many newcomers presented falsified accounts of their early lives. Some did so as a means of taking a few years off their age, or to conceal the fact that they were Jewish, or to hide a record of some sort of shame, such as prostitution. Others went further. Out of a belief that success depended on it, they completely reinvented themselves, either on their own initiative or at the instigation of studio strategists. The romantic makeovers of a bullet-headed young man from Austria and of a somewhat fleshy young woman from Cincinnati were two cases in point.

On the Fourth of July, 1914, on-location shooting of D. W. Griffith's *The Birth of a Nation* commenced in southern California fields. To assist with the squadrons of cavalry he had assembled, Griffith sent out a call for expert horse handlers. Among the respondents was Erich von Stroheim. He was, he said, the son of a German baroness and an Austrian count, a graduate of the Imperial Military Academy at Wienerneustadt, and a veteran of the war of the Bosnia-Herzegovina annexation in 1908—which he had entered upon horseback, he further claimed, and from which he had emerged in an ambulance with sixteen inches of lead in his body. The name of Erich von Stroheim does not appear, however, in the officer lists of the Austro-Hungarian army in 1908. Furthermore, the conflict of which he spoke had not occurred. In the words of Donald Kagan's *On the Origins of War and the Preservation of Peace* (1995), the Bosnian crisis of 1908–1909 represented "a crucial step on the road to war [in 1914]." At the time, however, war was averted when the Serbs and their Russian allies backed down in the face of the collective might of Austro-Hungary and Germany. The likely truth about Erich von Stroheim is that he was the son of a Viennese Jewish hat manufacturer named Benno Stroheim and that he had left his homeland for America without ever having heard a gun fired in anger.

In the same summer that this self-proclaimed war hero went to work for Griffith, Theodosia Goodman, the daughter of an Ohio tailor, was practicing how to shoot steamy looks out of heavy-lidded eyes. Nineteen fifteen witnessed her studio-assisted rebirth as Theda Bara (an anagram for Arab Death), the Sahara-born love child of a French artist and an Egyptian princess, and her rise to stardom in the role of the femme fatale who feeds on masculine sexual energies in the William Fox movie *A Fool There Was*. ("Kiss me, my fool" was Theda's most famous dialogue card.)[6]

Illusion-making, then, was a Hollywood business off the screen as well as on, and Jay Gatsbys abounded. In such a place at such a time, it is not surprising that a young comedian whose memories of the past were filled with horrors and fearful uncertainties also offered prevaricating answers when biographical questions were put to him.

E. V. Whitcomb of *Photoplay* spent nearly two hours with the "lovable lad" toward the end of Chaplin's first year in Hollywood, and in the February 1915 issue he declared that he had done his best to reproduce "exactly what he said in the way he said it." "I have always worked hard," Chaplin began,

> ever since my father died, when I was seven years old. My mother was a wonderful woman, highly cultivated, yet life was hard on her. We were so poor, she used to sew little blouses by hand, trying to earn enough to keep us. That was in England—she died there. Poverty is a cruel thing, and I sometimes think that if I had not worked so very hard as a child, I should be much stronger now than I am, because, you see, I am not at all strong, physically. I have never had a day's schooling in my life; my mother taught us [i.e., Charlie and his older half-brother, Sydney] what she could, but after she died, I was an apprentice to a company of traveling acrobats, jugglers and show-people. That was in England too, and oh, what hard work it was. I have never had a home worth the name. No associations that might have helped me when I was young. Looking back upon it is no joke, and that is why it seems so out of place when I am made much of now.[7]

His mother was not dead. At age forty-nine, physically vigorous but hopelessly insane, she was under nursing-home care in England. Perhaps Chaplin was motivated to lie about her by an awareness that many people believed that the mental illness of a family member was something to be ashamed of. Or he may have been trying to hold at bay memories of her suffering that he could not bear to think about. Still another possibility is that he wished she were dead. For his intense feelings about her were ambivalent, ranging from adoration to an aggrieved sense that she had betrayed him.

There were two more truths that lost out to fantasy in the *Photoplay* interview. Charles Chaplin, Senior, died when the boy who bore his name was twelve years old, not seven. And on various occasions in his childhood little Charlie had, in fact, attended school. As for Chaplin's evocation of a past scarred by Dickensian poverty and dependency for survival on his mother's meager earnings from hand sewing, he would cling to that claim for the rest of his life; nevertheless, it, too, was quite misleading. The description of his mother as highly cultivated was likewise unfounded. And in speaking of her and Charles Senior in back-to-back sentences, he neglected to point out that the two of them had separated long before he, little Charlie, was old enough to remember the event—possibly even before he was born.

Finally, he did not disclose his lack of certainty that Charles Senior really was his father. Eddie Sutherland, the assistant director of *A Woman of Paris* and *The Gold Rush*, later stated on the basis of confidential talks with the comedian that "Charlie Chaplin was born of a man named Chaplin, possibly. . . . Apparently the mother had strayed from the path with several men—at least she had romances with quite a number of men—and Chaplin told me, 'I don't know, actually, who my father was. There's some doubt about it.' He wasn't saying this against his mother, he said. 'This is what has been quoted to me.' "

Chaplin's distrust of the idea that he was Charles Senior's son raised the further question in his mind of whether he might be part-Jewish, as rumor mongers early and late have often claimed. "I think I might have Jewish blood," he confessed to Eddie Sutherland. "I notice that my characteristics are very Semitic, my gestures are, my thinking is certainly along money lines." But then he added, "As far as I formally know, I have no Jewish blood in my veins, although I have these characteristics."[8]

In an interview with another *Photoplay* writer, published in July 1915, Chaplin expanded upon his earlier tribute to his mother's high degree of cultivation. "It seems to me that my mother was the most splendid woman I ever knew. I can remember how charming and well-mannered she was. She spoke four languages and had a good education. I have never met a more thoroughly refined woman than my mother." These comments stand in solemn-serious contrast to a comic convention with which Chaplin and his mother were both familiar. Music hall audiences of the late-Victorian era had long been interested in aristocratic frauds, and songs about lazy good-for-nothings of either sex who had no funds but who dressed up and put on airs with the intention of being mistaken for ladies or gentlemen were sure-fire crowd pleasers.

In creating a tramp hero with a fastidious sensibility and the manner, oftentimes, of a fallen or a would-be gentleman, Chaplin paid homage to the mocking spirit of songs of this type. But in his assertion that his mother was a lady who spoke four languages, there was not a hint of mockery. Not for another half century would he be willing to make a public acknowledgment of Hannah Hill Chaplin's verbal adroitness in terms more in line with the reality of her South London Cockney upbringing. In one of the many fleeting scenes in the compound of fact and fiction that he solecistically entitled *My Autobiography* (1964), he re-created an exchange he had overheard in his boyhood between his mother and the hoity-toity daughter of the landlady she was currently renting from. Leaning over the banister, Hannah had shouted, "Who do you think you are? Lady Shit?" "Oh," the young woman had sniffed, "that's nice language, coming from a Christian." "Don't worry," Hannah shot back. "It's in the Bible, my dear; Deuteronomy, twenty-eighth chapter, thirty-seventh verse; only there's another word for it. However, shit will suit you." [9]

4

In the late spring of 1915, Chaplin talked at length on several occasions with an up-and-coming feature writer on the *San Francisco Bulletin*. It is altogether possible that his responsiveness to Rose Wilder Lane was sparked by a sexual attraction to her, for she was a good-looking, intelligent, and morally liberated young woman, recently separated from her husband. In the course of her future career as a journalist and novelist, she would be intellectually sustained by a close friendship with the foreign correspondent and subsequent columnist for the *New York Herald-Tribune*, Dorothy Thompson, and by the occasional company of such writers as Sinclair Lewis, Clarence Day, and Max Eastman. As a political writer of the libertarian persuasion, she would slowly assemble a small but well-thought-of body of work on civil-liberties questions. At the age of seventy-eight, she would cover the Vietnam War.

Her most interesting literary achievement, however, did not become public knowledge until after her death. As Professor William Holtz of the University of Missouri has demonstrated, Lane's mother, Laura Ingalls Wilder, was dependent on her daughter's ghostwriting skills in fashioning her classic Little House books. In the appendix to *The Ghost in the Little House* (1993), Holtz juxtaposed passages from the "Laura" manuscript of *Little Town on the Prairie* with the ghostwritten "Rose" versions that the world is familiar with. His comparison revealed the critical importance of Lane's contributions. While she retained her mother's story line and many of the incidents relating to it, her "fine touch," in Holtz's words, created a "shining fiction" out of a "tangle of fact." [10]

Prior to Lane's meetings with Chaplin, the *Bulletin*'s legendary chief, Fremont Older, had serialized other stories of hers about the lives of successful men, as well as the purported autobiography of a railroad engineer that identified her as the editor of the manuscript. But, in fact, she had composed the engineer's story out of a composite of interviews she had conducted with a number of old railroad hands. The story of Chaplin's life, ostensibly related in his own voice, appeared in the *Bulletin* in July and August 1915. Yet while Lane was the actual author of these pieces, she could not possibly have written them had she not been successful in persuading Chaplin to reminisce for hours and hours. Despite his busy schedule, he allowed himself to be drawn out by her —although not to the point of speaking straightforwardly about his remembrances of things past.

Toward the end of 1915, an Associated Press reporter named Guy Moyston, who later became Lane's lover, negotiated a contract with Bobbs-Merrill for hardback book publication of an expanded version of her Chaplin pieces. An advance copy of *Charlie Chaplin's Own Story* came into the possession of the purported author in September 1916. A note on the title page, Chaplin discovered, affirmed that the book was a "faithful recital" of his life, and to his stunned surprise it expressed his "obligations and thanks to Mrs. Rose Wilder Lane for invaluable editorial assistance." Surprise quickly gave way to outrage—accompanied quite possibly by alarm. He had made no protest when the *Bulletin* series ran. But ephemeral stories in a newspaper were one thing and a book was quite another. Conceivably, he felt that its publication posed a threat to his freedom to continue inventing himself. Or he may have feared that he had spoken too freely to Lane about certain details in his relationship with his mother. In any case, he immediately contacted his high-powered New York attorney Nathan Burkan, who numbered Vanderbilts among his clients, and instructed him to prevent the sale of the book. Two months later, Burkan's threats of legal action finally persuaded Bobbs-Merrill to abandon its distribution plans. Although a few copies made their way into the possession of readers and various libraries, the rest never left the publisher's warehouse and were eventually destroyed.[11]

While Nate Burkan was still tussling with Bobbs-Merrill's lawyers, Chaplin received a lengthy letter signed "Yours very sincerely, Rose Wilder Lane." That she really was sincere in her belief that the book was a "faithful recital" of the information he had given her was as clear as her anguish.

I'm sure you will feel, in recalling the information you gave me, that . . . I made the best possible use of it in writing the story. It not only disposed of any number of wild rumors which, as you know, were afloat about you, but in addition the sympathetic interest of the public in the little boy who had such a hard time to get started in London was greater than that of any of the other successful men whose life stories I have written.[12]

Charlie Chaplin's Own Story opens with a one-sentence sketch of the narrator as a street urchin. "When I was eleven, homeless and starving in London, I had big dreams." Next comes a cautiously phrased admission that at the moment the narrator's mother is "in an English hospital." But in the wake of this brief burst of candor, he returns to fantasyland. "I do not know my mother's real name. She came from a good respected family in London, and when she was sixteen she ran away and married my father, a music-hall actor. She never heard from her own people again. She drifted over England and the Continent with my father, and went on the music-hall stage herself." Although Chaplin was painfully aware that his half-brother Sydney had been born out of wedlock, *Charlie Chaplin's Own Story* avoids saying so: "My brother Sydney was four years old when I was born." And where did that blessed event occur? "In a little town in France, between music-hall engagements."[13]

To other interviewers early on, Chaplin identified the town as Fontainebleau. As the site of one of the largest and most sumptuous of royal residences in France, Fontainebleau might very well have caught Chaplin's fancy as he was having a daydream about himself as a descendant of titled personages. So successful was he in imposing the Fontainebleau notion on the thinking of film writers that in the 1920s his diligent French biographer, Édouard Ramond, took the trouble to check the town's registry of births. To the disappointment of a nation in which Charlot—little Charlie—was utterly adored, in which even Marcel Proust, *circa* 1915, had his mustache trimmed for a time in the Charlie Chaplin style,* the results of Ramond's investigation showed that the Fontainebleau registry had never been "enriched" by Chaplin's name. Eventually, the comedian changed his story about his birthplace. He was London-born as well as London-bred. Nevertheless, the contemplation of a French connection continued to give him pleasure. The truth of the matter, he was wont to say, was that he had been conceived in Fontainebleau. And years later, after taking up residence in Switzerland in the 1950s, he would make a movie about an exiled monarch who was Charlie Chaplin transparently disguised.[14]

"[My mother's] stage name was Lily Harley," the narrator of *Charlie Chaplin's Own Story* continues, "and she was very popular in English music halls, where she sang character songs. She had a beautiful sweet voice, but she hated the stage and the life. Sometimes at night she came

---

* "He was fond of asking for advice," according to Proust biographer Ronald Hayman, "and Celeste [his housekeeper], because she was always there, was often consulted. After following a suggestion from his barber (or someone else), he came home one day with a Charlie Chaplin moustache. Did she think he looked foolish with this little toothbrush under his nose? On the contrary, she said, it made him look younger." Ronald Hayman, *Proust: A Biography* (New York, 1992), p. 414.

into my bed and cried herself to sleep with her arms around me, and I was so miserable that I wanted to scream, but I did not dare, for fear of waking my father."[15] But it was his brother Sydney, not a long-since-gone father, who would have been awakened by his screaming. That Hannah did not elect to cry herself to sleep while embracing Sydney is significant. Like other young boys destined for fame, the truly gifted son was his mother's favorite.

One day when Charlie was about five years old, the narrative continues, he and Sydney were playing on the floor when their mother came in, staggering. Charlie thought she must be drunk. He had seen so many people drunk that the condition was commonplace to him, but seeing his mother in what he assumed was that kind of shape shocked him. "I screamed and screamed, it seemed as if I could not stop." His mother started across the room and tried to take off her hat. All her hair came tumbling down over her face and she fell on the bed. After a while Charlie crawled over and touched her hand, which hung down. It was cold and frightened him, so he backed under the bed until he reached the wall and there he stayed, still staring at his mother's hand. (Where Sydney was while all this was going on is not specified.)

The next thing that happened was that the door was flung open and a man whom the narrative refers to as the boy's father walked in. The boy heard him swearing. When he came over and stood by the bed, Charlie smelled whisky. His mother spoke, and the weak sound of her voice pierced her son's heart. "Don't be a hysterical fool," he heard his father reply. "You've got to work tonight. We need the money." "I can't," Charlie's mother cried. "I'm not up to it. I'm sick." Charlie's father stamped up and down the room. "Well, I'll take Charlie, then," he growled. "Where's the brat?"

Charlie backed closer to the wall and kept still. He was terrified. His father tramped out and down the stairs. Charlie's mother called to him, and slowly he came out from under the bed. His mother told him she wanted him to go on the stage in her place, and sing his very best. He said he would. Then she had him bring her a little new coat she had made for him and a fresh collar. It took her a long time to dress him and to get his hair combed to suit her. His father's boots sounded loud on the stairs. Charlie's mother kissed her son and told him to do his best.

His father took him to a music hall in Aldershot, a garrison town.* Soldiers were everywhere. Charlie had never seen a music hall before because his mother had always put him and Sydney to bed before she went to work. His father conducted him down a little alley, through a bare dim place, to one end of the stage. Charlie caught a glimpse of the crowd out front. Music and noise filled the air, and the stage was a glare of light. Then it was time for his mother's act. His father faced him toward the stage and gave him a little push. "Go out and sing 'Jack Jones,' " he said.

It was an old costermonger's song. Charlie sang one verse and started the second, hurrying to get through. He was not afraid of the crowd, but the stage got bigger and he got smaller every minute, and he wanted to be with his mother. Something hit him on the cheek, and something else hit the floor by his feet. Then a shower of things fell on the stage. The crowd was throwing money to him. Pennies and shillings covered the floor. " 'Oh! Wait, wait!' I shouted, and went down on my hands and knees to gather it up. 'It's money! Wait just a minute!' I got both hands full of it, and still there was more. I crawled around, picking it up and putting it in my pockets and shouted at the audience, 'Wait till I get it all and I'll sing a lot!' "

The excitement was tremendous. People laughed and shouted and climbed over their seats to throw more money. Charlie filled his pockets with it and put more in his hat. He stood up and sang the costermonger's song twice over and would have sung it again, but his father came out on the stage and led him off. At home, he poured the money over his mother, laughing all the while. His father took the money and bought them all a great feast. "I remember how I crowed over Sydney that night." [16]

My Autobiography recycles this story in considerably altered form, beginning with the fact that no father is present. Little Charlie's mother had been having trouble for some time with her voice. Never strong, it had been progressively weakened by constant use, to the point where it began to crack while she was onstage singing, as Charlie well knew, for

---

* The leading music halls in Aldershot were the Artillery, the Cavalry, Salter's Theatre of Varieties, and Billings's Concert Hall. The hall in *Charlie Chaplin's Own Story* has no name. In *My Autobiography* it is called the Canteen.

he often accompanied her to the theater. After being booed several times by disgruntled audiences, she fell into disfavor with the booking agents and her nervous system went haywire. At last she received an invitation to appear at the Canteen in Aldershot, a venue that many performers tried hard to avoid. Not only was the Canteen a grubby place, but Aldershot was the site of the most extensive military barracks in Britain, and the audiences there were notoriously rowdy.

Charlie was standing in the wings, raptly watching and listening to his mother, when her voice again betrayed her in the middle of a song and faded away to a whisper. The soldiers out front were outraged and mocked her with raucous catcalls and falsetto singing. Charlie's mother turned pale and fled into the wings. With the theater in turmoil, the stage manager had to think fast. Seizing Charlie's hand, he led him onstage and introduced him to the audience. Charlie had never before appeared in public, but behind the scenes he had more than once entertained stagehands with song-and-dance routines his mother had taught him. Once the orchestra had located the musical key he was most comfortable with, he launched into a song made popular by the coster comedian Gus Elen about the behavior of a Cockney bloke named Jack Jones who had inherited some money.

> Jack Jones well and known to everybody
> Round about the market, don't yer see,
> I've no fault to find with Jack at all,
> Not when 'e's as 'e used to be.
> But since 'e's 'ad the bullion left him
> 'E 'as altered for the worst.
> For to see the way 'e treats all his old pals
> Fills me with nothing but disgust.
> Each Sunday morning 'e reads the *Telegraph*,
> Once 'e was contented with the *Star.*
> Since Jones come into a little bit of cash
> Well, 'e don't know where 'e are!

Halfway through the song, Charlie was interrupted by a shower of coins hitting the stage. He responded by announcing that he would pick up the money first and continue singing afterwards.

This caused much laughter. The stage manager came on with a handkerchief and helped me to gather it up. I thought he was going to keep it.
This thought was conveyed to the audience and increased their laughter,
especially when he walked off with me anxiously following him. Not
until he handed it to Mother did I return to continue to sing. I was quite
at home. I talked to the audience, danced, and did several imitations,
including one of Mother singing her Irish march song.

But as he was repeating the chorus of the march song, he mischievously mimicked his mother's cracking voice and was surprised at the
impact it had on the soldiers. "There was laughter and cheers, then
more money throwing, and when Mother came on the stage to carry
me off, her presence evoked a tremendous applause." [17]

The rock on which the Aldershot story in both its versions founders
is *The Era*, the authoritative weekly journal of the British theatrical
profession. Through its exhaustive listings of theatrical presentations
and its "professional card" advertisements, Lily Harley's—Hannah Hill
Chaplin's—music hall career can be tracked from beginning to end. Her
first publicized engagements as a so-called serio-comedienne took place
at the Star in Dublin and the Buffalo in Belfast toward the close of 1885.
She was twenty years old, had been married for six months, and had a
nine-month-old child. During the next year and a half she enjoyed only
sporadic success in obtaining bookings, and her engagement at the Folly
Theater in Manchester on June 20, 1887, proved to be the last of
her recorded appearances. In his earliest years, Chaplin affirmed and
reaffirmed, his mother had been a music hall star. The evidence, however, forcefully indicates that by the time she gave birth to Charlie in
the spring of 1889, she had been retired from the halls for almost two
years.[18]*

The most successful serio-comediennes of the period, like Jenny
"The Electric Spark" Hill, projected enormous animal magnetism, as
did a petite, chesty, suggestive-voiced newcomer who was destined to
become, in T. S. Eliot's words, "the greatest music-hall artist of her time
in England." What Marie Lloyd could do, another of her admirers has

---

* Almost a decade later, she made one more public appearance, but at a political club,
not in a music hall. An advertisement for this event is reproduced in Charles Chaplin,
My Life in Pictures (New York, 1975), p. 43.

nostalgically written, "with the inanities of her song about 'walking rahnd the houses' with such a 'pair' that they had to be seen to be believed, and not even then, is now music-hall history." [19] In the highly competitive world of the halls, in which the top performers set a very high standard of entertainment, and in which the anterooms of the agents were crowded every day with scores of old-timers and young aspirants just waiting for the chance to take over from a performer who had faltered, Hannah had to be at her best to hold her position. The brevity of her career suggests, however, that she was seldom at her best, and for why this may have been so, there is no other explanation nearly as compelling as the gathering disorder of her mind. It is also plausible to assume that something like the tall tale of a little boy filling in for his stricken mother on the stage first took shape in Chaplin's imagination in early childhood, along with other rescue fantasies involving the two of them. For would not a sensitive youngster have wished with all his heart to deliver his mother from whatever torment was causing the terrifying lapses in her behavior?

Schizophrenia is the most severe and most baffling of mental illnesses. It has a vast range of socially, emotionally, and intellectually disabling symptoms that come and go unpredictably. In times of crisis, the symptoms can include delusions of grandeur or persecution; hallucinatory voices and visions full of threats and commands, meaningless giggling, outbursts of weeping and rage, incoherent and wandering speech, and violent, sometimes suicidal, impulses. To a normal person, a schizophrenic can appear to inhabit an entirely different universe; even sympathetic family members can feel separated from the sufferer by "a gulf which defies description," as Karl Jaspers has testified. Some psychiatrists speak of a sense of encountering someone who seems totally strange, puzzling, inconceivable, sinister, and frightening. Many schizophrenics are "object addicts" who cling to everybody and everything. Moved by an extreme fear of losing object relationships, they hold on to other people for dear life. Visitors to mental hospitals, as well as the physicians, social workers, and aides who work in them, sometimes find themselves the targets of tender, sensual, or hostile actions on the part of schizophrenic patients who are desperately attempting to maintain contact with the objective world. Many schizophrenics also turn with bizarre intensity to religious ideas, to messianic dreams, to obsessions and monomanias of any kind that promise connection to the real world, or, paradoxically, total transcendence of it.[20]

In time, Hannah Chaplin would become fervently religious, and an examining physician at Cane Hill Asylum would note her belief that she had been sent into the world on a mission by the Lord. What commands immediate attention, however, is the account of Hannah's distraught behavior in *Charlie Chaplin's Own Story:* ". . . She hated the stage and the life. Sometimes at night she came into my bed and cried herself to sleep with her arms around me, and I was so miserable that I wanted to scream. . . ." Chaplin's linkage of his mother's extraordinary behavior on these occasions to a hatred of the stage and its life makes much less sense than precisely the opposite possibility: that she was a washed-up performer overcome by a yearning for the stage and its life. Or perhaps she was missing her estranged husband, or was involved in some sort of sordid difficulty with one of her lovers. The gravest of all the possibilities is that she was in the grip of the chaotic emotions of her schizophrenia and desperate for someone to cling to.

Whatever her mental condition may have been at such times, there can be little doubt about how five-year-old Charlie felt. Not even the exhilaration of knowing that he was his mother's favorite son or the enthralling sensation of physical closeness to her could have compensated for the terrifying experience of trying to cope with her desperation. Instead of being able to call out in the night for parental comforting, he was having to assume that role himself, and since he did not know how to play it, he wanted to scream.

In speaking of Chaplin some ninety years later, his widow would aver that "Charlie loved women, but I sometimes thought he was frightened of them. He didn't understand them." Having listened for years to her husband's obsessive recollections of his childhood, perhaps Oona O'Neill Chaplin was aware of the congruence between the fright and incomprehension that she discerned and the fear and confusion that had overwhelmed him in the darkness of nightmarish nights long before.[21]

The description of the time when Hannah acted so strangely that little Charlie thought she must be drunk would also reverberate. As the boy was hiding beneath the bed with his back against the wall, he heard a man wearing boots brutally reply to his mother's plaint that she was sick by ordering her to stop behaving like a hysterical fool. On how many other occasions in Chaplin's childhood did he hear angry lovers or scornful neighbors fling language like that in his mother's face? As the insults were searing the young boy's soul with impotent rage and shame, the dragon's teeth of the shocking cruelty of Chaplin the man may well have been sown. "I saw myself," he recalled in conversation years later with the author Dana Burnet, "a scared, undersized, skinny kid, leading my mother by the hand, dragging her through the fog and the smells and the cold, towards our miserable home, while the other kids yelled and jeered at her." In this recollection, Burnet said, Hannah Chaplin became "a figure of tragic intensity . . . a woman of sorrows outlined vaguely against gray mist, gray death—in life." [22]

5

Symptoms of schizophrenia usually appear for the first time between the ages of fifteen and twenty-five, during the passage from adolescence to young adulthood. By the time Hannah Hill turned sixteen, Chaplin suggests in *My Autobiography*, she had left her family and struck out on her own. Was this action on her part an early-warning sign of her sickness? Quite possibly. But the questions connected with her departure that would hound her son down the years had to do with where she went when she left and how she supported herself.

2

"THAT BOY IS A BORN ACTOR"

*Pownall Terrace in South London. Hannah Chaplin
and her son Charlie lived here in early 1903.*

I N the rather surprising opinion of Chaplin's English friend Thomas
Burke, the author of *Limehouse Nights* (1917) and other popular works
of fiction that grew out of his intimate knowledge of London lowlife,
the "true land" of the Cockneys did not lie in the sprawling docklands
of the East End, or in the streets of Cheapside within the sound of the
bells of St. Mary-le-Bow, but in the districts on the south side of the
Thames. The most conspicuous of the Cockneys were, of course,
the costermongers, who hawked fruits, vegetables, and flowers, among

other wares, out of barrows in the streets. But on Sundays and holidays, if the weather was good, a walker in the streets of South London would have been more conscious of the passing parade of coster lads and lasses known as pearlies and fevvers, in tribute to the large pearl buttons and gorgeous clusters of feathers that respectively adorned their jackets and headdresses. The music hall stars who celebrated the costers and indeed all of the folkways of Cockney life were another colorful presence in South London, especially the leading men.

"When I was a boy," Burke remembered in *City of Encounters* (1932),

Camberwell, Kennington, Brixton and Stockwell were thick with music-hall artists, and on Sunday mornings they rallied upon a central point— the *White Horse* in Brixton—then the most completely Cockney public-house in London. In the lounge of that house you might see, at midday on a Sunday, most of those stars of the halls who were not on tour. . . . I myself, as a boy, sitting in a corner, arrayed with heart-cake and lemonade, saw most of the gods. . . . Some of them recur to me in image— George Lashwood, marvelously tailored. Dan Leno, in his old gardening suit. George Chirgwin, Witty Watty Walton, one of the Poluskis, Phil Ray, Harry Ford, Tom Costello, Joe Elvin.[1]

Among the worshippers at the feet of the gods in the middle 1880s was a quiet, brooding young man in his early twenties. His name was Charles Chaplin, known in this narrative as Charles Senior.

The son of a butcher from Ipswich who had migrated to London in the 1850s and settled in Marylebone, Charles Senior had been living in South London since the late winter of 1885, in a room he had rented in the comfortable home of a certain Joseph Hodges at 57 Brandon Street, Walworth. His move from Marylebone had been prompted by his decision to seek a career on the stage as a singer of dramatic and comic songs. From Brandon Street, he must have reasoned, he could easily get to Brixton on a Sunday, where he might become friends with some of the music hall headliners who frequented the White Horse. With equal ease, he could make the rounds of the music hall booking agents, all of whose offices were located along York Road in Lambeth. And in the Westminster Bridge Road, he could conveniently catch the shows at two of the liveliest of London's music halls, the Canterbury and Gatti's.

There was also a female lodger at Brandon Street that winter, a pertly attractive and obviously pregnant nineteen-year-old who shared Charles Senior's aspirations to a music hall career. On March 16, Hannah Hill gave birth to a baby boy. Three months later, she and Charles Senior were married, and the infant whom she had registered on his birth certificate as Sidney John Hill became Sidney Chaplin. In time, Sidney would decide that Sydney was a spelling that better suited him.

Neither his birth certificate nor his baptismal record at St. John's Church, Larcom Street, lists the name of Sydney's father. In later years, Hannah spoke of having eloped to South Africa with a rich bookmaker named Hawkes, and claimed that he was Sydney's father. Predictably, *My Autobiography* advanced a gaudier version of this idea:

> At eighteen Mother eloped with a middle-aged man to Africa. She often spoke of her life there; living in luxury amidst plantations, servants and saddle horses. In her eighteenth year my brother Sydney was born. I was told he was the son of a lord and that when he reached the age of twenty-one he would inherit a fortune of two thousand pounds.[2]

Chaplin's own son, however, Charles Chaplin, Jr., would not be the only person to remark on what he tactfully called the "chance resemblance" between his uncle Sydney and old photographs of Charles Senior.[3]

Hannah Hill grew up in poverty in South London. Her mother, born Mary Ann Terry, had had a son by a previous marriage to a sign writer who was killed when he fell off a London horse-bus and fractured his skull. As the wife of Charles Hill, Mary Ann gave birth to two daughters, Hannah in 1865 and Kate in 1870. To feed five mouths on his meager earnings as a cobbler was a constant struggle for Hill, even though his wife acquired sufficient skill as a boot binder to provide him with unpaid help.[4]

Once their daughters left home, the Hills had nothing to hold them together. Mary Ann, it is said, had an affair with another man that ended abruptly when she was caught in a compromising position by her husband; according to other gossip, she had a long history of infidelity. What seems beyond doubt is that the couple quarreled bitterly, until Mary Ann effectively ended the marriage by walking away from it. An investigator for the census of 1891 found her living with two other women on Barlow Street. Of her cohabitants the investigator remarked that "these 2 females were admitted Saturday night & turned out Monday without information being obtained," which suggests that they were whores. As for Mary Ann, she was listed as a "wardrobe dealer," which meant that she supported herself by selling old clothes in the streets. In the same way she financed a terrific thirst for gin that may well have hastened her mental collapse. She was being poisoned, she told a doctor, by the doctors in an infirmary, and her bed there was infested with beetles, rats, and mice. On February 23, 1893, having been officially certified as insane, she was committed to the London County Asylum at Banstead.[5]

2

What sort of life had Hannah led in the approximately four-year interval between her leaving home and showing up pregnant in Brandon Street? The direct answers that her son offered the world were romantic fabrications. At sixteen, he insisted, she had played the leading role in an Irish melodrama called *Shamus O'Brien* and had gone on tour with it; at eighteen, a life of luxury in South Africa was her fortunate lot; and so forth. But in the secret chambers of his mind, Chaplin had developed an appalling idea about his mother's activities during this period, and when he was in his sixties he wove it into the heroine's life story in *Limelight* (1952), his most overtly autobiographical film.

The drunken music hall has-been Calvero (played by Chaplin) saves a lovely young ballerina (played by Claire Bloom) from suicide. The troubled girl's name is Terry, which Chaplin took from the maiden name of his mad grandmother. When Terry is crippled by a hysterical paralysis of the legs, Calvero quizzes her about her background. Just as Kate Hill was her sister Hannah's junior by several years, so Terry had an older sister, named Louise. After the death of their mother, Terry tells Calvero, Louise had not only supported her, but had given her the money for dance lessons. The solution to the mystery of the source of her sister's income was brutally thrust upon Terry one evening as she made her way home from dancing class. In Piccadilly, she and a few of her classmates caught a glimpse of Louise in the obvious stance of a streetwalker. A short while later, Terry went away to boarding school, after which she landed a place in the ballet company of London's Empire Theater. The world was opening in glory for the young girl until the day the ballet company hired one of the dancers who had been with her on the evening she learned Louise's secret. As Calvero argues, this sudden reminder that her training as a ballerina had been paid for by a prostitute's earnings caused Terry to feel ashamed about her dancing, and the troubles with her legs began.

Chaplin was dramatizing through the characterization of Louise his suspicion that when his mother ran away from her parents she became a prostitute. And he further speculated through his recapitulation of the Louise-Terry relationship that Hannah had financially aided her younger sister after she, too, left their parents. The saucily pretty, temperamental Aunt Kate, whom Chaplin had dearly loved as a boy, was supposedly a successful actress known professionally as Kate Mowbray. "Actress," however, is a category that covers a multitude of sins. In all probability, Kate Mowbray was a woman of easy virtue who had learned as a girl how to get money from men, even as her sister had.

The English physician William Acton observed in 1870 in the expanded edition of his monumental treatise *Prostitution, considered in its Moral, Social and Sanitary Aspects, in London and other Large Cities and Garrison Towns* that "by far the larger number of women who have resorted to prostitution for a livelihood return sooner or later to a more or less regular course of life." In the main, Acton reiterated, "prostitution is a transitory state, through which an untold number of British women are ever on their passage."[6] If for a time Hannah Hill belonged to London's vast army of streetwalkers, it could have been because her first attempts to gain the attention of music hall booking agents were rebuffed and she felt she had no other choice. Yet one of the aspects of her mental illness was her inability to sustain a long-lasting relationship with a lover. For this sort of disturbed person, prostitution might not have been a hard expedient to accept.

3

Charles Senior had been married for two years before he finally aroused a booking agent's interest in his routines. His first recorded professional engagement took place by coincidence in the same June week in 1887 that marked the end of his wife's career.

Male singers who were able to create an individual character for themselves and a distinctive situation within each song had a great appeal in the halls. Often dressed in the fashion of men-about-town,

they swaggered across the stage, swinging a cane or adjusting a boutonniere as they trumpeted the superior virtues of Britannic civilization, or
recounted the woes of a husband with a roving eye and a vigilant,
scolding wife. Yet in more subdued moods, they also were capable of
communicating a touching vulnerability. Manifestly, Charles Senior was
never able to generate audience excitement in the way The Great
MacDermott could when he launched into "We don't want to fight, yet
by Jingo! if we do, We've got the ships, we've got the men, and got the
money too." Or George Leybourne, whose rendition of the drinking
song "Champagne Charlie" had inspired his nickname, or Albert Chevalier, the theatrical incarnation of the costermonger. In 1891 nineteen-
year-old Edward Gordon Craig, the pioneer-to-be of a completely new
movement in stage direction and stage decoration, saw Chevalier in
London. "[He] swept the town," Craig wrote years later,

> just as, nearly a century earlier, Edmund Kean had done with Shylock.
> The face, the figure, the voice, its words and its singing tunes, all this
> delighted us. Especially wonderful and lovely was the rhythm of the
> whole thing, a rhythm made up of tune and swinging limbs and of face,
> of buttons and tilted bowler—and of delightful words, full of fun and of
> power too. Never a moment's pause—all joy.

All the same, Charles Senior's pleasant baritone voice and sophisticated manner soon brought him top billings, both in London and on
the northern circuits. He became sought after as well by music publishers, who realized that having his name and photograph on their sheet
music strengthened sales.* Not until his self-destructively heavy drink-

---

* In 1893, for instance, a sketch of his smiling face and debonair figure appeared on the
front sheet of "Oui! Tray Bong!" The rhythm and words were well suited to his stage
personality:

> Through the streets we marched along
> Singing every comic song—
> Hip, hooray! Let's be gay!
> Boom diddy-ay, Ta-ra-ra!

> To each little French dove
> Standing drinks and making love
> We fairly smashed the ladies
> With our Oui! Tray Bong!

ing began to catch up with him (and that would cause his death, at age thirty-seven) did his considerable earnings decline.[7]

"Mother said [his drinking] was the cause of their separation," Chaplin declared in *My Autobiography*.

> It was difficult for vaudevillians not to drink in those days, for alcohol was sold in all the theatres, and after a performer's act he was expected to go to the theatre bar and drink with the customers. Some theatres made more profits from the bar than from the box office, and a number of stars were paid large salaries not alone for their talent but because they spent most of their money at the theatre bar. Thus many an artist was ruined by drink.

And many a marriage. His mother told stories of domestic strife with humor and sadness, Chaplin remembered. Charles Senior had a violent temper when drinking, she averred, and during one of his tantrums she ran off to Brighton with friends. In answer to his frantic telegram, "What are you up to? Answer at once!" she wired back, "Balls, parties and picnics, darling!"[8]

But could such anecdotes be taken as truths, or were they masks disguising the truth? The possibility that haunted Chaplin in his later years—as it presumably had in his childhood—was that Charles Senior and Hannah's marriage had been fatally damaged not by his drunken rages, but by her infidelity. In readying himself to film *Limelight*, Chaplin composed a background story on the drunken Calvero's earlier life that fleshed out this hypothesis.

Not too many years ago, in this scenario, Calvero had become deeply involved with a young woman named Eva Morton, whose mother he had loved a generation earlier and lost when she ran off to Africa with another man. Eventually he married Eva, only to discover that she was sexually promiscuous. In Chaplin's words, "Her desire was insatiable and verged on being pathological." From Eva's viewpoint, the desire that made it impossible for her to "be faithful to any man" was "something separate and apart from herself and her life with Calvero," but Calvero "would not tolerate any compromise. . . . His nature demanded the full possession of the thing it loved."

The story then depicts the showdown between the troubled couple,

on the night that Eva shamelessly accompanies her lover of the moment
—a rich Manchester factory owner—to the Drury Lane Theater, where
Calvero is playing the principal clown in a pantomime. From the stage,
he catches sight of his wife and her companion and attempts to deal
with his heartbreak by interpolating into his performance some bleakly
humorous comedy about a heartbroken cuckold. At the end of the evening, he accuses Eva of infidelity and they part bitterly. Calvero turns
to alcohol for solace, and when his drunkenness becomes habitual, he
pays heavily for it with the loss of his comic touch and then of his
mind. For three years he languishes in an institution. When he is finally
released he looks markedly older. He attempts to make a comeback, but
succumbs once more to drink. The last chapters of his life history are
enacted in *Limelight*.[9]

According to *My Autobiography*, Chaplin entered the world on the
sixteenth of April, 1889, at eight o'clock in the evening in East Lane,
Walworth. However, no birth certificate on file in the Office of Population Censuses and Surveys attests to this event, even though the census
law of 1874 made filing—by the parents—obligatory. Nor is there any
record that the Chaplin family ever lived in East Street, as East Lane
was officially called. Chaplin's statement that his grandfather Hill ran a
boot-repairing business in East Lane is likewise unsubstantiated. The
listing in *Kelly's Post Office Directory* of 1889 of fourteen boot-and-shoe-
repairing establishments in East Street makes no mention of a Charles
Hill as one of the proprietors. There is also no record that confirms
Chaplin's further assertion that "soon after" his birth "we moved to
West Square, St. George's Road, Lambeth."[10]

Only two certainties stand out in this fog. In the week of April 16,
Charles Senior was in the north, rather than at his wife's bedside, playing an engagement at the Empire Palace of Varieties in Hull. And on
May 11, a music hall paper called *The Magnet* published the following
item: "On the 15th [not the 16th] ultimo, the wife of Mr. Charles
Chaplin (*nee* Miss Lily Harley), of a beautiful boy. Mother and son
both doing well. Papers please copy."[11] As a single mother, Hannah
had dutifully filed a birth certificate for illegitimate Sydney in 1885.
Did she and Charles Senior, upon his return from Hull, really content
themselves with recording the arrival of baby Charlie in a music hall
paper?

My own efforts to find a birth certificate for Charles Chaplin filed somewhere else in England or, alternatively, at some other time during 1889, or a certificate that lists the baby's mother as Hannah Hill or Lily Harley and omits mention of the father's name, have all come to naught. The possibility still remains that a certificate was filed for him under some name other than Chaplin or Hill or Harley. At the same time, Hannah may have neglected to file a form for the simple reason that she was, psychologically, "not herself," and that Charles Senior disdained to do so because he and Hannah had already separated by the time of the birth, or were living together only now and then, or because he was not entirely sure that the baby was his. Whatever the truth may be, little Charlie grew up in the shadow of a fearful but fascinating ambiguity about the identity of his father, which could only have been strengthened by his realization that he bore no resemblance to Charles Senior. For he got a look at him one night on the stage at the Canterbury and on another occasion while out walking. And for two months during 1898, when Hannah was being cared for at Cane Hill Asylum, he and Sydney lived with Charles Senior and his mistress at 289 Kennington Road.

School-admission records relating to Sydney reflect Hannah's restlessness in the year of baby Charlie's first birthday. The register of the King and Queen Street School Walworth indicates in an entry on March 3 that a new student, Sydney Chaplin, lived at 68 Camden Street. In the space on the registry from opposite "Parent or Guardian," Charles Senior's name appears, but this does not necessarily mean that he, too, was living in Camden Street. By the middle of May, Sydney's address was 14 Lambeth Square and he had been switched to the Addington Street School Lambeth; this time, Hannah was listed as his parent or guardian. Shortly thereafter, Charles Senior left England for a tour of the United States (during which he scored a hit with the customers at the Union Square Theater in New York). The following November, Sydney was attending the Flint Street, East Street School Walworth. His new address was 94 Barlow Street, and Charles Senior was again listed as his parent or guardian, although it is all but certain that Barlow Street was not his residence. For in the census of 1891, conducted the following spring, Hannah and her two boys, but not Charles Senior, are described as the occupants of three rooms at 94

Barlow, the same building in which Hannah's gin-drinking mother also lived.[12]

Hannah's new lover that spring was a handsome singer out of the Limehouse slums named George Dryden Wheeler. Known to his fans as Leo Dryden, he was just about to strike it rich with a wonderfully dramatic composition, "The Miner's Dream of Home," about an English-born digger in the Australian goldfields who misses his native land. (Well into the twentieth century, homesick Englishmen around the world would sing "The Miner's Dream of Home" on New Year's Eve.)

In August 1892, Hannah gave birth to Dryden's son, but if she was dreaming of becoming Mrs. Dryden, she was doomed to disappointment. At some point in 1893, Dryden not only dropped out of her life but spirited away his son, out of concern, in all probability, about Hannah's stability as a mother. In 1912 young Wheeler Dryden went to India with his father's vaudeville company and remained there for several years, touring with theatrical companies.

Not until 1921, in southern California, was he reunited with his mother. All things considered, the reunion went very well. Young Dryden paused in the doorway of the room in which poor Hannah was sitting and dramatically asked, "Do you know who I am?" "Of course I do," replied Hannah. "You're my son. Sit down and have a cup of tea."[13]

4

In the earliest memories of his mother that Chaplin recorded in *My Autobiography*, she was in her late twenties. Among her most attractive features were a fair complexion, violet-blue eyes, and light-brown hair that she could sit on. Charlie and Sydney adored her and thought her "divine-looking," although she was "not an exceptional beauty." In later years people who had known her as a young woman assured Chaplin that she had been "dainty and attractive and had compelling charm."

On Sunday mornings, she took pride in dressing Sydney in an Eton suit with long trousers and Charlie in a blue velvet one with blue gloves to match, before setting out for family walks along the Kennington Road. In those "prosperous days," the three of them lived for a time, according to *My Autobiography*, in the Westminster Bridge Road. The gay and friendly atmosphere of the neighborhood, with its attractive shops, restaurants, and music halls, could not have been more different from the spell created by the solemn Houses of Parliament across the Thames. "This was the London," Chaplin wrote,

> of my moods and awakenings: memories of Lambeth in spring . . . of riding with Mother on top of a horse bus and trying to touch the lilac trees . . . of rubicund flower girls at the corner of Westminster Bridge, making gay *boutonnieres*, their adroit fingers manipulating tinsel and quivering fern—of the humid odor of freshly watered roses that affected me with a vague sadness. . . .*

The cut flowers that the child was conscious of in these precious moments of intimacy with his mother would appear and reappear years later in a long string of Chaplin movies, including *The Bank* (1915), *The Gold Rush* (1925), and *City Lights* (1931), as emblems of the lovely young woman who is loved by a lonely little man.

From the time he was three and a half, Chaplin also remembered that "each night before Mother went to the theatre Sydney and I were lovingly tucked up in a comfortable bed and left in the care of the housemaid," whom they could afford because Hannah was a music hall "star," earning "twenty-five pounds a week." No mention is made of the fact that in the fall of 1892, when Charlie was three and a half, a housemaid employed by Hannah had to have been taking care of her newborn son by Leo Dryden in addition to Sydney and Charlie. Furthermore, it was undoubtedly Dryden who was footing the cost of the maid and was paying the rent on the "three tastefully furnished rooms" in which this memory is set. For when Hannah left for the evening after tucking up her little boys, she was certainly not headed for theatrical engagements of her own. Listening to her lover work his musical magic on adoring fans was her most probable goal.

Another nighttime recollection, which Chaplin summons up in Pickwickian images, is of being wrapped in a traveling rug on top of a four-in-hand coach and of "driving with Mother and her theatrical friends, cosseted in their gaiety and laughter as our trumpeter, with

* The literary skill of this and other passages raises the question of whether Chaplin had covert help in writing his autobiography.

clarion braggadocio, heralds us along the Kennington Road to the rhythmic jingle of harness and the beat of horses' hoofs."

"Then something happened!" Chaplin melodramatically declares. He suddenly realized that "all was not well with Mother and the outside world."

> She had been away all the morning with a lady friend and had returned home in a state of excitement. I was playing on the floor and became conscious of intense agitation going on above me, as though I were listening from the bottom of a well. There were passionate exclamations and tears from Mother, who kept mentioning the name Armstrong— Armstrong said this, Armstrong said that, Armstrong was a brute! Her excitement was strange and intense so that I began to cry, so much so that Mother was obliged to pick me up and console me.

The reason she was upset, Chaplin explains, was that she had just returned from the law courts where she had been suing Charles Senior for nonsupport of her children, and the case—which was argued on her husband's side by a lawyer named Armstrong—had not gone too well for her.

While the lawsuit was quite possibly fictitious, the scene compellingly conveys a sense of the sick lability of Hannah's moods. Superimposed on her schizophrenia was an affective roller coaster. Her elevated moods were marked by euphoria, cheerful humor, enthusiastic renditions of music hall routines, and dramatic re-creations of historical incidents and biblical scenes. In her downcast periods, she was excitedly anxious, tearful, and angry. The fanciful details in *My Autobiography* about the trouble she started having with her voice in the months preceding the crisis on the stage at Aldershot add up symbolically to a description of a depressive crack-up.

> She had been having trouble with her voice. It was never strong, and the slightest cold brought on laryngitis which lasted for weeks; but she was obliged to keep on working, so that her voice grew progressively worse. She could not rely on it. In the middle of singing it would crack or suddenly disappear into a whisper, and the audience would laugh and start booing. The worry of it impaired her health and made her a nervous wreck.[14]

5

"When the fates deal in human destiny, they heed neither pity nor justice. Thus they dealt with Mother." With those sonorities, the author of *My Autobiography* launched into his fullest elaboration of the myth of bottom-of-the heap impoverishment that long had served him as a metaphor for the authentic nightmares of his childhood. It is a measure of the agony that the up-and-down, inexorably worsening nature of his mother's illness had put him through that he began *My Autobiography* with a portrait of her on the eve of a breakdown. Nevertheless, he could not bring himself to chronicle the history of her pathology in anything like its full detail. Nor did he possess either the self-knowledge or the will to analyze the psychic price he had paid, in either the short run or the long, as a result of growing up in the shadow of her suffering, or of being separated from her, or of missing the balance-wheel presence of a caring father. In lieu of painful confrontations with painful truths, the septuagenarian author resorted, as in his early Hollywood days, to sympathy-inducing allusions to abject poverty. It did not hurt, either, that such allusions perfectly complemented both his famous tramp persona and his leftist politics.

After Aldershot, he declared, "Mother . . . never regained her voice." Although she had a little money, that very soon vanished, along with her jewelry and other small possessions, for she had to pawn them "in order to live." From three comfortable rooms, she and Sydney and Charlie moved into two rooms and then into one, in progressively drabber neighborhoods, until finally they found themselves in the "cheerless twilight" of "wretched circumstances." Having learned to make her own theatrical costumes, Hannah had sewing skills that enabled her to earn a few shillings as a dressmaker. Alas, such an income was "barely enough" to meet their minimal needs.[15]

In 1883 the reform-minded secretary of the London Congregational Union, the Reverend Andrew Mearns, affixed an arresting title to the penny pamphlet he had just finished writing: *The Bitter Cry of Outcast London*. As the title page explained, the pamphlet represented "an Inquiry into the Condition of THE ABJECT POOR." Grounded in Mearns's personal investigations of slum life in South London and vibrating with his Christian outrage, *The Bitter Cry* is the most evocative account ever published of London's lower depths in the late-Victorian era.

Mearns's indignation was immediately apparent in his refusal to refer to the hovels of the abject poor as homes, "for how can these places be called homes," he asked, "compared with which the lair of a wild beast would be called a comfortable and healthy spot?" Few who will read these pages have any conception, the minister proclaimed, swinging into his full rhetorical stride, "of what these pestilential rookeries are, where tens of thousands are crowded together amidst horrors which call to mind what we have heard of the middle passage of the slave ship."

To get into them you have to penetrate courts reeking with poisonous and malodorous gases arising from accumulations of sewage and refuse scattered in all directions and often flowing beneath your feet; courts, many of which the sun never penetrates, which are never visited by a breath of fresh air, and which rarely know the virtues of a drop of cleansing water. You have to ascend rotten staircases, which threaten to give way beneath every step, and which, in some places, have already broken down, leaving gaps that imperil the limbs and lives of the unwary. You have to grope your way along dark and filthy passages swarming with vermin. Then, if you are not driven back by the intolerable stench, you may gain admittance to the dens in which these thousands of beings who belong, as much as you, to the race for whom Christ died, herd together.

Eight square feet was the average size of very many of these dens. Their walls and ceilings were black with secretions of filth. Holes in the windows were stuffed with rags or covered by boards to keep out wind and rain, and the panes were so begrimed and obscured that they scarcely admitted light. The furniture might consist of a broken chair, the tottering relics of an old bedstead, and the mere fragment of a table; but more commonly Mearns found rude substitutes for these things, rough boards resting upon bricks, an old hamper box turned upside down, or, more frequently still, nothing but rubbish and rags.

The suffering of the women and children was particularly appalling to Mearns. The children's bodies were alive with vermin, he reported.

Many of them had never seen a green field and they often passed a whole day without a morsel of food.

> Here is one of three years old picking up some dirty pieces of bread and eating them. We go in at the doorway . . . and find a little girl of twelve years old. "Where is your mother?" "In the madhouse." "How long has she been there?" "Fifteen months." "Who looks after you?" The child, who is sitting at an old table making match-boxes, replies, "I look after my little brothers and sisters as well as I can."

Perforce, the older children worked, when they did not turn to thievery, but the wages were miserable and the hours unspeakable. In order to earn, for instance, ten shillings sixpence a week, that twelve-year-old girl who was making matchboxes had to turn out fifty-six gross of them every seven days, or 1,296 a day. Many of the poor women whom Mearns came to know worked as seamstresses and were similarly exploited.

> We asked a woman who is making tweed trousers, how much she can earn in a day, and are told one shilling. But what does a day mean to this poor soul? *Seventeen hours!* From five in the morning to ten at night—no pause for meals. She eats her crust and drinks a little tea as she works, making in very truth, with her needle and thread, not her living only, but her shroud.[16]

The Bitter Cry sent a "thrill of horror through the land," a British newspaper of the period declared. But for all the lurid detail of its vignettes, its most shocking passage consisted of three flatly stated words: "Incest is common." Abject poverty, Mearns emphasized, generated many forms of vice and sensuality. Ask if the man and woman living together in a South London rookery were married, he said, and your simplicity would earn you a smile. Prostitution thrived in the slums as well, to the point where in one street of thirty-five houses thirty-two were known to be brothels. Incest, however, was the ultimate evil. In raising the specter of it, Mearns had mentioned the unmentionable, as Gertrude Himmelfarb has observed in *Poverty and Compassion: The Moral Imagination of the Late Victorians* (1991). Three years after he broke the conspiracy of silence, the poet laureate Lord Tennyson also dared to invoke incest, in a catalogue of shames in "Locksley Hall Sixty Years After":

Is it well that while we range with Science, glorifying in the Time,
City children soak and blacken soul and sense in city slime?
There among the looming alleys Progress halts on palsied feet,
Crime and hunger cast our maidens by the thousands on the street.
There the Master scrimps his haggard semptress of her daily bread,
There a single sordid attic holds the living and the dead.
There the smouldering fire of fever creeps across the rotted floor,
And the crowded couch of incest in the warrens of the poor.

In 1888 delicacy was renewed. Beatrice Potter (later, Beatrice Webb) published *The Pages of a Workgirl's Diary*, drawn almost verbatim from her own diary, but omitting a reference to incest in one-room flats.[17]

How widespread were the vistas of suffering and sordidness descried in *The Bitter Cry?* Who, precisely, were London's abject poor? Which particular streets and neighborhoods were their strongholds? Was the number of these unfortunates larger or smaller than that of the poor whose income levels made life difficult but not horrific? How and where did the latter groups live? Such questions were finessed by Mearns. But they held a fascination for a remarkable shipping-firm magnate from Liverpool, Charles Booth. In the mid-1880s he embarked on a dozen and a half years of scientifically methodical research and writing, out of which there emerged the seventeen masterful volumes of his *Life and Labour of the People in London* (1889–1903). His wife's cousin, Beatrice Webb, once said of Booth that he embodied the "Spirit" of his time. For the 1880s was a time of education and preparation, of accustoming people to new ways of seeing England and of interpreting human relationships. Had Chaplin known of the thickness of detail in *Life and Labour*, he might have refrained from speaking of specific streets or neighborhoods in the course of alluding to his allegedly wretched poverty in the final years of the nineteenth century and the first years of the twentieth.[18]

"By the word 'poor,'" said Booth, "I mean to describe those who have a sufficiently regular income, such as 18s. to 21s. per week for a moderate family, and by 'very poor' those who from any cause fall much below this standard." His paradigm of a moderate family was a "father, mother and three children of, say, 11, 8 and 6." By this standard, four of the eight classes in his alphabetical schema lived beneath the "line of poverty":

A. The lowest class—occasional labourers, loafers and semi-criminals.

B. The very poor—casual labour, hand-to-mouth existence, chronic want.

C and D. The poor—including alike those whose earnings are small, because of irregularity of employment, and those whose work, though regular, is ill-paid.

E and F. The regularly employed and fairly paid working class of all grades.

G and H. Lower and upper middle class and all above this level.

Class A made up 0.9 percent of the population of London; Class B, 7.5 percent; Classes C and D, 22.3 percent.

The following excerpt from Booth's description of a street in which most of the residents belonged to Classes C and D both illustrated the carefulness of his observations and enlarged his portrait of "the poor":

Bradford Street. A wide street of modern two-storeyed houses, each like its neighbour, leading from a busy thoroughfare into the midst of a number of dingy and uninviting streets. The houses contain four rooms and a small kitchen in the rear. In most cases there is a narrow strip of ground in front of the house, enclosed by railing, but trodden down by the many children who play in the street. In some of the houses windows are well kept, with curtains and ornaments carefully placed within the view of passers, and a general air of comfort, but the children, playing about, though fairly nourished, have a ragged appearance, pointing to a lack of any superfluous means. Paper, straw and refuse litter the gutters and sidewalk. There are 30 houses in all. . . .

Perhaps the most stunning of Booth's accomplishments was a volume of color-coded maps encompassing all streets in every section of the world's greatest city. Seven shades of color differentiated the social conditions of the inhabitants, as defined by the author's A-through-H classifications. At one end of the scale, black streets and dark-blue streets represented the respective lairs of the "elements of disorder" of class A and the "very poor" of class B. In the middle of the scale were streets colored purple, indicating a mixture of people living in poverty and comfort, "usually C and D with E and F." At the other end, yellow streets, "hardly found in East London and little found in South London," symbolized the presence of "families who keep three or more servants." [19]

From *My Autobiography* and other records we know that flighty Hannah Chaplin's various perches included a basement room in Oakley Street, a room at the back of Kennington Park (10 Farmers Road was the exact address), a room in one of the back streets behind Kennington Cross near Hayward's pickle factory (*i. e.*, 39 Methley Street), two rooms over a barber shop in Chester Street, and a place Chaplin described as a "small garret" in a "row of old derelict houses" set back off the Kennington Road on Pownall Terrace. None of these streets bore the somber colors of extreme poverty on Booth's maps. Despite the perfume from the pickle factory, the inhabitants of Methley Street lived, Booth's color code revealed, in "working class comfort" ("corresponding to Classes E and F, but containing also a large proportion of the lower middle class of small tradesmen and Class G"). The same was true of the inhabitants of Farmers Road, except for a small stretch in which the comfortable and the poor lived side by side.

As for Pownall Terrace, it, too, had a mixed population, according to Booth's maps, and elsewhere in *Life and Labour* he elaborated upon the mix that obtained throughout the whole area in which the Terrace was located: "A few stage professionals and good shopkeepers, but nearly all the people are working class; majority are truly comfortable, but there are many labourers, hawkers, carmen, &c., below the line of poverty. Some large houses let in tenements." That reference to large houses tenanted as separate dwellings might have been composed with the row houses of Pownall Terrace specifically in mind. Built as vertically organized, multistory homes, they were never allowed to degenerate into a derelict condition and were subsquently divided into rooms occupied by the "genteel poor," in the words of the keeper emeritus of the Museum of London, Colin Sorensen.[20] A pen drawing of the Terrace by an artist named Fletcher and a watercolor by an artist named Mills, both executed in the early 1960s, draw attention to details of the brickwork in the façade. Aesthetic values, however, meant nothing to the developer who bought and demolished the houses in 1966.[21]

6

After Leo Dryden left her, Hannah must have accepted money from other men. For how else could she have kept herself and her two boys above the social level of Booth's "very poor" or the Reverend Mearns's "abject poor"? She earned only pittances as a seamstress, after all, and there are good grounds for disbelieving Chaplin's assertion that Charles Senior gave her ten shillings a week. Furthermore, there were times— many times, apparently—when she would put aside her dressmaking, don a spangled costume she had managed to hold on to from her theatrical days, and regale her boys with "song successes and . . . the dances that went with them until she was breathless and exhausted." She gave imitations, too, of such famous actresses as Ellen Terry, and of Joe Elvin and other music hall stars. In narrating a story or recounting a historical anecdote, which she also was fond of doing, she took all the key parts. Thus, in an episode from the life of Napoleon, she was the emperor standing on tiptoe in his library to reach for a book, but she was Marshal Ney as well, as he intercepted his sovereign and said, "Sire, allow me to get it for you. I am higher." To which Napoleon replied with a scowl, "Higher? Taller!" As Nell Gwyn, Hannah leaned over the palace stairs, holding her baby and threatening Charles II: "Give this child a name, or I'll dash it to the ground!" and as Charles II she answered, "All right! The Duke of Saint Albans."

Following her turn to God, résumés and actings-out of New Testament passages assumed a much larger place in her repertoire. With tears welling up in her eyes, Chaplin recalled,

> she told of Simon helping to carry Christ's cross and the appealing look of gratitude Jesus gave him; she told of the repentant thief, dying with him on a cross and asking forgiveness, and of Jesus saying: "Today shalt thou be with me in Paradise." And from the cross looking down at his mother, saying: "Woman, behold thy son." And in his last dying agony crying out: "My God, why hast thou forsaken me?"

As little Charlie sat spellbound before her and then tried out imitations of her various acts, he acquired precocious skills.[22]

Harking back in his memory for incidents that would illustrate how pitifully poor he and his brother and mother had been, Chaplin came up with one involving clothes. Winter was approaching and Sydney had outgrown the coat he needed for school. "So Mother made him a coat from her old velvet jacket. It had red and black striped sleeves pleated at the shoulders." Sydney burst out crying when he was made to wear it. "What will the boys at school think?" "Who cares what people think?" said Hannah. "Besides, it looks very distinguished."[23] But the coat caused Sydney to have many a fight with jeering boys who called him "Joseph and his coat of many colors." Charlie, meantime, was being called "Sir Francis Drake" because of his appearances at school in a pair of his mother's red tights cut down for stockings. The story has an authentic ring to it. Yet Hannah's demand that her boys attend school in clownish costumes of her devising might have had less to do with economic hardship than with a recurrence of her mental illness.

In the spring of 1895, Hannah was overcome by a stress-related affliction that Chaplin would later describe as migraine headaches. For days she lay in a dark room with tea-leaf bandages over her eyes. Finally, on June 29, she was taken into the Lambeth Infirmary for what proved to be a monthlong stay. On or about July 1, John George Hodges, a prosperous artisan and a practicing Christian who was known to Hannah because he was the son of Joseph Hodges, in whose house she had lodged in the last months of her pregnancy with Sydney, welcomed six-year-old Charlie into his comfortable home in York Road. At the same time, the Lambeth authorities placed ten-year-old Sydney in the local workhouse for four days, after which they transferred him to a school in rural West Norwood for poor children from Lambeth. After being discharged from Norwood in mid-September, Sydney lived for a time with Charles Senior, which suggests that Hannah's stress had still not eased to the point where she was able to resume her maternal duties. The shadows of her tragedy of mind were growing longer.[24]

The following February, life momentarily brightened for her. Not only did she have her boys back with her, but on the eighth of that month she was able to make a one-night appearance as a serio-comedienne at the Hatcham Liberal Club. Three months later, she collapsed and was taken to the Champion Hill Infirmary, while Sydney and Charlie were placed in the Newington Workhouse, "owing to the absence of their father and the destitution and illness of their mother." (The authorities could speak of destitution because she told them that she was a "machinist"—*i.e.*, a sewing machinist; presumably, they concluded that she had no other means of support.) Eventually, the Southwark Board of Guardians, which had jurisdiction in the case, decided to send both Charlie and Sydney to the Hanwell poor-law school, located in a lovely stretch of countryside twelve miles out of London. Before doing so, however, the board obtained Charles Senior's promise that he would contribute fifteen shillings a week toward the cost of maintaining the boys there. Only gradually would the board realize that he had no intention of keeping his word.[25]

On June 18, Charlie and Sydney traveled to Hanwell in a horse-drawn bakery van. Horse chestnut trees lined the lanes they passed through as they neared the school, and the fields beyond were filled with ripening wheat and dotted with orchards. For Charlie, however, the beauty of the scene was no compensation for the pain of being separated from his mother for the second time in twelve months. "Only mother love lasts," he was once quoted as saying, but his oldest son, Charles Chaplin, Jr., sensed a lack of conviction on his part that he had truly possessed that love. In the opinion of Lillian McMurray Spicer, the mother of his second wife, Chaplin felt that his mother "had failed him when he had needed her the most."

The question of how the repeated ruptures in their relationship affected his emotional development also interested the tempestuous Polish actress Pola Negri during her highly publicized affair with Chaplin in the 1920s. "[His] ability to bring out maternal feelings was one of his greatest assets with the opposite sex," she later observed in *Memoirs of a Star* (1970), and one of the evidences of this was the thousands of letters he received from women all over the world who wanted to look after him. In Negri's view it was his need for a mother substitute that made him unconsciously solicit this reaction. "It was as if a part of Chaplin had never grown up. It was probably why he retained that marvelous child-like wonder and innocence that contributed so much to his genius. He was at his best when he created situations to which he could react with the confusion and bashful awkwardness of the young."[26]

7

Hanwell School was one of the shining achievements of the late-Victorian social conscience. The diet provided by its kitchen was wholesome, the dormitories were clean, and the health-care facilities included a doctor's dispensary and a dentist's office. In a Hanwell classroom, Charlie experienced the thrill of learning to write his name. Nevertheless, his underlying despondency was profound, as one of the school nurses came to realize. When an epidemic of ringworm broke out, he contracted an infection on his scalp, and the nurse who spotted it immediately shaved his head and painted the entire surface with iodine. But instead of being grateful to her for her vigilance, he gave way to paroxysms of weeping. Conceivably, his brother could have consoled him, but he and Sydney lived in different ward blocks and rarely saw each other.[27]

Not long before her untimely death in 1916, their aunt Kate expressed astonishment to a reporter (who obviously polished the style of her remarks in the course of writing them up) that anyone would "write about Charlie Chaplin without mentioning his brother Sydney. They have been inseparable all their lives, except when fate intervened at intervals. Syd, of quiet manner, clever brain and steady nerve, had been father and mother to Charlie. Charlie always looked up to Syd, and Sydney would suffer anything to spare Charlie." At Hanwell, unfortunately, the luck of the draw not only placed them in different wards, but in the fall of 1896 it presented Sydney with an opportunity to enlist in a seamanship and gunnery program aboard the naval training ship *Exmouth*. Not until January 1898, when Sydney was discharged from the *Exmouth* within days of Charlie's discharge from Hanwell, were the brothers at last reunited, in their mother's London room.[28]

Even worse for Charlie than Sydney's departure from Hanwell was Hannah's protracted failure to come to see him there. Where she lived, and how, and with whom, in the period following her release from Champion Hill is a mystery. Not until August 10, 1897, some fourteen months after Charlie's arrival at Hanwell, did she finally pay him a visit. For a self-conscious eight-year-old, it was an excruciating moment. Small children are easily embarrassed by anything out of the way about their parents' appearance or behavior, and their peers can be merciless in calling attention to deviations from the norm. In the story about Hannah's visit that Chaplin related to his San Francisco socialite friend and sometime assistant Harry Crocker, he admitted that "she caused me anguished embarrassment. What a traitor to her I felt!" The trouble was that she arrived at Hanwell "with an oil can—she'd been shopping —and the association of her with the oil can . . . and all the boys seeing her—was too much. I cried, 'Why do you come with that, mother?' I sobbed, pointing to the oil can. 'Why do you come at all? They'll all see you; they'll all see you!' "[29]

In the wake of this drama, another one unfolded, of which Charlie was unaware. On September 14, the Southwark Board of Guardians posted a reward for the arrest of Charles Senior "for neglecting to maintain his two children." Fortunately for him, he had a responsible older brother, Spencer, the proprietor of a prosperous London pub, the Queen's Head. To keep Charles Senior from being jailed, Spencer came up with the debt-clearing sum of forty-four pounds eight shillings. Yet in the closing months of 1897, Charles Senior again welshed on his payment obligations and the board again took steps to have him arrested.[30]

Of the early months of Hannah's reunion in London with both her boys, Chaplin asserted in his autobiography that "for a while she was able to support us." By what means, he did not say. In any case, 1898 soon devolved into a terrible year. On July 22, she glumly led her sons into the Lambeth Workhouse. On August 1, Charlie and Sydney were shipped off to Sydney's old school in West Norwood, a far more somber place, in Charlie's demoralized opinion, than Hanwell, by which he meant that the leaves on the trees were darker and the trees much taller. Ten days later, with an assurance born of an upswinging mood, Hannah insisted, and the workhouse authorities for some reason agreed, that she was quite capable of caring for her boys. On August 12, having been returned to the workhouse from West Norwood, Sydney and Charlie were released from custody in their mother's care. The three of them spent the day in Kennington Park. After a picnic lunch of a bloater and black cherries that Sydney paid for, the boys played catch while Hannah sat on a bench, doing crochet work. At teatime, she declared that the hour had arrived for a return to the workhouse, where she obtained readmission for all three of them. On August 15, the boys were remanded to West Norwood. Hannah remained at the workhouse.[31]

On September 6, aides transferred her to the Lambeth Infirmary, her body covered with bruises. Possibly she had had to be forcibly restrained; possibly she had been quarreling violently with other patients.* Her next stop, six days later, was the Cane Hill Asylum in Surrey. A physician recorded the stark facts of her psychotic break in a lunacy examination book:

> Has been very strange in manner—at one time abusive & noisy, at another using endearing terms. Has been confined in P R [padded room] repeatedly on a/c of sudden violence—threw a mug at another patient. Shouting, singing and talking incoherently. Complains of her head and depressed and crying this morning—dazed and unable to give any reliable information. Asks if she is dying. States she belongs to Christ Church (Congregation) which is Ch. of E. [Church of England]. She was sent here on a mission by the Lord. She says she wants to get out of the world.[32]

Two of the nurses on the Norwood staff called Sydney out of a soccer game and informed him that his mother had been adjudged insane and sent to Cane Hill. Sydney returned to the game, but at the end of it, he broke away from the other boys and wept. Chaplin remembered that when his distraught half-brother told him what had happened, he himself remained dry-eyed but was overcome with a baffling despair and sense of betrayal. "Why had she done this?" he asked himself. "Vaguely I felt that she had deliberately escaped from her mind and deserted us."[33]

---

* The fact that the infirmary authorities also described her as having dermatitis may explain their erroneous conclusion—which physicians who examined her in 1903 and 1905 would notably fail to endorse—that Hannah was suffering from syphilis. For certain cases of this dire disease, skin rashes that may imitate a variety of dermatologic conditions usually appear within six to twelve weeks after infection. These rashes, or secondary lesions, as they are more generally called, finally vanish without a trace and the patient again appears to be well. Without the aid of salvarsan, which the German bacteriologist Paul Ehrlich did not give the world until 1910, the syphilis sufferer eventually develops destructive tertiary lesions, the most severe of which are those that attack the brain, causing general paresis or dementia paralytica. Such attacks usually occur, however, when patients are in their forties or fifties, owing to the delay of years between the time of infection and the onset of its neurological consequences. See The Merck Manual of Diagnosis and Therapy, 14th edition. Robert Berkow, gen. ed. (Rahway, N.J., 1982), pp. 1616–24

8

The younger boy was Charles Senior's namesake and the older one was his stepson. That was all the Lambeth authorities were interested in considering as they faced the question of what to do with two suddenly motherless children. Twelve days after Hannah's collapse, they compelled Charles Senior to take both boys into his terraced, late-Georgian house in a section of Kennington Road that Charles Booth rated as "well-to-do; inhabited by middle-class families who keep one or two servants." [34]

The exterior of the house was handsome. The interior was another story. Ugly pieces of horsehair furniture were complemented by a glass case containing a stuffed pike that was engorging itself on another pike. Presiding over this gruesome scene was Charles Senior's mistress, Louise, a tall, shapely, full-lipped, morose-looking woman of thirty with an abusive tongue, a terrible temper, an interest in hard liquor that matched her lover's, and an illegitimate son whom Charles Senior acknowledged as his. Louise's sole act of humanity in regard to her unwanted guests, *My Autobiography* maintains, was that she did not prevent them from attending a neighborhood school. But in their free hours at the end of the week, she made them scrub floors and clean knives while she and a lady friend sat in the parlor and drank. From time to time she aimed barbed remarks at Sydney, for whom she had taken an active dislike, and threatened to report him to Charles Senior.

That gentleman's hours, however, were largely spent elsewhere. In the evenings he generally appeared in time to get ready for the theater. Before departing, he would swallow six raw eggs in port wine. Then in the middle of the night he would reappear, almost always drunk. Yet at the breakfast table on Sunday mornings, before it was time for him to meet some of his chums, he was often charming and tender with Louise and genially expansive with Charlie and Sydney. When he was in the mood, he performed some of his favorite vaudeville turns, and by watching him "like a hawk" and "absorbing every action," Charlie enhanced his theatrical know-how and enjoyed himself in the bargain. In the most memorable of these Sunday morning shows, Charles Senior would wrap a towel around his head and chase Charlie around the table, crying, "I'm King Turkey Rhubarb." [35]

One Saturday night, Charlie took a long walk by himself through gas-lit neighborhoods he scarcely knew. Upon his return around midnight through Kennington Cross, he suddenly heard a harmonium and a clarinet playing a gay and beautiful tune called "The Honeysuckle and the Bee." The music was coming from the vestibule of a corner pub. He had never before realized that a melody could be played with so much feeling. But as he approached the vestibule, the blissful sense of beauty the music had aroused in him was shattered by the sight of the harmonium player's hideously scarred face and empty eye sockets and the clarinetist's drunken, embittered look.[36]

9

In addition to groups of wandering musicians, the entertainers who earned money in the streets of nineteenth-century London included exhibitors of portable Punch-and-Judy shows, card-trick conjurers, sad-faced clowns, and dancers who either threw themselves about in Highland flings, with bagpipe accompaniment, or made a wonderful racket performing clog dances in wooden-soled shoes.[37] After Hannah came out of Cane Hill on November 12 and reclaimed her sons from Charles Senior, Sydney quit school and took a job as a telegraph boy in a post office, while Charlie skipped school and earned pennies as a street dancer.

As he was going through "an ordinary street Arab's contortions one day," Chaplin told an interviewer for the *Glasgow Weekly Herald* in 1921, he became aware of a man watching him intently. "That boy is a born actor," he heard him say, and then the man spoke to him directly. "Would you like to be an actor?" William Jackson was the man's name, his game was managing a troupe of young dancers known as the Eight Lancashire Lads, and his encounter with Charlie had not been accidental. Jackson was acquainted with Charles Senior, and it was his enthusiastic account of Charlie's talents that had interested the manager in recruiting the boy into his troupe. The only question was, how would Hannah react to yet another fracturing of her family?[38]

If the frequency of her changes of residence was any indication, the lovers who enabled Hannah to rent decent lodgings quickly became disillusioned with her erratic behavior and dropped out of sight, leaving her at the mercy of that awesome figure of late-Victorian urban culture, the landlady. Relations between landladies and their lodgers, as Charles Booth described them, were not very different from those between village and manor in medieval times. With one hand, the landlady dispensed kindnesses; with the other, she laid down the law. In *Limelight*, Chaplin called up childhood memories of this creature's readiness to rent a room out from under a tenant if she was not paid promptly, and of her nosy concern about respectability. After her release from Cane Hill, Hannah had begun life anew in the quiet and modestly attractive backwater of Methley Street, where, according to Booth's *Life and Labour,* "working class comfort" predominated, along with "a large proportion of the lower middle class of tradesmen."* There, however, she may have soon run into trouble about the rent.

The deal that William Jackson proposed to Hannah was that as a Lancashire Lad Charlie would receive free meals and free lodging while on the road, and that every week she would receive half a crown. That was as much as she could earn in forty-two hours of work as a seamstress. Furthermore, Jackson turned out to be a family man and devoutly religious, and he promised that Charlie could live with him and his wife during the time it would take for him to master the Lads' clog-dancing drills. And so Hannah said yes, he could have her son.[39]

---

* In the fall of 1994, I paid a visit to the Chaplins' address in Methley Street and found workmen engaged in refurbishing its apartments. Although the rooms are small, they are certainly pleasant. Outside, a plaque attests to the fact that Charlie Chaplin once lived there.

3

THE POISONOUS WOUND

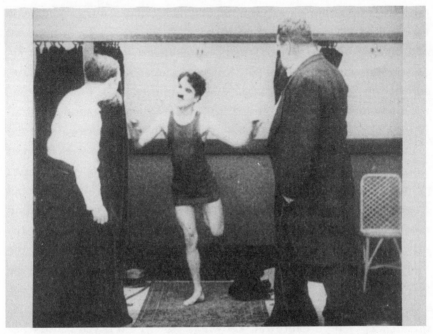

In The Cure *(1917), Chaplin made fun of the living-statue acts
that he recalled from his music hall days.*

Dᴜʀɪɴɢ the two years and four months that Charlie remained
with the Lancashire Lads, the troupe's tours took him into more music
halls than he could remember, where he learned far more than in the
schools he fleetingly attended here and there. Music halls, it might be
said, were his Eton College and his Harrow.

The years from 1890 to 1914 were the great era of the halls. Arthur
Symons was inspired to write poems about them, and Walter Sickert
did many paintings and pen-and-ink drawings of theaters in outlying

London locales, where the patrons were the "lads" of the district, the relations between the audience and the performers were closer and less formal, and the emotional atmosphere was warmer than in the glittering palaces of central London.[1] But no matter whether the hall was legendary, like the Argyle in Birkenhead, or lowly, like the Bedford in London, where audiences peered at the stage through clouds of foul-smelling tobacco smoke, the entertainment that was offered was prodigiously various.

Acrobats, high-wire performers, mesmerists, magicians, ventriloquists, musicians who could play thirty instruments in quick succession, animal acts, and men with astonishing memories—like the virtual automaton who spills out the answer to Robert Donat's question in Alfred Hitchcock's *The Thirty-nine Steps*—all had their moment of glory in the glare of the spotlight in one venue or another. Still other acts featured stern-faced Apache dancers, slick-as-grease escape artists (the greatest of whom was Harry Houdini, as he would prove in his sensational London debut at the Alhambra in 1901), and living statues, holding poses like the ones that Chaplin would parody while dressed in a bathing suit in *The Cure* (1917). And occasionally in some of the halls, the house lights were dimmed so that crude cinematographs could be shown.[2]

Among the many black-faced entertainers of the time, the most celebrated was George Chirgwin, known as "the White-Eyed Kaffir" because of the diamond-shaped patch of white makeup he wore across one of his eyes. A striking figure in black tights, knee-length white coat, and top hat tilted back, Chirgwin interlarded his patter with remarkably impolite asides. During Hannah's brief career as Lily Harley, she once appeared on the same bill with Chirgwin at the South London Palace. Her son Charlie seems to have been familiar with his work as well, especially with the routine in which he created an impression of a dancer by manipulating two clay pipes on a tin tray; in time that trick would evolve into the enduringly famous dance of the rolls in *The Gold Rush*.

Comic sketches set in pawnshops, lodging-house bedrooms, cheap restaurants, and seaside resorts were another standby of music hall entertainment. While many of them included verbal exchanges set to music, the actors depended mainly on dumbshow, or mumming. Some of the mummers also performed before family audiences in Christmas pantomimes, which had been a British institution for two hundred years. Typically, these entertainments began with a rather loose re-creation of a famous children's story—"Jack in the Beanstalk," perhaps, or "Babes in the Woods," or selected rhymes from *The Real Mother Goose*—in which music, spectacle, topical gags, and slapstick were fused. Some of the actors played women's roles, some of the actresses played men's, and children appeared as animals. With the conclusion of this extravaganza, the show evolved into a Harlequinade, featuring a cast of characters whose theatrical lineage could be traced in most cases to Italian masked comedy of the fifteenth century: Joey the Clown, an incorrigible thief; aged Pantaloon, who often was blamed for the Clown's misdeeds; a blustering Policeman; a handsome Swell; gay and spangled Harlequin, dancing about with the lightness of a gazelle, but walking with a peculiar, henlike hop that Charlie Chaplin surely found amusing, and forever brandishing his fabulous wooden bat, which not only possessed the transformative powers of a magic wand, but was useful as a weapon, just as the tramp's cane in Chaplin's comedies would prove to be; and last but not least, enchanting Columbine, Harlequin's fairylike companion.

Year after year, Christmas pantomimes were staged in theaters all over Britain. But their most hallowed home was London's Drury Lane. Two top-drawer music hall comedians, diminutive Dan Leno and large and beefy Herbert Campbell, worked together at the Drury Lane every year from 1888 to 1903, and would doubtless have continued to do so for many more years had they not both died in 1904, Campbell in an accident and Leno from a brain tumor. The contrast in physical type on which their comedy thrived would be milked for many a laugh by Chaplin in the movies he made with gigantic Eric Campbell and with hefty Mack Swain. As for the movie career of slender, pucker-faced Stan Laurel (known in his English music hall days as Stan Jefferson), it would not really take off until he teamed up with burly Oliver Hardy.[3]

The wild and inconsequent yet closely observant humor for which Dan Leno was famous, and the abrupt shifts of mood and tragicomic sense of life which reflected the mental anguish that left him fluttering, in his final years, just outside the cage of madness, were on the same wavelength as the young Chaplin's quivering imagination, notwithstanding the ungenerous attempt of the author of *My Autobiography* to convince the world that Leno had been of no importance to him. "I never saw Leno in his prime," he said; indeed, he insisted that his knowledge of him was largely secondhand, through his mother.

In Max Beerbohm's tribute to Leno, however, can be discerned the beleaguered but indomitable spirit of Chaplin's comic persona:

> The moment Dan Leno skipped upon the stage, we were aware that here was a man utterly unlike anyone else we had seen. Despite the rusty top hat and broken umbrella and red nose of tradition, here was a creature apart, radiating an ethereal essence all his own. He compelled us not to take our eyes off him, not to miss a word that he said. Not that we needed any compulsion. Dan Leno's was not one of those personalities which dominate us by awe, subjugating us against our will. He was of that other, finer kind: the lovable kind. He had, in a higher degree than any other actor that I have ever seen, the indefinable quality of being sympathetic. I defy any one not to have loved Dan Leno at first sight. The moment he capered on, with that air of wild determination, squirming in every limb with some deep grievance that must be outpoured, all hearts were his. That face puckered with cares, whether they were the cares of the small shopkeeper . . . or the lodger; that face of a baby-monkey, yet ever liable to relax its mouth into a sudden wide grin and to screw up its eyes to vanishing point over some little triumph wrested from Fate, the tyrant; that poor little battered personage, so "put upon," yet so plucky with his squeaking voice and his sweeping gestures; bent but not broken; faint but pursuing; incarnate of the will to live in a world not at all worth living in—surely all hearts went always out to Dan Leno, with warm corners in them reserved to him for ever and ever.[4]

A world not at all worth living in. Two other comedians whom young Charlie admired were bedeviled by that idea. Frank Coyne appeared gay and outgoing whenever Charlie spoke to him offstage. Unfortunately, his bonhomie was a mask. One afternoon in the bathroom of a rented flat, he cut his throat with such vehement strokes that he all but decapitated himself. The somewhat less bloody suicide of the celebrated French comic known as Marceline took place to the strains of a musical accompaniment, which was altogether typical of his Gallic flair.

Charlie became familiar with Marceline's work when the Lancashire Lads were picked to play the parts of the cats and dogs in a presentation of *Cinderella* at the splendidly proportioned Hippodrome in London. In the show's biggest production number, the stage floor sank from view and water flooded over it. Pretty girls marched into the pool in military formation and disappeared beneath the surface—or so it seemed. Next, Marceline entered, dressed in disheveled evening wear, sporting a top hat and carrying a fishing rod. He baited the hook with a diamond necklace and cast the line into the water. When nothing happened, he chucked in a few diamond bracelets and admired the splash. Finally, he felt a tug on the line. With an outburst of comic effort involving his entire body, he landed his inexplicable catch—a toy poodle. The poodle at once began to imitate everything Marceline did; if Marceline stood on his head, the poodle stood on its head. From first to last, the scene was utterly zany, and Charlie and the other Lads loved every moment of it. Beneath the surface of the pool in the Frenchman's mind, however, lay things that he was unable to laugh at. In a New York apartment in the 1920s, he finally put a pistol to his head and pulled the trigger, while a phonograph was playing "Moonlight and Roses."[5]

The handsome, dignified, surprisingly youthful Bransby Williams was yet another large figure in young Charlie's new life. With amazing dexterity, Williams transformed himself in the course of a program into Uriah Heep, Bill Sikes, and a host of other Dickens characters. As Charlie watched his performances from the wings, he resolved to ape them. Wearing an old gray wig and carrying a stick, he was soon tottering about backstage as if he were the old man in *The Old Curiosity Shop* who could not recognize the death of Little Nell. Eventually, he was allowed to present his act in front of paying customers. But the reception he received was derisive, and that was the end of that.

Bransby Williams also fired up his curiosity about Dickens's novels, especially *Oliver Twist*. Buying a copy of the book, he unexpectedly discovered the Cruikshank illustrations. That these "vividly terrible images," as Henry James called them, would always mean as much to him as Dickens's prose is evident in the reference in *My Autobiography* to "these sepia Dickens characters that moved in such a strange Cruikshankian world" and in a late characterization of the movies he had made as "caricatures of Cruikshank's drawings."[6]

2

With one of his companions in the Jackson troupe, Tommy Bristol, Charlie thought up a comedy act to be known as "Bristol and Chaplin, the Millionaire Tramps," in which both boys would wear tramp whiskers and diamond rings. When nothing came of the idea, Charlie came up with another. During a matinee performance of *Cinderella*, he improvised a bit of attention-getting business. Disguised as a cat, he sniffed at the rear end of one of the dogs and winked at the audience by pulling a string inside his costume. Then he smelled the proscenium and lifted his leg. To his chagrin, the stage manager forbade him to repeat these antics for fear that the Lord Chamberlain would close down the theater.[7]

Despite his abiding loneliness and his resentment of Jackson's stern discipline, a creative zest was driving young Charlie. Imagine, then, his astonishment when Jackson dropped him from the troupe on April 13, 1901, at the conclusion of *Cinderella*'s three-and-a-half-month run. He discovered he had his mother to thank. During weekend get-togethers, she had fussed about how pale and thin he looked, and in her madness she concluded that clog dancing was affecting his lungs. When she expressed her worries to Jackson, he became angry and took out his feelings by firing Charlie. Ordinarily, Charlie would have turned for sympathy to his brother. But on April 6, Sydney had shipped out as a steward on the first of half a dozen ocean voyages he would make in the course of the next two years.[8]

Perhaps it was because he missed Sydney that he looked for Charles Senior in The Three Stags one evening. This Kennington Road watering hole was one of the entertainer's favorite haunts.

> I opened the saloon door just a few inches [Chaplin would recall], and there he was, sitting in a corner! I was about to leave [out of last-minute uncertainty, presumably, about the sort of reception he might be given], but his face lit up and he beckoned me to him. I was surprised at such a welcome, for he had never been demonstrative. He looked very ill: his eyes were sunken, and his body had swollen to an enormous size. He rested one hand, Napoleon-like, in his waist coat, as if to ease his difficult breathing. That evening he was most solicitous, inquiring after Mother and Sydney, and before I left, took me in his arms and for the first time kissed me.

Three weeks later he was taken to St. Thomas's Hospital by a group of his friends, who had to reduce him to drunken befuddlement in order to entice him there. When he realized where he was, he struggled wildly to get away, but there was no strength left in him. Even though hospital attendants drained sixteen quarts of liquid from his knee, the relief it provided him from his dropsy was merely symptomatic. He was also suffering from cirrhosis of the liver, and within a few days he was dead.[9]

3

Hannah was now being helped by seamen's allotments from Sydney. Charlie, too, augmented her income with money earned in various ways. His first job after leaving the Jackson troupe consisted of walking through pubs with a wistful expression on his face that he hoped would persuade the customers to buy the flowers he was selling. Whenever he paused at a table, he always bowed and said, "Thank you, sir," no matter how rudely he was treated, even as Calvero would in the scene in *Limelight* in which the old entertainer is reduced to singing in pubs and then passing the hat. Although the money Charlie earned was surprisingly substantial, Hannah made him give up the work because, once again, she was worried about him. In the sort of seductively pleasant surroundings that Charles Senior had loved, a growing boy might develop a taste for strong drink.[10]

Between his twelfth and his fourteenth birthdays, Charlie's places of employment included a barbershop (where he absorbed the techniques that the Jewish barber would display *con brio* in *The Great Dictator*); a stationery store (did it resemble the one that figures in *Limelight?*); a doctor's office; a glass factory; a chandler's shop; and a printing plant, in which his fears of being swallowed by a gigantic Wharfedale press foreshadowed the fate of Charlie the factory worker in *Modern Times*. In addition to drawing pay from full-time jobs, Hannah's hustling son exhibited "the strong element of the merchant" in his personality by offering dance lessons on the side for five shillings a week. On other occasions he stood on a wooden box in the street and hawked old clothes, just as his drunken grandmother had. Old clothes played an important part in the class drama of Victorian life. Since the poor could not easily afford to buy new clothes, the coats and trousers, the dresses and stockings that had worn out their use in the upper classes were passed down to them via secondhand merchants, thence to the abject poor, and finally to the bums at the very bottom of the social heap, becoming ever more disreputable-looking in the process. The baggy pants, the tight coat, the oversized shoes, and the battered bowler that made up the most famous costume in movie history might have been culled from the heaps of hand-me-downs that Chaplin had sold as a boy in South London.[11]

4

Three Pownall Terrace: to no other address of his youth did Chaplin refer as often, either in conversation or in writing, and the main scene in *My Autobiography*'s artfully shaped, possibly ghost-assisted "Prelude" is set there. It was as if Pownall Terrace constituted the key to his formative years.

Inasmuch as "Prelude" bears a resemblance to the opening of a movie, it can be described in movie terminology. In a voice-over Chaplin says that in the days before Westminster Bridge was open, Kennington Road was only a bridle path. After 1750 a new road was laid down that connected the bridge to a direct link to Brighton, and some fine houses fronted by iron-grill balconies were erected. The occupants of these houses could at one time have glimpsed the royal coaches of George IV and his entourage en route to Brighton.

The first person to appear, however, is young Charlie Chaplin, standing outside a Kennington Road pub called the Tankard. It is Sunday, and he is watching some of the most illustrious music hall entertainers in England, resplendently dressed in checkered suits and gray bowlers, with diamond rings on their fingers and diamond pins in their ties, entering the lounge bar for a final quick one and then departing for their midday meal.

When the last of the entertainers has come and gone, Charlie returns to the "row of old derelict houses" on Pownall Terrace and mounts the "rickety" stairs at Number Three to his garret home. Charlie's mother is there, seated at the window, gazing out. She turns and smiles weakly at her son. The voice-over says that at this time she was not yet thirty-seven. But in fact the scene about to take place had to have occurred in the first days of May 1903, when Hannah was going on thirty eight and Charlie had just turned fourteen.

The camera eye reveals the room and all its telling details. It is a little over twelve feet square, but seems smaller. The ceiling is slanted and seems low. The table against the wall is crowded with dirty plates and teacups, and in the corner, snug against the lower wall, is an old bed that Hannah had painted white and that she and Charlie presumably shared. Between the bed and the window is a small fire grate, and at the foot of the bed is an old armchair. Chaplin's narrative voice declares that the armchair "unfolded and became a single bed upon which my brother Sydney slept. But now Sydney was away at sea."

Charlie is shocked by his mother's appearance. She is thin and haggard, and her eyes have the look of someone in torment. She speaks to her son apathetically. "Why don't you run along to the McCarthys'?" Charlie is on the verge of tears. "Because I want to stay with you," he says. Hannah turns and looks vacantly out of the window. "You run along to the McCarthys' and get your dinner—there's nothing here for you." Charlie feels the reproach in her tone. "I'll go if you want me to," he says weakly. She smiles wanly and strokes his hand. "Yes, yes, you run along." He pleads with her to let him stay. She insists on his going. "So I went with a feeling of guilt," Chaplin's narrative voice confesses, "leaving her sitting in that miserable garret alone, little realizing that within the next few days a terrible fate awaited her." [12]

The prominence that Chaplin accorded this scene by plucking it out of chronological order and placing it first in his life story lends decisive support to Thomas Burke's intuitive certainty, expressed more than thirty years before the appearance of *My Autobiography*, that at the age of fourteen his friend Charlie had suffered a blow of obsessionary importance to him. Burke's discussion of this belief would occur at the end of an exceptionally vivid piece of word portraiture in the stylish essay he published on Chaplin in 1932.

Tiny hands forever fluttering, a sweet smile forever flashing from a full-lipped, mobile mouth, a gentle voice forever sending out nervous, staccato sentences—these were some of the compelling characteristics that were bound together in Chaplin's electric personality, Burke began. After being exposed to his cascading bursts of agreeably acid and aerated talk, his million-volt energy, and his body movements as piquant and precise as a ballerina's, otherwise interesting and brilliant people seemed "unaccountably dull." Nevertheless, anyone who really studied Chaplin ultimately became conscious of "a dark, troubled quality." The comedian's gaiety was not spontaneous. For all of his exuberance, he could not escape being "difficult and reserved."

In photos of him as a youth, Burke continued, one could see in his eyes the same dark, haunted look that distinguished Chaplin the man. On the cause of the look Burke was unwilling to comment. But he was willing to pinpoint its origin in time, and to accord it a cinematic as well as a real-life importance.

> At some time of that first decade [of the century] he was in some way very dreadfully hurt . . . by some one blow; and the poison of the wound went right into his being. I have never asked him to tell me what the hurt was. I am certain that my guess is right. But out of that hurt has come something that all the world recognizes. It constitutes his knowledge; it is what, in every film, he is trying to tell us. On the screen he is still the wounded boy of fourteen, trying to hide his hurt by self-consolatory antics; and every film of his, from the early crude things . . . down to the more sensitive and considered productions . . . asks help for the young and the wounded.[13]

Hannah's collapse in the spring of the year that Charlie turned fourteen brought his disordered childhood to a horrifying climax. Only in periods of unpredictable length had he ever been able to rely on the loving attentiveness, the theatrical flair, and the other qualities that he worshipped in his mother. Always the specter of her instability, the embarrassment of her oddities, the sight and sound of her torment returned to haunt him. At some point he also lost faith in the romantic stories she had told about her late-adolescent years, and in her claim that the drunken entertainer for whom he was named was really his father. As for Charles Senior, he had steadfastly refused to assume parental responsibility for his putative son—except very briefly, when legally ordered to do so. Furthermore, no dependable father-substitute had emerged from the succession of men who temporarily took up with Hannah.

Constant changes of residence, occasional confinements in institutions, and exceedingly spotty schooling created additional incoherences in his life. While the degraded social conditions of the outcast poor of South London were only observed by him and not directly experienced, the psychological pressures he was placed under were appalling. That his zestful spirit and drive to succeed were not broken by his ordeal is a tribute to his mental hardihood.

But if he emerged unbroken from the treacherous world of his child-hood, he was not unscarred. The least attractive characteristics of Chaplin the man—his self-pity, his anger, his cruelty, his mania for taking total control of the lives of young women who caught his eye—must have been gathering strength within him all the while.

Total-control impulses can likewise be discerned in the way he ran his film studio and in his genial habit of giving performances as a means of managing social friendships. For decades, he dazzled dinner parties with his imitations of everything under the sun, whether animal, vegeta-ble, or mineral.* He was devoted as well to playing charades, and he helped his friend, Max Eastman, devise a fiendishly difficult speech-making game in which one had to choose one's identity from the slips of paper in one hat and the subject of the address one was obliged to give from the slips in another. To the end of his days, Eastman fondly recalled Chaplin's lecture, as Carrie Nation, on "Some Doubts as to the Origin of Species" and his discourse as a "Toothless Old Veteran" on "The Benefits of Birth Control." No matter how demanding the imita-tive task, he could bring it off wonderfully well.[14]

But who, exactly, was Charlie Chaplin? Behind the masks of his social performances, was anybody there? Thomas Burke addressed that ques-tion:

He is first and last an actor, possessed by this, that or other. He lives only in a role, and without it he is lost. As he cannot find the inner Chaplin, there is nothing for him, at grievous moments, to retire into; he is compelled to merge himself, or be merged, in an imagined and superimposed life.[15]

---

* Cf. movie director Michael Powell's recollection of a Hollywood party chez Chaplin in 1952: "Chaplin was a delightful host, and was acting all the time. He often got up to make a point, or to mimic somebody, or dance. At one point, he was hanging desperately on to the door handle, trying to keep an imaginary intruder outside, and barking like a West Highland terrier." Michael Powell, Million Dollar Movie (New York, 1995), p. 205.

Having been unable, as he was growing up, to count on the protection of his mother, or of his father, whoever he was, he had taken refuge within himself. Not, to be sure, in any core self, but in the assumption of roles, in the imagining of other lives. In his adulthood, these habits of mind persisted. And at the top of his creative form they led to the making over of the world in movies, featuring dramatic rescues, outbursts of madness, and other rearranged legacies of a heartbreaking childhood.

There is film evidence that suggests that no one in our own time has had a finer intuitive grasp of the transcendent nature of Chaplin's achievement than a comedian who for a number of reasons, ranging from multiple talents to personal notoriety, seems very like him. Thus in the last of the several instances that bear upon Chaplin's life in Woody Allen's superbly satirical fable about the psychotic Leonard Zelig and his multiple personalities, Allen has Saul Bellow speak as follows about Zelig's feat of flying over the Atlantic upside down, even though he had never before flown a plane: "The thing was paradoxical, because what enabled him to perform was his ability to transform himself; therefore his sickness was also at the root his salvation. And I think it's interesting to view the thing that way, that it was his very disorder that made a hero of him."

For a very long time—as children measure time—the young Chaplin's despair about his mother had been tempered by hope. Someday, by a miracle, she might get better. But then he came face-to-face with the shattering truth: her insanity was irremediable. Surely this realization constituted the dreadful hurt resulting from some one blow of which Burke spoke. Behind the appeals for help for the young and the wounded that would powerfully affect so many viewers of Chaplin's pictures over the years lay the tortured sessions in the night court of his sleep—or his sleeplessness—in which he shaped and reshaped the sickening sense of defeat and solitariness that swept over him in the spring of 1903.

5

Hannah's psychotic break occurred on May 5. Chapter 4 of *My Autobiography* sets forth an infinitely sorrowful, gently protective version of what happened. At the Pownall Terrace gate, Charlie was stopped by some children of the neighborhood, who informed him that his mother had gone mad. Apparently, she had been knocking at all the doors, giving away pieces of coal and saying that they were birthday presents for the children. Charlie ran to her, fell on his knees, buried his face in her lap, and burst into uncontrollable weeping. "What's wrong?" she said, stroking his head. "You're not well," Charlie burst out between sobs. "I was looking for Sydney," she said weakly. "They're keeping him away from me." "Oh, Mummy, don't talk like that! Don't! Don't!" Charlie sobbed.

Finally, he summoned a doctor, who examined Hannah and explained to Charlie that she was "suffering from malnutrition." In the infirmary, he said, she would be properly fed. The building was a mile away, and Charlie escorted his mother there. En route, she staggered from side to side of the road, and the people who passed them "must have thought Mother was drunk." Actually, her problem was "weakness." At the infirmary, a young doctor kindly said, "All right, Mrs. Chaplin, come this way." She submitted obediently.[16]

The lunacy-reception records of the Lambeth Board of Guardians tell a much less passive story. Charlie is quoted as having informed the doctor by way of background information that his mother had been "mentioning a lot of people who are dead," that she fancied she "could see them looking out of the window," that she had talked to "imaginary people" and had kept "going into strangers' rooms, etc." After examining her, the infirmary doctor stated: "She is very noisy and incoherent, praying and swearing by turns—singing and shouting—she says the floor is the river Jordan and she cannot cross it." The doctor emphasized in addition that at times she was "violent and destructive."[17]

Besides absorbing visions of his mother's violence and madness into his creative imagination, Chaplin at some point became convinced that in his personal life as well he was destined to reenact her tragedy. In *My Father, Charlie Chaplin* (1960), Charles Chaplin, Jr., revealed that Hannah's mental illness

preyed greatly on my father's mind, for he spoke of it often. . . . His light treatment of it did not deceive [either me or my brother]. "Thank God you're born with two hands and two feet and two legs and one head," he would say. "That you're normal, became something you know. . . . And of course you could have been this other way. There's something in the family, something. . . ." He spoke jokingly but he would then knock on wood as though the very mention of that family specter had brought it nearer than was comfortable to him.

Rollie Totheroh, who worked behind Chaplin's cameras for thirty-eight years, had a similar opinion. What old Charlie figured on for years and years, Totheroh told an interviewer in 1978, was that he, too, "would eventually go insane." [18]

6

Sydney's ship, the *Kinfairns Castle*, reached England on May 9, four days after Hannah's hospitalization, and Charlie met his train at Waterloo Station. After listening to the awful news about their mother, Sydney had some better news for Charlie. He intended to quit the sea and become a dramatic actor. Furthermore, his plans included his kid brother. With the twenty pounds he had made conducting sweepstakes and lotteries on shipboard, Sydney figured he could support both himself and Charlie for four months, while each of them looked for theatrical work. Charlie was elated. Since being fired from the Lancashire Lads, he had held many jobs, yet he had never abandoned his aim of becoming a theatrical headliner, one way or another.[19]

On learning that Hannah had again been transferred to Cane Hill, the two boys went to see her. She was very pale and deeply depressed. Not until January 1904 would she be sufficiently lucid to leave the asylum. But the light of her precarious sanity soon dimmed. On March 18, 1905, she reentered Cane Hill, for a stay that lasted seven and a half years. Charlie heard of her recommitment while on tour in the Midlands.

That he had managed to break out of the pack of England's unemployed actors was due first of all to his aggressiveness. Generally, he tried to avoid speaking to strangers. Nevertheless, he had had the gumption to launch his quest for employment on the stage by badgering the clerks in one of the best-known theatrical agencies in London, H. Blackmore's. Finally, the head of the firm gave him a letter of introduction that led to an interview in early June 1903 with C. E. Hamilton, the manager of the London offices of the internationally famous impresario Charles Frohman. As Stan Laurel later observed, "Charlie as a performer and as a person, too, was a wonderful mix—a shy, timid man who kept getting up courage to do the most wonderful, adventurous things." [20]

Hamilton could not help exclaiming at how small Chaplin was. It was a reaction which, over the years, countless numbers of people would have. Witness Alistair Cooke's description of him in the early 1930s: "Chaplin could [not] have been much over five feet. . . . He certainly is a tiny man." Actually, his full height was five feet four inches. But his astonishingly small feet and hands—"as exquisite as those of Madame la Marquise," in Thomas Burke's words—and the economical grace of his body movements combined to create a general impression of out-of-the-ordinary diminutiveness. [21]

His grace as well as his good looks and charm were presumably not lost on C. E. Hamilton. He offered Charlie the part of Billy the pageboy in a road-company revival, due to open in October, of an enormously popular dramatization of Sherlock Holmes's adventures by the renowned actor-director William Gillette and Holmes's creator, Sir Arthur Conan Doyle. In the meantime, Hamilton added, a suitable role for Charlie was available in a new play called *Jim: A Romance of Cockayne* that the Frohman organization was staging. The author was another actor-director, H. A. Saintsbury, whom the organization had also signed to play the title role in the new production of *Sherlock Holmes*. Hamilton then addressed the matter of Charlie's pay. If Saintsbury gave him a part in *Jim*, he told him, he would be paid two pounds ten shillings a week, and the same salary would obtain in *Sherlock Holmes*. Charlie never batted an eye. "I must consult my brother about the terms," he grandly announced, and Hamilton burst out laughing. [22]

Saintsbury met with Charlie in the quietly luxurious setting of the Green Room Club in Leicester Square, of which Saintsbury was a member. Born into a financially secure family, educated at St. John's College, Hurstpierpoint, and quite possibly homosexual, Saintsbury was so charmed by Charlie that he dispensed with a formal tryout. With Sydney's help, Charlie was able to memorize his lines in *Jim* within three days. Sydney also went to Hamilton's office and asked him—without success—to raise Charlie's salary. He had not had any luck in landing an acting job himself, so he became, in effect, Charlie's agent, and continued to play this role even after his own employment picture brightened. Indeed, his devotion to his younger brother's interests would never flag. In the acid opinion of the "hobo" author Jim Tully, who worked as a screenwriter on *The Gold Rush*, the proverbial closeness of the brothers Chaplin was based on Sydney's slavish acceptance of Charlie's tyranny. "Without Charlie's capacity," Tully said, "Sydney remained a varnished cockney. Unlike the Oriental Charlie, he was of light complexion with slick hair parted in the middle, and the manner of a promoted bank clerk." [23]

Jim was the cliché-riddled story of an aristocrat suffering from amnesia who finds himself living in a garret with a young flower girl and a newspaper boy. The play opened on July 6, was roasted to a fare-thee-well by the critics, and closed ten days later—at which point the Frohman organization speeded up the rehearsals of the *Sherlock Holmes* revival and gave it its pre-tour premiere in a London theater on July 27.

In the original presentation of the play on Broadway, as well as in the first London production, the title part had been taken by the thriller's Connecticut Yankee coauthor, William Gillette, whose distinguished Puritan forebears included the leader of the band of settlers who founded Hartford. Gillette's lean, handsome face, set off by a deerstalker cap, had established the quintessential image of Holmes's presence in both the English and the American minds. H. A. Saintsbury, however, had an equally long and sensitive face, while his high, domed forehead appeared to be bulging with deductive power. From the very start, his portrayal of Holmes played to packed houses. In the course of forty weeks on the road with the show, Charlie saw some parts of Britain that he had not visited with the Lancashire Lads and learned a lot from Saintsbury about the rudiments of "straight" acting. Yet his excited sense of widening horizons was punctuated by bouts of loneliness and melancholia. Without the comforting letters that he regularly received from the dutiful Sydney, who was working as a bartender in London, he might have been moved to quit. Thus when the actor who was playing Count Von Stalberg suddenly left the cast, Charlie at once suggested Sydney as his replacement. For the last six months of the tour, the two brothers rejoiced in being together again. [24]

The Saintsbury company disbanded in June 1904. This did not mean, however, that *Sherlock Holmes* was no longer considered a theatrical gold mine. The following fall, the Frohman office mounted three new productions of the play. Sydney failed to obtain a role in any of them, but Charlie played Billy in the so-called Midland Company until the end of its run in the spring of 1905. Four months later, a seedy impresario named Harry Yorke purchased the rights to *Sherlock Holmes* and on the cheap assembled a company. Both Charlie and Sydney were engaged by him, at sharply reduced salaries. For six weeks, the company did its inadequate best to entertain audiences in the industrial north. And with every passing day Charlie became progressively less popular with the rest of the cast as a result of his inability to restrain himself from telling the director how Saintsbury and the Frohman office had handled various dramatic problems. Had he not received an offer of another job that enabled him to quit the show at the end of September, the cast members whom he had most offended with his know-it-all manner might have taken steps to shut him up.[25]

While the terms of the new job were outlined in a telegram from William Postance, the stage manager of Frohman's prime London property, the Duke of York's Theater in St. Martin's Lane, the offer had been authorized by William Gillette, no less. Fresh from his latest triumph on Broadway in *The Admirable Crichton*, Gillette had come back to England and was currently appearing at the Duke of York's in a new comedy, *Clarice*. Because he himself was the author of the play as well as its star, and because of the presence in the title role of the enchantingly beautiful Marie Doro—who would later appear in movies—the advance ticket sales had been good. But the critics had not cared for the play, to put it mildly, and in an outburst of cultural superciliousness they had taken further exception to Gillette's New England twang. Justifiably offended, the actor-playwright fashioned a sarcastic rejoinder in the form of a curtain raiser to *Clarice* called *The Painful Predicament of Sherlock Holmes*, in which Holmes could not possibly have spoken like a New Englander because he had no lines.

As the curtain rises, a screaming madwoman is struggling to enter the detective's Baker Street lodgings. Billy the pageboy tries to keep her out, but when he is unable to do so, Holmes scribbles a note and hands it to him, and Billy goes off into the night. The woman pours out her grievances in a wild torrent of words while Holmes ruminatively puffs on his pipe and walks about. Finally, Billy returns with two policemen and exclaims to his employer, "It was the *right* asylum, sir." Besides assigning himself the role of Holmes, Gillette persuaded the famous actress Irene Vanbrugh to play the madwoman. But when it came to casting the part of Billy, he turned to Postance for advice. On the basis of Charlie's previous work under Frohman auspices, Postance recommended him. Conceivably, Postance also knew that Charlie was the son of a onetime music hall comedienne who had also been confined in an asylum.*

Although the critics professed to be charmed by *The Painful Predicament*, it did not change their minds about *Clarice*, so in mid-October the disappointed Gillette took both plays off the boards and substituted that tried-and-true crowd pleaser, *Sherlock Holmes*, with himself in the title role, Marie Doro as Alice Faulkner, and Charlie as Billy. Some of the dramatic techniques for which Gillette was renowned could hardly have failed to interest Charlie. In an age in which stylized modes of speaking still prevailed on the stage, whether the play was a drawing-room comedy, a thriller, or a Shakespearean tragedy, the laconic Gillette had pioneered a more natural delivery. He was an innovator, too, in his development of the "fade-out," a gradual lowering of the lights before the lowering of the curtain. This excitement-heightening stratagem would be exploited in years to come in countless plays by Gillette's rivals, while D. W. Griffith, whose youthful stage career had included an appearance in one of Gillette's plays, was only the most notable of the early movie directors who adapted the "fade-out" to cinematic uses and called it the "dissolve."

But it was for personal, not technical, reasons that Charlie was riveted by the final scene in the Gillette revival of *Sherlock Holmes*. The detective and Alice Faulkner are alone on stage, at long last. After brusquely assuring Alice that his relationship with her has been strictly business, Holmes starts to leave the room. Alice stops him by saying that she doesn't believe him. "Why not?" asks Holmes. "From the way you speak—from the way you—look—from all sorts of things!" she replies.

* In *Limelight*, the impresario Mr. Postant, played by Nigel Bruce, displays the same qualities of kindliness and understanding that Charlie seems to have valued in Postance.

Holmes moves a step closer to her. "Your powers—of observation—are somewhat remarkable, Miss Faulkner—and your deduction is quite correct! I suppose—indeed I know—that I love you. I love you." Alice draws near to him as Holmes continues, "I know that no such person as I, seared, drugged, poisoned, almost at an end, should ever dream of being a part of your sweet life! . . . There is every reason why we should say goodbye and farewell! There is every reason—" Alice interrupts him by placing her right hand on Holmes's breast. He slowly looks down into her face. His left arm gradually curves around her. As the lights fade, Alice is resting in Holmes's arms, her head on his breast.[26]

The detailed description in *My Autobiography* of Marie Doro's delicate, pouting lips, regular white teeth, adorable chin, raven hair, and dark-brown eyes would testify to the fact that Charlie's daily closeness to her at the Duke of York's had had a heady effect on his sixteen-year-old sensibility. But because he lacked the courage to say anything to her other than "Good evening" as they passed one another on the stairs backstage, she left England at the end of the two-month run of the play without any awareness that she had made a conquest. In the role of Alice Faulkner, on the other hand, her womanly intuition had enabled her to perceive how Holmes felt about her. The tongue-tied, lovesick Charlie, watching from the wings as Holmes and Alice embraced, must have been utterly miserable at the great detective's good fortune.

7

While struggling to forget Marie, Charlie turned for the first time to the consolations of paid sex. Whores, after all, were no challenge to his courage. Professionally speaking, he also had to lower his sights. Except for Harry Yorke, who was taking his third-rate production of *Sherlock Holmes* on tour again and who hired him to play Billy, not a single producer in the legitimate theater showed interest in his talents. Nevertheless, a sizable entry about his career appeared in 1906 in a prestigious stage directory called *The Green Room Book*. An actor as young and unknown as Charlie would not have been included unless he had an influential sponsor who vouched for his talents in no uncertain terms. Charlie's sponsor, almost surely, was H. A. Saintsbury, who had remained in close touch with him since the end of their professional association two years before. If there is a suggestion here that their relationship was sexual, there is no evidence to support it.

Thanks to Sydney, who had talked himself into a position with a newly formed music hall company that was mounting a sketch called *Repairs*, the company offered a part to Charlie. In the role of a spectacularly inept assistant plumber, he helped other awkward employees of the house-decorating firm of Spoiler and Messit wreak inadvertent havoc in a middle-class villa. This sort of situation was familiar to music hall patrons, but they laughed at *Repairs* all the same, even as movie audiences would appreciate Chaplin's replay of its farcical destructiveness in *Work* (1915).

Shortly after his seventeenth birthday, Charlie heard that the comedian Will Murray planned to tour the provinces with a collection of sketches called *Casey's Court Circus*, and that the impresario Harry Cadle, who was backing Murray, was looking for approximately a dozen boys who could sing and dance and had experience as pantomimists. As street urchins who clown around in the alley beside the home of a certain Mrs. Casey (played by Murray), the boys would poke fun at famous adults, living and dead. The crudeness of Murray's sense of humor clearly meant, Charlie realized, that *Casey's Court Circus* would never be booked into topflight halls, so when his bid to join the troupe was accepted, he had second thoughts, he told Rose Wilder Lane in 1915, about signing on. "I who had been a hit in a West End theater acting [in] a low vulgar comedy in dirty fourth-rate houses . . . I said savagely that I would not do it."[27] But in the end he could not resist a salary of two pounds five shillings a week, plus a promised increase of five shillings after the first month and a half.

There was not much he could do with his minor part in a parody of Dick Turpin's ride to York except to run and run and skid around corners with one leg raised, more or less as he would do in the movies. But when he was assigned the lead role in a takeoff on the current music hall sensation "Dr." Walford Bodie, he was able to transform the broadly sketched characterization that Murray had in mind into a more recognizable—and more devastating—portrait of a humbug. Bodie, an erstwhile ventriloquist and card-trick performer turned mesmerist and miracle healer, had brooding eyes that supposedly were the source of his hypnotic powers and a V-shaped waxed mustache with a wing span wider than his cheekbones. In nightly appearances on stage, he had "cured" hundreds of cases of seemingly hopeless paralysis, while in his hypnotic demonstrations he ordered the men and women who were his subjects to go cackling about the stage like barnyard fowl, deliver political stump speeches, or sing arias from *Madame Butterfly*.

Murray, who had caught Bodie's act more than once, was able to answer Charlie's probing questions about his mannerisms. Charlie then proceeded to get them down pat by practicing for hours in front of a mirror. Murray announced that he wanted him to wear burlesque makeup and a top hat that came down over his ears. Charlie, however, was determined to create a serious impression—for the first half a minute or so. After carefully studying a photograph of Bodie, he stealthily entered the theater on opening night and made up his face to resemble him exactly. He also stuffed paper in the brim of his top hat, so that it fit his head properly. Once on stage, he advanced slowly and majestically toward the footlights. Here was a deeply learned man, his movements proclaimed. Deliberately, he hung his cane over his arm—by the wrong end. The cane clattered to the floor. As if startled, Charlie stooped to pick it up, and as he did so his hat came off. He grasped it and put it on again, but not before the paper wadding in the brim fell out. The result was that virtually his entire head disappeared from view within the hat.

"A great burst of laughter came from the audience," Chaplin remembered. "When pushing the hat back, I went deliberately on with my serious lines, the crowd roared, held its sides, shrieked with mirth till it gasped. The more serious I was, the funnier it struck the audience. I came off at last, pursued by howls of laughter and wild applause, which called me back again. I had made a hit." From that point on, he was recognized as the most talented lad in the show and his salary was raised to three pounds a week. In a photograph of the troupe made for advertising purposes, he is sitting next to Murray near the center, wearing a three-piece suit, a bowler, and a calm, collected look on his face.[28]

The care that Charlie had invested in making his satirization of "Dr." Bodie's hypnotic manner as accurate as possible was indicative of something more than his superior understanding—as compared to Will Murray's—of the art of making people laugh. A painfully inhibited, sexually ravenous young man with a childhood history of feelings of helplessness about his mother was quite taken by the fantasy that a man of superior mind could utterly dominate members of the opposite sex by usurping their willpower. George du Maurier's novel about the Scotch-Irish artist's model Trilby O'Ferrall and the dirty, sinister musician who, with a wave of his hand and a look of his eye, could turn her into a singer capable of thrilling audiences the world over, and make her love him at his bidding with a strange, unreal, factitious love that was like his own love for himself turned inside out as if reflected from a mirror, had become a best-seller on both sides of the Atlantic upon its publication in 1894. But that response represented the mere beginning of the *Trilby* mania. A raging storm of controversial commentary that lasted for years made Svengali and Trilby household names throughout the English-speaking world. Advertisements and parodies also contributed to their fame, as did the theatrical companies that presented an author-approved adaptation of the novel to capacity audiences in New York, London, and elsewhere. Public enthusiasm kept the play on the boards in England until the end of the century, and in 1905 a new production opened in London to wonderful reviews.

At some point, a wide-eyed Charlie Chaplin saw a performance in which the eminent actor-manager Herbert Beerbohm Tree appeared as Svengali. In *My Autobiography* Chaplin said of Tree that "he was the subtlest of actors," that he appealed "to the mind as well as the emotions," and that his conception of character "was always brilliant." Thus his Fagin in *Oliver Twist* "was both humorous and horrific," while his portrayal of the "ridiculous" Svengali "made one believe in this absurd character and endowed him not only with humor but with poetry." Those distancing epithets "ridiculous" and "absurd" make it seem as if Chaplin saw no similarity between himself and Svengali. There is reason not to take him at his word. In his career as a filmmaker, he had played a Svengaliesque role in the lives of one untutored Trilby after another.[29]

8

Casey's Court Circus closed up shop on July 20, 1907. But capitalizing on his success in it proved more difficult for Charlie than he had anticipated. For several months he was forced to depend on handouts from his brother, who had been prospering as a pantomimist. In his capacity as Charlie's unofficial agent, Sydney also tried to get him a job with his own employer, Fred Karno, of the entertainment empire known as Karno's Speechless Comedians. But while Karno granted Charlie an interview, nothing came of it. In the impresario's words, "Syd brought his kid brother along—a pale, sullen-looking youngster. I must say that when I first saw him, I thought he looked much too shy to do any good in the theatre, particularly in the knockabout comedies that were my specialty."[30]

Inasmuch as Jewish comedians were currently popular, Charlie's next thought was to become one. With a loan from Sydney, he bought some musical arrangements of comic songs, an American jokebook entitled *Madison's Budget*, and a set of false whiskers. Thus armed, he obtained a trial booking without pay in a small theater off the Mile End Road in the heart of London's Jewish quarter. From there, he dreamed, the road to the top would be straight up. On opening night, everything went wrong. It was bad enough that he was unable to establish an intimate rapport with his audience and that his Jewish accent kept slipping out of control. But what really killed him was his failure to realize that some of the jokes he had lifted from *Madison's Budget* were anti-Semitic. After a minute or so, booing began, accompanied by barrages of orange peels and small coins. At the end of his turn, he did not even bother to pick up his musical arrangements as he headed for the stage door and disappeared into the merciful dark.[31]

Two more fiascoes swiftly followed. As the romantic lead in a domestic comedy, *The Merry Major*, he played opposite an actress of fifty who was supposed to be his wife. Each night he kissed her on the lips and each night he was all but overwhelmed by the smell of gin. The play closed within a week. He then wrote a comedy of his own—a sketch merely, not a full-length play—about the tribulations of jury duty on a breach-of-promise case. A vaudeville investor purchased it from him for three pounds on the condition that he direct it. A cast was assembled and rehearsals began, but on the third day the investor sent Charlie a note saying that he was withdrawing his support. The unpleasant task of breaking the bad news to the cast was clearly the director's responsibility, but Charlie could not face it. "I can't," he whimpered to Sydney, "I just can't." "Go and tell them," Sydney shouted in a rare burst of anger. Charlie began to weep. "What can I say?" he asked piteously. In

..e end, Sydney did his dirty work for him, as other men so often would in Hollywood.[32]

9

Fred Karno liked to be called "the Guv'nor," and virtually everyone of his acquaintance obliged him. The sobriquet seemed appropriate for one of the most powerful and influential figures in music hall history. In the three knocked-together residences in Vaughan Road that housed what he called his "Fun Factory," he maintained a scene dock, a costume and property store, and several rehearsal rooms for the use of the mimes, acrobats, and singers who had made his "Speechless Comedians" known in theaters throughout Britain and in foreign countries as well.

As the child of an itinerant cabinetmaker, Karno had grown up in disordered and impoverished circumstances. At the age of fourteen, he took a job in a lace factory in Nottingham. Later, he worked as a costermonger, a bricklayer, a barber's lather boy, a shop clerk, a plumber's apprentice, a glazier, and a gymnastic exhibitionist in traveling circuses—for his five-foot five-inch body was trim and hard. With two other acrobatic young men, he formed a vaudeville team in 1888. Seven years later, a pantomime sketch he had composed, called *Hilarity*, brought down the house in Birmingham with its circuslike rough-and-tumble and its quality of attention to details of gesture and manner in the midst of the violence. Another half decade of seasoning in the provinces ensued. In a make-or-break bid for big-time success, he then offered three new sketches, plus a revival of *Hilarity*, to London audiences. The year was 1901. Changes in the social and economic climate made the time ripe for the triumph of new talents.

Thanks to the steady climb in real income from the 1860s onward, critically important improvements in the British standard of living were readily discernible by the end of the century. Not only were middle-class wage earners noticeably better off than they had ever been before, but so were millions of skilled and semiskilled laborers. Even a portion of the unskilled no longer had to struggle along on earnings that permitted next to no purchases beyond the minimum necessities of life. In the years after 1900, another welcome change took place in the British economy. Weekly working hours declined from the total of sixty or seventy they had averaged in the nineteenth century to fifty-three by 1910. With the increase in leisure time came the question of how to make use of it. Holiday travel boomed, as did newspaper readership, ticket sales to sports events, organized betting, and music hall attendance.[33]

As never before, the music halls of the Edwardian era drew customers in strength from every class. "Ford Madox Ford edited his *English Review* in a box at the Shepherd's Bush Empire," the literary historian Samuel Hynes has noted, "and the King himself preferred an evening of variety at the Empire or the Gaiety to G. B. Shaw at the Royal Court." In the culture of the working classes, however, the music halls had traditionally occupied a position of unique importance, going back to the days when their entertainments had been staged in taverns. Humbly born Fred Karno never forgot this basic fact. Between 1904 and 1914, when he was operating at the peak of his powers, his comedies spoke to the mounting sense of outrage of working-class audiences.[34]

Their grievances were many. The long rise in real wages that they had enjoyed came to an abrupt halt in 1901, and thereafter the wage level remained stagnant or declined slightly. Not until 1918 did it resume an upward course. For many working-class families, the sudden short-circuiting of their rising expectations was an embittering and alienating experience. A revulsion against social hypocrisy and deceit and the hypertrophy of institutions began to build. As one year gave way to the next without alleviation of the tension, some observers became convinced that a social explosion was in the offing. In 1909, H. G. Wells likened the situation to an early day in a fine October. "The hand of change," he wrote in *Tono-Bungay*, "rests on it all, unfelt, unseen; resting for awhile, as it were half reluctantly, before it grips and ends the thing for ever. One frost and the whole face of things will be bare, links snap, patience end, our fine foliage of pretences lie glowing in the mire." In *The Condition of England*, published in the same year, the noted Liberal politician Charles Masterman assessed the mood of lower-class crowds in central London and foreboded evil days to come:

> There is a note of menace in it . . . possibilities of violence in its waywardness. . . . It will cheer the police which is scattering it like chaff and spray, mock openly at those who come with set purposes, idle and

sprawl on a summer afternoon at Hyde Park or an autumn evening in Parliament Square. But one feels that the smile might turn suddenly into a fierce snarl of savagery. . . .

Charlie Chaplin, who turned twenty in 1909, was a loner in the midst of these crowds. Nevertheless, he might readily have shared their sense of injustice. Indeed, it is not implausible to assume that his pro-Communist sympathies began to take shape during this portentous period.[35]

In the violence and wide scale of such disputes as the great South Wales strike of 1910–11 and the dockworkers' strikes of 1910–14, long-smoldering feelings of being cheated finally burst into flame. Some of the workers' more militant leaders, moreover, were committed to the syndicalist vision of a general strike that would eventuate in worker control of industries and services. In August 1911, an inflammatory speech in Liverpool by the syndicalist Tom Mann led strikers to stone the soldiers who were trying to maintain order. The following year, *The Times* of London warned that "the public must be prepared for a conflict between Labor and Capital, or between employers and employed, and upon a scale such as had never occurred before." Lord Devonport's counterattack on the London dockers and the call by a group of Welsh miners for producer control of the coal mines were two of the events of 1912 that bore out the *Times*'s prophecy. In the opinion of the exiled Lenin, the British proletariat had hardened wonderfully. "The workers have learned to fight," he asserted. "They have come to see the *path* that will lead them to victory." Among the militants there was talk of staging a general strike in November 1914.[36]

The guns of August blew the strike plans for the fall to kingdom come, and the "new energy" of England, as the historian George Dangerfield has called it, "rushed headlong onto the battlefields of Flanders and the bloodstained beaches of Gallipoli." Yet the chances are that even if Britain had not gone to war, the workers' movement that had unexpectedly taken a revolutionary course would finally have broken the hearts of the militants. For the prewar English workingman was no doctrinaire. Obeying the law and doing his duty were habits that were deeply ingrained in him. He was conscious, too, of how much better off he was than his forebears, and of how much he might lose if the existing society were violently overturned. As for undoing the capitalist order by peaceful, legislative means, that dream notably failed to materialize, despite the establishment of the Labour Party. The working classes may have been industrially strong, but politically they were disunited and inhibited. So torn were they between antithetical feelings of anger and acceptance that they did not as a whole become socialist.[37]

"Our people never formulates," Wells observed in *Tono-Bungay;* "it keeps words for jests and ironies." In the music halls of the period lay a proof of this observation. While workingmen could not speak with one voice about a political agenda, they were united in their enthusiasm for the humor of Fred Karno.[38]

In the comic world of this brilliant mass psychologist, some characters felt cheated and perpetrated acts of revenge; others flouted respectability and decorum; still others dreamed of escaping from England to distant lands. Yet at the same time that Karno's sketches emphasized reprisals and running away, a wryly defined fatalism pervaded them. Life, according to "the Guv'nor," was not a pathway to victory but a pitfall-strewn road to absurdity. British soldiers in World War I, conscious as they were of all that could go wrong in the military, consoled themselves with a derisive song that began, "We are Fred Karno's Army,/ A ragtime crowd are we. . . ."[39]

Mumming Birds, the most often performed of Karno's sketches, was a show within a show: a music hall audience is subjected to a perfectly dreadful variety program and responds by humiliating the performers, until finally one of the principal dissidents goes too far. The curtain rises on a false proscenium flanked by two double-decker theater boxes. A fat boy in an Eton suit, carrying a basket of buns and accompanied by his rather proper uncle, settles into one of the lower boxes. An inebriated swell is conducted to the lower box on the other side by a pretty usherette. A self-assured smile creases the swell's face as he removes his right glove with a flourish. In his drunken confusion, he attempts to repeat this gesture, and is struggling to do so when the usherette points out that he is tugging at his skin. After a failed attempt to light a cigarette from an electric bulb, the swell notices that the fat boy across the way is offering him a lighted match. He gratefully leans forward, cigarette in mouth, and promptly falls out of his box. As he clambers back in, the show begins.

A pair of skinny cancan girls comes on first, followed by two song-and-dance men, whose excruciatingly boring patter elicits groans from the fat boy and the swell. A ham actor succeeds them, but his overblown recital of "The Trail of the Yukon" is likewise punctuated by protests from the audience. A lady vocalist fares no better with her rendition of "Come Birdie, Come and Live with Me." A male quartet's offering of "Hail, Smiling Morn That Tips the Hills with Gold" is prematurely terminated by a volley of buns from the fat boy's basket. A soubrette tries to sing and dance her way through "You Naughty, Naughty Man," only to find that her come-on vulgarity inspires the swell to get out of his box and make a grab for her as she flees into the wings.

The final act features Marconi Ali, "The Terrible Turk, the Greatest Wrestler Ever to Appear Before the British Public." Just before this purportedly awesome creature comes on stage, the "Number Man," who has introduced all the acts, announces that a purse of one hundred pounds will be given to anyone in the theater who can throw Ali within fifteen minutes. In ludicrous contrast to his advance billing, Ali turns out to be a scrawny little fellow in a fez and droopy wrestling trunks who seems barely able to support the weight of his enormous mustache. The fat boy tosses a bun in his direction and the Turk leaps forward like a spaniel, catching it in midair and swallowing it as though he hasn't eaten in a week. Yet when a challenger jumps down from one of the upper boxes, Ali quickly dispatches him. The swell starts to strip off his clothing, having decided that he will be the next challenger, but is hustled offstage by the protective usherette. A few moments later, he reappears, dressed in long underpants decorated with red ribbons, and defeats the Turk by tickling him into a state of helplessness. The swell accepts the prize money with a gracious bow. The audience, in effect, has won its battle with the performers. But the victory is quickly kicked away. When the swell is asked if there is anything else he would like, he provocatively replies, "First bring on the girls!" The sort of anarchic denouement known as a "Karno picnic" ensues. Everyone in the show rushes toward the center of the stage. In a confused and purposeless melee, clothes are ripped, blows are exchanged, oranges and bananas are thrown, and imprecations fill the air. The curtain falls.[40]

Stan Laurel called *Mumming Birds* "one of the most fantastically funny acts ever known—probably the greatest ensemble of the cen-

tury."[41] At one time or another, he himself played a number o
in the sketch and apparently relished every one of them. The
swell, however, offered the richest possibilities for clowning. The origi-
nator of the role was Billy Ritchie, who later imitated Chaplin in a series
of Hollywood comedies—and justified his infringement on the grounds
that he had worn similar makeup as a music hall actor. Another mime
who took the part of the swell was Billie Reeves, whose brother, Alfred
Reeves, managed road companies in the Karno empire before becoming
the unflaggingly faithful general manager of the Chaplin film studio.
But in the summer of 1908 in London, and again in the fall of 1909 at
the Folies-Bergère in Paris, Karno put *Mumming Birds* on the boards
with Chaplin as the swell. On a tour of America with a Karno troupe
lasting from the fall of 1910 through the spring of 1912, Chaplin per-
fected his command of the part in theaters large and small. As one of
his American reviewers said of him, "Charles Chaplin . . . is an artist,
and even though doing the broadest burlesque, never gets out of the
part for an instant. His falls in and out of the boxes are wonderful and
were he not a skilled acrobat, he would break his neck."[42]

Two factors accounted for his acrobatic dexterity: the extraordinary
physical grace that he naturally possessed and the body-control discipline he learned at the "Fun Factory." Karno, the onetime circus performer, taught his actors to maintain total control of their movements at
all times, even when they had seemingly lost control. To this end he
insisted on hours and hours of rehearsals. Chaplin recalled that Karno
disparaged every new group he assembled as a "scratch crowd" until it
had gone through at least six months of intensive drills. "Each new man
working for Karno had to have perfect timing," he affirmed, "and had
to know the peculiarities of everyone else in the cast. . . . It took about
a year for an actor to get the repertoire of a dozen shows down pat.
Karno required us to know a number of parts so that players could be
interchanged. When one left the company it was like taking a screw or
a pin out of a very delicate piece of machinery." Stan Laurel, who joined
the "Speechless Comedians" in 1910, later said of "the Guv'nor" that
he "didn't teach Charlie and me all we know about comedy. He just
taught us most of it. If I had to pick an adjective to fit Karno, it would
be supple. That's what [he] was, mentally and physically. . . . Just as
importantly he taught us to be precise. Out of all that endless rehearsal

and performance came Charlie, the most supple and precise comedian of our time."[43]

At least a dozen of Chaplin's early comedies were enlivened by borrowings from Karno's work. In a popular Karno sketch called *The G.P.O.*, for instance, a middle-aged tumbler named Perkins—whom Chaplin played from time to time—finds work in a post office. A doctor enters and purchases a stamp. Turning from the counter, he sees Perkins, pulls out his watch, grabs hold of Perkins's wrist, takes his pulse, and orders him to stick out his tongue. When Perkins complies, the doctor uses his tongue to moisten the stamp he has bought. After sticking the stamp on the letter, he tips his hat and walks on. As the janitor in *The Bank* (1915), Chaplin victimizes a waiting customer in precisely this way.

The Bank also benefited from Chaplin's recollections of his starring role in *Jimmy the Fearless*. Jimmy is a working-class lad who arrives home late, after a date with a "bit o' skirt," and is severely reproved by his mother. The resentful youth eats his supper, picks up a trashy novel, falls asleep while reading it, and dreams that he is in the Rocky Mountains. At the end of a knockdown fight with a bunch of desperadoes, he frees the pretty girl whom they had captured. Later, he strikes it rich and he and the pretty girl move into a mansion. Life is a dream come true—until the dream ends. The youth awakens to the reality of a threatened beating from his father for staying out late with the "bit o' skirt." In *The Bank*, the janitor falls asleep and dreams of how he rescues the pretty office secretary, with whom he has fallen in love, from the robbers who have taken her hostage. Emboldened by her gratitude to him, he embraces her and caresses her hair—only to discover, as he regains consciousness, that he is stroking the strands of his mop.*

The lengths to which Karno was prepared to go in order to create realistic settings for his comedies likewise inspired Chaplin. On April 11, 1910, the most spectacular production of "the Guv'nor's" career opened at the Paragon Theater in London's East End. A look at life

---

* Stan Laurel believed that "you can see *Jimmy the Fearless* all over some of [Chaplin's] pictures—dream sequences, for instance. He was fond of them, especially in his early pictures. And when it comes right down to it, I've always thought that poor, brave, dreamy Jimmy one day grew up to be Charlie the Tramp." Quoted in John McCabe, *Charlie Chaplin* (Garden City, N. Y., 1978), p. 36.

aboard a transatlantic steamer, the sketch was called *Wontdetainia*, a humorous allusion to the Cunard Line's *Lusitania* and *Mauretania*, both of which had been launched in 1907. Karno's liner was 120 feet long and boasted a superstructure made of solid steel. Because it was powered by two hydraulic rams in the wings and a third concealed behind the rear curtain, it could roll from side to side and heave up and down. The passengers' horrendous bouts of *mal de mer* thus became hilariously believable. In two of his movies in the mid-teens, Chaplin made similarly grand efforts to achieve a compelling illusion of seasick-making conditions. Several of the shipboard sequences in *Shanghaied* (1915) and *The Immigrant* (1917) were filmed aboard real ships, but in order to satisfy Chaplin's insistence on the appearance of movement through heavy seas, his cameramen placed their cameras on pivots and controlled the swing with heavy counterweights. For interior shipboard shots, he had studio construction crews build rooms with rockers beneath them.[44]

Of the established stars in the Karno troupe whom he looked up to, Chaplin learned the most from Fred Kitchen. A huge but graceful man who had played Harlequin at the Drury Lane, Kitchen was famous for his shambling walk, halfway between a shuffle and a hop. Its incongruousness was further heightened when he started wearing a pair of outsized, ankle-high shoes that Karno found for him. Kitchen also had an engaging habit of throwing a cigarette over his shoulder and kicking it with his shoe. While Chaplin would not have dared to make immediate use of either of these foot tricks, in time he immortalized both of them.[45]

10

By and large the people at the "Fun Factory" were not fond of Syd Chaplin's younger brother. The personal assessment of him by the sharp-tongued proprietor himself was especially harsh. "He wasn't very likable," Karno flatly declared after Charlie left his employ. "I've known him to go whole weeks without saying a word to anyone in the company. Occasionally he would be quite chatty, but on the whole he was dour and unsociable. He lived like a monk, had a horror of drink, and put most of his salary away in the bank as soon as he got it."[46]

Even after he had millions in the bank, Chaplin never seemed to have any money on him, and when dining out with friends he always allowed someone else to pick up the tab. The young skinflint who offended Karno was not quite as monkish, however, as "the Guv'nor" believed. As soon as the brothers Chaplin could afford to do so, they rented a four-room flat at Glenshaw Mansions in the Brixton Road and spent forty pounds furnishing it with such items as a raised brass fender with red leather seating, an upholstered couch and two armchairs, a fretwork screen, an upright piano, and a picture of a nude model standing on a pedestal, looking over her shoulder at a bearded artist who is about to brush a fly off one of her buttocks. The result was that the place resembled, Chaplin realized in retrospect, "a combination of a Moorish cigarette shop and a French whorehouse."[47]

In the recollection of Stan Laurel, who roomed with Chaplin for a time on their first Karno tour of the United States, the future creator of the world's most famous tramp character was given to wearing exceedingly shabby clothes. On the other hand, Laurel added, there were occasions when he would astonish the rest of the company with his elegance. "At these times he would wear a derby hat (an expensive one), gloves, a smart suit, fancy vest, two-tone side button shoes, and carry a cane."[48]

While he was extremely moody and always would be, Karno's dismissal of Chaplin as dour and unsociable failed to take his shyness into account. Nor was Karno capable of appreciating the fact that unlike most comedians Chaplin wanted to improve his mind. Oftentimes, to be sure, his intellectual reach exceeded his grasp. Thus, on his first American tour, he bought several textbooks—Kellogg's *Rhetoric*, an English grammar, and a Latin-English dictionary—but lacked the resolve to study them. Not until his second tour to the States did he look into them again.[49]

During one of his *Sherlock Holmes* tours, Chaplin had imitated the detective's fondness for the violin by buying one himself, on which he had the strings reversed so that he could play left-handed. Practically everywhere he went, he took the instrument with him and practiced for hours at a time. This habit persisted into his Karno years. At some point he also learned to play the cello and the piano. Music helped to cheer him up when his mood was grim.[50]

It had been particularly grim in the late summer of 1908, for several reasons. The weather had been oppressively hot for weeks. Most of his

associates struck him as commonplace people. And the nightly work
schedule was physically and mentally exhausting. Following an early-
evening performance of *Mumming Birds* at the Empire Theater in suburban Streatham, he and the rest of the company were transported in
one of the big black buses that Karno had made his trademark to a
second engagement at the Canterbury and thence to a third at the
Tivoli. "Those were melancholy days," Chaplin would write in 1933,
"until one August night." [51]

At the Empire, he found that *Mumming Birds* came on after a song-
and-dance troupe called Bert Coutts's Yankee-Doodle Girls. One night,
as he was standing in the wings watching the troupe's performance, one
of the girls slipped and fell to the floor and the other girls began to
giggle. One of them glanced offstage to see if anyone else was amused.
Her big brown mischievous eyes caught Chaplin's attention, as did her
bewitchingly full mouth and her slim figure, which made him think of a
gazelle. [52] Hetty Kelly was her name, he quickly ascertained, and she was
fifteen years old. He himself was nineteen. Their brief romance stands
out in Chaplin's amorous history as the first known instance of his
attraction to a girl in whom there was a "childish something," as Humbert Humbert remarks in the early pages of *Lolita* (1955), à propos of a
"short, slim" sixteen- or seventeen-year-old Parisienne with a "small
agile rump" whom he accosts near the Madeleine on a spring afternoon
and who charges him one hundred francs for access to her "curiously
immature body." [53]

When Chaplin first spoke to Hetty, as she came offstage at the Empire, he was charmed by her sprightliness. He asked if she would consent
to spend some time with him the following Sunday and she replied, "I
don't even know what you look like without the red nose!" In preparation for his part in *Mumming Birds*, Chaplin had not only donned the
white tie and tails of a London swell, but had dusted his nose with red
powder to indicate the swell's intoxication. Finally, Hetty consented to
go out with him. At the tram stop where he met her on Sunday, the
simple sailor hat she was wearing and her lack of makeup made her
more beautiful than ever in his eyes. Perhaps he was also enchanted
because these touches made her look even younger and more innocent
and therefore less threatening. Almost immediately he launched into a
declaration of his affection for her. Amazed by his fervor, she permitted

him to take her to a posh restaurant in the West End. While he consumed an elaborate meal, she contented herself with a sandwich. The
next morning at seven o'clock, and again on Tuesday and Wednesday
mornings, they took a walk together before her schedule of rehearsals
began at eight. "These morning walks with hands clasped all the way to
the Underground were bliss," Chaplin would croon in *My Autobiography*.[54]

On Thursday morning, however, her manner was different. She
would not take his hand and walked straight ahead "with a schoolgirl
stride." He kept pressing her to say that she loved him. Would she
marry him, he finally asked, if she were compelled to marry someone?
Her answers betrayed embarrassment and confusion. At the entrance to
the underground, he took her hand and patted it tenderly. "Goodbye,"
he said. "It's better this way. Already you have too much of a power over
me." But, in truth, what he could not tolerate was the failure of his bid
to exert power over her. Following a night of "mental agony," he showed
up at her house. She had just washed her face with Sunlight soap and
"it smelled so fresh," he exclaimed in remembrance. Her eyes, however,
struck him as cold and objective. "Well," he said, "I've come to say
goodbye again." He extended his hand and smiled. "So goodbye again,"
he said. "Goodbye," she answered coldly. A year later, he encountered
her by chance. "Her figure had developed, and I noticed the contours
of her breasts and thought their protuberance small and not very allur-
ing. Would I marry her even if I could afford to? No, I did not want to
marry anyone."[55]

II

In the fall of 1909, Chaplin made his first trip to Paris. The manager
of the Folies-Bergère had asked Karno to send over a troupe for a
one-month run. On the night of Chaplin's arrival, he struck up a conversation backstage with a young ballerina who spoke English. The girl
informed him that Hetty Kelly had recently danced in Paris, but that
her troupe was now in Moscow. Suddenly, Chaplin would relate in *My
Autobiography*, a harsh voice came over the stairs: "Come here at once!
How dare you talk to strangers!" It was the girl's mother.

The mother was buxom, fortyish, and separated from her Scotsman husband, by whom she had had two daughters. The pretty thirteen-year-old, to whom Chaplin had been talking, was the *première danseuse* of the Folies-Bergère; her fifteen-year-old sister, on the other hand, possessed neither looks nor talent. Upon discovering that Chaplin had taken a room in the same hotel where she and her daughters were living, the mother began inviting him to their rooms for tea. One afternoon when the daughters were out, he noticed that Mama was acting rather strangely as she officiated at the tea table. Finally, she arose and stood in front of him. "You are sweet," she said, cupping his face in her hands and looking into his eyes. "Do you know, I love you like a son," she told him with a tremor in her voice. Still holding his face in her hands, she kissed him. "Thank you," he said, and kissed her back. She continued looking at him, her lips parted and her eyes glazed. She seemed to be waiting for something to happen, but nothing did; Chaplin simply stood there. Suddenly she returned to the tea table. Her manner changed. With a certain humor she said, "You are very sweet. I like you very much." Thinking back on her overtures and his own unresponsiveness, Chaplin wryly remarked, "I was incredibly innocent." [56]

If his erstwhile friend and associate Harry Crocker had lived long enough to read *My Autobiography*, he might have hooted at this story. For in the late 1920s Chaplin had offered him a very different account of his Parisian adventures. "I was with Charlie day and night for four years," Crocker later wrote in his unpublished biography of Chaplin, and "I kept notes [on everything he said about his personal life] which I set down at the earliest opportunity in typewritten form." It would appear from Crocker's manuscript that Chaplin talked to him a number of times about the young dancer in the Folies-Bergère who had informed him that Hetty Kelly was in Moscow.

Her name was Mabelle Fournier, and she was not thirteen, as in the version in *My Autobiography*. Nor was she merely pretty. And her relationship with Chaplin was not just an incidental part of a larger story. Mabelle was "marvelous," Chaplin exclaimed, "like Pavlova—dainty, graceful, beautiful—oh, how I fell! I was mad about her." She was "only ten or twelve," he told Crocker, and from this confession he hurried on to another. "I have always been in love with young girls, not in an amorous way—just as beautiful objects to look at. I like them young because they personify youth and beauty. There is something virginal in their slimness—in their slender arms and legs. And they are so feminine at that age—so wholly, girlishly young. They haven't developed the 'come on' stuff or discovered the power of their looks over men." "I suppose you might say," he continued, "that I had a crush on the little Parisienne. It was funny; not in a sex way—I just loved to caress and fondle her—not passionately—just to have her in my arms."

Her mother objected at first to his involvement with Mabelle. But then she began inviting him to dinner. Sometimes Mabelle had violent nosebleeds and had to lie down, and her mother would say to Chaplin, "She likes you. Go in and lie down on the bed and comfort her." Obediently, "I would go in and put my arms around her and pat her. No sex at all in it. . . . I'd lie there for hours until my arms would be numb from lying on them. I'd be spellbound with her beauty."[57]

With girls as young as Mabelle Fournier, Chaplin never had to worry about rejection, or betrayal, or about being adjudged inadequate. Never would he forget that his sense of not knowing what to do while gripped in his mother's frantic embraces had made him feel like screaming. But lying for hours with Mabelle's virginal slimness, her wholly girlish femininity, enveloped in his arms was very heaven.

4

"THIS IS WHERE I BELONG!"

*Mabel Normand, displaying the form that helped to make
her famous as "the Keystone Girl."*

C HAPLIN'S relationship with Karno had never been secure.
When the impresario assigned him the top part of Stiffy the Goalkeeper
in *The Football Match*, one of the dialogue sketches that were fast becoming an indispensable addition to the pantomimes in the Karno repertoire, he felt that his star was in the ascendant. But at the Oxford, a
prestigious London music hall, he was not effective in the role—because
of laryngitis, he pleaded, an excuse that he may have recycled in his story
about his mother's vocal crisis at Aldershot. When Karno peremptorily

removed him from the cast in favor of his understudy, the idea of going to America began to occupy his thoughts.[1]

In *Skating*, cowritten by his brother Sydney, he had better luck. Since 1906, England had been in the throes of a roller skating craze. Rinks had opened all over the place, and orchestra leaders were forever being asked to play "Rolling Round the Rink" and other catchy skating songs. Nevertheless, there were very few rinks that could boast abler—or more amusing—skaters than Charlie Chaplin. Thus when he notified Karno that his contract had run out and he wanted a raise, he did not expect to be greeted, as he was, with a brutal reminder of the "fiasco" of *The Football Match*. Even though Karno finally upped his pay from five pounds to six, the insulting nature of the negotiations stiffened his resolve to leave England.[2]

Being picked by Karno as one of the comedians to go to the States in the fall of 1910 was the first in a series of wonderful breaks that would come his way in the next few years. He assured his boss that he would return to England at the end of the tour—and, in fact, he did. Secretly, however, he was hoping to settle permanently in America. As he would confess to Thomas Burke during an all-night walk through London byways in 1921, he was convinced that in England he was "up against that social barrier that so impedes advancement and achievement—a barrier that only the very great or the very cunning can cross." In a magazine piece, Burke summarized the rest of his new friend's reasons for leaving the land of his birth:

America freely gave him what he could never have wrested from England —recognition and decent society. He spoke in chilly tones of his life in England as a touring vaudeville artist. Such a life is a succession of squalor and mean things. The company was his social circle, and he lived and moved only in that circle. . . . Altho he was then a youth with little learning, an undeveloped personality, and few graces, he had the instinctive feeling for fine things. Altho he had no key by which he might escape, no title to a place among the fresh, easy cultivated minds where he desired to be, he knew that he did not belong in the rude station of life in which he was placed. Had he remained in this country, he would have remained in that station. He would never have got out. But in America the questions are, "What do you know?" and "What can you do?" not "Where do you come from?" and "Who are your people?" "Are you public school?"[3]

2

On reaching New York in late September, Chaplin rented a back room above a cleaning and pressing establishment in a brownstone on West Forty-third Street. The building was repulsively smelly and dirty and made him homesick for the digs he and Sydney had occupied in Glenshaw Mansions. The rest of his first day in the city was largely devoted to surveying the scene and compiling reactions—which for the most part were negative. The accelerated tempo of New York's rhythms, the alacrity with which the shoeshine boy flipped his polishing rag, the bartender drew beer, and the soda jerk mixed a frappe, made him feel like a visitor from another planet. That evening, however, as he moved with the flow of the crowd on Broadway and watched the lights brightening on the theater marquees and in the tall buildings looming behind them in the Indian-summer dusk, his sense of not belonging dropped away. "That is it!" he said to himself. "This is where I belong!"[4]

Unfortunately, he and his fellow comedians got off to a faltering start at the Colonial Theater a few evenings later with a new and untested farce called *The Wow-Wows*. For a Karno comedy, it was an uncharacteristically wordy piece of work, largely devoted to demonstrating how the residents of a summer camp take their revenge on a blithering tightwad (played by Chaplin) by forming a secret society and initiating him into it. While its silly jokes were of the sort that sometimes tickle English funnybones, they evoked a tepid response on Broadway. As the reviewer for *Variety* succinctly put it, "The Colonial audience laughed at the show . . . but not enough."[5]*

Along with everyone else in the company, including the manager, Alf Reeves, Chaplin feared that poor press notices would kill their chances of being signed by a booking agency for a nationwide tour. But significantly enough, he did not share his colleagues' discouragement for long. As he later affirmed, America's immoderate optimism was rubbing off on him. Thus the paradoxical result of the company's theatrical failure was that "I began to feel light and unhampered. There were many other

---

* The audience seems to have included a twenty-eight-year-old theater-loving painter named Edward Hopper. Gail Levin, *Edward Hopper: An Intimate Biography* (New York, 1995), p. 47.

opportunities in America. Why should I stick to show business? I was not dedicated to art. Get into another racket!"[6]*

In a conversation one day with Alf Reeves, Chaplin proposed that the two of them should start filming and marketing "picture comedies" based on Karno sketches. Each man would ante up one thousand dollars so that they could purchase a motion picture camera. No further investment would be necessary, they naively agreed.[7] While the proposal was clearly not well thought out, the partners' basic premise was eminently sound: the movie business was the wave of the future in the entertainment industry.

As longtime troupers, Chaplin and Reeves could hardly have failed to notice how many music halls in Britain had added movies to their programs in order to meet the competition from theaters exclusively devoted to showing them.[8] Chaplin's sojourn in Paris in 1909 could have been the time that he learned something else about movies of interest to him. The one-reel comedies of a man named Max Linder were exceptionally funny.

The son of a wealthy family named Louville from the Bordeaux wine country, Linder had moved to Paris in 1904 at age twenty-one. Following a successful year as an actor in theatrical melodramas and as a stand-up entertainer in cabarets, he began making quickie pictures at the Pathé studios. By the end of 1907, he had appeared in no fewer than four hundred of them, at which point Pathé decided to give him more

---

* At some point in 1910, American hustle came to be personified for him by a good-looking, fast-talking thirteen-year-old school dropout who was currently appearing in an extravaganza called Gus Edwards's 1910 Song Revue. The song hits that had made Gus Edwards rich included "By the Light of the Silvery Moon," "In My Merry Oldsmobile," "If I Was a Millionaire," "Sunbonnet Sue," and, most notably, "School Days." Some of these songs were presented in the Revue by a group of boys, one of whom was the aforementioned school dropout. The name of this "scallywag," as Chaplin called him in My Autobiography, was Walter Winchell. In off hours, Chaplin remembered, the scalawag shot dice with the stagehands. But Chaplin may actually have been remembering an event that took place onstage, not off. For the opening curtain of the Revue went up to reveal seven newsboys, including young Winchell, shooting dice in the Bright Light District and singing "Dear Old East Side," followed by "If I Was a Millionaire." Chaplin, My Autobiography, p. 123; Walter Winchell, Winchell Exclusive (Englewood Cliffs, N.J., 1974), p. 11; Neal Gabler, Winchell: Gossip, Power and the Culture of Celebrity (New York, 1994), pp. 15, 17–18.

time and money for his work. Nevertheless, his productivity remained high. For several years a new Linder picture went into release every week. Both socially and sartorially, their hero, named Max, was a farcical version of the character whom Adolphe Menjou would play in Chaplin's *A Woman of Paris* (1923) and other movies of the 1920s and afterwards: an idle-rich rake, sporting a carefully trimmed mustache, evening clothes, an opera cloak, and a top hat. For all his impeccability, however, Max repeatedly became involved in physically upsetting situations, as the hyperkinetic tradition of early French filmmaking virtually guaranteed that he would.[9]

Hundreds of knockabout gags that the world would come to associate with American slapstick were first tried out in front of cameras in France. French comedies swarmed with comic stuntmen called *cascadeurs*, who, in film historian Nicole Védrès's words, "really did perform the plunge from the third storey into a tub of washing; and at the exact moment that the floor of a room fell through, each man knew precisely where to leap—one onto the piano, another onto the aspidistra—silk hats still in their hands, lorgnettes dangling, beards aquiver."[10] With magnificent ineptitude, the accident-prone Max took pratfalls on ice skates, all but broke his neck while climbing a mountain, and plunged headlong into a vat of vegetable dye in a vain effort to escape the vengeance of a husband he had cuckolded.

The *poursuites* in his comedies were particularly famous. Yet Linder thoroughly disliked them. Indeed, he had only a limited interest in any of the forms of purely physical humor of which he was a master. Even in his early appearances as Max, there are flashes of the sly, mordant wit that he would factor into his comedies after he won the right, in 1911, to direct them. There are hints, too, in all phases of his work of his personal troubles. Thus, in the midst of the frantic activity in *Troubles of a Grass Widower* (1908), the camera occasionally cuts in tight on Max's nervous half smiles and darting glances. In such moments of earnest befuddlement or desperately achieved calm, the lurking shadows of Linder's own spirit can be discerned.

Wherever it was that Chaplin first encountered Linder's comedies, did they cause him to realize that the motion picture camera had not only enlarged the playing field of a slam-bang humor of incident, but could also enormously enhance a humor based on character? Did the gentlemanly deliberateness, for instance, with which Max removed his gloves, finger by finger, before popping an adversary on the nose teach Chaplin something about the ways in which a gentlemanly tramp might conduct himself? To ask these questions is to answer them. But in *My Autobiography*, Linder is conspicuous by his absence. Only once did his famous student acknowledge a debt to him. Following his recovery from the horrors of service as a front-line soldier in World War I, Linder accepted an offer of work from a Hollywood studio. Upon his arrival in the movie capital, he visited the Chaplin Studio, and as he was leaving, his host gave him a photograph of himself on which he scribbled a salute to "The one and only Max, The Professor, From his Disciple, Charlie Chaplin." [11] Neither the memory of that kindness, however, nor the passionate devotion of his young wife, Madeleine Peters, could arrest his deepening depression. In a Paris hotel in 1925, Linder and Madeleine both committed suicide by taking poison and slashing their wrists. He was forty-five; she was twenty.

3

Two weeks after the dismal opening of *The Wow-Wows*, Alf Reeves moved the show to the Fifth Avenue Theater. By that time, its jokes had been substantially sharpened, to the point where a previously skeptical agent agreed to book the company into a twenty-week tour on the Sullivan and Considine circuit. Cleveland, Chicago, St. Louis, Minneapolis, and Denver would be on the comedians' itinerary, as well as towns in between and points west, along with a couple of side excursions into Canada.

Chicago "throbbed" with "masculine loneliness," Chaplin would recall in *My Autobiography*, in a phrase that could have been written by Dreiser. To deal with their "somatic ailment," men turned to burlesque shows, with their lineups of barely dressed chorus girls, dirty-mouthed comedians, and "smutty harem comedies." A number of chorines lived in the same seedy hotel on Wabash Avenue where the Karno troupe elected to stay—out of a "libidinous hope" on the part of some of the younger men in the troupe that liaisons would develop. One of these girls, Chaplin observed, was unlike the others in that she seemed very self-conscious and kept to herself. He heard that she was suffering from syphilis. Later he learned that she had been cured by injections of Salvarsan, a new drug at that time.[12]

The threat of venereal disease did not sway him, however, from joining half a dozen other horny troupers in making a beeline for the red-light district in every stop along the way. "Sometimes we won the affection of the madam of a bordel and she would close up the 'joint' for the night and we would take over. Occasionally some of the girls fell for the actors and would follow them to the next town." But in Butte, Montana, the tagalong girls had to compete with a "hundred cribs in which young girls were installed ranging in age from sixteen up for one dollar." The incredible supply of arrestingly good-looking whores was only one of Butte's surprises. Once a godforsaken mining camp, it was now the biggest city between Minneapolis and Spokane, thanks to the ore pits controlled by Anaconda Copper. With its theaters and opera houses, its foreign-born populations (Serbo-Croatian, Chinese, Irish, Italian, and Finnish, among others) and its Wild West barrooms, Butte was an improbable combination of elements, and the mix was volatile. Dashiell Hammett, who re-created his days in Butte as a Pinkerton agent in the pages of *Red Harvest* (1929), worked seventeen murders into the first twenty-one chapters. Chaplin, too, became conscious of Butte's gunplay when he saw a fat old sheriff shoot at the heels of an escaped prisoner before running him down in a blind alley.[13]

Early on in their tour, Reeves and company revived *Mumming Birds*, which Reeves renamed *A Night in an English Music Hall* so that American audiences could understand what it was about. To Chaplin's delight, he was awarded the role of the drunken swell. On reaching San Francisco, the troupe was booked into the Empress Theater, the jewel in the crown of Bay-area vaudeville theaters managed by young Sid Grauman and owned by his father. Young Grauman was on hand at the Empress on the day that *A Night in an English Music Hall* was scheduled to be on the evening bill. About two hours before showtime, he recalled years later, two waiters from a nightclub called the Black Cat dragged Chaplin into the theater. A whore had flirted with him, her pimp had smacked him, and now "he had a shiner like a small mountain." He said he could not go on that night. Grauman persuaded him that he could. Chaplin started to get undressed and peeled off his shirt. "His undershirt," Grauman noticed, "was covered with make-up stains." A purse was hanging between his shoulder blades, which he detached and opened. Four hundred dollars was inside. He walked over to a mirror, pointed to the purse, and addressed his image. "Some day, Charlie Chaplin, you will be a millionaire."

In the course of the tour, Chaplin had tried cocaine and opium. Coke, he discovered, had no effect on him, but opium made him feel as if he were floating. Possibly he had been floating that afternoon in San Francisco.[14]

4

At the end of the tour Chaplin's colleagues expected to return to England immediately, and he expected to accompany them, not having received an American job offer. At the last minute, however, Alf Reeves accepted an offer from the agent William Morris to book the troupe into a six-week engagement at a roof-garden theater in Manhattan. That engagement, in turn, led to another national tour on the Sullivan and Considine circuit.

The company arrived back in England in June 1912 after an absence of twenty-one months. Chaplin discovered to his shock that Sydney had married a Karno actress and had given up their Glenshaw Mansions flat in favor of a few furnished rooms in the Brixton Road. Bachelor Charlie no longer had a home, and the experience of having to cast about in a hurry for new accommodations left him feeling somewhat bitter toward Sydney. For the first time, there was a slight estrangement between the brothers.[15]

Nevertheless, they visited Cane Hill together. Their mother had been in an "obstreperous phase" of late, they were informed, and had had to be confined in a padded room. Charlie quailed at the thought of seeing her, so Sydney went to her room by himself. When he returned, he was visibly upset. In order to calm her down, the attendants had been giving her shock treatments in the form of ice-cold showers, he reported, and her face was blue. The brothers thereupon agreed to split the cost of placing her in Peckham House, a private institution, where the care would be less callous. Peckham House was known to them as the nursing home to which Dan Leno had been taken when he seemed to be losing his mind.[16]

At first, Karno kept everyone who had traveled with Reeves under his direct surveillance in music halls near London. Apparently satisfied that their work was up to snuff, he sent them off again in early July to the Channel Islands and France. On the island of Jersey the annual carnival of flowers had begun and the tourist crowds were at their peak. According to Reeves, Chaplin came back one day from one of the street pageants fairly bubbling with excitement about an idea for a movie. The pageant, it seems, had been filmed by a newsreel cameraman. The cameraman kept moving around, Reeves remembered Chaplin saying, yet

wherever he went a very pompous gentleman, who was apparently *chargé d'affaires*, would always be found in the foreground of the camera lens. He would shake hands with different dignitaries, but would always turn away from the person he was greeting and face the camera, bowing and registering his greetings to the camera, while his guests were in the background off to one side. Charlie was fascinated by this incident and told me that this bit of real comedy he would put in pictures should he ever be in a position to do so.[17]

On October 2, 1912, Chaplin sailed for America for a second time under Karno auspices. Only five members of the previous company were on board this time, and some of the new members were not at all fond of Charlie. His awareness of their animosity heightened his determination to sever his connection with the troupe at the first opportunity.

While crossing the country, he renewed his acquaintance with a cocaine-sniffing society lady in St. Paul, with an Irish bartender in Butte, and with Sid Grauman and his father in San Francisco. The Graumans loved vaudeville, they averred, but were not exclusively wedded to it—as Sid eventually proved. In 1918 he made headlines in Los Angeles by erecting, in an elaborate, Spanish-rococo style known as the Churrigueresque, a downtown movie house called the Million Dollar. As a result of his decision to locate it on Broadway, he established that street as a prime venue for motion pictures. By 1931, the blocks between Third and Ninth streets contained the highest concentration of movie palaces in the world. Yet the late 1920s also witnessed the emergence of Hollywood Boulevard as a first-run movie theater district, thanks in large part to the construction of Grauman's Egyptian and Chinese theaters.[18]

Female companionship and colorful friends only temporarily relieved Chaplin's despondency. If on his first trip to the States he had been exhilarated by the raw energy of towns he had barely heard of before, he was discouraged on the second by the grind of doing three or four shows a day in depressingly drab theaters in cities that repelled him. "Not for the love of knowledge, but as a defense against the world's contempt for the ignorant," so he later wrote, he began spending his mornings browsing in secondhand bookstores. Ingersoll's *Essays and Lectures*, Emerson's "Self-Reliance," and Whitman's *Leaves of Grass* were among the works he collected in this way. The discovery that meant the most to him, however, was a three-volume edition of Schopenhauer's *The World as Will and Idea* (1819), which he would "read on and off, never thoroughly, for over forty years."[19] At the very time that this lifelong infatuation was taking hold of Chaplin, the same philosopher was capturing the mind of another despondent outsider, a young Austrian living in Bavaria. In the fall of 1914, Adolf Hitler would carry a volume of Schopenhauer with him to the Western Front, where he managed to memorize long passages.[20]

Presumably, Chaplin and Hitler were both attracted to the key principle of Schopenhauer's philosophy: the primacy of the will. But for the erotic-minded Chaplin, nothing about Schopenhauer could have been more important than the fact that sexual passion had always had a strong attraction for him, and that in *The World as Will and Idea* he had made "this constant theme of all the poets his own." "Next to the love of life," Schopenhauer wrote, sexual love is "the strongest and most active of all motives, and incessantly

lays claim to half the powers and thoughts of the younger portion of mankind. It is the ultimate goal of almost all human effort; it has an unfavorable influence on the most important affairs, interrupts every hour the most serious occupations, and sometimes perplexes for a while even the greatest minds. It does not hesitate to intrude with its trash, and to interfere with the negotiations of statesmen and the investigations of the learned. . . . Every day it brews and hatches the worst and most perplexing quarrels and disputes, destroys the most valuable relationships, and breaks the strongest bonds. It demands the sacrifice sometimes of life or health, sometimes of wealth, position, and happiness. Indeed, it robs of all conscience those who were previously honorable and upright, and makes traitors of those who have hitherto been loyal and faithful. Accordingly, it appears on the whole as a malevolent demon, striving to pervert, to confuse, and to overthrow everything. If we consider all this, we are induced to exclaim: Why all this noise and fuss? Why all the urgency and uproar, anguish, and exertion? . . . The essential thing [of being in love] is not perhaps mutual affection, but possession, in other words, physical enjoyment. The certainty of the former, therefore, cannot in any way console us for the want of the latter; on the contrary, in such a situation many a man has shot himself. On the other hand, when those who are deeply in love cannot obtain mutual affection, they are easily satisfied with possession, *i.e.*, with physical enjoyment. This is proved by all forced marriages, and likewise by a woman's favor, so often purchased, in spite of her dislike, with large presents or other sacrifices, and also by cases of rape. . . . However loudly those persons of a lofty and sentimental soul, especially those in love, may raise an outcry over the gross realism of my view, they are nevertheless mistaken.[21]

Sexual love appears as a malevolent demon: Chaplin would draw on that dramatic idea in *The Kid* because of its immediate relevance to his private life.

5

The kingpin of the Keystone Film Company, Mack Sennett, boasted to the ghostwriter of his autobiography, *King of Comedy* (1954), that he and his girlfriend, Mabel Normand, had been so impressed by Chaplin's mime work in a performance in New York "in late 1912" of *A Night in an English Music Hall* that they had then and there discussed whether he was "good enough for pictures." *King of Comedy*, however, is filled to overflowing with apocryphal stories. Furthermore, other accounts allege that it was an ex-bookie named Adam Kessel who spotted Chaplin's cinematic potential. Kessel was in the habit of acting as a talent scout because he and another ex-bookie, Charles Baumann, controlled Keystone's parent organization, the New York Motion Picture Company.[22]

What is more certain than the identity of Chaplin's "discoverer" was that in the spring of 1913 Kessel and Baumann sent a telegram to Alf Reeves, in care of the Nixon Theater in Philadelphia, that read something like this:

IS THERE A MAN NAMED CHAFFIN IN YOUR COMPANY OR SOMETHING LIKE THAT STOP IF SO WILL HE COMMUNICATE WITH KESSEL AND BAUMANN 24 LONGACRE BUILDING BROADWAY.[23]

The next morning, Chaplin caught an early train to New York. In Kessel and Baumann's office he learned that Keystone's brightest star, Fred Mace, was leaving the company. Whether or not they really meant it, Kessel and Baumann flattered Chaplin into believing that they expected him to fill Mace's shoes. For his services for one year, he further learned, he would be paid a salary of one hundred and fifty dollars a week. Following a couple of weeks of dickering by mail about details, he signed the contract they sent him. The commencement date of his employment was set for December 16, 1913, since bookings did not permit him to leave the Karno troupe until the end of November.[24]

Chaplin was eager to stay in America, but he was not particularly fond of the sort of movies for which Keystone was known, as well as far from sure, when he came right down to it, that making movies was what he wanted to do with his life. At the same time he realized that working in films might make him famous. "A year at that racket," he told himself, "and I could return to vaudeville an international star." When he finally left for Hollywood in late November, he did so without any conviction that he would remain there for long.[25]

6

Mack Sennett—born Mikall Sinnott—was an immigrant from Canada who succeeded in escaping the harsh life of an iron puddler by parlaying his crude gifts as an entertainer into a so-so career as a burlesque comedian and chorus boy in Broadway musicals. New Year's Day 1908 found him out of work and down on his luck. Swallowing his pride, he applied for an acting job in a place of employment that he considered beneath his dignity: the brownstone mansion on East Fourteenth Street in lower Manhattan where the American Mutoscope and Biograph Company maintained its movie studios.*

Some weeks later, another man of the theater showed up on Fourteenth Street in a similarly chastened frame of mind. A native of Kentucky and a seasoned performer in touring company productions of nineteenth-century melodramas, he had a royal way of carrying himself, offstage as well as on, that served to remind his friends of his claim of descent from Welsh kings of old. Although he sometimes preferred to appear professionally under assumed names, his real name was David Wark Griffith.[26]

Biograph put both men to work as actors in such films as *The Sculptor's Nightmare*, a caricature of the various politicos who were hoping to gain the White House in 1908. But in the late summer of that year of change, Griffith was given the key job of directing all of Biograph's pictures, for the company had recently been reorganized and the Kentuckian's know-how about melodrama perfectly suited its new plans. Throughout the company's twelve-year history, the two specialties of the house had been partial-reel—known as split-reel—comedies and actualities. Only now and again were melodramas and sentimental love stories added to the menu. The actualities focused on simple things—on waves breaking on a shore, on the arrival of a train at a station, on the dedication of a public monument. As for the comedies, they were mainly built upon borrowings from other sources of mass entertainment. Chase comedies from Pathé and Méliès in France and from Gaumont in Britain were born again at Biograph, as were the comic-strip adventures of the Katzenjammer Kids and Happy Hooligan. Other inspirations for the Fourteenth Street filmmakers came from the humorous sequences of photographs that were mounted on cards and sold to the public for stereoscopic viewing. Somewhat less raunchy versions of burlesque-show playlets were also recycled in such films as *Soubrettes in a Bachelor's Flat* (1903) and *Peeping Tom in the Dressing Room* (1905).[27]

---

* The first half of the company's jawbreaking name stemmed from the fact that the bankers who funded the enterprise had been initially interested in manufacturing very brief films for individual viewing in hand-cranked peep-show machines known as mutoscopes. The machines could usually be found in penny arcades, and the films tended to be "blue."

The mastermind of the company's shift in production policy was Jeremiah J. Kennedy, a business executive with experience in reorganizing large enterprises. In 1907, the Empire Trust Company had sent him to Fourteenth Street to look into the failure of Biograph's officers to make interest payments on a $200,000 loan from Empire. The expectation was that Kennedy would find it necessary to liquidate the company. But after inspecting the books, he decided it was salvageable. Among the first steps he took thereafter was to reconsider the content of Biograph's pictures in the light of the increasingly ominous political situation in which the entire film industry now found itself.

Morally alarmed clergymen, social workers, and newspaper editors had begun to lash out at the salaciousness of the "flickers" to which viewers had easy access in thousands of nickelodeons, ten-cent vaudeville houses, and penny arcades across the country. Thus in March 1907 the *Chicago Tribune* declared editorially that the city's nickelodeons were "without a redeeming feature to warrant their existence." Because they ministered to "the lowest passions," the *Tribune* indignantly continued, there should be a law "absolutely forbidding" the admission of boys and girls under eighteen. Three months later in New York, the forces of morality found even more to cheer about in a report from the police commissioner to the mayor, George B. McClellan (the son of the Civil War commander), recommending the cancellation of the licenses of all the arcades and nickelodeons under his jurisdiction. Clearly, the movie companies had to clean up their act.[28]

The drive to endow a lucrative but raffish business with middle-class respectability also led to efforts to alter the atmosphere of the dark and often smelly rooms in which most exhibitors had set up their screens by providing sufficient lighting so that everyone in the audience was at all times visible, and by improving the circulation of the air. Further efforts in this period to upgrade the milieu of the moving-picture show eventually included the addition of restrooms, ushers, refreshment stands, and luxurious decorations and furnishings, and the elimination out front of garish posters, importuning barkers, and blaring music.[29]

The comedies that Biograph made after 1907 were not nearly as vulnerable to moralistic attack as *Peeping Tom in the Dressing Room*. But Jeremiah Kennedy regarded comedy of any kind as a much lower form of entertainment than melodrama, and actualities bored him completely.

His rearrangement of Biograph's budget gave D. W. Griffith a marvelous chance. Whereas in 1907 only four melodramas had come out of Fourteenth Street, the total topped one hundred in the first twelve months during which Griffith was in the director's chair. By the time another movie company lured him away from Biograph in 1913, approximately 450 films bore the stamp of his genius, most of them one-reel thrillers and sentimental dramas and the remainder comedies.[30]

Among the landmark achievements of his Biograph years was a thriller entitled *The Lonely Villa* (1909), based on a script by Mack Sennett about three villainous tramps who observe a gentleman's departure from the isolated house where he lives with his wife and daughters and promptly break into it with robbery and worse in mind. When the gentleman calls his wife some time later, he hears her horrified cries for help just before the phone wires are cut. Whereupon he frantically tries to reach her side before it is too late. The camera shifts back and forth from his transportation difficulties to the tramps' implacable, room-by-room pursuit of the wife and the utterly terrified children (one of whom is Mary Pickford, looking considerably younger than her seventeen years). Just as the intruders succeed in breaking down the last of the locked doors between them and their quarry, the husband arrives and rescues his family.[31]

Out of a need for techniques of storytelling that would not only convey but multiply the dramatic power inherent in the stories themselves, Griffith developed an entire vocabulary of cinematic expression. From the work of other filmmakers, he appropriated the close-up shot, and made such brilliant use of it that he was hailed as its inventor. The practice of cross-cutting from one scene of action to another, as in *The Lonely Villa*, essentially derived from his experience onstage, where an equivalent had been introduced by directors who had grown impatient with the lack of plasticity in the modern theater. Still other techniques, most notably backlighting and the spot-iris vignette, were developed with Griffith's encouragement by his gifted cameraman, Billy Bitzer.[32]

In the early evening Griffith could usually be found conducting a seminar in directing for the benefit of Mack Sennett, although at the time he was not conscious of doing so. All he knew was that as he walked home at the end of the day, his inexhaustibly energetic colleague caught up with him and began asking technical questions, which Griffith never failed to answer at length. In his growing excitement about his work, he was only too happy to talk about it. Notwithstanding the fact that Sennett had an ego as outsized as Griffith's, he would later pay homage to his walking companion for having served as "my adult education program, my university."[33] And when Griffith made a chase comedy in 1909 called *The Curtain Pole* (which he shot mainly on location in Fort Lee, New Jersey), he did Sennett a further favor by plucking him out of the ranks of Biograph's bit players and casting him in the leading role of a French fop who comes to grief in small-town America as a result of his attempt to earn a pretty girl's gratitude.

Comically decked out in a long formal coat, top hat, and spats, and played by Sennett in what he apparently hoped was Max Linder's style, the fop tries to upstage the hometown admirer of a pretty girl by offering to hang some curtains for her in her living room. Unfortunately, the pole breaks and he hurries off to buy a replacement. Along the way, he pauses at a saloon, from which he emerges the worse for wear. After purchasing a new pole, he carries it along the street athwart his body, bowling over other pedestrians as he blithely proceeds. Upon realizing at last the wrath of his victims, who have dusted themselves off and are running hard to catch up with him, he hails a horse-cab. With several feet of the pole sticking out of each of the side windows, the cab takes off at high speed. The pole smashes into everything from a cart full of vegetables to a man on a stepladder who is repairing a street lamp. More and more townsfolk join the chase. The eye of the camera alternately focuses on the pursuers and the pursued. At the girl's home, a different sort of misfortune confronts him. Someone else—quite possibly her hometown boyfriend—has already replaced the broken pole.

Griffith was not really comfortable with the crass humor of *The Curtain Pole*, even though it broke all Biograph records. The genteel "Jones family" comedies he subsequently made were much more to his taste.[34] For Sennett, on the other hand, the picture's opening moments of domestic slapstick and its relentless put-downs of a social outsider defined comic possibilities that he himself was determined to develop, once he was accorded directorial power. But what fascinated him above all about *The Curtain Pole* was its ballistics. The surrealistic automobile collisions and railroad crossing smashups of Sennett's Keystone comedies would become his trademark—but it was Griffith's treatment of a careening horse-cab that basically taught him how to film these demolition derbies.[35]

Not until 1911 did the Biograph brass place Sennett in charge of a production unit specializing in comedies. Even then, he was denied the freedom to test his contention that the formal gestures and preposterous uniforms of cops were funny. Nor was he encouraged, as he would be at Keystone, to find ways of getting around the new censorship of sexual humor. Finally, the absence of racial and ethnic minorities in his Biograph films suggests that he was not permitted to include them in his equality of ridicule, as he would be at Keystone in such films as *Cohen Collects a Debt* (1912) and *Rastus and the Game Cock* (1914).

Thus when Messrs. Kessel and Baumann approached him in August 1912 and offered him a part-ownership as well as the managing directorship of the film-comedy company they were setting up in a studio they owned in a southern California town called Edendale (now the southeastern part of Glendale), he had no difficulty in making up his mind.

7

Richard V. Spencer, who handled scripts for Kessel and Baumann's New York Motion Picture Company, noted in an article in *Moving Picture World* in April 1911 that "Los Angeles within the short period of two years has reached the position in the moving picture manufacturing field where it is second only to New York." A combination of climatic advantages and environmental diversity, Spencer correctly discerned, was primarily responsible for this development. Not only did southern California provide "320 days for good photography, out of the 365," but "within a twenty-mile radius of Los Angeles may be found conditions suitable for exteriors from a tropic to a frigid background, and from desert to jungle." In addition, "a score of high class beach resorts," conveniently connected to the city by trolley lines, lay twenty miles or so to the west. "There may be taken resort comedies with an Atlantic City or Coney Island background," Spencer observed in a prophetic sentence. As for movies that required residential backgrounds, Los Angeles offered a profusion of interestingly varied streets, while for Wild West settings Griffith Park was available, "the largest park in the world," situated "within a ten minutes' ride" of the city. A good many cowboy-and-Indian movies had already been shot there.[36]

An eminent modern-day chronicler of southern California history regards the movies that Mack Sennett made in his Keystone heyday as a wonderful resource for the study of Los Angeles in the process of becoming a notable American city. In the background of Sennett's scenes of hot pursuit, Kevin Starr has observed, Americans of the time

> caught glimpses of a city where everyone seemed to live in a bungalow on a broad avenue lined with palm, pepper or eucalyptus trees and there was never any snow on the ground or other evidence of bad weather. It is difficult to assess the public relations effect the Sennett imagery of sunny beaches, gardens, and homes had as it flickered before middle America in darkened movie halls, but Los Angeles was being announced subliminally by . . . [him] as a new American place with its own audience and visual signature, and Americans did emigrate there in droves, pushing the population to well over a million [by 1916].[37]

Fred Mace, Ford Sterling, Mabel Normand, and Henry Lehrman— all of whom had worked for Biograph—either accompanied Sennett to Los Angeles or joined him in Edendale after his arrival. By the time Chaplin came on board, Sennett had also gained big bruiser Mack Swain, as well as Slim Summerville, walrus-whiskered Chester Conklin, Phyllis Allen, Alice Davenport, Fatty Arbuckle, and Arbuckle's wife, Minta Durfee, and was about to pick up Edgar Kennedy (later renowned for his "slow burn" routine). Forty years later, Sennett would look back at this assemblage of talent and say of it that "never again in all his pictures . . . did Charlie Chaplin face up to such competition." Chaplin's worthiest rivals in the group were Fatty Arbuckle and Mabel Normand.[38]

Arbuckle carried close to 280 pounds on a five-foot ten-inch frame, yet his body, as his wife said, was hard as nails. Swift of foot and a good swimmer, as well as an accomplished tumbler and a marvelously agile ballroom dancer,* he was a master of the mad dashes and pratfalls that

---

* Dancing with Fatty, the actress Louise Brooks remembered, made her feel as if she were in the embrace of a floating doughnut. Quoted in Betty Harper Fussell, *Mabel* (New Haven, Conn., and New York, 1982), p. 65.

Sennett comedy required. Often cast as a lovesick suitor or a philandering husband, he nevertheless came across as sexually harmless, thanks to his baby face, goo-goo grin, and overgrown infant's girth. The occasional look of heartlessness in his light-colored eyes was scarcely noticed. But after eight years of fabulous success, he was suddenly caught up in a scandal that destroyed his career.

At a wild, drunken party he staged in a San Francisco hotel suite on Labor Day weekend in 1921, a twenty-five-year-old actress, Virginia Rappe (pronounced Rappay), whose primary claim to distinction was that her face had been featured on a sheet-music cover of the hit song "Let Me Call You Sweetheart," began screaming in pain and tearing at her clothes. Some of the guests clumsily tried to ease her agony by dumping her into a bathtub filled with ice. Later she was transported to a sanatorium, where she died the following Friday. Gonorrhea had been one of her problems, but the woe that had plagued her since childhood was cystitis. In drinking heavily at the party, as testimony indicated that she did, she had certainly risked a bad attack of bladder pain. It was by no means impossible that the pajama-clad Arbuckle had sexual intercourse with Rappe in the bedroom of the suite. But no proof was ever offered to substantiate the idea that he raped her, and that her bladder was ruptured by a combination of his great weight pressing down upon her and his insensate manipulation of a Coca-Cola bottle. Nevertheless, that was the gossip that spread across the nation like wildfire, fanned by hundreds of newspaper stories and headlines. TORTURE OF VIRGINIA RAPPE CHARGED (San Francisco Examiner); ARBUCKLE DRAGGED GIRL TO ROOM, WOMAN TESTIFIES (New York Times); ICE ON ACTRESS BIG JOKE TO ARBUCKLE (Los Angeles Examiner).

Despite Arbuckle's exoneration by the jury in the third of the trials he was forced to endure, a national outcry against him persisted, thereby compelling the movie industry's newly appointed front man and moral adviser, Will Hays, to ban him from the screen. As the New York Times angrily asserted, "Arbuckle has become, through mischance, a symbol of all the vice that has been indulged in by movie people," and "the only thing to do with a scapegoat is to chase him into the wilderness." Eventually he was permitted to direct pictures under another name. With macabre humor, he chose Will B. Goode as his pseudonym, but Will Hays made him change it to William Goodrich.[39]

If Arbuckle's tragedy testified to the reputation-destroying capabilities of the press, it was also a measure of the torrential emotions that movies could unleash. By 1921, millions of moviegoers had long since assumed that the cinematic Fatty and the real Fatty were essentially one and the same—and the fact that his nickname had frequently appeared in the titles of his films (*Fatty's Tintype Tangle, Fatty's Chance Acquaintance*, and so on) did nothing to discourage this view. In a violent reaction to the news of his indictment, many Americans replaced their shattered illusions about him with a devastatingly different one. In the popular mind, the image of an impotent, overweight sex maniac who had needed a Coke bottle to achieve penetration became a symbol of the moral squalor of a disordered postwar world—even as the story about a girl who had been raped with a corncob set off reverberations in the mind of a young writer named William Faulkner, when he heard about it one night from a hooker in a Memphis nightclub.

Petite Mabel Normand had the full bosom, tiny waist, and large-eyed, black-haired beauty of a Gibson Girl, which was why Charles Dana Gibson and other top-drawer magazine illustrators hired her, at age seventeen, to pose for them. Sex appeal alone, however, did not account for her subsequent success as an actress at Biograph, where she appeared in twenty-five comedy shorts between her nineteenth and twentieth birthdays, or for her emergence at Keystone as the premiere comedienne of silent movies. Like Arbuckle, she was wonderfully athletic, excelling in particular in water sports. She could also take a fall as well as a professional acrobat, while her feisty personality and repertoire of delightful grimaces enabled her to hold her own with male costars as different as Sennett, Arbuckle, and Chaplin.

Sexy-funny girls were the toast of American vaudeville in these years. But as Betty Harper Fussell has pointed out, Mabel Normand was the first sexy clown to become a film star. Among her many successors, the closest to her in spirit was the young Carole Lombard, who as a teenager in 1927 made a dozen shorts for Mack Sennett; but such varied figures as Clara Bow, Jean Arthur, Ginger Rogers, Rosalind Russell, Katharine Hepburn, Judy Holliday, Lucille Ball, and Goldie Hawn may also be claimed for the tradition she established.[40]

At Biograph, Normand wore whatever sort of costume struck her fancy and did whatever she pleased, from driving a racing car to hitching a ride beside the pilot in an open-seated airplane.[41] In her first Keystone movie, a split-reeler of late 1912 called *The Water Nymph*, she appeared in a black, form-fitting, leotardlike bathing suit known as "Kellerman tights," in tribute to the garment that had inspired the arrest in Boston some years earlier of the swimming and diving champion Annette Kellerman. Holding her hands high above her head to raise her breasts, she paused for a moment took a deep breath, and executed a perfect dive.* The following summer, in *A Noise from the Deep*, she hurled the first Keystone pie—and scored a direct hit on her target (Fatty Arbuckle's face). Thereafter, she herself became fair game for pie throwers. On other occasions, she was drenched with water while fully clothed and slapped half silly with whitewash-loaded paintbrushes. And by the time she staggered ashore at the end of a picture in which she had been marooned in a rowboat in the middle of a lake that had been suddenly and maliciously drained of water, she was totally covered with liquified mud.

Yet whenever she was kicked, Normand kicked back. In this respect, her comic persona resembled the undauntable and charmingly pugnacious youngsters whom Mary Pickford had begun to play. Although Normand's salary and other perquisites would never approach the magnitude of Pickford's, she did receive authorization from Sennett to direct some of her own pictures. Sennett was willing to jeopardize his romance with Normand by turning the sofa in his office into a casting couch, but he remained a faithful admirer of her comic intelligence. In her role as a director, she did not take her responsibilities lightly, as Chaplin would discover in a notable showdown between the two of them.

Off the set, however, her behavior was defiantly irresponsible, and after she realized that Sennett would never give up his sexual foragings

* Upon learning of Normand's death in February 1930, the eminent Hollywood director King Vidor would recall that when he had been a young ticket-taker in a Texas nickelodeon, "beautiful, lithe-figured Mabel Normand . . . had been my dream girl. I remembered her, black tights covering her body, as she walked to the end of the board and dived gracefully into the water below." King Vidor, *A Tree Is a Tree* (New York, 1951), pp. 190–91. It would be interesting to know if the audience for *The Water Nymph* in 1912 also included a twelve-year-old tomboy in Montgomery, Alabama, named Zelda Sayre. As a high school student a few years later, crazy, sexy-funny Zelda would delight in going off the high board to impress college boys.

among extra girls, it turned self-destructive. In the disapproving opinion of the producer Hal Roach, Normand was the "wildest girl in Hollywood" and "the dirtiest girl you ever heard."[42]* Roach also disapproved of her drug-taking and blamed her for corrupting the starlet Clarine Seymour and other younger actresses. Samuel Goldwyn, on the other hand, chose to remember her generosity. When receivership threatened his company during World War I, Normand gave the beleaguered producer $50,000 in Liberty bonds to help him through the crisis. He also saw her give a thousand-dollar check to "a poor girl stricken with tuberculosis, with a dependent family." In contrast to Pickford, whom Goldwyn, or rather his ghostwriter, termed "a systematized human being," Normand was "a creature of impulse."[43]

Nineteen eighteen marked the beginning of her pitiable decline. Attended only by a nurse, she gave birth in her bedroom to a stillborn baby boy. Perhaps the prematureness of the birth was related to her drug addiction, but in any case her dependency on narcotics, combined with a fondness for booze, inexorably affected her looks and her energy level. A leading director at Paramount, William Desmond Taylor, with whom Normand had fallen in love, put her in a hospital for a drug cure in late 1919. After her release, he continued to encourage her to live a drug-free life. In addition, he asked a federal narcotics prosecutor in Los Angeles for legal help in fighting the underworld pushers who were her suppliers. That Taylor's efforts to save her were of little avail was evident to a newspaperman who saw them together at a party on New Year's Eve 1921: "There was a weary droop to her once pert and vivacious gestures. She swayed a little, leaning on her escort's arm."[44]

A month later, Taylor was shot to death in his duplex apartment in Alvarado Court in the then-fashionable West Lake Park district of Hollywood. (Among the other residents of Alvarado Court was Edna Purviance, Chaplin's longtime leading lady and Mabel Normand's close friend.) Because Normand had been with Taylor in his apartment on the evening before his body was discovered and was the last known

---

* See the actress Miriam Cooper's description of Mabel in her autobiography. "Mabel . . . wasn't my type, as she was tough and dirty-talking, but all those girls who did comedy were tough." Miriam Cooper, *Dark Lady of the Silents* (Indianapolis, Ind., 1973), p. 181.

person to have seen him alive, she was immediately implicated in the case, as was another young actress who worshipped Taylor, Mary Miles Minter.

The movie executive Benjamin B. Hampton was exaggerating when he wrote in his *History of the Movies* (1931) that the Taylor case "sold more newspapers everywhere in America than were ever sold by any items of news, not excepting war news, before or since."[45] But there can be no doubt that the question of who killed William Desmond Taylor fascinated millions of people on both sides of the Atlantic,* or that it created a public relations headache for Hollywood that was exceeded only by the Arbuckle story.

The failure of the police to solve the murder meant that a number of reputations, among them Normand's, were shadowed by it forever after —and hers had already been damaged by her drug taking. Even the fan magazines betrayed her. The portrait of her in a punningly entitled piece, "The Inside Dope on Movie Stars," was especially savage: "Her eyes are bulging and have lost their old luster. Her voice is dull and, at times, wandering. . . . The old Mabel Normand of the serio-comic smile and quick wit is gone."[46] Afflicted by tuberculosis as well as by the ravages of her addiction, Normand could no longer kick back against the savageries of life.

8

If Mack Sennett was a "master" within his cinematic range, as Theodore Dreiser once said of him,[47] he was also an uneducated roughneck with apelike arms, oafish manners, and either a foul-smelling cigar clenched in his teeth or a chaw of tobacco in his cheek. The actors he hired were a tough bunch, too, and it was Chester Conklin's judgment that Chaplin was initially intimidated by them. Thanks to a mischievous decision by Sennett, said Conklin, "that little Englishman" had to share a dressing room with Fatty Arbuckle and Mack Swain, "the hardest-

---

* As Robert Giroux has reminded us, the murderer in Georges Simenon's *La Tête d'un Homme* tries to bait Inspector Maigret by bringing up the Taylor case. *A Deed of Death* (New York, 1990), p. 223. In the late 1940s *Tête d'un Homme* was made into the film *The Man on the Eiffel Tower*, starring Charles Laughton as Maigret.

boiled giants we had. For weeks he was scairt to change his clothes in their presence." A difficulty he had of another sort, Conklin continued, was that "he knew nothing at all about pictures. When he first saw himself on the screen he was all bowled over. 'It cawn't be. Is that possible? How extr'ordi'ry. Is it really me?' "[48]

An American wish to put an Englishman down could easily have been responsible for the animus in Conklin's remarks, as well as for the dubious if not outrageous contention of Arbuckle's wife, Minta Durfee, that Chaplin smelled. "He was a clever man," she later conceded, "but he was plenty dirty."[49] The principal reason, however, for his unpopularity at Keystone was that despite his humble manner he could be exceedingly disagreeable when he chose to be, and even before he made his first picture, he made clear his dislike of some of the studio's practices. Although Sennett occasionally depended on a detailed script, he usually went to the opposite extreme and began shooting a movie with only a general idea about what he wanted to do. At first, such an approach seemed all too casual, all too American, to Chaplin. He also did not care for the headlong chases, as he had known he would not, that Sennett never grew tired of. As Chaplin later explained, chases "dissipated one's personality; little as I knew about movies, I knew that nothing transcended personality."[50]

Perhaps to punish his recruit for his upstart opinions, Sennett gave him no assignments for weeks. With nothing to do except to check in every day, Chaplin spent his time wandering about the lot and exploring the neighborhood. Edendale, he discovered, was a tacky community, littered with small lumberyards and junkyards and woebegone farms, on some of which a small store or two had been built near the road. At first glance, the Keystone property was no less unattractive. A dilapidated green fence surrounded the lot. Inside the fence, a dirt path led to an old bungalow that housed the administrative offices and the actresses' dressing rooms. To one side of the bungalow were a nondescript barn and a harness room, where the actors had their dressing rooms. Yet Chaplin also found that the stage on which all the interior scenes of the comedies were shot was an enchanting place. Vertical sheets of white linen defined the peripheries of each set and horizontal sheets were suspended above. Beautifully diffused sunlight softly filtered through the linen, creating an ideal condition for daylight photography.[51]

Sennett finally tapped Chaplin for the role of an unscrupulous dude in a thousand-foot one-reeler called *Making a Living* and sent it before the cameras in the last days of January 1914, under the direction of Henry Lehrman. Known to everyone as "Pathé" Lehrman, he was not the person he claimed to be. In reality he was an Austrian immigrant who had kept himself alive after leaving Ellis Island by working as a streetcar conductor in one of New York City's outer boroughs. But when he presented himself one day at the Biograph studios and asked for a job, he introduced himself as M. Henri Lehrman from Pathé Frères, whose "wide and varied" cinematic experience could be of inestimable assistance to an ambitious American film company. Although D. W. Griffith at once saw through his pretenses, he hired him as an actor—and after he demonstrated a flair for thinking up gags, Griffith passed him on to Sennett's comedy unit. As a director at Keystone, he kept up the fiction that he was a Frenchman, even though the Gallic accent he affected was continually betrayed by his Viennese gutturals.[52]

Chaplin detested "Pathé" Lehrman, as did many other movie people, even though they recognized that he was talented. Among the more experienced actors on the Keystone lot, he was often referred to by a second nickname, "Mr. Suicide," because of his willingness to place them, for the sake of thrilling audiences, in physically dangerous situations. In addition, he was a dope addict and a deadbeat. Perhaps the only person in the entire Los Angeles area who genuinely cared for him was his new girlfriend, seventeen-year-old Virginia Rappe.[53]

The tension between Chaplin and Lehrman was exacerbated by Lehrman's contempt for a newcomer's claims to comedic know-how. Because of his burning desire to make his film debut a success, Chaplin crammed his performance in *Making a Living* with as many extra gags as he could think of—only to find that Lehrman left the bulk of them on the cutting-room floor. "When I saw the finished film," Chaplin remembered, "it broke my heart, for the cutter had butchered it beyond recognition." A bitter quarrel between the two men broke out, which Sennett settled by siding with his fellow director.[54]

Was the raw footage of *Making a Living* as good as Chaplin implied? On the evidence of the finished product, it is doubtful. Only in a few fleeting moments does Chaplin's overdressed but nonetheless seedy four-flusher, with his top hat and monocle, grotesquely long, double-breasted frock coat, droopy handlebar mustache, and histrionic, curses-foiled-again gestures, break free of the clichés of comic stage villainy. Sennett's view of his performance was that

> Chaplin was almost lost in the shuffle when Lehrman tried to put him through our fast paces. Virginia Kirtley, Alice Davenport, Minta Durfee, Chester Conklin and Pathé himself [in the role of the honest newspaper-man who is the seedy dude's professional and romantic rival] went into their routines like sprinters taking off from their marks. Chaplin was confused and plaintive. He couldn't understand what was going on, why everything went so fast, and why scenes were shot out of chronology.[55]

Kessel and Baumann hated *Making a Living*, Chaplin's performance in it above all. As Sennett recalled, both men "raised hell" with him for having hired "this silly cheap comedian"—although it was the two of them who had cut the deal. Mabel Normand vividly remembered how upset Sennett was. Inasmuch as she had turned down the chance to play the leading lady, on the ground that "I don't like [Chaplin] so good now that I've seen him," Sennett made no effort to conceal from her his sudden fear that bringing the little Englishman to Keystone had been an awful mistake. According to Normand, he "screamed" at her that "he had hooked himself up with a dead one." [56] The language in both of these recollections is so high-colored that it raises doubts about their accuracy. Yet they mesh with the overall impression of Chaplin at this point as a man without any allies. From self-pitying loneliness to self-important superiority, all of the feelings of alienation that he had displayed vis-à-vis professional associates in his theatrical years were eating into him once again as he nervously awaited his next assignment.

9

As settings for his pictures, Sennett often filmed real-life events—a Shriners' parade, perhaps, or a concert in a park, or a horse race. For very little cost, location shooting of this sort added visual interest and sometimes inspired the story line as well. Consequently, when he heard that a soapbox derby for kids had been scheduled in nearby Venice, he immediately began thinking of ways to make use of it.

A pleasant trolley ride away from downtown Los Angeles, Venice had been designed by a visionary developer as a residential community for an affluent and educated clientele. Initially it had offered the cultural activities of a Chautauqua and the romantic allure of an "Old World" setting. The Queen City of the Adriatic could boast of canals and distinguished hotels, and so could its namesake on the Pacific. Unfortunately, the developer overreached himself, and the dream town he had created dissolved into a West Coast version of Coney Island. Not far from the spectacular auditorium where symphony orchestras had played, eminent professors had lectured, and Sarah Bernhardt had performed in *Camille*, a bowling alley, a shooting gallery, a dance pavilion, and a Ferris wheel sprang up almost as rapidly as the weeds that had choked the canals.[57]

The plan that Sennett came up with in connection with the soapbox races called for Lehrman and Chaplin to attend them, along with two camera crews. Lehrman and the first crew would appear to be making a documentary about the derby, while the second crew filmed their efforts to do so—despite the annoying interferences that Chaplin would create. It was on one of the playgrounds, then, of modern America's nascent mass culture that a nameless comic figure—whom the public would decide soon enough to call Charlie—stepped out of a crowd and demanded photographic recognition.*

Shortly before the day of the shooting, Chaplin was told that he could choose his own costume and makeup. Lehrman later described the selections he made.

[He] borrowed Fatty's trousers, Chester Conklin's old shoes, and got the rest of his clothes from the dressing room he shared [with Arbuckle and Mack Swain] and from the studio wardrobe. A few days later, we were getting ready to go out to Venice, where there is an amusement park, like Coney Island but on a smaller scale, and I saw Chaplin arrive wearing the costume that would make him famous. His mustache consisted of a

---

* Although a generous amount of footage was shot, *Kid Auto Races at Venice* was released on February 7 as a split-reel film of 572 feet and a running time of approximately six minutes. The rest of the reel was filled by a factual film, *Olives and Their Oil*. Some historians have argued—unconvincingly in my judgment—that in spite of the fact that Chaplin's third picture, *Mabel's Strange Predicament*, went into release two days after *Kid Auto Races*, it was actually shot first.

rectangle of black crepe glued under his nose. He seemed delighted with his appearance and twirled his walking-stick with his fingers. . . . And that's how we got to see Charlie Chaplin for the first time in his "trampy" disguise.[58]

For all its precise detail, Lehrman's description does not jibe with the visual evidence of the movie. The trousers, first of all, do not envelop Chaplin, as Arbuckle's surely would have. Rather, they are unfashionably short, a little wide in the upper part of the legs but not at the ankles, somewhat outsized at the waist, although not overwhelmingly so, and fit snugly over the buttocks. Furthermore, the general effect of the costume is not "trampy." While the Edwardian-style jacket and vest create an odd impression because they are much too small for him, they appear to be in reasonably good condition. The collar and cuffs of his white shirt look clean and his shoes—which are large but not ludicrously so—and jauntily cocked derby hat seem only marginally the worse for wear.

Nor is the main character in *Kid Auto Races at Venice* a master of the Charlie Chaplin walk. He toes out, to be sure, but most of his strides are stiff-legged struts, not hitchy jogs. As he moves away from the cluster of spectators along the road that is serving as the raceway and assumes a self-conscious stance in front of Lehrman's camera, his features come into clear focus for the first time. They are considerably darker than the white mask of more famous appearances. In combination with his large nose and two locks of dark hair curling forward on either side of his forehead, his skin color suggests a Mediterranean provenance—south Italian, perhaps, or Greek.

As for the facial expressions of this strange bystander, they raise the question of whether he is crazy. When Lehrman orders him to stand aside, he responds with a glare, or with sardonically raised eyebrows, or with a blank look that conveys mock bewilderment about Lehrman's indignation. From his insouciant swaggerings about, his butt-sprung, cock-of-the-walk poses, and his habit of lighting a cigarette, throwing the dead match over his shoulder, and kicking it with his heel, to his schoolgirlish skipping down the hill from the starting line of the races, everything he does is designed to call attention to himself. "Look at me! Look at me!" is his silent cry.

In their work together on *Kid Auto Races*, Chaplin and Lehrman were both tied to a real-life subtext: the ugly knot of bad feelings between them. The knot served, however, to tighten the drama of their on-camera antagonism. Charlie infuriates Lehrman by repeatedly blocking his shots of the races, until finally the director gives his tormenter a violent shove that bowls him over. To his immense frustration, Charlie snaps back like a rubber band and resumes his interfering ways.

In a less egregious fashion, a number of the racing fans in the grand-stand—who are ordinary citizens, not Keystone hirelings—prove to be attention-seekers, too. As they become conscious of Lehrman's camera panning across the stands, they stare at it with a mesmeric intensity, as if willing it to remain focused on them—although one woman holds a paper in front of her face so that she cannot be identified. Her reaction exemplifies twentieth-century wariness about the power of mechanical devices to intrude and record. Yet it is also true that most people take a narcissistic delight in being eyed by cameras. Instead of feeling lost in the crowd at a beach or a ballgame, they achieve a sense of existential importance through having their presence registered on film. I have been photographed; therefore, I am. Drawing on memories of the camera-hogging public official he had noticed on the island of Jersey, Chaplin turned his loosely defined assignment in *Kid Auto Races* into a broadly exaggerated but remarkably perceptive commentary on the reactions that the presence of a camera can cause.[59]

10

The first of his appearances opposite Mabel Normand took place in Chaplin's third picture, *Mabel's Strange Predicament*. Lehrman had sketched out the script and expected to direct. But when his quarrel with Chaplin showed no signs of cooling off, Sennett decided to take the reins himself.

As an elegant young lady who suffers the embarrassment of being locked out of her hotel room while dressed in her pajamas, Normand was her usual sexy-clownish self. But as another member of the cast, Chester Conklin, was forced to admit, the little Englishman stole the show. A number of Keystone actors and actresses who were not involved in the picture came by to watch the filming of the first sequence. Charlie, a drunken masher, wanders into a hotel lobby; Mabel enters with a dog on a leash; Charlie tries to pick her up but has no success and becomes entangled with the dog's leash; flirtations with other females also fail; he falls down and gets his hand caught in a cuspidor. All this time, the onlookers on the edge of the set were chuckling appreciatively. Ford Sterling's laughter, however, was edged with envy. A heftily built "Dutch" comedian who had been a major Keystone player from the time the company was organized, Sterling built most of his jokes out of crude gesticulations and strenuous mugging, whereas the comedian he was watching garnered laughs through perfect timing, exquisite facial gestures, and an amazing command of his body. The material in *Mabel's Strange Predicament* could not have been more primitive. What counted, however, was that Chaplin was already the "supermarionette" actor of Marcel Marceau's admiring phrase, whose body seemed to be suspended in space as if "pulled by invisible strings" and whose artifice filled hearts and eyes "with the greatest admiration." "Dutch" Sterling, in sum, had been hopelessly outclassed, and he knew it. After making two more pictures for Sennett, he quit Keystone and founded his own company. Lehrman also left to form the L-Ko (Lehrman Knock-out) Company.[60]

Sixty-year-old George "Pop" Nichols was another Keystone director with whom Chaplin had trouble. The basic cause of the friction between them was that as early as mid-February, when Sennett made them a team, Chaplin was itching to direct his pictures himself. Stung by Sennett's belief that he lacked the technical competence to do so, he took out his anger in complaints about Nichols. As he summed them up in *My Autobiography*, old "Pop" had but one gag, which was to take his comedians by the neck and bounce them from one scene to another. Whenever Chaplin ventured to suggest slower-developing situations that would allow for subtle looks and charming bits of business, Nichols would cry, "We have no time, no time!" and an argument would break out. "Any three-dollar-a-day extra can do what you want me to do," Chaplin claims he declared at one point. "I want to do something with merit, not just be bounced around and fall off street cars." "What the hell do you know about it?" he remembered Nichols replying.[61] Yet the four pictures they made together reveal that the veteran director had an awareness of Chaplin's special gifts and that he also was willing to modify scenarios so that Chaplin could experiment with Charlie's character.

Thus in their first joint effort, *A Film Johnnie* (released on March 2), Chaplin took a step toward the ultimate identification of Charlie as a tramp by making him a panhandling loiterer, even though Nichols could have insisted with reason that the film studio equivalent of a stage-door Romeo ought to have been played in top hat and tails. Nichols also permitted him to experiment with a variety of comic tricks, such as putting on his derby in a way that enabled him to make it spring into the air, and a punctiliously polite habit (which he may have stolen from Fatty Arbuckle) of tipping his hat to someone before kicking him.

One of the reviewers of *A Film Johnnie* referred to Chaplin as Edgar English. A fair number of them, however, not only got his name right, but made clear that he was fast becoming the apple of their eye. "Another triumph for the old Karno comedian," said one commentator, and another averred that "the sensation of the year is the success of Chas. Chaplin. . . . One of his films is *A Film Johnny* [*sic*] which . . . is packed with indescribably funny incidents." [62] But while such praise tasted sweet in Chaplin's mouth, he continued to pick fights with "Pop" Nichols, as Sennett did not fail to notice. More than ever, Sennett was conscious that his "team of professional slam-bangers" did not like the little Englishman any better than he did. In addition to being a chronic complainer, he was an "oddball" who "*liked* to be lonely." At night, said Sennett, he walked the streets "peering at things and people," and despite his good salary kept right on living in "a shabby hotel." [63]

With grudging admiration, Sennett did admit that when it came to ambition, the oddball was the studio's pacesetter. Chaplin "was the most interested person where he himself, his future, the kind of thing he was trying to do, was concerned, I ever knew," Sennett later told Theodore Dreiser. "He wanted to work—and nearly all the time. We went to work at eight o'clock and he was there at seven. We quit at five, say, or later, but he'd still be around at six, and wanting to talk about his work to me all the time." He was eager, too, to survey the results of the day's work. "And if anything in the run didn't please him, he'd click his tongue or snap his fingers and twist and squirm. Now why did I do that that way? What was the matter with me anyhow?" [64]

Mabel Normand's opinion of Chaplin, which had been icy in December, quickly thawed. As a deft pantomimist in her own right, she admired all the quirky little gestures with which he filled out his performances, while off the set she found him funny and charming. Instead of scorning his company, as Sennett did, she started inviting him to her dressing room to talk things over. In a further indication of her wish to be friends, she agreed to join him in studying French.[65] Consequently, when spring came, Sennett saw no reason not to remove Chaplin from Nichols's direction and place him under Mabel's, in a picture in which she would also play the heroine.

There were two sorts of Keystone comedies, farces and burlesques. *Mabel at the Wheel* (released on April 18) was in the latter category. A takeoff on the serialized thriller movies of Pearl White, Ruth Roland, and other daredevil heroines, the picture called for Mabel to take the place of her kidnapped boyfriend in a motorcar race and emerge victorious, despite the efforts of the villain of the piece (played by Chaplin) to thwart her. Attired in a top hat and frock coat and sporting, in addition to a mustache, two satanic tufts of whiskers beneath his chin, Chaplin went before the cameras looking even more evil than he had in *Making a Living*. As he must have known from the start, the role did not suit him, and the realization did nothing to make him feel better about having to take orders from a director who was younger than he was, and a woman at that.

What he later described as "the inevitable blowup" occurred on the very first day of on-location shooting. He and his henchmen were supposed to hose down a portion of the racetrack so that Mabel's car would skid. Because he feared that the scene was not sufficiently incident-rich, he proposed to Mabel that he accidentally step on the hose. While examining the nozzle in a puzzled attempt to figure out why the water had ceased to flow, he would step off the hose, with predictable results. The gag was as old as the hills, but so were many others that had seen service in Keystone films. His proposal, in short, made good sense. Nevertheless, Mabel felt challenged by it and told him, in effect, to stop bothering her and do what he was told. Chaplin responded by sitting down on the side of the road and refusing to continue the filming. Such a display of insubordination would probably cause Sennett to fire him, he realized, but he was not about to let anybody shut him up about his work.[66]

Much to his surprise, Sennett greeted him cordially the following morning. After Mabel and Sennett had talked, she, too, seemed eager to forgive and forget. Just a day or so earlier, he later learned, Sennett had heard from Kessel and Baumann that exhibitors across the country were automatically booking every Keystone picture that featured the little fellow in the derby and that there was a huge demand for more of them.[67]

The first step Sennett took to placate his suddenly hot property was to remove Normand as the director of *Mabel at the Wheel* and assume the position himself. Once the picture was finished, he guided Chaplin through *Twenty Minutes of Love*, and then Chaplin and Normand showed everybody at the studio that they were friends once again by amicably codirecting *Caught in a Cabaret*. But beginning with *Caught in the Rain*, Chaplin alone devised and directed all but a handful of the two dozen comedies he appeared in between May and December of 1914.

II

Among the multitudes of Americans of all ages who fell in love with Chaplin's early work was a little boy in Knoxville, Tennessee, who turned five in November 1914. In his autobiographical novel, *A Death in the Family* (1957), James Agee recalled how much Charlie's antics had meant to him when he was growing up.

Following an enchanting prologue entitled "Knoxville: Summer, 1915," the first chapter opens with a proposal by the father of a little boy named Rufus (as a child, James Rufus Agee was always called by his middle name) that they go downtown after supper and see the picture show at the Majestic. Rufus's mother strenuously objects. "That horrid little man! . . . He's so nasty! . . . So *vulgar!* With his nasty little cane; hooking up skirts and things, and that nasty little walk!" Her husband dismisses her tirade with a laugh, "as he always did," and Rufus is cheered by the laughter, for he felt that it "enclosed him with his father."[68] The scene illustrates family tensions and alliances. In its larger meaning it arraigns the genteel tradition in American culture for its disdain of Charlie Chaplin movies.

At the Majestic, father and son make their way to their seats "in the exhilarating smell of stale tobacco, rank sweat, perfume and dirty drawers, while the piano played fast music." A William S. Hart Western was just finishing. Then the screen filled with images of a city, and there on a side street lined with palm trees was Charlie. After stealing a bag of eggs and hiding them in the seat of his pants—to Rufus's delight—he catches sight of a pretty woman and begins to twirl his cane and make silly faces, but she pays no attention to his overtures. When she stops at a corner to wait for a streetcar, she deliberately turns her back on Charlie. His response is to look at the audience and shrug his shoulders. As every ardent moviegoer would have known by the summer of 1915, that glance at them was a Chaplinian device for enlisting their complicity in whatever outrageous act Charlie was about to commit.

> He flicked hold of the straight end of his cane and, with the crooked end, hooked up her skirt to the knee, in exactly the way that disgusted Mama, looking very eagerly at her legs, and everybody laughed loudly; but she pretended she had not noticed. Then he twirled his cane and suddenly squatted, bending the cane and hitching up his pants, and again hooked her skirt so that you could see the panties she wore, ruffled almost like the edges of curtains, and everybody whooped with laughter.

Agee's childhood resistance to his mother's puritanism hardened in his teens into a lifelong rebellion against being forced to lead an existence governed by prohibitions and commandments.[69] Thus the rule-shattering impertinences of early Chaplin comedies were dear to him. In the picture evoked in *A Death in the Family*, he focused on the traditional "tease" relationship of women to men. What was the purpose of those ruffled panties if not to fill out that pretty woman's hips and to emphasize by contrast the slimness of her ankles? Having deliberately made herself attractive to the opposite sex, she inevitably hooked susceptible Charlie—and then was deservedly "hooked" herself when she pretended he did not even exist.

But Agee's remembrance of a night at the movies extends beyond the moment of Charlie's triumph to an exposure of his vulnerability. The humiliated young woman turns in rage and gives her tormenter a shove in the chest,

> and he sat down straight-legged, hard enough to hurt, and everybody whooped again; and . . . there was Charlie, flat on his bottom on the sidewalk, and the way he looked, kind of sickly and disgusted, you could

see that he suddenly remembered those eggs, and suddenly you remembered them too. The way his face looked, with the lip wrinkled off the teeth and the sickly little smile, it made you feel just the way those broken eggs must feel against your seat, as queer and awful as that time in the white pekay suit, when it ran down out of the pants-leg and showed all over your stockings and you had to walk home that way with people laughing. . . .[70]

Adult male exultation has abruptly dissolved into little boy embarrassment. Indeed, the spectacle of Charlie lying there amidst the squashed eggs reminds Rufus of the excruciating day when he, too, had had to cope with fouled pants. The finest thing in Agee's evocation of the effect on an audience of a crude early Chaplin comedy is the linkage he establishes between the sickly little smile on Charlie's face and the memories they stir in Rufus of his own helplessness. Agee's account of Chaplin in *A Death in the Family* fails in only one respect. While seeming to glory in Charlie's nastiness, the book actually blocks awareness of the vindictive extent of it.

The cruel sense of fun in the comedies Sennett directed was rendered unreal by the jerky, speeded-up, almost cartoonlike action, which the surrealist-minded Sennett deliberately fostered by instructing his cameramen to "undercrank" their cameras. For if a picture was "undercranked," the operators who manned the variable-speed projectors of the time would almost inevitably elect to exceed the taking speed in showing it. Chaplin, on the other hand, wanted to give audiences the time to take in the details of his jokes—including those that involved the infliction of pain. In such episodes as the entrapment of Mack Swain in *His Musical Career* (November 1914), the pace is slow and the agony prolonged.

Mountainous Mack is a piano mover and puny Charlie is his assistant. In a seeming effort to impress his burly boss with his strength, Charlie assumes a posture of struggling triumph as he hoists Mack's brimming pail of beer in one hand, then proceeds, uninvited, to tilt the pail to his lips. Mack claps him on the back and—to the big guy's vast amusement —a shower of suds spews out of Charlie's mouth. Once Mack's back is turned, Charlie replaces the pail of beer with a pail of varnish, and the generous swig that Mack takes is instantly followed by frantic spitting.

As if to help him subdue the fire in his throat, Charlie throws beer in his face.

At the point where Mack and Charlie's boss orders them to deliver a piano to a customer, the picture's rough-and-ready humor turns savage. Charlie lifts one end of the piano so that Mack can attach a couple of ropes to the underside. As soon as Mack has crawled beneath the instrument, Charlie lets it fall on him, pinning his upper body to the floor. Without appearing to be aware of his colleague's plight, Charlie nonchalantly walks across his backside. At long last, he bends down and asks Mack why he is screaming. Mack's thrashing arm catches him in the eye. Charlie retaliates with a cruelly aimed kick. Moving with an exquisite deliberateness, he takes off his shirt cuffs, after which he finally releases Mack and receives a roughing up in reprisal.

Charlie also picks on powerless old men in two other comedies from the second half of 1914, *His Trysting Place* and *The Property Man*. As he is waiting in the first of these pictures for a seat at a lunch counter, Charlie takes a bite from an elderly stranger's doughnut—and since the only napkin in sight is so filthy that it offends his fastidious sensibility, he wipes his sticky fingers in the old man's beard. The old man jumps to his feet and complains to the counterman. Quick as a wink, Charlie slides onto the vacated stool. The episode ends with his indicating with head, hand, and eyebrow movements that the old man's anger is a sign of insanity.

Much grimmer treatment befalls the oldster in *The Property Man*. Charlie is in charge of the props in a vaudeville theater, and a rather pathetic old man is his assistant. Their task is to carry a huge trunk down a flight of stairs. With minimal help from Charlie, the old man manages to balance the trunk on his back, at which point Charlie kicks him in the head as if he were a recalcitrant donkey. Jauntily carrying a hatbox in one hand and smoking a pipe, Charlie walks down the steps, followed by his staggering assistant. At the foot of the steps, the old man collapses under the weight he is bearing and the trunk falls on him. Charlie halfheartedly tries and fails to budge it. Calmly, he relights his pipe, climbs atop the trunk, and stretches out, exhausted by all the work he has not been doing. The vaudeville strong man's attractive bride, clad in a bathrobe, walks by and gives Charlie the eye. With no thought for the old man's excruciating situation, he pursues her. Later, he returns and makes a second halfhearted attempt to lift the trunk, but it remains where it is until the strong man happens by and frees the prisoner. The scene ends with Charlie kicking and slapping the old man.

That connoisseur of cruelty, Bertolt Brecht, may not have seen *The Property Man* when Chaplin's Keystone comedies were finally released in Germany in 1921. But he did take in *The Face on the Bar Room Floor*, with its drunken brawling and spitting, its coarsely exaggerated drama of romantic betrayal, and its attention to rumps, male and female, and was swept away by it. Having noted the enjoyment of the moviegoers around him, he wrote in his diary: "The film owes at least part of its effectiveness to the brutality of the audience."[71]

That many Americans found a tonic value in comic brutality had long been true. The torment-based pranks in Chaplin's comedies of the middle teens extended a tradition of exulting in the nasty side of existence that had surfaced again and again in the United States through most of the nineteenth century, from the malignant tall tales of the pre–Civil War southwestern humorists to the crippling jokes of the "bad boy" stories of George Wilbur Peck.

12

Moralists were especially appalled and disgusted by the viciousness of Chaplin's sense of fun. With equal vehemence, they disapproved of his preoccupation with sex. Thus the author of a letter to the editor of the *New Orleans American* asserted that Chaplin's films were unworthy of the attention of citizens of the "better class," inasmuch as they centered on what he inaccurately termed the "grotesque and vulgar antics" of a "product of the slums of Whitecastle." Meanwhile, a reviewer of *The Property Man*, who was apparently troubled by the number of gags involving undergarments and tights, felt impelled to warn his readers that "some of the funniest things in the picture are vulgar."[72]

The unhappiness of the moralists was understandable. In spite of the content restrictions that the movie industry had imposed on itself less than a decade earlier, and in spite of the surveillances instituted by municipal and state censors and by the National Board of Censorship, founded in 1909 under the leadership of a prominent reformer, Charles Sprague Smith, sex themes had not only crept back into American movies, but were being elaborated in ever bolder ways. Even prostitution had found its way to the screen. In 1913 the producer-director George L. Tucker had brought out a shocker called *Traffic in Souls*, based on the Rockefeller Commission's findings about the entrapment of women in white-slave rings in New York City. In the light of the astonishing popularity of Tucker's picture, other directors became aware that if they condemned the lusts of the flesh they, too, could get away with portraying them.

The two scenes of sexual terror in *The Birth of a Nation* (1915), far more sensational than those in *Traffic in Souls*, contributed mightily to the picture's unprecedented impact. As reviews both at home and abroad proclaimed, Griffith's re-creations of Civil War battles and his brilliantly orchestrated depiction of mounted Ku Klux Klansmen rushing to the defense of a postwar Southern community's moral order set a new standard of cinematic excitement. But when audiences in the North as well as the South became so wrought up with emotion that they actually arose from their seats to cheer the Klansmen's ride, they were responding to Griffith's masterful intercutting between the ride and an equally gripping scene in which a well-dressed but gorilla-like black politician has locked a young white woman (played by Lillian Gish) in a small room and is rapidly proceeding with plans for a forced marriage between them. The same volatile mixture of sex, race, and violence had also been stirred into an earlier scene in which a tomboyish blond teenager (played by Mae Marsh) had leaped to her death from the edge of a cliff rather than submit to the touch of the slavering, animalistic black man who had finally caught up with her after a hard run through dappled woods.

For millions of white moviegoers, these two episodes lent a fearsome credibility to the nightmarish figure of the black rapist. At the same time, they precipitated outbursts of protest against the film. The entire Negro population of the United States, cried the urban reformer Frederic C. Howe, had been "degraded" by Griffith's portrayal of Negroes as "lustful" and "depraved"; Chicago's Jane Addams declared that the movie was vicious; and the mayor of New York, John Purroy Mitchel, alarmed by mounting social tension in the city, persuaded the manager of the Liberty Theater, where *The Birth of a Nation* was playing, to censor both scenes. A short while later, a group of civil rights activists in Boston, led by the black newspaper editor William Monroe Trotter, entered a downtown theater during a screening of the picture and set off stink bombs. At the end of the show, fistfights between whites and blacks broke out in front of the theater and arrests were made. Emerging from a police station after being booked, Trotter told reporters that the movie "will make white women afraid of Negroes and will have white men all stirred up on their account." Such protests, however, were of little avail against a picture in which visions of moral anarchy had been combined with a triumphant reaffirmation of traditional family values. *The Birth of a Nation*, as Cecil B. DeMille would declare in 1948, "burst upon the world with atomic force." By the end of 1917, its earnings exceeded $60 million, an all but incredible amount that would have been even higher had not unscrupulous exhibitors like Louis B. Mayer of Haverhill, Massachusetts, underreported their earnings.[73]

When it came to making comic movies that circumvented the suffocations of sexual prudery, no studio in the business set a higher premium on doing so than Keystone. In 1914, the famous Bathing Beauties were still a year away from being organized; nevertheless, sexy actresses had always been a high-priority item on Sennett's recruitment list, as his pictures amply testified. In *Ambrose's First Falsehood* (1914), a happily married suburban husband, played by Ford Sterling, is tempted into joining a couple of pals on an afternoon fling and gets paired off, to his flustered embarrassment, with a stupefyingly well-endowed café singer who later shows up at his front door. Out of situations like this, Sennett made comedies by the dozen. Joking references to prostitution and other off-color facts of life were another feature of his pictures, but because he was adept at burying them within morally acceptable situations, it was difficult for the censors to justify the use of their scissors. Who could object, for instance, to a spoof of an amateur-talent show that paid particular attention to the ludicrously inept performance of a women's dance group? Only when the women held up cards, just before prancing offstage, on which they had printed their names and addresses, did it become clear— to dirty minds, at any rate—what their actual occupation was.

Sennett also gave Chaplin the green light as far as sexual jokes and sub-jokes were concerned. The result was the suggestiveness of such comedies as *Laughing Gas* and *Those Love Pangs*. When the dentist in *Laughing Gas* is summoned home one day, his assistant, Charlie, pretends that the office is his. Ignoring an older woman in the waiting room whose jaw is bandaged and clearly causing her pain, he ushers a shapely and much younger one in a form-fitting dress into the inner office and seats her in the chair. She expects him to tie a towel around her neck, but instead he polishes her shoes with it. While doing so, he begins to giggle and so does she, as if they are both aware that he is about to do something else surprising. Suddenly he throws his leg across her lap. She pushes him away and tries to show him her aching tooth, but when he leans across her body and looks down, it is her bosom that transfixes his gaze. More giggling occurs. Then, with a dancer's grace, Charlie pivots about and falls backward upon her, seemingly because it is the only way he can see into her mouth. Like a child at play, he spins the chair around, until finally he becomes dizzy and tumbles to the floor. Again he attempts to climb into her lap. After managing to kiss her, he repeatedly seizes her nose with a pair of forceps and swings her face around for more kisses. Her half-resisting complaisance at last gives way to unalloyed annoyance. He retaliates by collapsing the back of the chair. With a difficulty that makes for a nice look at her legs, she scrambles out of the chair and flees the office. Not until the scene in W. C. Fields's *The Dentist* (1932) in which Fields ends up on the floor of his office between the shapely thighs of a young lady from whose mouth he is attempting to extract a tooth by brute force would a Hollywood comedian get more mileage out of the priapic potentialities of a dental appointment than Chaplin did in *Laughing Gas*.

Romantic developments in *Those Love Pangs* culminate in transsexual jokes. In separate confrontations in the first part of the picture, a desperately horny Charlie puts to rout the two young men who have been monopolizing the affections of a bold-eyed brunette and an adorable blonde. Finding themselves at loose ends without their boyfriends, the two young women decide to go to a movie—but Charlie follows them into the theater and takes a seat between them. Spreading his arms wide in an embrace of both girls, he feels marvelous twice over. As his sexual excitement mounts, he raises his knees, splits his legs apart, and rocks back and forth. In their simulation of arousal, his movements are amazingly explicit. They are of the sort, however, associated with a woman's ecstasy, not a man's. Acting as if he has attained a climax and is now content, Charlie dozes off. The defeated boyfriends, intent on revenge, enter the theater and take the young women's places. Upon waking up, Charlie lazily fondles his seatmates' faces without looking at them. Several seconds pass before he realizes the mistake he has made. As far as the two men are concerned, homosexual insult has been added to heterosexual injury. They work Charlie over with considerable enthusiasm and finally throw him through the movie screen.

Sliding into a feminine mode was easy for Chaplin. From the Charlie comedies to *Monsieur Verdoux* and *Limelight* to *A King in New York*, his acting would be marked by a kittenish coyness and other feminine mannerisms, as well as by feelings of greater delicacy than the women playing opposite him displayed. Across the years, too, numerous observers of his directorial technique of conveying what he wanted from his actors and actresses by briefly assuming their roles would be amazed by the precision and style of his female impersonations. Thus the veteran actor Norman Lloyd, who had worked with Orson Welles and Alfred Hitchcock before landing a role in *Limelight*, could not get over the contrast between Chaplin's direction of his son, Sydney Chaplin, and his direction of Claire Bloom. "He played the leading man [Sydney] straightforwardly, but he acted the woman [Claire Bloom] fantastically; his body expressed everything about the meaning of the scene and its emotional level. . . ."

Female acquaintances early and late would be moved to make comparable comments about the private Chaplin. Oona Chaplin's longtime friend Carol Matthau said that he "had what only whole men have— certain feminine qualities," while to Mary Pickford he illustrated her general theory about the sexual makeup of the men and women in the arts who had achieved a great success. They were almost always endowed with more of the qualities of the opposite sex than of their own, she contended. "For instance, there is a great deal of the masculine in me, perhaps more than there 'is of the feminine. . . . [Of] Charlie Chaplin . . . one would never say he was effeminate, but I would consider that he is at least 60 per cent feminine. You can see it in his work; he has feminine intuition." And the artistically gifted Clare Sheridan, who did a portrait bust of Chaplin in the 1920s, came to the conclusion that "a feminine streak in Charlie" was evident in the fact that "his moods varied with the hours" and that "he suited his dressing-gowns to his moods." She herself, Sheridan continued, always regarded color as an expression of a mood—there are days when one feels like wearing red, other days when one is drawn to blue; there are white days and black days, and I have often wondered how men could bear to wear the same dismal-colored clothes perpetually. Charlie was comprehensible to me. He would start the morning in a brown silk robe lined with yellow, and as the day advanced and the sun glared he would change it for another brighter one. He had them of every shade—orange, blue, violet and emerald.[74]

By 1910 the destabilization of traditional relations between the sexes and the concomitant disruption of familiar assumptions about manliness and womanliness had become subjects of serious discussion both in Europe and the United States. As a result, Walter Lippmann felt able to say in *Drift and Mastery* (1914) that man's "sexual nature is chaotic through the immense change that has come into the relations of parent and child, husband and wife. Those changes distract him so deeply that the more 'advanced' he is, the more he flounders in the bogs of his own soul."[75]

If fear, incomprehension, and cruelty can be discerned in Chaplin's private relations with women, so can a vivid degree of identification with their sensibilities. And beginning with his work at Keystone, he made the sort of floundering of which Lippmann spoke an occasion for comedy.

13

The Keystone actress whom the success-emboldened comedian pursued most assiduously off camera was a slim, blond, eighteen-year-old beauty, Peggy Pearce. At the marvelous parties that producer-director Thomas Ince regularly gave at Inceville, as he called the studio he had established on an oceanside ranch in the wilds of northern Santa Monica, Chaplin and Peggy danced to an orchestra on an open-air stage within earshot of the waves breaking on the shore. But if each night was illuminated with avowals of their love, each night ended with a struggle between his importunings and her resistance. Peggy, it seemed, was determined to carry her virginity like a chalice to her wedding bed. But Chaplin had no desire to marry anyone. Finally, he gave up seeing her.

"Freedom was too much of an adventure," he later explained. "No woman could measure up to that vague image I had in my mind."[76]

He also made a run at Mabel Normand. One night in San Francisco, following a charity benefit in a downtown movie theater at which he and Mabel and Fatty Arbuckle had each made a personal appearance with great success, he accompanied her to the dressing room where she had left her coat. For a moment they were alone. With her large, heavy-lidded eyes and full lips, she was radiantly beautiful. As he placed her wrap around her shoulders, he kissed her, and she kissed him back. They might have gone further, but Arbuckle was waiting outside in a car. Later, he made a second overture, but without success. She wasn't his type, she informed him, and he wasn't hers. It was a shrewd assessment. Chaplin wanted women who would never stand up to him. Feisty Mabel Normand did not fit that description.[77]

5

THE MOB-GOD

Charlie with Edna Purviance in The Champion *(1915).*

Aₛ a member of the Los Angeles Athletic Club, Sennett had the right to give a business associate a temporary membership card, and in the summer of 1914 he gave one to Chaplin, much to the cost-conscious comedian's delight. For twelve dollars a week, which may have been less than he had been paying for his hall bedroom in an obscure hotel, he was able to rent an airy corner room that included a piano and an array of bookshelves and was just down the hall from the quarters of the millionaire owner of the May Company department store, Mose

Hamberger. Sennett's largesse also gave Chaplin access to all of the club's facilities, from its elaborate gymnasiums and swimming pool to its cocktail bar and dining room. "All told," he later declared, "I lived in a sumptuous style for seventy-five dollars a week, out of which I kept my end up in rounds of drinks and occasional dinners." (Chester Conklin remembered to the contrary that "Chaplin . . . was willing to let you buy him a drink . . . but I guess he had not spent much time in London pubs where he would have learned that it was up to him to knock for the next round.")[1]

On club stationery on August 9—five days after the outbreak of World War I—he penned a triumphant letter to his brother. Inasmuch as it represented his first communication with Sydney since leaving England twenty-two months earlier, he began by saying, "Yes. It really is your brother Chas. after all these years," before going on to give him, in slightly flawed spelling, the news. "Well, Sid, I have made good. All the theatres feature my name in big letters, i.e. 'Chas. Chaplin hear today.' " As a result, he had been receiving "all kinds of offers," including one from the theater chain magnate Marcus Loew, who wanted him to form his own comedy company and who proposed to give him, in lieu of salary, 50 percent of the stock, which "means thoullions," Chaplin expansively declared. He also wanted Sydney to know that he had been talking to various people about the comic talents of his older brother and that Sennett would shortly be communicating with him directly about coming to work for him for a hundred and fifty dollars a week—"but don't come for *less than 175 understand?*"

With that piece of advice out of his system, he returned to boasting about himself.

I have made a heap of good friends hear and go to all the partys ect. I stay at the best Club in the city where all the millionairs belong. . . . I have my own valet [strictly speaking, a club employee], some class to me eh what? I am still saving my money and since I have been hear I have 4000 dollars in one bank, 1200 in another, 1500 in London not so bad for 25 and still going strong thank God. Sid, we will be millionaires before long.

His achievement of that status would not occur, however, under Keystone auspices, the letter made clear. For although Sennett was "a lovely man and we are great pals," he had decided not to sign another contract with him. "Business," he explained, "is business."

Toward the end of the letter he inquired about Hannah and asked whether Sydney thought it was safe for him to send any money across the Atlantic for her nursing-home care "while the war is on." "This war is terrible," he thought to add, as he moved toward a concluding round of boasting. "I have just finished a six real picture with Marie Dressler the American star and myself. It cost 50,000 . . . and I have hog the whole picture. It is the best thing I ever did. I must draw to a close now as I am getting hungry. Just this second my valet tells me I have friends to take me out Automobiling so am going to the beach to dine."[2]

The movie with Marie Dressler was *Tillie's Punctured Romance* (November 1914). Directed by Mack Sennett, who also mapped out the scenario, it took fourteen weeks to film and edit and in the annals of the movies has since been celebrated as the first feature-length slapstick comedy as well as the vehicle that made Dressler a Hollywood star. A large woman with the low-hanging jowls and dark-circled eyes of a St. Bernard dog, the forty-five-year-old comedienne had appeared on stage before Chaplin was born, and in 1910, in *Tillie's Nightmare*, had achieved Broadway musical immortality with her rendition of "Heaven Will Protect the Working Girl." Sennett based the scenario for his *Tillie* on the musical *Tillie* and surrounded Dressler—to whom he was paying the staggering sum of $2,500 a week—with all of his top-drawer Keystone comedians, beginning with Chaplin and Mabel Normand and excluding only Fatty Arbuckle, who reputedly was barred at Dressler's request, on the grounds that his girth outrivaled her own.

In the role of a fortune-hunting city slicker, Chaplin danced an unforgettable tango amidst the potted palms in the mansion of the wealthy, empty-headed country bumpkin (Dressler) whom he has duped. As for his lovemaking scenes with Dressler, he carried them out with a cynicism that anticipated his performance as a seducer of well-heeled women in *Monsieur Verdoux* three decades later. Mabel Normand, too, did a memorable job in *Tillie* as the slicker's sidekick. Yet if anyone hogged the picture, it was Dressler. Talk about dancing! Following the bumpkin's first-ever drink of hard liquor, her rural demureness exploded into the eye-rolling, bum-swiveling cavortings of a mad elephant. Yet while Dressler reveled in the grotesqueries of Sennett slapstick, they also became a confinement for her. Not until her appearance with Greta Garbo in the early talkie *Anna Christie (1930)* was she at last able to show the world her capacity for serious drama.[3]

The enormous success of *Tillie* not only ensured Dressler's future as a movie comedienne; it also made Chaplin better known than ever. Even so, none of the filmmakers who kept phoning him to discuss contract terms were willing to satisfy his audacious insistence on a salary of a thousand dollars a week. Meanwhile, his brother—who by this time had arrived from England—was strenuously counseling him against the alternative strategy of setting up a comedy company of his own. With the termination of his association with Keystone looming dead ahead, Chaplin grew more nervous by the day—until the producer-director Jesse Robbins, of the Essanay Film Company of Chicago, called to say that even though he had heard through the grapevine that Chaplin was demanding a salary of $1,250 a week, plus a signing bonus of $10,000, he wanted him to know that Essanay was interested in talking to him. The salary figure substantially exceeded the amount that Chaplin had been thinking of and the idea of a bonus had never crossed his mind. Nevertheless, the terms mentioned by Robbins lay at the heart of the contract he signed with Essanay. When it came to bargaining-table adroitness, Mary Pickford (backed by her fearsome mother) was unequaled among movie stars, but Chaplin, too, knew how to play the game.[4]

The "S" of Essanay was the firm's financial brain, George K. Spoor. At one time, he had earned no more than a modest living operating a lunchroom and a newsstand in a Chicago train station, but shrewd investments in theaters and a film rental business had laid the basis for his participation in Essanay, which was now in the process of piling up a fortune for him of between seven and ten million dollars. Spoor's partner, G. M. Anderson, was a cowboy actor. Having changed his name from Max Aronson to conceal his Jewishness, Anderson got his start in films by telling Edwin S. Porter, the cameraman-director of *The Great Train Robbery* (1903), that he had been "born on a horse and raised in Missouri." Only after Porter hired him to play one of the mounted holdup men in the picture did his ineptitude in the saddle become painfully apparent. Yet by the time he and Spoor joined forces in 1907 and started making Wild West pictures about a cowboy named Broncho Billy, he had become a sufficiently capable rider to assume the leading role. In the spring of 1908, Anderson established a permanent base for his filmmaking in a studio in Niles, California, an hour's drive from San Francisco. For 376 consecutive weeks thereafter, a one-reel Broncho Billy picture came off his assembly line every seven days.[5]

At the wheel of a new green Mercedes, Anderson picked Chaplin up at the Los Angeles Athletic Club on a Monday morning in mid-December 1914—two days after Chaplin had walked off the Keystone lot without saying good-bye to anyone—and drove him up the coast to Niles. With a population of four hundred, the town was a tiny island of one- and two-story buildings in a sea of alfalfa fields and cattle ranches, Chaplin discovered to his disappointment, and the sets in the Essanay studio had a glass roof above them that had a greenhouse effect on their temperatures. The affable Anderson responded to the sour look on Chaplin's face by encouraging him to think that he would find Essanay's Chicago facilities much more to his liking. A few days later, Chaplin was aboard an eastbound train. For all of his worldly triumphs, he felt isolated and powerless. Perhaps he would be able to overcome these feelings in Chicago.[6]

But the frigidity of the Windy City in January did nothing to improve his mood. Furthermore, the studio manager who welcomed him to the Essanay plant promptly angered him by saying that he could pick up the script for his first picture from the head of the scenario department, Louella Parsons.* "I don't use other people's scripts," Chaplin snapped. "I write my own."[7] In the casting office, on the other hand, he was gratified to come upon two performers who perfectly suited his personnel needs for the comedy he wanted to make about life in a movie studio: cross-eyed, chicken-necked Ben Turpin and a comely extra girl, not yet sixteen years old, with enormous, ice-water-blue eyes, a petite, perfectly proportioned shape, and verve in every move.

---

* As the author of a number of well-regarded scripts and as a shrewd judge of the work of other scenarists, Parsons was well thought of at Essanay. Before the end of 1915, however, she left the studio and began writing a motion picture gossip column for the Chicago *Record-Herald*. In her glory days as a syndicated gossip columnist for Hearst, studio heads groveled before her and her birthday was unfailingly remembered by the stars. George Eells, *Hedda and Louella* (New York, 1972), pp. 45–46 and *passim*.

Chaplin was going to play an employee of a movie studio that he had decided to call the Lockstone Motion Picture Company, and his first thought was to assign the girl to the bit part of a stenographer in the studio's front office. But she was such an appealing creature that he quickly conceived of a grander plan for her. By the sheer force of his will and the power of his comic example, he would make her into his leading lady. The girl never forgot the morning he spent with her,

> trying to get me to work up routines with him. These all involved kicking each other in the pants, running into things and falling over each other. He kept laughing and making his eyes twinkle and talking to me in a light, gentle voice and encouraging me to let myself go and be silly. . . . All morning I felt like a cow trying to dance with a toy poodle. Moreover, I knew after an hour that I didn't want to spend the next month or so trying to be cute and elfish, so I made very little effort and finally told him I just didn't see the humor in many of the things he was asking me to do. We were both perfectly pleasant after that, but I could see that he was hurt and annoyed.[8]

Thus ended Chaplin's attempt to shape the career of Gloria Swanson.

The mistake he made about her lay in his assumption that she had no dramatic aims of her own and would therefore be willing to submit to his. But at the age of fifteen, Swanson was already armored with an icy independence, within which there burned the fire of an awesome ambition. As soon as she was able to get out of her Essanay contract, she joined the migration of midwestern beauties to the West Coast. Following a successful stint as a Mack Sennett comedienne, she finally caught the attention of Cecil B. DeMille, who in Swanson's grateful words was the sort of director who "gave an actress an initiative, got her to use her creative side." By casting her as the bored, dissatisfied wife in *Don't Change Your Husband* (1919), DeMille set the stage for her emergence as the poised, perfectly coifed, glamorously costumed incarnation of 1920s chic.[9] She also had a comic flair. In the role of a shop girl in *Manhandled* (1924), she amused the other guests at a swanky party with a first-rate imitation of Chaplin's Charlie character. Twenty-six years later, she staged another Chaplin performance for William Holden's benefit in *Sunset Boulevard*.

2

Chaplin bluntly told Spoor, whom he did not like, that he was un-happy in Chicago, and that if Spoor wanted satisfactory pictures from him, he should arrange for him to work in California. The millionaire producer was only too aware that advance orders for *His New Job*—Chaplin's movie studio picture—were pouring into the Essanay office at a rate that astounded the secretaries. "We'll do everything we can to make you happy," he unctuously replied. "How would you like to go to Niles?" In the absence of any other alternative, the disgruntled come-dian chose to return there at once.[10]

The chief cameraman on the Broncho Billy pictures, Roland H. (Rol-lie) Totheroh, met Chaplin's train in San Francisco and escorted him to a limousine driven by G. M. Anderson's chauffeur, Joe Flynn. En route to Niles, Totheroh explained that Anderson and all the other actors of consequence—one of whom was the oafish-looking Wallace Beery, who had made a name for himself by playing the part of a Swedish maid named Sweedie in a series of comedies—lived in little bungalows near the studio. Upon reaching town, Flynn drove to Anderson's bungalow, where a room had been set aside for Chaplin. "It was dark when we entered," Chaplin recalled,

> and when we switched on the light I was shocked. The place was empty and drab. In [Anderson's] room was an old iron bed with a light bulb hanging over the head of it. A rickety old table and one chair were the other furnishings. Near the bed was a wooden box upon which was a brass ashtray filled with cigarette butts. The room allotted to me was almost the same. . . . Nothing worked. The bathroom was unspeakable. One had to take a jug and fill it from the bath tap and empty it down the flush to make the toilet work. This was the home of G. M. Anderson, the multimillionaire cowboy. I came to the conclusion that Anderson was an eccentric.[11]

In an effort to ease Chaplin's distress, Totheroh and Flynn decided to help him settle in by emptying the bag he was carrying. It was one of those "canvas-like handbags," Totheroh told an interviewer in 1972, and all he had in it was "a pair of socks with the heels worn out and a couple of dirty undershirts, an old . . . shirt and an old worn out toothbrush. . . . Joe said, 'Jesus, he hasn't got much in this bag, has he?' "[12] Even a tramp might have had a spare pair of decent socks.

Despite the sparseness of his own effects, Chaplin rejected the bungalow as unsuitably Spartan and moved into a hotel on the other side of town. The next day, he got down to business. Having been impressed by the performances in *His New Job* of Ben Turpin, Leo White, and Bud Jamison, he invited all three of them to join the little company of regular players he had decided to form. The singular-looking Turpin had come to the movies from the savagely competitive world of burlesque comedy and was an accomplished scene-stealer. Unfortunately, that talent created difficulties for him in Niles. After being allotted juicy parts in the first two comedies that Chaplin made there, he discovered that the amount of press attention he was receiving had aroused his boss's envy. Only one more role in a Chaplin comedy came his way before he quit Essanay in disgust and signed on as the lead comic at another studio.

Leo White, on the other hand, was a veteran of the musical stage who for years had adeptly subordinated himself to Fritzi Scheff in Victor Herbert's *Mlle. Modiste* (the show in which Scheff made "Kiss Me Again" her signature tune). At Niles, White excelled in Frenchified roles, but he also endeared himself to Chaplin by never trying to upstage him. As for Bud Jamison, he was an amiable giant who dreamed of moving on to a career as a professional magician; Chaplin, however, liked to have him around because his size set off his own.[13]

Two other actors who hitched their wagons to Chaplin's star after his return to Niles were vaudeville acquaintances of his from England, Billy Armstrong and Fred Goodwins. His most critical recruitment problem, however, was to find a leading lady—who might also, if he was lucky, fill the void in his personal life. Totheroh recalled that Broncho Billy Anderson began to "ask around for a girl who would suit Chaplin. [He] spoke to Fritz Wintermayer, who was more or less a handyman for Charlie at Essanay. Fritz remembered Edna Purviance and . . . brought [her] over from San Francisco, where she was a secretary. Charlie met her and said, 'That's the girl!' "[14] Chaplin's own memory was that he and Anderson devoted a considerable amount of time to inspecting chorus girls around the Bay area, but that while it was nice work, none of the candidates proved to be photogenic. Finally, one of Essanay's cowboys, a handsome, young German-American named Carl Strauss, told Anderson that he knew of a lovely blond secretary in San Francisco who occasionally went to Tate's Café on Hill Street. Mr. Tate was quite well acquainted with her, apparently, for he said that she lived with her married sister and that she hailed from a little gold-mining town in Nevada called Lovelock.[15]

The nineteen-year-old Purviance (rhymes with reliance) met Chaplin in the lobby of the St. Francis Hotel. She was blessed with large eyes, beautiful teeth, and a sensitive mouth, he discovered, and there can be no doubt that he also took note of her lush figure. The only concern that occurred to him in the course of their interview—aside from whether or not her beauty would translate onto film—was inspired by the gravity of her facial expression. Was someone who looked so serious capable of laughing at life? The question seems to have lingered in his mind even after he learned that she had been down in the dumps that day at the St. Francis because she was just getting over a love affair. Not until the supper party that they both attended on the night before the filming of his leadoff movie at Niles was due to begin did he become fully appreciative of his new leading lady's sense of fun.

After the supper dishes had been cleared away, someone brought up the subject of hypnotism, and Chaplin responded with a boast about his own hypnotic powers. (Perhaps he saw himself doing his music hall imitation of "Dr." Walford Bodie, or was he recalling Beerbohm Tree in *Trilby?*) Edna told him he was talking nonsense, and when he offered to make a bet with her of ten dollars that he could hypnotize her within sixty seconds, she took him up on it. At his request, she stood up against a wall. When a timekeeper said, "Go!" Chaplin stared intensely into Edna's eyes and waved his hands in front of her face. Leaning closer to her, he whispered, "Fake it!" Almost at once she began to stagger, and Chaplin caught her in his arms. Two of the onlookers screamed. "Quick," said Chaplin. "Someone help me put her on the couch." After a moment, Edna stirred, and as she sat up, she feigned bewilderment and said she was tired. Chaplin's retrospective comment on the incident was that "for the sake of a good joke," Edna had relinquished the certain chance of winning her bet and in so doing "won . . . my esteem and affection." But her sacrifice meant more to him than that. It showed how willing she was to surrender herself to his domination. Like other young women whose lives he would bestride like a colossus in years to come, Edna had grown up in a fatherless household. After siring three daughters, her father had deserted the family, and he did not reappear until Edna started earning a Hollywood salary.[16]

At the same time that Purviance was prepared to comply with Chaplin's every desire, she offered him a rocklike security. Just as her blond beauty and Junoesque figure photographically complemented his darkness and slightness, so her calm, sweet, maternally accepting temperament matched up with his need for a haven he could count on.

3

A young French soldier, Jean Renoir, fell ardently in love with "Charlot's" comedies in 1915, while convalescing from a leg wound received at the front. Toward the end of his own notable career as a filmmaker, Renoir pooh-poohed the criticism of technical specialists that Chaplin's films had been "shot with poor technique" and were "poorly lit" and "poorly photographed."[17] But the specialists were by and large correct. In 1915, the year of the cinematographic daring of DeMille's *The Cheat* and Maurice Tourneur's *Alias Jimmy Valentine*, Chaplin's new work already had a behind-the-times look.

The first three of the five movies he made at Niles between February and April of 1915 displayed another sort of cautiousness in that they repeated comic formulas worked out at Keystone. The drunken misadventures of Charlie and Ben Turpin in *A Night Out* hardly differed from the revels of Charlie and Fatty Arbuckle in *The Rounders*. His slugfest with Bud Jamison in *The Champion* was a clever piece of work that instantly became a favorite with moviegoers; yet, as many of them must have recognized, his antic movements in the ring were merely an extension of his groggy stumblings about as the referee who gets caught in the line of fire between Fatty Arbuckle and Edgar Kennedy in *The Knockout*. As for *In the Park*, it offered the same combination of courtship overtures to ladies and trouble with rivalrous gents that had served him so well at Keystone in *Getting Acquainted, Twenty Minutes of Love,* and *His Trysting Place*. ("All I need to make a comedy," he once assured Mack Sennett, "is a park, a policeman and a pretty girl."[18])

With *A Jitney Elopement*, his fourth effort at Niles, he regained his forward stride. To begin with, it added a new dimension to his screen personality. Keystone Charlie had never really cared about the women he lusted after. But in *Jitney* a tenderness in his nature emerged, first of all in the shot of him sniffing and caressing a flower while standing beneath the window of an unhappy young woman, Edna Purviance, who is being pressured by her father into marrying a purported French count, and then in the long sequence in which he succeeds in freeing Edna from this situation.

Jitney also drew more freely than any of his previous pictures upon his memories of things past. If the flower that Charlie is caressing stands for the romantic happiness he is yearning for, it was also related in Chaplin's dreaming mind to the lost happiness of riding with his mother "on top of a horse-bus trying to touch passing lilac-trees" and of walking with her past "rubicund flower-girls at the corner of Westminster Bridge, making gay *boutonnieres.*" The jitney, too, carried him back to childhood times, despite its Model T modernity. In 1915, jitneys plying back and forth were a familiar sight on American streets and could be boarded for small fares; hence their function was analogous to a bus's. And when daredevil Charlie assumes the wheel of the flivver, remembrance took a wish-fulfillment turn. The picture's climactic car chase over bumpy roads and through mud puddles, ending triumphantly in Charlie and Edna's escape from her unwanted suitor, is a rescue fantasy. Psychologically if not circumstantially, Charlie's deliverance of Edna from her distress is akin to the story about a little boy filling in for his stricken mother on a music hall stage. That story, in all likelihood, was very much on Chaplin's mind at the time he made *Jitney*, inasmuch as he described it in graphic detail to Rose Wilder Lane a scant month and a half after the release of the picture.

The closing shots of *Jitney* track a joyous dash to a parsonage, where Charlie and Edna plan to get married. That footage also had a personal significance for Chaplin: he and Edna were in the first flush of their ardor for each other. "My heart throbbed this morning when I received your sweet letter," Edna adoringly wrote her lover in this period. "It could be nobody else in the world that could have given me so much joy. In a reply addressed to "My Own Darling Edna," Chaplin assured her that she had made him "the happiest person in the world."[19]

A Jitney Elopement was a forecast of future Chaplin achievements. So, most emphatically, was the two-reeler entitled *The Tramp*, which proved to be the last of his Niles productions. In the course of playing Charlie for another twenty years, Chaplin would appear as a janitor, a decorator's apprentice, a tailor's apprentice, a fireman, a street musician, a pawnbroker's assistant, a property man's assistant, a laborer, a waiter, and a guest at a spa, among other guises. These epiphenomenal identifications, however, did not affect the world's sense of Charlie's basic identity. That issue was settled forever, once *The Tramp* went into release.

4

Polite society continuously defines and redefines itself through the exclusion of what it marks out as "low"—as dirty, repulsive, contaminating. But as Peter Stallybrass and Allon White maintain in *The Politics and Poetics of Transgression* (1986), "Disgust always bears the imprint of desire. These low domains, apparently expelled as 'Other,' return as the object of nostalgia, longing and fascination." The theater, the slum, the circus, the seaside resort, the savage: "all these, placed at the outer limit of civil life, become symbolic contents of bourgeois desire."[20] So it was with the tramp phenomenon of the late nineteenth and early twentieth centuries.

In the late summer of 1877, an American writer then living in London who had failed to pack and leave in August and by so doing had "survived the departure of everything genteel," found that his attention was drawn to "studies of low life." Wherefore he took note in an essay he would publish in an American magazine of "the rough characters who are lying on their faces in the sheep-polluted grass." These men, Henry James continued, "are always tolerably numerous in the Green Park, through which I frequently pass, and are always an occasion for deep wonder." Within the span of a long paragraph, James moved from voicing his belief that most tramps not only resembled "stage-villains of realistic melodrama" but had served time in prison for "stamping on some weaker human head with those huge square heels that [at the moment] are turned up to the summer sky" to a pitying recognition of "their look of having walked over half of England and of being pennilessly hungry and thirsty." In expressing the prayerful hope in his closing words that they "might sleep for ever and go nowhere else at all," the novelist seemed to waver between compassion for them and his dreadful sense of their history of violence.[21]

That sense was shared by the vast majority of James's countrymen, many of whom had ugly stories to tell about encounters with tramps. The Panic of 1873 had ushered in five years of economic depression in the United States, with the result that record numbers of footloose men had been forced onto the nation's roads and byways. The reigning judgment of these wayward figures was that congenital character defects were responsible for their condition, that they were lazy by nature, and improvident, and shamelessly addicted to drink. Furthermore, the judgment continued, they had little or no respect for law and were therefore a threat to the social order. From all over the East, in particular, came reports of thefts, incendiary fires, rapes, and even murders committed by vagrants. Alternately begging and stealing, they moved through the countryside like locusts, in the indignant words of the *New York Times*; among their victims, the *Times* averred, were a widow in Millertown, New York, who apparently was so frightened by the bullying manner of a tramp who came to her door that she collapsed and died, and two young girls who were "waylaid" and "outraged" while out for a walk.[22]

During the winter months, the tramps of the 1870s tended to congregate in cities, where they placed a terrible pressure on the religious missions that attempted to feed them and on the shelters that were sometimes provided for them in police station houses. In one miserably crowded room in New York City's Tenth Precinct, a reporter for the *New York Herald* disclosed, sixty or seventy ragged lodgers slept on planks a few inches apart. Yet if expressions of compassion for the lot of such men were not unheard of, they tended to be laced with evidences of extreme aversion to them. "As we utter the word *tramp*," the dean of the Yale Law School, Francis Wayland, declared, "there arises straightway before us the spectacle of a lazy, shiftless, sauntering or swaggering, ill-conditioned, irreclaimable, incorrigible, cowardly, utterly depraved savage."

A writer whose nom de plume was "Agile Penne" let loose an even lengthier barrage of pejorative language in a short story in the weekly

Saturday Journal about a New York newspaper reporter who discovers, while waiting for the Staten Island ferry one warm summer evening, a sleeping tramp at the end of the pier.

> As I stood by the sleeping outcast I speculated idly as to who and what he was. A wanderer, evidently; that was plain both from his dress and his face. One of those human wolves—pariahs of the world—whose hand is against all men and whom all men's hands are against. An outcast from his kind; a modern Wandering Jew, who can find rest in one place only, Potter's Field.

An outcast, a human wolf, a pariah, a Wandering Jew: "Agile Penne" could hardly contain his revulsion. Only in the writings of such dissidents as the single-tax theorist Henry George and various commentators in the radical labor press was the argument forcefully—if rather too confidently—made that social and economic calamities beyond the control of the tramps were the cause of their degradation and could be eliminated by proper planning.[23]

The major depression of nineteenth-century America began in May 1893. For the next several years, tramps were even more visible than they had been two decades earlier, and many people were afraid of them. Thus when dwindling funds compelled the twenty-four-year-old D. W. Griffith to bed down in flophouses during an extended search for theatrical employment in New York, he was terrified by the prospect of being set upon and robbed by the rough-looking customers he encountered. Griffith's apprehensiveness was further inflamed by his familiarity with the theater. Playwrights in the 1890s often included evil tramp characters in their work as a means of manipulating the latent anxieties of their audiences. In setting up situations in his early movies—e.g., *The Lonely Villa*—in which innocent women and children are imperiled by tramps, Griffith drew just as heavily on a fund of melodramatic precedents as he did on his flophouse memories.[24]

Yet it was indicative of a growing sympathy for tramps within the mainstream public in the 1890s that some of the most popular commentators on their allegedly incorrigible laziness handled the subject humorously. In the highly successful *Weary Willie* comic strip, as well as in the vaudeville skits and movie shorts that were inspired by it, a total aversion to honest labor on the part of the sleepy-faced, tin-can-hatted title character served to define his delightfulness, and the "happy tramp" monologues of the vaudeville comedian Nat M. Wills were similarly indulgent.[25]

However he may have felt at the time, Jack London invested his reminiscences of his tramp adventures in the summer of 1892, when he was sixteen years old, and in 1894, when he joined a protest march on Washington by a West Coast affiliate of "General" Jacob Coxey's "army" of the unemployed, with a glowing nostalgia.* San Francisco's most famous literary son—still alive at the time that Chaplin was making pictures at nearby Niles—regarded tramps as men like himself who relished the release from society's routinized ways.

> Perhaps the greatest charm of tramp-life is the absence of monotony. In Hobo Land the face of life is protean—an ever changing phantasmagoria, where the impossible happens and the unexpected jumps out of the bushes at every turn of the road. . . . Every once in a while in newspapers and magazines, and biographical dictionaries, I run upon sketches of my life, wherein, delicately phrased, I learned that it was in order to study sociology that I became a tramp. This is very nice and thoughtful of the biographers, but it is inaccurate. I became a tramp—well, because of the life that was in me, of the wanderlust in my blood that would not let me rest. Sociology was merely incidental, it came afterward, in the same manner that a wet skin follows a ducking. I went on "The Road" because I couldn't keep away from it. . . .[26]

En route to Washington, London and "two thousand hungry hoboes" crossed the length of Iowa. Some Iowans resented their incursion and formed committees to harass them. But the welcomers far outnumbered the harassers. "They turned out with their wagons and carried our

---

* Inasmuch as most of the men in the protest march of 1894 had not deliberately opted out of the workforce, they were not, strictly speaking, tramps. For these men who desperately wanted work, "hoboes" is a more accurate term. Yet the fact is that Jack London used "tramp" and "hobo" interchangeably, as did millions of his contemporaries. And this habit of mind would persist for at least half a century. Cf. the definition of "hobo" in Webster's *Seventh New Collegiate Dictionary:* "1. a migratory worker. 2. *a*: a homeless and usually penniless vagrant: TRAMP *b*: BUM."

baggage, gave us hot lunches at noon by the wayside; mayors of comfortable little towns made speeches of welcome and hastened us on our way; deputations of little girls and maidens came out to meet us, and the good citizens turned out by hundreds, locked arms, and marched with us down their main streets. It was a circus day when we came to town, and every day was circus day, for there were many towns." *Every day was circus day.* For the good people of Iowa, the strangers in their midst constituted a romantic excitement.[27]

By 1912, the year in which Chaplin completed the first of his Karno tours of America and returned for his second, a long period of prosperity had substantially diminished the vagrancy problem. Reminders of its continued existence, however, could easily stir slumbering fears. As he walked away from the Grandview, Missouri, train depot on a spring night in 1912, a young farmer named Harry S. Truman noticed that another man was tracking his footsteps through the dark streets. In a letter the next day to his sweetheart, Bess Wallace, Truman admitted how scared he had been.

> I had the livin' scared out of me as I came through the burg. Some guy evidently got off the train as I did. He followed me clear through town a quarter of a mile. Every time I'd whip up he would, too, and if I slowed down so did he. I guess he thought I was a bum and I'm sure he was. He finally went south and I went north. I was very much relieved when he did.[28]

Had Truman been shadowed in this way two years later, he might have felt even more uneasy. For in the course of the winter of 1914, there was a sudden upswing in the number of press reports about tramps and their menacing ways. Certain events further suggested that in New York and other cities radical political agitators had gained control of them.

In late February, for example, a mob of seven hundred homeless men —whom the newspapers referred to as tramps—burst into the Second Avenue Baptist Church in Manhattan. The minister who came out to meet them was informed by their leaders that the speakers at a mass rally in Union Square had exhorted them to satisfy their need for food and shelter by breaking into grocery stores and occupying churches without permission. Whether this statement intimidated the minister is unclear, but in any event he did not attempt to evict the intruders. In the course of the next three nights, they took over three other churches in a similar fashion. These invasions, said an alarmed citizen in a letter to the city's mayor, John Purroy Mitchel, were "evidence of the volcano beneath us."

On a snowy evening not long afterwards, Frank Tannenbaum of the revolutionary Industrial Workers of the World (IWW) shepherded five hundred so-called tramps into one of New York's better-known Catholic churches, St. Alphonsus. The rector of the church rejected Tannenbaum's demand for overnight sanctuary for the group and summoned the police. With the arrival of the bluecoats, the men began to leave the building. Suddenly, the sound of an explosion reverberated in the high-vaulted nave. A newspaper photographer, it seems, had set off a flashbulb, but the men believed that they were being shot at and turned on the police. A bruising battle with fists and billy clubs ensued. The police took almost two hundred of the rioters into custody, including Tannenbaum, who subsequently received a sentence of a year in prison.[29]

The following October, on the anniversary of the death of the Spanish anarchist Francisco Ferrer, a bomb exploded in St. Patrick's Cathedral and another wrecked the rectory of St. Alphonsus—as a retaliation, it was widely believed, against the priest who had refused to give sanctuary to Tannenbaum and his band.[30]

Nineteen fourteen was a year of politically symbolic acts of violence, and many citizens ascribed at least some of them to tramps who had been radicalized by the IWW. In the cities where the violence occurred, the police reacted to alarmed calls for increased protection by stiffening the enforcement of vagrancy laws. Tramps, it seemed, had again become a threat to the social order.[31]

It was in an atmosphere, then, of resurgent fears about ragged outcasts that Chaplin presented his comic alter ego in the guise of a tramp. Perhaps he was moved by a sympathy for society's outcasts. Perhaps it was Jack London's belief that "the greatest charm of tramp-life is the absence of monotony" that motivated him. Perhaps there were more factors at work in Chaplin's mind than he himself could have sorted out. In any event, he made his choice without any indication to anyone that a permanent commitment might be involved. His luck was that he tapped into a historic accumulation of nostalgia, longing, and fascination of far greater depth and emotional potency than he could have gauged. From coast to coast, audiences responded instantly to his new persona, although not all in the same way. For silent films were much more like dreams than talking pictures would be, and their pantomimes lent themselves to different interpretations.

5

The title character of *The Tramp* (April 1915) is a free spirit who lives by his own rules. Getting a job on a farm, he promptly disrupts its discipline. While he despises the trio of rough-looking itinerants who sneak out of the woods on the edge of the farm with mayhem and robbery in mind, he himself is not above opportunistic filching. In years to come, Charlie the tramp's resistance to the intimidations of work settings and of time-hallowed traditions and beliefs would become legendary; even the sight of the Statue of Liberty, in a comedy released two months after the United States entered World War I, would inspire him to question the continued validity of the statue's promises. Yet to many—possibly almost all—moviegoers in the United States, his stance as an outsider did not mark him as a foreigner; on the contrary, his don't-tread-on-me spirit seemed quintessentially American.

Charlie was especially delightful in *The Tramp* when putting on the manners of a swell. His jauntiness, however, made him seem more knowable than he actually was. Evidences of the darkness within him had their enigmatic aspects as well, and moviegoers became involved in defining their meaning. To the many men and women, for example, whom the decline of authentic forms of community had left floating free of the anchoring bonds of kinship and tradition,[32] images of the tramp's alienation and loneliness may have seemed like projections of their own inner lives.

Still unknown in 1915 was a man who was an exact contemporary of the creator of *The Tramp** and who possessed a like ability to uncover tendencies in the age and dramatize them in public performances. Adolf

---

* Indeed, the two men were born within a few days of each other.

Hitler's very first speech, delivered in Munich in the fall of 1919, exemplified the political style that would come to haunt the world, and it would have fascinated the future creator of *The Great Dictator* if he had known of it. For the speaker's stunningly angry rhetoric was distilled from his memories of the tramps and other outcasts of society among whom he had lived in the bitterest years of his young manhood.

6

In November 1909, the weather in Vienna had turned unpleasantly cold, and there was a good deal of icy rain mixed with snow. Unfortunately for him, the twenty-year-old Hitler had by that time spent the last of his inheritance from his father, as well as his share in the sale of his parents' home. His one remaining source of income was an orphan's pension, which he continued to receive as a result of his claim that he was enrolled as a student in the imperial capital's Academy of Fine Arts, although the truth of the matter was that the academy had twice denied him entrance, mainly because of the clumsiness of the drawings he had submitted with his application.[33]

Having reached the point where he could no longer afford to rent a room anywhere, Hitler spent several nights shivering on park benches in the freezing air, or fitfully dozing in smoky cafés. On the morning, then, that he finally joined the line in front of the refuge for homeless men in Meidling, a Vienna suburb, he was thoroughly miserable. A vagabond named Reinhold Hanisch, who showed up at the refuge after extensive wanderings on the roads of Germany and Austria, later recalled his first meeting with Hitler. "On the wire cot to my left was a gaunt young man whose feet were quite sore from tramping the streets. Since I still had some bread that peasants had given me, I shared it with him." The contradiction between Hitler's longing for middle-class respectability and his actual situation, Joachim C. Fest observes in his searching biography of the Nazi leader, "certainly never appeared more plainly than during the weeks in the flophouse, surrounded by broken-down derelicts, befriended by no one but the crudely cunning Reinhold Hanisch."[34]

A few days before Christmas, Hitler and Hanisch moved into another home for men, on Meldemann Strasse in the Twentieth District of Vienna. Here Hitler remained for three and a half years. Long afterwards, he still shuddered with horror at the memory of the "sordid scenes of garbage, repulsive filth, and worse." [35] As for the home's inhabitants, they were, in Fest's words, "the shipwrecked of various kinds, adventurers, bankrupt businessmen, gamblers, beggars, moneylenders, discharged army officers—flotsam and jetsam from all the provinces of the multinational state. What linked them all was common wretchedness; what separated them was the desperate determination to escape that world—to scramble out even at the expense of all others." [36]

Service in the army in World War I supplied Hitler with a social niche and a gratifying sense of belonging. But in postwar Munich, terrible feelings of superfluousness swept over him again. During the winter following the Armistice, he occasionally attended a political rally, but that kind of involvement really did not interest him. Nineteen nineteen, however, was a tumultuous year, and in the course of it he changed his mind—and his appearance as well. For at some point in the spring he trimmed the inverted V-shaped mustache he had affected since adolescence, in the hope that it made him look like an artist, into the squared-off brush of a military officer. The change made some observers think that he looked like Chaplin's tramp. But that resemblance was belied by the glitter in his eyes. The historian Karl Alexander von Muller, who saw him at a lecture in June 1919, described his appearance: "a pale thin face beneath a drooping, unsoldierly strand of hair, with close cropped mustache and strikingly large, light blue eyes coldly glistening with fanaticism." [37] Three months later, the fanatic began attending the weekly meetings in the Sternecker beer hall of a minuscule political group that grandiosely referred to itself as the German Workers' Party. In short order, he was named to the party's governing board and placed in charge of recruitment and propaganda. His fellow board members were amazed by the fervor with which he attempted to push the party into the public eye.

At a party-sponsored public meeting on October 16, he inspired even more amazement. Although he had long been accustomed to dominating conversations, he had no experience as a public speaker and was filled with doubts about his oratorical abilities. Nevertheless, he felt moved to address the crowd. "For thirty minutes," Fest relates, "in a furious stream of verbiage, he poured out the hatreds that ever since his days in the home for men had been stored up within him or discharged only in fruitless monologues. As if bursting through the silence and human barriers of many years, the sentences, the delusions, the accusations came tumbling out."[38]

The iconoclastic film critic David Thomson has posed the question, "Was Chaplin's common man so far from Hitler?" In Thomson's opinion, the answer is no. Chaplin, he says, "spoke to disappointment, brutalised feelings and failures and saw that through movies he could concoct a daydream world in which the tramp thrives and in which his whole ethos of self-pity is vindicated."[39] While that brilliantly hostile formulation is worth thinking about, it delineates a much closer resemblance to Hitler's appeal than is warranted. The lonely spirit of Chaplin's tramp is unquestionably susceptible to self-pity. Yet if Charlie takes a masochistic pleasure in his brutalized feelings, there are no shadows in them of the hatreds that blossomed in Hitler's brain in the home for broken men on Meldemann Strasse. Furthermore, in the final moments of *The Tramp*—the master model for so many later pictures—a spirit of American optimism prevails. Hitler, too, spoke to feelings of hope, renewal, and transformation, but they were of a different order than the tramp evokes.

7

In the distance, as *The Tramp* begins, a lone man is seen walking along a dusty road with a hitchy stride. Two automobiles speed past in quick succession. Each time, the vehicle comes so close to Charlie that he is forced to jump out of the way, and in doing so he loses his balance and tumbles head over heels. On regaining his feet the second time, he produces a whisk broom and dusts himself off; by bending down and putting the broom between his legs, he even manages to attend to the seat of his pants. Yet at the same time that such fastidiousness is laughable there is something melancholy about it. For the little tramp's derby is dented, his shoes don't fit, and the bagginess of his pants is grotesque —as he proceeds to demonstrate. While somberly gazing straight at us, he hunches up the excess material in the front of his pants and folds it back and forth from one side of his waist to the other. His daunted mood does not prevent him, however, from making a sexual boast. Holding the excess material away from his waist, he peers down inside his pants, and after a long look glances back at us with a satisfied leer.

In the next episode, it is lunchtime. Charlie walks a few feet away from the road, tips his hat to a tree, and sits down in its shade. But instead of immediately devouring the sandwich that he fishes out of his belongings, he puts it aside. He has noticed that his fingernails need attention, and while he is meticulously buffing them and cleaning under the tips with a paring knife, another tramp sneaks up behind him and steals the sandwich. By the time Charlie discovers what has happened, the thief has vanished. Charlie's substitute lunch consists of a handful of wild grass, which he judiciously salts. Finally, having finished eating, he dips his fingers in a tin of water and dabs at his mouth. The latter gestures climax a marvelously executed parody of a gentleman's adherence to the proprieties of polite-society dining. Once again, however, a certain melancholy is apparent in Charlie's conduct, the causes of which are conceivably rooted in painful recollections of a vanished respectability. But that is not certain, for the little tramp's past is mysterious, and will remain so.

The eye of the camera shifts to the tramp who has stolen Charlie's sandwich. He is spying on a farmer's daughter—played by Edna Purviance—as she stands alone in a field, counting a sheaf of dollar bills that her father has given her. The tramp tries to take the bills from her, but Edna breaks away and is not overtaken until she reaches the shady spot where Charlie is taking his postprandial ease. With a brief display of pugilistic razzmatazz, Charlie puts the thief to rout, much to Edna's relief. But Charlie, it turns out, is not above a little thievery himself now and then, and this is one of those times, as Edna sadly realizes. The only trouble is that he finds he can't stand the sight of her unhappiness. Whereupon he gives the money back to her—except for two or three bills that he slyly reserves for himself. Meantime, the other tramp has rejoined two hard-faced companions at their bivouac in the woods and informed them about the girl with the money. These men immediately launch assaults of their own upon Edna, but in each case Charlie manages to hit the miscreant on the head with a brick wrapped up in his kerchief. Gratefully, Edna takes Charlie home with her and introduces him to her father, who promptly hires him to pitch hay in his barnyard. His seeming delight in the assignment suggests that he is ready to reintegrate himself into society.

The next several minutes of the picture expose the sadistic pranksterism in Charlie's personality. He repeatedly thrusts the tines of a pitchfork into the backside of another workman on the farm. He also drops a bag of flour from atop a ladder onto the farmer's head, and then clambers down and sits on the bag while the farmer is still beneath it. His most insulting pranks, however, are those that give vent to the dislike of clergymen for which he would continue to be known.

The first prank takes place when Charlie notices a minister standing outside the barnyard with an open prayer book before him and a look of reverential rapture on his upturned face. Charlie purposely wipes animal droppings off his shoes as he passes by, and the stink abruptly terminates the minister's musings. A minute or two later, Charlie finds two eggs in the barn. He cracks open one of them on the forehead of the workman. The other, however, is rotten, so he holds on to it until he can surreptitiously drop it into the minister's prayer book.

The task of milking a cow gives Charlie the chance to get off another sex joke. Milk pail in hand, he approaches a bull; but this demonstration of biological ignorance is as nothing compared to his wide-eyed response to the sight of the creature's genital equipment. Eventually, a cow appears and Charlie tips his hat to her (as a gentleman should, upon encountering a lady). When his Weary Willie–like stratagem of pumping the cow's tail does not accomplish anything, he picks up a full pail of milk and carries it back to the admiring Edna, who readily accepts his implication that he has done the squeezing.

From the moment he plucks a flower from a bush and coyly throws it at Edna, it is clear that he is falling in love with her. Thus when the three tramps in the woods inform him that they would like his help in invading the farmer's house and stealing all his money, he pretends to go along with the scheme—but his intention is to protect Edna and her father. Thanks to a warning from Charlie, the farmer is able to repel the attack with a blast or two from his shotgun. Unfortunately, one of the marauders shoots Charlie in the leg as he is giving chase to them. This shocking and naturalistically enacted scene alters the very nature of *The Tramp*. Instead of continuing in the vein of knockabout comedy, it finishes as a tragicomic romance in which a fair amount of the acting is remarkably straight. A comparison comes to mind. With the composition of "The Overcoat," Gogol began a new chapter in Russian literature by treating an underdog and social misfit not as a figure of fun but as a human being who has as much right to happiness as anyone else.[40] With the wounding of Charlie in *The Tramp*, Chaplin brought a similarly historic innovation into movies.

Which is not to say that during his convalescence in the farmer's home Charlie is not amusing. The languid pose he strikes as he semireclines on a chaise next to Edna parodies the lounging attitudes of young Edwardian aesthetes, whom Chaplin might have observed firsthand on more than one occasion while having a drink at the bar in a music hall in central London. The way Charlie raises his eyebrows also conveys his aptitude for the good life, as does his exquisite response to the aroma of the cigar he is smoking. But the most charming moment in this sequence occurs when he expresses his appreciation for the taste of a mouthful of whisky by gargling it.

His love for Edna, on the other hand, is serious business. Consequently, the arrival of a well-dressed, good-looking young man who turns out to be her fiancé does not bring any smiles of welcome to Charlie's face. Since his leg has healed, he can see no reason to remain at the farm any longer. With a great effort, he masks his heartbreak as he wishes Edna and her sweetheart all the best. Once again the glints of personal history shine through the action. Chaplin learned as a child not to count on his mother, and thereafter his distrust of women was striking. In *The Tramp* and elsewhere, this habit of mind led to agonized portrayals of romantic disappointment.

The shot of Charlie walking down the dusty road away from the farmhouse brings the story back to its beginning—except that his pace is slower now and his shoulders sag with the weight of his sense of loss. Here indeed was something new under the cinematic sun: a comedy with a sad and self-pitying ending. But the show is not quite over. Suddenly Charlie burlesques a ballet step and then moves on with an unmistakable eagerness. He is still, after all, a free man, and an open road unwinds ambiguously before him. Who knows what lies around the bend? Implicit in this epochal picture is the proposition that as long as you can count on humor, you must not entirely despair of life.

8

Shortly after the release of *The Tramp* on April 11, Chaplin returned to Los Angeles and went to work in a mansion on North Hill Street that Essanay rented for his use until a lease could be worked out on a proper studio on Fairview Avenue. The hick-town tranquillity of Niles had lacerated his nerves, and the Essanay facilities there had proved to be too small to accommodate his demands upon them in addition to Broncho Billy Anderson's, not to mention Wallace Beery's. Having to share the studio had irked Anderson, too, so he was only too glad to see the little comedian go.

In his last days at Niles, Chaplin submitted to an interview by Charles J. McGuirk of *Motion Picture Magazine* and at the end of it had a question for the reporter. "Say, did you see *The Tramp?*" he asked. "I know that I took an awful chance. But did it get across?"[41] Actually he already knew the answer from newspaper and magazine reports. As a sardonic contributor to the highbrow *Little Review* had just proclaimed in a piece of overripe prose laced with elitist sneering, Charlie Chaplin was having an electrifying effect on audiences.

The seats creak expectantly. The white whirr of the movie machine takes on a special significance. In the murky gloom of the theater you can watch row on row of backs becoming suddenly enthusiastic, necks growing suddenly alive, heads rising to a fresh angle. Turning around you can see the stupid masks falling, vacant eyes lighting up, lips parting and waiting to smile. . . . The lights dance on the screen in front. Letters appear in two short words [*i.e., The Tramp*] and a gasp sweeps from mouth to mouth.

The name of a Mob-God flashes before the eyes. Suddenly the screen in front vanishes. In its place appears a road stretching away to the sky and lined with trees. . . . The road smiles like an old friend. And far in the distance a speck appears and moves slowly and jerkily. . . . It takes the form of a man, a little man with a thin cane. . . .

Charlie Chaplin is before them, Charles Chaplin with the wit of a vulgar buffoon and the soul of a world artist. He walks, he stumbles, he dances, he falls. His inimitable gyrations release torrents of mirth clean as spring freshets. He is cruel. He is absurd; unmanly; tawdry; cheap; artificial. And yet behind his crudities, his obscenities, his inartistic and outrageous contortions, his "divinity" shines. He is the Mob-God. He is a child and a clown. He is a gutter snipe and an artist. He is the incarnation of the latent, imperfect, and childlike genius that lies buried under the fiberless flesh of his worshippers. They have created Him in their image. He is the Mob on two legs. They love him and laugh.

"Fruits to Om."
"Glory to Zeus."
"Mercy, Jesus."
"Praised be Allah."
"Hats off to Charlie Chaplin."[42]

From Los Angeles, Chaplin began phoning Essanay headquarters in Chicago about altering the terms of his contract. As a preparation for future dealings with other studios, he also hired his wily brother as his full-time business manager. At Sydney's insistence, he took the further step of hiring an extra secretary, because the secretary whom Essanay had assigned to him was unable to cope with the stacks and stacks of fan mail that were being delivered to his office every day. In addition, there were letters from companies that wanted him to license various products, and when the price was right he did so.

Meantime, other moviemakers were cashing in on Chaplin's colossal success by copying him. Among the most determined of these imitators were Hal Roach and Harold Lloyd. Two months after the appearance of *The Tramp*, Roach released the first of his Lonesome Luke comedies. The costume devised for the title character (played by Lloyd) was the obverse of Charlie's getup—trousers that were too tight and too short, a jacket that was inappropriately long, and so on. But in addition, Luke sported a cane and a mustache consisting of two dots of greasepaint, and he had a habit of tipping his top hat (in later films, a light-colored derby) at odd moments.

For two and a half years, Roach and Lloyd ground out Luke comedies —perhaps as many as sixty in all. But one night in a neighborhood movie house, Lloyd heard a small boy say to a friend, just as a Luke two-reeler was about to begin, "Oh, here's that fellow who tries to do like Chaplin." When Lloyd subsequently told Roach that he had no intention of "going on being a third-rate imitation of anybody, even a genius like Chaplin," the producer was upset, but he did not attempt to discourage Lloyd from developing a new persona. By the end of 1918, Lloyd's "glass character," as he called him, had become world famous and sales of black frames for eyeglasses were booming. In later years, the multimillionaire comedian refused to admit his early indebtedness to Chaplin. "I never did, really, even in the slightest sense, try to imitate Charlie," he insisted.[43]

9

The first film that the star of *The Tramp* turned out after his reappearance in Los Angeles was *By the Sea*, a one-reel account of Charlie's nervously aggressive efforts to pick up Edna on a sunny, windswept, late April day at the seashore. While it had its delightful moments, the constraints of the one-reel format left Chaplin feeling dissatisfied and he never again resorted to it.

His itch to upgrade the quality of his work also drove him to discard possibilities for gags that probably would have passed muster with him at Keystone. The result was that only five of his comedies reached the market between the end of April and the end of the year, whereas in the comparable period the year before he had been involved in twenty-three. Yet if he was determined to become a more discriminating film-maker, he was also in a gambling mood. Having taken chances in *The Tramp* and won, he felt emboldened to take others. In *Work* and in *Life* his experimentalism was breathtaking. Unfortunately, both pictures failed, for different reasons.

The first part of *Work*, which he made in June, is almost surreal. In the middle of a busy Los Angeles street, a familiarly dressed figure—complete with derby—is straining forward like a beast of burden between the shafts of a top-heavy cart. Ensconced on the seat behind Charlie is a beefy, sullen-faced driver, and heaped up behind him in perilous balance are the ladders, planks, and other accoutrements of the house decorator's trade. When the cart gets stuck in streetcar tracks, the driver methodically beats his bent-over, sweating assistant with a whip-like cane. At other junctures, he repeats this exercise, adding for good measure a few vicious jabs with the point of the cane.

A shortcut up a steeply inclined grassy hill presents Charlie with an even greater physical challenge, and he keeps sliding back onto the right-of-way of fast-moving interurban trolleys. At last, he makes the grade, but not before the screen is filled with a cinematically stunning shot, something relatively unusual in the Chaplin canon. The cart lies motionless on the steepest part of the hillside against the backdrop of an enormous sky, its rear end resting on the ground, its shafts pointed upward at an angle of forty-five degrees. Holding on to the crossbar between the shafts and flailing at the air with frantic motions that resemble the convulsions of an insect impaled upon a pin is Charlie. As a comic recognition of the pointlessness of most human strivings and of the ultimate mystery of existence, the shot anticipates the bizarre settings, the physical constraints placed upon actors, and the focus on tramps and cripples in Beckett's plays.*

The idea for opening *Work* in this way, Chaplin declared in the magazine called *The Theatre* in September 1915, "came to me from a scene I witnessed, one that was not funny to the assistant, but very laughable to the bystanders."[44] Although his translation of this scene to the screen was brilliant, he was unable to sustain its poetic evocation of existential absurdity and instead filled out the film with standard music hall nihilism. The model he worked from was the house-decorating sketch called *Repairs*, in which he had played, in 1906, a hopelessly awkward plumber's helper. Charlie has the comparable role of a contractor's assistant, and with help from his feckless boss he makes an utter mess of a suburban household with indiscriminate applications of wallpaper and paste and buckets of house paint. The farcical sideshows that accompany this spectacle include angry protests by the head of the household, attempts by his wife to conceal her romance with a French count, and Charlie's discovery—after prudishly placing a lampshade over the private parts of a statuette of a naked woman—that he can create the illusion of a hootchy-kootchy dance by setting the lampshade in motion. An explosion in a gas oven brings these goings-on to an end with a bang. In the final shot, Charlie emerges from the explosion with a battered smile and is promptly hit by falling plaster. But the true victim of *Work*'s destructiveness is the promise of the picture's unforgettable beginning.

Life was apparently designed to be a feature-length examination, from a savagely satirical point of view, of the nature of life in the lowest of

---

* In the 1920s, young Samuel Beckett (born 1906) "was fascinated with the developing cinema," his biographer Deirdre Bair has pointed out, "and never missed a film starring Charlie Chaplin, Laurel and Hardy (who became the 'hardy Laurel' in the novel *Watt*), or Harold Lloyd. Later, when the Marx Brothers began to make movies, Beckett saw every one." In casting the Beckett movie called *Film* in the 1960s, the director Alan Schneider wanted Chaplin for O (or the object), but never received an answer to the barrages of letters he sent to the comedian's home in Switzerland. So Schneider finally turned to Buster Keaton. Deirdre Bair, *Samuel Beckett* (New York, 1978), pp. 48, 570–71.

the lower depths of an unnamed city. But the Essanay front office, in all likelihood in the person of George Spoor himself, forced him to pull the plug on the project in the midst of production, which was tragic, albeit understandable.

In the renegotiated contract that Chaplin had signed in July, he had promised to produce ten two-reel comedies before January 1, 1916. He himself volunteered the further assurance that he would turn them out at the rate of one every three weeks. When he quickly fell behind schedule, it was no laughing matter to Essanay, for the company was paying him $1,250 a week on the assumption that it would make a profit of $125,000 on each two-reeler. Thus when Spoor learned that Chaplin had embarked upon a feature film called *Life*, he protested that there was no time for it. Two-reel pictures were what he wanted, and had contracted for.[45]*

During his last days at Essanay, Chaplin incorporated the flophouse footage he had shot for *Life* into a three-reeler called *Police*. After he left the company, however, Essanay made cuts in *Police*, including a considerable portion of the flophouse footage, in order to reduce it to the standard two-reel format. When Chaplin saw *Police* in the spring of 1916, he assumed that the excised footage had been destroyed. His former associates, however, were nothing if not thrifty.

In 1918 Essanay put out a "Chaplin picture" called *Triple Trouble*. German spies appear in it, along with a nutty inventor named Colonel Nutt—and two episodes from the unfinished *Life*. In one Charlie is a kitchen boy, working under the surveillance of a demonic cook in a rich man's home, and Edna Purviance is a housemaid, fiercely scrubbing floors. The other takes place in the flophouse. Only in recent years has it at last been possible to see all of Chaplin's flophouse footage under one roof, so to speak, in producer-director Don McGlynn's documentary, *The Chaplin Puzzle* (1993).

The proprietor of the flophouse is a scrawny character, quite likely a Jew, with a long straggly beard and a skullcap on his head. To ward off the stink of unwashed flesh, he holds his nose once or twice as he takes

---

* Eventually Essanay instituted a legal claim against Chaplin based on an estimated lost profit of half a million dollars on four pictures not made. The claim was settled out of court in 1922.

coins from the men who are filing into the awful room behind him with two rows of narrow beds jammed side by side. One of the men has a patch on his eye and is popping pills into his mouth. Another is a consumptive who is admitted free of charge because of his hacking cough. Still another, a big man, has the exaggerated mannerisms of a homosexual queen. All of the entrants are nauseatingly ragged and dirty, except Charlie, who by comparison looks almost respectable.

These derelicts are as repulsive to Charlie as the human flotsam and jetsam in the Meidling refuge for the homeless were to Hitler. Initially, Charlie makes a brave show of his revulsion by means of sadistic humor. The sight—and the smell—of the bare feet of a man who is out cold on one of the beds prompts him to place a lighted match between his toes. Next, he knocks out a woebegone drunk whose psychotic caterwauling is bothering him. Any thoughts, however, of inflicting pain on other unfortunates not able to fight back are driven from his head by the abrupt appearance of a hideous, wild-eyed, bent-over figure with a great gap between his teeth, a ruined hat on his head, and a clear case of galloping insanity. This jackal from hell immediately robs the homosexual, who has fallen asleep. With fiendish glee interrupted by body spasms, he adds up his loot. The daunted Charlie slides under the blanket on his bed with his head facing toward the opposite row of beds and his hands in his shoes, which he carefully positions beyond the edge of the blanket. As a way of enabling him to keep an eye on a potential assailant whom he is afraid of, it is an altogether charming stratagem, and Chaplin would make use of it again in *The Gold Rush*. This light moment, however, only temporarily eases the tense atmosphere of the scene. At the close, a fight breaks out among several of the inmates that threatens to engulf the entire shelter, and Charlie flees into the night.

Because Chaplin chose to make his comic persona a tramp, many critics—especially leftist critics—have assumed that he thereafter became an attorney for the wretched of the earth. Chaplin, however, was more complicated than that. He unquestionably resented the class-bound restrictions of British society and may well have hoped, *circa* 1910, that the militant trade union leaders who were calling for vast strikes would succeed in overturning the existing order. The fact that his choice of a tramp disguise was made in the aftermath of a wave of violence by homeless men who had supposedly been listening to Frank

Tannenbaum and other agitators may not have been mere coincidence. And yet . . .

The flophouse nightmare came straight out of Chaplin's childhood experience—but not in a direct way. After being forced to give up three-room, middle-class comfort, Hannah and her two boys did not sink nearly as far as Chaplin implied; rather, they ended up living either just above or just below the poverty line. For marginal people who have experienced status loss, there is always the fear of the abyss beneath them, as well as a compulsion to keep up appearances, to dress respectably, to speak properly. "Living as we did in the lower strata," Chaplin would write in *My Autobiography*, "it was very easy to fall into the habit of not caring about our diction. But Mother always stood outside her environment and kept an alert ear on the way we talked, correcting our grammar, and making us feel that we were distinguished."[46] And in the *Life* fragments the satirical savagery of Chaplin's presentation of the poor devils in a squalid flophouse leaves little doubt that he had a horror of such people.

10

The last weeks of 1915 found Chaplin living by himself in a house in Santa Monica facing the sea. In the evenings he sometimes arranged to have dinner with the proprietor of Nat Goodwin's Café on the Santa Monica pier. A Bostonian by birth, the fifty-eight-year-old Goodwin had earned his first paychecks as a vaudeville performer in a Boston theater that later became the Old Howard burlesque house. During his many years of stardom on the legitimate stage, Goodwin had been known for his ability to play any sort of role, but in his own opinion his finest achievement was his interpretation of Fagin in a 1912 dramatization of *Oliver Twist*, in which the love of Chaplin's mooncalf adolescence, Marie Doro, also appeared. Inasmuch as Goodwin had been married eight times, some of his fellow actors thought of him as personally difficult, but Chaplin was not one of them. In his view, his new friend was "an amiable, cultured man" with a "profound sense of humor." After dinner, they would talk for hours while strolling along the deserted oceanfront. Chaplin was grateful for Goodwin's advice. The topic that came up on their most memorable walk had to do with Chaplin's personal relations with his admirers.

Chaplin began the conversation by saying that he would shortly be leaving for New York to talk to his brother Sydney about the contract terms that Sydney had been discussing on his behalf with the heads of various companies, all of whom seemed very anxious to make his personal acquaintance as well. According to Chaplin, Goodwin's reply went something like this:

> You've made a remarkable success, and there's a wonderful life ahead of you, if you know how to handle yourself. When you get to New York keep off Broadway, keep out of the public's eye. The mistake with many successful actors is that they want to be seen and admired—it only destroys the illusion.

The depth and resonance of Goodwin's voice underscored his seriousness. "You'll be invited everywhere," he continued,

> but don't accept. Pick out one or two friends and be satisfied to imagine the rest. Many a great actor has made the mistake of accepting every social invitation. John Drew was an example; he was a great favorite with society and went to all their houses, but they would not go to his theatre. They had had him in their drawing rooms. You've captivated the world, and you can continue doing so if you stand outside it.[47]

That Chaplin was pantingly eager to make a splash in Manhattan may have seemed obvious to Goodwin because of his young friend's self-improvement program. Every day, Chaplin looked up new words in the dictionary. He read—or dipped into—serious books. He was rapidly eliminating all traces of Cockneyism from his accent. And as pictures of him in this period attest, he had taken to wearing expensive-looking, conservatively cut, three-piece suits with his old-fashioned button shoes. As he himself said, he was "young, rich and celebrated" and ready for "the pleasures of Vanity Fair." In the weeks and months immediately ahead, however, he would discover that mere acquaintances "were willing to enter into the warmest of friendships and share my problems as though they were relatives." While this was all very flattering, his shy, moody, work-absorbed nature did not respond to such intimacy. As he would arrogantly confess, "I like friends as I like music—when I am in the mood."[48]

In New York in early 1916, Chaplin certainly made waves in the social swim. But he did not remain immersed for long. Even though he regarded loneliness as a "repellent" condition that implied an "inadequacy to attract or interest" and left him feeling "slightly ashamed," social involvement quickly tired him. For perhaps two hours, Thomas Burke would later remark, "[Chaplin] will be the sweetest fellow you have ever sat with; then without apparent cause, he will be all petulance and asperity." In this respect he reminded Burke of Charles Dickens, "a man of querulous outlook, self-centered, moody, and vaguely dissatisfied with life." [49]

6

"SHEER PERSEVERANCE TO
THE POINT OF MADNESS"

Skating with balletic grace in The Rink *(1916).*

T H E train Chaplin took to Chicago went by the southern route. Just before boarding, he sent Sydney a telegram, stating the time of his arrival in the Windy City, where he would stay overnight before proceeding on to New York.

Through Arizona and New Mexico and on into the Texas Panhandle, the other passengers failed to recognize the wavy-haired, well-dressed young man in their midst who seemed too shy to say much of anything to them. As the train pulled into Amarillo, he was in the washroom in his underwear, shaving and freshening up before supper. On peering out of the window, he was surprised to see a large crowd milling about on the platform in an obvious state of excitement. Every stanchion was wrapped in bunting, flags flapped in the evening breeze, and several long tables were set up with refreshments. "Where is he? Where's Charlie Chaplin?" he heard people shouting, and inside the train there was the sound of running feet and slamming doors.

Suddenly the door of the washroom burst open. "On behalf of the mayor of Amarillo, Texas, and of all your fans," a man said, "we invite you to have a drink and a light refreshment with us." Somewhat reluctantly, Chaplin got dressed and followed the man outside. Cheers saluted his appearance, drowning out the formal greetings of the city's mayor. The crowd surged forward, pressing the object of its affection against the train. "Get back!" shouted several policemen as they shouldered their way forward. When the tumult had subsided, the mayor made a speech, Chaplin thought of something to say in reply, and the crowd made short work of the sandwiches and bottles of soft drinks on the refreshment tables. Chaplin asked the mayor how he had known he was on the train. Through the telegraph operators, the mayor explained. The telegram that Chaplin had sent to Sydney had been relayed through operators all across the country, and some of them had divulged its contents to the press.

The crowds awaiting him in Kansas City and Chicago were huge, while at railroad junctions and in fields in between he saw people standing and waving at the speeding train. But instead of being pleased by their adulation, it left him feeling trapped, and this sensation overcame him again during his stopover in Chicago at the Blackstone Hotel. A bellboy brought a telegram to his room from the chief of police in New York, advising him that upon reaching the city, he should leave the train at 125th Street, rather than at Grand Central Station. The chief, it seems, doubted his ability to hold back the sea of humanity that would surely be on hand at the terminal.[1]

2

The talented publicist Terry Ramsaye, who got to know Chaplin in 1916, described how the financial heads of Universal, Vitagraph, Famous Players, and Fox went after the comedian when he reached New York. "All the delights of Manhattan, with considerable frankincense and myrrh, were laid before him," and in the wee hours of the morning "verbal millions were ... tossed about like confetti in the standard cabaret scene."[2] Chaplin, for his part, did not trust these offers, or the big shots who made them. The only executive in whom he did have faith was John R. Freuler of the Mutual Film Corporation, mainly because, unlike his rivals, he was not interested in nightclub entertaining and had confined his sales pitches to business hours.

An imposingly tall, white-haired Milwaukeean, Freuler had built Mutual, with its winged-clock trademark and accompanying announcement that "Mutual Movies Make Time Fly," into one of the great film-distribution concerns. A fair chunk of the company's profits in 1914 and 1915 had come from meeting the ceaseless demand of movie houses for prints of Chaplin's Keystone pictures. But these prints had now begun to wear out from constant use, and Freuler was unable to obtain new ones because of his strained relations with a former business associate, Harry E. Aitken, of the Triangle Film Corporation. Having acquired ownership of the nitrate negatives of all of Chaplin's work for Mack Sennett, Aitken was in a position to supply Freuler's company with more prints if he wanted to—but he emphatically did not. Another problem confronting Mutual was competition from outlaw suppliers who had illegally imported prints of Chaplin's early comedies that had been sold abroad to foreign distributors. Compounding this headache was the considerable and equally illegal traffic in "duped" copies of Chaplin's work, the manufacture of which involved making a negative from a positive print.[3] Thus the only means by which Mutual could again assemble an impressive inventory of Chaplin's work and at the same time fend off its lawbreaking competitors, Freuler concluded, was by contracting with the comedian to make more pictures. To sign him, however, would take a major effort.

Mutual's final and successful offer was stupendous: a salary of $10,000 a week for a year of Chaplin's services, plus a signing bonus of $150,000.* Furthermore, the company promised to equip a new studio and to pay all the filmmaking costs, which Freuler rather optimistically

---

* To translate these amounts into mid-1990s dollars, multiply them by fourteen.

estimated would come to no more than $10,000 a picture. In exchange, Chaplin agreed that beginning in the spring, when the contract would take effect, he would supply a newly formed Mutual subsidiary, the Lone Star Film Corporation (the name referred to him, not to Texas), with twelve two-reel pictures, at the rate of one picture every four weeks. (After producing eight pictures between May and December of 1916, Chaplin would successfully insist on a considerably looser production schedule for the final four, with the result that the last of his Mutual pictures was not released to exhibitors until October 1917.)

Freuler staged the contract-signing ceremony in front of reporters and cameramen on a February evening on the mezzanine floor of the Hotel Astor. With a dramatic flourish, he wrote out a check for the full amount of the bonus and handed it to Chaplin, who raised his eyebrows and rapidly blinked his eyes as he verified the amount. Later that night, the star stood with the crowd in Times Square and watched the news of his triumph unfold like a ribbon on the electric sign running around the Times Building: "Chaplin signs with Mutual at $670,000 a year." So exhausted was he by the emotional wear and tear of a month of hard bargaining that he read the bulletin "objectively, as though it were about someone else."[4]

Public reaction to the news was decidedly mixed. A writer in *Photoplay* did manage to affirm that if Chaplin was now a "millionaire-elect," he deserved to be, for his contract fell "into its proper relation in the scale of receipts and disbursements when the profits made out of Chaplin's pictures are considered." Nevertheless, it clearly offended the writer to think that with the exception of the president of U.S. Steel, a movie comedian in his middle twenties was probably now receiving the biggest salary "grabbed off by any public person outside of royalty," and that the total combined earnings of the nine justices of the U.S. Supreme Court came to only 19.5 percent of Chaplin's.[5] Even as ardent a Chaplin enthusiast as the veteran entertainment writer Robert Grau, who considered the creator of Charlie "the most extraordinary figure the Motion Picture has ever revealed," could not refrain from sarcastically declaring that the entire film world was convulsed with laughter by the "truly funny spectacle of a screen star, two years ago hardly known by name, inducing a half-dozen sane film barons to pay him more money per week (and every week of the fifty-two in the year) than was ever meted out to Edwin Booth, Patti, Caruso and Paderewski in a job lot."[6]

Meanwhile, newspaper and magazine cartoonists were working off their own disgust by drawing attention to the disparities between the lonely, shabbily dressed Little Tramp and the dapper, much-sought-after, incipiently rich young man who was playing him. In all likelihood, the widespread belief that Chaplin was Jewish also inspired anti-Semitic comments about his bargaining skills, although they never surfaced in public and probably did not have a significant influence on the disturbing attitude toward him that *Motion Picture Magazine* reported in the May 1916 issue. So many of the respondents to the magazine's "Popular Players" contest simply ignored him that he finished in thirty-sixth place, and in another polling a month later his popularity rating was even lower.[7]

At the same time that hostile commentators were predicting the imminent collapse of the Chaplin boom in the United States, he was having problems in his homeland as well. Britain's love affair with Charlie Chaplin had begun almost as propitiously as America's. By 1915, schoolchildren were singing songs about him, and Charlie Chaplin lookalikes had become a standard attraction in musical revues. Yet it was also true that Chaplin's decision, in August 1914, not to return home at once and join the army had engendered a fair amount of ill will among his compatriots, some of whom sent him letters with white feathers enclosed. With the subsequent passage of the Military Service Act, Britain began to train its first conscript army, and hostility toward young men who were still civilians markedly intensified. Thus when the British public learned that a clause in Chaplin's new contract forbade him to leave the United States during the period of his employment without Mutual's express permission, a huge outcry erupted. Signs appeared outside local cinemas saying "No Chaplin Here." The press ran headlines about Chaplin the Slacker. And a sheet-music firm published a set of ominous lyrics, to the tune of "Redwing," that "scared the daylights" out of Chaplin when he heard about them:

> The moon shines bright on Charlie Chaplin
> His boots are cracking,
> For want of blacking,
> And his little baggy trousers
> They want mending
> Before we send him
> To the Dardanelles.[8]

Had these attacks been echoed by the nation's fighting men, Chaplin's hold on the affections of British civilians would have been seriously compromised. But in the year of the Battle of the Somme, in which, on the first day alone, sixty thousand British troops were either killed or wounded, the movie tents behind the lines in France continued to be filled with laughter whenever Charlie Chaplin comedies were shown. Inasmuch as Chaplin had long since ceased to feel any nationalistic identification with Britain, he was lying in his teeth when he told an English correspondent that "I only wish that I could join the English army and fight for my mother country." * Yet there was nothing exaggerated about his further comment to the same correspondent that he had received "many letters" from "soldiers at the front . . . asking me to continue making pictures." The British embassy in Washington felt the same way. His pictures were such an important factor in keeping up the morale of the troops in the trenches, a top official assured him, that sending along an occasional new one was the most valuable service he could possibly perform for his country.

New ones continued to be sent to Britain all through the war and were, indeed, a morale booster for soldiers and civilians alike—including a disgruntled eleven-year-old boy at All Saints, a highly exclusive choir school (fourteen boarding students all told) located near Oxford Circus in London. In 1918 the boy was earning only average grades; but whenever he entertained school assemblies with impromptu impersonations of Charlie Chaplin and other film actors, his classmates knew that Larry Olivier was special.[9]

3

At loose ends in Manhattan, once the negotiations with Mutual were behind him, Chaplin felt the need of applause from an audience of one, namely, Hetty Kelly, whose adorableness still lingered in his mind, even though their eleven-day love affair in 1908 had ended in bitterness.

* That Chaplin maintained his British citizenship throughout his Hollywood years had less to do with lingering loyalty to the "mother country" than with his calculated hope that someday he might be knighted. So, at least, his English-born friend Eddie Sutherland believed. Edward Sutherland tape, Columbia University Oral History Project.

Rumor had it that she was living in a grand house in New York as a guest of her sister, who had married an American millionaire, Frank Gould. Upon discovering that the Gould mansion on Fifth Avenue was only a few blocks away from the Plaza Hotel where he was staying, Chaplin strolled past its stately windows one morning, wondering whether Hetty was inside. If she happened to be, perhaps she would come out and he could pretend that their meeting was an accident. After a fruitless half hour of continued patrolling, he walked across Central Park and ate a lonely meal of pancakes washed down with coffee at a Childs Restaurant on Columbus Circle.[10]

The incident illustrated how little thought he had been giving to Edna Purviance. Ever since his departure from Los Angeles, she had been miserably unhappy, as he must have known she would be. He had promised to keep in touch on a regular basis, but all he had vouchsafed her was one economically worded telegram. Finally, she went to visit her family in Nevada, and during her stay she wrote him a reproachful letter.

I really don't know why you don't send me some word. . . . How much longer do you expect to stay. Please, Hon, don't forget your "Modie" and hurry back. Have been home for over a week and believe me my feet are itching to get back [to Los Angeles].[11]

Whether they were reunited on the day he returned is not clear, but in any case he retired to his hotel room at an early hour. By way of celebrating his new affluence, he had decided to treat himself to a week's sojourn at the swankiest hostelry in town, the Alexandria, at Fifth Street and Main. Marble columns framed the spacious lobby, and spread across the floor was the legendary rug known as the "million-dollar carpet," in tribute to all the profitable schemes that Hollywood wheeler-dealers had hatched upon it. As Chaplin was inspecting the comforts of his room and getting undressed—so he would relate in *My Autobiography*— he started humming one of the show tunes he had heard in New York. Occasionally he paused, and whenever he did so, a woman's voice in the next room took up the song where he had left it. This interchange led to a conversation at the keyhole of the connecting door to her room, and when the woman finally yielded to his blandishments and unlocked the door on her side, he was gratified to see that she was a ravishing young blonde in a silky negligee.

"Don't come in or I'll beat you up!" she said, showing her pretty white teeth, but it soon became apparent that she already knew who he was and that she had no intention of sleeping alone that night. The next night, she tapped on the door and once again proved ready for lovemaking. But while in bed with her on the third night, Chaplin realized that he was "getting rather weary; besides, I had work and a career to think about." On the fourth night, he ignored her tapping. On the fifth night, no tapping was heard, but as he quietly watched, the doorknob slowly turned. Fortunately, he had made sure that the door was locked. A furious knocking followed, interspersed by violent turns of the doorknob. The next morning, he checked out of the hotel.[12]

Apparently he had tired of the tireless blonde and was eager to get back to work. But in all probability that episode and everything else that Chaplin said about sex in *My Autobiography* were written out of a distressed awareness that years of adverse publicity about his relations with women had seriously damaged his reputation in the United States. Eddie Sutherland once said of him, "He always liked gals," but *My Autobiography* hardly began to suggest the phenomenal extent of his appetite for them. "As for sex," Chaplin depreciatingly declared,

> most of it went in to my work. When it did rear its delightful head, life was so inopportune that it was either a glut on the market or a serious shortage. However, I was a disciplinarian and took my work seriously. Like Balzac, who believed that a night of sex meant the loss of a good page of his novel, so I believed it meant the loss of a good day's work at the studio.
>
> A well-known lady novelist, hearing I was writing my autobiography, said, "I hope you have the courage to tell the truth." I thought she meant politically, but she was referring to my sex life. I suppose a dissertation on one's libido is expected in an autobiography, although I do not know why. To me it contributes little to the understanding or revealing of character. Unlike Freud, I do not believe sex is the most important element in the complexity of behavior. Cold, hunger and the shame of poverty are more likely to affect one's psychology.
>
> Like everybody else's my sex life went in cycles. Sometimes I was potent, other times disappointing. But it was not the all-absorbing inter-

est in my life. I had creative interests which were just as absorbing.
However, in this book I do not intend to give a blow-by-blow description
of a sex bout; I find them inartistic, clinical and unpoetic. The circumstances that lead up to sex I find more interesting.[13]

I had creative interests which were just as absorbing. Even though he read
and reread *My Autobiography* before publication, Chaplin never caught
the slip. Close to the end of an elaborate disavowal of sexual addiction,
he inadvertently rated his interest in sex on a par with his famous absorption in his work. In spite of himself, he told the truth after all.

Throughout 1916 and well into 1917, Edna saw Chaplin more often
than did any other woman. She rented an apartment in a hotel near the
Los Angeles Athletic Club, where he was living, and almost every night
he would bring her to the club for dinner. We were "serious about each
other," he later insisted; indeed, at the back of his mind he "had an idea
that we might marry." Yet he also admitted to having had "reservations"
about her, although he did not specify what they were. At the fêtes and
galas to which he took her, he lavished his charm and wit on other
women. When he did so for too long, however, Edna "would get jealous
and had an insidious way of showing it." Without warning, she would
disappear; a short while later, he would receive a message saying that
she had regained consciousness after having fainted and was asking for
him. At which point he would reluctantly leave the dance floor and
spend the rest of the evening by her side.

However, at a Red Cross benefit in the summer or fall of 1917—by
which time America's entrance into the war in Europe had made this
sort of event socially fashionable—Edna's fainting act had a different
outcome. Upon regaining consciousness, she appealed for the comforting presence of another actor, the tall, masterful-looking Thomas
Meighan, Paramount's most consistently popular male star. Presumably
because Chaplin was preoccupied by the "galaxy" of pretty girls whom
he remembered from that evening, he was unaware of this surprising
event—until a fabulous if somewhat faded Hollywood beauty, Fannie
Ward, whose enormous home, the largest in the movie colony, had been
the scene of the party, filled him in the following day. Chaplin instantly
flew into a rage. Yet when Edna vigorously denounced the story as a
pack of lies, he accepted her word without question and they were

reconciled. Several weeks later, he encountered her at the studio as she was picking up her paycheck and discovered that Meighan was with her. "In that brief moment," he would dramatically proclaim in *My Autobiography*, "Edna became a stranger." [14] It would not have taken much of a mental effort to figure out that he was the grand love of Edna's life and that she had been making a play for Meighan merely to demonstrate to her errant lover that he could not take her for granted. Nevertheless, the idea seems never to have entered Chaplin's head. Edna's show of independence was an affront and a betrayal. Nothing else figured in his reaction.

Although he immediately demoted her from official girlfriend to occasional sexual convenience, he continued until 1923 to present her in starring roles in his movies. Three years later, he financed a Josef von Sternberg melodrama called *Sea Gulls*, on the condition that Edna would be given the female lead. But when the picture was finished, he refused to release it, in all likelihood because he believed that the critics would laugh at her timid performance. By the end of the 1920s she was living in a little house he had bought her and subsisting on the monthly retainer he had instructed his payroll office to send her.

In 1932 a cascade of bills impelled her to appeal to Chaplin for help in paying for an operation for a perforated ulcer and for a decent burial for her ne'er-do-well father. Apparently he provided it. To the surprise of her family, she eventually married an airplane pilot, Jack Squires, and when he became a Pan Am executive they lived for some years in Rio de Janeiro. After his death, she returned to Los Angeles. Through all the years of her separation from Chaplin, she faithfully assembled a file of newspaper and magazine clippings about him and occasionally wrote him an amiable letter. Her last one was composed, in pain, in November 1956, two years before her death at the Motion Picture Home in Woodland Hills, California:

Dear Charlie,

Here I am again . . . back in hospital (Cedars of Lebanon), taking cobalt X-ray treatment on my neck. . . . It is the best known treatment for what ails me. . . . Am thankful my innards are O. K., this is purely and simply local, so they say—all of which reminds me of the fellow standing on the corner of Seventh and Broadway tearing up little bits of paper, throwing them to the four winds. A cop comes along and asks him, what was the big idea. He answers: "Just keeping elephants away." The cop says: "There aren't any elephants in this district." The fellow answers: "Well, it works, doesn't it?" This is my silly for the day, so forgive me.

Hope you and the family are well and enjoying everything you have worked for.

Love always, Edna.[15]*

4

As the weekly checks for $10,000 mounted up in his savings accounts and his investments mushroomed into holdings of hundreds of thousands of dollars, the twenty-seven-year-old comedian began to think about living in a somewhat grander style. Nineteen sixteen had all but ended, however, before he finally decided to hire a valet and a chauffeur and to purchase—for cash, right off the showroom floor—a seven-passenger Locomobile. When he inquired about the price of the car, the salesman said it could be his for $4,000. "Wrap it up," Chaplin replied.[16]

Chaplin's valet, Tom Harrington, was a gentle soul with a high-domed brow, downcast eyes, and the asceticism of a monk. For several years he had worked as a dresser for the English-born vaudevillian Bert Clark and had accompanied him to Hollywood when Clark became a Keystone comedian. In addition to his comic talents, Clark was an excellent pianist, a fact that persuaded Chaplin to enter into a partnership with him in a music-publishing venture. At Clark's suggestion, they put Harrington in charge of the quarters they rented in a Los Angeles office building. The erstwhile valet's first task was to peddle two thousand copies of the words and music of a couple of songs that Chaplin had composed. But while Chaplin was by this time a fairly accomplished pianist in his own right (and an able fiddler as well), he still had a long way to go as a composer. It was not for a lack of trying that Harrington

---

* For a film tribute to her and to Mabel Normand, see Paolo and Vittorio Taviani's *Good Morning Babylon* (1987). Two young Italian film workers in Hollywood in the 1920s meet two lovely extras named Edna and Mabel.

was able to dispose of only three copies of the songs before the partnership between his employers collapsed.

When Clark left Los Angeles for a new assignment in vaudeville, Harrington stayed behind, saying that he would prefer to serve as Chaplin's dresser. His new duties soon became secretarial as well. In the morning he would appear at the Athletic Club with mail from the studio and a sheaf of newspapers and order his master's breakfast. Sometimes, without having been asked to do so, he also left books by Chaplin's bedside, by authors whom Chaplin had either never heard of—Lafcadio Hearn, for instance, and Frank Harris—or had not read, such as Boswell. Although Harrington had been raised in poverty on the Lower East Side of New York and had not had much schooling, he was an indefatigable reader. For years he would serve Chaplin as a model of the possibilities of self-education.[17]

Twenty-eight-year-old Japanese-born Toraichi Kono, whom Chaplin took on as his chauffeur, was the undutiful son of a well-to-do family in Hiroshima. In defiance of his father's plans for him, he had emigrated to the United States and attended an engineering school in Seattle, in preparation for pursuing his dream of a career in aviation. But after sending for and marrying his Japanese sweetheart, he discovered that she was just as independent-minded as he was. Instead of meekly submitting to his authority, she declared that flying was too risky an occupation for a husband and father and insisted that he give it up. A consular friend in California advised him that if he wished to avoid becoming just another addition to the thousands of Japanese gardeners in the state, he should learn to drive a car. After serving as Chaplin's chauffeur for a few years, Kono assumed the roles of household manager and personal emissary in various crises, even though he never learned to speak English without a virtually impenetrable accent. His private opinion of his employer, behind which there lay a proud consciousness of his own distinguished ancestry, was that he was little more than a Cockney upstart and that the riches he had earned at the box office merely proved that the general public was imbecilic.[18]

5

A new friend who encouraged Chaplin to be more free with the money that Mutual was paying him was Julian Eltinge, for whom the

Eltinge Theater on Broadway had been named. Fresh from his latest triumph in New York as the star of the Jerome Kern musical *Cousin Lucy*, Eltinge had come to Hollywood to make three pictures for Jesse Lasky: *The Widow's Mite*, *Countess Charming*, and *The Clever Mrs. Carfax*. On the way back to his hotel one night from a bar he had become fond of, he saw a little man standing in front of the window of a secondhand store, his hands clasped behind his back. Eltinge realized that this inconspicuous figure was Chaplin and went up and spoke to him. Over a drink they had no difficulty in thinking of something to talk about. In two of his Keystone pictures and one at Essanay, Chaplin had appeared in drag, while Eltinge was America's premier female impersonator. In 1916 that was saying quite a bit.[19]

In early-nineteenth-century American minstrel shows, the head comedian would often "do a wench" in one of the blackface afterpieces. By the late 1880s, "female imps" in first-run vaudeville houses were doing everything from toe dances to imitations of Sarah Bernhardt, while their lowly counterparts in honky-tonks and wine rooms were staging less discreet performances and working the boxes as hostesses as well without ever removing their wigs. But it was in the unsettled years after 1910, when "the amusements of the city, the jokes that pass for jokes, the blare that stands for beauty [and] the folksongs of Broadway" were evidence, in Walter Lippmann's phrase, that America was being blown "hither and thither like litter before the wind," that transvestites reached the apex of their popularity on the American stage. An entertainer billing himself as "the male Patti" charmed audiences of both men and women from coast to coast, as did "the male Soprano," Herbert Clifton. Karyl Norman, who appeared as a gaudily dressed "high-yaller" gal from Creole country, and a clothes horse known as "the Divine Dodson" had a particular appeal to women because of the splendor of their costumes. In 1914 two out-of-work chorus boys, Bert Savoy and Jay Brennan, teamed up as a male-female duo, with Savoy in the female role; two years later, they were headliners on Broadway earning $1,500 a week. One of the hallmarks of Savoy's impersonations was the swishy sway of his hips as he walked, and another was his insinuating way of saying, "You must come over." (If the latter invitation seems uncannily like Mae West's "Come up and see me sometime," it is no wonder. As a rising star on Broadway *circa* 1915, the young West deliberately added elements of Savoy's campy repartee to her "enchanting, seductive, sin-promising wriggle," as she herself described her hip-swaying walk.)[20]*

In contrast to the flamboyant Savoy, most impersonators opted for a low-keyed satirical style, and more than a few of them made offstage efforts to prove that they were not in the least effeminate. Both these characteristics marked the most celebrated of the lot. In front of the footlights, Eltinge projected a faultlessly but not exaggeratedly feminine image, whether he was modeling a bathing suit, doing an "Incense Dance" in an exotic Oriental costume, or singing a ballad in a low, sweet voice while wearing an evening gown over a corset of the sort that Lillian Russell had favored until her retirement in 1912. Behind the scenes, however, he was ready to demonstrate to any stage-door heckler who dared to scoff at him as a "Miss Nancy" that he was formidably quick with his fists. Did he protest too much? There were those who thought so.[21]

The most notable of Chaplin's female impersonations was his campy performance in *A Woman* (1915), as the disturbed reactions of moral custodians attested. Mischief-making Charlie disrupts the efforts of a couple of lechers to pick up a pretty girl in a park. He himself picks up Edna, who is swayed by his charm to the point of taking him home with her and her mother to have dinner. Her father and a friend show up. They are the lechers from the park and, on recognizing Charlie, they start to give him a good going-over. He runs upstairs, slips into some of Edna's clothes, shaves off his mustache, and sways his way back downstairs. His lovely face, pincushion-enhanced embonpoint, and fluttery gestures drive the lechers wild. Swedish censors were so upset by the kinky psychodynamics of *A Woman* that in 1917 they placed a nation-wide ban on the picture's distribution and did not lift it until 1931. Two weeks after its release in the United States, the founding editor of

---

* West also absorbed lessons from Savoy and other famous impersonators in the theater about the significance of costumes; many impersonators even changed their glamorous clothes on stage, just as West would in her hit play *Diamond Lil* (1928). Carol M. Ward, *Mae West: A Bio-Bibliography* (Westport, Conn., 1989), p. 9. Yet for all of her exaggeratedly female getups and her forty-three-inch bust, Ward shrewdly noted, West's intelligence and control came across as the signs of a masculine toughness. "While [Marilyn] Monroe seemed a child trapped in an all-too-adult body, West seemed a man masquerading as a woman." *Ibid.*, pp. 74–75.

Variety, Sime Silverman, complained in print that "the Censor Board is passing matter in the Chaplin films that could not possibly get by in other pictures."[22]

6

From Paderewski, Pavlova, Godowsky, and Melba to Somerset Maugham, Harry Lauder, Helen Keller, and Nijinsky, dozens of distinguished visitors to Hollywood in the later teens were eager to meet Chaplin, and in spite of how busy he was, he made time for all of them. What a delight it was to kid around at the piano with Godowsky, or to make a little movie with Harry Lauder! What a thrill to be told by Nijinsky that "your comedy is *balletique*, you are a dancer"![23]

Yet in this period of his life, Chaplin still had time for less glamorous friends. On Tuesday nights, he generally attended the prizefights at Doyle's sports palace, out in Vernon, along with his cameraman, Rollie Totheroh, and a couple of his actors. "Charlie was the center of attention," Totheroh recalled, "especially among the fighters. . . . Before the fight would start, the first thing they'd go over there—they knew where he sat—and they'd reach out and shake hands with him. They all got to know who he was." At baseball games, it was the same story. The players would spot him and then everybody in the crowd, Totheroh affirmed, would be

> looking down in the box seats—Charlie's there. He was one of the bunch, meeting down at Barney Oldfield's [saloon] or any place where [the players] all hung out after. Charlie coined a phrase, he'd say, "How's the light, Rollie?" and I would say, "Well, maybe we can shoot another scene, couple of scenes. I think the light is better down at Barney Oldfield's." Meaning that the light beer is better.

Totheroh was nevertheless aware of the depths of reserve beneath his boss's bonhomie. In the cameraman's nicely calibrated expression, Chaplin "more or less mingled" with his Mutual employes, and when he was "tired, or ran out of ideas," then "he'd dismiss the crew."[24]

One evening at Levy's Café, where Chaplin occasionally ate dinner by himself, the English stage star Constance Collier sent him a note from her table, asking him to join her, which he was pleased to do. In his London youth, he had seen her in a number of plays with Herbert Beerbohm Tree at His Majesty's Theater, and while it was Tree's performances that he could still recall in detail, he also admired Collier's work. She had come to Hollywood, she explained, to appear opposite Sir Herbert in a movie adaptation of *Macbeth*. Chaplin's warm response to the information that Tree was in town was not lost on Collier, and a few days later she brought the two men together at a small dinner at the Alexandria Hotel, where the famous actor-manager and his eighteen-year-old daughter, Iris, were staying.

The dinner, as it turned out, had to proceed without the hostess. A costume fitting for her part as Lady Macbeth did not end in time for Collier to attend. Fortunately, Tree and Chaplin got along quite well, and Chaplin found the precociously sophisticated Iris enormously amusing, even though she confessed to him that she was probably "the only person in the world who hasn't seen you on the screen." In the 1920s, he would link up with her again in Paris.[25]

The indefatigably social Collier also wanted Chaplin to meet a new American friend of hers, Douglas Fairbanks, so she arranged for him to be invited to a dinner party at Fairbanks's home. At the last minute, however, one of Chaplin's reclusive moods overtook him, and he phoned Collier and hoarsely announced he was ill. The excuse did not wash with her. Faced with her insistence that he honor the engagement, he decided to feign a headache midway in the evening and leave early. Meanwhile, Fairbanks was suffering a case of nerves about meeting the famous Charlie Chaplin. Instead of greeting him upon his arrival, he bolted down the basement stairs and began practicing shots in the billiard room. So began the closest friendship of Chaplin's American life.[26]

7

Artful camera work caused moviegoers to assume that Fairbanks was a six-footer, but in fact he was only three inches taller than Chaplin. In ironic reference to his size as well as to his tobacco-colored skin—which Fairbanks constantly sought to darken still further by sunbaths in the nude—a Hollywood wit once observed that if hollowed out, he would have made a dandy golf bag.[27] A hyperactive extrovert and a superbly well-conditioned athlete, Fairbanks filled idle moments on movie sets by performing difficult exercises, such as handstands on chair arms, and enlivened social occasions with killingly exact imitations of the speech mannerisms of Sam Goldwyn and other satirizable characters in the Hollywood community. He also was a practical joker who liked to discomfit his guests with animal imitations. As the New York hotelkeeper Frank Case discovered on the visits he paid in the 1920s to the former hunting lodge in Beverly Hills that Fairbanks had remodeled into "Pickfair" as a wedding present to his second wife, Mary Pickford, formal dinners held there in honor of titled Englishmen and other dignitaries were apt to be disrupted by the restless host's habit of crawling under the table "to where a duke, a prince, or a financier, or one of their ladies, was seated, and with a nip and a very enthusiastic bark," starting something. Lest anyone think that this sort of fun was somewhat tiresome, Case added that Fairbanks "never scored a failure and no one ever objected; on the contrary [everyone] loved it. . . . Mary's only remonstrance was a gentle, 'Now, Douglas.' "[28]

On Sunday mornings before the sun came up, Fairbanks would often organize a posse of cowboys, roust Chaplin out of bed, and ride horseback over the hills with him to meet the dawn. "The cowboys would stake the horses and make a campfire," Chaplin remembered,

> and prepare breakfast of coffee, hot cakes and "sowbelly." While we watched the dawn break, Doug would wax eloquent and I would joke about loss of sleep and argue that the only dawn worth seeing was with the opposite sex. Nevertheless, those early morning sorties were romantic. Douglas was the only man who could get me on a horse, in spite of my complaints that the world oversentimentalized the beast and that it was mean and cantankerous with the mind of a halfwit.

The two friends also indulged in a good deal of clichéd philosophizing. Fairbanks believed that human lives were foreordained, but his mystic ebullience on the subject usually had a cynical effect on Chaplin. The comedian recalled with special delight one starry summer night when the two of them climbed to the top of a large water tank and sat there talking. Chaplin argued that life was without reason.

"Look!" said Douglas, fervently, making an arc gesture taking in all the heavens. "The moon! And those myriads of stars! Surely there must be a reason for all this beauty? It must be fulfilling some destiny!" . . . Then he turned to me, suddenly inspired. "Why are you given this talent, this wonderful medium of motion pictures that reaches millions of people throughout the world?"

"Why is it given to Louis B. Mayer and the Warner brothers?" I said. And Douglas laughed.

Yet if Fairbanks was incurably romantic, there sometimes were sharp breaks in his manic high-spiritedness. "Doug could be serious, moody, sensitive as any woman," one of his early directors, Allan Dwan, said. "Every now and then I'd see signs of depression coming, something inside gnawing at him. All of a sudden he'd just disappear, take his anguish and hole up with it. He hid his black moods well. I doubt if a handful of people ever noticed it."[29]

In 1930 young Douglas Fairbanks, Jr., described his father as "a series of masks," and half a century later he said of him that "he designed the living of his life, almost from the start, coloring it as he went along. He did it so successfully that his best friends and biographers were seldom able to see him accurately."[30] Indeed, in Douglas Jr.'s summaries of his father's early years there are indications that he, too, had been deceived by him, at least in part. Whether or not Fairbanks gave Chaplin an accurate account of his background, or whether or not Chaplin confessed to Fairbanks the ambiguities about his own, perhaps both men knew instinctively that they were brothers in prevarication.

The Fairbanks story began sometime after the Civil War, when a ladylike but somewhat mysterious young woman named Ella Marsh, who may have grown up in Virginia or possibly in New York, met and married an even more mysterious southern gentleman, John Fairbanks, and accompanied him to his home in New Orleans. Supposedly, Fairbanks owned a plantation and a sugar mill—although no mention of him appears in the land ownership records of postbellum Louisiana, or even in New Orleans city directories of the period. Their son, John Jr., was born in 1873, the year in which, Ella would always insist, her husband suddenly died of natural causes. In the unsuccessful claim she made to Fairbanks's estate, she was assisted by a New York lawyer, H.

Charles Ulman. A year or so later, Ella and her little boy surfaced in Georgia, where she married a certain Edward Wilcox, by whom she had another son. Wilcox, however, was a lush and she soon divorced him, again with the legal help of H. Charles Ulman.

In 1880 Ella arrived in Denver, along with Ulman and the older of her two sons, the younger having been left with his father. A handsome, flamboyantly mannered Jew who loved the theater and who strongly resembled the famous Shakespearean actor Edwin Booth, the forty-nine-year-old Ulman was a member in good standing of the New York bar. But when he moved to Denver, he forsook his legal clientele—as well as his wife—and did not return to the practice of law, electing instead to invest in speculative mining properties. Ella gave birth to the first of her two illegitimate sons by Ulman in 1882, and to the second, whom she named Douglas, in 1883. Although Douglas was a good-looking baby, he became convinced as he grew up that his unusually dark skin was an embarrassment to his mother, and as an adult he often recited the story of how she used to reach down into his baby carriage, whenever she saw someone coming along the street whom she recognized, and pull the blanket over his head. Whether or not the story was true, it symbolized Ella's cover-ups of other unpleasant facts about her family.[31]

By the time Douglas was four or five, his father was drinking heavily. Finally, he deserted Ella and left town, thereby condemning her and her boys to a life of shabby-genteel pretenses. Several years later, he reappeared in Denver, apparently in the hope of a reconciliation with his abandoned progeny. Ella, however, would not hear of it; she had long since given the name of Fairbanks to both of her Ulman sons in order to conceal their illegitimacy as well as their Jewishness. In his relations with the world at large, Douglas Fairbanks would perpetuate these concealments; even with his three wives and his son, he drew a blackout curtain across the subject of his bastardy. Throughout his life he also maintained the fiction that he had received a splendid education, although the truth is that when he arrived in New York as a stagestruck youth of sixteen, he had not graduated from high school, nor would he ever. Nevertheless, his circumstantial accounts of bright college years fooled a great many people. Thus a reporter for *Theatre Magazine* who interviewed him in his Broadway dressing room in 1912, when he was at the height of his career on the stage as a juvenile lead in light comedies, came away convinced that "at the Colorado School of Mines and later at Harvard University he was popular for his fun-loving spirit and his irresistible sense of humor." Sixty years later, the myth of Fairbanks's higher education still had its adherents. David Niven, for instance, in his ghostwritten memoir, *Bring on the Empty Horses* (1974), referred to the father of his close friend of many years, Douglas Fairbanks, Jr., as "an ex-Harvard graduate."[32]

Fairbanks's hugely successful costume pictures, set in foreign locales and centered on the exploits of D'Artagnan, Robin Hood, the thief of Baghdad, and other dashing figures, belong to the history of the 1920s. But beginning with his first film in 1915 and for half a decade thereafter, he mainly appeared in modern American roles. Inspired by the self-hardening accomplishments of his idol, Theodore Roosevelt, Fairbanks took particular delight in playing a frustrated office worker or a soft socialite who responds to the impact of a change of scene to the West by turning into an "all-around chap" and celebrating his newborn masculinity with breathtaking leaps and bounds and deeds of derring-do. Thematically and visually, his pictures were knockouts. Fairbanks Jr. later said of his father that he and Chaplin "both felt . . . that the silent screen was their proper medium. They could express themselves in mime and tell the story in action . . . and in visual effect."[33]

At the time that Fairbanks first met Chaplin, he and Mary Pickford had been lovers for almost a year. Yet they were acting, in Chaplin's opinion, "like frightened rabbits about it," for they feared that public exposure of their unfaithfulness to their respective spouses would destroy their careers.[34] Even the prospect of taking the requisite steps to legalize their relationship filled them with foreboding. As Pickford worriedly inquired of her favorite screenwriter, Frances Marion, "If I get a divorce and marry Douglas, will anyone ever go to see my pictures again?"[35] In public places, they endeavored to act as though they were just friends, while most of their assignations were held in the less-than-satisfactory confines of studio dressing rooms. (As Pickford exclaimed to Frances Marion after at last becoming Mrs. Douglas Fairbanks, "You can't imagine the luxury of a comfortable bed after the hurly-burly of the couch.")[36]

In order not to upset the assumption of her fans that her usual on-screen portrayal of an innocent between twelve and sixteen years of age was firmly related to the person she really was, she had been compelled for years—mainly by that *stupor mundi* of movie moguls, Adolph Zukor —to conceal the unhappy truth that, far from being satisfactorily married to the movie actor Owen Moore, she was irrevocably estranged from him, if only because of his alcoholism. At some point in 1914, moreover, she had probably succumbed to the seductive wiles of one of the most accomplished of movieland's Don Juans, the director James Kirkwood. Naturally, this relationship, too, had to be kept a dark secret, along with her fondness for wearing long fingernails and smoking cigarettes. Smoking was "taboo," Zukor emphatically recalled. "In public— for example in a box at the theater—she could not be permitted to toy with a lipstick, a pencil or a bit of paper. From a distance it might be taken for a cigarette. Occasionally she did so thoughtlessly, and I have seen her mother or my wife take the object gently from her fingers."[37] If you are to be "the queen of motion pictures," Zukor once admonished her, "you must pay the penalties of royalty."[38] There were also no reprieves from her constant assignment to curly-locked, young-girl roles. I am in a "dramatic rut," she cried out to a confidant in 1917. "And I hate curls," she fiercely added. "I loathe them—loathe them!"[39]*

Small wonder, then, that Little Mary and handsome Doug desperately pretended in front of strangers that their passionate attachment was nothing more than a friendship, or that she, in particular, was angered by Chaplin's advice—the unsympathetic nature of which reflected his rivalrous relationship with her—that instead of getting married, they should live together until they had gotten their lust for each other out of their systems.[40] In the end, the decision in favor of candor that they

---

* Money was Pickford's consolation. Because of her obsessive need to prove that she, not Chaplin, was the super-luminary in the Hollywood heavens, she had been extremely upset by the news of his contract with Mutual. She made six or eight feature pictures a year; Chaplin made two-reel shorts. Yet she was earning "only" $2,000 a week, plus a $10,000 bonus for each picture. Backed by her iron-fisted mother, Pickford compelled Zukor to construct a new contract that would give her 50 percent of the net profits from her films. A guarantee that the 50 percent would not amount to less than $1,040,000 was also built into the agreement. In the words of one of her biographers, this contract was "a small masterpiece of employee demand and employer humiliation." Scott Eyman, *Mary Pickford: America's Sweetheart* (New York, 1990), p. 86.

themselves could not bear to make was made for them. On April 11, 1918, shortly after the two of them, plus Chaplin, arrived in New York in the course of a public appearance tour to promote the sale of war bonds, Fairbanks's long-suffering wife, Beth Sully, a Watch Hill, Rhode Island, socialite, summoned a group of reporters to her suite in the Algonquin Hotel. The burden of her message to the press was that her husband was in love with another woman, that she and her son, Doug Jr., no longer mattered to him in comparison, and that she had finally realized that "he must go his way while I went mine."

In front of reporters in her suite at the Plaza, Mary frantically attempted a cover-up, declaring that she did not have "the remotest idea that my name has been brought into any difference between any man and his wife." "I am sorry," Beth was duly quoted as saying in reply, that "the woman who has caused all this unhappiness in our home is not willing to acknowledge to the world, as she has acknowledged to her friends and her family, her love for Mr. Fairbanks." Stunned by the magnitude of this public relations disaster, Fairbanks the war-bond salesman darkly hinted to newsmen that reports of difficulties between him and his wife were the work of German propagandists.[41]

Six months later, he and Beth were divorced. An affair he had had with "an unknown woman" was cited as the cause of the breakup. Under pressure from Fairbanks, Mary finally sought a Nevada divorce from Owen Moore, and on March 2, 1920, she obtained it. To the press she announced her intention not to marry again; instead she would devote the remainder of her life to motion pictures. Three weeks later, she and her lover were married in Los Angeles.[42] The fan magazines had never acknowledged that in the divorce proceedings against him Fairbanks had been accused of adultery, and even the general press had not identified Mary Pickford as his inamorata. With the announcement of their marriage, however, all their prevarications about their affair were exposed as disingenuous, and they braced themselves for retribution from disillusioned fans.

To their amazement, the public quickly forgave and forgot about their deceits. Two months after the wedding announcement, the *New York Times* saluted Mary as a truly wonderful homemaker. "Out in Hollywood, California," breathed the *Times*, "a little woman with golden hair puts the chops on the stove and wonders with a sigh if her adorable fellow will be late. The telephone rings and he tells her he will be on hand for dinner in twenty minutes accompanied by fourteen guests. . . . Married life under such conditions is more than art. It's work." The fan magazines dispensed an even more syrupy treacle. In the June 1920 issue of *Photoplay*, an article entitled "The Wooing of Mary Pickford" hailed her romance with Fairbanks as "one of the great love stories of all time."[43]

8

No matter how often Fairbanks visited the set of a Chaplin picture, he voiced enthusiastic approval of everything his pal Charlie was doing. That kind of talk made Roland Totheroh smile. A quiet, tough-minded man who had played a few seasons of minor-league baseball before it occurred to him that grinding a movie camera was a congenial way of making a living, Totheroh was an efficient and uncomplaining worker. Chaplin had learned that while living in Niles and watching him in action on the set of one or two Broncho Billy Anderson Westerns. Consequently, when Totheroh dropped by to ask Chaplin for a job shortly before Mutual opened its Lone Star Studio on a spacious lot in Los Angeles on March 27, 1916, the comedian immediately hired him as the assistant to his new head cameraman, William C. Foster. Three pictures later, Foster quit—quite possibly because he had reached the limits of his patience with Chaplin's habit of repeatedly changing his mind about what he wanted to do—and Totheroh replaced him. It was typical of the bright side of Chaplin's relations with his employees that his association with Totheroh lasted until 1954. And the dark side was exemplified by *My Autobiography*, which contains only one passing reference to "Rollie."

In concocting the scenarios of the Mutual pictures, the studio's press chief, Terry Ramsaye, noted, Chaplin was aided and abetted by a couple of unsung writers, backed by a retinue of secretaries.[44] Yet these team efforts rarely resulted in a finished script before the cameras rolled. According to Totheroh, virtually every Chaplin picture prior to *The Great Dictator* ended up being guided by a script that developed as the filming proceeded, and at every step of the way these developments were attended, in Ramsaye's words, by "the severest mental suffering" on Chaplin's part.[45]

On a typical morning, he might arrive for work with a basic idea for a piece of comic business in mind, but only an unclear idea of how to elaborate it. If he was lucky—and a lot of the time he was not—he was able to solve this problem in the course of a day or two, after many false starts and with suggestions coming at him from all sides, although no one on the set was ever so foolhardy as to tell Chaplin bluntly what he ought to do. Whenever a thought occurred to Totheroh, he would come around in front of his camera and say, "Gee, Charlie, you could do this," or "Are you going to do that?" in as nice a way as he knew how. He also was careful not to take credit for any of his suggestions that Chaplin happened to adopt, unlike a bluff-mannered graduate of the Karno factory, Albert Austin, who had joined the Chaplin troupe at the same time that Totheroh had. "I gave Charlie that gag," Austin would boast, and when remarks of this sort got back to headquarters, fireworks ensued.[46]

A process of painfully achieved, incremental improvements, then, was the modus operandi at Mutual, and one consequence was that huge quantities of film were exposed. Thus in shooting *The Immigrant*, Chaplin used up, so rumor had it, slightly more than ninety thousand feet of raw film stock, an amount that came close to equaling the footage consumed by Griffith in filming *The Birth of a Nation;* yet when the film finally emerged from the cutting room, it was a two-reeler measuring 1,809 feet. Further costs were incurred by production postponements. On days when nothing suited Charles-the-Expensive, as Ramsaye dubbed him, he would halt the shooting and retire to his dressing-room study, or go for a long drive in his car, or closet himself in the carpenter's shop in the sole company of his violin, while an army of extras and other personnel sat idle.[47]

During rehearsals, Chaplin adhered to his usual practice of showing his fellow actors what he wanted from them by assuming their roles. With astonishing ease, he could become a sweet old lady in one minute and a neighborhood bully in the next. But the unfortunate result of his chameleonism was that at the end of a day he had sometimes introduced his actors to so many interpretive possibilities that they were confused. He was fickle, too, about makeup, so that an actor might show up on the set with a beard, as requested, only to be ordered to appear without it the next day. And he took personal charge of the wardrobe and hair style of Edna Purviance, as he would with all his leading ladies to come.

"He loved even doing the actors' hair," Totheroh recalled. "He loved to cut hair and trim. In fact, he used to cut his own hair at home; he didn't want to sit around in a barbershop."[48]

Inasmuch as the Lone Star Studio was, in effect, a royal court headed by an absolute monarch, it was inevitable that a number of the courtiers could not resist becoming yes-men, or "Charlie's Stooges," as they were covertly called. One of the most eager of them was an overweight opera singer of days gone by named Henry Bergman. A lifelong bachelor who loved the chance the movies gave him to play both male and female roles, Bergman adored Chaplin and stood ready to do anything to please him, including serving as his bodyguard—for as Totheroh, among others, was aware, "Chaplin always wanted somebody with him, as a protector." Much to Totheroh's annoyance, Bergman "would come around and shout—'Mr. Chaplin's busy—please,' and he'd push people away."[49]

Another of Chaplin's protectors whom Totheroh disliked was the comedian's half-brother Sydney, who was "always around," who was "always suspicious someone was going to do something to Charlie," and who "always used to tell Charlie, 'Don't hold your crew [including, presumably, Totheroh] too long. Get rid of them before they get to know much about you.' " Because "Sid . . . was crooked himself," in Totheroh's opinion, he thought everybody else was. "He used to watch the guys on location. He'd think maybe they'd steal a few pieces of lumber that were hanging around. . . . If they'd load it on the truck to take it home, for kindling wood . . . he'd go chasing after them. And he'd hire kids, a couple of kids to straighten out nails."

But a far more significant instance of Sydney's sharp practices was that he made off with as many feet of film of unused scenes and sequences from his brother's Mutual pictures as he could lay his hands on. By so doing he broke the law, for these so-called outtakes did not belong to Chaplin, in whose name Sydney took them; they belonged to his employer. But Sydney was calculating, according to Totheroh, that "at the time Charlie passed away . . . there'd be nobody to object."[50] After Chaplin founded his own movie company, the purloined outtakes were housed in the company's vaults, along with a rapidly growing assemblage of other bits and pieces of film. In 1952, when Chaplin shut down his studio and left the United States, he instructed Totheroh to destroy a mass of cinematic material, including all the outtakes. Fortunately, the cameraman botched the job, thus making possible, some thirty years later, the fascinating portrait of a self-doubting perfectionist at work in a three-part British television series, *The Unknown Chaplin*, edited by Kevin Brownlow and David Gill.

Turning out publicity stories about Mutual's premier star was originally the responsibility of a young graduate of the English vaudeville stage, Fred Goodwins, who had performed the same function for Chaplin at Essanay, as well as making appearances in several of his comedies, most notably *The Tramp*, in which he played the farmer who is Edna Purviance's father. In June 1917 he was supplanted by an erstwhile newspaperman from Brooklyn, Carlyle T. Robinson, who possessed a savvy about the press that Goodwins had lacked. Thus Robinson was almost surely a hearty supporter of the idea of bringing Hannah to the United States, lest the world gain the impression from inquiring reporters that Chaplin was keeping his mother stashed in an English nursing home because he was ashamed of her condition.

Initially scheduled for the fall of 1917, her journey was thwarted by the refusal of paper-shuffling bureaucrats in Britain to issue the necessary permits for her release. The hazards created by the intensification of German submarine warfare in 1918 caused the postponement of her rescheduled crossing until early 1919. But at the last minute that crossing, too, was called off, this time by Chaplin himself, out of fear that his mother's presence in California might depress him at a time when personal and professional unhappiness had already strained his nerves to the breaking point.

Not until the spring of 1921 did Hannah finally arrive in New York, under the care of Chaplin's secretary, Tom Harrington, and a pair of nurses. Neither Chaplin nor Sydney chose to be on hand to greet her, so Harrington guided her through the Ellis Island maze. Despite the inevitable confusions of the immigration process, she seemed quite normal—until an immigration official chanced to say to her, "So you're the mother of the famous Charlie." "Yes," Hannah sweetly replied, "and you are Jesus Christ." When the kindly Harrington duly reported this story to Chaplin, he may not have fully appreciated, unlike the toughminded Rollie Totheroh, that he was talking to a man who lived in fear of becoming like his mother.[51]

Perhaps that fear was the cardinal reason why, in the seven remaining years of Hannah's life, Chaplin seldom appeared at the pleasant bungalow he purchased for her in the San Fernando Valley and only rarely invited her to his studio or his home. Her day-to-day care was left to a housekeeping couple and a trained nurse, while for sociable diversions she mainly depended on visits from the Sydney Chaplins and from Amy Reeves and her husband, Alf, the erstwhile Karno-tour manager whom Chaplin hired in 1918 as general manager of his film corporation. In lieu of loving personal attention to Hannah, in sum, her famous son simply paid her bills.

9

No other series of Chaplin shorts is as consistently engaging as the pictures he made for Mutual. In *My Autobiography* he looked back on the year and a half in which he came up with such winners as *Easy Street, The Pawnshop, The Floorwalker, The Immigrant,* and *The Cure,* and pronounced that period of activity the happiest of his career. At the same time, he dropped hints of the mental price he had paid for his creativity. Writing, acting, and directing required "an exorbitant expenditure of nervous energy," he confessed. "At the completion of a picture I would be left depressed and exhausted, so that I would have to rest in bed for a day." In an even more revealing moment he posed the question "How does one get ideas?" and his answer was "By sheer perseverance to the point of madness. One must have a capacity to suffer anguish and sustain enthusiasm over a long period of time."[52] In these same words, he might have been describing the tenacity that he had been forced to develop in order to survive the tests of his childhood.

Thanks to the number of times he restaged his acrobatics in front of Rollie Totheroh's live camera,* the tumbling and balancing feats in the Mutual shorts are flawlessly executed. As a store employee in *The Pawn-*

---

* Back at Mutual headquarters, John Freuler did not complain too loudly about the cost overruns resulting from retakes because Chaplin's pictures were coining money for the company. "Unprecedented in the annals of motion picture history are the bookings through the country and Canada for the first-run pictures of . . . Chaplin-Mutual," *Variety* reported in May 1916. "At price asked, the Chaplin-Mutual *Floorwalker* picture will earn $10,000 a day for the first week, $7000 for the second and $5000 for the third."

shop, he falls backwards off the top of a ten-foot stepladder, bounces to his feet, and checks his watch. As an affluent drunk in black tie in a tour de force called *One A.M.*, he weaves his way into his house and comes close to breaking his neck on a slippery floor, a treacherous rug, and a flight of stairs. Once he has made it up the staircase, he faces further hazards to life and limb in the form of a wall clock with a gigantic, wide-swinging pendulum straight out of an Edgar Allan Poe nightmare and a folding bed with a fiendish mind of its own. And as a roller-skating enthusiast in *The Rink*, he did his Karno training proud by holding one of his legs straight out in front of him and exactly parallel to the floor while agilely gliding around less accomplished skaters. Flawless execution also marks the frantic chases in the Mutual shorts, such as the wonderful one in *The Floorwalker* in which department store detectives join the manager in giving chase to Charlie from the second floor to the first and back again, mainly by means of an escalator that perversely tends to be moving in the opposite direction to the flow of the traffic. On seeing this scene, Mack Sennett groaned with envy that he had not thought of it.

Charles-the-Expensive spent further amounts of John Freuler's money on solidly built sets. (Onstage, Marcel Marceau has observed, a mime's illusions create reality, whereas in movies reality creates illusions.[53]) For instance, the escalator in *The Floorwalker* has a thoroughly authentic look, as do the display cases on either side of the main aisle and the shelves full of shoe boxes that go up to the ceiling and have a movable ladder in front of them. But the comedian who was adding "things" to his pictures in the name of reality was also partial to gags in which his hero converts objects into arbitrarily framed notions of the mind, even as Hannah Chaplin had once treated pieces of coal as Christmas presents and passed them out to the children in the neighborhood. In the kitchen scene in *The Pawnshop*, Charlie drapes a roll of dough around his neck as if it were a lei and strums on a large wooden spoon as if it were a ukulele. But by far the most memorable of *The Pawnshop*'s transpositions is precipitated by a customer who brings an alarm clock into the shop at a moment when Charlie is working as the clerk behind the counter. In the *New Republic* for February 3, 1917, the playwright Harvey O'Higgins seized on the episode as a quintessential illustration of "Charlie Chaplin's Art." "A man brings in an alarm clock to pledge it," wrote O'Higgins, and Charlie has to decide how much it is worth. He sees it first as a patient to be examined diagnostically. He taps it, percusses it, puts his ear to its chest, listens to its heartbeat with a stethoscope, and while he listens, fixes a thoughtful medical eye on space, looking inscrutably wise and professionally self-confident. He begins to operate on it—with a can-opener. And immediately the round tin clock becomes a round tin can whose contents are under suspicion. He cuts around the circular top of the can, bends back the flap of tin with a kitchen thumb then, gingerly approaching his nose to it, sniffs with the melancholy expression of the packing-houses. The imagination is accurate. The acting is restrained and naturalistic. The result is a scream.

"And do not believe that such acting is a matter of crude and simple means," O'Higgins added. "It is as subtle in its naturalness as the shades of intonation in a really tragic speech."[54]

10

While still on the Essanay payroll, Chaplin had had a talk with a member of the executive staff of the National Board of Review, W. W. Barrett. He had agreed to the meeting because he wanted to smooth the board's ruffled feathers. In response to the disapproval implicit in Barrett's pious expression of hope that in the future his comedies would prove to be "a helpful influence in the community and . . . a factor in the artistic development of the Motion Picture," the canny comedian explained that "the little threads of vulgarisms" in his pictures were entirely the product of his music hall training. But in spite of his heritage, he hastened to add, he was already endeavoring to steer clear of the "Elizabethan style of humor" and to adapt himself to "a more subtle and finer shade of acting."[55] He really had no intention, however, of making his Mutual pictures less offensive to moralists than his earlier work had been.

Homosexual flamboyance, for instance, was a sourcebook of entertainment that he refused to pass up. A generation and more before Franklin Pangborn, Edward Everett Horton, and Billy De Wolfe intensified the delightfulness of smart, sophisticated movie comedies with their "eye-rolling concierges and mincing maître d's," as the filmmaker Bruce LaBruce has fondly described the characters they played, Chaplin was stepping up the outbursts of balletic pirouettes and other ambiguously masculine mannerisms in Charlie's behavioral style. At the same time, paradoxically, he poked fun at homosexuality in such comedies as *Behind the Screen*.[56]

The picture takes place behind the scenes at a movie studio. Charlie is the property boss's assistant, and Edna is an aspiring actress who has disguised herself as a workman in order to gain access to the studio. Sex is very much on Charlie's mind as he wanders through the prop shop past a statue of a nude woman who is clutching one of her breasts in one hand and one of her ample buttocks in the other. Yet when he encounters Edna powdering her face, he somehow fails to notice the swelling curves beneath her overalls. On the assumption that he has caught out a homosexual, he mockingly plays up to "him." Only when Edna's capacious cloth cap comes off and her lovely blond hair is briefly exposed to view does Charlie launch a love campaign in earnest. As they are smooching, the prop boss, played by Eric Campbell, comes upon them.

Another Karno veteran and a former member as well of the D'Oyly Carte Opera Company, the thirty-seven-year-old Campbell had a heavyweight wrestler's build and hypnotically furious eyes, which he made even more menacing by making himself up with the flaring eyebrows of a D'Oyly Carte Mikado. Juicy roles in all but one of Chaplin's Mutual comedies catapulted him to fame. Unfortunately, his personal life was a mess, and on December 20, 1917, he died violently when he and the two young women who were with him were thrown from their seats in a high-speed automobile collision on Wilshire Boulevard. As the prop boss in *Behind the Screen*, Campbell reacts to the sight of an embrace between what he thinks are two male workers by sticking out his rear end and flouncing about with baby steps, all the while exclaiming (as the title card tells us), "Oh! You Naughty Boys!"

Sexual deviance of a different nature comes into play in the episode in *The Floorwalker* in which Charlie, in the newly assumed role of a store employee, takes it upon himself to wait on a lady customer in the shoe department and finds such a degree of fetishistic pleasure in fondling her foot that he all but jumps out of his skin. But the most intense moment of erotic arousal in the Mutual comedies occurs in *The Rink*, when Charlie sits down on a bench beside a pretty girl and discovers that she is masturbating by rapidly swinging one of her crossed legs back and forth in an exaggeratedly wide arc. As a lecherous smile creases Charlie's face, he leans his head against the wall behind him so that the front end of his derby tips upward, in a transposed indication that he is experiencing a phallic erection.

In *The Floorwalker* and *The Rink*, Chaplin almost seemed to be daring the censors to take action against him. In *The Immigrant,* on the other hand, a sudden onset of prudence about making sex jokes may have been the reason that he scrapped his original plan for the picture. As the silent-film historian Kevin Brownlow has noted, surviving rushes of *The Immigrant* reveal that it began as "a kind of skit on *Trilby,* set in the bohemian quarter of Paris."[57] Conceivably Chaplin became convinced that a comical treatment of bohemian manners and morals was bound to get him into trouble with official bluenoses. In any event, he turned to another idea, which eventuated in what Brownlow justly called "his most beautifully constructed two-reeler."[58] The emotional inspiration for its story of a romance between two immigrants to the United States probably came from the plans that Chaplin had just been working out with his brother for bringing their mother across the Atlantic.

Charlie is a deck passenger on a barely seaworthy tub. Head down and shoulders quivering, he is bending over the rail. But it is not mal de mer that is responsible for his posture, as he reveals when he turns around and triumphantly displays the fish he has caught. Among the other passengers huddled together in the open air—most of whom resemble the figures seen in photos of turn-of-the-century immigrants from southern and eastern Europe—are a young woman, Edna Purviance, and her ailing mother. While all of these people are hoping to make a new life for themselves in the New World, the mood of some of them has been obviously affected by their dislocation and their poverty. Edna and her mother are especially downcast after they are robbed of their meager savings by a fellow passenger. Charlie does his gallant best to ease their plight by slipping the coins he has won in a crap game into Edna's pocket. Her tearful thanks when she discovers the coins are his ample reward.

The specter of deprivation also hangs over the accidental reunion of Charlie and Edna a few months later. On the strength of his discovery of a twenty-five-cent piece on the pavement outside, Charlie musters the courage to enter a restaurant. As he is eating a plate of beans, he notices Edna sitting nearby without any food in front of her. He asks her to join him. The black-bordered handkerchief she uses to dab her eyes makes him think that her mother must have died, and Edna sadly confirms this. As for herself, her New World adventure has been a "failure," to use the bleak word that Chaplin applied to her, and to Charlie as well, in a retrospective commentary on the movie.[59]

Nevertheless, their reunion is a delight to both of them. As they share his simple repast, he begins to woo her, and her responses are encouraging. In his winsome awkwardness, he comes across as very young, whereas Edna's innate dignity and physical solidity—for in the two years since becoming Chaplin's leading lady, she had clearly begun to put on weight—make her seem matronly. Within the gravitational attraction between them lies a mother-son pull.

The nervousness in Charlie's manner reflects his panicky realization that somehow he has lost the coin he had found, and that the ferociously suspicious and aggressive waiter (Eric Campbell) will surely wipe the floor with him if he proves to be a deadbeat. Deliverance from danger finally materializes in the form of a well-to-do artist at the next table who has been amusing himself during his meal by studying Charlie and Edna and who now proposes that they allow him to employ them as models. By surreptitiously picking up the tip that the artist puts down for the waiter, Charlie is able to pay his own bill. Another lucky break comes when the artist offers his newly hired models a two-dollar down payment for their work. An exultant Charlie thereupon carries Edna off to the nearest marriage-license bureau.

In the last view of them, Charlie has picked Edna up in his arms and they are both laughing. Yet there is a mournful reminder of how poor they still are. Rain is pouring down and both of them, inadequately dressed for such weather, are soaked to the skin. Even in his early comedies, Chaplin later wrote, "I strove for a mood; usually music created it. An old song called 'Mrs. Grundy' created the mood for *The Immigrant*. The tune had a wistful tenderness that suggested two lonely derelicts getting married on a rainy day."[60]

The vision of hardship in *The Immigrant* has a political dimension as well. At the end of the first part of the picture—which Chaplin did not film until May 1917, after he had completed the second part—the arrival of the immigrants' ship in New York harbor occasions an ironic comment. Just as the Statue of Liberty comes thrillingly into view and a title card announces, "Arrival in the Land of Liberty," immigration inspectors who have come aboard herd the passengers against a rail on the deck and rope them off as if they were cattle. The faces of the confined are solemn. Welcome to the Land of Liberty!

The inclusion of this scene took a certain amount of courage on Chaplin's part. Even before the assaults on civil liberties that followed on the heels of Woodrow Wilson's request to the Congress on April 2, 1917, for a declaration of war against Germany, a wave of repressive sentiment had been building.[61] Thus a xenophobic literacy-test bill had passed the Congress in February 1917, amid confident predictions that it would effectively shut off the flow of immigration from southern and eastern Europe. As for the so-called hyphenated Americans who still felt tied to the "old country," President Wilson had bitterly denounced them the year before for having "poured the poison of disloyalty into the very arteries of our national life. . . . Such creatures of passion, disloyalty and anarchy must be crushed out."[62] Consequently, it was no surprise when he warned German-Americans in his declaration-of-war request that expressions of disloyalty on their part would "be dealt with with a firm hand of repression."

Nor was it surprising that within hours of his departure from Capitol Hill, members of Congress introduced legislation designed in the name of espionage control to censor the press and prevent the use of the mails for the dissemination of allegedly treasonable (*i.e.*, antiwar) materials.[63] With the Espionage Act of June 15, 1917, in hand, Wilson's postmaster general proceeded to block all mail distribution of a wide variety of journals that had dared to criticize the government, including more than a dozen socialist publications, ranging from the earnest *Appeal to Reason*, with its subscription list of half a million, to Max Eastman's mixture in *The Masses* of proletarian revolutionism and literary and artistic avant-gardism.

Meanwhile, the federal Committee on Public Information had busied itself with the task of persuading the public that the war was an expression of one-hundred-percent Americanism from which no true patriot would utter a word of dissent.[64] In the same tyrannical spirit, the American Defense Society, the American Protective League, and other hyperpatriotic organizations began making life difficult for German-Americans who merely took pride in their cultural heritage, for Irish-Americans who deplored the U.S. alliance with perfidious Albion, and for Polish- and Jewish-Americans whose hatred of the czar made it impossible for them to root for a Russian victory against the Central Powers on the Eastern Front. The acquiescence of academia in these shameful developments was typified by the announcement of Columbia University president Nicholas Murray Butler, at commencement cere-monies on Morningside Heights in June 1917, that in times of peace the policy of the university was to offer refuge to dissidents, but that conditions had "sharply changed" with the coming of war. "What had been wrongheadedness was now sedition," said Butler. "What had been folly was now treason." [65]

Those who spoke out against intolerance in wartime America often came under attack themselves. It was admirable and more than a little surprising that Chaplin was willing to take that risk, in view of his vulnerability as a foreigner who had worked in the United States since 1913 without evincing the slightest interest in applying for citizenship, and who seemed quite content, furthermore, to forgo military service. To counteract his image as a slacker and the critical sting of *The Immi-grant*, he steeled himself against his nervousness about public speaking and spent part of the spring of 1918 promoting the sale of war bonds before huge outdoor gatherings in New York City, Washington, D.C., and seven southern states. And the following August he produced a ten-minute propaganda movie called *The Bond*.

II

The look and feel of *Easy Street*—the most famous of the Mutual comedies—indicate the London of Chaplin's childhood.* Although some of the subjects the story touches on—religious ecstasy, violent

---

* For all of its London atmospherics, the scene of the picture becomes unmistakably Californian at one point. As Charlie is being chased around the block by the neighbor-hood bully, a body of water and an empty field come into view, along with a low-lying building with a huge sign painted on one side. Only a portion of what the sign says can be discerned. "L. A. City W." It can be presumed that the building belonged to the Los Angeles City Water Works.

insanity, marital discord—were painful ones for the comedian to think about, he knew how to guard himself against an overload of anguish. As he would assert in an essay of 1922, humor is a "gentle and benevolent custodian of the mind which prevents one from being overwhelmed and driven to the point of insanity by the apparent seriousness of life." [66]

On one level, the title of the picture is ironic—for life is hard on Easy Street; on another, it constitutes a wordplay on East Lane, Walworth, where Chaplin liked to believe he was born. Easy Street, however, is not crowded with vendors' carts, as the actual East Lane almost always was. On the contrary, the setting is bleak; a few bricks and other debris litter the largely deserted roadway, and laundry lines overhang it. The film historian and biographer David Robinson has compared this mise-en-scène to Methley Street, where Hannah Chaplin went with her two boys in the period following her release from Cane Hill Asylum in November 1898. But the inhabitants of Easy Street are clearly of a lower class than the people whom the sociological scholarship of Charles Booth identified at the time as typical Methley Street residents.

In the cast of characters listed at the outset of the picture, Charlie is grimly referred to as "The Derelict." The ensuing shot of his shabbily clad figure lying half asleep on the ground outside a charitable mission further testifies to his desperate condition. From his curled-up posture we can tell how cold and uncomfortable he is, while his painfully slow movements, once he gets to his feet and begins to climb the flight of steps to the mission entrance, suggest that he is faint with hunger as well. Inside the building, a religious service has begun. A sternly admonitory clergyman, assisted by a lovely mission worker (Edna Purviance), is addressing a small band of humbly dressed worshippers who apparently have been hoping to achieve a sense of self-worth through a conversion experience.

A member of the tiny congregation hands Charlie a vest-pocket hymnal, but the print in it is so minuscule that he is unable to figure out which end of the book is up and keeps turning it around. The next item that comes his way is the wooden collection box, which he immediately holds to his ear and shakes to determine how full it is and thus to decide whether he should steal it. This fleeting disclosure of his larcenous instincts is followed by an incident that gives him a chance to show how good-hearted he is. As a favor to the woman seated beside him, he agrees to hold her baby for her, along with the bottle of milk that the infant has been sucking on. A look of Christian sweetness illuminates Charlie's face, only to vanish behind a dark cloud as he suddenly realizes that his lap is becoming damp. But it is not the fault of the baby— whom he immediately hands back to the mother—that he is getting wet; the source of the leak is the bottle of milk, which Charlie has been holding upside down. At the end of the service, both Edna and the minister approach Charlie and urge him to turn over a new leaf. Already half in love with Edna, he says he will. With shoulders squared and eyes wet with exaltation, he starts for the door, where he pauses for a moment, reaches into the inner folds of his trousers, and surrenders the collection box. He had stolen it after all.

A giant bully (Eric Campbell) is terrorizing Easy Street, and attempts by the police to subdue him have proved exceedingly hazardous to their health. Small wonder, then, that the local police station has a help-wanted sign posted outside, or that the morally rejuvenated Charlie, having applied for the job, is immediately given a uniform and dispatched to the combat zone. Belaboring the bully's head with his nightstick, he discovers to his horror, merely induces a tickling sensation in the big fellow's ear. Before carrying out his threat to tear Charlie apart, the bully demonstrates how strong he is by bending a lamppost so far over that its gas-fed lamp is within six feet of the ground. In a fear-driven burst of resourcefulness, Charlie quickly pulls the lamp over the bully's head, turns up the gas, and sends him off to dreamland. With superb nonchalance, as if this sort of victory were familiar to him, he then proceeds to walk his beat, sometimes with his hands clasped behind him and sometimes swinging his nightstick. So impressed are all the other toughs on Easy Street that they abandon their own plans to drive him out of the neighborhood.

In the course of making her social work rounds, Edna appears on Easy Street, and is surprised and delighted to see Charlie in uniform. At her invitation, he accompanies her on a visit to a family with nine children, all of whom have been fathered by a bantam rooster of a man. After looking him over, and then looking again at all his progeny, Charlie takes off his badge and pins it on the little fellow's chest.* The visit

* Chaplin himself, it is worth noting, would father eight children by Oona O'Neill.

ends on a mock-pastoral note, as Charlie moves among the children casting grains of cereal down to them as though he were feeding a flock of chickens.

The camera switches back to the story of the bully. Taking advantage of his unconsciousness, several police officers have carted him off to the station house and placed him in handcuffs. But when he comes to, he immediately breaks the handcuffs apart and manhandles an entire squad of bluecoats, despite the flailing nightsticks that are beating a tattoo on his skull. Upon his truculent return to Easy Street, he picks a fight with his wife. As pieces of crockery come sailing out of their windows, patrolman Charlie decides to intervene—without any awareness of whom he will be dealing with. Once the bully catches sight of him, one of the most intricate, most hilarious chases in all of Chaplin's films unfolds. Up and down stairs, in and out of buildings and around the block, our hero somehow manages to stay a step ahead of his maddened pursuer. Finally, he gives him the slip just long enough to gain access to the bully's now-ruined flat. Straining with all his might, he shoves a heavy iron stove close to a window and tips it over the sill, exactly above the spot on the sidewalk where the bully is standing. For the second time, the tyrant of the neighborhood goes down for the count, like a conked-out predator in an animated cartoon.

At the very same moment, a new problem for Charlie is materializing. A bearded anarchist who despises all embodiments of authority over-powers Edna and thrusts her down a flight of stairs into a squalid base-ment room where a drug addict is shooting up on a corner bench. Once the drugs start working in his system, the addict sidles up to Edna with obviously lascivious intentions. But in this parody of the scenes of sexual menace in *The Birth of a Nation* (which Chaplin apparently went to see almost every week during its long Los Angeles run), the fiend is barely able to lay a paw on his blond victim before Charlie involuntarily arrives on the scene, thanks to another staircase propulsion by the anarchist. Charlie's fight to defend Edna is a losing battle—until he is knocked backwards onto the bench where the addict has propped up a drug-loaded syringe. The needle penetrates his buttock and the drug blows his mind. In one of Hannah Chaplin's outbursts of psychotic violence in the late summer of 1898, she had thrown a mug at another patient. Psychotic Charlie does better than that. He floors the drug addict in nothing flat, roars up the stairs from the basement, bursts into the barroom frequented by the anarchist and a collection of other nasty characters, and cleans out the place single-handedly. The fair-haired Edna shows up to thank her rescuer; still riding his drug-induced high, Charlie greets her with an open-armed ballet pose, rushes toward her —and falls down a manhole.

The final episode of the picture opens with a shot of the relocated and much enlarged mission at the top of Easy Street. Other changes in the life of the neighborhood are even more impressive. The roadway has been cleared of debris and no longer has laundry lines suspended above it, while the men and women streaming toward the mission in impressive numbers are wearing clothes that bespeak a startlingly augmented respectability. The bully and his wife emerge from their building and join the throng. Reconciled with his wife and as meek as a lamb, the bully deferentially tips his sleek top hat to the cop on the corner, who is Charlie. Finally, Edna appears, and as she and Charlie head for the mission, he ceremoniously takes her arm.

"Love Backed by Force" is the title-card commentary at the close. The phrase puts an explicit law-and-order spin on this very clever, deeply felt picture. Yet how could this be? That Charlie Chaplin, of all people, had celebrated the use of strong-arm tactics by a policeman and had portrayed his hero as fully adjusted to playing the enforcer's role has never made much sense to the critics, and a few of them have denounced the ending as aberrant and abominable. But in fact it can be easily explained. Chaos was the law of life in the madness-haunted domiciles of Chaplin's boyhood; order, *Easy Street* declares, was the boy's abiding dream.

"A PICTURE WITH A SMILE— AND PERHAPS A TEAR"

Talking to Jackie Coogan on the set of The Kid *in 1919.*

A N outburst of revulsion by Oona O'Neill Chaplin about her cock-strutting husband's reminiscences of "scoring" is recalled in detail in Carol Matthau's salty-sugary memoir *Among the Porcupines* (1992). "All those old bags he slept with!" Oona exclaimed to old friend Carol in the ladies' room at El Morocco. "Jesus Christ, I'm sick of hearing about them. And you'd think maybe by now he'd be sick of even thinking about them. What am I supposed to do when he's talking like that? Sit there and smile and simper?"

It was an evening in 1947. Carol and her then-husband, William Saroyan,* had driven in to New York from their house on Long Island to have drinks at the Stork Club with the Chaplins, who had come east for the premiere of *Monsieur Verdoux*. The four of them then went on to supper in the Champagne Room at El Morocco, and while they were eating the two men got to talking about Rebecca West.

As a nineteen-year-old of uncommon intelligence and considerable wit, West had captivated H. G. Wells. For ten years, from 1913 to 1923, they were lovers, and West bore the novelist a son. Chaplin seemed impressed by all that. When West came to Hollywood in 1924, he wanted Saroyan to know, he himself had seduced her. With ease, he emphasized. "Bill, she was a piece of cake," he kept saying. Whereupon Saroyan admitted that he had once chased West around a bed for several hours without success. "Dear boy," Chaplin chided him, "that is not how it is done. You do not chase anyone around the bed. You do it from the moment you say 'How do you do?' "[1] But if Oona was disgusted by all this, West would have a very different story to tell of her amatory encounters with Chaplin.

Another woman to whom the comedian spoke in romantically flattering terms from the instant of being introduced to her—or rather, in this case, reintroduced—was Marie Doro. As William Gillette's costar in *Sherlock Holmes*, Marie not only had not noticed the effect of her looks on the youth who was playing Billy the pageboy, but after the show closed she quickly forgot his name. Eleven years later, in the early summer of 1916, the actress—now thirty-seven—arrived in Hollywood to make a movie called *The Heart of Nora Flynn* for Cecil B. DeMille. At a large evening party, Constance Collier brought her together with Chaplin. "But we've met before," he began by saying. "You broke my heart. I was silently in love with you." When dinner was served, they sat at the same table in the garden, and in the glow of candlelight Chaplin went on talking about "the frustration of a youth silently in love with her." Almost two years elapsed before they met again, this time in New York. Marie was appearing in a Broadway play that spring, and when she learned that Chaplin was in town for a bond-campaign appearance with Douglas Fairbanks, she sent a note to him at his hotel, suggesting

---

* After twice marrying and divorcing Saroyan, the former Carol Marcus married the actor Walter Matthau.

that they go out for dinner and then take a drive through Central Park. "However," Chaplin recalled in *My Autobiography*, in a sentence reverberating with the hollow sound of omitted details, we "just dined quietly in Marie's apartment alone."[2]

Is it possible that he went to her apartment with vindictive thoughts in mind about her husband, Elliott Dexter? A number of young women in Hollywood had secret crushes on the handsome actor. Gossip had it that one of them was Mildred Harris, whom Chaplin first met in the latter part of 1917 at a swimming party at Sam Goldwyn's beach house. Mildred spent the "whole afternoon," he noticed, "ogling" Dexter.[3] How Chaplin felt about this is evident from his account of what he said to Mildred in his car, after she asked him for a ride back to town. She had quarreled with the friend who brought her to the party and he had already left, she explained. Perhaps her friend was jealous of Elliott Dexter, Chaplin huffily replied. But it was he who was jealous. Six months later in a New York hotel suite, he had the chance to work his seductive charms on Dexter's wife. Chaplin would not have been Chaplin if he had simply dined quietly with Marie.

2

An article on Mildred Harris in the February 1914 *Photoplay* was illustrated by a photograph of her that certainly gave credibility to the contention of the author, Jean Darnell, that little Mildred was "one of the most perfect children playing before the camera today." Gushing on, Darnell praised her "gorgeous head of natural flaxen curls and large expressive blue eyes, [her] perfect nose and mouth and, in all, one of the most classic profiles that I have ever seen." In thrillers produced by the Ince Studios, where her mother worked as the wardrobe mistress, Mildred repeatedly played little girls who were mistreated or kidnapped and yet could melt the heart of a villain. Moviegoers in 1914–15 encountered her as Dorothy in a *Wizard of Oz* series. In 1916—if they looked carefully—they could find her in D. W. Griffith's outsized epic *Intolerance*. The following year, the most influential woman director in Hollywood, Lois Weber, gave her the chance to show what she could do with an adult role by casting her as a pathetic young shop girl in the suggestively titled *The Price of a Good Time*.[4]

How old was she in February 1914? Mildred told her *Photoplay* interviewer that she was "just a little girl, for I am but nine years old."[5] If that was true, then she could not have been more than thirteen at the time she met Chaplin. But understating one's age was common in movieland. Furthermore, there are modern résumés of Harris's career that declare she was born in 1901. If so, that means she turned sixteen in the year of the Goldwyn party. The only certain fact is that although Mildred played an adult role in a picture about the wages of sin in 1917, she could look remarkably childlike whenever she wished to. As Theodore Dreiser would say of her in 1920, she was "very small, very babydollish."[6]

When Chaplin attempted in the 1960s to detoxify his sexual history, he insisted that he would never have become involved with Mildred had it not been for her aggressiveness. His chauffeur, he affirmed in *My Autobiography*, drove them straight from the Goldwyn party to the Cadillac Hotel in Venice, where Mildred was living with her mother. After dropping her off, Chaplin returned to his digs in the Los Angeles Athletic Club "with a sense of relief, for I was glad to be alone." Five minutes later, the phone rang, according to Chaplin. It was Mildred. (Was her mother aware of the call?) "I just wanted to know what you were doing," she said. Chaplin informed her that he was going to have a bite to eat in his room and then get into bed and read a book. What kind of a book and what is your room like? she inquired. No sooner had he answered these questions than she boldly asked, "When am I going to see you again?" Chaplin chided her for betraying Elliott Dexter. Mildred said that she really didn't care for Dexter. This "swept away my resolutions for the evening," Chaplin's version of the story continued, "and I invited her out for dinner."

In the middle of the following week, having heard nothing from him since their dinner date, Mildred phoned the studio and left a message with Tom Harrington. In relaying it to Chaplin, Harrington chanced to say that the chauffeur had told him that Mildred Harris was the most beautiful girl he had ever seen. As Chaplin professed to remember it, this passing remark so appealed to his vanity that he suddenly became eager to see her. "There were dinners, dances, moonlit nights and ocean drives." Whether out of naïveté or malicious knowingness, Mildred later made a more revealing comment than he ever would about the ties that had lassoed him and bound him to her. He was "wonderful" and "so fatherly," she exclaimed, and "acted to me as though I had been a mere child."[7]

At the height of their affair, Chaplin would sit for hours in his car outside Universal Studios, where Mildred was making another picture with Lois Weber, waiting for her to emerge. It was as though he were a parent picking up a child after school. One day, D. W. Griffith saw them together and asked, "Mildred, why don't you marry Charlie? He'd make a nice husband for you." Without pausing, he then turned to Chaplin and said, "Charlie, wouldn't she make a wonderful wife for you?"[8] Griffith's comments reflected his own attraction to child-women. His ideal of the feminine film star, he told an interviewer for *Photoplay*, had "nothing of the flesh, nothing of the note of sensuousness,"[9] and he demonstrated this preference time and again in the casting assignments he made. In *The Birth of a Nation* he assigned the most important female role to the slightly built, seventeen-year-old Lillian Gish, whose fugitive hands and agitated body gestures satisfied Griffith's supplementary taste for "the nervous type,"[10] and the second most important role to the coltish, tomboyish Mae Marsh, age eighteen.

Off the set, the fatherly director courted both Gish and Marsh; indeed, the silent-film star Colleen Moore once said that Gish confided in her that Griffith asked her to marry him. His love for her, however, did not prompt him to terminate his pursuit of other young women, for as Griffith had made clear to his first wife years before, he was highly sexed and incorrigibly promiscuous. At the same time, he considered the opposite sex dangerous. "He admired and loved women," Lillian Gish recalled,

> yet he seemed afraid of them. He never saw a girl in his office without a third person present. . . . Hollywood was already filled with ambitious girls, who would stop at nothing to get into films. Some unscrupulous young girls, having obtained an interview with a producer, would threaten to remove their clothes and accuse him of rape if he didn't promise them a role in a movie.[11]

Entrapment, in short, was a familiar tactic in the Hollywood war of the sexes, and Griffith lived in dread of it.

At some point Mildred popped the key question: when did Chaplin intend to marry her? Chaplin bluntly said, "Never," and assumed that the discussion was closed.[12] But it had merely been postponed. In the late summer of 1918, Mildred announced she was pregnant. He did not need to have it spelled out that if he refused to marry her, she and her mother would crucify him in the press, and that every reporter who was covering the story would portray her as a wronged innocent—even though there were rumors around town that she had previously tried to entrap D. W. Griffith and after him the French-born director Maurice Tourneur.[13] The question of her age was especially perilous. Would she say, under duress, that she was sixteen, or thirteen? Either way, Chaplin would be exposed as having broken the law, and accused of committing statutory rape.* He could serve time for that, and as a resident alien he could be deported. In sum, there were reasons enough to marry her, despite his certainty that she and her mother had deliberately set out to snag him.

Dejectedly, Chaplin instructed Tom Harrington to make arrangements for an unpublicized marriage ceremony at the home of a justice of the peace. Harrington was likewise put in charge of purchasing a wedding ring. The ceremony took place on October 23, and at the end of it the groom had to be reminded to kiss the bride. At work the next day—for Chaplin had no interest in a honeymoon—a further ordeal awaited him. As he was walking to his dressing room, he encountered Edna Purviance. "Congratulations," she said softly. "Thank you," Chaplin replied in an agony of embarrassment.[14]

The newlyweds moved into a house that Chaplin leased for six months at 200 DeMille Drive in the Laughlin Park section of North Hollywood. Almost immediately, Mildred's pregnancy proved to be a false alarm. More than likely she had lied to him about her condition. Nevertheless, he went on living with his baby doll as man and wife, with the result that by late November she really was pregnant. Unfortunately, the news did nothing to soften Chaplin's surging disdain for the "pink-ribboned foolishness" cluttering Mildred's mind. He tried very hard, he plaintively recalled, to talk seriously with her about their future, only to find that she "had no sense of reality." Marriage to her, he claimed, was

---

* Chaplin would claim in *My Autobiography* that at the time of their marriage Mildred was "not quite nineteen" (p. 230).

"an adventure as thrilling as winning a beauty contest. It was something she had read about in storybooks. . . . She was in a continual state of dazzlement." To top everything off, she had no understanding of how committed he was to his work, and complained when he failed to come home at the same time that other husbands did.[15]

Out of a wish to portray her as a cipher, Chaplin neglected to mention her strong points as a wife. Her talkativeness included a sense of humor; her imaginative decoration of the DeMille Drive house won the praise of a Los Angeles newspaper; and like her mother she was a stylish dresser.[16] For better and for worse, in short, she bore a resemblance to the classic child-wife personality, as described in a psychoanalytic paper in 1947 by Dr. Phyllis Greenacre of the New York Psychoanalytic Institute:

Such women almost invariably marry, and generally quite young. Even in the years of their marriage and motherhood they seem successfully to resist maturity, and eventually fade rather than mature or age. They are often chatterboxes who "run on" in their talk . . . but have a flair for clothes and sometimes for household decoration. Their speech or flow of talk often gives the impression of being essentially an autoerotic discharge rather than a means of communication, much in the fashion of young children whose prattle shows a sensual pleasure in the sound and mouthing of the words. They are not infrequently witty, but again in the way of a child who flutteringly makes risqué remarks with seemingly literal-minded innocence; and they present a peculiar mixture of worldly competitiveness and apparent naïveté. . . . They give the superficial impression of always having been protected; yet in their difficulty in learning from experience they resemble to a mild degree the psychopathic personality.[17]

3

John Freuler had dearly wanted Chaplin to remain with Mutual, as he made clear in the spring of 1917 by offering him a million dollars for eight pictures. Chaplin, however, wanted to feel free to take all the time and spend all the money that making top-notch pictures required. As Sydney Chaplin remarked at a press conference in Chicago, prior to a series of high-level business meetings in New York, "No more of this sixty-mile-an-hour producing stuff will be seen in the Chaplin films from now on. . . . Hereafter the Chaplin pictures will take from two to three times longer to produce than they do now. The settings and stage properties will be the finest. It is quality, not quantity that we are after." A bid for monopolistic power by Adolph Zukor was the fortuitous development that enabled the Chaplin brothers to work out the arrangement they were seeking.[18]

In addition to showing his Famous Players pictures in the theaters that he himself owned, Zukor had signed an agreement to distribute them through Paramount, the nation's leading distributor of movies and the corporate proprietor to boot of a number of choice theaters in various cities (including the Paramount in New York). Thus he was already a figure to be reckoned with on the exhibition side of the movie business when he walked into a meeting of Paramount's stockholders on June 13, 1916. By the end of the day, he had outmaneuvered the company's founder, W. W. Hodkinson, and installed his own representative in the driver's seat. Other moves followed. He merged Famous Players with Jesse L. Lasky's Feature Play Company and brought twelve other producing companies under their amalgamated umbrella. He pressured Lasky into buying out his partner, Sam Goldwyn—still known as Sam Goldfish—for $900,000. And in a coup that rocked the industry to its foundations, he used the assets of Famous Players–Lasky to purchase outright control of Paramount. Having integrated production and distribution and augmented his movie theater holdings, he now was in a position to raise rental rates without restraint on the independent exhibitors who still owned the bulk of America's first-run movie houses.[19]

Fighting off Zukor's chokehold became the exhibitors' obsession. In April 1917, a group of them headed by Thomas L. Tally and J. D. Williams founded the First National Exhibitors' Circuit for the purpose of buying and making pictures and distributing them. First National's first goal was to work out a deal with Chaplin, which it succeeded in doing in June. As an independent, Chaplin would bear all of the production costs on the eight two-reel pictures he agreed to deliver every year. First National would advance him $125,000 on each of them, plus $15,000 for each additional reel if the pictures ran longer. Furthermore, First National would foot the bills for trade-publication advertising and assorted other expenses. After all costs were recovered, Chaplin and First National would split the net profits fifty-fifty. On the day of the signing, neither party could have foreseen that it would take Chaplin five years to bring eight pictures into release, or that one of them would be of feature length, or that of the remaining seven only three would be limited to two reels.[20]*

Construction work on a home for Chaplin's filmmaking got under way in the fall of 1917, on a five-acre site at the corner of Sunset Boulevard and La Brea Avenue. When completed the following January, the façade of the studio looked like a linked row of English workers' brick-and-stucco cottages, with chimney stacks and imitation half-timbers of brown-painted wood on the Tudor gables. Chaplin's office occupied the central room of a small bungalow and was far more modest than the headquarters of other Hollywood chieftains. Indeed, when the young Alistair Cooke saw the room some fifteen years later, he was struck by its tackiness.

> It had worn oilcloth on the floor, and if it was ever wallpapered, the paper had rotted in the fungi of mildew. There was one small window, three straight-back wooden chairs, an old table, about half a dozen books with peeling spines, and an ancient upright piano hideously out of tune. It was probably about as luxurious as any of the rooms Chaplin had rented in the boardinghouses of prewar England, and as I was to learn, in working there the following year, it reflected Chaplin's deep distrust of elegant surroundings whenever there was serious work on hand.[21]

To run the studio, Chaplin turned to an old friend, Alf Reeves, the former manager of Fred Karno's American tours. A wiry sparrow with Cockney mannerisms that he would never lose, Reeves had been un-happy about living in Britain since his return there in 1913. The primary reason was that he could not abide the climate. Consequently, he leaped at the chance to settle in sunny California. Vociferous arguments soon

---

* Having landed Chaplin, First National went after Zukor's own superstar, Mary Pickford. For making three four-to-six-reel pictures, which she had to deliver—and did, in fact—within nine months, the company agreed to pay her $750,000, with a $150,000 advance. The terms enabled her to go on telling her mirror that she was still the most sought-after player in the land.

became a feature of his relationship with Chaplin. "You're a bloody slut!" one of them would cry. "You're a bigger bloody slut!" the other would yell in reply. To which the inevitable counterreply was, "You're a double bloody slut!" Nevertheless, the rock-solid tenure and considerable influence that Reeves enjoyed at the studio until his death in 1946 constituted the most impressive example of the comedian's loyalty to old-time staff. In this respect, Alistair Cooke once said, Chaplin was like "a sergeant who has been through years of trench warfare with a motley pack of privates and ever afterward uses them as a protective base of sanity."[22]

4

In an article called "Charles Not Charlie" in the September 1918 *Photoplay*, one of the most cultivated of the early movie writers, Julian Johnson, argued in effect that Chaplin's rude, untutored genius had finally been tamed by his absorption of the civilized values of people like Johnson himself. The comedian's new studio, Johnson's paean began, is the "most artistic" ever built in the movie colony. But this was only one of the ways in which Chaplin had demonstrated that he had "the innate taste and refinement of a man slowly rising to self-won culture after early vicissitudes and almost no schooling." He dresses, said Johnson, with "the unostentatious attire of good breeding." He talks with "the clean, well-bred speech of an Englishman." He supports "carefully chosen" charities. Most tellingly of all, "the serious bits in all his plays are the ones he likes most," especially the episode in *The Bank* (1915) in which Charlie, in the role of a janitor, discovers that the bouquet of flowers he has given to a beautiful secretary, Edna Purviance, as a token of his love for her has been tossed into a wastebasket. "In the ensuing bit of pantomime," Johnson proclaimed, "Chaplin struck a note of tragedy which in its depth and universality was really Shakespearean."[23]

Five months prior to the appearance of this testament, Chaplin released the first of his Sunset and La Brea productions, a three-reel story about the tramp and a stray pooch named Scraps who becomes his constant companion, just as little Jackie Coogan would in *The Kid*. Chaplin's belief that *A Dog's Life* was more carefully crafted than anything he had done before is set forth in one of the all-too-brief, all-too-infrequent discussions of his filmmaking in *My Autobiography*. In the course of the picture he had achieved a thematic unity, he said, by dint of paralleling the life of the dog with that of the tramp.

> This leitmotif was the structure upon which I built sundry gags and slapstick routines. I was beginning to think of comedy in a structural sense, and to become conscious of its architectural form. Each sequence implied the next sequence, all of them relating to the whole. The first sequence was rescuing a dog from a fight with other dogs. The next was rescuing a girl in a dance hall [Edna Purviance] who was also leading "a dog's life." There were many other sequences, all of which followed in a logical concatenation of events.

Yet while he was proud of his newfound skill in story construction, Chaplin had to admit that architecture "restricted my comedy freedom." In the early days, "the tramp had been freer and less confined to plot," and "his instincts" had been much more active than "his brain." Behind these references to "comedy freedom" and "instincts" lay the autobiographer's nostalgic recall of the wild spirit of his Keystone and Essanay comedies. In them he had uncovered repressed feelings, confronted taboos, and confounded moralists. Now, however, his hero was growing "more complex" as he placed his portraits of personal suffering in more complicated contexts.[24]

The humor in *A Dog's Life* rises out of the midst of hunger, homelessness, and violence in a nameless city. The first scene finds vagabond Charlie rolling back and forth beneath a board fence on a vacant lot in order to steal a hot dog and elude the cop who has witnessed the theft. The second takes place in an employment office, where he is consistently beaten out in the race to the application windows by more ruthless job-seekers. In the uproariously funny third scene, he plays a cat-and-mouse game with the cook (played by Sydney Chaplin) who runs an outdoor lunch stand. Every time the cook turns to the stove, Charlie gobbles down one of the goodies heaped up on a plate on the counter. The cook tries to catch him at his thievery by quick-as-a-wink swervings around, but Charlie is even quicker, and soon enough the plate is virtually empty.

Yet in spite of his filching successes, Charlie's face is pale and haggard, and once he begins sleeping, on bare ground in the cold outdoors, cuddled up to a hungry mutt that he has adopted and named Scraps, he feels the pinch of fleas. Accompanied by Scraps, he goes to a miserably run-down tavern called the Green Lantern in search of cheer on the cheap, only to encounter the rule that dogs are not welcome. Where-upon Charlie conceals Scraps inside his clothing and bluffs his way in—without awareness that Scraps's tail is sticking out of a hole in his pants. The point is clear. Charlie, too, is leading a dog's life.

In a parody of a gangster-film rivalry, the Green Lantern experience leads this unlikely candidate for a hero's role into involvement with a couple of gun-toting—eventually gun-firing—thugs in a contest for possession of a stolen wallet bulging with money. Moreover, he manages to rescue Edna Purviance from a life more degrading than his own. "Logically it was difficult," Chaplin would admit in *My Autobiography*, "to get a beautiful girl interested in a tramp."[25] But in *A Dog's Life* he accounts for Edna's interest in Charlie by emphasizing her down-and-out desperation. For some time she has been working as a dance hostess at the Green Lantern, but one night a free-spending customer makes advances to her, which she repels. In a furious reaction to her recalci-trance, the owner of the tavern fires her on the spot and refuses to pay her back wages. The intensity of her distress implies a fear that the only recourse left to her is prostitution. Thus when Charlie shows her the stolen wallet, which Scraps has unearthed by accident from the hole where the thugs had buried it, she listens without protest to his glowing description of how happy the two of them will be as a married couple living on a farm and raising a family of five children.

A comedy grounded in grim urban facts ends in a sudden blaze of rural sweetness and light, and only a mocking humor enables Chaplin to get away with such a heavy dose of sentimentality. Farmer Charlie is shown poking holes in the earth and carefully planting seeds one at a time, but when the camera pulls back for a panoramic shot, the absurdity of his efforts is revealed: the field in which he is standing stretches to the horizon. Charlie then joins Edna in their picture-postcard cottage. Very quietly, they approach the cradle that is standing in front of the fireplace. Two proud parents are about to take a peek at their firstborn child—or so it is assumed, until a close-up shot of the cradle shows Scraps inside with a litter of puppies. Having come up with this last-second laugh-getter, Chaplin sincerely hoped that audiences would not remember the clear indications of male identity in earlier shots of Scraps.

5

A comedy about Charlie as an American soldier fighting the Germans in France became the next order of business at the Chaplin Studio, despite warnings from knowledgeable acquaintances in the Hollywood community that the public would be angered by it. "It's dangerous at this time to make fun of the war," Cecil B. DeMille opined.[26] *Shoulder Arms* went into production on May 29, 1918. For the next four weeks, Chaplin spent most of his time and a significant amount of money filming a two-part introductory sequence about the domestic tensions in Charlie's life as a civilian and the discomforts and embarrassments he suffers during his induction physical exam. In late June, he junked all this footage, along with the idea of including a postwar sequence. After working ferociously hard all summer long, he finished the picture in the midst of a mid-September heat wave. At which point he decided that all his efforts had been in vain. On top of the grim probability that he was going to have to marry Mildred Harris in a few weeks, he now had to contend with a sickening sense of professional failure. Had it not been for Douglas Fairbanks's roars of laughter at a special screening, he might have consigned *Shoulder Arms* to the ash can. "Sweet Douglas," he fondly recalled, "he was my greatest audience."[27]

American and Canadian exhibitors began showing the picture in the last ten days of October, and by the time of the Armistice on November 11, it was clear that a box-office bonanza was in the making. Today, the reputation of *Shoulder Arms* as a masterwork has faded badly, mainly because most of its ideas derived from short-lived, news-of-the-day associations in the public mind. Walter Kerr offered a sample list of these ideas in his perceptive book *The Silent Clowns* (1975):

. . . wet trenches with street signs marked "Broadway and Rotten Row," omnipresent cooties, gift packages, the new taboo of three-on-a-match, the French nation pictured as a woman with head bowed low before her shattered home, fat Germans and pint-sized ones all equipped with spike mustaches, leering enemy officers apt to do anything at all to available women, the Kaiser himself, Limburger cheese.[28]

Three scenes, however, will always be worth recalling for the humanity of their humor. In the first of them, Chaplin thought of a fresh and compelling way to dramatize the demoralizing loneliness of men at the front.* Having received no mail himself, Private Charlie steals up behind another doughboy who is standing in a trench in the rain perusing a letter from home and surreptitiously reads it along with him. As the pages are turned, the perfectly synchronized facial expressions of the two men successively register joy, concern, and finally contentment. From *The Floorwalker* to *The Circus* to *The Great Dictator*, Chaplin focused again and again on ideas involving mirror images and doubles; the letter-reading scene in *Shoulder Arms* is a particularly enchanting example of what his split-screen imagination could accomplish.

That cold, frightened, battle-weary men were given to regressive dreams of childhood security was an aspect of the psychology of war that Chaplin instinctively understood. Private Charlie finds a womb with a view on the deserted second floor of a bombed-out house. The walls and ceiling of the room he enters have been destroyed, and while the window frame is still standing, not a single pane of glass remains. Nevertheless, when he wants to check whether German soldiers are in the area, he raises the sash before looking out. Having satisfied himself that he is not in danger, he lowers the sash, pulls down the shade, and curls up on the bed like a child. As in a dream, a beautiful young Frenchwoman (Edna Purviance) enters the room and, out of a belief that this sleeping man has been wounded, does her motherly best to comfort him.

Breaking free of comic clichés about combat, as purveyed most successfully on the English-speaking side of the war by the British cartoonist Bruce *(The Better 'Ole)* Bairnsfather, proved largely impossible for Chaplin. The grand exception was the spy-mission caper, filmed on location in a California woodland. Essentially, it was another manifestation of its creator's fascination with transposed identities. For reconnoitering purposes, Charlie encases himself in papier-mâché bark and becomes a tree. His camouflage enables him to position himself near three German soldiers who happen by and start to build a campfire.

---

* In 1925 King Vidor would use this scene as the model for one of the incidents in his World War I epic, *The Big Parade*.

Inevitably, they find that they need more wood. One of them grabs an ax and volunteers to get some. After taking a healthy lick or two at another tree, he decides that he prefers the looks of the Charlie-tree. Terrified but resolute, Charlie knocks the ax-wielder out with a sneak blow from one of his branchlike arms and similarly disposes of his two companions. While still camouflaged, he then saves the life of an American sergeant who has been apprehended for spying. This exploit exposes his subterfuge, however, to an overstuffed sausage of a German soldier and he is forced to flee into dense woods, with his fat enemy in puffily sweaty pursuit. In his uncertainty as to which of the surrounding trees is the fake one, the German begins to bayonet trunks right and left. The scene could hardly be more absurd. Yet the imminent horror of a bayoneting also endows Charlie's peril with a reality that can compel audiences to identify with him, so that when he finally escapes unscathed, they experience a personal sense of relief.

6

Less than two weeks after his marriage, Chaplin started work on another picture, but making progress on it turned out to be agonizingly difficult. Having to live with Mildred, he brooded, had adversely affected his creative faculties.[29] Time and again he shut down the studio and went off on excursions with congenial companions, leaving Mildred behind. On one occasion, he took an automobile trip with the actor Carter DeHaven; on another, he invited all his employees to be his guests for three days at an air show in San Diego. There was nothing that he and Mildred seemed to have in common. Thus when Max Eastman arrived in Los Angeles in February 1919 to make a political speech, Chaplin attended it without his wife.

Borne down by a combination of economic pressures and political hysteria, the Eastman-edited *Masses* had died, but he had quickly raised his revolutionary banner in another magazine, *The Liberator.* Following a vehement protest in its pages against the Allies' placement of troops in the northern reaches of Soviet Russia for what Eastman construed to be the obvious purpose of bringing down the Bolshevik government, he had begun delivering a speech entitled "Hands Off Russia!" in cities from coast to coast. A tall, sleekly handsome man and a master of low-keyed oratory, Eastman had a spellbinding effect on audiences. As the ovation at the end of his Los Angeles address subsided, an acquaintance of his named Rob Wagner came to the front of the auditorium and gave him a message from Chaplin.

Wagner was a striking figure himself. A flamboyantly dressed bohemian and an outspoken radical intellectual who had worked for a time as a stage designer for Ziegfeld, he had come to Los Angeles in 1912 and taken a job as a teacher of art history and drawing at Manual Arts High School. After school, he supervised those students (between 1913 and 1915, one of them was Frank Capra) who were interested in painting scenery and designing sets for school plays. In the evenings and on weekends, he researched and wrote articles. One of his more ambitious efforts was a series of pieces for the *Saturday Evening Post* that examined the lives of various "film folk," as he called them, as a means of answering the question of how to make it in Hollywood. For Wagner was fascinated by the movies and had resolved that someday he would break into the business himself as a writer and director. His dream finally started to come true in 1920. But well before then he had struck up friendships with a number of prominent people in Hollywood and had become especially close to Chaplin, who showed his faith in their like-mindedness by entrusting him with the task of ghostwriting an article explaining his ideas about comedy to the readers of *American Magazine*.[30] It was only natural, then, that Chaplin invited Wagner to accompany him to the Eastman speech and that afterwards he asked him to inform Eastman of his wish to meet him.

The encounter was one of the grand moments in Eastman's life. "Charlie Chaplin," he later wrote, "was then the most famous man in the world, not excepting President Wilson, Lloyd George, General Foch, not excepting anybody." After shaking the editor's hand, Chaplin thrilled him again by commenting favorably on his speech. "You have what I consider the essence of all art—even of mine, if I may call myself an artist—restraint."[31] The two men continued their conversation during supper at a nearby tavern and renewed it the following morning at the Chaplin Studio. By the time they parted, each of them was sure that he had found a new friend. They had loved talking about the theories of humor that Eastman was working up into a book. Equally important to both men was the continuing story of the Russian Revolution. In

1943 Chaplin would sum up in a public statement what that stupendous event had meant to him.

> Twenty-six years ago a brave new world was born that gave hope and inspiration to the common man. That world was Soviet Russia, imbued with a dream that would give its people, no matter what race or color, their natural rights to equal liberty, equal justice, and equal opportunity in the pursuit of food and shelter and the life beautiful.[32]

Perhaps Chaplin had been on the political left since his young manhood in prewar England. But even if he had sided at the time with the most militant strike leaders, his enthusiasm about the triumph of the Bolsheviks seems incongruous. On his first night in New York in the fall of 1910, he had been stirred by the promises of American life symbolized by the tall buildings and bright lights. In contrast to England, where the class-based constrictions of society had filled him with resentment, America was wide open and dynamic. "This is where I belong!" he had exclaimed to himself. Since then, his breathtakingly rapid accumulation of wealth, his increasingly expensive tastes, his fondness for the company of other movieland millionaires, his satisfaction in becoming the master of a movie studio of his own, and his need as an artist for untrammeled freedom of expression should have made his stake in the survival of capitalist democracy so clear to him as to render him immune to collectivist dreams.

Chaplin, however, craved the acquaintance of intellectuals, in part because he enjoyed their company and in part because their acceptance of him as an equal enhanced his self-esteem. Rob Wagner and Max Eastman were convinced, as were many of their most articulate counterparts across America, that the Russian upheavals of 1917 had ushered in a new era of social deliverance for the suffering masses of the world, and their certainty served to intensify Chaplin's own response to that thrilling vision. Through interaction with his brilliant but gullible friends, he came to believe that he was in touch with the reality of the Red Revolution, whereas actually he was estranged from it.

How he felt about World War I once the Bolsheviks seized power is a subsidiary question, but nonetheless interesting. On November 9, 1917, the new leadership in the Kremlin issued a "Decree of Peace," declaring the war to be a conspiracy by the international ruling class against the workers of the world. A month later, Germany announced that it had reached an agreement with Russia about an armistice. With Russia's sudden departure from the war, the troops of the Western allies faced a foe that no longer had to fight on two fronts. At the prospect of a sudden surge in American casualties, a bitterness arose in the United States about Eugene V. Debs, Big Bill Haywood, and other American radical leaders who were openly rejoicing, in Haywood's phrase, in the "breaking of the glorious Red Dawn" in Russia. As one historian of the era has observed, "the Bolshevik Revolution pushed an already alienated radical community far outside the mainstream of American politics so that, in its imagination, America's radical left now inhabited a different world than the rest of the nation: its heart was in another country—Russia."[33] While Chaplin's heart lay in his work, it is quite possible that his admiration for the Russian Revolution alienated him as well from America's will to win the war. In which event he would have secretly regarded his Liberty Bond tour in 1918 as nothing more than a necessary exercise in public relations.

With the end of the conflict, the idea of an American revolution emerged. When Chaplin met Eastman in February 1919, Eastman had just come from Seattle, where he had addressed, in his words, "a 'mob' of proletarian thousands in the public square" on the subject of the city's already legendary general strike. The strike had originated in a vote on January 21 of 35,000 shipyard workers to walk off the job. The Seattle Central Labor Council, headed by a hard-edged pro-Bolshevik, had thereupon demanded that labor union members throughout the metropolitan area demonstrate their solidarity with their shipyard brothers. For five long days, Seattle lay paralyzed. Although forces called in by the mayor, Ole Hanson, handily crushed the strike, its breathtaking scope emboldened labor radicals elsewhere. A huge wave of strikes, involving more workers than ever before in American history, swept the nation, climaxing in the walkout in September of 365,000 steelworkers, led by the Communists' future candidate for President, William Z. Foster—for whom Chaplin would give a reception at the Chaplin Studio in 1922—and in the downing of tools by 400,000 coal miners on November 1.[34]

Both the American Communist Party and the rival Communist Labor

Party* were explicitly dedicated to the violent overthrow of the American state. As the Communist newspaper editor Carl Päiviö proclaimed, "A rioting mob is the one and only possible means for organizing a fight ... in these last open and decisive blood-battles between the capitalists and the working classes. . . . To hell with the teachings of peaceful revolution. The bloody seizure of power by the working classes is the only possible way." The combined membership of the two parties numbered between twenty-five thousand and forty thousand. These figures were paltry, to be sure. But some labor militants took encouragement from the thought that in the spring preceding the October revolution in Russia, the Bolshevik party had contained only eleven thousand members.[35]

A number of left-liberal intellectuals also came to believe in a new social order in America, and prophetic essays on the subject appeared in the *New Republic* and the *Nation*. Thirteen years later, John Dos Passos recalled the mood of revolutionary hope as he had experienced it in the spring of 1919:

> Any spring is a time of overturn, but then Lenin was alive, the Seattle general strike had seemed the beginning of the flood instead of the beginning of the ebb, Americans in Paris were groggy with theatre and painting and music; Picasso was to rebuild the eye, Stravinski was cramming the Russian steppes into our ears, currents of energy seemed breaking out everywhere as young guys climbed out of their uniforms, imperial America was all shiny with the new idea of Ritz, in every direction the countries of the world stretched out starving and angry, ready for anything turbulent and new, whenever you went to the movies you saw Charlie Chaplin.[36]

Most Americans, however, were in a different mood that spring. They had come out of the war nursing a grievance against Bolshevik Russia because of the separate peace it had signed with Germany, and in the months just after the war they were alarmed to see Reds playing key roles in high-profile strikes. Chaplin, it came to be perceived, was on the left, too. When he had crossed the country in 1916, waves of adula-

---

* The two parties merged at the Kremlin's insistence in 1921.

tion had washed over him at every stop. But between 1919 and 1921 his friendships with Eastman and Rob Wagner and other radicals aroused talk about his Red sympathies. The reporters who hurled pointed questions at him about his politics voiced the first faint indications of the suspicion and anger that he would incur with a vengeance in the aftermath of another world war.

7

Sunnyside was the misleading title of the strange picture that Chaplin finally finished in the spring of 1919. The public was puzzled by it, the reviewers panned it, and there was whispered speculation in Hollywood that in the fast-changing postwar world the "Master," as Chaplin was known to other comedians, had lost his touch.

Nineteen nineteen was a year of unparalleled growth in the film industry. Larger and gaudier theaters were going up, box-office receipts in America were soaring, the world market was expanding exponentially, and the demand for comedy films had never been greater. Fatty Arbuckle's *A Desert Hero* and *Backstage* (each of them featuring the up-and-coming Buster Keaton in an important supporting role) furnished new proof that the fat man still knew how to lick the lollipop of life, while the maniacally productive Harold Lloyd, the third most popular screen comedian and gaining fast on both Chaplin and Arbuckle, put his tortoise-shell-rimmed "glass" character on view in thirty-three shorts.[37] By comparison with his rivals, the creator of *Sunnyside* seemed paralyzed.

The picture's two dream sequences revealed the bleak state of his mind about his private life. Charlie is a man-of-all-work for a hotelkeeper-*cum*-farmer in the village of Sunnyside. One of the farmer's unruly cows, on whose back the lazy Charlie has been riding, bucks him off, and in hitting the ground he is knocked unconscious. In the dream sequence that follows, he awakens to find himself being cooed over by four woodland nymphs, bare-armed, flimsily dressed in costumes recalling ancient Greece, and gloriously young. Their graceful poses and swirlings about entice him into dancing with them. After rearranging his hair in Pan-like horns, he and the maidens prance about an Arcadian clearing with suggestively erotic abandon. Suddenly Charlie trips and falls into a bed of cactus and his buttocks are punctured by needles. The pain goads him into dancing at an ever more furious pace. His earlier rapture has been lost, however, and the dream inexorably fades away. On one level, this scene constituted a burlesque homage to "the mystic world" of Nijinsky's *L'Après-midi d'un Faune*, which the great dancer had conjured up in front of Chaplin's ravished eyes at a performance in Los Angeles in the spring of 1917.[38] On another, less pleasant level, the scene enabled a self-pitying prisoner of sex to act out his initial excitement in becoming involved with a baby doll and the painful disillusionment he had subsequently suffered.

The second dream sequence is not identified as such until the end of the picture. Only then does it become apparent that, during an episode in which a handsome, urbane, obviously wealthy young man is involved in an automobile accident outside Sunnyside's only hotel and is carried inside, Charlie had sat down in the lobby and dozed off. In his dream, his courtship of the prettiest girl in the village, played by Edna Purviance, cannot compete with the romantic finesse of the stranger. In a last-ditch attempt to win Edna back, Charlie does his best to emulate the sartorial splendor of his affluent rival by pulling a pair of old socks over his shoes as makeshift spats. But when he calls on Edna at her home, one of the socks unravels and he is humiliated. In despair at having lost Edna's love, he deliberately walks into the path of an on-rushing automobile. A close-up shot shows him bracing himself for the crash that will end his life. In the next shot, he is being shaken out of a sound sleep by his highly annoyed employer. In the world of reality he discovers that the stranger has no interest whatsoever in Edna. As the picture ends, she and Charlie are reunited.

Marital bitterness and fears about his creative faculties had finally driven Chaplin into acting out, through his tramp counterpart, a suicide attempt. Two events thereafter, one of them involving the death of a comic idea and the other the death of someone he expected to love, made life even more difficult for him. On May 23 he had hurled himself into a new picture, provisionally entitled *Charlie's Picnic*. It was no accident that the story centered on the trials and tribulations encountered by Charlie and his wife and five small children on an outing in the country. For as the end of Mildred's pregnancy approached, Chaplin had begun spinning out fantasies of what it would be like to be a parent. The fantasies, unfortunately, were not very funny, as he despairingly sensed. In mid-June, therefore, he quietly buried his hopes for *Charlie's Picnic* and paid off the child actors he had hired. At the end of the month, he abruptly changed his mind, called the actors back to the set, and ordered Totheroh to start shooting. But this desperate effort to revive the dead picture lasted less than a week.[39]

Norman Spencer Chaplin was born on July 7. Three days later, he died. On the afternoon of the 11th, the remains were buried in Inglewood Cemetery under a gravestone inscribed with Mildred's pet name for the pitifully malformed infant, "The Little Mouse." Chaplin subsequently told a friend that even though his son had never smiled, the undertaker had manipulated his facial expression into a ghastly grin.[40]

According to Sydney Chaplin, the loss of the boy plunged his brother into a "terrible depression."[41] Only work promised relief from it. The assignment the comedian set himself began with the surprising decision to make a feature-length film. In 1914 *Tillie's Punctured Romance* had been a Mack Sennett project; only in the abortive *Life* in 1915 had Chaplin himself undertaken a picture of that amplitude. Shorter inspirations, it seemed, better suited him. But just as novels generally earned their authors more money than short stories, so the really big profits in the movie business were being raked in by the makers of full-length pictures. For Chaplin, the gamble was worth the imaginative and financial risks. Only three weeks after burying his son, he started filming a six-reel picture called *The Waif*—in time, the title would be changed to *The Kid*—about Charlie's discovery in a slum alley of an abandoned baby, whom he decides to raise.

Happenstance also figured in his stunning recovery of creative power. "After *Sunnyside* I was at my wits' end for an idea," Chaplin would recall in *My Autobiography*. "It was a relief in this state of despair to go to the Orpheum for distraction." One of the acts featured an eccentric dancer, who was "nothing extraordinary." But at the end of his performance, the dancer brought out his four-year-old son and namesake and shared the applause with him. After bowing to the audience, the boy broke into an amusing dance step. Shooting a knowing look across the footlights as he finished it, he waved his hand and ran off the stage. Prolonged applause compelled him to return. This time, he did a quite different dance. Like everyone in the audience, Chaplin found the boy unusually engaging. Indeed, his recollection of him was so like his fanciful accounts of his own debut at Aldershot as to leave no doubt that Chaplin identified with young Jackie Coogan.[42]

A few days after the visit to the Orpheum, someone at the Chaplin Studio called the comedian's attention to a report in the morning paper that Jackie Coogan had just been signed to a film contract by Fatty Arbuckle. Suddenly Chaplin realized that the boy was a natural for the movies. As he was kicking himself for not having thought of hiring him, ideas for scenes with the boy kept popping into his mind. For the rest of the day and well into the evening, he could think of nothing but the possibilities of a comedy involving Jackie. Someone finally suggested that he should try to find another boy, but Chaplin disconsolately shook his head. It was Jackie he wanted. And when Chaplin's publicity man, Carlyle Robinson, called Arbuckle's office and found that Fatty had actually signed the boy's father, Jack Coogan, Sr., it was young Jackie whom Chaplin got. ("Why, of course you can have the little punk," said Jack Sr. when Chaplin asked him if he would allow his boy to work for him.[43])

Production of *The Kid* began on July 21 and for two months it moved forward at quite a fast clip, in part because movie acting came so easily to Jackie, as Chaplin would graciously acknowledge in *My Autobiography*. "There were a few basic rules to learn in pantomime and Jackie very soon mastered them. He could apply emotion to the action and action to the emotion, and could repeat it time and again without losing the effect of spontaneity."[44]

8

Not counting *The Bond*, the ten-minute propaganda film he had turned out for the Liberty Bond campaign, and an even briefer film for charity made in collaboration with the great Scottish star of British music halls, Harry Lauder, Chaplin entered the fall of 1919 having finished only three pictures since joining forces with First National. The officers of the company were unhappy about this, and it distressed them still further to learn that the temperamental comedian could give them no idea when he expected to complete *The Kid*. In response to their pleas for a product to supply to exhibitors, Chaplin put *The Kid* on hold in early October and produced a quickie two-reeler called *A Day's*

Pleasure. Like the abandoned *Charlie's Picnic*, it dealt with a family out-ing. The bulk of the picture was shot in seven days on an excursion steamer in San Pedro harbor and focused on jokes about collapsing deck chairs and various cases of seasickness (including the curious case of a black trombonist who turns white from feeling green). While editing this footage, Chaplin added leftover material from *Charlie's Picnic* deal-ing with the difficulties of starting and steering a Ford car. On October 19, he threw this bone in front of First National's ravenous officers and went back to work on *The Kid.* While his eagerness to finish it was evident in the hours he put in, he would not succeed in doing so for another nine months, in all probability because of the emotional cost of deep delvings into his past.

9

He and Mildred—and Mildred's mother—were now living in a house on South Oxford Drive in Beverly Hills. But the sad fact was that they seldom saw one another. Cut to the quick by his contempt for her, Mildred paid him back with studied neglect. After a long day at the studio, Chaplin would come home to find the dinner table laid for one and would eat alone. Every now and then, Mildred went off on weeklong trips with her mother, leaving no indication that she had gone other than the open door of her empty bedroom.[45] When she was in town, she usually spent her weekends with her friends Lillian and Doro-thy Gish, while Chaplin hung out with Douglas Fairbanks.[46]

These were the harvest days, too, as Max Eastman phrased it, of the friendship that he and Chaplin had formed the previous winter.[47] East-man had returned to Hollywood at the end of September to be with the aspiring stage and screen actress Florence Deshon, who had recently signed a contract with Samuel Goldwyn. A wayward-spirited, sculptur-esquely beautiful young woman, Florence had first caught Eastman's eye at the *Masses* ball in Greenwich Village three years before.[48] Flor-ence "could be like a little girl, and was so always toward my superior knowledge," Eastman would later write. Yet she possessed more poise and self-confidence than he did (or so he thought), and he periodically suspected that she was drifting away from him. As for his commitment to her, it was constrained by his self-centeredness, as he himself recog-nized. Even though he was enthralled by her, there were times when he thought about other women and still others when he actively preferred to be alone.[49]

In Hollywood the lovers found an apartment on De Longpre Avenue, just across from an expanse of meadow, for the movie capital still possessed many open spaces. Once they were settled, Eastman called on Chaplin at his studio and took Florence with him, surmising that her beauty would ensure that her welcome was no less cordial than his. When Chaplin greeted them both as though they were intimate friends whom he had been aching to see, Eastman thought it was a reflection of the lonesomeness of his life as Mildred's husband.[50] In the weeks that followed, Eastman and Florence both felt that they became Chaplin's intimates, although Eastman also realized that this warm and friendly man "carried a remoteness within him, however close he came to you."[51]

On his way back to New York in late November, Eastman stopped off in San Francisco to make the acquaintance of a young woman whose poems he had been publishing in *The Liberator*—and ended up going to bed with her. He feared Florence would take another lover herself but was not sure, and he felt unable to ask her because of the agreement about mutual independence they had reached before his departure.[52] Yet he could not help noticing in his perusal of her letters that while she had numerous male friends in Hollywood—Theodore Dreiser, for instance, who later created around her image his memorable portrait of the "sensuously and disturbingly beautiful and magnetic" Ernestine De Jongh in *A Gallery of Women* (1929)—the only man she mentioned being with was Chaplin:

Charlie is always very sweet to me.

I dined with Charlie on Christmas Eve, and he gave me a Christmas present.

Charlie speaks of going away, but it all depends on this picture [*The Kid*] and at the rate he is working, he will never finish it. I know I am naughty, but I become tired of Charlie's matrimonial troubles. He stays in that frightful situation at his home, and his powerlessness to move wears me out.[53]

Not until Florence went east in August 1920 would Eastman learn the story of her involvement with Chaplin. Following his departure from Los Angeles, Chaplin had started going around to her apartment every day after work to spend the evening with her, and eventually the night as well. While he succeeded in seducing her, there had been no arrogance in his courtship, Florence assured Eastman; in fact, Charlie used to tell her, she said, that he had sneaked in where a better man belonged.[54]

As soon as Chaplin moved out of the house he shared with Mildred and returned to the Los Angeles Athletic Club, every gossip in Hollywood began talking about his romance with Florence, with the result that she attracted the interest of more movie producers than she ever had before. Thus when Goldwyn informed her, after holding her for six months in salaried idleness, that he wished to break her contract, she promptly received three offers at twice the Goldwyn salary.[55] The same phenomenon had occurred in Mildred Harris's career. Once she was able to add Chaplin to her professional name, Louis B. Mayer signed her up with the expectation of building her into a major star. But after she filed for divorce on March 17, 1920, on the grounds of desertion (later changed to cruelty), it became clear to Mayer that the pictures in which he was planning to star her were not likely to become big successes.*

This realization did nothing to improve the truculent producer's mood a month later when he looked across the Hotel Alexandria dining room and saw that Chaplin and a group of friends were among the other diners. In his frustration, Mayer sent a note to Chaplin's table, rebuking him for his treatment of Mildred. Outraged by his cutting words, Chaplin sent him a rejoinder in kind, and when the note did not seem to bother Mayer, he walked over to his table. Mayer arose and Chaplin hit him, with little effect. Before getting into the movie business as a theater owner in Haverhill, Massachusetts, Mayer had owned a junkyard and had handled a lot of heavy metal. So powerful was the

---

*One of these pictures, *The Woman in His House*, was the story of an anguished young mother (played by Harris) whose child's life is threatened by poliomyelitis. Apparently it was designed to evoke moviegoers' memories of the death of the baby born to Harris and Chaplin in July 1919.

punch he packed that in a fight one night he had fractured his opponent's skull. When Chaplin was foolish enough to take him on, Mayer
decked him with a single blow.[56] The newspaper accounts of the incident
were even more painful for the bruised comedian. For, like the stories
that had reported Mildred's charges of cruelty, they created an impression of him as a hothead who could not control himself.

To Florence he voiced a dream of getting out of town. As she duly
reported to Eastman,

> Charlie is all excited about buying a yacht. He said, "Let's you and Max
> and Elmer [the young playwright Elmer Rice] and I go off together." I
> said we would make movies in all the countries we touched, and he is
> enthusiastic about your acting in them. Well, we had a wonderful time.
> Anyhow as soon as he finishes the picture he asked me if I wouldn't take
> a trip in his car. We all had the wanderlust very strongly and were flying
> all over the world. . . .[57]

Production of *The Kid* came to an end on July 30. At Chaplin's invitation, Florence attended a screening of the picture, and even though she
had not been feeling well for quite a few weeks for some mysterious
reason, she was tremendously enthusiastic about it, as she indicated in a
letter to Eastman: "Beloved, Charlie came to dinner last night and I
gave him your book. He was happy to get it. I saw his picture *The Kid*
in the projection room. It is wonderful, wonderful. I cried and laughed
and smiled and worried. It was the most exciting thing I ever saw."[58]

The task of editing *The Kid* remained. But Chaplin feared that if he
undertook it at the studio, First National's lawyers would join forces
with Mildred's in a legal attempt to attach the negative, along with all
the rest of his business assets. He was involved in a dispute with both
parties. On the one hand, Mildred had suddenly rejected the grudging
divorce settlement of $100,000 that she had previously agreed to accept.
On the other, the officers of First National were defending their belief
that they were obligated to fork over no more than $405,000 for the
picture, whereas Chaplin contended that they owed him considerably
more. He had already invested $500,000 of his own money, he pointed
out, as well as a year of intensely demanding work. In order to thwart
the legal moves he was sure were in the offing, he and Rollie Totheroh

and Alf Reeves sneaked out of town aboard a train bound for Salt Lake City; in the baggage car were the cans containing the negative of *The Kid.*[59]

It was a sign of his passion for Florence as well as of his concern about the state of her health that Chaplin invited her to meet him in Utah and accompany him and his associates eastward. Perhaps when they got to New York she could find a more enlightening physician than the baffled internist she had consulted in Los Angeles. Upon arriving in Salt Lake City, Reeves and Totheroh had the cans of film transported to a hotel room, where Chaplin began cutting and splicing. Once the 400,000 feet of raw film had been shaped into a picture of 5,300 feet, Reeves arranged for a preview performance at a local movie house. The audience's overwhelmingly favorable reaction helped to damp down Chaplin's high anxiety. With the edited negative in hand, the four travelers headed for New York. Additional editing tasks were carried out in a vacant movie studio in Fort Lee, New Jersey.

The ailing Florence joined Eastman at his country place in Croton-on-Hudson. She had a fever, he realized as they embraced, so without delay he phoned his friend, Dr. Herman Lorber, who took care of most of the intellectual and artistic rebels of Greenwich Village, and arranged for an appointment the following morning, August 21. "You came just in time," Lorber told Eastman after examining her. "Only an immediate operation can save her from a blood-poisoning that might be fatal. I wonder what kind of a doctor she had out there [in Los Angeles]." Since Eastman seemed not to grasp the import of what he was saying, Lorber made his diagnosis specific: "Florence has been pregnant for three months and the fetus is dead. I don't know how long ago it died, but any delay might be fatal." Left unstated was the fact that the child she had been carrying must have been Chaplin's.[60]

She underwent an operation that afternoon and spent the next several days convalescing in Croton, although she recovered so quickly, Eastman recalled, that his nursing of her amounted almost to nothing. When she felt well enough, she took the train down to New York to be with Chaplin. A period now ensued in which this lovely young woman, in Eastman's words, "commuted between two lovers." Neither man was jealous, or so Eastman would claim, for each of them had a sense of humor and an ironic awareness of the vagaries of human experience. As for their opinion of Florence, "We both admired her extravagantly. There was something royal in her nature that gave her the right to have things as she pleased."[61]

Chaplin came to Croton once and took a room at a fashionable road-house on the Albany Post Road. Florence spent many hours with him there, but could not persuade him to accompany her to Eastman's house. Four decades later, Eastman called on Chaplin at his estate in Switzerland and inquired whether he would mind his telling about their dual attachment to Florence in a memoir he was writing. "You ought to see what I'm telling here!" Chaplin answered, holding up the manuscript of his autobiography. "Florence was a noble girl!" he added. But *My Autobiography* would, in fact, contain no mention of her.[62]

In the same month that Florence was operated on, Mildred Harris finally acceded to Chaplin's settlement terms and promised in addition that she would not attempt to prevent his marketing of *The Kid*. Once this agreement was signed, divorce proceedings commenced. Within a few months, Chaplin assured Florence, he would be a free man. Nevertheless, when it came time for her to choose between going back to the West Coast with him or staying on with Eastman, she chose the latter course, much to Chaplin's distress. At the end of her last day in his company in New York, she took a late train back to Croton and he saw her off at the station. If the story that Florence told Eastman was accurate, Chaplin said, "Don't mind these tears. I'll be all right." In Eastman's opinion, Florence meant more to Chaplin than any young woman he was ever involved with, except Oona O'Neill.[63]

In choosing Eastman, Florence had temporarily forgotten how much she hated the supremely high value he placed on being independent. Throughout the first thirty days of her sole devotion to him, her outbursts of rage against his withdrawnness were by her own admission "absolutely insane." Finally they agreed that only by parting could they bring to an end the destructive warfare that their love entailed. And so, on the sixth of October, she took the train back to Hollywood.[64]

In trying to revive the career that her *Jules et Jim* love affair had interrupted, Florence discovered that it was not her talent or her beauty that the movie moguls had valued, but the glamour deriving from her liaison with the world's most famous man. As her stock declined on the Hollywood exchange, she turned to Chaplin for comfort—and found him friendly but impersonal. While waiting for his divorce to become final in November, he was amusing himself with another young actress, May Collins. A rather desperate sonnet that Florence composed and mailed off to Eastman, expressing a yearning to recapture the "summer days" of their first perfect union, brought him to her side in January 1921. Although he resisted her proposal that he move into her apartment, they saw each other constantly. Through the good offices of Chaplin's factotum, Tom Harrington, Florence bought a new Buick at a bargain price, and she and Eastman took many long drives together, a particular favorite being the drive to Santa Monica through orange and avocado groves and black-earth vegetable gardens. Punctuating these moments of exaltation, however, were tigerlike quarrels, the basic significance of which Eastman did not comprehend until much later. In her certainty that she did not wish to marry him, Florence was deceiving herself. Eastman's leave of absence from his editorial duties expired in June and he returned to New York alone. His romance with Florence appeared to have ended.[65]

Within the month, renewed correspondence brought their relationship back from the dead. Indeed, it achieved a considerable warmth, until Florence suddenly denounced him for his neurotic selfishness and declared that she would neither write him again nor read any letters he might send to her.[66]

At the time she wrote, she was acting with the Pasadena Playhouse, her movie career having ended. In the autumn of 1921, she arrived in New York, hoping to find a part in a Broadway play. Eastman sent a copy of his book *The Sense of Humor*, which he had dedicated to her, to her room at the Algonquin Hotel. The thank-you note he received opened the way to their becoming friends again. To save money—for she was still unemployed—she left the Algonquin in December and took a one-room apartment on West Eleventh Street in Greenwich Village. Two months later, she turned on the gas in her room and lay down to die. Another tenant in the building smelled the fumes and forced open the locked door of the apartment. When he saw her lying unconscious on the bed, he phoned the emergency room at St. Vincent's Hospital.

Eastman arrived at the hospital and was told that she was dying, but that it was just possible that a blood transfusion would save her. Because his blood type was the same as hers, he became the donor. While lying on a white table beside her, with his blood mingling with hers, he could hear her raucous and ragged breathing, as her body struggled to get air. Yet he was sure that in spite of her body's effort, her will to die would triumph, and it did. She was twenty-six. Eastman would recapitulate the circumstances of her suicide in *Love and Revolution* (1964), and Chaplin, too, would hark back to them—although he made the outcome a happy one—in the scene in *Limelight* in which the tortured young ballerina, Terry, turns on the gas in her London flat, but is saved from death by another tenant in the building, the aging and drunken Calvero.[67]

10

The agreement that Chaplin's persistence and the response of preview audiences to *The Kid* finally forced out of First National called for an advance of $1.5 million.[68] To the further disappointment of the prophets of his decline and fall—of whom the most outspoken was the reviewer for *Theater Review*, who had confidently predicted in 1919 that "in the natural course of events, the Chaplin vogue in five years will be a thing of remote antiquity"—*The Kid* racked up record receipts in America from the moment of its opening in New York on January 6, 1921. Between 1921 and 1924, its reception in fifty other countries around the world was no less remarkable.[69]

In a magazine piece in 1922, Thomas Burke described Chaplin as a man who works in a fury, as though "seeking distraction or respite from his troubled inner life."[70] But if his work on *The Kid* was a distraction for him, it is also true that the picture was forged in the crucible of his inner life. In its comedy, its melodrama, and its pathos, *The Kid* is a fantasy-charged essay in his own personal history.

In the first minute of the story, it becomes apparent that a young woman has given birth to a baby out of wedlock. This projection of Chaplin's longtime anxiety about the circumstances of his own birth is accompanied, however, by an insistence on the moral immaculateness of the mother. Not even D. W. Griffith's film version of that notorious Victorian tearjerker *Way Down East* (1920) applies a heavier sugar coating to the image of a fallen woman than does the opening sequence in *The Kid*. "A picture with a smile—and perhaps a tear," the first title card announces. Next we see the mother, played by a quite matronly looking Edna Purviance (whose battle with weight problems had not been helped by her growing dependence on finding happiness in alcohol), being let out of the prisonlike gate of a charity hospital with a newborn in her arms. "The woman—whose sin was motherhood," the second card declares, just before a frozen image of Christ carrying the Cross appears on the screen as a symbol of the woman's purity and martyrdom.

The father of her child, a handsome artist, is depicted next, taking his pipe-smoking ease in a romantically bohemian studio. As he steps back to admire one of his paintings, he knocks a photograph of Edna from its propped-up position on the mantelpiece and it falls into the fire. When he finally notices what has happened, he retrieves the photo. But it is somewhat scorched, and after debating with himself for a moment or two, he throws it back in the flames. That Edna has borne his child means nothing to him. For Chaplin, such cool indifference was analogous to Charles Senior's shirking of parental responsibility—and to the failure of any other man in his mother's life to own up to being his father. Seven years after *The Kid*, he would again reveal his raw feelings on this score in the wake of an encounter with an old man who was looking for his son. "What is it, fatherly love?" the comedian bitterly remarked to the writer Konrad Bercovici. "No father of mine has been looking for me so assiduously."[71]

The sentimentalization of the mother resumes. On her pathetic wanderings, babe in arms, she passes a church and pauses to watch a wedding party coming out. The bride is in the bloom of youth but sad-looking, while the elderly groom seems full of himself; when a flower falls from her bouquet, he heedlessly crushes it beneath his foot. The camera cuts back to the forlorn Edna. From behind her, the light reflected in one of the church's stained-glass windows creates the illusion of a halo around her head.

This additional bit of sainted-martyr symbolism was necessary, Chaplin may have felt, in order to inoculate audiences against the moral horror of the mother's next act, which is to abandon her baby. An unlocked limousine parked in front of the perfectly manicured lawn of a large house (in what is quite undisguisedly an affluent neighborhood in southern California) gives her the opportunity. After scribbling a note, "Please love and care for this child," she deposits the baby in the backseat and hurries away. Scarcely is she out of sight when two thieves appear and speed off in the car, past a row of palm trees. While taking a breather in a dismal slum alley sometime later, they are startled to hear a baby cry. After deciding against killing their unwanted passenger, they leave him beside a trash can and drive on.

As the picture gradually makes clear from this point, the baby has been dumped in what seems like a London slum, where coin deposits are required for gas usage and some of the humblest dwellings have courtyards (albeit the policemen aren't bobbies). From the other end of the dismal alley, Charlie ambles into view, picking his way past accumulations of trash and dodging others that are being hurled from windows on high. With all the aplomb of a Mayfair swell, he stops for a moment to remove his fingerless gloves and select a butt from a lozenge tin with a neat-fitting lid. (Lozenge-tin-as-cigarette-case is the first of the beguiling transposition jokes that are one of the charms of *The Kid*.) In an instinctive reaction to his first sight of the baby, Charlie glances at the windows above the spot where the baby is lying, as though trying to determine from which of them he has been tossed (transposition joke number two: baby-as-trash). Compassion prompts him to pick up the baby—to his immediate regret. After frantic efforts to pass on his embarrassing burden to a witch of a woman pushing a baby buggy and a gaga old man have ended in failure, he sits down on a curbstone and is briefly tempted by the thought of pushing the baby into the sewer beneath his feet. Not until he discovers the mother's scribbled plea for someone to love and care for the child does he decide to assume the responsibility himself.

In his garret home, the look of which calls to mind the description in *My Autobiography* of Hannah and Charlie's little room at 3 Pownall Terrace, Charlie in effect becomes a mother. The baby sleeps in a hammock of Charlie's devising and sucks milk from a coffee pot that has been ingeniously fitted with a nipple. To amuse the little fellow, Charlie makes funny faces at him and pats his bottom, until he realizes that his hand is getting damp. In the hope of avoiding further accidents of this nature, he hastily makes diapers out of pieces of cloth and—in anticipation of the toilet training to come—manufactures a potty chair by cutting out a portion of the wicker bottom of a chair and placing the chair above a cuspidor.

Five years elapse. Jackie Coogan is discovered by the camera sitting on a curbstone cleaning and buffing his nails and critically admiring them. Like all of Jackie's imitations of famous Charlie-isms, this one lights up the screen with its gesture-perfect accuracy. Little Jackie was indeed a gifted mime. All he lacked was dramatic experience, so on long walks with him through orange groves as well as on more formal occasions on the set, Chaplin patiently schooled him in the art of conveying the abrupt shifts in mood that his role demanded. In keeping with his usual directorial practice, the "Master" taught by example. Thus in the scene in which the Kid starts to throw a stone at a window but does not follow through, because in bringing his hand back in a windup he feels the presence of a policeman who has stolen up behind him, Chaplin instructed his pupil to watch how he himself would express surprise and embarrassment. When he was finished, Jackie took over and acted out the scene three or four times. "[It] was one of Jackie's best," Chaplin recalled, and "one of the high spots of the picture."[72]*

The at-home relationship of Charlie and the Kid has the mother-and-child quality of the earlier scene with the baby. With brusque but loving efficiency, Charlie examines the Kid's ears and hair to see if they are free of dirt and lice and teaches him how to eat his food with a knife; and when the Kid gives him a quick kiss on the cheek, he responds in a flustered, quite feminine way. Through the looking-glass of this interplay, Chaplin was surely glancing back to his own childhood.

Even in the late years at Pownall Terrace there had been days when Hannah had been bright and cheerful and she had made that "miserable garret glow with golden comfort," as Chaplin would recall in *My Autobiography*. "Especially on a wintry Sunday morning when she would give me my breakfast in bed and I would awaken to a tidy little room with a small fire glowing and see the steaming kettle on the hob and a haddock or a bloater by the fender being kept kept warm while she made toast

---

* With the release of *The Kid*, Jackie became an overnight sensation, and his father immediately formed Jackie Coogan Productions. In the course of the next four years, the boy played starring roles in nine pictures, including the title roles in *Peck's Bad Boy* and *Oliver Twist*, and earned upwards of $2 million. Thereafter, his popularity declined precipitously. Not until the television era did Coogan again acquire instantaneous recognizability in American households—as the overweight, bald-headed Uncle Fester in *The Addams Family*.

... [and] I read my weekly comic."[73] This memory, too, is acted out in
The Kid, although it was typical of Chaplin's imagination that he reversed the positions in it of the parent and the child. While Charlie
lingers in the bed that he and the Kid share, smoking a cigarette, reading
a newspaper, and stretching luxuriously, diminutive Jackie is busy at the
stove preparing pancakes for their breakfast.

Outside the confines of the garret, the dealings between Charlie and
the Kid are established in father-and-son terms. Thus when the Kid
becomes embroiled in a street fight with a somewhat older boy, Charlie
takes him aside in between rounds, as it were, and shows him how to
feint and jab. A more elaborately developed petty-crime caper is likewise
built upon a father/son collaboration. As soon as the Kid, working under
Charlie's instructions, has deliberately broken a window in someone's
home by throwing a stone through it, Charlie—a glazier by trade—
happens by with a pane of glass on his back and offers to fix the window,
for a fee. One morning a policeman becomes suspicious of Jackie's
stone-throwing propensities and decides to follow him. When the policeman comes upon Charlie as he is completing a repair job, he is all
but convinced that he has uncovered a conspiracy. As Charlie is has-
tening away from the vicinity of the policeman, Jackie scoots up to him
and tries to take his hand. In an effort to prevent the policeman from
putting two and two together, Charlie keeps shooing Jackie away with
covertly delivered kicks. Chaplin as a child had been denied the companionship and the guidance of a father. In *The Kid*, paternal denial is
turned into an endearing joke.

While the Kid has been growing up, Edna, his real mother, has
achieved worldly success as an opera star. To assuage her guilt about
giving up her child, she also devotes considerable time to charity work
in the slums. One day she encounters the Kid in an alley. He has fallen
ill with fever and is barely conscious. She sends for a doctor and promises to return at a later date to find out how he is faring. The doctor
who examines the boy sternly quizzes Charlie about their relationship.
Charlie not only confesses that he is not the father, but hands the
doctor the note he had found on the baby five years before. The doctor
thereupon informs the appropriate public authorities and an orphan-
asylum truck is dispatched to Charlie's address.

The forcible restraint of the struggling Charlie by a policeman and the driver of the truck, the brutal dumping of the screaming Kid in the open back of the vehicle, and the imploring, desperate way in which the Kid stretches out his arms, first to the pompous official who is in charge of his removal and then to the heavens above, are heartrending. As for the succeeding rescue scene, it is far more modest in scale than what D. W. Griffith was capable of in this genre (in, for instance, the ride-to-the-rescue by the mounted cavalry of the Ku Klux Klan in *The Birth of a Nation*), but it is thrilling all the same. After a daring rooftop pursuit of the speeding truck, Charlie catches up with it, scares off the driver, and recovers the Kid. With tears streaming down his face, he clutches the boy to him, covering his face and mouth with kisses. Through the conversion into melodramatic action of anguishing memories of being separated from his mother and of ecstatic memories of London reunions with her, Chaplin attained a pitch of emotional intensity in these back-to-back scenes that would be outrivaled in his later feature pictures only by the ending of *City Lights*.

The reunion of Charlie and the Kid does not last the night. The doctor has passed on the note in the mother's handwriting to the very person who will recognize it: Edna. Aware at last that the Kid is her own child, she posts a reward for his return to her. The proprietor of the flophouse in which Charlie and the Kid seek refuge reads the reward notice and spirits the boy away while he and Charlie are sleeping. At the police station, mother and child embrace, and she carries him off. Charlie, meantime, has discovered the Kid's absence from their flop-house bed and has spent the rest of the night wandering through the streets searching for him. Overcome by exhaustion and grief, he finally sinks down on the front steps of the building where he lives and falls asleep. Sometime later, he is awakened by a policeman and escorted to a waiting limousine. At the door of a suburban mansion (once again, the setting of the picture has become Californian), he is greeted warmly by the Kid and his mother. The front door closes behind him and the picture ends. The camera does not reveal even the look on his face at the sight of the interior and, presumably, the prospect of a prosperous new life.

There was a very considerable comic potential, of course, in the idea of a down-and-outer being welcomed into the home of a wealthy patron and then repaying hospitality with rip-offs. But the presentation of that kind of comedy was out of the question here. Like certain heroes of American fiction in the 1920s—like Jake Barnes and Gatsby, for instance—the hero of *The Kid* is a faithful, suffering figure. In 1932, however, the rip-off idea would finally be explored—by a Chaplin admirer. Jean Renoir's *Boudu Sauvé des Eaux (Boudu Saved from Drowning)* is the story of a tramp, played by the celebrated French actor Michel Simon, who is saved from an attempt to drown himself and is taken home by a prosperous Parisian bookseller. Far from being grateful to his benefactor, Boudu proves to be an irascible and abrasive guest. Furthermore, he seduces the bookseller's wife and proposes marriage to the maid, with whom the bookseller has been accustomed to sleeping. When Boudu wins a fortune in a lottery, he is tempted to shed his rags and turn respectable. But in the end he renounces his bourgeois dreams and returns to tramping—a free soul once more.*

* Paul Mazursky's *Down and Out in Beverly Hills* (1986) is essentially a remake of Renoir's picture.

8

"STICK TO ME! FOR GOD'S SAKE, STICK TO ME!"

With Pola Negri in Berlin, 1921.

T H E responsibility for hiring several children to appear as street urchins in *The Kid* fell to Chaplin's assistant, Chuck Riesner. One of Riesner's first recruits was a big-boned girl of twelve whose remarkably Nabokovesque name, Lillita McMurray, reflected her partly Scottish, partly Mexican heritage. Even though Lita, as she was usually called, was only moderately attractive, she immediately caught Chaplin's roving eye, while the fact that she had grown up without a father and was looking, however unconsciously, for a replacement figure to revere made his quick capture of her youthful heart all the easier. Four and a half decades later, a chronic need for money, a wish to publicize a nightclub act she was trying to get together, and an indignation born of the insultingly brief reference to her in *My Autobiography* that did not even mention her by name spurred Lita Chaplin to start shopping for a publisher for the story she had to tell.

Bernard Geis Associates was a high-roller company, much given to aggressive promotions of exposé books. *Sex and the Single Girl*, *Valley of the Dolls*, and a roman-à-clef novel about Frank Sinatra called *The King* paid off handsomely for the company either just before or just after Lita Chaplin signed on. An intelligent and experienced editor, Don Preston, and a well-known ghostwriter, Morton Cooper, whom Preston respected for his ability to listen, his worldly understanding, and his writing skills, took on the task of turning the wandering memories of a recovered alcoholic into a coherent manuscript.

Neither man had any faith in Lita's insistence that for quite some time she managed to keep her mother in the dark about her intimacies with Chaplin when she was fifteen; to the contrary, they were of the opinion that her mother had encouraged the liaison right from the start. Nevertheless, they had to accept Lita's word in this matter in order to get her name on the book. Another fault in *My Life with Chaplin* (1966) is that the conversations are much too detailed to be fully believable and consequently must be handled judiciously.[1]

During the first few days that the gawky twelve-year-old and her twice-divorced mother spent at the Chaplin Studio, its busy chieftain seemed to be unaware of her existence, even though he directed a scene in which she and the other urchins figured. She was therefore very surprised one morning to hear him speak to an illustrator about painting a likeness of her in what he called an "Age of Innocence" pose. His next step, some days later, was to take her by the arm and escort her to his dressing room, where Toraichi Kono was waiting to assist him in putting on his tramp costume. As soon as he had seated her in a chair beside his dressing table, he pulled out the painting that the illustrator had dashed off and demanded to know whether she liked it. When she said that it made her better looking than she really was, he retorted that she was talking nonsense. The painting was a delight, he said. Not only had the illustrator given her a perfect "Age of Innocence" expression, but he had caught what Chaplin called "the elusive quality in your eyes." "Elusive?" Lita asked. Her puzzlement merely caused him to press his contention more strongly. "I've been peeking at you, my dear, when you haven't been looking. I've been more and more drawn to those fascinating eyes of yours."

With this confession, Chaplin swung around in his chair and began applying his tramp makeup, a task that now included darkening the streak of premature gray in his hair. While staring at his reflection in the dressing-table mirror, he urged Lita to tell him whether she had ever thought about pursuing a movie career. When she said that she wasn't sure that she had the talent for it, he again swept her modesty aside and asked if she would like to take a screen test. Suddenly there was a sharp knock on the door. Kono answered it and admitted Lita's mother. She had been looking everywhere for her daughter, she angrily asserted. A deep frown creased Chaplin's brow as he let her know that he did not appreciate her accusatory attitude. "I am not in the habit," he icily huffed, "of seducing twelve-year-old girls."[2]

Lita left the dressing room convinced that she would be dismissed before the day was over. But that afternoon, Chaplin summoned the studio hairdresser and instructed her to arrange Lita's hair so that she looked eighteen. After a similar instruction was given to the makeup department, a screen test was scheduled for her. The high heels she was forced to wear caused her to lose her balance so many times that she was sure she had failed the test. Chaplin, however, was jubilant about the results and turned to Rollie Totheroh for a confirmation of his opinion. Instead of giving it to him, the cameraman shot back a taunting question: "So now you've got the test, what're you gonna do with it?"

Chaplin left the studio for the weekend a few hours later and remained away through the following Monday. On the morning of his return, he announced to his staff that he had drawn up a plan for an addition to the movie in the form of a dream sequence, which he intended to interpolate into Charlie's exhausted snooze following his fruitless, nightlong search for the Kid. Looking straight at Lita, he then went on to say that the dream sequence would contain an important part for her and that he intended to terminate her status as a temporary employee and sign her to a one-year contract. To everyone's surprise (and disapproval, in all probability), he also installed her in Edna Purviance's dressing room.[3]

As the dream sequence begins, Charlie awakens to an astonishing sight. The walls and gateway of the drab courtyard outside his home have been transformed by garlands of flowers into a corner of heaven. A party with free food and drink is going on and music fills the air. All of Charlie's old neighbors are on hand, wearing clothes of paradisiacal white and pairs of wings. The Kid appears, grinning shyly. Charlie embraces him and admires his wings. After being outfitted with a pair himself, he takes a practice flight around the courtyard. Heaven, in short, suits Charlie just fine—until erotic temptation leads to disaster.

"Sin creeps in," a prefatory title card announces. A devil with a pitchfork slips past the watchman at the courtyard gate. Immediately thereafter, a saucy-faced angel with carefully coifed hair and painted lips—*i.e.*, Lita—flits into view and is welcomed with a kiss by her boyfriend, a hugely muscled young tough (Chuck Riesner) with whom Charlie had come to blows at an earlier point in the picture. Following the devil's instruction to "vamp him," the angel starts flirting with Charlie. "Innocence" is the sarcastic comment inscribed on another title card. By hiking up the hem on one side of her skirt, the angel arouses Charlie's admiration of her ankle, but as soon as she sees that he has become interested in her, she darts out of sight around the corner. A moment later, she reappears, raises her leg straight out from her body, and in a blatantly inviting way wiggles her ankle at Charlie. Although she darts away again, Charlie catches her without too much trouble and kisses her. Her muscular boyfriend rejoins her and she greets him with a lover's kiss—but keeps Charlie on the hook by winking at him.

As a result of the jealousy she has stimulated in both her admirers, they trade vicious punches. A winged policeman breaks up the fight and starts to arrest Charlie for disturbing the peace. But before he can haul him in, Charlie flaps his wings and soars into the air. The policeman takes out his pistol and fires a shot at the fugitive. Charlie plummets to the ground in front of the steps of his home. The policeman roughly turns his motionless body around. As the dream ends and Charlie's conscious life resumes, the same policeman (sans wings) is trying to arouse him by shaking his shoulder.

Beginning with his commissioning of the "Age of Innocence" painting, Chaplin had done his best to draw Lita into the web of his power. Yet in the utterly bizarre fantasy that he insisted on interpolating into his story about a tramp and a boy, he proposed that angelic Lita was a creature of the devil and that he was doomed to fall victim to her wiles, even as he had to Mildred Harris's. What he dramatized was a prophetic fear.

After completing *The Kid*, Chaplin did not see Lita again until after his tearful breakup in New York with his and Max Eastman's girlfriend-in-common, Florence Deshon, and the commencement of his affair with actress May Collins. During one of the talks he had with Lita at the studio in the late fall, he asked her out, in effect. He wanted her, he breathed, to come to a party he was holding at his house on Friday night in honor of a dear friend of his, Miss Collins. Lita told him that she would love to come but would have to ask her mother's permission. Chaplin seemed annoyed. Couldn't she, he irritably asked, sneak away for a few hours without being missed? Before she could answer, her mother appeared out of nowhere. According to *My Life with Chaplin*, her blazing words left no doubt that she had grasped the gist of what Chaplin had been saying and that she was furious. My daughter, she cried, will be doing homework on Friday night and on every other night for a long time to come.

Lita's book further alleges that Chaplin reacted angrily, and that she expected once again to be fired forthwith. But once again he surprised her. Not only was she kept on, but at the end of January 1921, she and her mother were both assigned bit parts in a Chaplin two-reeler called *The Idle Class*. The following summer, however, her one-year contract was not renewed. As she left the studio on her final day, she had the awful feeling that she had seen Mr. Chaplin—as she still called him—for the last time. Two and a half years would pass before she took steps to prove herself wrong.[4]

2

As of January 1, 1921, Chaplin still owed First National three pieces of work, and the New Year's wish of Mary Pickford, Douglas Fairbanks, and D. W. Griffith was that in the coming year he would show a little of the productive speed of his Keystone days. Two years earlier, in January 1919, the four of them had formed a company, United Artists, under whose auspices they planned to distribute their own independently produced pictures. The plan was a great idea, marred only by the fact that Chaplin could not begin to release his accomplishments through the company until he had fulfilled the terms of his contract with First National.

The thought of joining forces with his fellow luminaries had first entered his mind when Oscar Price, the press agent for the Secretary of the Treasury, William Gibbs McAdoo, put a question to him during the Fairbanks-Pickford-Chaplin Liberty Bond tour in the spring of 1918. "Why don't you folks get together and distribute your own pictures?" Price had asked. "You are big enough to do that."[5] Nine months later, a disturbing experience at a convention of First National exhibitors at the Alexandria Hotel in Los Angeles caused Chaplin to think harder about Price's remark. In a personal appearance before the exhibitors' governing board, he had urged First National to give him larger advances, so that he could further upgrade the quality of the work he was doing. The members of the board had rejected his appeal with an abruptness that was almost rude. It was as though they had forgotten that *Shoulder Arms* and *A Dog's Life* had filled the coffers of First National exhibitors in every section of the country.

Chaplin was angered and mystified by the board's action. The next day he learned that Douglas Fairbanks and Mary Pickford were similarly at a loss to explain recent developments in their own careers. Zukor's Famous Players–Lasky and First National had displayed a strange lack of interest in renewing their respective contracts. To find out whether some sort of plot against them was afoot, Fairbanks proposed to Chaplin that the two of them hire a private detective. The clever young woman whom they engaged spent the next couple of evenings in the company of a lecherous conventioneer whom she had contrived to pick up in the lobby of the Alexandria. Perhaps because he wished to appear important in her eyes, the delegate told her he knew for sure that the rumors involving First National and Adolph Zukor's sprawling empire were true: a merger of powerhouse production companies was in the works, and along with it the hookup of a superb network of premier exhibition outlets.[6]

In the view of many movie industry moguls, the only cloud on the golden horizon of the postwar dawn was rising production costs. Audiences had developed an overwhelming preference for feature-length pictures, which meant that producers had to spend more money on the purchase of the movie rights to plays and novels, as well as on bigger staffs, more expensive sets, and more lavish costumes. The costs that

bothered the moguls the most, however, were the salaries of their famous employees. Beginning the task of lowering their levels of remu-
neration would require an awesome concentration of managerial muscle
—which the prospective alliance between Zukor and First National
would manifestly possess. It was a widespread front-office presumption
that the alliance's inevitable triumphs over overcompensated actors and
directors* would set a beneficial precedent for the entire industry.[7]

First National's rebuff of Chaplin's budget request and the absence of
renewal offers for Fairbanks and Pickford were portents, the three stars
concluded, of much graver developments ahead. The time had come for
taking personal charge of their destinies. On January 15, 1919, the three
of them appeared at a press conference, along with two other Hollywood giants, D. W. Griffith and stone-faced cowboy star William S.
Hart, to announce their plans for United Artists. The corporation
would function as the distributor of their films. As far as production
was concerned, each of them would be his own employer and his own
financier.

At the heart of the organizers' formal statement lay an attack on the
moguls' block-booking practices.

> We believe [United Artists] is necessary to protect the exhibitor and the
> industry itself, [and will enable] the exhibitor to book only pictures he
> wishes to play and not . . . other programs which he does not desire. . . .
> We also think that this step is positively and absolutely necessary to
> protect the great motion picture public from threatening combinations
> and trusts that would force upon them mediocre productions and ma-
> chine-made entertainment."[8]

Behind this idealistic rhetoric lay a self-serving calculation. If the
U.A. partners could uncouple the pictures they expected to make from
the block-booking system, if their pictures could be marketed, that
is, on an individual basis, rather than as the lead items on locked-in,

---

* Like the moguls themselves, the top performers and directors lived "like potentates,"
Adolphe Menjou observed upon his arrival in Hollywood in 1921. "Unless a person
earned $1000 a week he was a mendicant. If he didn't have a swimming pool, three
saddle horses, four servants, and an Isotta-Franchini town car, he was a peasant."
Adolphe Menjou and M. M. Musselman, *It Took Nine Tailors* (New York, 1948), p. 85.

qualitatively uneven lists, then they could compel the exhibitors to pay sky-high prices for them.[9]

The agreement that was drawn up and signed three weeks later called for each of the four principals—Bill Hart had quit the group by then—to subscribe to $100,000 of common stock. To keep the ownership from passing into other investors' hands, the company was given the right to repurchase any holdings that came up for sale. A further stipulation called for each principal to deliver nine pictures to the company, and as a guarantee that the company would indeed have pictures to distribute, the shares of each owner were divided into ninths and placed in escrow. Every time one of them submitted a picture for distribution, one-ninth of his stock was released to him.[10]

With the filing of incorporation papers in Delaware on April 17, United Artists was in business. But three and a half years would elapse before Chaplin finally became an active partner. The first of the three pictures that he still owed First National went into production on January 29, 1921. Although the picture was less than two thousand feet long, he kept tinkering with it until nearly the end of June. For all the time spent on it, *The Idle Class* turned out to be a mediocre imitation of the classic Mutual shorts. Its most interesting feature is Chaplin's dual appearance in the lookalike roles of a tramp and a wealthy fop. In *The Great Dictator* (1940), his abiding interest in doubleness would again take this form. On August 6, he started shooting another two-reeler, only to abandon it a day or so later and shut down the studio. For weeks, he had been "feeling very tired, weak and depressed," and the "specter of a nervous breakdown" appeared ready to pounce. The arrival of a cablegram announcing that *The Kid* was about to have its premiere in Britain precipitated his decision. He would devote the bulk of the extended vacation he clearly needed to a visit to the land of his birth.[11]

3

On the train between Los Angeles and Chicago, Chaplin played cards with his traveling companions, Carlyle Robinson and Tom Harrington. After an overnight stop at the Blackstone Hotel and a pleasant chat with Carl Sandburg, he proceeded on to New York. The crowd on hand at

Grand Central tore at his clothes and might have done him bodily harm had not Douglas Fairbanks showed up to run interference for him. At his hotel, he faced the onslaught of another crowd, as well as the shouted questions of the gentlemen of the press, who wanted to know if he was a Bolshevik. "I am an artist," Chaplin evasively replied. "I am interested in life. Bolshevism is a new phase of life. I must be interested in it."

His gallant friend Doug and wife Mary joined him in his suite. They were in town for the premiere of one of Fairbanks's most engaging pictures, *The Three Musketeers*, and much against his will, Chaplin agreed to attend the premiere. Upon arriving at the theater, he was approached by a woman with a pair of scissors. She cut a piece of material from the seat of his trousers, while another fan started pulling on his tie. In the next few minutes, he lost his collar and the buttons on his vest and someone scratched his face. Policemen intervened at this point. Grabbing him by the shoulders and ankles, they lifted him above the crowd and carried him through the lobby. In the Fairbankses' box, Mary added insult to injury by criticizing his tattered appearance in the steely-polite tones with which he was becoming familiar in their business dealings.[12]

His other experiences in New York were more rewarding. He had lunch one day with Max Eastman and went to a party that night at his house, where he met all sorts of interesting people, all of whom were eager to talk with him. This was not surprising. Chaplin had not only reached new heights of prodigious fame with *The Kid*, but he had the gift, Eastman later remarked, "of admiring others, and the rarer gift of listening to them with vivid and prolonged interest." Furthermore, said Eastman, his "endless . . . and fertile interest in thinking" was genuine. "He never had any schoolroom discipline to speak of, and he read a big book like Spengler's *Decline of the West*, for instance, by a hop-skip-and-jump process that [was] remote from scholarship. But he [made] no bluff to the contrary, not with me at least."[13]

Several of his initial contacts with Greenwich Village intellectuals had occurred when he had been in New York the year before. On a visit to the editorial offices of *Vanity Fair* to have a photograph made, he had showed the magazine's young managing editor and premier essayist, Edmund Wilson, how to perform the trick of pulling his derby down on his head and having it pop up into the air. Although it was clear that Chaplin liked doing this trick, Wilson was impressed that "he had none of the exhibitionism peculiar to professional clowns. He was good-mannered and perfectly natural." At parties in the Village, he had made the acquaintance of other magazine writers, as well as of a number of painters, sculptors, and theater people, including several members of the Provincetown Players.* In the wake of these encounters, the word spread among the New York intelligentsia that Charlie Chaplin was a delightful man.

On his return to the city in 1921, he solidified this reputation, first of all at Eastman's party, then at a gathering of the Coffee House Club attended by *Vanity Fair* editor Frank Crowninshield, the publisher Condé Nast, and such influential journalists as Heywood Broun and Alexander Woollcott, and finally at a dinner for thirteen that he himself gave. On the last of these occasions, he topped off the evening by joining the actress Georgette Leblanc, who at one time had been married to Maurice Maeterlinck, in a burlesque of the dying scene in *Camille*. Mademoiselle Leblanc coughed, but the gag was that it was Chaplin who contracted the disease, lapsed into convulsions, and died.[14]

Aboard the liner *Olympic*, which left New York for Cherbourg and Southampton on September 3, he again had Carlyle Robinson and Tom Harrington at his beck and call. He spent most of his time, however, with the British-born actor Edward Knoblock. Having also been present at the *Three Musketeers* premiere, Knoblock was aware of Chaplin's exciting effect on crowds. Nevertheless, he was unprepared for the crush of delirious humanity awaiting the comedian's arrival in London.

[The] crowd at Waterloo was a thing not to be believed. Wild as the enthusiasm had been on the first night of *The Musketeers* in New York, it was nothing to the frenzy with which Charlie was greeted by thousands and thousands of his admirers. He himself was completely bewildered. It must have seemed to him like a fantastic dream. . . . He kept turning to me and shouting through the din: "Stick to me! For God's sake, stick to me!"[15]

Once he had settled into a suite at the Ritz, he had a chance to review what he wanted to do. There were two ways in which he could measure

---

* He was not, however, fated to meet his close contemporary and future father-in-law, Eugene O'Neill.

his storybook rise in the world. One was to revisit the haunts of his childhood and the other was to hobnob with the celebrated people who were clamoring to meet him. Neither way seemed to him to be dispensable.

Exiting through the service doors of the Ritz to avoid his fans out front, he taxied across the Thames and spent an entire day on his own in South London. Among the places he sought out was the Canterbury Music Hall, where for the first time he had laid eyes on Charles Senior, prancing about the stage. He also inspected the church in the Westminster Bridge Road in which Hannah had worshipped and the barbershop in Chester Street that had taken him on as a lather boy, and walked around Kennington Cross, where a clarinetist's rendition of "The Honeysuckle and the Bee" had opened his soul to music. Accompanied by Carlyle Robinson and three other movieland friends and acquaintances, of whom the most prominent was the Scottish-born actor Donald Crisp,* he paid a second visit to South London late one night. To the astonishment of his entourage, he proceeded to interrupt the sleep of the widow who now lived in the garret at 3 Pownall Terrace. "I should like to sleep here again for a night," he informed her. "It's not like your hotel," the widow parried. "Never mind about my hotel," Chaplin replied. "This is my old room and I am much more interested in that than my hotel."[16] Clearly he was just joking about staying there, but his strained jocularity suggests that his mood was not really light. It was as if he were fighting off upsetting memories.

He conspicuously did not inquire about the current addresses of any of the neighborhood lads he had known in yesteryear. On the other hand, he spoke eagerly of his wish to see his first love, Hetty Kelly— until Hetty's brother, Arthur "Sonny" Kelly, somberly informed him

---

* In 1921 Crisp was best known for his glowering performance in D. W. Griffith's psychosexual thriller, *Broken Blossoms* (1919), as the Cockney boxer whose incestuous jealousy of his teenage daughter (Lillian Gish) for becoming involved with a young Chinese shopkeeper in London's East End leads him to beat her to death. Griffith based this remarkable movie on the story "The Chink and the Child," in Thomas Burke's *Limehouse Nights* (1917), which Griffith read at Mary Pickford's recommendation. "I read a great story," she told him, when he asked her one day whether she had any story ideas for him, "but it would take a lot of courage to do it." Scott Eyman, *Mary Pickford: America's Sweetheart* (New York, 1990), p. 130.

that Hetty had died in the flu epidemic of 1918.* Thus his only confrontation with a female acquaintance from his past occurred by accident as he was walking the streets of Lambeth. A narrow-chested, white-faced woman came up to him and said that as a girl she had worked in a lodging house in which he and his mother had lived. Chaplin remembered her—and remembered, too, that she had gotten pregnant and had left the lodging house in disgrace. He also had an interesting encounter one night with three young prostitutes, as he was walking back to the Ritz. They hailed him and his male companions with a familiar "Hello, boys," but as soon as they recognized who he was, they became quite respectful and called him "Mr. Chaplin." One of them said that she had loved him in *Shoulder Arms* and another, who had just seen *The Kid*, confessed that it had made her cry.[17]

From the thousands of invitations he received, his secretary, Tom Harrington, selected those that he thought looked interesting and Chaplin then decided which ones to accept. But whenever it suited him to shun human contact, he cavalierly broke appointments he had agreed to, despite Knoblock's warnings that his countrymen did not take kindly to such fickleness. Here in England, Knoblock later wrote, "where the whole social system is run on punctuality and a sense of obligation to others, his neglect of all such rules caused offence. I fear he hurt himself a great deal with many of his greatest admirers by turning up late when he was expected, or at times not even turning up at all." Yet whenever he did appear, Knoblock conceded, he triumphed.[18] At a reception in his honor at the Garrick Club, for instance, E. V. Lucas, Sir James Barrie, and other literary and theatrical figures hung on his every word and lavished compliments upon his pictures, although the author of *Peter Pan* opined that the dream sequence in *The Kid* had been entirely unnecessary. In a further demonstration of Barrie's lack of understanding of Chaplin, he wondered why the mother in the picture had been given such a prominent role.

The first of the comedian's several encounters with H. G. Wells— during one of which he also met Wells's lively, liquid-eyed mistress,

---

* "Sonny" Kelly, a onetime music hall performer, was now a movie company executive. In time, he became a vice president of United Artists, thanks to Chaplin's confidence in his acumen.

Rebecca West*—took place at the premiere of a British filmmaker's adaptation of Wells's novel *Kipps*. During the dinner that Wells hosted after the show, he and Chaplin talked about Russia. Wells had recently been there and had interviewed Lenin. In an article about his visit, he had taken a middle position between the propaganda of Communist apologists in the West and the rigorous anti-Communism of Winston Churchill and other mainstream politicians, but his temperance had only earned him wholesale abuse. The apologists were infuriated by his contention that the new regime was on the verge of collapse, while the anti-Communists could not abide his insistence that he had also seen signs of vitality in the nation and that the power of Lenin's personality could not be discounted.[19] In the face of Wells's omniscient air, Chaplin was mainly content to ask questions of his host. A decade later, he would be much more outspoken about his political and economic opinions.[20]

At yet another London party in honor of the native son's return, a group of his new friends announced that someday soon they hoped to take a walk with him through the Limehouse district and that they had asked the author of *Limehouse Nights* to act as guide. To their surprise, he resented their plan and refused to go along with it. As he heatedly explained to Carlyle Robinson, Thomas Burke was the one writer "who sees London through the same kind of glasses as myself," and he wanted to be by himself when he met with him. Upon phoning Burke, which he did immediately, Robinson found him more than willing to meet with Chaplin at his home that evening.[21]

Chaplin's awareness of the "elemental lusts, passions and emotions" in Burke's stories led him to assume that the author must be built like a heavyweight boxer. He was therefore slightly startled to be greeted in the front parlor by a little man with a thin, peaked face and sensitive features. As Burke resumed his seat beside the fireplace, in which a lump of coal was burning, he motioned to Chaplin to sit down as well. The author's taciturnity, and his long looks into the fire, as though he were too shy to look at his guest, had the effect on Chaplin of making him feel socially obligated. It was up to him, he felt, to take charge of the conversation. Only later did he wonder whether the author's reticence

---

* West's verdict on Chaplin at this time was that he was "a darling . . . a very serious little Cockney" with "a serious little soul." Victoria Glendinning, *Rebecca West: A Life* (London, 1987), p. 94.

had been a clever trick for getting him to open up. In any event, he started talking, and went right on doing so as they left the house on a prodigious five-hour ramble through the misty streets and squares and alleyways of Stepney, Highgate, Spitalfields, and other purlieus. From this workout Chaplin learned a lot about London that he hadn't known before—while Burke assembled out of Chaplin's torrential unburdenings of himself a fund of psychological insights, on which he would eventually base the perspicacious assessments he would later make about him.[22]

On that first visit, Burke would recall a decade later, Chaplin at times affected the sad remoteness of a Byronic hero; if he was the friend of millions, he was also the loneliest man in the world. But on his next trip to England, in 1931, it suited his fancy to play the sadistic prankster. "Tyl Eulenspiegel himself," said Burke, "never achieved so superb a prank as Charles did when he set the whole Mayfair mob struggling for invitations to his *City Lights* supper party, and made them give him all the amusement that his films gave them." That he really did not care for the socialites whose hospitality he avidly accepted and whose famous names he loved to drop was an illustration, too, of Burke's judgment that Chaplin was "not much interested in people, either individually, or as humanity. The spectacle of life amuses or disturbs him. There is nothing, I think, that he deeply cares about." All sparkle and mettle he may seem, "but catch him in repose, and you will catch a drawn, weary mouth and those eyes of steel."

The conclusion that Chaplin "has found nothing in life to hold on to" obviously saddened Burke. Yet he also wondered whether the comedian's personal confusions did not bear a relation to the fantastic popularity of his pictures. They might explain, Burke tentatively proposed, why Chaplin, alone of all film actors, "has made a conquest of all the peoples of the world—because he is, like so many obscure millions, still the pilgrim; still looking for something and not knowing what it is."[23]

4

Paris was the next stop on the traveler's itinerary. In the course of a week, pursuing photographers recorded his get-togethers with the heavyweight boxer Georges Carpentier, the visiting Lady Astor, the caricaturist Cami, and other celebrities. But it was the lunch he had one day with a lesser-known American who was just his age that led to his most memorable experiences in the French capital.

As one of the editors, in 1917, of the brilliant but short-lived *Seven Arts* magazine, and as the author, in 1919, of a manifesto of artistic rebellion entitled *Our America*, Waldo Frank had vigorously promoted the idea that a revitalized American culture, breaking free at long last from the suffocating grip of the genteel tradition, was in the early stages of a remarkable revival in literature and the arts. Edgar Lee Masters, Theodore Dreiser, Robert Frost, H. L. Mencken, Sherwood Anderson, and Van Wyck Brooks headed the list of writers whom Frank had hailed. Moving beyond traditional definitions of culture, he had also made room in *Our America* for praise of Chaplin. "Our most significant and most authentic dramatic figure," he had called him, "our sweetest play-boy, our classic clown, [and] sprite of our buried loves."[24] Even though Frank had added that "there are sophistications in [the comedian's] work that are not healthy," his comments thrilled Chaplin. An authentic highbrow had taken his work seriously. "Naturally, we became very good friends," he said later.[25]

Over lunch they talked at length, and the next morning at the crack of dawn they started talking again while sitting on a bench on the Champs-Élysées and watching the produce wagons go by on their way to market. One evening, Frank and Chaplin had dinner with Jacques Copeau, the director of the Théâtre du Vieux Colombier and an editor as well of the *Nouvelle Revue Française*. Ever since its founding in 1909, the *NRF* had opened its pages to new French writers. In so doing, the review had inspired Frank's dream of what the *Seven Arts* might do for American letters. Copeau had three tickets in his pocket for the Cirque Médrano, where the fabulously talented Fratellini brothers were currently cavorting in the sawdust. Without any difficulty, he persuaded Frank and Chaplin to come along with him. During the first intermission, Copeau guided his guests to the Fratellinis' dressing room. The eyes of both brothers filled with tears and their hands trembled as Copeau introduced them to Chaplin, and since they could not speak English, they simply hugged him.

During the last part of the Fratellinis' act, the audience finally realized that Chaplin was in the stands. As soon as the Fratellinis had finished, Frank recalled four years later in a *New Yorker* profile, a high-tiered human monster, suddenly shouting *Charlot!* with a thousand throats, avalanched down upon a single spot of the arena rail, where a little man in a dapper dining coat sat blinking. . . . A score of gendarmes broke into the delirious maze of men and women, pressing on Chaplin as if they were hungry to devour him. The police . . . formed a phalanx about him and he was shuffled out into the Place Pigalle.

But the cry *Charlot!* had got there first. The square, the boulevards that lead to it, turned into a magnetized mob; thousands came pouring, pushing, shouting. Men touched him; women tried to kiss him. At last, with his London-tailored garments reduced to the state of a rummage sale in the Bronx, Charlie was swept into a strategic taxi. And as the car maneuvered him into a side street and the voice of Paris shouting *Charlot!* had dimmed, he shook himself; he smoothed his hat; and he said:

"It's *all—nothing!* It's all a joke! It can all be *explained*, I tell you. It's all —nothing."[26]

Later that night, after Chaplin had changed his ruined clothes, Copeau escorted him and Frank to the large back room in the Brasserie Lipp in Saint-Germain-des-Prés, where a number of the *NRF*'s stellar contributors and all the leading performers of the Théâtre du Vieux Colombier, from Louis Jouvet and Charles Dullin on down, were waiting to meet him. In Frank's opinion, the attitude of these writers and actors was more understandingly reverential than any of the homages accorded Chaplin in either England or America. Only in a few of the writers—for instance, Jules Romains—did Frank sense a hypocrisy that masked an envy of a creative genius whose public was so much greater than their own.[27]

At one point in the evening, Frank decided in retrospect, Chaplin, too, had been guilty of hypocrisy. When he had dismissed the frenzied scene in the Place Pigalle as meaningless, he had sounded utterly sincere. But unlike Burke, Frank came to believe that Chaplin cared with a passion about the adulation of the mob. Take away his magical popularity, dim it even for an hour, and "Charlie's latent melancholy flames into hysteric rage." At breakfast with him one morning in 1923 in a Greenwich Village "box," Frank was stunned by his reaction when the waiters and other guests failed to recognize him. He was fretful at first and then furious. "I'm going home," he finally exclaimed. "Do you want a taxi?" Frank asked. "One taxi?" Chaplin cried. "Call me twelve! I'll go

home in twelve taxis. The first I'll ride in. The others will be my escort."
Suddenly, he burst out laughing.[28]

5

When Chaplin and Carlyle Robinson walked into the Palais Heinroth, the smartest nightclub in Berlin, and asked for a table, the manager
shrugged his shoulders and announced that he could seat them only in
the obscurest part of the room. His indifference bore out Robinson's
warning to Chaplin during their train ride from Paris that because his
pictures were only now being shown in Germany, he was not universally
known there. Chaplin suggested in his chronicle *My Trip Abroad* (1922)
that he would have left the Palais Heinroth without further ado had not
Albert Kaufman, the jovial German representative for Famous Players–
Lasky, come up to him. Slapping Chaplin on the back, Kaufman said,
"Come over to our table. Pola Negri wants to meet you."[29] In the
memoirs she published in 1970, Negri told a different story.

Earlier that evening, the imperious, Polish-born beauty had attended
the premiere of her latest German film, *Madame Du Barry*, directed by
Ernst Lubitsch and also starring the great Emil Jannings, at the newly
opened UFA Palace, the largest motion picture theater in Europe. At
the conclusion of the picture, the four thousand men and women in the
audience had given Lubitsch and his two stars a standing ovation that
went on endlessly. UFA officials then staged a huge party of celebration
at the Palais Heinroth. As Negri entered the club, she received a tumultuous welcome,

> and a little man with a sad sensitive face fought his way up to our table.
> Were it not for his odd appearance, so dapper and so pathetic, I would
> not have noticed him. He had such a strange physiognomy, with tiny
> feet, elegantly encased in black patent leather and gray suede button
> shoes, and an enormous head that made him seem top-heavy. . . . The
> only physically attractive thing about him were his hands, which were
> never without a cigarette.[30]

Because she spoke no more than a few words of English, Negri was
content, she claimed, to let Chaplin monopolize their conversation,
even though her lover of the moment, a tall and handsome German

businessman named Wolfgang Schleber, was annoyed by the comedian's volubility. Yet it was Schleber who inspired Chaplin to say something self-revealing. To the German's question of why he had developed a tramp character, he replied, "Herr Schleber, if I was as tall and handsome as you, there never would have been a tramp. You see, there would have been no need to hide."[31]

6

In the hectic last phase of his vacation, Chaplin kept darting back and forth across the English Channel, mainly by plane. A weekend in the country with H. G. Wells and his family, a garden party at Sir Philip Sassoon's estate in Kent, and a glittering convocation in Paris, at which the French government made him an Officier de l'Instruction Publique, were the occasions that excited him the most, even though the French award was a paltry honor. But finally, celebrity could give him no more, and with the realization that this was so there came an abrupt change in his mood. As he boarded the *Olympic* in Southampton a few days later, he still felt "miserable and depressed."[32]

On deck, a lovely eight-year-old girl with a smile on her lips and a bubbling voice came up to him and made a startling request. She wanted him, she said, to adopt her, "like you did Jackie Coogan." In the way he responded there were elements of a wooing. To avoid being overheard by the reporters who immediately clustered around them, he walked her around the deck, and the more serious she grew, he was pleased to note, the more tender and full of childish love she became. "You must be Spanish," he ventured at last, glancing appreciatively at her dark hair and beautiful profile of the Spanish type. No, she was Jewish, she said. "That accounts for your genius," Chaplin replied. "Oh, do you think Jewish people are clever?" she asked. "Of course," said Chaplin. "All great geniuses had Jewish blood in them." Before she could ask whether he himself was Jewish, he interjected, "No, I am not . . . but I am sure there must be some somewhere in me. I hope so."[33]

As the ship was pulling away from land, the girl's mother came forward and her daughter introduced her "without any embarrassment," Chaplin would assert in the closing pages of *My Trip Abroad*. "Come along, dear," said the mother, "we must go down to the second class. We cannot stay here." But Chaplin was not to be outmaneuvered. Before letting the little girl go, he made an appointment to have lunch with her two days later. During the lunch, "she [had] a great time." She told Chaplin that he simply had to visit her father. "He is so much like me. He has the same temperament, and is such a great daddy." For the rest of the voyage they continued to meet, and for Chaplin these moments with her made the days aboard pass quickly and pleasantly.

On deck on the morning of their landing in New York, his "little friend" was full of excitement as she handed him a present—a silver stamp box. In remembering the scene, Chaplin seemed to think of it as a movie scenario.

> She shakes hands. We are real lovers and must be careful. She tells me not to overwork, "Don't forget to come and see us; you must meet daddy. Good-by Charlie." She curtsies and is gone. I go to my cabin to wait until we can land. There is a tiny knock. She comes in. "Charlie, I couldn't kiss you out there in front of all those people. Good-by, dear. Take care of yourself." This is real love. She kisses my cheek and then runs out on deck.[34]

For this man of many moods, downcast at the end of a triumphant return and beset by anxieties about the changes that the times might soon impose upon his movie future, it had been a relief and a comfort to bask in the attentions of a loving little girl.

7

On the train back to Hollywood, an erstwhile reporter for the *Washington Post* named Monta Bell took copious notes as Chaplin paced back and forth in his Pullman car, pouring out recollections of his trip. Whether Bell eventually burst the bounds of his amanuensis role and actually wrote *My Trip Abroad* is a question that has never been satisfactorily answered. In any event, it did not seem to bother him when only Chaplin's name appeared on the title page, for he had no wish to become known as a ghostwriter. After a two-year stint in the Chaplin Studio as a general assistant, bit-part player, and story editor, Bell went on to become the director of a number of movies in both the silent and the sound eras, of which the most memorable was *Man, Woman and Sin*

(1927), starring the dissolutely beautiful Jeanne Eagels and John Gilbert.*

Chaplin would later convince himself that when he left England he was eager to get back to work. In work there was orientation, and all else was chimerical, he would proclaim in *My Autobiography*. But once he reached home he could not resist the plea of a visiting sculptress, Clare Sheridan, that she be allowed to add him to the list of illustrious men for whom she had made portrait busts. Clare was a tall, attractive blonde, four years older than Chaplin and the widowed mother of a delightful six-year-old boy named Dickie, whom she had brought with her to the Coast. Dickie was a direct descendant, through his late father, of Richard Brinsley Sheridan. Each day, Clare arrived in the forenoon at Chaplin's fantastically designed, pseudo-Moorish rented house on Beechwood Drive and set to work to catch his multitudinous personality in clay. Now and then, they took time out for tea, or for a tune on the piano by Chaplin, or for a breath of air on the sunbathed balcony, where, as she remembered, "Charlie with his wild hair standing on end, and his orange dressing gown dazzling against the walls of his Moorish house, either philosophized or did impersonations."[35] Soon the two of them were spending their evenings together as well, dining and dancing at the Hotel Ambassador, and one fine morning the sculptress and her famous model, plus Dickie, a chauffeur, and a chef, drove up the coast, found a secluded wood of eucalyptus trees within sound of the sea, ordered five tents set up, and settled in for a week of camping.[36]

As a dilettante radical, Chaplin had undoubtedly been thrilled to learn upon being introduced to Clare that she was pro-Bolshevik and had made busts of those awesome giants, Lenin and Trotsky. But the key biographical element in her appeal to him was her lineage. Clare's

---

* The film historian James Card once raised the question of how much influence Bell had in his capacity as story editor on the making of Chaplin's *A Woman of Paris* (1923). For one of the male principals in that picture bears a resemblance to the typical Monta Bell protagonist, as described by Card: "a mother-obsessed misfit, an unadmirable, immature character who invariably brought grief and embarrassment, sometimes tragedy, to any woman foolish enough to allow herself to become involved with him." The most plausible answer to Card's question is that Bell and Chaplin in some respects had kindred imaginations. James Card, *Seductive Cinema: The Art of Silent Film* (New York, 1994), p. 266.

mother had been one of the three celebrated Jerome sisters of New York, all of whom had married into distinguished families in Edwardian Britain and had mothered unusually interesting children. Clare's aunt Jennie was Winston Churchill's mother, and the journalist and writer Shane Leslie was one of the four talented sons of her aunt Leonie. While Chaplin may have secretly disliked many of the upper-class English people whom he knew and may have sought to punish them on occasion, as Thomas Burke suggested, he also poured all of his charm into courting them and was not averse to dropping their names in his autobiography. Thus he found it immensely gratifying to be on intimate terms—precisely how intimate, neither he nor she ever said—with a lady as well connected as Clare Sheridan.

According to her memoir, *Naked Truth* (1928), Chaplin had some bad moments on their camping trip. "I must get back to work, but I don't feel like it," he exclaimed one day. "I don't feel funny. Think—think of it, if I could never be funny again." [37] What he was talking about was his utter lack of interest in finishing *Pay Day*, the picture that he had begun and then abandoned just before his European vacation. After Clare left Hollywood, he ground out another fifteen hundred feet or so of lame jokes about laziness, drunkenness, and the horrors of living with a virago wife and called the results a comedy.

With *The Pilgrim*, in four reels, which he completed in a mere forty-two working days from the time the cameras began to turn on April 10, 1922, he terminated his relationship with First National. His assistant on the picture, the well-read Monta Bell, was partially responsible in all likelihood for its resemblances to the religious masquerade of the King and the Duke in *Huckleberry Finn*, its Menckenesque portrayals of the pomposity of latter-day Puritans, and its Sinclair Lewis-like satirization of a small-town tea party. In a considerable departure from his customary getup, Chaplin milked the humor out of these scenes while dressed in a black suit buttoned up to the collar and a broad-brimmed black hat.

For Pilgrim Charlie is actually a prison escapee who has had to disguise himself in the stolen clothes of a clergyman in order to avoid recapture. A train ride brings him to the dreary town of Dead Man's Gulch near the Mexican border. To his horror, he is forced to deliver a sermon in the local church by a welcoming committee of obtuse parishioners who have taken him for their new minister. As he stands behind the lectern all but paralyzed with fright, his familiarity as a criminal with courts of law and his total ignorance of church practices lead him to think that the singers in the choir must be the members of a jury, and when a deacon (played by Mack Swain) offers him a hymnbook, he raises his right hand as if he were being asked to take an oath. A few seconds later, the bar of justice is transposed into a barroom in his erratic imagination, for as he takes a sip from the glass of water on the lectern he raises his foot as though to rest it on a brass rail. In the scene's most hilarious moment, he devotes his sermon to the story of David and Goliath, which he acts out with music hall éclat. At the conclusion of his performance, a young boy seated in the otherwise stunned congregation gives him a round of applause, to which Charlie responds by taking a couple of curtain calls.

At a tea party after church, Charlie's efforts to live up to the pious requirements of his disguise are taxed beyond endurance by the snotty behavior of the sort of brat who would arouse the ire of W. C. Fields in the marvelous movie comedies he made in the 1930s. At a moment when no one is watching, Charlie takes his revenge on his youthful tormenter with a covertly delivered kick. Ultimately he is identified and arrested, although the sheriff who takes him into custody has no desire to remand him to prison. On a lonely stretch of road, he orders him to walk across the border into Mexico and pick some flowers. His assumption is that Charlie will understand that he is being given an opportunity to escape. But as the sheriff is riding away on his horse, his uncomprehending prisoner comes running after him. The sheriff drags him back to the border and boots him across it. Charlie is immediately pinned down by an exchange of gunfire between rival gangs of bandits. On one side of the border, he faces prison; on the other, the danger of death. In the last glimpse of him, he is walking away in a wide-legged waddle, planting one foot in the United States and the other in Mexico. For a comedian whose mind was divided about so many things, it was the perfect image of his everlasting ambivalence about America. He loved living in the United States, but disdained the thought of becoming a citizen.

8

As a working partner, at last, in United Artists, Chaplin was free to make any sort of picture he wished. His first thought was to retire the tramp temporarily and try something different. In the aftermath of his work on *The Kid*, he had confessed to a *New York Times* interviewer, Benjamin De Casseres, that he was suffering from a "disgust of the character that circumstances . . . forced me to create," and this feeling had persisted.[38] Furthermore, the mind-bending adulation he had received in New York, London, and Paris had tempted him into believing that he was a man of destiny who ought to be searching for grander means of communicating with the world. Pola Negri, who spent many days and nights with Chaplin in the months following her arrival in Hollywood in September 1922, would remember an evening at the Fairbankses' during which the other guests burst out laughing at him, on the mistaken assumption that he must have been joking when he told them that he was thinking of playing Hamlet or Napoleon.[39]* But in the serious drama he began filming in November, he restricted himself to the walk-on part of a railway porter.

The love-triangle situation in *A Woman of Paris* was inspired by Peggy Hopkins Joyce's recollections of her Parisian love affairs, which she passed on to Chaplin during their "bizarre, though brief" romance in the summer of 1922.[40] A former Ziegfeld Follies girl and now a would-be movie star, the flamboyantly bejeweled Peggy had enjoyed liaisons with a great many men since leaving her native Virginia for Chicago in the early days of World War I, as well as the largesse of the five millionaires she had married. (Not for nothing was it believed that the term "gold digger" was coined in her honor, *circa* 1920.) Chaplin found the denouement of the first of her Parisian affairs a fascinating commentary on the violent temper of postwar life. So, unbeknownst to him, had the Paris-based correspondent of a Canadian newspaper. In one of the six concentrated sentences in "Paris 1922" where he sought to distill the experience of five months of residence in the French capital, Ernest Hemingway had recently declared that "I have seen Peggy Joyce at 2 A.M. in a Dancing in the Rue Camartin quarrelling with the shellac haired young Chilean who had manicured finger nails, blew a puff of cigarette smoke into her face, wrote something in a notebook,

---

* Orson Welles would tell a similar story about the effect of Chaplin's solemn-serious grandiosity on Winston Churchill. "Churchill asked him what his next part was going to be, and Chaplin said Jesus Christ. There was a long pause and Churchill said, 'Uh—have you—uh—cleared the rights?' " Orson Welles and Peter Bogdanovich, *This Is Orson Welles* (New York, 1992), p. 137.

and shot himself at 3:30 the same morning."[41] Chaplin's imagination was also stirred by Peggy's account of her involvement with the prominent and wealthy French publisher Henri Letellier, with whose suavity of manner Chaplin was familiar, for Letellier had attended the ceremony at which he had been honored by the French government.

Although the author of *My Autobiography* would not speak of them, other considerations besides the glamorous appeal of Peggy Joyce's anecdotes influenced the making of *A Woman of Paris*. Thus the picture gave Chaplin the chance to take a long look—a long, guilt-stricken, valedictory look—at seven years of association with Edna Purviance. With the completion of the picture, he planned to discard her as his leading lady, and he hoped that her performance would be good enough to launch her on a new career as a serious actress at some other studio. As for the two men in the triangular story, Chaplin regarded them as mirrors in which he could examine his own divided self.

One of the men, Jean Millet, is a young, dedicated, mother-dominated artist of provincial origin; the other, Pierre Revel, is an elegantly tailored, cynically self-indulgent boulevardier. To play Millet, Chaplin made the mistake of picking the lackluster Carl Miller. But his choice of Adolphe Menjou for the role of Revel could hardly have been improved upon. The son of a French-born hotelkeeper in Pittsburgh, the dapper, mustachioed Menjou had established a reputation for sartorial perfection and cynical sophistication in *The Sheik* (1921) with Rudolph Valentino and in *The Eternal Flame* (1922) with Norma Talmadge. But it was his responsiveness to Chaplin's intention to combine the melodramatic plot of *A Woman of Paris* with restrained, subtly nuanced, psychologically suggestive acting that catapulted him to stardom. "Not until we started shooting," the grateful actor remembered,

did I begin to realize that we were making a novel and exciting picture. It was Chaplin's genius that transformed the very ordinary story. Aside from his own great talent as an actor he had the ability to inspire other actors to perform their best. Within a few days I realized that I was going to learn more about acting from Chaplin than I had ever learned from any director. He had one wonderful, unforgettable line that he kept repeating over and over throughout the picture. "Don't sell it," he would say. "Remember, they're peeking at you." . . . In [other] movies I had been schooled in the exaggerated gestures and reactions that were thought necessary to tell a story in pantomime. But when I, or any other actor, would give out with one of those big takes, Chaplin would just shake his head and say, "They're peeking at you." That did it. I knew that I had just cut myself a large slice of ham and had tossed the scene out of the window.[42]

Ernst Lubitsch, who came to America in 1923, the year in which *A Woman of Paris* was released, claimed the picture's style as a precedent for the laconic touches that would mark all of his Hollywood-made comedies about marital and extramarital tensions.* Chaplin himself would claim that *A Woman of Paris* was "the first of the silent pictures to articulate irony and psychology." While Lubitsch's remarks may have been too generous, given his previous work in Germany, and Chaplin's somewhat exaggerated, the picture did have a major influence on a number of future filmmakers, including the four young men who worked as Chaplin's assistants during the filming: Edward Sutherland, Monta Bell, and a pair of talented Frenchmen, Comte Jean de Limur and Henri d'Abbadie d'Arrast.[43]

When Chaplin asked Edna Purviance to play the part of the "woman of Paris," Marie St. Clair, whose heart is broken by male fickleness, he was really asking her to play herself. The parallels that Edna in all likelihood also saw between Marie and herself began with the fact that Marie had spent her formative years in an obscure French village, even as she had grown up in a lost Nevada town. Because Marie's romance with a local painter, Jean Millet, is being thwarted by parental resistance on both sides, the lovers make plans to elope to Paris. On the appointed evening, Jean fails to appear at the train station at the agreed-on time. In the parlor of his parents' home, his father has suffered a deadly stroke. Instead of fulfilling his promise to Marie, Jean elects to remain with his possessive mother. His inability to break free of her is the first indication of his final fate.

The train arrives at the station. Embittered but undaunted, Marie elects to board it. When the camera finds her again, a year has passed and she is ensconced in a fashionable Paris apartment as the mistress of

* In the first of them, *The Marriage Circle* (1924), Adolphe Menjou would play the most important male part.

Pierre Revel, whose mercenary values and womanizing compulsions mirror Chaplin's voluptuary side.

The problem that Chaplin faced in portraying Marie's illicit relationship with Revel is that Hollywood was currently in the throes of reconstructing its badly damaged moral image. To counteract a succession of public relations disasters, of which the Fatty Arbuckle scandal had been the most horrendous, and to avoid the threat of federal censorship of motion pictures, of which there had recently been talk in Washington, the studios had formed the Motion Picture Producers and Distributors Association (MPPDA) and brought in Will Hays as its president.

Hays was a Presbyterian, an Elk, a Moose, a Rotarian, a Mason, and a political conservative who had served as national chairman of the Republican Party in 1920 and as postmaster general in the Harding administration. In the judgment of the newspaper columnist O. O. McIntyre, he was also a "slicker among the worldly" who could wear "the most meticulously knotted evening tie on Broadway" and yet "outwhittle anyone" in his home town of Sullivan, Indiana. As a front man for a Jewish-dominated industry under attack from an antimovie lobby made up mainly of outraged Protestants (the Women's Christian Temperance Union, the Reverend William H. Short's Motion Picture Research Council, Canon William Shaefe Chase's Federal Motion Picture Council, et al.), Hays was, in sum, ideal.

To the horror of civil libertarians, he immediately established a "morals clause" in Hollywood contracts and urged the studios to tone down their publicity about the high-on-the-hog style of life of the stars. But while he requested that a synopsis of every story that was under consideration for a film be sent to his office so that he could judge its moral suitability, he really had no means of enforcing his cautionary counsels. Essentially, he was a public relations agent and a lobbyist.[44]

Although Chaplin hated Hays,* he knew that his opinions reflected the judgments of mainstream America. Therefore he repeatedly tried to come up with an ingeniously indirect way of making clear that Revel and Marie were living together. His resourcefulness greatly impressed Adolphe Menjou:

---

* In 1922 the sign over the door of the men's toilet at the Chaplin Studio said, "Welcome to Will Hays." FBI report, Charles Chaplin file, August 15, 1922.

Revel came to [Marie's] luxurious apartment and was admitted by a maid. The audience had no idea who or what this man was in her life. Apparently he was just an admirer calling to take her out to dinner. Chaplin wanted to find some casual piece of business that would suddenly reveal that Revel was a frequent and privileged caller. A good many devices were discussed. First Chaplin had me pick up a pipe from the table and light it, but that was no good because Revel was not the pipe-smoking type. Then he considered having the maid bring me a pair of slippers, but that was out of key because I had called to take Marie out to dinner.

Finally Chaplin thought of the handkerchief business, which solved the problem. I went to a liquor cabinet, took out a bottle of sherry and poured a drink, then sipped it. But when I started to take a handkerchief from my pocket I discovered that I had none, so I turned casually and walked into the bedroom. Edna was at her dressing table, fully dressed but still fussing over her coiffure. I didn't look at her and she paid no attention to me as I crossed to a chiffonier. There I opened a top drawer and took out a large gentleman's handkerchief, put it in my pocket, and walked out. Immediately the relationship was established: we were living together and had been for some time.[45]

In 1918, Edna Purviance had had to learn from a newspaper story that Chaplin had married Mildred Harris the day before. No less brutally, the information reaches Marie that Pierre Revel has become engaged to a socially prominent heiress. Two women friends pay a call on Marie, and one of them shows her a magazine in which the engagement is noted. In a subtly staged sequence, Marie glances at the story and tries to conceal her anguish by tossing the magazine aside with a laugh and casually lighting a cigarette. But as soon as her friends take their leave, she agitatedly rereads the story.

By accident, Marie discovers that Jean Millet and his mother have moved to Paris. While Marie is posing for him in his studio, they fall in love again and agree to marry. Revel is amazed. His worldly assumption had been that in spite of his plans to marry for money Marie would continue to be his mistress. Although he tries to convince her that she is making a mistake, she won't listen to him. Other events, however, seem to be conspiring to aid his cause.

"An eternal problem—mother and son," a title card reads. The hysterical reaction of Jean's mother to her son's confession that he has proposed marriage to Marie intimidates him in short order. "All right," he says, "I won't marry her." While posing for Jean, Marie had worn the clothes of a courtesan. But as Eric Bentley emphasized some years ago in an appreciative commentary on *A Woman of Paris*, Jean had depicted her exactly as she had been, clothes and all, in the days of her provincial innocence. By marrying her, said Bentley, he would restore her virginity; otherwise, he fears that by renouncing her he will drive her back to Revel.

In an apparent confirmation of this intuition, Marie accompanies Revel to a cabaret. They are trailed by Jean, and following an inconclusive confrontation with them in the anteroom of the cabaret, Jean shoots himself and falls dead. The nearby statue of a naked woman appears to be mocking his corpse. On hearing the news of her son's death, Jean's mother arms herself with a revolver and swears she will murder Marie. (As Eric Bentley wisely remarked, the appeal of melodrama is wholly to those who can accept it for what it is.) At the last minute, fortunately, the realization that her rival for her son's love is as grief-stricken as she is keeps her from carrying out her revenge.[46]

Another time shift occurs. Jean's mother and Marie have rebuilt their lives by caring for a group of orphans in a country setting (shades of Hanwell!). One day, Revel and a friend of his happen to drive down the same dusty road on which Marie and a little boy are taking a walk behind a slow-moving hay wagon. "By the way," the friend asks, "whatever became of Marie St. Clair?" Revel answers with an indifferent shrug of his shoulders. Neither man recognizes Marie as they sweep past. That she is equally unaware of the identity of the motorists is evident from the unruffled look of contentment on her face. With this prayerful vision of Edna Purviance's future happiness, the screen goes dark.

9

Pola Negri's nine-month-long affair with Sharlie, as she called him, was a comedy of conflicting aims. Chaplin was interested in sexual conquest, as always, but not in marriage, whereas Negri saw herself as the second Mrs. Charles Chaplin. By snagging the most eligible bachelor in the nation as her husband, she would increase her leverage with her new bosses at Paramount. At a press conference that she and Chaplin held at the Del Monte Lodge on January 28, 1923, Negri declared that they were engaged and destined to wed—but as she was speaking, Chaplin's body

English indicated his acute embarrassment. In addition to being extremely skittish about the very idea of marrying again, he was absorbed in the making of *A Woman of Paris* and did not want a big Hollywood wedding and an obligatory honeymoon to interfere with it.

So persistent, however, were Negri's wifely fantasies that she took charge of selecting the sites for tree plantings on the Summit Drive hillside below the Fairbankses' Pickfair estate (and just above Harold Lloyd's), where Chaplin was building a new house. In February a newspaper quoted him as saying that at the moment he was too poor to get married. His outraged inamorata immediately issued a statement to the press in which she dramatically declared that "the happy days are dead for me. It is all over." Although Chaplin at once effected a reunion by claiming he had been misquoted, he continued to elude matrimonial capture. In June Negri appeared at the glittering reopening of the Coconut Grove nightclub in the Hotel Ambassador on the arm of the tennis star Bill Tilden (whose homosexual affairs with young boys were not yet a matter of public knowledge). It was a signal to the press that she had finally had her fill of Sharlie's indecisiveness. "In my opinion Mr. Chaplin should never marry," she subsequently told the *Los Angeles Examiner.* "He has not any quality for matrimony."[47]

10

The New York premiere of *A Woman of Paris* took place at the Lyric Theater on October 1, 1923, and Chaplin was in the audience. Among the critics on hand for the occasion was the aspiring playwright and future author of *Waterloo Bridge* (1930), *The Petrified Forest* (1934), and *Idiot's Delight* (1936), Robert Sherwood, who would assert in his review the next day in the *New York Herald* that "there is more real genius in Charles Chaplin's *A Woman of Paris* than in any picture I have ever seen."[48] After the show, Waldo Frank took Chaplin to dinner in a Greenwich Village restaurant and then guided him by the elbow to a one-room apartment on Grove Street, where they found a young friend of Frank's from Garrettsville, Ohio, in pajamas playing a Victrola. "I opened [the door] and in walked Waldo Frank," Hart Crane wrote to his mother the next day. "Behind him came a most pleasant-looking, twinkling little man in a black derby—'Let me introduce you to Mr. Charles Chaplin,' said Waldo."[49]

Crane was so surprised and excited that "I acted natural," he told his mother. He had seen *The Kid* two years before in Cleveland and loved it. "I must tell you that my greatest dramatic treat . . . was recently enjoyed when Charlie Chaplin's *The Kid* was shown here," he had exclaimed to his closest literary friend Gorham Munson.

> Comedy, I may say, has never reached a higher level in this country before. We have (I cannot be too sure of this for my own satisfaction) in Chaplin a dramatic genius that truly approaches the fabulous sort. I could write pages on the overtones and brilliant subtleties of this picture, for which nobody but Chaplin can be responsible, as he wrote it, directed it,—and I am quite sure had much to do with the settings which are unusually fine.

Crane had enclosed in the letter some lines of a poem, "Chaplinesque," that seeing *The Kid* had inspired him to write. "My poem," he explained to Munson, "is a sympathetic attempt to put in words some of the Chaplin pantomime, so beautiful, and so full of eloquence, and so modern." Before Munson found the time to answer, another letter from Crane arrived.

> Here you are with the rest of the Chaplin poem. I know not if you will like it—but to me it has a real appeal. I have made that "infinitely gentle, infinitely suffering thing" of [T. S.] Eliot's into the symbol of a kitten. I feel that, from my standpoint, the pantomime of Charlie represents fairly well the futile gesture of the poet in U.S.A. today, perhaps elsewhere too. And yet the heart lives on.[50]

Chaplinesque

> We make our meek adjustments,
> Contented with such random consolations
> As the wind deposits
> In slithered and too ample pockets.
>
> For we can still love the world, who find
> A famished kitten on the step, and know
> Recesses for it from the fury of the street,
> Or warm torn elbow coverts. . . .

And yet these fine collapses are not lies
More than the pirouettes of any pliant cane;
Our obsequies are, in a way, no enterprise.
We can evade you, and all else but the heart:
What blame to us if the heart live on.

The game enforces smirks; but we have seen
The moon in lonely alleys make
A grail of laughter of an empty ash can,
And through all sound of gaiety and quest
Have heard a kitten in the wilderness.*

Standing in the doorway of the Grove Street apartment, Frank and Chaplin persuaded Crane to put on his street clothes again. After walking back arm in arm to Frank's apartment, the three men talked nonstop until breakfast time. Crane wrote his mother, "I can't begin to tell you what an evening, night and *morning* it was"—but then proceeded to tell her everything about his new friend.

> Our talk was very intimate—Charlie told us the complete Pola Negri story—which "romance" is now ended. And there were other things about his life, his hopes and spiritual desires which were fine & interesting.... Stories (marvelous ones he knows!) told with such subtle mimicry that you rolled on the floor. Such graceful wit, too—O that man has a mind.... I am very happy in the intense clarity of spirit that a man like Chaplin gives one if he is honest enough to receive it.[51]

* If literary critics have sometimes failed to appreciate the imagistic originality of Crane's poem, it may be because of their unfamiliarity with *The Kid*. See Warner Berthoff's comment in *Hart Crane: A Re-Introduction* (Minneapolis, 1989), p. 10: "My own sense of 'Chaplinesque' is that it has the immediately accessible virtues but also the limitations of the merely occasional poem, the more so as its own particular occasion—Charlie Chaplin's extraordinary film presence—was one already so worked over by media publicity and bathed in clichés of little-guy compensation and release that it held out a special temptation to sentimentalize.... His ... decision ... to round out the poem with a second allusion to the rescued kitten in Chaplin's film *The Kid* seems too patly arrived at, too merely given him by his fashionable subject." But there is no kitten in *The Kid*. As Crane indicated to Munson, the kitten was a symbol, and he alone had thought of the "infinitely gentle, infinitely suffering thing" in that way.

9

"WHY DON'T YOU JUMP?"

Dining on boiled shoe in The Gold Rush *(1925).*

IN 1923 a young office worker in Britain threw over his job after seeing *A Woman of Paris* and went looking for employment in a movie studio. Fifty-seven years later, the superlatively versatile director of *I Know Where I'm Going* (1945), *The Red Shoes* (1948), and *Peeping Tom* (1960) explained why Chaplin's picture had affected him so strongly. "I reckoned," said Michael Powell, "that if . . . film was capable of this sort of subtlety, it was the medium for me."[1] The broad public, on the other hand, did not take to the picture, on either side of the Atlantic. For the first time ever, Chaplin had concocted a flop *d'estime* that failed to recover its production costs. No exhibitor is known to have protested when he quietly withdrew it from circulation.

Moviegoers, in sum, sent him a message—he should stop dabbling in worldly dramas and go back to making pictures about the tramp. But even before the release of *A Woman of Paris*, he had decided to do just that. The feelings of depression, the boredom with comedy, and the disgust with the mask of the tramp that had dogged him ever since the filming of *The Kid* had evaporated. All he needed to get going was a story idea.

He found it at Pickfair in the summer of 1923. One Sunday morning after breakfast, he and Fairbanks idled away an hour looking at stereoscopic slides. The most interesting of them showed a long file of prospectors struggling up the Chilkoot Pass in the Klondike River district of the Yukon; on the back was a caption describing the hardships that these gold-crazed men—and thousands of others like them—had endured in their wild rush into this almost inaccessible region, following the discovery of rich, gold-bearing gravel in Bonanza Creek in 1896. Here was a "wonderful theme" for a movie, Chaplin realized.[2] By the time his preparations for production got under way in December, his imagination had also fastened on an account he had happened to read about the Donner party. This, too, was a story of madness. High in the Sierra Nevadas in the late autumn of 1846, eighty-two California-bound pioneers, under the patriarchal leadership of George Donner, were repeatedly delayed by minor calamities. Wintry storms finally broke upon them, and both of the groups into which the party had divided became imprisoned within walls of snow, some of them as high as thirty feet. Thirty-five men, women, and children died. The remaining forty-seven held on to life by eating their oxen, their dogs, the rawhide in their showshoes, and the flesh and inner organs of fallen companions. Some of those who died went crazy in the course of their ordeal, and a few of the survivors were similarly afflicted.[3]

Out of this gruesome tragedy the mastermind of *The Gold Rush* fashioned two of the most memorable food scenes in movie history. In the first of them, the famished prospector, Big Jim McKay (played by Mack Swain), consumes the entire top side of a boiled shoe that the equally hungry Charlie has prepared and served with cordon-bleu care on carefully wiped plates, leaving the chef to satisfy himself with the spaghetti-like shoelaces and the nails in the sole, which he sucks on as though they were the bones of a juicy capon. Except for a belch or two indicating a mild amount of gastric discomfort, all of Charlie's gestures—from finger wiggles to shoulder hunchings—bespeak his appreciation of the succulence of his cooking. The second scene takes place several food-deprived days later. The transformation of Charlie in Big Jim's hunger-maddened eyes into a toothsomely plump barnyard chicken would have been funny no matter what. But it is Chaplin's uncannily accurate imitation of the leg, wing, and head movements of a chicken that makes Big Jim's hallucination so marvelous.

In all likelihood, two Hollywood sources, Harold Lloyd's *Safety Last* and the flood of gossip about Erich von Stroheim's *Greed*, also had an effect on *The Gold Rush*, although Chaplin never publicly acknowledged either debt. On April Fool's Day of 1923, *Safety Last* began playing to capacity crowds. The experience of witnessing the vertiginous climb of an eager, ambitious, all-American go-getter up the face of a tall building and the awful problem he has in holding on to the minute hand of a huge clock as his weight inexorably pulls the clock face away from the wall was hair-raising, and audiences loved it. Chaplin's all but mandated response to this challenge was a fear-of-falling scene of his own, in which Charlie and Big Jim are confronted with the fact that their cabin refuge has been blown halfway off the edge of a cliff during a violent nocturnal storm.*

When stacked up against Lloyd's technical tricks, in particular his clever use of a concealed platform on the façade of the skyscraper his hero is scaling, Chaplin's reliance on shots of a miniature replica of the cabin seems primitive. The greatness of *The Gold Rush* scene resides first of all in its psychology. Prefatory to a comic treatment of naked fear that almost matches the hilariousness of Lloyd's, Chaplin established a Melvillean sense of disquietude. On awaking the morning after the storm, neither Charlie nor Big Jim is aware of the change in the position of the cabin, and its frosted-over windowpanes keep them from realizing

---

* Lloyd's man on the clock fixed an image in the American mind, and as the 1920s wore on and the Bull Market boomed, it acquired a larger significance. Here was an emblem if ever there was one of the perils of dizzying prosperity.

why it is that whenever they both move to the right side of the room (as viewed from the audience's perspective) the cabin tips downward like the heavy end of a seesaw. Initially, Charlie ascribes the sinking feeling in his stomach to alcoholic indulgence the night before and resolutely tries to ignore it. Furthermore, the cabin floor levels off again when the two men are on opposite sides of the room from each other, or both are on the side underpinned by solid ground, so that a fair amount of time elapses before their fits of alarm coalesce.

To determine the precise extent of the trouble they are in, Charlie finally steps out the door on the overhanging side and instantaneously hurtles downward; only by clinging to the doorknob does he manage to break his fall. Big Jim reaches out to save him, but their combined weight in that far-out position tips the cabin so far over that it begins to slide. Fortunately, an anchor rope gets caught in a rock and holds fast. The cabin is now pitched at a terrible angle, and any sudden movement —even a sneeze—by its occupants causes it to slide a little bit more. After a series of ever more desperate acrobatics, both men manage the perilous ascent to safety just before the cabin plunges into the abyss below.

Safety Last was an example set before Chaplin's eyes. But initially all he knew about von Stroheim's *Greed* came from the talk about it on the Hollywood grapevine. Closely based on Frank Norris's famous novel *McTeague* (1899) and filmed for the most part in three distinctly different locales—the Polk Street district of San Francisco, the area around the historic Big Dipper mine in Placer County, and stretches of baking desert in Death Valley—*Greed* told a relentless, doom-driven tale of gold and madness, and took seven hours to do so. Again and again, movieland conversation kept coming back to that well-nigh incredible statistic. The shooting had taken no more than a reasonable length of time, from March 1923 to the following October. But the length of the picture was utterly unreasonable. Von Stroheim believed that he had created a masterpiece. The betting among the wiseacres, however, was that it would never be released.*

* Eventually, von Stroheim reduced its running time to five hours and proposed that exhibitors show it in two parts, with a light supper served in between. When *Wunderkind* producer Irving Thalberg finally released the picture in December 1924, its running time was two and a half hours.

While piecing together his vision of *The Gold Rush*, Chaplin could easily have gained a sense of *Greed* by glancing through a copy of *McTeague*, for all of the high points of the picture were in the novel: the passion that the brutish "Doc" McTeague conceives for a new patient of his, the lissome Trina, as she lies before him in his dentist's chair; McTeague's loss of his practice, following a tip to San Francisco authorities from an estranged friend, Marcus Schouler, that he is unlicensed; the ex-dentist's degeneration into a shiftless alcoholic, and the refusal of Trina to succor him by dipping into the hoard of $5,000 in gold coins she has won in a lottery; the pathological fondness Trina develops for going to bed with the gold coins spread out on the sheet so that they touch the entire length of her body; the animal fear of her husband's sadistic reprisals that makes sleep impossible for her; McTeague's murder of Trina and his flight with her gold back to Placer County, where in his youth he had worked as a carboy in the Big Dipper mine; his second flight, still carrying the gold, into the pitiless heat and vast vacancy of Death Valley; the fugitive's encounter there with the vengeful Schouler, now a member of the posse that is searching for McTeague; and finally, the hate-maddened struggle between the two men, climaxing in the death of Schouler and McTeague's discovery that in a last convulsive act his antagonist has handcuffed them together.

Toward the end of the filming of *Greed*, von Stroheim explained to a reporter from *Picture Play* that his purpose had been to make the picture "a sinister and lasting triumph of sordid, though intense and magnificent, naturalism."[4] Obsessed by atmospheric authenticity, he had not only shot most of the picture on location, but had insisted on accurate renderings of all the turn-of-the-century details in Norris's novel, from costumes and house furnishings to haircuts. "The screen must be life's mirror," he paused to tell a *New York Times* interviewer in the midst of his Death Valley work, but in recent Hollywood films he had found precious few approximations of this ideal. Among the outstanding examples in his opinion were two comedies, Chaplin's *The Kid* and Harold Lloyd's *Grandma's Boy* (1922). Because they were rooted in settings familiar to their makers, they revealed more about real life than the majority of Hollywood's so-called serious pictures.[5]

The praise that von Stroheim bestowed upon *The Kid*, and his exemplary pursuit of authenticity even into the inferno of Death Valley, may have led Chaplin to film a portion of his own story of gold in the snows of the Sierra Nevadas. Accompanied by Rollie Totheroh, Chuck Riesner, and his set designer, Charles D. Hall, he paid a reconnoitering visit to Truckee, California, in bitterly cold weather in February 1924. Upon his return there in April with a full complement of actors and technicians, the temperatures were still uncomfortably low and a recent blizzard had added a few more inches to the considerable accumulations of snow on the ground. Von Stroheim had had logistical headaches in Death Valley; those in the Sierras required Chaplin (that is to say, Alf Reeves) to bring in a construction gang from Sacramento to break a nine-mile trail through dense woods and snowdrifts to a railroad line.[6] The drafty windows and the shortage of bathrooms in Truckee's only hotel placed an additional strain on the comedian's temper. Nevertheless, these trials were eminently worth enduring. Footage shot in the Sierras enabled Chaplin to endow the opening of *The Gold Rush* with the epical vision of the stereoscopic slide of Chilkoot Pass that had inspired him at Pickfair. After marshaling scores of men into a closely bunched file, he sent them trudging and stumbling up the pass that his construction gang had gouged out of the snow on a mountainside.

The experience of confronting a wilderness may also have inspired Chaplin to make a richly suggestive alteration in the classic British laugh-getter with which he introduced Charlie in the picture. A lone figure, wearing exceedingly baggy trousers and twirling a cane to keep himself company, comes into view, clambering gingerly along a snowy ledge. A bear emerges and begins to follow him. This is a situation, as Edmund Wilson would point out, that derived from an oldtime Christmas pantomime involving a bear and a gaggle of comedians lost in a forest. Eventually the comedians always became aware of the bear and a helter-skelter chase developed. Chaplin opted for a quieter denouement —with ominous overtones. The bear behind Charlie eventually turns off into a cave. "Only then," Wilson would write, "does Charlie think he hears something: he turns around, but there is nothing there. And he sets off again, still fearless, toward the dreadful ordeals that await him."[7]

2

In between searches for gold across trackless white wastes, the fortune hunters of *The Gold Rush* foregather in a combination saloon and dance hall that Chaplin may have modeled on the establishments that he and his girl-hungry companions in the Karno troupe had frequented in wide-open Butte, Montana. Charlie wanders into the two-story-high room and comes to a dead stop on the periphery of the crowded dance floor. Even though in the weeks just past he has experienced blizzards, near-starvation, the mad attacks of Big Jim, and life-threatening encounters with a cold-blooded killer named Black Larson (who himself is killed when a crevasse opens beneath his feet), this convivial social situation daunts him. As he shifts uncertainly about, the camera eye travels through the crowd, picking out interesting faces here and there and finally focusing on a confrontation between a conceited roughneck named Jack and a beautiful dance hall girl. Like the dance costume that Hannah Chaplin had held on to from her music hall days and had liked to wear again while performing in front of little Charlie and Sydney, the dance hall girl's cheap finery is spangled. A vision of the glamour and seductiveness of a sequined dancer had been programmed into Chaplin's sensibility since childhood.

As recently as *The Kid*, a glimmering of Keystone-era lechery had still been evident in Charlie's conduct. While plying his trade as an itinerant glazier, he had put some fast moves on a buxom housewife. In *The Gold Rush*, by contrast, he cannot even bring himself to introduce himself to the dance hall girl, despite being so smitten by her that upon discovering a torn and discarded photograph of her lovely face and figure he pockets it as a keepsake. Not until she beckons him to approach her does he haltingly do so. Haltingly and uncomprehendingly. For even though she and Jack have been having a violent quarrel more or less under Charlie's nose, he fails to appreciate that in summoning him to her side and indicating her wish to dance, she is merely striking back at Jack for his bullying treatment of her. Whereas the Charlie of old had been slyly aware of the foibles of women, the salient fact about the romantic instincts of the hero of *The Gold Rush* is that he is a thoroughgoing naïf. During his first turns around the dance floor with the girl, his eyes are brimming with wonderment. A ragged tramp has somehow attracted the reigning beauty of the house![8] After a few more turns, a look of casual sophistication—through which innocence shines clear—comes over his face, and as he sweeps his partner past a disbelieving miner at the bar, he tips his derby to him. Memorable dance scenes abound in the Chaplin canon; but only the "Emperor of the World" ballet in *The Great Dictator* ranks with this one as a revelation of the character of a human soul.

At the conclusion of the dance, Charlie picks up a flower that has fallen out of the girl's hair and presents it to her with a formal bow. When she rather dramatically hands it back to him, her motivation once again is to make Jack jealous. Innocent Charlie doesn't understand this either. To him, the bruised flower is an emblem of her unhappy state of mind. Someday, he dreams, he will enable her to escape to a better life.

In the scenes involving true love in Chaplin's pictures, as the writer John Peale Bishop would trenchantly observe in the *New Republic* in 1927, "the girls . . . remain remote and mysterious." ("So vague, so preoccupied" were the roughly parallel terms in which Chaplin would describe the Ur-model for all these girls, his schizophrenic mother.[9]) In the dance hall girl's case, remoteness is exemplified by the faraway looks on her face and mysteriousness by the unpredictability of her mood shifts. At times, she leaves no doubt of her profound dissatisfaction with her situation; on other occasions, she seems no less pleased with its superficiality than the other hostesses who are her friends.

One day she and her giggly colleagues are having a snowball fight in the street in front of the cozy cabin that an acquaintance of Charlie's has lent to him. Charlie invites them inside, and the girl of his dreams sits down on his bed. Enshrined beneath his pillow, she discovers, are the bruised flower she had given back to him and the discarded photo of herself. A look of awe washes over her face at the sight of these things, but this flash flood of soft emotion is quickly superseded by a mean playfulness. After making room for him to sit on the bed beside her, she touches his hair and holds his hand, all for the purpose of amusing herself and her friends at his nervously trembling expense. In her soulful good-bye to him at the doorway, however, she seems less certain of how she feels, as she promises to return with her friends to have dinner with him on New Year's Eve. Has she again been touched by the nakedness of his devotion to her, or is she simply carrying her mockery of him to a cruel extreme? Perhaps she herself doesn't know for sure— until she rejoins her friends outside and doubles over with laughter.

In the New Year's Eve scene in the cabin, a spiffed-up Charlie distributes presents around the dinner table, lights the candles, and sits down to wait for the girls, who never arrive. When he finally falls asleep, they

materialize in his dream, laughing and talking in their contentment at
being with him. Just as Chaplin—and his mother before him—liked to
stage performances at home, so Charlie amuses his guests with his version of a famous music hall routine. Performed with bread rolls impaled
upon forks and presided over by his hovering, expressive face, the nifty
footwork of "the dance of the rolls" creates a magical spell.

In the midst of her New Year's Eve reveling, the girl happens to
remember the ridiculous little tramp who had invited her to dinner.
Along with a group of her high-spirited friends, she decides to drop by
his cabin. On arriving, she finds that he is not there, but since the door
is unlocked she glances inside—and sees the place settings and the party
favors still laid out. A pang of conscience punctures the balloon of her
mischievous mood. When Jack, who has accompanied her, asks for a
New Year's kiss, she refuses to cooperate. Jack presses her for it and she
slaps him. Should it be assumed from her anger at Jack that she feels a
seed of guilt about the tramp?

The author of *My Autobiography* affirmed that this was the case. "In
The Gold Rush," he wrote, "the girl's interest in the tramp is started by
her playing a joke on him which later [*i.e.*, on New Year's night] moves
her to pity, which he mistakes for love."[10] But the expression of pity
which he mistakes for love occurs only in the sound-enhanced rerelease
of the picture in 1942.* In the 1925 version, the New Year's night scene
does not contain any indication of regret by the girl for her treatment
of the tramp the night before. That it does not is not surprising. For in
September 1924, when the filming of *The Gold Rush* was still months
away from completion, Chaplin had been compelled to shut down production by the whore—as he called her in raging self-pity—whom he
had cast in the role of the dance hall girl. Again he had been foolish—
and careless—and now she had to be replaced because of her adamant
refusal to get an abortion. The whore had spoiled everything! She had
spoiled the publicity buildup he had given her as his new leading lady.
She had spoiled the scenes he had already shot in which she had figured.
And by threatening to ruin his precariously reestablished personal reputation unless he married her at once, she was blackmailing him. Thus
when he finally was able to resume filming with a new actress in the

---

* The rerelease also features an original musical score and a running commentary by
Chaplin.

role of the dance hall girl, his anger about scheming women kept intruding into his storytelling. In the New Year's night scene, the girl displays not a scintilla of pity about Charlie's wounded feelings. Her sole concern is to renew her affair with oafish Jack.

As the camera picks her up, she is writing a note to Jack, which she dispatches via a waiter to his table in the dance hall. The note says, "I'm sorry for what I did last night. Please forgive me. I love you." From the balcony above the dance floor, she watches Jack react to the note with a contemptuous laugh. She turns away in disappointment. Prankster Jack passes the note on to Charlie. Charlie thinks that the declaration of love is meant for him.* Rushing up to the balcony, he embraces the girl, kisses her hand, and grandiloquently proclaims—in total unawareness of her clearly exhibited physical recoil from him—that he will return very soon and rescue her. But first he must guide his amnesiac friend Big Jim to the vicinity of the "mountain of gold" that Jim had discovered earlier but can no longer locate without Charlie's help. Little does he know that she won't wait for him.

The picture's final sequence takes place on a ship bound for the United States. Charlie and Big Jim are traveling first class and are dressed in the top-hatted style of Wall Street tycoons. Having struck it rich, they are living it up. A newspaper reporter urges Charlie to put on his tramp costume so that a photographer can take some human-interest shots of him. While posing on the deck some minutes later, Charlie falls backwards down a ladder and lands on the third-class deck, more or less at the feet of the dance hall girl. Up to this moment, he had had no idea that she was on board. Two ship's officers assume from Charlie's ragged clothes that he must be the stowaway they have been looking for and collar him. The girl—who is amazed to see him—makes the same assumption and tells the officers that if they let him go she will pay for his passage. With this gesture, which Charlie interprets as another sign that she loves him, his romantic dreams seem at last to have taken over the story. All ambiguities, however, have not been resolved.

The ship's captain shows up, along with the newspaper reporter, and identifies Charlie as a multimillionaire. The reporter asks Charlie about

---

* In 1942 Chaplin cut the girl's love note to Jack and spliced in instead a shot of a note addressed to Charlie: "Please forgive me for not coming to dinner. I'd like to see you and explain."

his relationship with the girl. Charlie whispers that they are going to be married. Never has the girl, however, seemed more remote and mysterious than at this moment. Although she voices no objection to Charlie's statement, she voices no satisfaction in it either, while her face is almost wooden in its lack of any display of emotion. The information that Charlie is now a rich man has not been lost on her, of course. Is it possible that a deadness in her heart has been superseded by a crass calculation of self-interest? Unfortunately, Chaplin could not bring himself to pursue this question, even though at that very moment he was commiserating with himself for having been entrapped by another fortune-hunting mother-daughter duo.

Yet as he was topping off the picture's saccharine finale, he suddenly took a swipe at it. The photographer poses Charlie and the girl in old-fashioned tintype intimacy. In the instant that he snaps his shutter, Charlie kisses her. A dialogue card registers the photographer's protest: "Oh! You've spoilt the picture."[11]* The oddity of the comment suggests that it bears a symbolic load. One possibility is that Chaplin was sending a mocking message to the erstwhile leading lady of the picture who was now, to his unutterable disgust, his wife. Because for a time at least—in his savage opinion—she really *had* spoiled the picture. And a second possibility is that the photographer's protest was Chaplin's way of expressing his awareness that the conventional happy-sappy ending he had just contrived was a travesty. For the truth of *The Gold Rush* lay elsewhere, in its epic-comic revelations of avarice, cruelty, madness, and blind striving in a universe ruled by cosmic chance.

3

The announcement appeared in a Los Angeles newspaper in the first days of 1924. Charlie Chaplin was about to start filming a full-length picture about the Klondike gold rush and was looking for a new leading lady. Although young hopefuls by the hundreds immediately applied for the position, Lillita McMurray wondered whether she might have a

---

* In the sound-version *Gold Rush*, Chaplin cut this remark. Instead, his running commentary says that the reporter replies to Charlie's announcement of impending marriage by exclaiming, "Hey, this will make a great story, with a happy ending." "And so it was, a happy ending," Chaplin's commentary sentimentally concludes, as Charlie escorts the girl up the ladder to the first-class deck.

chance. At age fifteen, she had developed into a fairly good-looking, fairly serious student of acting in a halfway decent drama school. Encouraged by her boy-crazy best friend, Merna Kennedy, who had learned the aggressive ways of the world as a child dancer on the Pantages vaudeville circuit, she finally made up her mind. Without seeking prior approval from either her mother or her grandparents (in whose house she and her mother were currently living), she would go after the Chaplin job.

Merna accompanied her to bolster her courage. At the studio, Lita asked for Chuck Riesner, who had befriended her before. As one of the three assistant directors assigned to *The Gold Rush*, Riesner was able to grant both girls immediate access to his boss. Chaplin greeted Lita as his "Age of Innocence" girl, as he broke off what he was doing and vigorously shook her hand. After a quick appraisal of redheaded Merna, he redirected his attention to Lita. "My word, what a young lady you've become," she would claim to remember him saying. "Oh, splendid, splendid!" he rather incoherently added.

A screen test followed. Rollie Totheroh was no more impressed with the way she photographed than he had been three years before. The hobo author, Jim Tully, who was now the studio's publicity man, also weighed in with some negative comments. Nothing that either man said made any difference. Chaplin imperiously summoned Alf Reeves and ordered him to draw up a contract. At the signing on March 2, Chaplin informed Lita that thenceforward she would be known as Lita Grey.* That he had given her a new identity lent a further excitement to the daydream of a father-lover that had been filling her thoughts for weeks. "I was scared of my shadow, scared of most men, scared even to be near most boys—yet I was consumed by the fantasy of being held and kissed and protected by Charlie." [12]

During the filming at Truckee, Chaplin caught the flu and had to take to his bed. Through the actor Henry Bergman, ever eager to serve Chaplin in no matter how demeaning a capacity, Lita learned that her

---

* In Woody Allen's Chaplin-haunted *Zelig*, the first name of the first woman who comes forward and embarrasses the beleaguered hero by claiming that he is her husband and the father of her child is Lita, and the last name of the second woman who claims to be his spouse is Grey.

As a boy, Chaplin thought that his mother, Hannah, was "divine-looking." But her mental illness, culminating in psychotic breakdowns and institutionalization, cast a huge shadow across his life.

In the 1890s, Charles Chaplin, Senior, was a popular music hall star. A self-destructively heavy drinker, he lived apart from his wife and the two boys she was raising, Charlie and his half-brother Sydney. His namesake was never sure that Charles Senior really was his father.

In 1906, seventeen-year-old Charlie (center) was already exhibiting extraordinarily keen comic instincts as a member of the music hall act called Casey's Court Circus.

4

Exuberant early days in Hollywood. Left to right, the producer Thomas Ince, Chaplin, Mack Sennett, and D. W. Griffith. From Sennett, his first boss, Chaplin learned a lot about movie-making, even as Sennett had learned from Griffith.

5

For all the self-consciousness of this pose, Chaplin actually played the cello—and the violin and piano as well—with considerable dexterity. Note the left-handed bowing.

A scene from *The Knockout* (1914), in which Chaplin played the referee. The talented cast also included, left to right, Mack Swain, Fatty Arbuckle, and Edgar Kennedy.

In February 1916, Chaplin signed a contract with John R. Freuler (seated, left) of the Mutual Film Corporation for $670,000, the equivalent of about ten million dollars today. Between the signatories is Chaplin's adoring half-brother Sydney.

In the guise of a shoe salesman in *The Floorwalker* (1916), Charlie cops a feel.

The evaluation—and evisceration— of an alarm clock
in *The Pawnshop* (1916).

The Chaplin Studio on La Brea Avenue in Hollywood, completed in January 1918. Already the author, director, and star of his pictures, Chaplin was now to become his own producer as well.

To promote the sale of Liberty Bonds during World War I, Douglas Fairbanks holds Chaplin aloft in front of a huge crowd in lower Manhattan in April 1918.

Dubbed "Charlot" by the French, Chaplin was regarded by them, in the words of this poster, as "the ace of comic actors."

Left to right, Douglas Fairbanks, Chaplin, and Mary Pickford, kidding around during a break in the shooting of Pickford's *Pollyanna* (1920). Along with D. W. Griffith, the three stars were now partners in United Artists Corporation.

14

Mildred Harris (center), Chaplin's first wife, at the premiere in October 1920 of her latest picture, *The Woman in His House*. A few weeks later, their divorce became final.

15

The actress Florence Deshon, who committed suicide following simultaneous romantic involvements with Chaplin and Max Eastman. Chaplin would recall her fate in the opening minutes of *Limelight* (1952).

16

Mothering Jackie Coogan in *The Kid* (1921), a film that was permeated with memories of Chaplin's own childhood.

Lita Grey, with her mother at her elbow, signs a contract to be Chaplin's leading lady in *The Gold Rush*, March 2, 1924.

18

Chaplin picked Georgia Hale to replace Lita Grey as the dance hall girl in *The Gold Rush* (1925) when Lita became pregnant, spurned the idea of an abortion, and compelled Chaplin to marry her.

19

In August 1927, after three years of marriage and two children, Charles, Jr., and Sydney, Lita Grey Chaplin takes the oath on the witness stand in her divorce suit. The settlement she won made headlines.

Chaplin and his mentally unbalanced mother, in a picture taken shortly before her death in 1928.

Posing, in 1930, with the novelist Upton Sinclair, whose visionary thinking about economic matters appealed to Chaplin, as did other dubious solutions to the problems of the Great Depression.

22

Chaplin sat for this sequence of photographs by Edward Steichen
in 1931. The story it tells quite possibly reflected

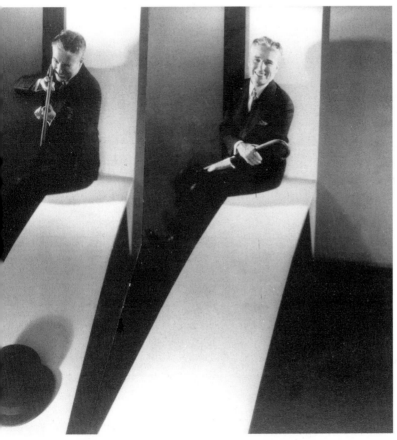

the comedian's awareness that the advent of talking pictures would eventually force him to abandon the speechless Tramp.

23

At the unveiling of a public monument in *City Lights* (1931), Charlie's compromising posture suits him fine, but it outrages the crowd of onlookers.

24

In *City Lights* Virginia Cherrill plays the blind flower girl whose sight will be restored in the most poignant rescue drama in all of the Tramp pictures.

On his visit to England in 1931, Chaplin attended a charity dinner at Grosvenor House. So celebrated was he that the sponsors seated him next to the Prince of Wales.

At their meeting in a house in the East India Dock Road, Chaplin asked Mahatma Gandhi why he hated machinery. Perhaps the comedian was already thinking about the assembly-line scenes he would film in *Modern Times* (1936).

On reaching
Berlin, where his
reception was
tumultuous,
Chaplin met with
the glamorous
Marlene Dietrich
in his suite at the
Hotel Adlon.

With his half-brother Sydney in
Switzerland in February 1932.
Sydney's resemblance in this
photo to Charles Chaplin
Senior—who, supposedly, was
not his father—is striking.

With Paulette Goddard in the garden of Chaplin's Summit Drive mansion in Beverly Hills in 1936. Her performance as his plucky leading lady in *Modern Times* launched her on the road to stardom.

Goddard had been Chaplin's live-in mistress since 1932. Yet in 1935 he made no effort to disguise his interest in the popular comedienne Thelma Todd. A few months after this photo was taken, Todd was found in her car dead from asphyxiation by carbon monoxide fumes.

The apotheosis of the Tramp.
With this famous shot of Charlie and his beloved (Paulette Goddard)
at the close of *Modern Times*, Chaplin bade farewell to his iconic hero.

With Goddard at
the Trocadero,
January 1941.
A relationship of
almost nine years was
at an end. Goddard's
vanity case and ring
reflect her lifelong
passion for acquiring
jewelry.

In June 1943, following a romance with
Chaplin that had left her obsessed with him,
Joan Barry learns that he has just married
Oona O'Neill in Carpinteria, California.

Eighteen-year-old
Oona and the
fifty-four-year-old
Chaplin in a
Hollywood nightclub
two months after
their marriage.

Chaplin being booked on February 14, 1944, on a grand jury indictment charging violation of the Mann Act by paying for the transportation of Joan Barry across state lines for sexual purposes, and conspiracy to defraud Barry of her civil rights.

36

Chaplin on the witness stand in April 1945, during the second of his trials on the paternity charge brought by Joan Barry.

Barry's reaction to the news that a Superior Court judge had ordered Chaplin to pay child support for her year-and-a-half-old baby, Carol Ann, until she was twenty-one, even though blood-test evidence (inadmissible in California courts at the time) indicated that he was not her father.

Chaplin and Oona waving dollar bills at a Henry Wallace for President rally
in Los Angeles, 1948. In the wake of the financial and critical failure
of *Monsieur Verdoux* (1947), the comedian was now facing
a mounting outcry against his pro-Soviet politics.

In September 1952, Chaplin took his family abroad
and Attorney General James P. McGranery revoked
his re-entry permit. This meant Chaplin would have
to face questioning by the Immigration and
Naturalization Service about his politics and morals
before being permitted back in the country.
He chose not to confront the INS.

Chaplin and Oona bidding goodnight to Ingrid Bergman (left) at a dinner party
in the comedian's honor in Rome, December 1952.
During the dinner he had received the Italian Legion of Merit.

41

The elegant, 37-acre Manoir de Ban in Corsier-sur-Vevey,
Switzerland, which Chaplin purchased in 1953 as a home for
his growing family. It was hardly coincidental that in his next
picture, *A King in New York*, shot in England in 1956,
he would play an exiled monarch.

42

In 1954, Chaplin was awarded the "World Peace Prize" of the Communist-sponsored World Peace Council, and announced he would use the prize money of five thousand pounds to foster international peace and understanding.

43

44

Chaplin's well-publicized meetings with Chinese premier Chou En-lai in Geneva, Switzerland, in 1954 and with the Soviet Union's premier Nikolai Bulganin in London in 1956 further testified to his willingness to allow his name to be exploited for Communist propaganda purposes.

The Chaplin family on vacation at Cap Ferrat on the Riviera in 1957.
From left: Oona, Geraldine, Chaplin, Eugene, Victoria, Josephine,
and Michael. Two-month-old Jane is not pictured,
and Annette and Christopher were yet to be born.

Marlon Brando listens and watches as Chaplin shows him how to act in one of his scenes in *A Countess from Hong Kong* (1967). The tension that had developed between these two towering talents was fierce. And the film—Chaplin's last—was a box-office flop.

After Chaplin received a special Oscar at the close of the Academy Awards ceremony
in April 1972, admirers swarmed onto the stage and surrounded him.
From left: Jack Nicholson (in flowered shirt); singer Johnny Mathis;
Jane Fonda, who had been named "Best Actress";
and the emcee of the evening, Sammy Davis, Jr.

On his arrival in London
with Oona on a flight from
Los Angeles, Chaplin proudly
displayed his Oscar to reporters
and photographers.

With Oona at the Savoy Hotel
in London on March 4, 1975,
after being knighted at
Buckingham Place
by Queen Elizabeth II.

Sir Charles Chaplin, with Lady Chaplin and their daughter Josephine, at a circus
performance in Vevey in November 1976. Thirteen months later,
on Christmas morning 1977, he would die in his sleep at the Manoir de Ban.

employer expected her to drop by his room. She found him reclining in red silk pajamas reading a book about Napoleon. He told her that she resembled Josephine. Following a few more idle remarks, he ceased talking and threw himself upon her. Whether because she was frightened and disgusted, as she later claimed, by the crudity and "almost brutal force" of his attack, or because she had coolly figured out that the best way to inflame his interest in her was to resist him, she struggled to get away and repeatedly pleaded with him to stop. Abruptly, he pulled back. Apparently her cries had reached the ears of other guests in the hotel, for the murmur of voices could be heard in the hallway outside the room. Chaplin cursed. Before Lita left, he tried to get her to agree to submit to him at some later date. "I'll be your teacher," Svengali proposed. But to no avail. The only promise she was willing to make— so she would emphasize to her disbelieving ghostwriter, Morton Cooper —was that she would not tell her mother what had happened.[13]

By the time the work in the Sierras was wrapped up and filming had resumed at Sunset and La Brea, Lita's thwarted lover had settled on a more methodical plan for having his way with her. Whenever he was invited to a dinner party or a movie premiere, he made sure that he could bring her along—as a means of gaining publicity for his new leading lady, he explained to one and all. Yet he never allowed himself to be seen in public with Lita without a lady on his other arm. Sometimes it was Lita's mother whom he asked to join them, but their more frequent companion was a striking-looking divorcée, Thelma Morgan Converse, who like many socialites in the 1920s aspired to movie stardom. Another of her hopes was that Chaplin was romantically interested in her.*

---

* Thelma was the twin sister of Gloria Morgan Vanderbilt and the aunt, therefore, of the Gloria Vanderbilt who was born in February 1924. In the early 1930s, Little Gloria —"the poor little rich girl," as the press called her—became the object of a headline-making custody battle between Big Gloria and her dead husband's formidable sister, Gertrude Vanderbilt Whitney, who regarded Big Gloria as morally unfit to raise the child. Thelma meantime had married into the British aristocracy and as Lady Furness had had an affair with the Prince of Wales. It was either in the latter part of 1930 or early 1931 that she brought Wallis Simpson and her husband into the prince's life. In the period just before Oona O'Neill met Chaplin, Oona and young Gloria Vanderbilt were both splash hits in the social swim in New York. Gloria was later married for a time to Leopold Stokowski, who was seven years older than Oona's white-haired choice of a husband.

Despite the chaperonage, Chaplin found occasions to be alone with his quarry. On weekends, he and Lita and Thelma were usually to be seen at the Santa Monica Swimming Club. In this favorite haunt of the biggest names in Hollywood, there were always people on hand to whom Chaplin enjoyed talking—for a time. Late in the day he would stroll off with Lita to a lonely stretch of beach, where he would sit her down on the water's edge and hold her enthralled with his latest ideas for their scenes together in *The Gold Rush*. On the dusky afternoon that he at last abandoned talk for action, she was eager to give herself to him, until the pain of the experience proved too much for her and her whimperings coerced him into withdrawing. At the moment of penetration, he had mumbled something odd, she remembered: "Born . . . we're both being born. . . ."[14]

It was at a table for three at Musso & Frank's fashionable restaurant that Thelma lost her temper. She had been in the way long enough, she flung at Chaplin, as she pushed her plate forward, thrust her chair back, and flounced out of the room. Later that night, in the backseat of Chaplin's Locomobile, with the black divider curtain drawn so that Frank Kawa, the Japanese chauffeur, could not look in the mirror and see what was going on, the comedian made another attempt to consummate his passion for his "Age of Innocence" girl. As her cries of pain rang out in the darkness, he again felt compelled to desist, leaving her "distantly conscious" of the "insanity" of his having mounted her in such awkward circumstances.[15]

Three days passed. Chaplin quit work at noon, saying that he was suffering from a terrible headache. With Frank at the wheel of the Locomobile, they picked up Lita at a prearranged point some distance away and roared off to Chaplin's Summit Drive estate. En route, Lita desperately wanted to throw herself in her lover's arms and implore him to hold her, but somehow she guessed what she would later know for sure, that while Chaplin feasted on her bursts of emotion he "would go into a momentary state of shock if these bursts were directed squarely at him without his having intentionally prompted them."[16] For reasons that Lita never showed any signs of comprehending, the son of Hannah Chaplin had to have total control.

Toraichi Kono, who was now serving as Chaplin's general assistant, admitted them by the front door with "that semi-smirking grin of his" that Lita would learn to hate. Chaplin's first move was to take her on a

tour of the house. The two-story-high room in which he screened motion pictures was dominated by great rafters of solid oak and a massive
pipe organ. The living room contained a pleasant clutter of books and
pieces of jade, most of them nude figures. Chaplin picked up a cherub
and said that it was his favorite piece. Cherubs were special with him,
he explained, because there was no wickedness in them; I think of you
as a cherub, he added. In the walnut-paneled dining room, six chairs
were drawn up to a heavy carved table. The master chair had an exceptionally high back, ornately carved arms and legs, and thick velvet arm-
rests. Opposite this veritable throne was another outsized chair. Chaplin
pulled it back and invited Lita to sit down, addressing her as Josephine
as he did so.[17]

On the second floor, the costliness of the furnishings in the master
bedroom and of the tilework and other appointments in the master
bathroom took Lita's breath away, while the steam room beyond with
its built-in marble slab struck her as absolutely the last word in *luxe*.
"Here's the place to relax, Empress Josephine," Chaplin murmured.
After showing her the handle that controlled the flow of steam, he
suggested that she take advantage of the facility, inasmuch as he needed
to attend to some correspondence. Some minutes later, as she was lying
naked on the marble slab, enveloped in billowing clouds of steam, she
suddenly became aware of Chaplin's presence beside her. In motion
pictures in the Jazz Age, William de Mille once wrote of his famous
brother, "[C. B.] made of the bathroom a delightful resort which undoubtedly had its effect upon bathrooms of the whole nation. The bath
became a mystic shrine dedicated to Venus. . . ." It was in the adjoining
sanctum, then, of the sort of dream setting in which Cecil B. DeMille
had enveloped Gloria Swanson and other beauties in foam that Lita
finally surrendered without protest to her thirty-five-year-old pursuer.
The circumstances were so cinematic, indeed, that upon hearing Lita's
story, her editor at Bernard Geis, Don Preston, indicated doubts of its
authenticity. But she swore up and down, Preston remembered, that
every word of what she said was true.[18]

4

Behind Lita's back, Chaplin was also wooing Rebecca West in early
1924, West later wrote her sister Lettie. So pressing did his seduction

attempts become that she finally moved up the coast to Santa Barbara in order to escape him. When they met again three years later, he offered her a poignant explanation for his conduct, West reported to Lettie on April 3, 1927. He had wanted to sleep with her, he said, "because he had suddenly become terrified of impotence and wanted to see if it were so." And when she ran away from him, West's letter to her sister continued, he "experienced one of the regressive movements he had had at intervals all his life, and became interested in young children —I mean little girls of 13 or 14." Then he married Lita Grey, she added, and "for six months afterward he was impotent with mature women and remained so until he took up with Marion Davies."[19]*

Caught up in a sex-powered delirium, Chaplin could not imagine that he might end up having to marry again. But to keep Lita's devotion to him secure, he lavished praise and encouragement on her throughout the rest of the spring and summer of 1924. The most beautiful form of human life, he told her, is the very young girl just starting to bloom. In an effort to fill the beautiful blankness of her mind, he brought her books with pages and passages marked on subjects ranging from ballet to anthropology. By her own admission, Lita found most of his assignments rough going, although she did manage to keep her attention fixed on the biography of Napoleon he had been reading at Truckee. He intended to make a movie about Napoleon, he said, and to her distress —for she knew her limitations as an actress—he spoke of casting her as Josephine.[20]

The possibility that he might get her with child he dismissed with a wave of his hand, even though his policy of not taking any precautions had previously led to his shotgun marriage to Mildred Harris and to Florence Deshon's pregnancy. Toward the end of September, his foolishness caught up with him. On the day of the filming of the scene in which the tramp first sees the dance hall girl and is smitten by her, Lita asked Chuck Riesner to ask Chaplin if she could be excused from work on the early side. Inasmuch as the "Master" had pronounced himself satisfied with the scene after the fourth take, she thought he might grant her request, and he did. In a nearby doctor's office, she underwent a test

* West was mistaken about the timing of Chaplin's affair with Davies, which began before his marriage to Lita.

to determine the validity of her fears (or her hopes?) that she was pregnant. The next day the doctor confirmed that she was.[21]

The following Monday, her mother accompanied her to the studio and demanded to see Chaplin alone in his office. When they emerged after a quarter of an hour, he began bellowing at Alf Reeves to close down the set for the day and send everybody home. He was stomping about "like an insane man," Lita recalled. On the way back to her grandparents' home, she learned from her mother what had happened in the office. Chaplin was so angry, her mother said, that she thought he was going to strike her. Besides absolving himself of all blame for the calamity of her pregnancy, he insisted that Lita would have to prove that the baby was his, and he accused her of being involved with another man.

The next time she and her mother saw him, he was somewhat calmer. Upon receiving proof from the doctor that Lita was indeed pregnant, he would pay for an abortion, he said, but he could not possibly marry her. He had married a girl in her teens once before, he continued, and the press had been rough on him; if he did so again the press would destroy him.

His argument failed to move Lita's mother. Marriage was the only option she would consider. An abortion was morally repugnant to her, she said, and she would not permit her daughter to bear an illegitimate child. Chaplin countered with another proposition. If she would find a young man for Lita and persuade him to marry her, he, Chaplin, would give Lita $10,000 in cash. Lita's mother scoffed at the idea—for she, presumably, was thinking of Chaplin's millions—and the interview ended with Chaplin in a rage. Lita was "a little whore," he cried, as he ordered her as well as her mother to leave the studio premises.[22]

Consolation awaited him in the arms of William Randolph Hearst's blond, blue-eyed, and fun-loving mistress of almost nine years, Marion Davies. Chaplin had often been Hearst's guest at the publisher's San Simeon pleasure dome up the coast and had been even more frequently entertained by Marion in the seventy-room Santa Monica beach house that Hearst had given her after making her a film star, thanks to his control of Cosmopolitan Productions. Chaplin liked everything about Marion—her wit, her intelligence, her infectious laughter, even her stammer. But apparently it was not until the late summer of 1924, when he was shooting *The Gold Rush* and she was making a circus story called

Zander the Great that he began picking her up in his limousine after work. "All of the cast and crew of *Zander* were aware that something was going on," according to Davies's biographer Fred Lawrence Guiles, and in the course of the fall partially veiled references to the affair cropped up in the press. On November 16, a gossip columnist for the *New York Daily News*—the tabloid rival of Hearst's *Mirror*—took pleasure in saying: "Charlie Chaplin continues to pay ardent attention to Marion Davies. He spent the evening at Montmartre dining and dancing with the fair Marion the other night. There was a lovely young dancer entertaining that evening. And Charlie applauded but with his back turned. He never took his eyes off Marion's blonde beauty."[23]

Behind his mask of pleasure at the Montmartre, Chaplin was desperate. Within days of his showdown with Lita's mother, Lita's uncle, Edwin McMurray, a successful San Francisco attorney, had entered the fray. His first step had been to write Chaplin a letter, reminding him that statutory rape was a criminal offense punishable in the state of California by a thirty-year prison sentence. Following a few more lawyerly maneuvers on McMurray's part, Chaplin caved in and agreed to marry Lita. He also suspended work on *The Gold Rush* until he could find a replacement leading lady. For in addition to his personal reasons for being furious at her, there were professional considerations. As of the end of September, he had accumulated no more than half of the footage he had in mind, and most of the sequences involving the dance hall girl remained to be shot. Had he kept Lita in the cast, her condition would have been hard to conceal by the time her final scenes were enacted.[24]

In an effort to shield the wedding ceremony from the surveillance of the press, Chaplin devised a plan that smacked, as Lita's *My Life with Chaplin* would say with some justice, of "the peculiar inspiration of someone deranged." Accompanied by a full technical crew, assorted actors, and Lita and her mother, he took a train to Guaymas, Mexico, on November 24. The explanation that he directed his publicist, Jim Tully, to hand out was that he was broadening the scope of *The Gold Rush* to include south-of-the-border scenes as well as the Klondike. The reporters who followed him were suspicious at first about what he was up to, but gradually let down their guard. On an afternoon when they were hanging out in a bar, rather than maintaining a vigil outside the comedian's hotel, he sped off in an automobile with Lita, her mother, and Chuck Riesner. A wild ride across bumpy back roads brought them at last to a dusty town called Empalme and the odoriferous living room of a justice of the peace who knew no English; but Chaplin's imagination was apparently in the grip of a crazy movie scenario and he could not be swayed from acting it out.[25]

On the train back to California, the newlyweds occupied a drawing room. In Lita's memory of that nightmare trip, Chaplin denounced her, her mother, her grandparents, and her uncle as a "bloody bunch of money-hungry scum." These terrible words heightened the nausea the pregnant bride was experiencing, and when she complained about not feeling well, Chaplin suggested with seeming politeness that she walk out on the platform of the observation car and get some fresh air. She took his advice. As she was standing beside the waist-high guard door, breathing in the chilly night breezes, her husband came up behind her. In mocking tones he asked, "Why don't you jump?"[26]

5

The news that Chaplin had married a girl of sixteen made headlines across America. Three weeks later, a studio handout crafted by Jim Tully announced that the new Mrs. Chaplin wanted to devote every moment of her time to her husband and was consequently withdrawing from *The Gold Rush*. No mention was made of her pregnancy, of course. Just before Christmas there was a further announcement to the effect that the role of the dance hall girl would be assumed by a delicately beautiful brunette named Georgia Hale. Among Georgia's possessions was a copy of a birth certificate, dated 1909, which appeared to prove that she was fifteen years old when she met Chaplin. Her school record, however, makes it clear that she was born in 1900.[27]

For most of her childhood she had lived in a working-class neighborhood on the south side of Chicago. Her mother, she remembered in a memoir that would not be published until long after her death, was "very loving," but like other young women in Chaplin's life, she suffered from an absence of paternal guidance. Her father, she declared, was "like a boarder," who would "come and go, mostly go." Every month he gave his wife a small part of his salary, which would "all be spent in the first couple of weeks." The last days of the month invariably left his wife and three daughters "broke and hungry." Mr. Hale "very seldom" spoke to Georgia directly, although he often complained to Mrs. Hale about their beautiful girl's downcast attitude toward life. When Georgia was sixteen, he suddenly broke out of this pattern one day and called her to him and said, "You're so darn sad. What's wrong with you? I wish you'd been a boy, then you wouldn't be worried about trifles." Then, to her vast surprise, he added, "Here's some money. Take this and go to the movies. There's some comedy playing. It might, just by chance, do you some good."[28]

At the Bona-Venture Theater the show had already started when she crept to her seat. Finally, the comedy started.*

Onto the screen came a funny little fellow. He was a pathetic character, like the rest of us. His clothes were castoffs and much too large for his small frame. His shoes were way out in front of his feet. He did wear a collar and a tie, but no shirt, and on his head a classy, dirty derby. His hand whirled a cane, jauntily, as if in defiance of his lot.

I could see him skating with the skill and precision of a ballet dancer, twisting, whirling majestically around and through the crowd. . . . Courage and joy were the qualities he industriously used in his busy little life, for keeping body and soul together. . . . The kids near me wildly laughed and applauded this tiny comic, yelling, "Charlie Chaplin . . . more . . . more." His funny gags and clothes had sent them into the aisles rolling and screaming.

But I saw something different, something invisible. I felt something beautiful. A gentle beam of light had stolen into my dark world. "What was it?" I was silent. When the picture was over, I left the show quickly and ran ahead of the kids. I wanted to be alone. I wanted to hold it closely. Charlie Chaplin had said something to me . . . he had spoken to me directly.[29]

After being crowned Queen of the Pageant in a Chicago beauty contest in 1922, Georgia appeared in a number of pictures that were made in New York and then moved on to Hollywood. A bit part in a benighted film starring the fast-fading Mildred Harris led to her being picked to play the female lead in Josef von Sternberg's *The Salvation Hunters*. The male lead, George K. Arthur, sought to build Hollywood interest in the picture by persuading Chaplin's factotum, Kono, to show it in the

---

* It was *The Rink*, released in December 1916.

comedian's screening room at home. Chaplin was enormously taken with Georgia's performance and told her so when they subsequently met. By the time he decided that she would be right for *The Gold Rush*, Douglas Fairbanks had cast her in *Don Q. Son of Zorro*. But because his pal Charlie wanted her so badly, Fairbanks agreed to release her so that she could sign with him.

Almost immediately, Chaplin evinced a desire to add a personal dimension to their professional relationship, but because he was married Georgia held him at arm's length. Only after his divorce from Lita in 1928 did she become romantically involved with him. The man she loved with such a passion that marriage to someone else became, in her words, "impossible after knowing him" was a warm, humble, utterly delightful person whom she thought of as "Charlie." Yet hovering around and darkening their relationship, she quickly came to realize, was a cold, cruel, but fundamentally frightened shadow figure, whom she dubbed "Mr. Chaplin." Instead of hating "Mr. Chaplin," however, she felt compassion for him, for he was so clearly "in need of help."[30]

Lita Grey, on the other hand, rarely saw her husband's delightful side. Whenever Chaplin came home at night from wherever he had been, his lovelorn bride observed in anguish, he immediately went to his room to work on *Gold Rush* problems. Sometimes he would remain at his desk until dawn, then take a brief nap and hurry off to the studio. In time, he called off his cold war against her, but for the most part it was in ways that she found degrading. If they had dinner together at a bridge table beside the living room fireplace, he was apt to ask her questions at some point about the reading assignments he had resumed giving her. Then he would prop up a newspaper in front of him and read for the rest of the meal. And on the nights that he summoned her to his bed, he would expend his passion in repeated "bouts," as he called them, with remarkably few minutes in between,* after which he would send her away, as if she were a call girl.[31]

He also compelled her to participate in a scheme he had concocted

* When Max Eastman and his wife, Yvette, visited Chaplin and Oona in their home in Vevey, Switzerland, Chaplin told them "with a touch of bitterness" that when Lita first became pregnant she had said to him, "You'll marry me! I've never gotten a kick out of you, but you'll marry me!" Yvette Eastman, unpublished memoir, p. 455. During a long interview with me in Los Angeles in February 1994, Lita remarked that Chaplin was "not a good lover but often."

for deceiving the public. The scheme was against the law but that did not faze him, for psychological reasons that Clare Sheridan's *Naked Truth* helps to clarify. Making a portrait bust of Chaplin proved to be a difficult task, Sheridan found, for "it had been very hard to collect his varying personalities and crystallize them into one interpretation." On the day that she completed the bust and showed it to him, "he looked at the clay through half-closed eyes and finally said: 'It might be the head of a criminal, mightn't it?' and proceeded to elaborate a theory that criminals and artists are psychologically akin . . . 'both have a flame, a burning flame, of impulse, vision—a side-tracked mind and deep sense of unlawfulness.' "[32] Over the years, Chaplin would, in fact, have recurrent troubles with the law.

The illegality in which Chaplin enmeshed Lita grew out of his determination to conceal the damning fact that she had been pregnant on the day of their marriage. Lita gave birth to a baby boy on the night of May 5, 1925, in a corner of the Chaplin mansion that had been specially outfitted as a delivery room. Chaplin gave the doctor who attended her $25,000 to falsify the birth certificate. His next step was to send Lita into hiding, along with the baby, in an isolated cabin in the San Bernardino Mountains. Not until mid-July was she given the green light to return to Los Angeles. The birth certificate that was duly filed stated that Charles Spencer Chaplin, Jr., had been born on June 28.[33]

Within days of settling in again in Beverly Hills, Lita realized soon enough, her contraceptive-scorning husband had made her pregnant a second time.

6

The raw version of *The Gold Rush* was 231,505 feet long. After Chaplin finished readying it for release, it measured 8,498 feet. The premiere took place on June 26 at Grauman's Egyptian Theater, an eighteen-hundred-seat temple with cast heads of pharaohs mounted on pylons on either side of the entrance and Tut-mask wall sconces along the interior walls. Prior to the showing of the picture, an overture by Grauman's Egyptian Orchestra, with Julius K. Johnson at the "Mighty Egyptian Organ," was followed by the appearance of a group of dancing girls, some of them richly gowned, some of them garbed as Eskimos, who assumed either "artistic" or frolicsome postures in a setting of Arctic snows. Thereafter, a lineup of dancing ice skaters, a balloonist, and another group of dancing girls, dressed in skimpy "Monte Carlo" costumes, came on seriatim. After the film, Chaplin came to the front of the theater and made a speech that reflected a quiet contentment with his accomplishment. As Georgia Hale said, "He really felt it was the greatest picture he had made."[34]

On July 29, Chaplin left Los Angeles by train to attend the New York opening at the Strand Theater. In *My Autobiography* he would recall that the audience at the Strand began yelling and shouting from the moment it got its first glimpse of Charlie gimpily walking along in blithe unawareness of the bear behind him. When the lights came up at the end of the evening, the United Artists sales manager, Hiram Abrams, embraced Chaplin and predicted that the picture would gross at least $6 million—which it did.[35]

On returning to his hotel suite, Chaplin collapsed. The doctor who was summoned to treat him said that he was suffering from a case of nerves and recommended a few days of relaxation by the sea. En route to a hotel at Brighton Beach, he broke down and wept, for no reason that he could think of. In his room overlooking the water, he opened the windows and inhaled great drafts of fresh air, but his spirits failed to revive. As he studied the beach, he saw a lifeguard drag a drowning man from the surf and give him first aid, without success. "I was in a worse state than ever," his account concludes, "so I decided to return to New York. Two days later I was well enough to return to California."[36]

But in fact he did not return for another eight weeks. Why should he go home when that would mean living under the same roof with a wife he did not love and a crying baby? Far better to remain in New York, where he could pay pleasant visits to the East Sixty-first Street apartment of his increasingly dear friend Ralph Barton and the third of his wives, Carlotta Monterey.

Along with John Held, Jr., and Miguel Covarrubias, Barton was one of the premier illustrators of the 1920s. A smartly dressed bon vivant, with "the French Legion of Honor in his buttonhole, a cynic's wit on permanent tap and a philanderer's reputation with women," in the words of his discerning biographer, Bruce Kellner, Barton knew hundreds of the people who helped to give the decade its flavor, from his fellow Missourian Thomas Hart Benton and the actor William Powell to H. L. Mencken, Theodore Dreiser, Paul Robeson, and Hizzoner, the mayor of New York, Jimmy Walker. By authorial demand, Barton was chosen to provide the illustrations for Anita Loos's *Gentlemen Prefer Blondes* and the dust-jacket design for Carl Van Vechten's *The Tattooed Countess*. At the request of the theatrical producer Morris Gest, he decorated the intermission curtain for Gest's import from an émigré Russian cabaret in Paris of Nikita Balieff's *Chauve-Souris*, or Bat Theater, with cartoon portraits of Chaplin, John Barrymore, Al Jolson, Irving Berlin, Lillian Gish, Herbert Hoover, Ring Lardner, Lynn Fontanne, George M. Cohan, and Sergei Rachmaninoff, among other celebrities. As for the magazines that were eager to publish his wiry, fluent drawings, as John Updike has called them, they included *Judge*, *Puck*, *Collier's*, *Vanity Fair*, and Harold Ross's upstart *New Yorker*. Yet if the wit and the humor of his executions brought him fame and a fat income, they also functioned as mechanisms of self-defense against an encroaching darkness. Plagued by periodic waves of depression, chronic insomnia, and, as the decade wore on, a mounting paranoia, Barton exemplified Scott Fitzgerald's darkly romantic vision of the beautiful and damned.[37]

He and Chaplin had first met in Los Angeles in the spring of 1921, and when the creator of *The Kid* passed through New York the following September on his way to England, Barton took two days off from a pressing assignment so that the two of them could be together. In a letter, the illustrator described his new friend as "fine, modest, intelligent . . . quite frank about himself, and absolutely unaffected by his fame and so on, a very charming person altogether, well-read, and of a rather somber turn of mind." At the dinner party that Chaplin gave just before he sailed, at which he and Georgette Leblanc had reenacted Camille's death scene, Barton was among the favored few on hand.

Thereafter, Chaplin had a standing invitation, whenever he was in town, to join the social gatherings that Barton loved to assemble. If the comedian was in the mood, he would entertain the party, Barton recalled, by speaking in double-talk in several languages, or playing the piano or reenacting the "dance of the rolls" (which Barton recorded in a home movie), or doing imitations of everybody from a YMCA secretary to an organist who has killed a little girl in a church belfry to "the way Lillian Gish would come if she ever went to bed with anybody." In the afternoons, Chaplin was given to dropping by Barton's place at teatime and staying as late as five the following morning, talking "about books like a bibliophile, about music like a musician, about art like an artist." To the novelist Louis Bromfield, Barton affirmed that Chaplin was "the most marvelous person on earth—I am afraid, the greatest man of our times."[38]

Carlotta Monterey's snooty profile, as Bruce Kellner has wittily observed, looked like a Ralph Barton drawing. Born Hazel Neilson Taasinge in 1898 and unwanted by either the California fruit farmer who was her father or her eighteen-year-old mother, she was raised after the age of four by an aunt who ran rooming houses in San Francisco and accepted money in exchange for sex from an Oakland businessman. On the wings of being named Miss California in a beauty contest, Hazel went to London and briefly studied acting with Sir Herbert Beerbohm Tree, had an even briefer career on the stage, and got married and divorced. Back in America again following the outbreak of World War I, she changed her name to Carlotta Monterey, after the California town, and returned to the stage. Unfortunately, she was universally adjudged "an appallingly bad actress," as one of her first reviewers bluntly put it, although no one contested the fact that she possessed an unusual beauty.[39]

Barton and Carlotta became lovers in 1922 but did not marry until March 1925. By the time the creator of *The Gold Rush* arrived in New York in August, the Bartons were caught between their continuing passion for each other and a mutual disenchantment that felt like revulsion. Perhaps Chaplin witnessed a variation on the scene that Carl Van Vechten evoked in his diary in late September: "—& after the Bartons have talked for 3 hours about whether they will live together any more they take off their clothes & give a remarkable performance." The end came just before Chaplin returned to the West Coast. Carlotta arrived home unexpectedly from an out-of-town tryout, found Barton in bed with "a golfing Country Club type" named Ruth Goldbeck, and fled to the Madison Hotel, leaving Barton to discover at his agonized leisure that the woman he had just lost forever was the love of his life.[40]

7

Around the corner from the Strand Theater lay the New Amsterdam Theater, the site in the summer of 1925 of the new edition of the

Ziegfeld Follies. Edmund Wilson had dropped in on a Follies rehearsal some months earlier and had found Flo Ziegfeld in a ranting mood about his beauty chorus. "No brains! no beauty! no personality! Can't sing—can't dance—can't act!—stand 'em on their heads and they're all alike—you know! Who's fucking her?—I don't know."[41] Yet his scathing tongue helped to whip the new edition into "the most lavish, the most beautiful and the most humorous of all the Follies Ziegfeld has ever done," according to the rave review of the *New York American*'s critic. The headliners included Will Rogers, who mixed lariat tricks with surgically incisive comments on the Scopes "monkey trial" and other topics of the time, and W. C. Fields, juggler extraordinaire and hero of a series of playlets in which he was forced to deal with a nagging wife, an obnoxious kid in a baby buggy, and the idiots who were interrupting his afternoon nap.

As for the beauty chorus, Ziegfeld had "glorified" it with six new girls, two of whom were truly spectacular: the seductive Hilda Ferguson, known to her admirers as "The Body" (and known to the New York Police Department's Homicide Squad as the roommate of chorine Dot King, who was murdered in their apartment in 1923 under circumstances that four years later would be recalled in S. S. Van Dine's *The Canary Murder Case*), and eighteen-year-old Louise Brooks, a china doll with alabaster skin, a helmet of black hair, and a magnificent pair of legs, who danced up a storm in a number called "Syncopating Baby." New York that summer offered some marvelous shows to the ticket buyer who wanted songs, laughter, and pretty girls—Jerome Kern's *Sunny*, *The Cocoanuts* with the Marx Brothers (music by Irving Berlin, book by George S. Kaufman), George and Ira Gershwin's *Tip-Toes*, *George White's Scandals* and *Earl Carroll's Vanities*—but the Ziegfeld Follies more than held its own.[42]

The big dressing room on the top floor of the New Amsterdam that Louise Brooks shared with another girl quickly became the "cultural drop-in," as Brooks described it in one of her elegantly phrased remembrances, "of such clowning gentlemen as Walter Wanger, Herman Manckiewicz, Michael Arlen, Charlie Chaplin." She had met Chaplin shortly after the Strand premiere at a crowded cocktail party given by Wanger. A widely respected producer at Paramount, Wanger had assumed the role of Louise's protector and was giving her advice about how to handle the movie offers she had begun to receive. He also was going to bed with her whenever he got the chance, for she had many men-about-town tailing her in New York. And now here was Chaplin, singling her out of the crowd and clearly making plans to see her again. "Submerged in my own fascinating being," Brooks would remember, "I was only vaguely aware that *The Gold Rush* had brought Chaplin his greatest triumph; that he was the toast of all intellectual, cultural and social New York; and that for a week the tabloids ran front-page pictures of Broadway beauties, asking 'Who bit Charlie's lip?' " By the end of Wanger's party and forever afterwards, she considered him "the most bafflingly complex man who ever lived." As for his physical presence, it had "an exquisiteness the screen could not reflect. Small, perfectly made, meticulously dressed, with his fine grey hair and ivory skin and white teeth he was as clean as a pearl and glowed all over."[43]

A strikingly similar impression of his appearance was captured that summer by Edward Steichen in a black-and-white studio photograph of Chaplin standing in front of a long, narrow white shade that symbolically suggests a movie screen. A flood of light, coming from in front and low down, washes upward across him. He is wearing a dark, beautifully tailored, double-breasted suit, a lighter-colored tie that looks gray in the photograph, a white shirt, and buttoned shoes with cloth tops. In his right hand and close to his thigh, he holds a perfectly blocked gray Homburg; in his left he grips a jauntily angled and clearly expensive walking stick. The dynamism he conveys is enhanced by the slightly tipped-forward position of his head and the grin on his face. Above and behind him on the white shade looms the gigantic shadow he has cast. As Steichen brilliantly calculated, the shadow of the Homburg makes it look like a derby, while the shadow of the walking stick gives us no clue of its cost. The photograph, in other words, gives a double image—of Charlie the tramp as well as of Chaplin the toast of the town. Nor was this the end of Steichen's magic. The curls on the top of Chaplin's graying head endow the shadow figure behind with a pair of satyr's horns.

Chaplin had been accompanied to New York by Henri (Harry) d'Arrast, the young Frenchman who had served as one of his assistants on both *A Woman of Paris* and *The Gold Rush*. On double dates, d'Arrast paired off with Louise's closest friend in the Follies, Peggy Fears, and Chaplin squired Louise. "Swirling in chiffons of pink and blue," Louise later wrote, "Peggy and I danced the tango with them at the Montmartre where the head waiters bowed reverently before Chaplin and the haughty patrons pretended that they were not thrilled at the sight of him." At the Lido, to which Peggy wore crystal beads and Louise gold lace, the four of them watched the great dancer Maurice Mouvet punish his nervous new partner, Barbara Bennett, for a misstep at the outset of their Apache finale by throwing her—to Chaplin's delight—clear across the floor.* And at a new play called *Cradle Snatchers*, they "sat in a box . . . looking at Mary Boland, Edna May Oliver and a young actor, Humphrey Bogart, on the stage, while the rest of the audience looked at Charlie."[44]

After d'Arrast left for Hollywood, Chaplin took a suite at the Ambassador Hotel and Louise left her own swank apartment and moved in with him. One night they went to Greenwich Village to see a performance of Maxwell Anderson's *Outside Looking In*, "a play about tramps which Charlie had already seen twice." James Cagney, a former hoofer, but now, at age twenty-six, a rapid-talking, altogether exciting dramatic actor, headed a strong cast that also included Charles Bickford and Blyth Daly, in the role of a fugitive who disguises herself as a boy. Such a play would obviously have interested Chaplin, but what Louise did not realize and Chaplin did not tell her was that Blyth Daly had been responsible for his celebrated—by the tabloids—swollen lip. She had taken offense at his sexual importunings and had bitten him in reprisal.[45]

As a new partner for Peggy Fears, Chaplin and Louise recruited a fellow resident of the Ambassador, the movie theater financier A. C. Blumenthal. Inasmuch as his penthouse was far grander than Chaplin's suite, the four of them spent most of their time together there, according to Louise. "Blumie played the piano, Peggy sang, I danced, and Charlie returned to reality—the world of his creative imagination." Events in his London youth were summoned up in pantomime, Louise told the readers of *Film Culture* in 1966. In addition, he

> acted out countless scenes for countless films . . . [and did] imitations of everybody. Isadora Duncan danced in a storm of toilet paper. John

---

* A comic re-creation of their tough dancing would appear in the nightclub scene in *City Lights*.

Barrymore picked his nose and brooded over Hamlet's soliloquy. A Follies girl swished across the room; and I began to cry while Charlie denied
absolutely that he was imitating me. Nevertheless, as he patted my hand,
I determined to abandon that silly walk forthwith.[46]

To a few close friends, Louise confided less discreet details of the
goings-on in the Blumenthal penthouse. On one orgiastic weekend, the
two couples rarely took the trouble to get dressed, although they did
order in food from room service from time to time. Because Chaplin
was "afraid of contracting certain diseases," according to Barry Paris's
source-rich and valuable biography of Louise, "[he] had studied the
matter and was firmly convinced that iodine was a reliable VD preven-
tive. Normally he employed only a small local application, but one night
. . . he was inspired to paint the sum of his private parts with iodine and
come running with a great bright-red erection toward the squealing
Peggy and Louise."[47]

Chaplin's affair with Louise lasted for two months. Most of her evenings were committed to the Follies, of course, but after the show they
would take tremendously long walks before going on to a nightclub or
returning to the Ambassador. On a Lower East Side street one night,
Chaplin was recognized and all but overwhelmed by a sea of admirers,
so that he and Louise had to take refuge in a modest restaurant. "Four
hours passed before we came out," Louise would claim, "because inside
Chaplin had found a wild Hungarian torturing a violin, and Chaplin's
absorption in his performance kept us there until closing time. Twenty-
seven years later I saw the Hungarian violinist come to life again in the
person of Chaplin in his variety act with Buster Keaton at the piano in
Limelight." When their "joyful summer" finally ended, because Chaplin
was itching to get back to Hollywood and start work on another picture,
"he didn't give me a fur from Jaeckel or a bangle from Cartier," said
Louise, "so that I could flash them around, saying, 'Look what I got
from Chaplin.' The day after he left town I got a nice check in the mail
signed 'Charlie.' And then I didn't even write him a thank-you note.
Damn me."[48]

That she had no inclination to pursue the most famous man in the
world, either by letter or in person, was utterly characteristic of Brooks's
enigmatically passive personality. Although the long list of her lovers

included a number of millionaires, she was not like Peggy Fears and other Follies girls who were on the hunt for a sugar daddy to marry. She would be drawn to the District of Columbia laundry tycoon (and future owner of the Washington Redskins) George Marshall, and to CBS's William Paley, because they were such commanding figures, and in later life she came to attribute this preference to the fact that as a child of nine she had been sexually molested by an older man. "For me, nice, soft, easy men were never enough—there had to be an element of domination—and I'm sure that's all tied up with [my molester] Mr. Feathers." From a movie he saw her in, the brilliant German director G. W. Pabst could sense that she was a reckless, don't-give-a-damn hedonist, which is one of the reasons he chose her over Marlene Dietrich and all other German candidates for the role of Lulu in *Pandora's Box* (1929), the film that made her a screen legend. "It was clever of Pabst," she told Kenneth Tynan long afterwards, "to know even before he met me that I possessed the tramp essence of Lulu."[49]

Produced at Nero-Film in Berlin in the fall of 1928, *Pandora's Box* was based on two harshly erotic plays by Frank Wedekind, *Earth Spirit* (1895) and *Pandora's Box* (1904). Behind these plays lay Wedekind's obsession with the prostitute murders of Jack the Ripper, which he regarded as the overt expression of a sick society's subconscious fear of uninhibited freedom. In Pabst's surpassing version of Wedekind's tales, the primitively sexual Lulu, meaning no particular harm, either destroys or degrades the weak and lustful men who cluster about her. But ultimately, Lulu is herself destroyed. Having fled from her Art Deco apartment in Berlin in order to avoid serving a five-year prison sentence for manslaughter, she is reduced to working as a prostitute in the East End of London. On a foggy night, Jack the Ripper (played by Gustav Diessl) accosts her. He tells her he has no money, but because she likes him she leads him to her miserable garret.

"There was no complexity in Pabst's direction of the Jack the Ripper scenes," Brooks would write in one of the essays she collected in *Lulu in Hollywood* (1982). "He made them a tender love passage, until that terrible moment when Diessl saw the knife on the edge of the table, gleaming in the candlelight." Moving into the present tense as she imaginatively reentered Lulu's spirit, Brooks added, "It is Christmas Eve, and she is about to receive the gift that has been her dream since

childhood: death by a sexual maniac." Two decades later, Chaplin probably had this scene in mind while filming the episode in *Monsieur Verdoux*
in which Verdoux takes a young woman he has picked up in the street
back to his apartment with the intention of killing her.

8

According to Lita Grey, Chaplin reacted to the news of her second
pregnancy, which she broke to him upon his return from New York, by
ranting and raving "like a madman" that she was plotting to ruin his
career and by demanding—futilely—that she seek an abortion. In an
abrupt mood shift, he quieted down for a spell, only to flare up again in
new and alarming ways. In Lita's experience he had always been an avid
bather, but now he began taking as many as eight to ten baths and
showers a day. And in the dead of night, unable to sleep, he would arise
from his bed and patrol the grounds of his estate with a revolver in
hand, searching for prowlers. Lita's despair finally reached the point
where she broached the idea of divorce. By way of reply, she claimed,
Chaplin sprang to his desk, pulled out his revolver, and aimed it at
her, while spewing out "insane charges and threats." The thought of
being vilified in the press as a profligate who had abandoned a teenage
wife with a babe in arms and another on the way simply drove him
crazy.[50]

"One always writes comedy at the moments of deepest hysteria,"
V. S. Naipaul remarked in 1994 in a résumé of his own career.[51] In the
midst of Chaplin's frenzies in the fall of 1925, a nightmarish image of
his infant-bedeviled, exposure-threatened situation became fixed in his
mind. Miraculously, he was able to detect within that image the possibilities of a gag, and out of this imaginative coup an entire comedy struggled into the light. Henry Bergman would always remember the night
that his beloved boss sought him out and said, "Henry, I have an idea I
would like to do a gag placing me in a position I can't get away from for
some reason. I'm on a high place troubled by something else, monkeys
or things that come to me and I can't get away from them."[52] When the
details of the gag were filled in, Chaplin saw himself, or rather, Charlie,
as a neophyte tightrope performer near the top of a circus tent crowded
with onlookers. Not only is there no net beneath him, but his safety

harness comes loose. As he desperately strives to retain his balance on the swaying rope, circus monkeys, accidentally freed from confinement —and that surely represent the babies Chaplin did not want—come after him. As Charlie's terror mounts, the monkeys crawl over his shoulders and across his face and pull down his formal trousers, thereby exposing the fact that prior to his performance he had failed to put on a pair of tights. (Was Chaplin thinking here, however unconsciously, of his failure to wear a condom in his bouts with Lita?)

The young and intelligent assistant Chaplin hired to help him work out the ideas for *The Circus*—and whom he eventually tapped for the role of Rex the tightrope performer—was an aspiring actor and Yale graduate named Harry Crocker, of the wealthy San Francisco Crockers. A handsome six-footer, Crocker may have been one of Marion Davies's bedmates when Hearst was not around. In any event, it was Marion who introduced Crocker to Chaplin. But the scoop on the character of his new employer came from Eddie Sutherland and Harry d'Arrast. "If you're smart," said Sutherland, "you enter Chaplin on your books as a son-of-a-bitch. He isn't always one, but he can be one on occasion." D'Arrast voiced a similar warning. "Charlie has a sadistic streak in him. Even if he's very fond of you he'll try and lick you mentally, to cow you, to get your goat. He can't help it. You'll be surprised how many friends he's alienated through that one trait." [53]

With Frank Kawa at the wheel of the Locomobile, Chaplin and Crocker drove to Pearl Lodge in Del Monte, California, on November 9 for ten days of protracted brainstorming sessions about *The Circus*. On their return, Chaplin surprised a number of his staffers by not renewing Georgia Hale's contract—and surprised his wife by accepting her recommendation of her old friend Merna Kennedy as his new leading lady. Everything relating to the picture was now in readiness. Or so it seemed until December 6, when a violent wind and rain storm badly damaged the circus tent that the studio crew had erected. As a result, the first shooting date was postponed until January 11.

Sydney Earle Chaplin was born prematurely on March 30, 1926, into a household in which the film-anxious father could not tolerate the disruptions that a new baby caused. Although Lita tried her best to maintain an atmosphere of tranquillity, her efforts earned her nothing but threats and insults. Chaplin mocked her family ancestry by sneering that he knew how to handle "Mexican tramps."* In ominous tones he informed her—Lita recalled—that he could easily have her killed if he wanted to, inasmuch as he had contacts who could "do the job quickly and quietly and not think twice about it." The gibes that hurt the most, however, had to do with their sons' legitimacy. "I only wish I could find out," he cried, "if I'm really their father."[54]

Six months after little Sydney's disruptive arrival, catastrophe struck the Chaplin Studio. A fire broke out on the set of *The Circus* and completely consumed it. Adjoining prop rooms went up in flames as well. The studio's electric systems were put out of commission, and thousands of panes of glass were shattered by the firemen who battled the blaze. Although round-the-clock work by studio crews restored partial operations within five days, the shock to Chaplin's nervous system was not so quickly repaired.[55]

In November, Lita and her mother and baby Charlie went off to Hawaii for a vacation, leaving baby Sydney behind in the care of nursemaids. Among the hundreds of bitter thoughts that Lita took with her was an awareness that Merna Kennedy was now sleeping with Chaplin. Perhaps it was on the return voyage from the islands that she made up her mind to end the marriage. On December 2, front-page newspaper stories announced that she had left her husband and had taken their children with her. On the following day, the newspapers reported that she was demanding the stunning sum of $1.25 million in alimony. Chaplin was so upset by these events that he suspended work on *The Circus* and sent all but a handful of his employees home until further notice.[56]

A month later, Lita's uncle, Edwin McMurray, filed a forty-two-page divorce complaint against Chaplin, his studio, his business manager, Alf Reeves, four California banks that held Chaplin assets, and United Artists. The complaint could hardly have been more sensationally phrased. During her meetings with her uncle, Lita had told him that Chaplin's requests for oral sex had offended her and that he had also suggested, in

---

* Captain Lionel Krisel, U.S. Navy (Retired), who grew up on Summit Drive and was a close friend of young Charlie and Sydney Chaplin, says that Chaplin's prejudice against Mexicans served to diminish his respect for both boys as well as for their mother. Interview with Lionel Krisel, January 30, 1995.

the course of a weekend at San Simeon, that they invite another of Hearst's guests, a plain-looking young woman with a reputation for sexual ambidexterity, to join them in their bed. Lawyer McMurray inflated these accusations by couching them in richly denunciatory language of a high moral cast. A single sentence will suffice to convey the reverberant tenor of the whole: "Plaintiff alleges with regard to the sexual relations heretofore existing between said parties that the defendant's attitude, conduct and manifestations of interest therein have been abnormal, unnatural, perverted, degenerate and indecent." When such tidbits were reproduced in the press, they aroused enormous reader interest. In Los Angeles, meanwhile, a huckster who had somehow obtained all forty-two pages of the complaint made a small killing hawking mimeographed copies on street corners.[57]

On January 15, 1927, five days after being raked by McMurray's rhetorical shellfire, Chaplin suffered "a serious nervous breakdown," according to his physician. Three days later, the broken comedian learned from a story in the New York Times that the U.S. government was about to place a lien on his assets. On the 22nd, a government spokesman spelled out the Internal Revenue Service's contention that as a result of consistent underpayments stretching as far back as 1918, Chaplin owed $1.35 million in federal income taxes. Besides blocking access to his own money, the government succeeded in making it impossible for him to tap into United Artists funds.[58]

Chaplin's tax problems did him no good in the court of public opinion. Most of his critics, however, concentrated their disgust on his conduct as a husband and father. Reacting to a report that, with the paltry exception of one milk bill of twenty-seven dollars, he had not paid any child support from the moment his wife walked out on him and that he had not even bothered to visit his children at Christmas, a number of women's clubs across the country sought to embarrass him by raising money to "properly feed and care for Mrs. Chaplin's little boys." The La Salle, Illinois, League of Women Voters reacted to Lita's divorce complaint by recommending that all of Chaplin's films be banned from exhibition, and the mayor of Lynn, Massachusetts, issued an order declaring that none of Chaplin's films could be shown in the city until the resolution of his legal fight with his wife. But the distinction of formulating the question that was destined to come up again in the 1940s belonged to a certain Mrs. R. T. Niles. Chaplin, she said in a letter to the *New York Herald-Tribune*, "has an unfortunate habit of getting himself mixed up with young women whom he subsequently marries— probably to keep out of prison or from being deported. Is this man to be permitted to run riot for the rest of his life amid the foolish little girls of this country?"[59]

To Chaplin's infinite relief, he discovered that he also had defenders in 1927. Jimmy Walker and other big-city mayors laughed at the idea of banning his pictures. The Women's Club of Miami Beach appealed to local theater owners to show what they thought of the "silly agitation which women's clubs have taken in regard to Chaplin's pictures" by staging Chaplin film festivals. Another letter writer to the *New York Herald-Tribune*, Alice Carpenter, declared that "there is no one, man or woman, in the movie world who has done more to lift the pictures to a high plane, or who deserves to a greater extent the loyal sympathy and support of our people, than Mr. Chaplin, now suffering from the unbalanced actions of a willful girl."

Although a suggestion by the film columnist Harriet Underhill that "Mr. Chaplin never should marry" seemed to imply that there was something wrong with him psychologically, her explanation of the popularity of his pictures was that they were photographs of his "superior soul." Mr. Chaplin, she affirmed, "is filled with ideals." H. L. Mencken mordantly observed in the *Baltimore Sun*: "The very morons who worshipped Charlie Chaplin six weeks ago now prepare to dance around the stake while he is burned; he is learning something of the psychology of the mob. . . . A public trial involving sexual accusations is made a carnival everywhere in the United States." *Moving Picture World* stuck up for him on the grounds that he was an artist, as did *Theatre Arts*, and in a January 23 *New Yorker* piece called "Picking on Charlie Chaplin," his friend Ralph Barton rhetorically asked, "What other man on earth has been loved, respected and admired, at the same time, by French intellectuals, isolated Esquimaux, Iowa Babbitts, jazz-maddened New Yorkers, Bulgarian peasants, Scotch Presbyterians, New Guinea cannibals, German scientists, English statesmen, real estate brokers, dentists, kindergarten teachers and the entire race of artists?"[60]

Once he felt able to travel, Chaplin fled California and holed up in the Great Neck, Long Island, home of his lawyer, Nate Burkan, where he placed himself under the care of an eminent nerve specialist, Dr. Gustav Tiek. By the spring he was well enough to venture out into public again. On June 2, Burkan filed an answer to Lita's complaint. Two months later, Lita's implacable uncle struck again. He was ready, he let it be known, to release a list of five prominent women with whom Chaplin had allegedly been intimate during the period in which he and Lita had been living together as man and wife. Lita took it upon herself to pay a call on Marion Davies in order to inform her that she was on the list (along with Merna Kennedy, Edna Purviance, the actress Claire Windsor, and either Pola Negri or Peggy Hopkins Joyce). Davies was terrified by the thought of how Hearst would react to such a disclosure. As soon as Lita left, she appealed to Chaplin to settle his divorce difficulties before more people were hurt by them. He agreed to do so because he feared the fallout from the release of lawyer McMurray's list just as much as she did. Accordingly, at a courtroom hearing on August 22, at which he was not present, Lita was awarded $825,000, of which $200,000 was reserved for trust funds for her two sons. Chaplin also was ordered to pay $10,000 to Lita for the separation period, $22,000 in receivers' costs, $2,100 in court costs, and $1,000 a month to little Charlie and Sydney for five years while their trust funds were being organized. His own legal expenses amounted to almost a million dollars.[61]

9

Work on *The Circus* resumed on September 4, and a month later the final scene, in which the circus wagons depart and lonely Charlie remains behind, was shot—and repeatedly reshot—in the slanting sunlight and long shadows of early morning in a flat and dusty expanse of empty land in Glendale. Nothing about the activity that Chaplin brought into being there was lost on an observant reporter:

> Cameras grind. Circus wagons move across the vast stretch of open space. There is a beautiful haze in the background. The horses and the wagon wheels cause clouds of dust. The picture is gorgeous. No artist would be believed should he paint it. Twenty times the scene is taken.
> The cameras move in close to the ring. Carefully the operators mea-

sure the distance. From the lens to the tramp. He is alone in the center
of the ring.

He rehearses. Then action for camera. Eighty feet. The business is
done again. And again! And again! Fifty persons are looking on. All
members of the company. There are few eyes that are not moist. Most
of them know the story. They knew the meaning of this final "shot."

"How was that?" came inquiring from the Tramp. Fifty heads nodded
in affirmation. "Then we'll take it again; just once more," spoke the man
in the baggy pants and derby hat and misfit coat and dreadnought shoes.
The sun was getting high. The long shadows became shorter and
shorter. "Call it a day," said the Tramp, "we'll be here again tomorrow
at four [A.M.]." [62]

The fashionable people who turned out in force for the premiere at
the Strand Theater in New York on January 6, 1928, and for the Los
Angeles opening three weeks later at Grauman's Chinese Theater, rejoiced in the picture, as did almost all of the reviewers. While the
authoritative Stark Young, writing in the *New Republic*, had reservations
about its pathos, he reveled in its "old-style" Chaplin humor. The *New
York Times*'s Mordaunt Hall also waxed nostalgic about its resemblance
to "[Chaplin's] earlier films." As the *Literary Digest* said in summation
of the reviewers' delight, "[Chaplin's] critical admirers are killing the
fatted calf to celebrate his return to his own field of pure clowning."
The general public also demonstrated that it had not outgrown its taste
for the little tramp of old. In spite of having to compete with the success
of the sound-film revolution, *The Circus* earned close to $2 million by
1931. [63]

10

The long sequence that begins with the first glimpse of Charlie wandering about an amusement park somewhere in America (on Venice
Beach, in fact) is one of the classics of American slapstick humor. In an
aggressive gag that may have been grounded in Chaplin's anger about
infant feeding times on Summit Drive, Charlie devours a baby's hot dog
in wolfish bites while keeping the little darling amused with kittenish
grins and moues. Before taking an especially greedy chomp, he slathers

the dog with mustard. And when he has finished gorging, he fastidiously wipes the baby's mouth with a napkin, so as to allay parental suspicions about where the dog has gone. Trouble, however, is not so easily averted when a policeman concludes that Charlie is a pickpocket. And while he takes off lickety-split, the policeman proves to be just as fast a stepper. At last the fugitive dodges into a fun-house hall of mirrors, where a dozen reflections of his derby-hatted self disorient him as well as his pursuer. (For cameraman Rollie Totheroh, this scene may have been his proudest cinematographic moment.) Emerging into daylight again, Charlie takes a position among the wood-carved, mechanically powered figures on the fun house's arklike façade and, in a transpositional feat that by itself would have earned Chaplin enshrinement in a comedy hall of fame if there were such a thing, turns himself into a glockenspiel automaton. For a minute or two, the policeman is taken in by the performance, but then the chase resumes. Charlie runs into a circus tent, jumps on a revolving platform in the center of the ring, and keeps on running, with the policeman right behind him. Round and round they go, like a couple of squirrels in a cage, as the circus crowd roars with laughter. In a final attempt to elude the policeman, Charlie takes refuge in the hidden passageway beneath the platform on which a magician is about to stage a disappearing act. His inconvenient reappearances completely discombobulate the magician—and delight the crowd.

Once the real pickpocket has been arrested, Charlie is free to accept a surprising job offer. The circus, it turns out, is losing money because its clown acts are boring. To improve them, the owner-ringmaster hires Charlie, on the assumption that he is a very funny man. But in fact he is capable of provoking laughter only when he does not intend to. Every time he tries to be funny, he fails. With the introduction of this tricky premise, *The Circus* itself falters. The scene that proves that indeed he can't hack it as a conscious comedian is—inevitably—boring. As for the instances thereafter in which he appears in front of the crowd in a dead-serious frame of mind and tickles its funnybone by dint of unintentional fecklessness—or terrifies it, in the case of his pinch-hit performance as a tightrope walker—they are too few and far between to sustain the sublimely comic level of the first part of the picture.

While talking with an interviewer one day about the movie comics whose work he had learned by heart in his boyhood, Federico Fellini criticized Chaplin for his "emotional or ideological blackmail." How grateful we were, Fellini added, for "that carefree laughter with no purpose behind it" of Laurel and Hardy. Even though *The Circus* was undoubtedly one of the films that Fellini the circus lover had in mind when he referred to Chaplin as "a sort of Adam from whom we are all descended,"[64] it just as surely was one of the examples of the emotional extortion that he resented.

At first, the pathos is not unusual by Chaplin standards. Not for the first time, Charlie falls in love with a pretty girl who has no romantic interest in him. She is the daughter of the ringmaster and is herself employed in the circus as an equestrienne.* Eventually she develops a secret crush on a new addition to the troupe, a handsome tightrope walker named Rex, and Charlie makes it painfully clear to us that he is devastated. From this point onward, the portrayal of his suffering becomes somewhat embarrassing. Instead of binding up his broken heart and hitting the road, Charlie lingers on in the role of matchmaker between the girl and Rex. So masochistic is his selflessness that he even makes a gift to Rex of the ring he had purchased in the hope of presenting it to the girl himself.

By the final scene, fortunately, he has regained his dignity. As the circus horses are being hitched to the wagons for a move to another town, Rex and the girl, now happily married, urge Charlie to stick with the show, as they have decided to do. He knows, however, that the time has come for him to cut his ties with them and he remains behind. The camera shows him sitting motionless on a forgotten box in the center of the deserted grounds, his face shadowed with pain. Slowly he crumples a large piece of tissue paper with a star printed on it, of the sort that the ringmaster's daughter had used in her equestrienne act. At last, he gets to his feet and slowly walks away across the vast field. A sudden break in his stride is followed by a hitchy half-step, as in *The Tramp*. The last shot of his receding figure, in early-morning light, looking toward big trees in the hazy distance, is uncommonly beautiful.

---

* In almost all the scenes the girl wears a tutu. As Chaplin had already demonstrated in *The Gold Rush* and would again in the penultimate scene of *Modern Times* and in *Limelight*, he loved to cast his heroines as entertainers and to dress them in dance costumes. Behind all of these incarnations lay memories of his mother dressed as a serio-comedienne.

II

Chaplin's near-insane abuses of Lita, taking the form in his maddest moments of revolver brandishings and threatening remarks about an arranged killing, are translated in *The Circus* into the cruelties of the ringmaster. Given the real-life "Master's" contempt for Lita and her family as south-of-the-border scum, it is interesting that he chose a Mexican-American actor, Allan Garcia, to play the role.

The ringmaster's face is harsh and his eyes glare, and these indications of his nature are reinforced by every detail of the outfit that Chaplin had him wear, from his arrogantly cocked top hat to his riding breeches, high leather boots, and the whip he clutches in his hand. While there is no question that he knows his business, the way he runs it must have put Harry Crocker in mind of Eddie Sutherland's advice to "enter Chaplin on your books as a son-of-a-bitch" and of Harry d'Arrast's warning that "Charlie has a sadistic streak in him." Instead of offering helpful advice to the clowns when their cavortings in the ring fail to draw laughs, the ringmaster taunts them so harshly that he comes close to breaking their spirit. As for his treatment of his equestrienne daughter, it is so abusive as to suggest that he is being goaded by a physical attraction to her. In a characteristic outburst, he hurls her to the ground, threatens to strike her with his whip, and banishes her to her room without any supper, simply for committing an error in her performance.

When he physically assaults her toward the end of the story, Charlie retaliates by smashing him in the face, bruising it severely. Whether this chastisement begins the process of changing the ringmaster's heart is unclear, but in any event he subsequently makes peace with his daughter. His reformation, however, did not mean that Chaplin had no further use for him. For a power figure dressed in breeches and boots would reappear more than once in his cinematic world.

10

"YOU WANNA HEAR
'TOOT-TOOT-TOOTSIE'?"

With Harry Myers as the schizoid millionaire in City Lights *(1931).*

*T*HE *BIG PARADE* and *Ben Hur,* two of the most lavish movies
of 1925, boasted original musical scores. The task of playing them,
however, was in the hands of the thousands of musical ensembles (some
of which were full-scale orchestras) and solitary pianists or organists in
the employ of the theaters. Chaplin had earlier counted on the presence
of these musicians, and he continued to do so in the 1920s. For each of
the four silent films of feature length that he released in the course of
the decade—*The Kid, A Woman of Paris, The Gold Rush,* and *The Circus*

—he assembled a list of musical accompaniments out of a variety of published sources and supervised the preparation of cue sheets indicating when the numbers were to be played, which he then supplied free of charge to all the theaters that were booking the films. Admittedly, the procedure was cumbersome.

In the spring of 1926, the owners of a marginally successful Hollywood studio whose only dependable stars were Rin-Tin-Tin and John Barrymore came to the conclusion that a new technology could render theater accompaniments obsolete. Backed by the money that a high-flying Wall Street figure, Waddill Catchings, had recently invested in their company, the Warner brothers acquired the rights to a process developed by Bell Labs and manufactured by Western Electric that enabled disc-recorded sound to be played in synchronization with projected film images. The Warners' next step was to provide their newest Barrymore film, *Don Juan*, with a sound track of musical themes, played by the New York Philharmonic. When the picture opened in August at the studio's flagship theater in New York City, no other movie house in the country possessed the capability to handle Vitaphone, as the disc system was called, for an installation of Western Electric amplifiers and other necessary equipment cost $16,000 in an average-sized theater. Yet by the end of 1926, the Warners' gamble on Vitaphone looked like a winner. *Don Juan* had attracted markedly larger crowds to those theaters that had converted to the new technology than to those that had not. Furthermore, a series of Vitaphone shorts in which famous vocalists and instrumentalists had simply done their thing on a bare stage had also made a hit with audiences, while the sounds of bomb explosions, pistol shots, and neighing horses had enlivened an otherwise dated war comedy, starring Sydney Chaplin, entitled *The Better 'Ole*.

A hastily constructed sound stage on the Warner Brothers lot on Sunset Boulevard became the setting for their next enterprise, a film version of Samson Raphaelson's well-known play, *The Jazz Singer*, with Al Jolson, the most electrifying entertainer in Broadway history, in the title role.* The disc system, it was planned, would pick up Jolson's renderings of half a dozen Tin Pan Alley tunes, as well as excerpts sung

---

* Jolson's power over audiences was "supernatural," Robert Benchley wrote in the old *Life*. It was "as if an electric current had been run along wires under the seats where the hats are stuck." Quoted in Alexander Walker, *The Shattered Silents* (London, 1978), p. 29.

in Hebrew from "Kol Nidre" and the "Yahrzeit." No dialogue was to be recorded, however, for the Warners were leery of tinkering with the mimetic fundamentals of silent pictures.

At the outset of the movie, the hero, Jakie Rabinowitz (played by the child actor Bobbie Gordon), is a thirteen-year-old kid on the Lower East Side of New York. Because he wants to be a jazz singer, Jakie runs away from home, in defiance of the wishes of his rabbinical father (played by Warner Oland) that he become a cantor. Ten years later and three thousand miles away in San Francisco, the young singer, now known as Jack Robin (and played by Jolson), is down on his luck on the night that he wanders into Coffee Dan's nightclub. Given a chance to sing, he leaps in front of the band and offers a rousing version of "Dirty Hands, Dirty Face." The script called for Robin's performance to end with the enthusiastic applause of the audience, but the irrepressible Jolson could not resist the temptation to show off a little. "Wait a minute," he ad-libbed into the open mike, holding up his hands to quiet the applause. "Wait a minute. You ain't heard nothin' yet! Wait a minute, I tell you. You ain't heard nothin.' You wanna hear 'Toot-Toot-Tootsie'? All right. Hold on." Following a few instructions to the band, Jolson belted out the number. Had his spoken words sounded natural? Of course they had. And did they generate excitement? Of course they did. "You ain't heard nothin' yet" was a signature line that Jolson had used thousands of times to charge up his fans. Small wonder, then, that Sam Warner, the oldest of the studio's owners, not only ruled against cutting the ad lib, but sanctioned the inclusion of a second interpolation of sound speech.

As the movie continues, Robin, at long last, lands a part in a Broadway show and returns to his parents' home for the first time since his flight a decade earlier. There he finds his mother (played by Eugenie Besserer) in the parlor, and sitting down at the piano, he plays and sings Irving Berlin's "Blue Skies." In between the first and second verses, Jolson again speaks to his audience—in this case, his audience of one. "Mama darlin'," he cries, "if I'm a success in this show, well, we're gonna move from here. Oh, yes, we're—we're gonna move up in the Bronx. A lot of nice green grass up there. A whole lot of people you know. There's the Ginsburgs, the Guttenbergs and the Goldbergs. Oh, a whole lot of bergs. I dunno 'em all. And I'm gonna buy you a nice black silk dress, Mama. You see, Mrs. Freedman, the butcher's wife, she'll be jealous of you." Eugenie Besserer mumbled a brief reply. Jolson laughed—and immediately promised to take her to Coney Island for a ride on the Chute-the-Chute. "Oh, no!—I wouldn't . . ." Besserer exclaimed in protest. "Well, with me it's all right," Jolson rejoined. "I'll kiss ya and hug ya. You see if I don't. Oh Mama, Mama! Stop now! Will you? Kiss me!" After finishing off "Blue Skies" Jolson grinningly asked, "You like that slap in the tune?" For the rest of the picture, the dialogue, such as it was, appeared on cards, in normal silent-era fashion.

"One of the most delightful bits in the photoplay," declared the critic for *Moving Picture World*, "is an episode of gentle repartee between [Jolson] and Eugenie Besserer." Robert Sherwood's review expressed a larger appreciation. The jazz singer's scene with his mother, he announced, "was fraught with tremendous significance," by which he meant that "the end of the silent drama is in sight." Perhaps Sherwood's historical awareness was aided by the spectacle he had encountered outside the Warner Theater in New York when *The Jazz Singer* opened there on the evening of October 6, 1927. Jolson was on hand, having just returned from the Dempsey-Tunney rematch in Chicago. But the reporters who covered the opening were less interested in him—for a change—than they were in the size and behavior of the crowd. It was a mob, said the *New York Herald-Tribune*'s man, "one of those milling, battling mobs that used to blockade cinema premieres to watch the stars pass by in the days before they moved all the studios to Hollywood."

Although Samson Raphaelson detested the mawkishness of the Warner Brothers version of his story and condemned Jolson for ignoring the character of Jack Robin and playing himself, *The Jazz Singer* was the cinematic sensation of 1927. In theaters that were properly wired, it did a colossal business, and it cued a wave of conversions in theaters that were not. At the outset of 1928, only 157 of the 20,000 movie theaters in the United States had been able to present sound pictures; at the end of the year, more than a thousand could.

Warner Brothers was scrambling meantime to exploit the public's interest in movie talk that it could hear. Three music-oriented Vitaphone features already in production in early 1928 were turned into part-talkies, and on July 8, 1928, a melodrama about crooks called *Lights of New York*, in which all the dialogue was recorded, had its premiere at the Strand in New York. Although the story line was ludicrous, the dialogue had a certain rough-cut authenticity that inspired the *New York*

Times to hail it as "the alpha of what may develop as the new language of the screen."

To meet Warner Brothers' upstart challenge, Fox, Paramount, and other studios adopted an optical process of sound recording, while General Electric and RCA entered into competition with Western Electric as suppliers of sound equipment to theaters. By the end of 1929, more than eight thousand theaters had been wired, most of them with equipment that could present either disc- or optical-system sound. Attendance figures tell the story of why the industry's resistance to the sound revolution collapsed as rapidly as it did, in spite of the heavy costs it entailed, not to mention the headaches suffered on the set by directors, cameramen, and actors alike as a consequence of the primitive nature of some of the technology (*e.g.*, large stationary microphones that were hard to conceal). In 1926, the last year of a completely silent cinema, fifty million people a week went to the movies in the United States; in 1930, the first year of sound technology's domination, paid admissions soared to ninety million a week. America bought into a new deal in motion pictures before it did in politics.[1]

2

Chaplin feared and hated these developments. In early 1929, Gladys Hall, a reporter for *Motion Picture*, asked him, "What shall I tell our readers you think of the talkies?" "You can tell 'em I loathe them," Chaplin replied.

> They are spoiling the oldest art in the world—the art of pantomime. They are ruining the great beauty of silence. They are defeating the meaning of the screen, the appeal that has created the star system, the fan system, the vast popularity of the whole. . . . The screen is pictorial. Pictures! Lovely looking girls, handsome young men. . . . What if the girls can't act? Of course they can't. Who has cared?. . . Certainly I prefer to see, say, Dolores Costello, in a thin tale than some aged actress of the stage doing dialogue with revolting close-ups.

From now on, he added, his own pictures would feature synchronized music, but talk was out of the question. "For me, it would be fatal."[2]

"The great beauty of silence!" Jolson mockingly began in his published reply to Chaplin's lament.

I was at a party the other night, and from eight-thirty till around five A.M. Charlie never stopped talking and singing. . . . If Charlie wants to keep what he calls "the great beauty of silence," let him go lock himself in a room—become a nun's brother, or something. . . . Charlie goes on record as loathing talkies. Well, I'm just the opposite. I think he'd better get to like 'em—or he'll find out the public don't like him. . . . What he's really got is a gentleman complex. He's afraid he talks too nice to fit in with the characterization he had built up on the screen.[3]

Strictly speaking, Jolson's closing sneer made no sense. An actor as gifted as Chaplin would have had no more trouble imposing some sort of lower-class English or American accent upon the tramp than in allowing him to speak in the somewhat mincing manner that he himself had affected since coming to Hollywood. But the awful truth underlying Jolson's words was that no voice of any sort would have fitted the appeal of the tramp character. Charlie was a universal little man with whom many different peoples around the world identified. Betraying a specific national origin through recorded speech would have disastrously nar-rowed the range of this intimacy. Short of abandoning the role, Chaplin had no choice but to continue his reliance on pantomimed communica-tion. Despite mounting concern about a sudden and ominous decline in his mother's health, he began constructing plans for a tramp picture in which recorded music and comic sound effects would have considerable importance, but which would compromise no further with the sound revolution.

In the ensuing months, however, Hannah's protracted suffering from an infected gall bladder culminated in her miserable death on August 28, 1928, and paralyzing memories of all that she had been through made work very difficult. Ever since her arrival in California, Chaplin had been too distressed by her schizophrenic behavior to spend much time with her.* But in Glendale Hospital in the final weeks of her life,

---

* Sydney Chaplin (the younger) vividly remembers the family lore about his grand-mother Hannah. On a supervised visit to a Los Angeles department store one day, she asked the clerk for "shit-brown gloves." When pairs were brought out for her approval, she vehemently protested, "No, no! that's not shit-brown!" During rare appearances at Summit Drive, she was apt at some point to raise her skirt sufficiently high as to leave no doubt that she was not wearing underpants. Interview with Sydney Chaplin, February 6, 1995.

he showed up every day and did his best to make her laugh. On coming away from these visits he immediately sank into melancholy, and her death precipitated a long fit of depression. At the burial in Hollywood Cemetery it was expected that he would step forward and bid farewell to her before the lid on the coffin was lowered. But "I said no: I couldn't," he told the interviewer Richard Meryman years afterward. "Suddenly seeing somebody beloved and small, you think of all the events of life. . . . It's really moving. . . . I couldn't. . . . I couldn't touch her. No, I couldn't touch her."[4]

He also was distracted during this difficult year by financial worries, about the risk first of all of committing himself to a picture in which recorded dialogue would be shunned, and second, about the costly settlement in February of his personal and corporate income-tax troubles, which required him to pay the federal government a resounding $1.67 million.[5]* A far greater strain on his nerves, however, came from his prep work for his new picture. Never before had he faced the task of organizing such painful personal-history material. So slow was his progress in working out the details of the story that it was not until December 27 that the shooting of *City Lights* commenced.

3

The picture focuses on the tramp's involvement in two different cases of mind-darkening illness, madness and blindness. Double identities, grand illusions and disillusions, and stirring rescues are the stuff out of which the drama is elaborated. In the first strand of the story, Charlie meets a beautiful flower girl who is blind. That he is amorously attracted to her because of her affliction and not in spite of it has been derided by some critics as a sentimentality, but not by Evelyn Waugh. And if Waugh had known of mentally ill Hannah Chaplin's ability to attract men sexually—at least for a time—he again would have understood. As he observed in the early 1950s to the beautiful Diana Cooper, in a letter written in capital letters because Cooper's eyesight was fading,

---

* A happy consequence of his sudden need for cash is that he sold his stock holdings a year before the Great Crash.

"BLINDNESS AND MADNESS IN WOMEN HAS [sic] ALWAYS HAD PRODIGIOUS EROTIC APPEAL FROM EARLIEST RO-MANCE TO OUR DAY. CHARLIE'S HEROINE ... CITY LIGHTS AND M. ARLENS LILY CHRISTINE (I THINK) IN MY DAY QUO VADIS OR LAST DAYS OF POMPEII HAD BLIND HEROINE."[6]

Initially, Chaplin imagined that in the second strand of his story two members of a rich men's club would pick up the tramp one evening for the purposes of demonstrating the instability of human consciousness. After conducting him to their palatial apartment, they would wine and dine him and introduce him to pretty girls. When he was too exhausted to stay awake any longer, they would return him to his usual haunts. On waking up, he would be plagued by the disturbing uncertainty of whether or not his brush with high life had actually occurred.[7] But at some point in Chaplin's thinking, the tramp ceased to be the unstable character and the two rich men metamorphosed into a millionaire "Jek-yll and Hyde inebriate," as the comedian described him in an interview with the New York Times's Mordaunt Hall.[8] When drunk, the millionaire would be one sort of person; when sober, quite another.*

As the setting for the picture, Chaplin imagined an amalgam of urban locales. The public square and the principal shopping streets would have an American downtown look; the paved embankment of the river running through the city would call London to mind, or possibly Paris; and the courtyard below the apartment where the flower girl and her grandmother live would have a Mediterranean air. To work out the practical problems of set design, he hired a clever Australian, Henry Clive. Convinced by Clive's histrionic personality that he had acting talent, too, he asked him if he would be willing to take the part of the millionaire, and Clive said he would.

---

* Some years after the release of City Lights, the Finnish Madame de Staël, Hella Wuoli-joki, told Bertolt Brecht a story about a big landowner named Puntila who was divided against himself by the effects on the one hand of drinking and on the other of abstinence. Brecht reworked this material into Puntila and His Servant Matti. In his cups, Puntila is morally expansive to the point of becoming engaged to four different lower-class girls; on sobering up, an alienated, uptight Puntila disowns the girls and drives them away. It is possible that Chaplin's schizoid millionaire also influenced Brecht's conception of Puntila.

Finding an actress who could play the flower girl proved to be a much more difficult task. Of the many applicants whom Chaplin interviewed, not one seemed right for the part, and in his discouragement he began to think of expanding his search beyond Los Angeles. Then one night at a prizefight, he noticed a young woman sitting near him whose radiantly lovely face, framed by lightly marcelled blond hair, reminded him of Edna Purviance at nineteen. Her name was Virginia Cherrill. In *My Autobiography*, Chaplin would insist that he had encountered her on the beach at Santa Monica, where she and several other pretty girls, all of them dressed in bathing suits, were disporting themselves in between takes for a movie. Virginia waved to him and called, "When am I going to work for you?"

In truth, the twenty-year-old Cherrill, a somewhat spoiled socialite from Chicago, had never worked in the movies before meeting Chaplin and did not particularly wish to. Her only reason for coming to California had been to forget the emotionally draining divorce she had just gone through. Among the romantic landmarks in her future lay marriages to Cary Grant and William Rhinelander Stewart, and in 1937 she would move into the British aristocracy as the Countess of Jersey.[9] From the start, Chaplin disliked Cherrill, in all likelihood because of her independent spirit, and she, in turn, did not like him. Nevertheless, he hired her. The explanation he would give in *My Autobiography* was that she had the ability to look blind without looking repulsive, unlike the young women he had previously screen-tested who kept rolling their eyes upward and showing the whites.[10]

The filming of *City Lights* proceeded by nervous fits and starts. In the first 534 working days after the cameras started rolling, shooting occurred on a meager 166 of them. Chaplin's tension-riddled drive for perfection also led to a maniacal concentration on the smallest defects in Cherrill's acting. Hours, days, and ultimately weeks went by as he vainly tried to teach her how to offer a flower to Charlie for his buttonhole in precisely the way that he wanted. Figuring out a plausible reason why the flower girl should assume that Charlie was a rich man was another problem that plagued him. Given such travails, it is not surprising that on February 25, 1929, he was felled by stomach cramps. Immediately thereafter, he came down with flu and remained *hors de combat* until April 1. On his first day back at work, Cherrill was made to realize that he still did not approve of the way she offered the boutonniere to Charlie.[11]

In mid-May the stormy weather on the set temporarily improved, thanks to the Academy of Motion Picture Arts and Sciences. At a banquet on the evening of the 16th in the Blossom Room of Hollywood's Roosevelt Hotel, the Academy handed out its very first Oscars, as its honors were subsequently nicknamed for reasons that remain in doubt. The best-actor winner was Emil Jannings for *The Way of All Flesh* and *The Last Command*. The comedy direction award went to Lewis Milestone for *Two Arabian Knights*, a farce about two warring buddies in World War I. But neither of these narrowly defined awards aroused envy in the industry's one-man band. For the Academy bestowed a comprehensive Special Award upon Chaplin "for versatility and genius in writing, acting, directing and producing *The Circus.*"[12]

Ten days later, Henry Clive ran afoul of ringmaster Chaplin's mercurial temper. On the morning of the filming of the river scene that called for the moody millionaire to attempt to drown himself, Clive told Chaplin that he was just recovering from a bad cold and did not want to plunge into the chilly water (of the swimming pool that was serving as a section of the river) until a few more hours of sunlight had warmed it. Chaplin stalked off in a rage, hunted up Carl Robinson, and ordered him to fire Clive immediately. He then hired Harry Myers, a vaudeville and movie veteran best known for his fine work in the Hollywood version of *A Connecticut Yankee in King Arthur's Court* (1921) and spent the better part of a week—and a fair amount of money—reshooting the scenes in which Clive had already appeared.

The following September, another outburst shook the studio. Chaplin phoned Alf Reeves from home and informed him that he would not set foot in the studio again as long as Harry Crocker remained in his employ. What had angered him he refused to say, nor did Crocker ever shed any light on their difficulties. Not until the filming of *Limelight* in 1951 would the socialite be permitted to rejoin Chaplin's staff, as a business manager.[13]

The suspension of Virginia Cherrill, after ten months of shooting, was the clearest measure of the emotional toll that the picture was making Chaplin pay. For quite some time, he had been disgusted by Cherrill's off-the-set behavior. Very much of a good-time girl, she loved going to parties and often reported for work after having been on the town until the wee hours. On the mornings when she was somewhat the worse for wear, Chaplin never failed to pick up on the evidences of her dissipation. As the time approached for filming the climactic scene of the picture, in which the flower girl, her sight restored, at long last realizes that her supposedly rich benefactor is a tramp, Chaplin became terribly tense. In close-ups of Cherrill's face as well as of his, surges of conflicting emotion would have to be registered, and he was not at all sure that she was equal to the challenge. Thus when she came to him one morning and asked to be excused a little early that day so that she could keep a hair appointment, his nerves went haywire. Through Carl Robinson, the carrier of bad tidings in the Clive dismissal, he informed her that she was not to come to work until further notice.

During her absence from the studio, an excited Georgia Hale came close to convincing Chaplin that if he fired Cherrill she could handle the part of the flower girl. Carl Robinson, however, persuaded him that she could not. The next candidate to be considered was a beautiful blonde known professionally as Marilyn Morgan. Since she had just turned sixteen, she arrived at the studio accompanied by her mother. But while Chaplin was thrilling her with his enthusiasm about the outcome of her screen test, Reeves and Robinson were agreeing that their employer's reputation could not survive another scandal involving a teenage actress and her mother. Because the hour was late, only one typist was still on duty at the studio. After quietly instructing her to go home at once, Reeves and Robinson informed Chaplin that a contract for his new leading lady could not be prepared until the next day. By then, Chaplin had changed his mind about her, and a few days later he swallowed his pride and had a talk with Cherrill. To his surprise, she told him that she would not go on working for him unless he doubled her salary to $150 a week. As everyone in Hollywood knew, Charlie Chaplin could hang tough in negotiations. But when Cherrill emerged from his office after an hourlong confrontation, her face was wet with the tears of victory.[14]

In early November she returned to the set, against a backdrop of disastrous events. On October 24—"Black Thursday"—panic selling had overwhelmed the New York Stock Exchange, and five days later another spectacular drop in stock prices occurred. Within a month, a large part of the paper values of the preceding decade was wiped out. During the nine months of additional camera work and the two months of cutting and editing that were required to ready *City Lights* for its premiere at the grand opening of the Los Angeles Theater* on January 30, 1931, the Great Depression overtook the world.

4

To a fanfare of jazz trumpets, an electric sign spells out "City Lights" across a nighttime shot of a city square. With this dramatic flourish, Chaplin proclaimed that the picture, which in many ways is the finest he ever made, would be distinguished by the sound of music, as compellingly performed by a thirty-five-piece orchestra under the expert direction of Alfred Newman. With the exception of a few familiar tunes, most notably Padilla's "La Violetera" ("Who'll Buy My Violets"), which serves as the principal leitmotif for the blind girl, the melodies were composed by Chaplin and arranged by another musical expert, Arthur Johnston.

The camera remains focused on the square as night turns into day. In the foreground, a crowd of respectably dressed citizens has gathered beneath a podium; in the rear looms a large monument, covered with a sheet. Clearly, a dedication is about to take place. Although at this point the speaker is too far away to be identifiable, a title card conveys his opening comment: "To the people of this city we donate this monument, 'Peace and Prosperity.' " While the scene that follows was filmed well before the crash of the stock market, Chaplin added the title card

---

* The Los Angeles was the last of the great movie palaces to be erected in the Broadway theater district of the city. Although the independent film exhibitor H. L. Gumbiner supplied most of the financing, Chaplin was an investor, too, in order to ensure himself a showcase outlet for the silent pictures he intended to keep making. The theater cost more than a million dollars. From the lavish French-baroque lobby, with its chandeliers, fluted columns, mirrored walls, bronze banisters, and Louis XIV sunburst motif, ticketholders could walk up the central staircase to a crystal fountain and a mural "in the style of" Fragonard. Mothers with fretful babies could try to calm them in one of the soundproof crying rooms above the loge, and a supervised playroom in the basement was available to older children. A restaurant, a designated smoking room (with built-in cigarette lighters), a walnut-paneled lounge, and multicolored marble restrooms were also among the theater's amenities. "Broadway Historic Theater District," pp. 7–8.

afterwards and through its sarcastic reference to prosperity, he threw the shadow of a wider suffering across the picture's tormented personal stories.

The speaker is the city's mayor (Henry Bergman). As a close-in shot dwells on his cartoonlike embodiment of fat-cat pomposity (morning coat, striped pants, swelling paunch, and quivering jowls), the sound track mocks the triumph of the talkies by offering the vibrations of a kazoo in lieu of his voice. The mayor's successor at the podium, a hawk-faced clubwoman whose equally unintelligible remarks sound like the cluckings of a chicken, concludes the speechifying by releasing the covering on the monument. Three gigantic white figures are revealed. In the center of the group is an enthroned female figure with the grand bearing of a goddess; to her right is a kneeling male figure with his right hand upraised, palm out, in a gesture of peace; and at the goddess's feet is a recumbent and obviously defeated warrior, pointing a sword in her direction. Curled up asleep in the goddess's capacious lap is Charlie, looking for all the world like a little boy nestled against his mother, but also constituting a dark stain on the whiteness of the monument. The covering that has concealed him from view is one of the more literal veils of illusion that get stripped away in *City Lights*.

In response to the bellowed (in pantomime) commands of the mayor and the fire chief that he vacate the premises at once, Charlie tips his derby, turns around so that his backside is toward the crowd, and starts to lower himself to the ground, only to catch the hole in the seat of his pants on the warrior's sword. A band strikes up "The Star-Spangled Banner" and the crowd snaps to attention. With transparently insincere reverence, Charlie straightens up as best he can and presses his hat against his heart. But because his pants have become firmly hooked on the sword, he has an excuse to keep losing his balance and falling forward. The incident is amusing enough, but it is also an intentional sneer.

In the interwar decades, George Orwell once declared in a famously damning indictment, leftist intellectuals in Britain were

ashamed of their own nationality. In left-wing circles it is always felt that there is something slightly disgraceful in being an Englishman. . . . It is a strange fact, but it is unquestionably true, that almost any English intellectual would feel more ashamed of standing to attention during "God Save the King" than of stealing from a poor box. All through the critical years [of the 1920s and 1930s] many left-wingers were chipping away at English morale, trying to spread an outlook that was sometimes squashily pacific, sometimes violently pro-Russian, but always anti-British.[15]

As a leftist who liked to think of himself as a citizen of the world, Chaplin was also given to disparaging the idea of national pride. "Patriotism," he declared to a reporter as he came off the tennis courts at a posh hotel in Juan-les-Pins in the summer following the release of *City Lights*, "is the greatest insanity that the world has ever suffered."[16] Small wonder, then, that in the public-monument scene in the picture he drew a mocking contrast between Charlie's disruptive figure and the bunch of stuffed shirts standing stiffly at attention during "The Star-Spangled Banner."

5

To compete with the anarchic antics that the Marx Brothers were successfully importing into the movies from their musical-comedy triumphs, Chaplin relied on his own brands of that sort of behavior. Some of his samples harked back to Keystone and Essanay days. Thus when Charlie takes on a professional prizefight in order to earn money for the blind girl, he avoids the blows of his opponent by hiding behind the referee, at which point all three men begin to sidestep in unison in a zombielike ballet.

As a counterchallenge to Groucho's innuendos about sex and the libidinal rambunctiousness of Harpo, the old pro reached into his bag of tricks a second time and pulled out "Elizabethan" humor. The first instance of it occurs as the strains of "The Star-Spangled Banner" fade away. Charlie lifts his pants off the recumbent warrior's sword, slides backwards down the statue's extended arm, and comes to rest on the face. From the podium below, it appears that the warrior's nose is buried deep in the crack between Charlie's buttocks. For a couple of seconds, the little fellow sits motionless. Then he heaves a sigh that suggests how reluctant he is to move on. As cries of outrage arise from the dignitaries, a blank look comes over his face. What on earth is all the fuss about? he seems to be asking—to the further infuriation of the onlookers.

During the locker-room prelude to the prize-ring face-off, Charlie's fear of a beating again leads to homosexual joking. In the first glimpse of him in his cute boxing shorts, he is only slightly nervous. After all, the crooked boxer he is slated to fight has agreed not only to pull his punches but to split the purse with him fifty-fifty. The fix, in short, is in —until the boxer abruptly disappears, after being tipped off that the police are looking for him. As a last-minute replacement, the promoter picks a pug who makes it abundantly clear that he has mayhem on his mind. In a panicky attempt to ingratiate himself with this unsmiling ruffian, Charlie crosses his bare knees, arches his eyebrows, and revolves his derby—which he is unaccountably still wearing—one hundred and eighty degrees, all the while flashing a silly smile at his antagonist and coyly hunching up his shoulders. The ruffian for his part is so discomfited by these attentions that he retreats behind a curtain before stepping out of his pants and preparing for the ring.

The cleverest of the picture's sex scenes involves a naked female figure of sinuous proportions that dominates the display of sculptures in an art-store window. As Charlie strides along a fashionable downtown street after quitting the dedication ceremony, the nude catches his eye and he stops. As he does so, the camera switches to a viewpoint inside the window looking out at the street, just as it would at a critical point in the flower-shop scene at the close of the picture. Expectations of how the blatant vulgarian of the dedication ceremony is going to behave as he moves closer to the window are not fulfilled. Instead of staring at the statue with pornographic enthusiasm, he fixes his gaze on a Remington-like miniature of a mounted cowboy. At last, the nude receives his careful scrutiny, which Charlie attempts to mask by raising his arm and casually scratching his head. Quickly adopting a new mask, he becomes an art connoisseur whose concern with every last detail of the nude is prompted by aesthetic considerations. He moves smack up against the glass for a micro-inspection of the sculptor's achievement; he backs off to appreciate it in perspective; he twirls his cane; he crosses his feet; he coughs discreetly; his hypocrisy is exquisite.

And while he is moving back and forth, a freight elevator in the rectangle of sidewalk behind him is moving up and down, its platform

CHARLIE CHAPLIN AND HIS TIMES

coming flush with the sidewalk only when he unknowingly steps back onto it. Just as his air of connoisseurship is a veil, so the sidewalk is nothing more than a membrane, as he finally realizes. Gazing into the hole in which he might have broken his neck, he begins to berate a workman who is riding the platform back to street level. As the workman's head and shoulders come into view, Charlie's remonstrances become more vehement—up to the point where they abruptly cease. For the rising elevator destroys another illusion. The workman is not a little guy, as he had appeared to be, but a hulking giant. With an anxious tip of his hat, Charlie hastily retreats. Unwittingly, he is on his way to a rendezvous with exalted passion.

6

Cars are parked three deep on a curving street corner skirting the edge of a park in a prosperous part of town. As jaywalking Charlie is zigzagging through the maze of these vehicles, he comes up behind a cop straddling a motorcycle. To avoid attracting the attention of the law, he scoots into the back of a limousine parked against the curb and steps out on the other side. The slamming of the heavy door creates an illusion in the mind of a blind girl who is offering flowers for sale. Believing that a wealthy gentleman has just gotten out of his car, she hails Charlie as "Sir," holds up a posey in each hand, and asks if he would like to buy one. Since he is unaware of her disability, he is surprised and slightly annoyed that she would make her pitch to a tramp. Upon deciding after all to give her a little business, he looks off into space while she readies the boutonniere he has chosen and puts aside the other one. As his twitchily impatient gestures indicate, he is completely absorbed in himself. Only when he sees that she is blind does his attitude change, and the change is profound.

At nose-to-nose range, he stares into her eyes, as if seeking to plumb a mystery behind their blankness. Slowly and formally, he raises his hat to her, in a silent expression of understanding. He finds excuses to touch her hand and forearm. A strange, stricken look comes over his face as she pins the boutonniere to his lapel. Fishing a coin from his pocket, he presses it into her palm and assists her to sit down. Suddenly, the owner of the limousine (who looks rather like the Pittsburgh tycoon Andrew

Mellon) reappears and is driven away by his chauffeur. The blind girl calls, "Wait for your change, sir," and Charlie, realizing the mistake she has made, tiptoes around the corner, thus leaving her with a sizable tip. His gesture confirms her initial mistake about him. In the dark world of her mind, Charlie has an identity that is drastically at odds with the tattered truth. At the end of their next meeting, her benefactor will kiss her hand on the stairway beneath her apartment and ask if he may see her home again, and as she dreams on about his wealth she will reply, "Whenever you wish, sir."

In the quiet of the night, a drunken millionaire, dressed in a tuxedo, stumbles down the steps of a river embankment. He is a man of two minds in more ways than one. At the moment he is depressively intent on "ending it all" by drowning himself. Luckily for him, Charlie is on hand, sniffing the flower he has purchased from the blind girl. With a combination of physical effort and inspirational talk about the wonders of life ("Tomorrow the birds will sing"), he manages to rescue this nut case from the folly of self-destruction. The latter's gratitude knows no bounds. Following several dripping-wet bear hugs, the millionaire takes his new best friend home with him, plies him with booze, lends him a tuxedo, foots the bills that the two of them rack up in a fancy nightclub, and ends the evening by telling Charlie that he can have his Rolls-Royce. Unfortunately, his generous impulses are a sometime thing. On sobering up, he does not even recognize his buddy and bars him from his house. Only when he is soused again does he remember how much he owes Charlie.

The millionaire's inner turmoil is related to his feelings about his wife. When he pointedly asks his butler if there is any news of her, he learns that she "has sent for her baggage, sir." "Good!" exclaims the millionaire. The overwhelming likelihood, however, is that he still loves her. For when he happens upon a glamorously posed photograph of her dark-haired beauty, he furiously smashes it to the floor, and a minute or so later seizes a revolver from a table drawer and makes a halfhearted effort to shoot himself in the head.

Behind his insanely erratic behavior lay the shadow of Hannah Chaplin's. But in filling in the details of the millionaire's personality, Chaplin drew on Ralph Barton's bon-vivant appetites and thirsts—and fits of lovelorn depression about a dark-haired beauty. That Barton's psychological malaise was worsening in the late 1920s was common knowledge in the circles in which he traveled. All his artistic sensibilities had responded to Carlotta Monterey's lustrous black hair, smoldering eyes, and startlingly white skin. But because of infidelities he had lost her. In a half-joking way, he spoke to friends of killing himself, and as he became more and more disillusioned about his rebound marriage to a Frenchwoman, Germaine Tailleferre, the number of his veiled warnings of self-destruction increased. In mid-1929, he and Tailleferre came to a bitter parting of the ways. The event, however, that really crushed him that summer was Carlotta's marriage—in the teeth of his pleas to her to come back to him—to Eugene O'Neill.

A year and a half later, the news that he had actually made a suicide attempt moved Chaplin to intervene in his life, much as Charlie had in the millionaire's. Upon reaching New York for the opening of *City Lights* at the Cohan Theater, he persuaded Barton to accompany him to England. The change of scenery failed to raise the illustrator's spirits. Shortly after cutting his trip short and returning to New York, he ended it all with a single shot to the head from a .25-caliber revolver.[17]

The millionaire's spiritual desperation, evident in his Bartonesque, let's-have-a-party highs as well as in his suicidal lows, is an oddly engaging trait. Indeed, he is just as sympathetic as Charlie, when the two of them play off each other like a Chaplinian answer to Laurel and Hardy (who had become a team in 1926 in *Forty-five Minutes from Hollywood*). During their first encounter on the riverfront, the millionaire ties one end of a rope around a large stone and knots the other end into a loop, which he intends to secure around his neck just before tossing the stone into the water. By mistake, he loops the rope around Charlie's neck, so that it is he who gets jerked into the drink. Before the scene is over, each of them has all but drowned in the course of trying to save the other. Further confusions arise at the nightclub, where upon arrival they are already three sheets to the wind. Charlie consumes forkfuls of confetti under the illusion that it is spaghetti and cannot figure out why his cigar won't draw, because he does not see that the cigar he keeps lighting is in the millionaire's hand. And in a marvelous moment on the way home in the millionaire's Rolls-Royce, Charlie offers a word of caution to his boozy pal about driving across sidewalks when rounding corners, to which the millionaire replies, "Am I driving?"

The pivotal moment in the picture occurs in the last of the scenes in the millionaire's living room. Charlie is despondent about his failure to raise enough money to pay for an eye operation for the blind girl. The millionaire replies by taking out his wallet and handing him a thousand dollars. Alas for Charlie, a robbery attempt by two thugs who have been hiding behind the living-room curtains triggers a chain of events that ultimately lands him in jail. For by the time a policeman arrives, a blow to the millionaire's head from one of the thugs has catapulted him into his sobersidedly mean personality, with predictable results. He has no idea who Charlie is and cannot remember giving him the bundle of cash that the policeman has discovered in his pocket. Faced with arrest for thievery, Charlie grabs the money and runs. While he succeeds in passing it on to the blind girl, he is apprehended by detectives the next day.

7

The wind-riffled pages of a desk calendar indicate that Charlie entered prison in January 1930, and a title card announces that the time is now the following autumn. The girl he loves—but whose whereabouts are unknown to him—has regained her sight and is running an upscale flower shop. With her smart clothes and carefully styled hair, she seems like a product of the same privileged world that Virginia Cherrill came from in real life. Yet for all of her reasons for happiness, she is haunted by the inexplicable disappearance of her benefactor. A limousine stops at the curb and an imperiously handsome young man wearing an ascot at his throat and a silk topper on his head gets out and enters the shop. For a fleeting moment the girl believes that he is the gallant who once kissed her hand; when it turns out he is not, her disappointment is so intense that she has to sit down.

At that very moment, Charlie is shambling along the edge of the park where he first met her. Even though he has just been let out of prison, his appearance is shocking. In no previous Chaplin picture, going all the way back to 1914, had he ever looked so beaten down. His cane is gone, as is his tie. There are large rips in his pants and several holes as well in the dirty jacket that he clutches to him with the collar turned up. His derby, too, is a wreck.

Two newsboys at a busy corner begin to harass him. But instead of saucily snapping his fingers underneath their noses, as he had during an earlier confrontation with them, he shouts futile warnings from a distance and looks hurt; in fact, he *is* hurt, by the pellets that one of the boys aims at him with a peashooter.* Turning away from his tormenters, he notices a flower lying in the gutter. As he is bending over to pick up this talisman, the other boy tears off a portion of his underwear that a rip in his pants has made all too visible. In a burst of fury, the worm finally turns. Charlie rips the piece of cloth from the boy's hands and with a karate kick sends him and his companion fleeing, much to the amusement of the young woman seated in the window of the flower shop behind him. Just before Charlie turns around and sees her, the camera moves to a viewpoint inside the window looking out. The shock of recognizing the girl transfixes him. He cannot stop grinning at her like an idiot, he cannot stop staring, and he cannot move, except to squeeze the flower in his hand so hard that the petals fall off. His paralysis creates another ironic parallel in a picture that is replete with them; in this case it is to the hypocritical prancings of the "art connoisseur" in front of the nude statue in the art-store window.

"I've made a conquest!" the girl laughingly remarks to another woman in the shop. Out of a wish to give something to her battered admirer, she picks up a rose and by dumb show lets him know that he may have it as a replacement for the ruined flower in his hand. The thought then crosses her mind that she should offer him a coin as well. But when she stands up and moves toward the door of the shop, he becomes frightened and starts to hurry away. Something she says to him from the doorway causes him to stop and look back at her. And the formal, arm's-length way in which she holds out the rose persuades him to reach back and pluck it from her hand. The secret of his identity has thus far been preserved. But now she moves close to him. Taking hold

---

* The boy was Robert Parrish, who would have a notable career in films as an editor, director, and producer. His memories of Chaplin's directorial frenzies were detailed. "Charlie promptly stopped being the tramp and became two newsboys shooting peashooters. He would blow a pea and then run over and pretend to be hit by it, then back to blow another pea. He became a kind of dervish, playing all the parts, using all the props. . . . He really wanted to do it all. I don't think he ever fully accepted the idea of not being able to be behind the camera and in front of it at the same time." Robert Parrish, *Growing Up in Hollywood* (New York, 1976), pp. 43, 45.

of his wrist, she places the coin in his palm and closes his hand upon it with both of hers. The stirrings of memory induced by that touch—of the time he had placed a coin in her palm, of the time he had kissed her hand at the foot of the staircase—are reflected in the puzzled look on her face.

The camera tracks her hand as it caresses the sleeve of his jacket and the lapel where she had pinned the boutonniere, and then flies to her cheek in a gesture of stunned certainty. She looks steadily into his eyes, as he had looked into hers when she was blind. "You?" she asks gravely. Unable to trust himself to say anything without breaking down in tears, he briefly nods his head in reply. Yet a moment later, he, too, poses a question, at once despairing and joyful, in which the word "see" refers to the end of her illusion about his social status as well as to the restoration of her sight. "You can see now?" he says. Clasping his left hand with both of hers, she presses it to her chest. But the social gap between them is unbridgeable. A huge close-up of Charlie's glinting eyes, tremulous smile, and clenched right hand, in which he is holding the rose so close to his mouth that one of his fingers is touching his teeth, fills the screen until it goes blank. Swelling music underscores nothingness for another half minute.

An early indication of the extraordinary emotional power of the ending's double vision of miraculous recovery and devastating loss came from the famous scientist seated next to Chaplin at the premiere in the Los Angeles Theater. "During the final scene," Chaplin later wrote, "I noticed Einstein wiping his eyes." Many, many other people in many places have done the same since. "[That ending] is enough to shrivel the heart to see," James Agee justly said in 1949, although in his extravagant way, he went too far when he added that "it is the greatest piece of acting and the highest moment in movies." [18]

8

Despite the fact that the final scene and some other bits of *City Lights* still remained to be filmed, Chaplin took time during the summer of 1930 to get to know Luis Buñuel, freshly arrived in Hollywood under a rather surprising sponsorship. As a treat for his Surrealist friends, Buñuel had recently held a private screening in Paris of his second and still-unreleased film, *L'Âge d'or.* A representative of MGM had also been on hand, and was mystified and put off by the film. Nevertheless, he could not get it out of his mind. "So let me offer you a deal," he told Buñuel. "You go to Hollywood and learn some good American technical skills. I pay your way, you stay six months, you make two hundred and fifty dollars a month, and all you do is learn how to make a movie. When you get it, we'll see what we can do for you." Buñuel had been planning to go to Kharkov for a meeting of the Congress of Intellectuals for the Revolution, but the MGM offer was too good to refuse.[19]

After "five dazzling days" at the Algonquin in New York, he sped by train across the "most beautiful [country] in the world" to Los Angeles, where he was met at the station by three Spanish writers who had already been hired by the studios. That night, the four of them had dinner in a restaurant with an attractive young woman and her gray-haired escort, whom Buñuel's friends mischievously introduced to him as "the man you'll be working for." Not until the dinner was nearly over did Buñuel realize that he had been breaking bread with Chaplin and that his eye-catching companion was Georgia Hale, of *Gold Rush* fame. Chaplin claimed, Buñuel remembered, that he adored Spain, although he knew no Spanish and his idea of the country was "strictly folkloric, composed as it was of foot stomping and a lot of *olés*."[20]

Every Saturday for the rest of the summer, Chaplin invited Buñuel and his Spanish colleagues to play tennis, swim, and use the steam room on Summit Drive. As a further favor to his new friend, Chaplin also set up a sex orgy for him. To Buñuel, the idea of an orgy was "tremendously exciting," for like many Spaniards of his generation, he knew of only two ways to make love—"in a brothel or in marriage." In his "impotent" old age, he would look back with "equanimity" on all the whores he had known in Madrid, Paris, and New York, and he had vivid memories as well of a pornographic film called *Sister Vaseline*:

> I remember a nun in a convent garden being fucked by the gardener, who was being sodomized by a monk, until all three merged into one figure. . . . René Char and I once plotted to sneak into a children's movie matinée, tie up the projectionist, and show *Sister Vaseline* to the young audience. *O tempora! O mores!* . . . (Needless to say, we never got beyond the planning stage.)

The orgy promised him by Chaplin never came off either. For when three call girls arrived from Pasadena, they immediately began arguing over which of them would service Chaplin, and when they couldn't resolve the dispute they left.[21]

More often than not, Buñuel encountered Sergei M. Eisenstein at Chaplin's place, which probably did not surprise either of them. As a giver of dinner parties, Chaplin was still a reluctant and somewhat parsimonious host. But in the years when Red Hollywood was acquiring a critical mass, Summit Drive was famous for providing prominent leftists from home and abroad with politically *engagé* conversations, long cool drinks, splendid tennis, and pleasant dips in a pool that an architect had shaped into an exact copy of a derby. Eisenstein arrived in Hollywood in June, and immediately made contact with an English friend, Ivor Montagu, formerly of the Film Society of London, currently an associate producer at Paramount. Eisenstein, too, had signed on with Paramount, although the contract simply represented an agreement by the studio to pay his expenses for six months and did not call for services from him.

Hollywood at this time was attracting moviemakers from all over the world who were interested in the new techniques of sound film. Just as MGM subsidized Buñuel while he absorbed Hollywood know-how, so Paramount anted up five hundred dollars a week for Eisenstein. In addition to his Paramount tutorials, Eisenstein and his assistant, Grigory Alexandrov, spent long hours with Montagu in a three-way collaboration on two notable film scripts, *Sutter's Gold* and *An American Tragedy*, based—respectively—on notable novels by Blaise Cendrars and Theodore Dreiser. The Eisenstein-Montagu relationship may also have had a surveillance aspect. Although Eisenstein's masterful *Battleship Potemkin* (1925) had enormously enhanced the prestige of Soviet filmmaking, the paranoid master of the Kremlin regarded his political reliability as suspect. In 1927 Stalin intervened in the filming of *October* (or *Ten Days That Shook the World*) and forced him to cut every reference to Trotsky, Zinoviev, and Kamenev. And in 1929 Eisenstein was not permitted to show the true nature of the "liquidation of the kulaks as a class" in *The General Line*. Conceivably, it became Montagu's task to monitor his associates while in Hollywood. For in addition to being a brilliant screenwriter, a charming social companion, and a superlatively good tennis player, Montagu may have been subject to "guidance" by the NKVD.[22]

This versatile Englishman's first invitation to Summit Drive was to an afternoon tea party in the garden, where "all was incredibly decorous and English county." The sight of Constance Bennett with her pinky crooked stuck in his mind, as he later made clear in his memoir, *With Eisenstein in Hollywood* (1969), and so did the self-conscious sense of power emanating from David Selznick's brother Myron, the feared head of Hollywood's most important film agency. Prior to the serving of tea, Montagu also remembered, the focus of the party was on the tennis court, which he was delighted to find had an asphalt surface that took a spin beautifully, unlike the concrete courts he had played on elsewhere in southern California. In singles that day, he handily beat everyone who took him on, including Selznick, six-love, and Chaplin, six-three. Nevertheless, Chaplin's play impressed him. "He could run indefinitely, being superbly fit, and hit steadily, hard and accurately, forehand and backhand." Indeed, he was so good an athlete, said Montagu, that that wonderful figure of a man, the eternally bronzed Douglas Fairbanks, was unable to defeat him in any competitive exercise except golf, which Chaplin refused to play. At the baseline on a tennis court, where steadiness counted, he was formidable, but if you drew him toward the net, Montagu observed, he would become too excited to volley properly.[23]

Off the court, Chaplin's moods soared and crashed. At times, his pride in his achievements was boundless; at others, he experienced terrible doubts about them. Toward the end of his work on *City Lights*, he seemed on top of the world. There were passages in it that profoundly satisfied him; they had come right; they would be remembered; they could be likened to moments in Shakespeare. But when his mood downshifted, he moaned that the picture had not come off, that it was a failure, that no one would pay to see it. During one such crisis, Montagu and Georgia Hale were with him in his car. "I shall be ruined!" Chaplin cried in despair. Georgia attempted to buck him up: "It's not as bad as that, Charlie, you'll still have a million dollars left." Chaplin, however, was not to be consoled. "What is a million dollars?" he groaned. "What can you do with a million dollars?"[24]

Fears about diminished income also reinforced his longtime unwillingness to give the Soviet Union a special price on his pictures. The Soviet film-importing agency in New York kept bombarding Montagu with requests that he do something about Chaplin's lack of cooperation in this regard. Whenever Montagu brought up the subject, however, Chaplin would simply reiterate that he was not in any way anti-Soviet, but that business was business and the Soviets were offering him less money for nationwide rights to *The Gold Rush*, for example, than he had obtained from a single middle-sized town in the United States. Montagu would thereupon "explain all about the five-year plan, the need of the Soviet Union to import machinery, the shortage of valuta." But none of these appeals wore down the comedian's resolve. "It is the principle of the thing," he would say. "Pictures are worth something. They give Henry Ford valuta for tractors and my pictures must be worth at least as much as several tractors." [25]

Eisenstein had no better luck with an appeal of his own. Shortly after Paramount broke its contract with him in October 1930, he came to Chaplin and announced that he dearly wanted to make a film in Mexico —if he could find a backer, he meaningfully added. Chaplin did not take the hint. You ought to discuss your project with Upton Sinclair, he replied. At least the answer proved to be a good lead. When the filming of *Que Viva Mexico!* finally got under way, it was with funds supplied by the writer whom Ivor Montagu would apotheosize in his Eisenstein memoir as "the Red David who had challenged Goliath with *The Jungle* and *The Brass Check*." [26]

Chaplin and Sinclair had been friends since 1918. There was a sweetness in Sinclair's nature that beguiled Chaplin, and while he could not resist giving imitations of him at Hollywood dinner parties, the main point of them was that the novelist always spoke through a smile. In *My Autobiography*, Chaplin declared that it was not until he met Sinclair that he became interested in the economics of socialism.

We were driving to his house ... for lunch and he asked me in his soft-spoken way if I believed in the profit system. I said facetiously that it required an accountant to answer that. It was a disarming question, but instinctively I felt it went to the very root of the matter, and from that moment I became interested and saw politics not as history but as an economic problem.

In addition, he was captivated by the colorful tales about his life that the soft-spoken novelist liked to spin. As a young man, he had reenacted the utopian dreams of the nineteenth-century settlers of Brook Farm and Fruitlands by founding the Helicon Hall Colony in New Jersey, and he had sampled the felicities of communal living in several single-tax colonies as well. While his account in *The Jungle* (1906) of the horrors of the meatpacking industry had made him rich and famous, his success had certainly not made him either indolent or conservative. In an endless stream of novels and articles, he had continued to expose situations that he regarded as symptoms of the capitalist system's fundamental corruption.[27]

The Sinclair-Chaplin connection did not receive much of a play from American commentators in the 1920s, but in Europe it was regarded as important, especially in Weimar Germany, where Sinclair's novels were tremendously popular and Chaplin's pictures had had a "quite extraordinary" impact on the culture, according to the historian John Willett in *Art and Politics in the Weimar Period* (1978). Chaplin's "enormous influence," Fred Miller Robinson adds in his charming book, *The Man in the Bowler Hat* (1993), was one of the reasons why Weimar artists gave the bowler an iconic importance in their work and why bowler-hatted "little men" appeared as protagonists in such novels as Alfred Döblin's *Berlin Alexanderplatz* and Hans Fallada's *Little Man, What Now?* Sinclair and Chaplin appealed to the imaginations of German men and women in many walks of life. But it was the writers, artists, and journalists, the physicians and lawyers, and the scientists and philosophers of the left intelligentsia who were their most prominent devotees. To these cohorts, Sinclair and Chaplin were not only superlatively talented entertainers, they were also heroes of the fight for a socially just tomorrow. A captioned composite photo on a 1929 cover of the widely read radical weekly *AIZ (Arbeiter Illustrierte Zeitung)* said it all. The photo showed Chaplin in his tramp getup, flanked by Sinclair and the Czech Communist journalist Egon Kisch, and the caption read, "Three people pulling in the same direction."[28]

Not until 1934, when Sinclair won the Democratic nomination for governor of California and waged a spirited campaign against the lackluster Republican Frank Merriam, did the Sinclair-Chaplin connection make a splash in American publications. Sinclair had twice run for governor and once for senator on the Socialist ticket; when he registered as a Democrat in the late summer of 1933, in preparation for his third try for the governorship, it was because he sensed that he might win if only he would bow to the realities of American two-party politics. His prescriptions, however, for dealing with the Depression were chimerical, as he could not help revealing in a pamphlet entitled *I, Governor of California and How I Ended Poverty: A True Story of the Future.*

Under his governorship, the pamphlet foretold, the state of California had allowed the unemployed in various regions to grow their own food on unworked land acquired by the state through tax-delinquency proceedings, and had enabled them to manufacture their own clothing by throwing open the gates of idle factories that the state had either purchased or rented. The issuance of scrip within each regional system facilitated exchanges of goods with other systems. Gradually, an interlocking quasi-socialist economy came to rival and eventually surpass the economy of capitalism. By 1938, the pamphlet proclaimed, the Cooperative Commonwealth of California had completely eliminated the ills of poverty, at which point Governor Sinclair "considered his job done, and . . . purposed to go home and write a novel."[29]

As Billy Wilder, a newcomer from Austria, noted, Sinclair's EPIC (End Poverty in California) program "scared the hell out of the movie community. They all thought him to be a most dangerous Bolshevik beast." The studio moguls spread the rumor that they would be compelled to move the entire movie community to Florida if Sinclair were elected. "They couldn't move out if they wanted to," Sinclair rejoined. And in an aside that the press picked up on with particular relish, he declared that he just might "put the state into making pictures. . . . I'll ask Charlie Chaplin to run that part of the show."[30]

Besides Chaplin, Sinclair's supporters in the movie colony included Dorothy Parker, Nunnally Johnson, Jean Harlow (an extra girl in *City Lights*, incidentally), James Cagney, Morrie Ryskind, and Gene Fowler. But the vast majority of the best-known actors, writers, and directors were either sincerely pro-Merriam or so intimidated by the moguls that they pretended to be. Backed by a war chest of half a million dollars, which the moguls raised by assessing their highest-paid employees a day's salary, Louis B. Mayer of MGM commissioned his screen-test director to turn out a series of "newsreels" and distributed them gratis to California exhibitors. In one of these confections, the *New York Times* reported, a demure old lady, sitting on her front porch in a rocking chair, declared that she was voting for Merriam "because I want to save my little home." In another, a shaggy man with bristling Russian whiskers and a menacing look in his eye was asked by an interviewer why he was voting for Sinclair. "Vell, his system worked well in Russia," Mr. Whiskers replied, "vy can't it work here?"

The *Los Angeles Evening Herald* added to the discrediting of Sinclair by printing a photo of a mob of young hoboes in front of a freight car; apparently, these sinister fellows had become so inflamed by Sinclair's rhetoric that they had come to southern California to create revolutionary disturbances. Film buffs, however, identified Frankie Darrow and several other actors in the mob—for the photo was, in fact, a still from a Warner Brothers picture, *Wild Boys of the Road*. But the dirtiest trick of all was the flier calling for Sinclair's election that bore the imprimatur of Vladimir Kosloff, secretary of the Young People's Communist League. Kosloff and his organization did not exist.[31]

At one time, odds makers in Nevada had rated Sinclair's chances of election at even money; in the end, Merriam won by 250,000 votes. Sinclair accepted defeat with his customary cheerfulness—and a stern warning. Upon learning that some of his supporters were proposing that the EPIC movement ally itself in future contests with Communist militants, the movement's defeated paladin blasted the idea. "No EPIC worker," he declared, "can have anything to do with the Communists, or with any of the camouflage organizations into which the Communists seek to lure the workers."[32] The statement abetted the anti-Communism of leftists like the lawyer Culbert L. Olson and the ex-socialist schoolteacher Jerry Voorhis, who would be instrumental in reinvigorating the Democratic Party in California. Sinclair's words were aimed as well at his friends in the arts, of whom Chaplin was the most famous. But while Chaplin greatly respected his old friend, he did not share his anti-Communism. Indeed, the eagerness with which he sought out Communist friends and hired Communist associates led people to wonder whether he was under Communist discipline. On the other hand, no one could doubt the lack of ideological discipline in his socioeconomic ideas. With a relish that testified to his delight in hearing himself talk, he advanced arguments that were as ill-assorted as his tramp costume.

11

"STRIKES AND RIOTS!"

Going mad on the assembly line in Modern Times *(1936).*

WHILE at heart his friend Charlie was "the reddest of Reds," Thomas Burke remarked in 1932, in recollection of the comedian's visit to England the preceding year, he "likes to enjoy the best of the current social system." Most certainly he did. For his February crossing aboard the *Mauretania*, his staff had booked him as a matter of course into one of the ship's most luxurious suites, and in London his accommodations at the Carlton Hotel included sleeping quarters for his three companions—Ralph Barton, Carlyle Robinson, and Kono—as well as a splendidly appointed master bedroom for himself. "How many times I have looked through [the Carlton's] doors as a boy and wondered at its grandeur," he self-satisfiedly exclaimed in the account of his trip that he later sold for a whopping $50,000 to *Woman's Home Companion.*[1]

The first entertainment bid he accepted was from Lady Astor, who wanted him to come to lunch at her London home. Although words failed him upon being introduced to Bernard Shaw,* he pressed his opinions upon his hostess about the prospects for survival of Prime Minister Ramsay MacDonald's shaky government. Shortly thereafter, he had dinner at Chequers, the prime minister's official country house, where he tried to draw MacDonald into a discussion of his economic policies by proposing to him that the dole had been the saving grace of England because it had kept the wheels of industry turning and money in circulation, but MacDonald would have none of it. "He just nodded with an 'Is that so?' expression," Chaplin recalled with exasperation, unaware of the obvious fact that the beleaguered Scotsman had had no wish to ruin an evening's respite from his excruciating responsibilities by arguing with a *naïf*. When Sir Philip Sassoon took Chaplin to tea in Lloyd George's private chambers in the House of Commons a few days later, Chaplin immediately began to bend the former P.M.'s ear with descriptions of "all sorts of projects and enterprises for the relief of the unemployed," but again failed to realize that his host was not paying attention. "In spite of [Lloyd George's] interest I could not help noticing a stifled yawn and then I saw Sir Philip look at his watch."

Finally, Lady Astor gave him the chance to play the role of a political leader. At a dinner for twenty attended by Lloyd George, a brawny Communist named Kirkwood, and other politicos of various persua-

---

* G.B.S. was a Chaplin fan. See his letter of January 16, 1928, to Thomas Hardy's widow about the magnificent funeral ceremony in Westminster Abbey in which the novelist's remains had been laid to rest. Although he had tried to look solemn, Shaw told her, that was not how the occasion had struck him. For he had felt sure "all the time that he was there—up in the lantern somewhere— laughing like anything at Kipling and me and Galsworthy and the rest of us. Probably he shook hands with Handel at the end: his only link with that sort of thing now. If you only knew how I wanted at the end to swoop on you; tear off all that villainous crape (you should have been like the lilies of the field); and make you come off, *with him*, to see a Charlie Chaplin film!" *Bernard Shaw: Collected Letters, 1926–1950*, Dan H. Laurence, ed. (New York, 1988), p. 84.

sions, everyone was asked to outline in an after-dinner speech what he would do if he had "the power of Mussolini to help England in her present crisis." Chaplin was the first of the guests to get to his feet. Judging by his extensive quotation of his remarks in his *Woman's Home Companion* serial, he was proud of what he had to say. It was, in fact, a curious speech that successively voiced a libertarian belief in the virtues of reducing the size of government, an excitement about Major C. H. Douglas's social-credit philosophy (which also appealed to Ezra Pound and, for many years, to the voters of the Canadian province of Alberta), a state-socialist faith in "a governmental Bureau of Economics, which would control prices, interests and profits," and a capitalistic commitment to private enterprise—"so far as it would not deter the progress or well-being of the majority."[2]

Obsessed, as always, with his childhood, he had a driver take him to the poor-law school at Hanwell. The yard, the tailor's shop, the punishment room, the blacking hole in which the boys had shined their shoes on frosty mornings, and the dormitories with their depressing wash sinks made of slate were exactly as he remembered them. Back in London he confessed to Thomas Burke that "being among those buildings and connecting with everything—with the misery and something that wasn't misery" had been a wonderful experience. Burke rather bluntly told him that making such an emotional fuss about the place was "maudlin and morbid," but Chaplin refused to accept his rebuke. "I like being morbid," he said. "It does me good. I thrive on it."[3]

The multitudes that turned out to meet his train in Berlin on a snowy evening in March and that lined the streets in hopes of a glimpse of him as he sped past in a limousine en route to the Hotel Adlon were the largest he had ever seen anywhere. What he had been told was true: Germany adored him. A day or so after a meeting with Marlene Dietrich, which did not go particularly well, he had tea with several members of the Reichstag. One of the legislators predicted to him that the German economy would collapse within the year. Although Chaplin apparently refrained from offering the group his own assessment of the nation's economic ailments, he more than made up for this show of restraint with a torrent of pontification in the Albert Einsteins' modest flat. At the table, he complimented Mrs. Einstein on the delicious tart she had made and traded personal anecdotes with her and her husband.

But when the conversation at last came around to world problems, he / launched into a detailed recital of C. H. Douglas's ideas about the inelasticity of gold as a medium of exchange and offered a few comments as well about the threat posed to the employment of workers in industry by the increasing reliance of factory owners on modern machinery. "You're not a comedian," Einstein told him with a smile that took the edge off his irony, "you're an economist." There was a cinematic significance, however, in Chaplin's remarks about machinery that Einstein did not grasp. The lineaments of the most memorable scenes in *Modern Times* had already entered his consciousness.[4]

2

In London the popular press had excitedly noted his attentions to a would-be actress, Sari Maritsa. In Berlin his principal playmate was a beautiful interpretive dancer, romantically referred to as "G" in the *Woman's Home Companion* serial, but known to her rising number of fans in Germany as La Jana. On their last night together, the lovers had dinner at the Adlon and danced the tango. For the benefit of the *Companion*'s palpitating readers, Chaplin offered a version of their climactic conversation. "In your dance," he murmured, "you seem to express an exotic loneliness—to be in pursuit of some strange beauty." Hesitatingly, she replied, "Charlie, I love you—you're so appreciative. Although we may never see each other again, I will not regret it. For we have met in our pilgrimage. It is good to know that you are in life, and a living part of it." Whether by that time she had had too much wine to drink, Chaplin did not say.[5]

His next stop was Vienna, where the throng at the train station carried him out to the street shoulder-high, the obsequious manager of the Hotel Imperial assigned him the royal suite, and his sight-seeing subsequently inspired the most pretentious pair of sentences that he would ever conjure up from his incessant explorations of thesauruses and dictionaries: "Were I addicted to *cacoëthes scribendi* I should go into pages of rhetorical rapture extolling the beauties of Vienna. Therefore I shall spare you all too suffering readers any conscious pleonasms on my part." At the usual round of parties held in his honor, he took the opportunity to pursue an attractive concert pianist, Jenny Rothstein, and one night in a cabaret he had a wonderful time dancing the tango with the sexy if somewhat matronly (as well as married) Hungarian musical-comedy star Irene Palasthy. Unfortunately, Palasthy's passion for him suddenly demanded expression right then and there. Falling to her knees, she grabbed his hand and kissed it. What followed was even more embarrassing. In thrusting Chaplin's hand away from her in a gesture of romantic despair, Palasthy yanked on it with such force that he toppled over on her. Or so he insisted, despite the suspicious resemblance of his embarrassment to certain tumbledown situations in Chaplin comedies.[6]

"In the last few days Charlie Chaplin has been in Vienna," Sigmund Freud duly reported to a friend in a letter from his home at Berggasse 19. "I, too, would have seen him, but it was too cold for him and he left again quickly." Then the doctor proceeded to set forth his conclusions about the departed celebrity:

He is undoubtedly a great artist; certainly he always portrays one and the same figure; only the weakly, poor, helpless, clumsy youngster for whom, however, things turn out well in the end. Now do you think that for this role he has to forget about his own ego? On the contrary, he always plays only himself as he was in his early dismal youth. He cannot get away from those impressions and to this day he obtains for himself the compensation for the frustrations and humiliations of that past period of his life. He is, so-to-speak, an exceptionally simple and transparent case. The idea that the achievements of artists are intimately bound up with their childhood memories, impressions, repressions and disappointments has already brought much enlightenment and has, for that reason, become very precious to us. . . .[7]

It was not so much the cold as restless fatigue that drove Chaplin from Vienna. *City Lights* had left him more exhausted than he had realized. In Venice his shot nerves caught up with him, and his holiday took on "an aspect of utter futility." After two days of sight-seeing, he fled the glories of the city aboard a train for Paris. On arriving there, he quickly picked an ugly, friendship-terminating quarrel about nothing of importance with Cami, the humorous cartoonist who had worshipped him since their first meeting a decade earlier. An invitation from the Duke of Westminster to take part in a boar hunt on his beautiful estate in the Normandy countryside also turned out badly, for the fashion-conscious guest of honor felt humiliated at having to wear the outsized hunting costume lent to him by the six-foot-three, thickset duke.[8]

In the south of France his spirits began to revive, first of all because of his happiness at being reunited with his brother Sydney, whom he had not seen for several years. As an actor in films made in England, Sydney had enjoyed a certain success. On the other hand, his attempts to establish himself as a film producer had not worked out, and so finally he had settled into a life of very comfortable retirement in Nice. For all of his delight in Sydney's company, Chaplin did not move in with him, opting instead to occupy the suite that the millionaire owner of the Majestic Hotel, Frank Jay Gould, who had once been married to Hetty Kelly's sister, had made available to him at cost. Long workouts on the tennis court took up most of his mornings, while at lunch there were always important people to meet, from English dukes to Emil Ludwig, the biographer of Napoleon; Elsa Maxwell, the professional party-giver; and Sir Oswald Mosley. In regard to Mosley, Chaplin would opine in *Woman's Home Companion* that he was "one of the most promising young men in English politics." But thirty years later, hindsight familiarity with Mosley's record as the founder and leader of the British Union of Fascists, known as Blackshirts, would prompt him to say instead that Sir Oswald's eyes "with the whites showing over the pupils and [his] broad grinning mouth stand out in my memory vividly as an expression most peculiar—if not a little frightening."[9]

Inevitably, Chaplin found a new girlfriend, May Reeves (a.k.a. Mizzi Muller), a cheerful, round-faced brunette who had won nine beauty contests in her native Czechoslovakia, captured prizes for ballroom dancing in Nice, and mastered conversational ease in half a dozen languages. On Sydney's recommendation, Carlyle Robinson had hired her to help translate the flood of letters that Chaplin was receiving from continental European correspondents, but once Chaplin spotted her in the little office that Robinson had set up, Robinson had to start looking for another helper. Sydney feared that May would eventually sell a kiss-and-tell memoir to a scandal magazine, and when Chaplin's infatuation with her led him to take her on a side trip to Algeria, Sydney's anxiety soared. In the course of a worried discussion with Carl Robinson about his brother's foolhardiness about sex, Sydney confessed—quite possibly with his fingers crossed—that he, too, had had an affair with May. If Charlie were to find out about this, he predicted, his pride would lead him to dump the girl immediately.

Unfortunately for Robinson, Sydney's crystal ball was cloudy. When Robinson told him of Sydney's confession, Chaplin took out his anger on his hapless informant. As Robinson recalled, "Chaplin went white. Then he exploded. It was a filthy lie! A trick!" A week later, Robinson had lost his job and was on his way back to the United States, where he was given a far less important position in the Chaplin Studio's New York office. At the end of the year, Alf Reeves fired him in a one-sentence letter. After fifteen years in Chaplin's employ, Robinson was out on the street. And in the "merry" spring of 1932, he later wrote in ironic reference to the difficulties of finding a job in the Depression, he saw Chaplin one night as he was eating supper in a Hollywood restaurant. What impressed him was his ex-boss's cowardice.

> At the sight of me he fumbled with his napkin and pretended he hadn't seen me. A moment later he hurried off to an anteroom in the rear.
>
> After a few minutes he reappeared, waved his hands high above his head, and called my name the length of [the] restaurant! Then he came hurrying to my table, his hand outstretched. I rose and clasped it.
>
> "You're looking great, Charlie," I said.
>
> He assured me he was in perfect health—and then scuttled out of the place into the street.[10]

With May Reeves beside him, Chaplin finally left the tennis courts and social swim of Nice for the tennis courts and social swim of Juan-les-Pins, and she was with him still when he moved on to Biarritz. Here he lunched with Winston Churchill and met the Prince of Wales through Lady Furness (Thelma Morgan Converse), who had apparently forgiven him for turning her into the unwitting chaperone of his early dates with Lita Grey. Not until his return to Paris did he and May seemingly come to a parting of the ways, on a late-summer day in the garden at Malmaison, "where Josephine had lived and died after Napoleon had divorced her," as Chaplin did not fail to note. The little emperor and his consort were often in his thoughts as he acted out the scenarios of his private life.[11]

Invitations from Margot Asquith and Lady Cunard, among others, called Chaplin back to England in September. The bitterly contested general election that ended MacDonald's Labour ministry also held a fascination for him, as did the meeting he had with Mohandas Gandhi in a humble little house in the East India Dock Road. Adopting a very different attitude toward machine culture than he had voiced to Einstein —but again revealing that *Modern Times* was on his mind—he remarked to the Mahatma that while he was sympathetic with India's struggle for freedom, he was "somewhat confused by your abhorrence of machinery." "After all," he continued, "if machinery is used in the altruistic sense, it should help to release man from the bondage of slavery, and give him shorter hours of labor and time to improve his mind and enjoy life." Gandhi calmly replied that India's first task was to rid itself of English rule. "Machinery in the past has made us dependent on England, and the way we can rid ourselves of that dependence is to boycott all goods made by machinery. That is why we have made it the patriotic duty of every Indian to spin his own cotton and weave his own cloth." What Chaplin had in mind in his reference to the use of machinery "in the altruistic sense" was left unexplored.[12]

Shortly before Christmas, Chaplin received a telegram from Switzerland signed by Douglas Fairbanks—but not by Mary Pickford as well, for filmdom's "royal marriage" was on the rocks and Fairbanks had for some time been covertly courting Sylvia Ashley-Cooper, the estranged wife of the elder son of the Earl of Shaftesbury. Fairbanks's telegram urged his old friend to join him in St. Moritz for an extended skiing vacation. As Chaplin was pondering the invitation in his London hotel room, someone knocked on the door. It was May Reeves. Later, they went shopping at Harrods for skiing outfits, and after a considerable discussion with a jeweler in Bond Street, May walked out with a new bracelet. In St. Moritz, the vacationers saw in the new year and were joined for a time, to Chaplin's delight, by his brother Sydney. That May was utterly devoted to Chaplin and wanted to marry him was obvious to everyone, as was his lack of any sense of obligation to her. When he and Sydney made plans for a trip to the Orient, she was conspicuously left out of them. In March she accompanied her restless lover to Rome, where a tentatively scheduled meeting with Mussolini failed to materialize. On a dock in Naples the moment she had been dreading finally arrived. Years later, Chaplin comforted himself with the absurd belief that her mood that day was "gay."

There were no tears. I think she was resigned and somewhat relieved, for since our sojourn in Switzerland our alchemy of attraction had become somewhat diluted, and we both knew it. So we parted good friends. As the boat pulled out [on which Chaplin and Sydney were sailing for Singapore], she was imitating my tramp walk along the quay.[13]

3

In south Bali the travelers checked into the only hotel in the region. Almost immediately they met a young American painter currently living in the village of Den Pasar and bubbling with excitement about his recent discovery that his true métier was caricature. Al Hirschfeld and Chaplin hit it off straightaway. "The motion picture was unknown in Bali," Hirschfeld would later write, so on discovering that no one knew who he was, "Charlie decided to carry out an experiment." An experiment, that is, in comedy, and since a derby was unavailable he used a pith helmet. His native audience consisted of the seven houseboys who worked for Hirschfeld.

Charlie . . . put the pith helmet on his head and it sprang crazily into the air, seemingly with a will of its own. Undaunted, and with a wide-eyed look of nonchalance, he tried it again. And again the hat flew off his head. The natives howled with laughter, thinking his hat possessed demoniac powers.

"Movement is liberated thought," Chaplin told Hirschfeld on Summit Drive some years later. "For instance," he said, standing up to clarify his point, "a Balinese dancing girl is like this."

With the elegance of a ballet dancer he hopped about in staccato movement, his eyes wide and shifting back and forth like those of a spectator at a tennis match, his fingers nervously describing a Chinese fan, his head imitating the detached, boneless, easy rhythm of a cobra. There she was, the little Balinese dancing girl, clear as a drawing.[14]

4

Chaplin's announcement that he wanted to spend more time in Japan than anywhere else in the Far East brought joy to his Japanese major-domo. Kono had left the land of his birth at the age of eighteen and had not seen it since. Yet no sooner did he have the chance to talk with some of his countrymen aboard the special train from Kobe to Tokyo that the government had laid on for Chaplin than he began to look worried. Once they reached Tokyo, his behavior became even stranger. The chauffeur of the limousine in which they were traveling to their hotel unaccountably stopped the car in a quiet, out-of-the-way quarter near the emperor's palace. Kono cast an anxious glance out of the back window. When Chaplin asked him what was the matter, Kono responded with an odd request. Would Chaplin please get out of the car and bow in the direction of the palace? Although Chaplin agreed to do so, he did not really believe Kono's assurance that such a gesture from visiting dignitaries was customary.[15]

The next morning, Sydney reported that his bags had been searched and his papers rifled. A government agent appeared at the door of the Chaplin suite and informed the brothers that if they wished to go any-where they should inform him through Kono of their destination. With every passing hour, Kono betrayed more and more signs of nervousness, but did not explain why. That night, as Chaplin, Sydney, and Kono were dining in a secluded room in a restaurant, six young men abruptly approached their table. One of them sat down next to Kono and folded his arms; the others remained standing. The seated man talked to Kono in Japanese. His tone was angry. Kono's face registered alarm. Chaplin told Sydney that he wanted to leave and ordered Kono to call a cab. The cab came and they returned to their hotel.[16]

On the following day—Sunday, May 15, 1932—a historic "incident" occurred, and Chaplin was among the first foreigners to learn of it. Ken Inukai, the son of the prime minister, Tsuyoshi Inukai, invited him and Sydney to be his guests at a Sumo wrestling arena. The matches were proceeding when an attendant approached young Inukai and whispered in his ear. He excused himself and left his seat; when he returned, he looked ill. "My father has just been assassinated!" he cried. Nine naval and military officers, it developed, all of them between the ages of twenty-four and twenty-eight, had forced their way into the prime minister's residence and gunned him down. More or less simultaneously, the main offices of the Bank of Japan and the headquarters of the Seiyukai, the prime minister's conservative political party, were damaged by bomb blasts. As Hugh Byas, the *New York Times* reporter in Japan, later wrote in *Government by Assassination* (1942), the Inukai murder was the third political killing in Tokyo in the space of a few months. On February 9, the finance minister, Junnosuke Inouye, had been fatally shot, and four weeks thereafter, the same fate befell the managing director of the holding company that controlled the immense Mitsui corporation. By the time Chaplin arrived, the whole country was buzzing with rumors about further assassinations of prominent people. Presumably, Kono had picked up some of this talk aboard the train from Kobe to Tokyo and became concerned, as his odd behavior showed, about Chaplin's safety.[17]

Forty-one military and civilian conspirators involved in the "incident" were apprehended by the police. At their trial, the outlines of a multi-level plot, encompassing various schemes for creating social disorder as a means of overthrowing the government and for murdering such figures as Chaplin and U.S. Ambassador Joseph Clark Grew in the hope of provoking war with the United States, emerged. According to the testimony of the naval officers' ringleader, Lieutenant Seishi Koga, the conspirators had dreamed of precipitating a declaration of martial law by the war minister, General Sadao Araki, by throwing bombs onto the floor of the house of representatives from the gallery above; when the surviving legislators rushed out of the chamber, young officers in the lobby would await them with drawn guns. At one point the conspirators had also considered invading Prime Minister Inukai's residence while a scheduled meeting between the prime minister and Chaplin was in progress and pulling off a double murder.

Judge: What was the significance of killing Chaplin?
Koga: Chaplin is a popular figure in the United States and the darling of the capitalist class. We believed that killing him would cause a war with America, and thus we could kill two birds with a single stone.

Subsequently, Koga explained that the Chaplin murder scheme had been abandoned because "it was disputed whether it was advisable to kill the comedian on the slight chance that it might bring about war with the United States and increase the power of the military."[18]

Hugh Byas argued that the ideology of the young officers "was created by the impact of Marxism upon native chauvinism. Its result had been the establishment of a Japanese form of national socialism." The officers wished to take power from the capitalists and the politicians, whom they regarded as weak-willed and corrupt, and offer it to Emperor Hirohito, who in turn would entrust it, they felt sure, to patriots like themselves. Under the new order, huge national defense budgets would be enacted, the means of production, distribution, and exchange would be nationalized, and the Japanese people would collectively dedicate themselves to working for the greater glory of the state. The Japanese army's invasion of Manchuria in 1931 represented the first sign of the rightists' strength, and the assassinations and other terrorist acts of early 1932 represented the second. For the moment, however, their most grandiose dream of destiny had been put on hold. Murdering "the darling of the capitalist class" would do nothing more than give the American people a temporary jolt. Something considerably bloodier would be required to provoke the United States into declaring war on Japan.[19]

When Chaplin and Kono sailed from Yokohama for Seattle on June 2, 1932, leaving Sydney to await transportation to France, the trial of the May 15 conspirators was still a year away. Nevertheless, Chaplin had already learned all that a comic genius needed to know about them. Half a dozen years later, memories of the political madness of Lieutenant Koga and his associates probably gave a boost to the demonism in his portrayal of Adolf Hitler in *The Great Dictator.*

5

The 138-foot yacht owned by the president and chairman of the board of United Artists, Joe Schenck, could easily accommodate the swarm of poker-playing cronies and pretty girls with whom Schenck liked to surround himself on weekend cruises to Catalina Island.* It was

---

* Schenck could not have afforded a pleasure craft of this size had he simply been the CEO of a company that did nothing but distribute the films of the original UA partners. At his instigation, UA had started the Arts Cinema Corporation to finance and produce other films for UA distribution. In addition, he had formed the United Artists Theatre Circuit to secure suitable outlets for UA films. Tino Balio, *United Artists: The Company That Changed the Film Industry* (Madison, Wis., 1987), pp. 9–16.

unusual therefore for Chaplin to find, when he stepped on board one bright morning in July 1932, that there were only two other guests besides himself, a cutie whom the legendarily lecherous Schenck had obviously marked for personal use and a bit-part player named Paulette Goddard who had just signed on with the Hal Roach studio after finishing her work for Samuel Goldwyn in *The Kid from Spain*, starring Eddie Cantor and featuring a dynamite chorus that included, in addition to Goddard, Lucille Ball, Betty Grable, and Anita Louise. Goddard had a piquant, heart-shaped face, sparkling blue-green eyes, and hair dyed a Harlowesque platinum blond. By suppertime she was confiding in Chaplin. She wanted his advice about the financial soundness of a certain movie company in which she was thinking of investing the remaining half of a $375,000 divorce settlement she had received three years before. Was it simply blind luck that prompted her to seek guidance from a man who loved taking total charge of young women's lives? The question is an insult to the intelligence, wit, and material ambition that Goddard brought to all her relationships with famous and/or wealthy men.[20]

After examining the documents she had not by accident brought with her, Chaplin "almost took her by the throat" to prevent her from signing them. Before too long, he was advising her to return her hair to its natural color. By the end of the year, he had bought up her obligation to Hal Roach, signed her to a contract with the Chaplin Studio, and installed her as the mistress of Summit Drive. Now that his two boys were no longer babies (in 1932 little Charlie turned seven and little Sydney six), they more often than not spent their weekends with him, and if those occasions were a joy, it was mainly Paulette who made them so. Their father, they discovered, was a "constipated" man, as Sydney would say of him many years later, always correct—and correcting!— and closed in, whereas Paulette was gay-spirited and willing to play with them. "They look upon her as a sister," Alf Reeves observed in the summer of 1935, "and in shorts she looks like a little girl"—as the boys' father had undoubtedly noticed right off. Sydney, however, told an interviewer in 1995 that he and his brother looked upon Paulette as a wonderful stepmother who allowed them to sleep with her until Chaplin forbade it.[21]

Goddard herself was given to saying that she was seventeen when she and the forty-three-year-old Chaplin met. Hollywood know-it-alls guffawed at her audacity and said she was twenty-seven. The probable truth is that she had just celebrated her twenty-second birthday. Her parents, who were still precariously together at the time of the birth of Marion Levy (as the baby's name appeared on her birth certificate), were Joe R. and Alta Levy (sometimes spelled Levee, or LeeVee) of Whitestone Landing, Long Island. After the marriage broke up, Alta and Pauline (not Paulette), as Alta had taken to calling her little girl, lived on the edge of poverty and moved frequently, on one occasion as far west as Kansas. In the recollections of her sexually knowing childhood that Goddard later shared with her secretary Lois Granato, she talked of the marketing game she dreamed up. On rainy days she would stand on a street corner under an umbrella. When she had selected a likely looking man, she would sidle up to him and say, "If you give me a dime, I'll cover you with my umbrella, and if you give me a quarter, I'll let you look under my skirt."[22]

By early 1923 Alta and twelve-year-old Paulette were back in New York, and the following summer they lived well for a change as the house guests of Paulette's rich and fun-loving uncle, Charlie Goddard, in Great Neck, Long Island. To Hedda Hopper, Paulette later talked nostalgically of the thrilling times she had had at "his beautiful house on the edge of the grounds of a country club, of which he was president (the Soundview)."

In front of the house was a permanent dance floor; and each Saturday night meant a party to which were invited the biggest theatrical stars of that time: Marilyn Miller, Jack Hazzard, Jack Donohue, the Dolly sisters, Harry Pilzer, the Frank Cravens, the Arthur Hopkinses, and occasionally a Barrymore.

Then and there Paulette made up her mind that some day she was going to be a star. "I watched the biggest ones—how they walked, danced, dressed, behaved. And I kept saying, 'I can do it much better.'"[23]

In the fall, she began earning fifty dollars a week modeling Hattie Carnegie fashions. Three years later, her Broadway career began when she landed a role as a scantily clad showgirl in Ziegfeld's summer revue, *No Foolin'*, which led to her becoming the smiling lovely perched in the cutout moon to whom the baritone sang in Ziegfeld's big-budget musical, *Rio Rita*. On nightclubbing forays after the show, she appeared on the arm of a succession of sugar daddies, and on June 28, 1927, she married one of them. Handsome, patrician Edgar William James was twice her age and the president of the Southern States Lumber Company of Asheville, North Carolina. In a late-in-life reminiscence, Goddard described her life with him:

> He was from North Carolina and we went there to live. In Biltmore Forest. That's where I learned to hunt and jump and so forth. I was sixteen [seventeen, in all likelihood] when we were married. And we had a *beautiful* house there and I—I didn't know how to live that way. It was suburban but with corn whiskey, you know, for breakfast. They'd give you a big shot before you got on the horse, you know? It's supposed to be elegant and chic to do that, but I didn't get it at all. I couldn't live that way.

In 1929 she divorced him and, alimony in hand, headed for Hollywood, where she bought a Duesenberg roadster for $18,000 and appeared as an extra girl in a Laurel and Hardy two-reeler, *Berth Marks*.[24]

When making the Hollywood party scene with Chaplin, she loved talking about the yacht he had purchased at her urging. It pleased her, too, to show off the jewels that he was lavishing upon her and that set the standard for the remarkable pieces other lovers would be enticed into giving her in years to come. (At Paramount in the 1940s, she kept her glittering trophies heaped up in cigar boxes in her dressing room. According to the studio's highly talented costume designer, Edith Head, "she would open a cigar box, pass it around temptingly for all the seamstresses to see—but no, don't touch, they're not cigars, they're precious gems, jerks." It was her way, Head concluded, "of tormenting my staff.")

Tormenting the press was another of her pleasures. Whenever a cameraman wanted a shot of her at the movie premieres, the racetrack meetings, and other social functions she and Chaplin attended, she was the soul of cooperation, but to the reporters who asked her about her marital status, she offered nothing but cat-and-mouse games—and then laughed at their frustration. What was less amusing for her was the sharp curtailment in their party life that Chaplin enforced, once his program for making her over moved into high gear; indeed, it bred a resentment in her, for she was a much tougher cookie than Lita Grey. Thus on a cruise one day on someone else's boat, Chaplin overheard her say of him in contempt, as she was talking with another man, "Oh, he's just like a grandmother." But while he was wounded by her remark, it did not sway him. Dancing and singing lessons loomed large in his prescriptions for her, along with acting lessons, reading assignments, and discourses by him on everything under the sun. For her role as a street urchin in *Modern Times*, on which camera work finally began in the fall of 1934, he rehearsed her for hours at the studio and then resumed doing so at home. "Try it again, try it again," he kept repeating, even when she broke down and wept. "Oh, Charlie, I'm not an actress, I'm just not an actress," she would wail. Nevertheless he never let up.[25]

6

Charles Chaplin, Jr., would stress in *My Father, Charlie Chaplin* that "when Dad was happy he sang. How he would sing! Snatches from operas, from his favorite ditties, or stand-bys from his old music-hall days." One of the numbers he liked best betrayed his endless fascination with insanity. "Oh, ever since that fatal night/Me wife's gone mad,/ Awfully queer, touched just here"—when singing that line, Charles Jr. recalled, his father would always point to his head—"Bad, bad, bad! In the middle of the night/She'd sneak the sheets and walk round my bed post,/Singing 'Hamlet, Hamlet,/I am thy father's ghost.'" But in 1933–34 these impromptu performances ceased. Instead, his "dark moods became more pronounced," and his "flashes of anger more frequent." A fear of failure was plaguing him, his son realized.[26]

To begin with, there was his continuing holdout against full acceptance of the sound revolution. Other producers shook their heads at this and predicted disaster at the box office, and Charles Jr. guessed that "sometimes he must have been appalled himself at his . . . conservatism." The severe assessments of his achievement by a pair of young Marxist critics, Lorenzo Turrent Rozas and Harry Alan Potamkin, must also have upset him. They raised the issue of his outmodedness in a particularly stinging way, by talking about the social and political irrelevance of his work.[27]

In the pages of *The New Freeman* in 1931, Potamkin denounced the critics of the 1920s for creating a "cult of Charlie Chaplin which has never allowed a decent study of a man of talent who has not realized the great work that might have been expected of him." The following year, he derided *The Gold Rush*, *The Circus*, and *City Lights* for their "overdose of maudlin pathos," their "aimlessness," and their "directional looseness." *City Lights* came in for especially heavy abuse for its "unleavened procession" of narrative events, "now and then enlivened with a brief episode or gag of quality." Instead of sticking with its "major motif," the relation between the millionaire and the tramp, Chaplin had subordinated it to the "minor [!] motif" involving the blind girl. In *The Kid*, Potamkin granted, Chaplin had given indications of a capacity for social satire; unfortunately, his subsequent work had "fallen far beneath [those] indications."[28]

Rozas's essay, "Charlie Chaplin's Decline," orginally published in Spanish in a Mexican Communist magazine, was translated into English and republished in *Living Age* in June 1934. Chaplin, like Prince Kropotkin, was an anarchist, said Rozas, and anarchism was a philosophy that led "inexorably to defeat" because the anarchist "finally becomes involved with the society he repudiates." Thus Chaplin had become "an accomplice of capitalism" as a result of his failure to meet the artistic challenge of the Great Depression by moving past his commitment to pathos and the outmoded individualism of the tramp. Today, Rozas continued, Chaplin is "in his decadence—alone, seated in the limited arena of his art. He explores the horizon. There is no road for him to follow. To insist on the old one is impossible, and to go where the workers are now marching is also impossible. To do that he would have to throw away the ballast of his millions." In a final thrust, Rozas called Chaplin's pictures harmful to audiences, inasmuch as they "disorientate and confuse men who are struggling for the final victory of the disinherited."[29]

Yet another strain on the nerves of the racked comedian was the ironic result of the salute to him by the president and general manager of the Soviet film industry, Boris Z. Shumiatsky. During a visit to Hollywood in the late summer of 1935, Shumiatsky had come to the Sunset and La Brea studio. Chaplin had not only done him the courtesy of showing him a preliminary cut of *Modern Times*, so Shumiatsky told a *Pravda* interviewer upon his return to the Soviet Union, but had proved receptive to his criticism that its pessimistic ending was a mistake. "I am happy we met," he quoted Chaplin as saying when they parted. "But this meeting will cost me many weeks of labor on my picture." Those words convinced me, said Shumiatsky, that a new ending was going to be devised, that it would be infused by an awareness of how important it is to "fight for a better life for all humanity with a conviction of the necessity for active struggle," and that such an ending would mark "a stage in the ideological growth of a remarkable artist."[30]

On learning that the gist of this interview had been reported in the *New York Times*,* Chaplin realized he was in deep trouble. The original ending had been designed by Chaplin in 1933 for the purpose of ingratiating himself with the Catholic prelates who were becoming more and more unhappy about the political and moral complexion of Hollywood movies. If the prelates now came to believe that this ending had been discarded in response to the judgment of a top Soviet Communist official that it was "pessimistic," there was no telling how that devout Catholic, Joseph I. Breen, of the all-powerful Production Code Administration, might react.

7

It was in the summer of 1929 that Will Hays decided that the time had come for him to ally himself with Catholic reformers in pushing for a clear-cut code of production principles for the movie industry. If the practice of self-regulation was to survive, if federal interference was to be averted, the moguls would have to agree to the establishment of a truly serious control over the content of their offerings. More and more editorial writers across the country were attack-

---

* "The last reel of Charles Chaplin's forthcoming picture," the lead paragraph in the *Times* story declared, "has been materially affected by a conversation between the producer and B. Z. Shumiatsky, head of the Russian film industry, according to a statement made by the latter in Moscow immediately following his return from his recent visit to Hollywood." *New York Times*, September 29, 1935, sec. X, p. 4.

ing the Hays Office as a sham, while the temper of the censorship boards in certain communities and states was becoming alarmingly angry. Catholic officials who wanted to clean and disinfect the Hollywood pest hole—as some of them called it—became aware of Hays's wish to reach out to them when he dispatched his chief counsel to Chicago to talk with Father FitzGeorge Dineen, a frequent critic of the "immorality" of the films being exhibited in the large Granada Theater in his parish.

Archbishop (later Cardinal) George W. Mundelein of Chicago had meanwhile been exchanging thoughts with a prominent Catholic layman in the city, Martin Quigley, about the threat posed to the preservation of a healthy society arising out of a morally and politically unbridled entertainment. Mundelein liked Quigley's idea that the Church should become involved in drawing up a regulatory code for movies. Material deemed unacceptable by code standards could be eliminated either prior to or during production, Quigley argued. Instead of constituting a threat to family values and respect for government, movies made in America could be shaped into appealing reinforcements of these vital ideals. At the suggestion of Father Dineen, whom he had also consulted, Mundelein picked a professor of dramatics at St. Louis University, Father Daniel Lord, to draft the code. A prolific writer, Lord was known for his excoriations of Darwinian biology, abortion, birth control, Soviet Communism, the eroticism of modern dance, and the decadence of modern literature.

Lord formulated the code with Quigley's assistance, and then Quigley took it to Hays. "My eyes nearly popped out when I read it," Hays recalled in the 1950s. "This was the very thing I had been looking for." Naturally, he also approved of Quigley's proposal that the task of implementing the code be carried out through the Hays Office. On February 10, 1930, Hays, Quigley, and Lord met with Irving Thalberg, Jack Warner, and three other producers representing the movie industry as a whole to work out an agreement, if possible. All five members of the Hollywood group believed that the commandments in the code and its vision of a "correct entertainment" that would raise "the whole standards of a nation" denied reality. In their view, movies had long been, and ought to continue to be, "one vast reflection of every image in the stream of contemporary life." Nevertheless, on the second day of their meeting with Hays and his Catholic confreres, they accepted the code with only the mildest of reservations.[31]

To the outraged surprise of the reformers whom Mundelein had mobilized, it quickly developed that Hollywood had not really committed itself to changing its ways and that the Production Code was hamstrung by a lack of enforcement power, even as the Hays Office had been in the 1920s. Lord and Quigley were appalled by Howard Hughes's *Hell's Angels* (1930), in which Jean Harlow attempts to seduce a pilot "in the most candid and detailed fashion," Lord complained, as well as by Paramount's *Confessions of a Co-ed* (1931), MGM's *Just a Gigolo* (1931), and Columbia's *Good Bad Girl* (1931). Equally distressing to them was the presentation of crime in a wide array of pictures, of which Paramount's *Vice Squad* (1931), with its veritable "catechism," said Lord, "of blackmailing, framing, seduction, hotel prostitution . . . evil police, etc." was typical.[32]

Another Irish Catholic activist, Joe Breen, of the public relations department in the Hollywood branch of the Hays Office,* became convinced by the fall of 1932 that the Production Code had failed. To his friend Father Wilfrid Parsons, editor of the Catholic publication *America*, Breen confided his opinion that Will Hays lacked "guts" and that the Jews who managed most of the studios were contemptible. "Hays sold us a first-class bill of goods when he put over the Code on us," he irrationally burst out to Parsons on October 10. "It may be that Hays thought these lousy Jews out here would abide by the Code's provisions but if he did then he should be censured for his lack of proper knowledge of the breed." These Jews, he continued, "are simply a rotten bunch of vile people with no respect for anything beyond the making of money. . . . Here we have Paganism rampant and in its most virulent form. . . . These Jews seem to think of nothing but money making and sexual indulgence. . . . They are, probably, the scum of the scum of the earth."[33]

During the summer of 1933, Breen's West Coast confidant, Bishop John Cantwell, asked an abrasive-tongued, beetle-browed Los Angeles attorney, Joseph Scott—who in the mid-1940s would serve as Joan Barry's lawyer in her paternity-suit trials against Chaplin—to convey a

---

* Hays himself lived and worked in New York.

message to the Hollywood producers. The Catholic bishops of America, Cantwell told Scott to tell them, had run out of patience with a "vile industry" that was doing "untold harm" to the nation's children. Unless the producers recognized the moral significance of entertainment and reformed at once, the bishops would unleash the power of their church against them. Rhetorically if not substantively, the messenger considerably exceeded his instructions.

At a meeting arranged by Breen and attended by Jack Warner, Louis B. Mayer, Adolph Zukor, and Joe Schenck, among other Hollywood movers and shakers, Scott "lashed into the Jews furiously," so Breen wrote to Quigley on August 4. Characterizing his listeners as "disloyal" Americans, Scott accused them of having been engaged for years in "a conspiracy to debauch the . . . youth of the land." A recent trial in California had exposed "communistic" radicals as "100 per cent Jews," he further contended, as he segued into a warning that the connection between "dirty motion pictures" and radical Jews who had nothing but contempt for the bourgeois convention of moral distinctions was "serving to build up an enormous case against the Jews in the eyes of the American people." Cease your "damnable" practices, Scott raged, which have brought "disgrace upon the Jews and upon America."[34]

Zukor jumped to his feet as soon as Scott had finished and abjectly apologized for the "dirt and filth" that the reformers had found in Paramount's pictures and promised to do his best to keep the studio's future work free of pollution. Similar promises were made by the politically conservative Mayer and other producers. Only Joe Schenck argued to the contrary that serious pictures on serious subjects, such as RKO's forthcoming version of Somerset Maugham's *Of Human Bondage* (1934), should not be condemned out of hand because of their subject matter. In biting tones, Schenck also referred to religious critics of the movie business as "narrow-minded and bigoted," and he scorned his fellow moguls as self-abasing cowards who had allowed a histrionic lawyer to stampede them with anti-Semitic invective.

Breen's report of the meeting to Bishop Cantwell did not mention Schenck's remarks. Instead, he declared that the producers had been in "almost unanimous" agreement that they had erred and had to change. But the bishop had "no faith" in mere vows. Only concrete, specific, and immediate evidence of reforms undertaken would convince him of the movie industry's sincerity. When it was not forthcoming, he delivered a lengthy address about the need for forceful action against Hollywood at a November gathering of bishops at Catholic University in Washington, D.C. The bishops thereupon launched a Legion of Decency campaign that called upon the 20 million American Catholics —most of whom were concentrated in Boston, Chicago, New York, Philadelphia, Pittsburgh, Cleveland, Detroit, and other urban centers where movie theaters flourished—to pledge to boycott movies that Catholic officials condemned. In December everything fell into place for the reformers. With the suppliant approval of the moguls, the Hays Office created a Production Code Administration and appointed Joe Breen as director. From preliminary script to finished product, Breen and his staff were empowered to review and rule upon the ideas and images of every Hollywood film. If a film failed to receive a PCA certificate of approval, no mainstream theater in America would exhibit it.[35]

In the name of freeing the nation from the oppression of morally corrupting and degrading films, the PCA banned profanity, nudity, seminudity, provocatively sexual postures, amoral presentations of adultery and prostitution, glamorizations of gangsters, excessive violence, drug trafficking, white slavery, explicit plans for committing bank robberies and other crimes, and recipes for concocting lethal poisons. An early memo from Breen to his staff made clear that he also regarded the code as a mandate for enforcing respect "for all *law* and *lawful* authority." Films that undermined faith in the American government, or the free-enterprise system, or the police, or the courts, were to be considered as "Communist propaganda" and "banned from the screen." It soon became apparent as well that bloody confrontations between labor and management had to be toned down before Breen would approve them and that he expected a similar restraint in dramatizations of poverty and racial discrimination.[36]

Yet while he was proud of his record of reducing political and social criticism in movies, every now and again Breen displayed a degree of tolerance that confounded all expectations. Although he was convinced that the Soviet conspiracy was making a major effort to infiltrate the film industry in the United States and that the striking number of Reds in Hollywood was no accident, there were times when he refused to withhold his approval of movies for ideological reasons. It was as if he were constrained by the errant thought that the censorship of expression was a cure that was worse than the disease.

Thus in the light of announced PCA policy, Walter Wanger's chances for approval did not appear to be very good when he submitted a script to Breen in September 1934 of an antiwar film he wanted to make called *The President Vanishes*. For the script told the story of a sinister cabal of steel and oil tycoons, munitions makers, fat-cat bankers, and press lords that corrupts congressmen and senators, funds an army of fascistic street demonstrators, and sells the American people on the slogan "Save America's honor," all for the purpose of plunging the nation into another war in Europe. Furthermore, the script honored the Communist Party as the only political movement with the guts to stand up to the cabal. At the peak of a dramatic crowd scene, an idealistic young Red put it this way:

Fellow workers, it is your blood—my blood—the workers' blood they are after. For what—so the capitalistic bloodsuckers [the crowd boos at this point], yes yes, the capitalist bloodsuckers can grow richer. Tomorrow . . . Congress will say we must go to war to protect our honor. Only one thing can stop it—join the Communist party.

Although the picture could hardly have been more provocative, Breen confined himself in his response to Wanger to describing a few minor changes that would have to be made in an otherwise acceptable treatment.

A few weeks after the filming of *The President Vanishes* was completed, Will Hays and his board of directors attended a private screening in New York. They were horrified by it, and furious at Breen for having given it a certificate of approval. In Hays's view, the film was "communist propaganda, subversive in its portrait of American government, contrary to the accepted principles of established law and order, and perhaps treasonable." In a rare intervention, Hays ordered Breen to rescind the PCA certificate and arranged to meet with Adolph Zukor, for although Wanger had his own production company, he had made *The President Vanishes* under Paramount's auspices. The upshot was that the most inflammatory details in the picture, including the young Communist's "bloodsuckers" speech, were excised in exchange for a new PCA certificate.[37]

At the time that this little drama was playing out, Hollywood's most celebrated independent producer had just begun shooting *Modern Times*.

8

Originally, Chaplin had planned to call his new picture *The Masses*.[38] The proletarian sound of that title testified to his new resolve to align his art with his politics. Through a transformation of the tramp into a pathetic symbol of industrial man, dehumanized and dominated by the machinery of a cruelly exploitative factory system, he would give the lie to upstart critics who accused him of aimlessness and decadence. His decision, however, to change the title to *Modern Times* reflected the caution that led him to balance every scene in the picture that was on the left with a scene that was not. Thus the drama he tentatively devised for the ending offered a Catholic vision of life.

Charlie has fallen in love with a girl of the streets, a gamine, whom Chaplin ignorantly insisted on referring to as "the Gamin." After many adventures, the little fellow suffers a nervous breakdown and is confined to a hospital. Just as he is about to be discharged, he receives a surprise visit from "the Gamin," dressed in a nun's habit and accompanied by a Mother Superior. In the words of Chaplin's scenario, the Gamin greets him, "smiling wistfully," and seizes his hand. Twice he attempts to speak to her, but is unable to say anything. Finally, he

> releases his hand and walks slowly down the hospital steps, she gazing after him. He turns and waves a last farewell and goes towards the city's skyline. She stands immobile, watching him as he fades away.
>
> There is something inscrutable in her expression, something of resignation and regret. She stands as though lost in a dream, watching after him and her spirit goes with him, for out of herself the ghost of the Gamin appears and runs rampant down the hospital steps, dancing and bounding after him. . . .
>
> She is standing on the hospital steps. She is awakened from her revelry [*sic*] by a light touch, the hand of the Mother Superior. She starts, then turns and . . . together they depart into the portals of the hospital again. FADE OUT.[39]

Perhaps the ending in the preliminary cut of the picture that Shumiatsky saw at the Chaplin Studio did not fully adhere to the "nun scenario" and its imagery of the Catholic Church as a refuge in a stormy world. But even if this was so, the very fact that Chaplin took the trouble to write it reveals how concerned he was about staying in the good graces of Catholic America. Correspondingly, it measures the intensity of his wish to disabuse Joe Breen of the idea set forth in the *New York Times* story that his final revisions of *Modern Times* were undertaken to please a Soviet official. Otherwise, Breen might be prompted to take a second look at all of the left-wing material in the picture that he had originally not made a fuss about.

At Chaplin's frantic instruction, Alf Reeves called a press conference. While granting that the final reel of the picture had been significantly changed since Shumiatsky's visit to the studio, Reeves vigorously denied that anybody could "ever tell Chaplin anything about such matters— he, as you know, has very much his own way and he has his own ideas —always." He also attempted to discredit Shumiatsky's characterization of *Modern Times* as a film that revealed "honestly and truthfully how the American working class is carrying on the struggle against capitalism." The Russian, said Reeves, "reads deep, terrible social meaning [into] sequences that Mr. Chaplin considers funny." For good measure Reeves added that "I can assure you that this picture is intended as entertainment, and perhaps it might be said, too, that Mr. Chaplin's purpose in making this picture is to make money." [40]

Reeves's reassurances, plus the altogether familiar character of the new ending that Chaplin prepared, apparently sufficed to calm any storm that might have been brewing in the PCA office. On January 6, 1936, Breen composed a most cordial letter to Reeves:

As you know, we had the very great pleasure, this afternoon, of witnessing a projection room showing of your production of CHARLIE CHAPLIN IN MODERN TIMES, and I am sending you this to advise you that it is our judgment that the basic story is acceptable under the Provisions of the Production Code adopted by the industry, and, with the exceptions noted hereinafter, reasonably free from any serious difficulties at the hands of political censor boards.

In accordance with our verbal recommendations to you, we respectfully urge upon you the following eliminations:

1) The first part of the "pansy" gag [involving Charlie's hulking and presumably homosexual cellmate in prison];

2) The word "dope" in the printed title [in reference to the smuggling of cocaine into the prison];

3) Most of the business of the stomach rumblings on the part of the minister's wife and Charlie;

4) The entire brassiere gag in the department store; and

5) The close-up shot of the udders of the cow.

I wish again to recommend most earnestly that you make these eliminations here in Hollywood before the picture is finally completed and shipped east. Because of the outstanding entertainment quality of this picture, it is our judgment that you can well afford to "lean backward" in your efforts to make the finished picture completely acceptable to the untold millions of patrons who will surely view it and enjoy it thoroughly.

If you will advise us when you have made these eliminations, we shall be glad to issue this Association's formal certificate of approval thereon.

A week later, Reeves replied, "I am now able to inform you definitely that all of the five recommendations you made have been carried out in full, and in view of this fact we shall be pleased to receive your Association's formal certificate of approval thereon at the earliest possible moment."[41]

Chaplin suffered suppressions of the picture only outside the United States. The Vatican offered no objection to it,* but Mussolini's police would not permit it to be shown anywhere in Italy, on the grounds that it "incline[d] toward bolshevism," and Nazi Germany banned it as well. Indeed, German consuls around the world were instructed to do their best to discourage its exhibition in the countries in which they were stationed. This effort, however, was overwhelmed by the popular response to it, especially in the non-English-speaking parts of the world, as a United Artists report of its success in China vividly illustrated. "Despite bad weather and rickshaw strike compelling thousands walk

---

* In 1995 the Vatican's Pontifical Council for Social Communications observed the one hundredth anniversary of the cinema by singling out forty-five movies, from the United States, Europe, and Asia, that it said possessed special artistic or religious merit. *Modern Times* was one of them.

miles MODERN TIMES had brilliant premiere simultaneous Nanking Metropol theatres [also] creating new record gross for Shanghai breaking previous record held by CITY LIGHTS."[42]

In the American market, its earnings fell well short of the splendid totals accumulated by *City Lights, The Circus,* and *The Gold Rush.* For while Joe Breen's approval shielded the picture from organized resistance, countless moviegoers decided on their own to let it go by. After all, it was a silent picture. In the list of box-office champions of the mid-1930s, *Modern Times* was outclassed not only by the champion of champions, *Snow White and the Seven Dwarfs* (1937), but by *Mutiny on the Bounty* (1935) and *San Francisco* (1936), among other films.[43]

9

A huge timepiece with a swordlike second hand fills the screen. A few seconds later, the title of the picture and the opening credits are superimposed upon it. As an image of the tyranny of time in modern life, that remorseless second hand sticks in the mind, even though it possesses only a fraction of the imaginative power of Fritz Lang's depiction in *Metropolis* (1926) of a man nailed to a clock like Christ on the cross. In orotund officialese, a title card announces the theme of *Modern Times.* "A story of industry, of individual enterprise, of humanity crusading in the pursuit of happiness." A montage composed of a herd of sheep jostling one another on a runway and a throng of fedora-wearing workers surging up the steps of a subway station makes an additional promise about subject matter. This picture is going to portray the reduction of human beings to the level of animals.

The next shot, of an immense factory on the far side of an overpass and of the streams of men hurrying toward it, might have been plucked from a documentary about Detroit, whose automobile assembly lines had inspired Chaplin—or so he said—to make *Modern Times.* During an interview with a reporter from the *New York World,* he asserts in *My Autobiography,* his questioner happened to tell him about Detroit's "factory-belt system . . . a harrowing story of big industry luring healthy young men off the farms who, after four or five years at the belt system, became nervous wrecks. It was that conversation that gave me the idea for *Modern Times.*"[44] But in saying this Chaplin may simply have been

npting to scotch the widely held and well-founded suspicion that
he had lifted his basic ideas for the picture's assembly-line scenes from
René Clair's satire of the machine age, *À Nous la Liberté* (1931).

The Detroit-like look of the factory ends at its doors. Inside the
plant is the world of Chaplin's imagination. The camera eye glides past
glistening turbines and gleaming floors to a futuristic control room run
by a heavily built young man, stripped to the waist, who seems more
like a cadet in a Jules Verne fantasy than an industrial foreman of the
1930s, and thence to the office of the president of the company. The
president, played by the glaring-eyed, grim-visaged Allan Garcia of
circus-master fame, is hard at work—putting together a jigsaw puzzle;
and when he tires of it, as he quickly does, he switches his attention to
the comic strips, only one of which is discernible: *Tarzan of the Apes*. A
door opens and his secretary enters, bringing him a glass of water.
When he pops a pill in his mouth, the suspicion is left that he has an
ulcer.

What turns this *Daily Worker* caricature of a business executive into a
riveting figure is a flight of fancy on Chaplin's part, stemming from his
continuing search for ways to avoid a straightforward use of sound-
recorded speech. Just before the president barks his first audible command, the view of him shifts from his office to a wall in the control
room that is actually a closed-circuit video screen. The angry face of the
president looms in front of the foreman and his voice booms out. Unlike
the kazoo squeaks in *City Lights*, his message is intelligible. Nevertheless, sound-film "realism" is once again being subverted, for the voice is
an electronic transmission spewing out words in lip-synch with a televised image. In a further extension of the president's artificial reach, his
TV hookup has a two-way capability that enables him to spy on what is
happening anywhere in the plant, including the washroom—which is
where he catches the overall-clad Charlie enjoying a smoke. Well before
Orwell—and at a time, moreover, when television was hardly more than
a toy—Chaplin conjured up a prototype of Big Brother's monitoring
apparatus.

Another encroachment upon human freedom in the brave new world
of *Modern Times* is the feeding machine, an exploitative device for sup-
plying workers with lunch while they continue working. As Chaplin
would note in the picture book *My Life in Pictures* (1975), which he

helped to assemble in his final years, the idea of the feeding machine had been on his mind before the 1920s.[45] The machine's inventor, a crazy-professor type, brings a model to the president's office and attempts to sell it to him. "Real" talk, however, is again avoided. While the inventor stands mute and his eyeballs excitedly roll, a so-called mechanical salesman on a phonograph record makes the pitch, in laminated, Madison Avenue lingo, about the machine's "aerodynamic" design and "synchromesh" transmission.

The critical test of the contraption's workability takes place on the temporarily shut-down assembly line, with Charlie, inevitably, in the role of the guinea pig. The inventor's assistants strap him into a seat that places him at chin level with a rotating tray on which he notices, with a slightly alarmed look on his face, a bowl of soup, a plateful of bite-sized pieces of meat, a charlotte russe, and an ear of corn on a revolving skewer that also has the capacity to move back and forth like a typewriter carriage. In lieu of a napkin, a large white buffer swings forward at periodic intervals and painstakingly wipes the diner's lips. At first, the demonstration works like a charm. But when electrical problems erupt in a blaze of shorted switches, the machine goes berserk, and Charlie's face takes on the wild look of a trapped animal. In a high-tech, supremely funny update of slapstick sadism, his chest is drenched with hot soup, whipped cream from the charlotte russe is smeared across his face and neck, roundhouse swings from the napkin buffer all but knock him out, two metal bolts inadvertently set down on the plate of meat are shoved into his mouth and a maniacally revved-up cob of corn scours his teeth, his mustache, and the underneath part of his nose, as kernels fly in all directions.

Charlie's normal task is to use long wrenches to tighten the nuts on bolted metal plates traveling rapidly past him on a conveyor belt. The repetitiveness of the work and the hectic pace of it—which the president of the company keeps stepping up as the day proceeds—serve to reduce him to a textbook example of Henri Bergson's argument in his essay on laughter: "The attitudes, gestures and movements of the human body are laughable in exact proportion as that body reminds us of a mere machine."[46] Whenever Charlie walks away from the belt, the herky-jerky, tightening motions of his arms and shoulders involuntarily continue, and when a good-looking secretary happens by and bends over to retrieve something from the floor, he automatically tightens the large black buttons on the back of her skirt. The only way in which he can regain control of himself is to close his eyes and wrap his arms tightly about himself until the tics cease. Yet while his suffering is aimed at teaching a social lesson, it does not radicalize Charlie. Indeed, his quarrels with the worker toiling beside him and his adroitness in shifting the blame to him for a mistake of his own forecast the lack of worker-solidarity sentiment that he will manifest later on in the story.

A massive breakdown in Charlie's sanity occurs toward the end of the afternoon, when the president's latest call for more speed proves too much for him. Just before he hurls himself down the chute at the foot of the conveyor belt, the worker next to him cries out (as a title card announces), "He's crazy!!!" The ceiling-high wall of machinery on the floor below is dominated by sprocketed wheels and spools that look like the component parts of a gigantic movie projector. With arms outstretched in front of him, Charlie appears at the top of this system and is slowly threaded up and down through it, as though he were a strip of film. There are two images in *Modern Times*, of which this is one—the other is the road shot at the conclusion—that have become legendary, and both of them flowered out of Chaplin's sense of the end of an era in his career. *Modern Times* was to be the Tramp's last picture. From now on, Chaplin knew, he would no longer be able to resist the sort of use of the sound revolution that he considered alien to Charlie's universality as well as actively hostile to his dream-creating power. Imagining him as a film strip in a movie projector was one of the ways he chose to say good-bye to him.

A foreman finally manages to throw the movement of the wheels and spools into reverse and Charlie is propelled backwards onto the conveyor belt once again. From this launch pad a mad prankster takes off into the wild blue yonder. As he pirouettes and skips about, he uses his wrenches to tweak the noses and nipples of the workers. With the reappearance of the good-looking secretary, he goes into a pelvis-tilted crouch and comes on to her as though he were a hound dog, with wrenches for ears; when the wrenches flip upwards with the suddenness of phallic erections, he comes on to her again as a woodland satyr and she flees in terror.

Seized by a Luddite frenzy but still maintaining balletic grace, he disrupts production all over the plant by spinning valve wheels and reversing master gears in the control room and temporarily blinding whoever challenges him with squirts from an oilcan. Managers as well as workers try to catch him. Ever resourceful, he takes to the air, via a traveling pulley and a sling suspended from a giant hook, and triumphantly soars over the heads of his pursuers. But once he reaches the literal end of his rope and slides to the ground, he is hustled outside to an ambulance that has been summoned to take him to a psychiatric hospital. Before clambering into the vehicle, he covers a few more faces with squirts of oil. By this time, however, his antics are no longer funny. In the final moments of a truly remarkable outburst of the humor of madness, the comedian could not keep the lurking horror in his material from showing through.

10

During a conversation with Jean Cocteau, a fellow passenger on a tour of the western Pacific in the winter and spring of 1936, Chaplin admitted that the various parts of *Modern Times* "existed in their own right. I could show them separately, one by one, like my early one-reelers."[47] While their self-containment enabled him to shuffle them like cards into different sequences before deciding on the one he preferred, he paid a price for this convenience in narrative coherence. The contradictions in political outlook between the various parts also contributed to the picture's broken quality, as did Chaplin's quaintly out-of-date directorial methods, which called for crowds to gather out of nowhere and key players to move stiffly front and center. Even so, *Modern Times* is one of his enduring achievements.

After being released from the hospital, Charlie walks past a factory with a "Closed" sign on its doors. The doctor who attended him during his nervous breakdown has warned him to avoid excitement, but in an atmosphere of mass unemployment and social unrest he soon finds himself in the midst of it. While he is standing on a curb wondering what to do, the red "danger" flag on a piece of lumber hanging out of the back of a passing truck falls off. Charlie snatches up the flag and waves it back and forth in a vain attempt to get the driver's attention. As he walks slowly forward in the middle of the street, a crowd of unemployed workmen, carrying placards bearing such slogans as "Unity" and "Libertad," rounds the corner and comes up behind him, so that he appears to be the leader. Policemen move in, a violent scuffle ensues, and Charlie—who has offered no resistance whatsoever, but who is still holding the red flag—is arrested and taken away. A title card describes the injustice of his fate: "Held as a Communist leader, our innocent victim languishes in jail."

The scene reflected the familiar protestations of innocence in the 1930s by members of idealistically named Communist fronts. While they often waved red flags, in a manner of speaking, this did not mean that they were doing the bidding of Communists. On the contrary, they maintained, they were simply conscientious human beings who were moved by a sense of responsibility to their fellow man.

The family drama that follows likewise leads to politically motivated police brutality. On a crowded waterfront dock the camera picks up the Paulette Goddard character, "the gamin who refuses to go hungry," as a title card euphemistically describes her habitual thievery. A barefoot, wild-eyed creature, clothed in a rag of a dress and given to spread-legged stances, impulsive skippings about, and other tomboyish mannerisms, she is Chaplin's version of the tackily dressed, dirty-faced, feisty child-woman played by Mary Pickford in *Tess of the Storm Country* (1914), the picture that confirmed her position as America's Sweetheart. In the first glimpse of her, the gamin is rapidly cutting bananas off a huge stem of them that she has stolen. Occasionally she places the knife she is wielding between her teeth and tosses portions of the fruit to a group of young children, and her quick-darting eyes gleam with outlaw pleasure. Her main concerns, however, are the people who are awaiting her at home: her two little sisters, to whom she has been a surrogate mother ever since the death of their real mother, and her father, who is unemployed.

Defeat is written all over this man as he enters the shack where he and his daughters live. When the gamin appears with a bunch of bananas to share with him and her sisters, he chides her for her thievish ways—but oh! so gently. While industrial capitalism may have robbed him of his role as family provider, he still retains his fatherly sweetness. The next time he appears, he is lying dead from a bullet wound in a nearby street and the gamin is bending over his body and sobbing. The firing of the fatal shot has taken place within hearing but out of sight. Nevertheless, it is obvious that the deed was the work of one of the policemen who are running after and scattering the angry gathering of jobless men that the father had joined.*

The declaration on a title card that "the law takes charge of . . . orphans" has a lineage that traces back through a similar assumption of authority in *The Kid* to the decision of the Lambeth District Relief Committee to enroll Sydney and Charlie Chaplin in the poor-law school at Hanwell. While nothing is known directly about the institution to which the gamin and her sisters are slated to be sent, the brusque impersonality of the juvenile officers who come to take them into custody casts a shadow upon it, as does the gamin's rebellious preference for a life in the streets. As the officers are completing their paperwork, she tiptoes out of the room and escapes.

Charlie's arrest on false charges, the violent death of the gamin's father, and her refusal to submit to incarceration in an asylum of dubious quality are events that indict the social order. Meantime, however, a counteraffirmation of conservative values has been building. The central event of Charlie's jail term is an attempted breakout by a bunch of ruthless toughs—which Charlie all but single-handedly foils by banging iron doors against their heads, taking away the cell keys they have seized, and releasing the guards they have imprisoned. The panache he displays throughout this sequence is a joy to behold. In gratitude for his good citizenship, the warden gives him a cell of his own and fills it with

---

* Chaplin probably modeled this scene on the events of "Bloody Thursday." On the morning of July 5, 1934, at the height of the maritime strike that had crippled every port facility on the West Coast, a violent clash broke out on the Embarcadero in San Francisco. On one side were thousands of hard-fisted longshoremen, led by Harry Bridges and armed with bricks, cobblestones, and spikes; ranged against them and moving forward were hundreds of policemen carrying extra-heavy riot sticks and covered by rifle and pistol fire and tear-gas barrages. "By late afternoon the San Francisco newspapers were recapping the statistics for Bloody Thursday: two dead, thirty suffering gunshot wounds, forty-three clubbed, gassed, or hit by projectiles. The emergency ward of the county hospital was overflowing. One patient: *San Francisco News* photographer Joe Rosenthal, shot through the ear by a stray bullet. A decade later, Rosenthal would win the Pulitzer Prize for his photograph of the Marines raising the flag on Iwo Jima. He was more frightened on Bloody Thursday, Rosenthal insisted." Kevin Starr, *Endangered Dreams: The Great Depression in California* (New York, 1996), p. 108.

so many creature comforts that it looks like a bed-sitting room in a middle-class boardinghouse. As he lies stretched out at his ease on his bunk, he picks up a newspaper. The front-page headline reads, "Strikes and Riots!" and the subhead declares, "Breadlines Broken by Unruly Mob." Of all the critics who have written about *Modern Times* across the years, only Charles J. Maland, in *Chaplin and American Culture* (1989), has had the independence of mind to note that Charlie does not manifest the slightest degree of partisan sympathy with the actions of the mob. "He looks toward the camera and shakes his head disapprovingly in a way that many Americans did during the depression, trying to shake away the negative effect of the 'news.' "[48]

After being released from jail, he meets the ragged, barefoot gamin, and when she beckons him with an insistent wave of her arm to come along with her, he does so. But instead of hurrying, in the name of her martyred father, to the front lines of proletarian protest, they wander away from the city into a rawly new suburban development, where they chance to observe the early-morning farewell embrace between a young businessman and his wife in front of their cottage home. Following a vigorous kiss-kiss, hubby goes off to his job and wifey skips back indoors with such an exaggerated display of connubial bliss that Charlie cannot resist imitating her, much to the gamin's amusement. Could you imagine us living in such a house? he mockingly asks. Yet when the fantasy he conjures up comes to life on the screen, the striking fact about it is that its absurd features—such as the cute-as-the-dickens outfit that the gamin is wearing and the cow that comes by the side door on command, so that she and Charlie can have fresh milk with their meals—are outweighed by its straightforward resemblances to suburban living. Moreover, Charlie's desire to poke fun dissolves into an expression of middle-class aspiration. "I'll do it!" he finally cries, as the gamin thrills to his words. "We'll get a home even if I have to work for it." Cut to the department store that hires him as a night watchman.

For this nighttime scene, Chaplin may have drawn on a serious novel of 1934, James Gould Cozzens's *Castaway*, in which a certain Mr. Lecky is apparently the sole survivor of a colossal urban disaster and a department store that has also survived the destruction becomes his refuge. Like Cozzens's latter-day Crusoe on his island of plenty, Charlie and the gamin explore floor after floor of the deserted emporium he is supposedly guarding. Perhaps because Goddard was such a material girl, Chaplin primarily relied on her in these episodes to make the really excited responses to "things." On one floor, the gamin jumps up and down with the glee of a ten-year-old at being able to play with a stuffed Mickey Mouse and a toy truck, while on another she models the full-length ermine coat she has donned with all the slinky, self-loving moves of a sugar daddy's sugar.

A subsequent experiment in homemaking—during which it is made clear that the two adventurers are not sleeping together—serves to breathe new life into the picture's social criticism. For neither Charlie nor the gamin has a job at this point and their tumbledown domicile is a comic version of the Hooverville shanties of the period. Thus when Charlie learns that several factories are being reopened, he is elated. "Work at last!" he exclaims to his comely housemate. "Now we'll get a real home." It is a prophecy that will not be fulfilled. On his very first day on the job, a fellow worker comes by and announces, "We're on strike." That Charlie is reluctant to walk out is unmistakable. Earning money fast is his priority. Although he finally obeys the strike order, and even manages to get arrested (as a result of accidentally stepping on a plank that propels a brick toward a policeman's head), he remains, in the midst of his comrades, an isolated figure. The ambivalence of the promise that Chaplin extended at the beginning of the picture has now become completely clear. At one and the same time, Modern Times is a story of "humanity crusading in the pursuit of happiness" and of "individual enterprise."

Other socially conscious pictures of the 1930s can be interpreted in more than one way. For instance, in Mr. Deeds Goes to Town (1936), directed by Frank Capra—who voted that year for the Republican candidate for President, Alf Landon—but written by the left-liberal Robert Riskin, does the wealth giveaway scheme dreamed up by the eccentric millionaire Longfellow Deeds (played by Gary Cooper) tacitly celebrate the social programs of Franklin D. Roosevelt or the philanthropic impulses of big businessmen? Without much question, however, Modern Times was more at odds with itself than any other picture of the decade.

The deliciously funny café scene that unfolds just before the picture's legend-sealing finale features Charlie as an inept waiter who is trying to carry a roast duck on a tray across a crowded dance floor. The curvilinear patterns of his movements through the wheels and spools of the factory's machinery are retraced here in more intricate form in his revolving progress—or rather, lack of it—through the throng of milling dancers. But while this spectacle is a visual delight, it is Charlie's audible —yes! audible—performance as a singing waiter that makes the café scene historic. The jabber he offers the customers is improvised right in front of them, in a panicky reaction to his discovery that he has lost the shirt cuff on which the gamin had written the lyrics he was supposed to sing. In the tantalizing relationship of its nonsense to sense, his verbal adroitness calls to mind an interesting discussion of painterly deceptiveness in E. H. Gombrich's *The Sense of Order: A Study in the Psychology of Decorative Art* (1979).

There are many paintings by artists as different as Hogarth and Botticelli, Gombrich pointed out, that show a page of a book or a letter covered with squiggles indicating print or writing; as long as we do not attend to them, they strike us as fully convincing. Saul Steinberg, Gombrich continued, is a past master of the art of perceptual generalization. "He likes producing spoof documents and signatures which look at first glance like real writing but turn out to be a mere sequence of loops and strokes so cunningly distributed that they capture the general appearance without containing any genuine letter form." Among the achievements in other arts that Gombrich singled out as analogous examples of deceptiveness is the café scene in *Modern Times*. "When Charlie Chaplin was forced to make the painful transition from silent films to the talkies, he looked at first for an idiom that would be acceptable to all audiences and composed a song of nonsense words which convincingly sounds like a real text in an unknown language."[49]

Actually, Charlie's blurred "text" does tell a comprehensible tale— with Chaplinian and Goddardian overtones, moreover—about sex and jewelry. A paunchy, mustachioed rake successfully seeks to cajole a voluptuous maiden into stepping into a taxicab ("Ce rakish spagoletto, si la tu, la tu, la tua!/Señora pelafima, voulez-vous le taximeter?") and then persuades her to submit to him by offering her the flashy ring on his finger. Between bursts of song, Charlie dances, and his backward foot slides, curvy hand movements, and amazingly twitchy buttocks considerably heighten the suggestiveness of his lyrics.

Having pulled off the fabulous trick of giving Charlie a voice at long last while still clinging to the principle of his speechless universality,

Chaplin was ready to end his hero's career with pantomime and word cards, just as he had begun it. The end begins with a shot of Charlie and the lovely gamin resting their weary feet on the side of a deserted California highway, after having eluded the asylum officers who had come to the café to nab her for vagrancy. Tired and upset, she breaks down and weeps. "What's the use of trying?" "Buck up," says Charlie. "We'll get along." "You betcha," she cries, her face brightening. "Let's go." Beneath their linked arms as they walk away is the paint stripe in the middle of the road. Dead ahead of them lies an elephantine clump of treeless California hills, looking slightly mysterious in the misty dawn light. For a time Charlie carries the kerchief containing his belongings in front of him, as he and his perky companion move farther and farther away. But finally, he slings it over his shoulder, in the immemorial manner of a tramp on the open road.

With its deliberate evocation of the signature finishes of *The Tramp* and *The Circus*, the valedictory salute of Chaplin to Charlie seemed to illustrate the contention of the comedian's young Marxist critics that he was hopelessly old-fashioned. But in fact it was their criticisms, enunciated between 1931 and 1934, that history had rendered out of date. With the creation of the Popular Front in 1935, the Kremlin had temporarily set aside its official aim of overthrowing capitalism. Communists in every country were instructed to demonstrate due regard for their respective national traditions and to cooperate with all men and women of good will, regardless of their party affiliation. The slavishly obedient CPUSA forthwith abandoned its political and cultural militancy. Where before it had called for celebrations of the working class, the party now sought, as Diana Trilling trenchantly observes in her memoir, *The Beginning of the Journey* (1993), "a more common denominator and found it in the figure of the 'little man,' a virtually classless representative of the democratic hope but also of the failed promises of capitalism." [50] Wherever Boris Shumiatsky caught up with *Modern Times* again, he was bound to have approved of its "little man" ending.

II

Chaplin's musical skills did not include the essential techniques that the scoring of *Modern Times* required. On the recommendation of the orchestrator of music at United Artists, Alfred Newman, he hired the gifted David Raksin as his arranger. On the day of Raksin's arrival at the Chaplin Studio in September 1935, his new boss was there to meet him. The comedian's appearance struck Raksin as "exotic," from his "abundant white hair to his anachronistic shoes with their high suede tops and mother-of-pearl buttons." As for Chaplin's reaction to Raksin, he could not get over how young he was. Newman's recommendation of him, which Newman's co-orchestrator, Eddie Powell, had enthusiastically seconded, had made no mention of the fact that he was only twenty-three. According to the playwright Bayard Veiller, who wrote *Within the Law* and *The Trial of Mary Dugan*, Chaplin introduced Raksin to him one day at lunch at the Brown Derby by saying, "They tell you, 'I've got just the man for you—brilliant, experienced, a composer, orchestrator and arranger, with several big shows in his arranging cap'—and this infant shows up!"*

Despite his misgivings about Raksin's age, Chaplin at once invited him to have a look at *Modern Times*. The picture was then in a first-final edit, which meant that further changes of major proportions were now unlikely. Raksin—whose politics were "Red . . . very red"—loved the picture, laughing his head off at scene after scene, most especially at the food-machine sequence. Before the screening ended, Chaplin had begun to wonder whether this hyperenthusiastic young man was sincere. When he fired him a week and a half later, it was not because of any suspicion of that nature, however, but because a serious difference of opinion had arisen between them about the nature of Raksin's responsibilities and authority. "Like many self-made autocrats," Raksin later observed,

> Chaplin demanded unquestioning obedience from his associates; years of instant deference to his point of view had persuaded him that it was the only one that mattered. And he seemed unable, or unwilling, to understand the paradox that his imposition of will over his studio had been achieved in a manner akin to that which he professed to deplore in *Modern Times* [in the capitalist head of the factory]. I, on the other hand, have never accepted the notion that it is my job merely to echo the ideas of those who employ me.

* A decade later, Raksin showed Hollywood just how adept he could be at enhancing a movie by writing the music for *Laura* (1944).

Chaplin was a magpie, Raksin added, with a veritable attic full of memories and scraps of ideas, and "in the area of music, the influence of the English music hall was very strong." In Raksin's view, *Modern Times* was a "remarkable film" that deserved to be enhanced by a fine score. In Chaplin's view, Raksin was guilty of insubordination and had to go.

As usual, Chaplin delegated the painful task of making the severance announcement to someone else, in this case to Eddie Powell. Powell's words "just about broke my heart," Raksin recalled. But by that time Alfred Newman had got wind of the firing. He told Alf Reeves that Chaplin would be crazy to let go of Raksin. The cannily diplomatic Reeves thereupon persuaded Chaplin to rehire him. And so began what Raksin would always think of as four and a half of the happiest months of his life.

Chaplin would show up at the studio in mid-morning, armed with a couple of musical phrases he had thought of for the sequence at hand. Raksin would duly write them down. Then they would run the footage over and over and discuss how the music might relate to it. Sometimes they decided to go with Chaplin's melody. On other occasions they would modify it, or one of them would invent a new melody. Some of the phrases they began with were extensive, while others consisted of only a handful of notes. Again and again, Chaplin would whistle the tune, or hum it, or pick it out on the piano as they developed and varied it in accordance with the action on the screen. The work was hard. "We spent hours, days, months in that projection room," Raksin recalled,

> running scenes and bits of action over and over, and we had a marvelous time—shaping the music until it was exactly the way we wanted it. . . . Sometimes in the course of our work when the need for a new piece of thematic material arose, Charlie might say, "A bit of 'Gershwin' might be nice there" . . . and indeed there is one phrase that makes a very clear genuflection toward one of the themes in *Rhapsody in Blue*. Another instance would be the tune that later became a pop song called "Smile." Here Charlie said something like, "What we need here is one of those 'Puccini' melodies."

Chaplin and Raksin achieved, in sum, a degree of collaboration that neither of them had believed possible at the outset.

And that ended, unfortunately, in a renewed estrangement. At one of the recording sessions, Alfred Newman and Chaplin had a fierce argument. Chaplin accused some of the members of the orchestra of "dogging it." Newman's hair-trigger temper exploded. After throwing down his baton and breaking it, he stalked off the stage, vowing he would never again work for Chaplin. Raksin was asked to take Newman's place on the podium but he refused, and he further angered Chaplin by letting it be known that in his view the comedian owed Newman and the orchestra an apology. Thanks to an emergency clause in Eddie Powell's contract, Alf Reeves succeeded in compelling him to pinch-hit for Newman, and Raksin obliged Powell by filling in the uncompleted orchestrations. At the end of the recording session, Powell and Raksin threw a party at the Vendome. Everyone was in high spirits. Nevertheless, the farewell between Chaplin and his young arranger was not amicable. Not for many years would they become friends again.[51]

12

Five days after the Hollywood premiere of *Modern Times* at Grauman's Chinese Theater on February 12, 1936, Chaplin took Paulette and her mother and his new majordomo, Frank Yonamori (Kono having resigned from Chaplin's employ, out of resentment of Paulette's usurpation of his household authority), on a trip to Hawaii on the Matson Line's *President Coolidge*. On reaching the islands, where Chaplin was startled to find George Bernard Shaw among the flower-shirted tourists, he and Paulette decided to extend their stay aboard the *Coolidge* as it continued on to ports of call on the farther side of the Pacific Rim. A wire-service bulletin not long thereafter informed the world that they had become man and wife in Singapore, and thirty years later the author of *My Autobiography* would affirm that they were indeed married in the Orient, although Singapore would not be identified as the location of the ceremony.

Yet when the alleged honeymooners returned to California in June, Goddard resumed her game with reporters.

"Are you and Mr. Chaplin married?"

"It's never been announced officially."

"But is it so?"

"It's been rumored so much! Sometimes the rumors have us married, sometimes they have us not married. Back and forth."

"Would you deny you are Mrs. Chaplin?"

"I never discuss my private life. I find that my private life is one thing and my career another."

Those who doubted that she was or would ever become Mrs. Chaplin found further significance in the fact that during the winter of 1936–37 she allowed the writer Charles Lederer to pursue her. In March, moreover, at the home of Edward G. Robinson and his wife, she used all of her wiles to charm George Gershwin when she found herself seated next to him at a celebrity-studded dinner in honor of Igor Stravinsky. (Perhaps it was on this occasion that she made him laugh by asking, "Why don't you compose music people will hiss to?") Gershwin's worshipful and self-mocking friend, the pianist Oscar Levant, soon became conscious that his idol had fallen "madly in love with Paulette," and Anita Loos remembered that the composer "came to life in her presence as nobody had ever seen him before." But having aroused him to the point where he was ready to forsake his whoremaster ways and marry her, Paulette broke off the affair in May, two months before Gershwin's shocking death from a brain tumor.[52]

Remarkably enough, Chaplin's involvement with Paulette had already lasted longer than his courtship of Edna Purviance or either of his two marriages. Many of the news photos of the two of them together testify to the good times they had had. Despite her spirit of independence, she had almost always submitted to his often tediously didactic tutorials. Furthermore, in obfuscating the issue of whether or not they were married, she may also have been obeying his wishes. When, however, she two-timed him with Gershwin, she aroused the sleeping dogs of his fixed idea that women were not to be trusted, and thereafter their quarrels became more drastic.*

* In Goddard's defense it should be noted that in 1935 Chaplin had been quite taken with the curvaceous blond comedienne Thelma Todd. A few months after a photographer snapped the two of them, arm in arm and clad in bathing suits, Todd was found dead in her car of carbon monoxide poisoning. The circumstances that led to her death have never been explained.

12

"WHEREVER YOU ARE, LOOK UP, HANNAH!"

As Adenoid Hynkel in The Great Dictator *(1940).*

For fifteen years if not longer, Chaplin had dreamed of making a movie about the little conqueror with whom he identified. Alf Reeves and other old hands at the studio could not have been too surprised, therefore, when he announced in the summer of 1934 that he had hired a young reporter from the *Manchester Guardian*, Alistair Cooke, to help him turn out a scenario on the life and loves of Napoleon. Two months later, he announced to Cooke's chagrin that he was no longer interested in the idea. This was the assertion, however, of a man with a highly volatile mind.

In July 1935, he spent every minute he could spare from the making of *Modern Times* in brainstorming sessions about the entirely new outline of a Napoleon movie that his English house guest of the moment, John Strachey, had agreed to write. A socialist politician and a prolific author as well, the thirty-four-year-old Strachey had captured international attention two years before with a bold work of social prophecy, *The Coming Struggle for Power* (1933). Upon returning to England in August, he strengthened the plot of his Napoleon story by incorporating into it the romantic thesis of a novel by a popular French writer, Jean-Paul Weber, that the emperor had escaped from exile a second time with the aid of a double. That Strachey felt free to borrow from Weber's book was because Chaplin had recently obtained the film rights to it. Doubles, of course, had a powerful appeal to Chaplin's divided nature.[1]

Yet while he was on the Oriental leg of his Pacific trip with Paulette, he put all thoughts of Napoleon on hold and knocked out a ten-thousand-word story about a down-on-her-luck Russian countess who stows away on an ocean liner and falls in love with an American millionaire. As a vehicle for Paulette and himself, the story had real possibilities, he felt. Or did it? Once again, doubts triumphed over initial certainty. But with the magpie instincts that David Raksin had noted, he shelved the manuscript of "Stowaway" instead of tearing it up. Thirty years later, it would serve as the basis for the second of the two cinematic fiascoes of his twilight years, *A Countess from Hong Kong* (1967), starring Marlon Brando and Sophia Loren.

On getting back to Los Angeles, on June 3, 1936, he commissioned a soldier-writer of his acquaintance, Major Ronald Bodley, to fashion a movie scenario out of a new David Leslie Murray novel, entitled *Regency: A Quadruple Portrait* (1936), in which a well-born and willful young woman in Regency England gets caught in an emotional cross fire between her feelings of loyalty to the Regent and her growing attraction to a politically radical, lower-class outlaw. The role of the young woman seemed to Chaplin to be just right for headstrong Paulette, and he saw himself in the role of the outlaw and possibly of the Regent as well. Bodley completed his work in the spring of 1937. But by that time, Chaplin no longer believed in the project.[2]

2

Paulette's frustration was intense. Although all of Chaplin's filmmaking plans included her, he was apparently incapable of making a firm commitment to any of them. *Modern Times* had launched her toward stardom, but Chaplin's indecisiveness and continuing dread about bowing to the sound revolution kept blocking her attainment of it. So at last she signed a contract with David O. Selznick—a Summit Drive neighbor—to appear in Selznick International's *The Young in Heart* (1938), opposite Douglas Fairbanks, Jr. While the picture seemed promising, that was not the point. Her aim in going to work for Selznick was to beguile him into casting her as Scarlett O'Hara in *Gone With the Wind*.

Thirty-five actresses were tested for the role, ranging from second-magnitude stars—Jean Arthur and Joan Bennett—to a nineteen-year-old boutique model from New York, Edythe Marrener, later known as Susan Hayward. The originally designated director of *GWTW*, George Cukor, personally supervised a good many of these tests. In February 1938, he reported to Selznick that

> Frances Dee reads absolutely thrillingly with great temperament and fire. She is a most accomplished and technically efficient actress. I have only one reservation about her for Scarlett . . .—has she the shallow eternal minx quality that Mrs. Chaplin [*sic*] realizes so brilliantly in private life?

The very idea of Paulette as an actress, let alone as a serious candidate to play Scarlett, was "a joke" in the incisive opinion of Selznick's wife, Irene, the beautiful and hardheaded daughter of hardfisted Louis B. Mayer. But Irene Selznick underestimated Paulette's drive. She was taking acting lessons from Chaplin's friend Constance Collier, and she kept pressuring her agent, Myron Selznick, to make the case for her with his brother. Cukor may have sarcastically characterized her personality, but in the same month in which he did so he screen-tested her three times for Scarlett, and every time she came across as funny and full of energy.[3]

On the chilly evening of December 10, 1938, Selznick paused in the midst of the burning of Atlanta to send a telegram to Irene in New York: "Sound the trumpets. The Big Wind started shooting at eight twenty tonight." Even though he still had not decided on his Scarlett, he had been forced to start shooting by fears of what would happen to his picture if he could not manage to stay within the time limit that MGM had placed on its loan-out of Clark Gable for the part of Rhett Butler. As the dying fires of the torched city were still glowing in the nighttime California sky, legend has it, Myron Selznick appeared out of the darkness and approached his brother arm in arm with Vivien Leigh, freshly arrived from Britain and wearing a hat and a fur coat against the cold. In presenting Leigh to David, Myron said, "David, I'd like you to meet Scarlett O'Hara." Or perhaps he put it more briefly: "I want you to meet Scarlett O'Hara." Or perhaps he exclaimed, "Hey, genius, here she is!" There is always the possibility, of course, that all three of these accounts were the figments of Hollywood imaginations and that the introduction was, in fact, made the next day under more humdrum circumstances.[4]

What is certain is that two days later Irene Selznick received another communication from her husband in which he made mention of Leigh. "Shhhh: she's the Scarlett dark horse and looks damned good. (Not for anybody's ears but your own: it's narrowed down to Paulette, Jean Arthur, Joan Bennett and Vivien Leigh.)" A last round of tests, involving all four finalists, began on December 17 and ended on the 22nd. Leigh was the last to be tested and Paulette the second last.[5]

It is hard to imagine Leigh losing this competition. Paulette's cause was not helped, however, by her failure to dispel Selznick's public relations qualms, in this period of Legion of Decency vigilance, about her private life. In an interview in his office one day, he asked her point-blank whether or not she was married to Chaplin. She assured him she was. Where had the ceremony been performed and by whom? he wanted to know. On Catalina Island by the mayor, she replied. According to the authors of the first Goddard biography, Catalina Island did not have a mayor. They also say that Selznick realized before the interview ended that Paulette would not be able to produce a marriage license.[6]*

---

* In fact, the island did have a mayor. Nevertheless, Selznick would have been correct in concluding that Goddard was lying, because the mayor could not perform marriages. Interview with Catalina Island city hall clerk, August 16, 1995.

3

Because of her ambition, she risked Chaplin's ire, and she received it. Charles Chaplin, Jr.'s recollection of the situation on Summit Drive in the winter of 1937–38 was that "the dissension between Dad and Paulette had become so strong by February that Dad left town one weekend [for Pebble Beach, California]" and stayed away for "five long months."[7]

He was accompanied by another new socialite friend, Tim Durant, a young, clean-cut easterner, recently divorced from E. F. Hutton's daughter. Chaplin made his acquaintance when someone brought him to one of the Sunday tennis parties on Summit Drive. Durant was an excellent player, and he and Chaplin began having regular matches. Tennis helped Durant get his mind off bad memories of his marriage.[8]

Chaplin found Pebble Beach to be wild, beautiful, and slightly sinister. He called it "the abode of stranded souls." While the so-called Gold Coast section facing the ocean was thick with millionaires, many of the houses in the wooded sections away from the water were unoccupied, and the numerous fallen trees around them were full of wood ticks and overrun by growths of poison ivy and deadly nightshade. The house Chaplin rented, half a mile from the ocean, was dank and miserable; furthermore, the fireplace simply would not draw.[9]

Through Durant and a New York society friend of his, Peggy Brokaw, who had married one of Harry Crocker's San Francisco relatives, Chaplin was introduced into the continuous party life of the community. Soon he was being seen with Geraldine Spreckels, and the sugar heiress was learning to cope with reporters' questions. "We've never discussed marriage," she told a covey of them. "A tea here, a luncheon there, a little time aboard a yacht . . . that's all I've seen of him recently. . . . Yes, I like Mr. Chaplin very much. I think it would be nice for anyone to be Mrs. Chaplin."[10]

4

Chaplin was frequently the guest of the millionaire D. L. James at his cliffside mansion in Carmel. It was here that he came to delight in long talks with his host's twenty-six-year-old son, Dan, a would-be writer and an ardent Communist whom he later would employ as an assistant director on *The Great Dictator.* Chaplin "was always fascinated with people of the left," the younger James would recall. "One of the people he wanted to meet was Harry Bridges of the Longshoremen's Union. I fixed up a meeting and they took to one another immediately."[11] A card-carrying Communist[12] whose steadfast denials of the affiliation thwarted the U.S. government's repeated efforts to deport him, Bridges had the swaggering manner of an outlaw, and it stirred up the outlaw in Chaplin.

When questioned by reporters about rumors of his own affiliation with the Communist Party, Chaplin invariably said that he was a human being, not a Communist, or an artist, not a Communist. Paul Crouch, on the other hand, a former district organizer of the Communist Party for North and South Carolina, a former member of the Trade Union Commission and the Agricultural Negro Commission of the Central Committee of the Communist Party, and a former consultant to a number of other Central Committee commissions, presented a different picture of Chaplin's allegiances in the mid-1930s in an interview many years later with the Immigration and Naturalization Service.

The interview took place on October 2, 1952. Crouch began by recalling a meeting of the Central Committee at Communist Party headquarters on East Thirteenth Street in New York in 1935. Among those present were Jack Johnstone, V. J. Jerome, Alexander Trachten-berg, and J. Peters. Johnstone was a veteran member of the Committee and had served as William Z. Foster's assistant in the 1919 steel strike. Jerome and Trachtenberg were cultural commissars, it might be said, and well known in both Hollywood and New York. J. Peters, a man of many aliases, was an underground spymaster.* There was a general discussion, Crouch continued, of the program of the Communist Party in connection with Hollywood. The aim of the program was to recruit stars, directors, and writers into the party "for the purpose of using the names of these well-known people in Communist front activities, . . .

---

* In an executive session of the House Committee on Un-American Activities (HUAC) on August 7, 1948, Congressman Richard M. Nixon asked Whittaker Chambers how he knew that Alger Hiss was a member of the Communist Party, and Chambers replied, "I was told that by Mr. Peters . . . [who] was head of the entire underground, as far as I know . . . [of] the Communist Party in the United States." Quoted in Allen Weinstein, *Perjury: The Hiss-Chambers Case* (New York, 1978), p. 19.

[of obtaining] financial contributions for the Party . . . and [of] attempting to influence the content of moving pictures." Crouch also asserted that there was talk about Chaplin's Communism.

Q To the best of your recollection what was said and by whom regarding CHARLES CHAPLIN?

A JACK JOHNSTONE said that CHAPLIN was a devoted and loyal member of the Party, but that to protect him and to protect the best interests of the Party, he should remain a member at large and not be affiliated with the Party units being set up in Hollywood.

Q Was anything else said about CHARLES CHAPLIN?

A He used the term temperamental but loyal in reference to CHAPLIN.

Q Who said that—JACK JOHNSTONE?

A JACK JOHNSTONE.

Q Did any of the other persons present at this meeting say anything about CHARLES CHAPLIN?

A JEROME expressed agreement with what JOHNSTONE had said and stated that he must remain a member at large.

Q Who was JEROME at that time and what position did he officially occupy in the Communist Party?

A V. J. JEROME was the head of the Cultural Commission of the Central Committee of the Communist Party and was a writer for the Party press and the Party's acknowledged authority on literary and cultural fields. . . .

Q Do you recall any reason or purpose for which JOHNSTONE would have mentioned CHARLES CHAPLIN as he did? Mr. CROUCH, let me repeat this question. Do you know of any reason or reasons why JACK JOHNSTONE would have mentioned or discussed CHARLES CHAPLIN as he did at this meeting?.

A Yes; CHAPLIN was one of the best known actors in the United States and the question of how he should be used by the Communist Party was a very important question to determine. It was particularly important in connection with the fact that a large apparatus was just being set up in Hollywood and the relationship of nationally prominent people like CHAPLIN to the local organization was a very important policy question.

Q Was any decision reached at that meeting with respect to CHARLES CHAPLIN?

A While a formal vote was not taken the unanimity of opinion especially the absence of any disagreement made it clear that so far as the
position of those present were [*sic*] concerned it was unanimous. A
matter of that kind ... obviously had to be decided by the highest
authority of the Party, the Politburo.

Crouch was then asked whether there was any other occasion during
the period of his membership and activity in the Communist Party when
he participated in an official discussion about Chaplin, and he said:

A The ... occasion was a long series of discussions with V. J. JEROME
at Chapel Hill, North Carolina, following a return by JEROME from
Hollywood. JEROME spent about one month in the district of which
I was the head and we had long and very detailed discussions regard-
ing Communist work in Hollywood and the personalities of some of
the leading Party members there.
Q To the best of your recollection when did these discussions with V. J.
JEROME at Chapel Hill, North Carolina, take place?
A During the spring of 1937....
Q What was the occasion of JEROME coming to see you at Chapel
Hill?
A JEROME came to Chapel Hill to spend what was partly a vacation
and partly a period of work in cultivating the acquaintance of writers,
intellectuals and others at the University of North Carolina, and in
aiding me and the Party leadership in formulating plans for activities
in the cultural fields....
Q Mr. CROUCH, to the best of your recollection what did Mr.
JEROME tell you with respect to CHARLES CHAPLIN?
A He stated that CHAPLIN remained a member at large directly responsible to the Central Committee and that he had no organiza-
tional connections with the local Party organization in Hollywood.
Q Now, just for the sake of the record I want you to explain very briefly
the meaning of JEROME's statement....
A It was a policy of the Party at that time to have people of more than
ordinary importance placed on the status of a member at large in
which they would pay their dues and financial contributions to the
Party to designated representatives of a higher committee, receive
assignments for Party work from such contacts and would not be

carried on the ordinary rolls and would not be subject to the local Party organization or have any contact with it.

Q Now, was there any other topic or discussion by JEROME with you which would have been the basis for his statements to you that CHAPLIN was remaining a member at large and was responsible only to the Central Committee?

A Yes, he referred to some desertions from the Party at [*sic*] Hollywood and referred in this connection to CHAPLIN's absolute loyalty and devotion to the Party and to the fact that he had not been influenced by others in Hollywood who had left the Party. . . .

Q What else did JEROME say?

A JEROME referred to the necessity of taking no chances in exposing CHAPLIN. . . . Reference was made by JEROME to the citizenship status of CHAPLIN and the fact that he would be liable to deportation if he should be identified with the Communist party. . . .

Q In the course of the conversations and discussion which you had with JEROME . . . did JEROME tell you or indicate to you that he had personally contacted or had discussions or conversations with CHAPLIN with respect to CHAPLIN's membership or activity in the Communist party?

A Yes; he referred to his conversations with CHAPLIN.

Q To the best of your recollection what did JEROME say to you?

A He spoke of CHAPLIN in reference to the conversations as showing . . . loyalty and complete devotion to the Communist movement. . . . He stated that CHAPLIN was pained by desertions from the Party of people he had believed to be loyal Communists, but that nothing could shake his own faith in Communism.[13]

The satanic whirlwind of show trials, mass murders, and unprecedentedly large-scale deportations to Siberian gulags that Stalin set in motion in the USSR in the mid-1930s cost the CPUSA the support of a number of prominent Americans. If Paul Crouch can be believed, Chaplin was not only a member of the party at the outset of this period, but remained unshakably loyal to it. But can Crouch be believed? His testimony, although detailed, was hearsay. Furthermore, despite energetic efforts by its Los Angeles bureau, the FBI never uncovered documentary proof of Chaplin's affiliation with the Communist Party. One possible explanation is that he was indeed a member at large who was "directly responsible to the Central Committee" and therefore "not

... carried on the ordinary rolls" and "not subject to the local Party organization." Yet it is no less possible that Crouch was lying, and it does not help his credibility that the preliminary searches conducted at my behest in archives in Moscow came up dry. The truth about Chaplin's politics has to be sought, it would seem, in the words and images of his films, in the speeches he gave in the 1940s, and in the influences exerted on him. The evidence of *Modern Times* suggests that in the mid-1930s, at least, he was adrift between political worlds.

5

From Germany, Sergei Eisenstein's friend and associate (and NKVD supervisor?) Ivor Montagu mailed Chaplin a volume of photographs of Jews put out by the Nazis, *Juden Sehen Dich An (Jews Are Looking at You)*. The collection included a photograph of Chaplin labeled "the little Jewish tumbler, as disgusting as he is boring." Montagu's purpose in sending the book was to kindle the comedian's interest in making an anti-Nazi movie. Further encouragement of this idea came from the Hungarian-born head of London Film Productions, Alexander Korda, whom Chaplin had seen something of in the 1920s when Korda was working in Hollywood; in fact, Korda made the specific suggestion that he imitate Hitler in a satirical comedy about mistaken identity.

The writer Konrad Bercovici not only offered a similar suggestion, but fleshed it out in a six-page "treatment" about a little fellow—a barber, perhaps, or a peddler, Bercovici proposed—who is taken for Hitler. In a number of other telling respects, the Bercovici synopsis anticipated the picture that Chaplin finally shot. He suggested that the little fellow might have been sick for a long time and and consequently did not know about the terrible developments that had been taking place in the world. He imagined a scene depicting Hitler's performance of a ballet dance with a globe, and still another in which he stripped Hermann Göring of his medals. For his pains, the writer received neither financial compensation nor an acknowledgment in the screen credits. In a rage, he hired Louis Nizer as his lawyer and filed a plagiarism suit against Chaplin for $5 million. But the suit made claims that went beyond the evidence, and in the end Bercovici took Nizer's advice and settled out of court for a payment from Chaplin of $90,000.[14]

The most compelling outside influence on the decision to film *The*

Great Dictator was the political climate of opinion in Hollywood. Ever since Hitler's accession to power, a steady stream of artistically talented anti-Nazi émigrés had been arriving in southern California. Fritz Lang was a representative figure. As a director at Nero Films in 1933, he had had the audacity to interpolate anti-Nazi sentiments into *The Testament of Dr. Mabuse (Das Testament des Dr. Mabuse)*. Hitler's propaganda minister, Josef Goebbels, banned the film and ordered Lang to report to his office. To Lang's astonishment, Goebbels offered to place him in charge of the entire German film industry. Lang asked for time to think about it—and fled the country that night.

Like many other anti-Nazi émigrés to America, Lang sought to lecture his new homeland about its own fascistic tendencies, even though the examples he thought of bore no connection, as Germany's and Italy's demonstrably did, to the explosive forces of nationalism. Thus in 1936 he set out to explore American racism in an antilynching film for MGM called *Fury*, until Louis Mayer, with Joe Breen's concurrence, insisted that the victim had to be a white man (Spencer Tracy). Even so, the supercharged emotionalism of the crowd images proved to be so powerful that the film received rave reviews, including one from Graham Greene that called it "great," a word of praise that Greene seldom used.[15]

"Film and politics," Erika Mann noted in her diary in 1938, were the main topics of conversation on which the émigrés relied in social get-togethers with established Hollywood figures that often took place at the Santa Monica home of the outspokenly pro-Soviet—and unashamedly bisexual—Salka Viertel, who had arrived from Europe in the late 1920s and quickly became one of movieland's leading script writers, working primarily on Garbo films.* As the film writer James K. McGuiness later stressed in testimony before a congressional investigating committee, the émigrés were "vocal, articulate people" who "brought home very forcibly to Hollywood the dangers of the Fascist and Nazi regimes." Out of this cross-pollination came the idea of a Hollywood Anti-Nazi League.[16]

The founding members of the League—Dorothy Parker, Donald Ogden Stewart, Fredric March, Fritz Lang, and Oscar Hammerstein

---

* In *My Autobiography*, Chaplin would fondly remember "interesting supper parties" at Salka's.

II—were Popular Front leftists of varying degrees of sympathy with the Communist Party. In compiling a masthead list of sponsors, however, they sought a more ecumenical lineup. If they picked John Howard Lawson and Sam Ornitz out of the large pool of Communist screenwriters who worked for the studios in the late 1930s and early 1940s,* they also persuaded the conservative mogul Carl Laemmle to sign on. Behind the window dressing of famous names, a lesser-known figure did the scut work of organization. Had it not been for the drive, astuteness, and suavity of Otto Katz, known also as Rudolf Breda, the League might never have gotten off the ground.

A member of the German Communist Party since 1922, the Czech-born Katz had moved to Moscow in the 1930s, where he worked for the Swiss-German Willi Munzenberg, the Communist International's slickest propagandist and promoter of Communist fronts. In 1933 Munzenberg sent Katz to the United States to raise funds for both open and clandestine antifascist activities. Munzenberg's widow, Babette Gross, has written of Katz that he was "quick, imaginative, entertaining, witty and loyal. . . . In Hollywood he charmed German émigré actors, directors, and writers. Katz had an extraordinary fascination for women, a quality which greatly helped him in organizing committees and campaigns." Lillian Hellman took him as a model for the resistance hero of her play *Watch on the Rhine* (1941). But Hellman would have no comment a decade later when Katz was executed in the purge of the Jewish leadership of the Czech Communist Party.[17]

It was at Katz's instigation that a white-tie dinner was held at the Victor Hugo restaurant in April 1936 to raise money for the relief of victims of Nazism. The huge success of the dinner constituted the turning point for the still-nebulous League. Two months later, its formation was officially announced at a theater on Wilshire Boulevard before an audience of five hundred invited guests. By the fall, the League had the funds to run full-page ads in Hollywood trade publications and to engineer a mass meeting at the Shrine auditorium that drew an audience of ten thousand. At its peak, the historians Larry Ceplair and Steven Englund have estimated, the League

---

* In the early 1940s, 25 to 30 percent of the most regularly employed members of the Screen Writers Guild were members of the CPUSA. Larry Ceplair and Steven Englund, *The Inquisition in Hollywood: Politics and the Film Community* (New York, 1980), p. 68.

probably enrolled between four and five thousand members, including
... many famous film personalities.... Screenwriters of every persuasion joined the League: liberals like Jo Swerling, Wells Root, Robert
Benchley, Julius and Philip Epstein ... [and] Philip Dunne; radicals like
Dudley Nichols; Communists like Robert Rossen, ... Ring Lardner, Jr.
[and] John Bright. Even ultra-conservatives like Herman Mankiewicz
and Rupert Hughes joined, albeit the latter spent a large part of his time
trying to persuade the members to change the name of the group to the
Hollywood Anti-Nazi and Anti-Communist League.[18]

League-sponsored meetings, banquets, parties, and demonstrations
became a way of life in Hollywood. The League raised money for the
Loyalists in Spain, published the newspaper *Hollywood Now*, and paid for
two weekly radio shows. The screenwriter Mary McCall complained in
a humorous piece in *Screen Guilds' Magazine* that "nobody goes to anybody's house any more to sit and have fun. . . . [We] listen to speeches,
and sign pledges, and feel that warming glow which comes from being
packed in close with a lot of people who agree with you—a mild hypnotism, an exhilarating, pleasurable hysteria."[19]

To a comedian who was experiencing grave difficulty in deciding on
the subject of his first sound-dialogue film, a community of think-alikes
sent an unmistakably clear signal. He should—he must—make a fool of
Hitler, and throw in a burlesque of Mussolini for good measure. Alf
Reeves and his other subordinates at last received the go-ahead from
him in the early fall of 1938, either just before or just after the meeting
in Munich at which the leaders of Britain and France caved in to Hitler's
territorial demand for Czechoslovakia's Sudetenland. Not until September 9, 1939, however, at a moment when the world was still reeling
from the realization that Hitler had invaded Poland and that Britain and
France had declared war on Germany, did the shooting of the picture
begin.

My Autobiography contains an account of the making of *The Great
Dictator*. Sandwiched in between a remembrance that the construction
of miniature models and props cost him $500,000 even "before I began
turning the camera" and a valedictory salute to Douglas Fairbanks,
whom he saw for the last time when his stout and aged-looking old
friend stopped by the set "near the completion of *The Dictator*," is a

paragraph that established a historical backdrop to a portion of the filming: "Then Hitler decided to invade Russia! This was proof that his inevitable dementia had set in. The United States had not yet entered the war, but there was a feeling of great relief both in England and America."[20]

The facts were otherwise. Sixteen days before the filming commenced, Joachim von Ribbentrop on behalf of Nazi Germany and V. M. Molotov on behalf of the Soviet Union signed a nonaggression pact, and when *The Great Dictator*'s double premiere took place at the Capitol and Astor Theaters in New York on October 15, 1940, the two nations were still at peace with each other. Chaplin's damage-repair efforts in *My Autobiography* included his political as well as his sexual reputation. He placed part of the filming of *The Great Dictator* within the time frame of the war between Germany and the Soviet Union as an implicit justification of the movie's glaring failure to poke fun at the pocket Caligula in the Kremlin, as Boris Pasternak called Stalin.

The signing of the Nazi-Soviet pact had a devastating effect on Popular Front unity. For years, non-Communists had shared the faith of their Communist brethren in the Kremlin's will to resist Hitler. Overnight, the world turned upside down. Communist parties everywhere became defenders of peace, on orders from Moscow, and when war came between Hitler and the West, party loyalists dutifully defined it as a struggle between bourgeois imperialisms. Fascism, said Molotov, was simply a matter of taste.[21]

In the ranks of the Hollywood Anti-Nazi League, the pleasurable hysteria of close harmony gave way to distrust, disagreements, and defections. Thus the actor Melvyn Douglas, a high-profile liberal activist, tried to bring the organization into line with his political outrage by making a motion at a meeting in January 1940 that called on the League to denounce "Soviet perfidy" as well as "Nazi aggression." All he got for his pains was further cause for outrage. Not only was his motion decisively defeated by Stalinist loyalists, but he became the target for volleys of personal insult from the floor. Shortly thereafter Douglas resigned, and two months later he publicly confessed his painful realization that "a number of our most vocal liberals and liberal organizations [here in California] seem to be directly or indirectly under the influence of the Stalin Internationale."[22]

Young Dan James, who had come down from Carmel to work on *The Great Dictator*, discovered that Chaplin was "horrified by the Soviet-German pact." Among the many Communists worldwide who had similar reactions was Kim Philby, then engaged in espionage activity for Soviet intelligence in Paris. The pact "shocked" Philby, and in the early months of the war, when British troops and French troops on one side and German troops on the other stood facing one another idly and the air was thick with jeering remarks about "the phony war," he put puzzled questions to his London "contact." "Why was this [pact] necessary?" "What will happen to the single-front struggle against fascism now?" But after several talks on the subject, the chief of the Soviets' London residency noted, the youthful Englishman "seemed to grasp the significance of the pact."[23]

Perhaps Dan James and another young Communist at the Chaplin Studio named Bob Meltzer played the same role in regard to Chaplin's attitude toward the pact that Philby's London "contact" had in his. James himself would suggest this in an interview in the 1980s, in which he recalled that he and Meltzer finally succeeded but only after some difficulty in persuading Chaplin not to make critical reference to Stalin in "the last speech in *The Great Dictator*."[24] If James had been more candid, he would also have acknowledged that, as delivered, the speech perfectly complemented the Communist line in the pact period. For Chaplin did not end his picture with a call to arms against Hitler, whose megalomania and vicious anti-Semitism he had just finished pillorying. Instead, he made a plea for universal "kindness and gentleness." Without these qualities, Chaplin warned the world from behind the mask of the Jewish barber, "life will be violent and all will be lost."

The speech was recorded in the Chaplin Studio on June 24, 1940, precisely one week after the fall of France. Now only Britain stood between Hitler and total victory in the west. Stalin and his supporters worldwide were caught between fear and denial of the prospect that the conqueror might turn his legions eastward. Is it any wonder that the Communist parties in the United States and other countries where *The Great Dictator* was exhibited found useful propaganda in its peace message?

The message also appealed to traditional American isolationists. The political clout that this constituency possessed was made evident by the disingenuous political tactics of Franklin D. Roosevelt in 1940. Roosevelt fully understood how imperative it was that the United States enter the war on Britain's side. But in order to bring this about, he first had to be reelected, which meant that he had to damp down isolationist suspicions of his intentions. Thus he saw to it that the Democratic Party at its nominating convention in Chicago in July included a peace plank in its platform: "We will not participate in foreign wars. We will not send our armed forces to fight in lands across the seas, except in case of attack." In a speech broadcast from the Boston Garden on October 29, he said: "And while I am talking to you mothers and fathers [of America], I give you one more assurance. I have said this before but I shall say it again and again and again: Your boys are not going to be sent into any foreign war." And in the course of extemporaneous remarks in Buffalo on November 2, he flatly stated, "Your President says this country is not going to war." [25]

Chaplin supported FDR's reelection. There were profound differences, however, between their endorsements of peace. Chaplin's reflected the antiwar stance of Hollywood Stalinists, whereas Roosevelt's represented calculated advances toward war, in a chess game in which the stakes were nothing less than the future of Western democracy.

6

Turning his tramp persona into a German Jewish barber and allowing his speaking voice to be heard were only the most notable of the new departures that Chaplin undertook in *The Great Dictator*. At a considerable cost, he hired a number of well-known actors from outside the Chaplin Studio, including Jack Oakie, Henry Daniell, Reginald Gardiner, and—for the fat-slob, Hermann Göring role of Herring—Billy Gilbert. In Karl Struss, who had worked with Cecil B. DeMille, he found a more sophisticated director of photography than Rollie Totheroh. By adding the clothing-business veteran, Ted Tetrick, to his staff, he boosted the quality of the wardrobe department. And the arranger, conductor, and composer Meredith Willson, who later wrote the book, the lyrics, and the music for *The Music Man* (1957), finally consented after much persuasion to work for him on the music. [26]*

---

* In a gesture of filial loyalty, Chaplin also hired his half-brother Wheeler Dryden as an assistant director.

Chaplin got along wonderfully well with Willson. Such was not the case, unfortunately, in all his new relationships on the set. Much to his disgust, Karl Struss kept trying for "mood" effects by including arty objects like tree branches in his shots, while the script girl, whose very existence seemed to annoy him, drove him to distraction with her demonstrations of his directorial inconsistency in regard to entrance and exit doors and other details that were not important, in Chaplin's old-fashioned view.[27]

With Paulette, whom he cast as the barber's Jewish girlfriend, Hannah (named, of course, in honor of Hannah Chaplin), there were difficulties right from the start. Rumor had it that in MGM's not-yet-released production of Clare Boothe Luce's hit play, *The Women* (1939), she had held her own against four formidable attention-grabbers—Joan Crawford, Norma Shearer, Joan Fontaine, and Rosalind Russell—and that studio executives at Paramount were very pleased with the rushes of her performance opposite Bob Hope in *The Cat and the Canary* (1939). On the strength of these impending successes, she brought her agent, Myron Selznick, to Chaplin's office one day. In his account of the interview in *My Autobiography*, Chaplin left the agent nameless, as though he were a stranger instead of a familiar tennis-court opponent. This "slick, well-tailored young man [in fact, Selznick was forty-four at the time], who looked poured into his clothes, . . . spoke rapidly with clipped enunciation." Paulette's current pay, Selznick needlessly reminded Chaplin, was $2,500 a week. "But what we haven't straightened out with you, Mr. Chaplin, is her billing, which should be featured seventy-five percent on all posters—" He got no further. "What the hell is this?" Chaplin shouted. "Don't tell me what billing she's to get! I have her interests at heart more than you have! Get out, the pair of you!"[28]

To the Heinrich Himmler-*cum*-Josef Goebbels role of Garbitsch, the great dictator's minister of the interior and propaganda adviser, Henry Daniell brought the resources of a highly trained stage actor. His icy way of speaking, however, and his meticulous manners made it impossible for Chaplin to integrate him into any of the picture's comic sequences. In Dan James's opinion, Chaplin "developed a hatred for Daniell," of which Daniell was aware. If such was the case, it must have been very painful for him to observe Chaplin's easy relationship with Billy Gilbert and Reginald Gardiner, and above all with Jack Oakie.[29]

Chaplin had gone after Oakie because there was no one in Hollywood whose appearance and personality were better suited for the blustering, jut-jawed, cock-strutting role of the great dictator's rivalrous ally, Benzino Napaloni, the ruler of Bacteria (capital city: Aroma). Along with his peerless mastery of the double take, Oakie's comic trademark was the electric-lightbulb shine on his beefy face, for he never powdered it. If Chaplin were to order him to do so, he privately vowed, he would refuse to comply, no matter how serious a quarrel might ensue. To his surprise, Chaplin proved to be a most deferential boss, on this and all other issues that might have divided them. "I want you to do everything your own way, just as you always do," Chaplin told him.[30]

Oakie's on-the-set impression of Chaplin was of an actor-director who knew very little about the mechanics of sound pictures, but did not want any instruction from experts. Off the set, Oakie noted, he wanted to talk about the past in words that went something like this: "You know, Muscles [Chaplin's nickname for Oakie], I miss the click, click, click of those good, old-fashioned, hand-cranked cameras. I could hear the beat of the camera and time every one of my movements to its rhythm." He was also given to bragging about his comic achievements, which was all right with Oakie, for in his hero-worshipping opinion Chaplin had invented "every worthwhile trick in comedy." To Oakie as he had to others, Chaplin emphasized that his first achievement had been to slow the tempo of Mack Sennett's comedies and to individualize their indiscriminate violence. "First I'd find the target, like the villain's head," Chaplin would remind Oakie, "then I'd take off his hat and, picking a good spot, I'd aim before hitting it with my club. . . . Then I'd turn the head a little and hit it again, then turn it again to an even better spot and hit it again." Such conversations heightened Oakie's awareness of how carefully calculated Chaplin's performances had always been. As the "master mathematician of comedy," he had known how to draw two, three, or four laughs out of moments in which other comedians would have been satisfied with extracting one.[31]

7

The first reports that Chaplin was planning to play Hitler reached the German government in the fall of 1938. Upon receiving instructions from Berlin, Dr. Georg Gyssling, the German consul in Los Angeles,

wrote a letter to Joe Breen, warning of "serious troubles and complica-
tions if the reports were true."[32] The British for their part did not relish
the prospect of being offered a Hitler movie at a time when the peace
of the world was hanging in the balance. On March 2, 1939—some
six months after Neville Chamberlain's shameful trip to Munich—the
secretary of the British Board of Film Censors, J. Brooke Wilkinson,
sent a cable to Breen in which he spoke of "the delicate situation that
might arise in this country if personal attacks were made on any living
European statesman. You are aware of our stringent rule that the representation of any living personage without their written consent is disal-
lowed on the [British] screen."[33]

Breen was unmoved by these communications. When he and his staff
reviewed Chaplin's picture for the PCA a month before its scheduled
release, his only objection was that the word "lousy" had been used. As
he wrote to Alf Reeves, he was "considerably embarrassed" at having to
request the removal of the word, but the fact was that "lousy" was
specifically blacklisted in one of the Code's resolutions. With that detail
out of the way, he went on to tell Reeves "how very, very much we
enjoyed THE GREAT DICTATOR. It is superb screen entertainment
and marks Mr. Chaplin, I think, as our greatest artist."[34]

The general public, if not the critics, heartily agreed. In New York,
the Astor and the Capitol theaters were packed on opening night and
continued to be for fifteen weeks; nationwide, the picture also proved
to have impressive pulling power. In 1942, Bosley Crowther of the *New
York Times* compiled a list of the ten biggest moneymakers of recent
years; *Gone With the Wind* ranked number one and *The Great Dictator*
number three. When augmented by the belated receipts from those
countries in Europe and Asia—notably the Axis powers, Germany, Italy,
and Japan—in which it was not shown until after World War II, its
earnings exceeded $5 million, a new record for a Chaplin picture.[35]

Except for the prologue's rather dreary run-through of the Jewish
barber's misadventures as a German private at the front in World War I
and his subsequent hospitalization, the entire story is framed within two
speeches, both of them staged outdoors before huge crowds. In the first
of them, the speaker is the sweet-tempered barber's savage look-alike,
the dictator of Tomainia, Adenoid Hynkel. With his military boots and
breeches, his hate-filled face, and his penchant for humiliating subordi-

nates, he is the circus master redivivus—a circus master who would rule
the world. At a Nuremberg-style rally, he addresses the faithful of his
Double Cross party, the swastikalike emblem of which Hynkel wears as
an armband on his military shirt. His harangue is a tour de force of
mock-Hitlerian rant that sounds like German but mainly consists of
such bastardized phrases as "free sprachen stunk." As clever as some
of this rhetoric is, it is the accompanying pantomime that is the humor's
main engine. From the voluptuous gestures with which Hynkel celebrates the lactiferousness of Aryan mothers, to the demonic flarings of
his nostrils and the wild-eyed looks that convulse his visage as he speaks
of "the Juden," to his spastic fits of coughing and pauses for refreshment
from a glass of water (some of which he pours down the inside of his
waistband, as if to cool his testicles), Chaplin's facial and body language
is unfailingly brilliant.

No sooner has Hynkel finished speaking than he launches into a
second tirade—against Field Marshal Herring, for the accidental crime
of knocking him down a flight of stairs. In a picture in which the
Jewish barber is the gentlest character that Chaplin had ever played, he
funneled his brutal comic impulses through the character he despised.
Instead of forgiving Herring for his error, Hynkel strips medal after
medal off his paunchy front, as the somewhat womanish field marshal
struggles to hold back tears.

At bottom, all of the memorable scenes in *The Great Dictator* are built
on pantomime. Instead of taking full advantage of Oakie's delightful
ability to reduce Mussolini's bombast to a parody version of Italian-
immigrant English ("You gotama carpet," Naploni cries at the train
station, when there is a foul-up in laying a red carpet in front of the
door of his railroad car. "Well putama down!"), Chaplin kept involving
him in silent-film-style enactments, such as the hilarious competition in
the barbershop in Hynkel's palatial residence in which each of the dictators tries to jack up his chair to a higher position than the other.

In a deadly drama acted out in pantomime in the ghetto, several
peace-loving Jews, including the barber, reluctantly agree to choose one
of their number by lot for the dangerous task of blowing up Hynkel's
palace. Each man is given a small cake, but only one of the cakes,
presumably, has had a coin baked into it. By eating the cakes the men
will discover which one of them is to be the bomb thrower. The ginger-

liness with which the barber bites into his, the look of consternation on his face upon realizing that he has a coin in his mouth, and the relief he feels after hiding the coin in the cake of his unsuspecting neighbor at the table make for a wry dramatization of human nature—and the longer it lasts the wryer it gets. For every man in the room has a coin in his cake, and, with the exception of their dignified leader (played by the veteran Jewish actor Maurice Moscovich), every one of them proves to be as anxious as the barber to avoid the hero's role.

The most celebrated pantomime in the picture, and justly so, is Hynkel's performance in front of the Double Cross wall banner in his office of the "Emperor of the World" ballet. At the outset, the dictator is clinging to the twenty-foot-high window drape that he has shinnied up in half-enthralled, half-fearful reaction to Garbitsch's prophecy that once the citizenry of Tomainia has been purified into a blue-eyed, blond-haired Aryan super race, a mastery of the world will be within his grasp. With a faraway look on his face, he slides down the drape and dismisses Garbitsch from his presence. "I want to be alone," he says. To the strains of the Prelude to Wagner's *Lohengrin*, he approaches the globe beside his desk. Arms akimbo and eyes glittering, he contemplates it. "Emperor of the World," he murmurs. He lifts the globe; it becomes a balloon. Again and again he sends it soaring above him with high-booted kicks and thrusts of his head and buttocks. Pulling the balloon back to him, he balances it in perilous equilibrium on the tip of his finger and revolves it. As he holds the spinning world directly in front of the sick-wolf smile on his face, it becomes a metaphor of his tenuous psychological stability. An overly ecstatic embrace of the bubble finally bursts it. Hynkel breaks into tears and collapses across his desk. A dancer's physical grace; deliberate, almost slow-motion pacing; an ominously decorated office; Wagnerian music; and a madman's fantasy of global conquest: through this dreamlike combination of elements, Chaplin created an awed hush in movie theaters in the United States, Britain, and elsewhere in the year in which Hitler became the overlord of Europe from Norway to the Pyrenees.

The *New York Herald-Tribune*'s reviewer declared that *"The Great Dictator* is aflame with Chaplin's genius but the flame flickers badly." Among the picture's worst mistakes are the storm troopers who terrorize the ghetto. Thanks to sound-film technology, their wise-guy American accents and their adherence to the cadences if not the words of U.S. Army marching songs ("The Aryans, the Aryans, the airy, airy Aryans, as we go marching by") destroy the illusion that they are Germans, while their overweight, out-of-shape physiques make them seem more like Keystone Kops than Nazi bullyboys. And then there is the saucy Jewish girl, Hannah, who taunts the troopers as gutless and knocks two of them silly by smacking their noodles with a frying pan. It is sickeningly easy to imagine what such acts would have cost her in real life; therefore, to see her getting away with her defiance does not exhilarate or amuse us, as Chaplin intended it would. To the contrary, we are nauseated, as the émigré sociologist Theodor Adorno was, by the idiocy of making anti-Semitic persecution an occasion for slapstick jokes.[36]*

The barber's visionary speech—in Hynkel's guise—at the end of the picture is flapdoodle, above all because Chaplin failed to recognize the fundamental distinction between the moral and social behavior of individuals and "the brutal character of the behavior of all human collectives, and the power of self-interest and collective egoism in all intergroup relations," to borrow the hardheaded words of Reinhold Niebuhr in *Moral Man and Immoral Society* (1932).[37] "I'm sorry," the barber tells the crowd in front of him and his radio audience of millions,

> but I don't want to be an emperor, that's not my business. I don't want to rule or conquer anyone. I should like to help everyone—if possible—Jew, Gentile, black man, white. We all want to help one another—human beings are like that. We want to live by each other's happiness, not by each other's misery. We don't want to hate and despise one another. In this world there is room for everyone. . . . The inventions of

---

* Another émigré, Thomas Mann, who had come to know Chaplin fairly well, was of two minds about the picture. To Agnes Meyer on November 26, 1940, he reported, "We have seen Chaplin's somewhat weak, but in parts still very funny, travesty on dictators." In person, however, Chaplin completely enchanted him. See his letter to Fritz Strich from Pacific Palisades on November 27, 1945: "Day before yesterday we spent an evening at the home of [Hanns] Eisler, the composer, with Chaplin. For three hours I laughed till the tears came at his imitations, scenes, and clowning, and was still rubbing my eyes as we were getting into our car. Nobody so enlivens society as the gifted actor. They always want to perform, and so one is safe." Thomas Mann, *Letters of Thomas Mann, 1889–1955*, tr. by Richard and Clara Winston (Berkeley and Los Angeles, 1975), pp. 274, 358.

the airplane and the radio have brought us closer together. The very nature of these inventions cries out for the goodness in men, for universal brotherhood, for the unity of us all.

One of the concomitant purposes of Chaplin's rhetoric was to link the material values of capitalism with the military values of fascism, as in the barber's assertion that "greed . . . has goose-stepped us into misery and bloodshed." His left-wing utopianism is also evident in the little fellow's celebration of "the people" and his exhortation of them to "fight for a new world . . . a world of reason . . . a world of science . . . where progress will lead to the happiness of us all." Trying to pin down meanings in such swollen lines, however, is finally a fool's game.

As the barber moves into his peroration, the camera picks up Hannah lying on the ground outside a farmhouse. A storm trooper has roughed her up and she has been sobbing. In wonderment at the extraordinary message coming over the radio, she slowly raises her head and listens more intently. Not until the radio voice whispers "Hannah, can you hear me?" does she finally recognize it. The voice continues, but the camera remains focused on her transfixed, tear-stained face. The close-up exalts her into a symbol of all humanity. "Wherever you are, look up, Hannah!" the voice cries.

> The clouds are lifting—the sun is breaking through, we are coming out of the darkness into a new world—where men will rise above their hate, their greed, and their brutality. Look up, Hannah! The soul of man has been given wings and at last he is beginning to fly. He is flying into the rainbow—into the light of hope—into the future, into the glorious future that belongs to you—to me—and to all of us.—Look up, Hannah, look up!

At the close of *The Great Dictator,* Chaplin fused a dreamy politics with sentimental thoughts about his mother into a single ecstatic spasm.

In England, the Communist Party duly put out the entire speech as a special pamphlet.[38]

8

Although Paulette Goddard smiled for the news cameras as she stood at Chaplin's side at the New York openings of their second—and last—

film together, she had not traveled from the coast with him. In fact, her trip had originated in Mexico City, where she had been the guest for the second time in six months of Diego Rivera. On the first occasion, the great muralist and ardent Trotskyite had painted a couple of portraits of her, had welcomed her into his bed—which was all right with his wife, Frida Kahlo, who had been having an affair with Trotsky—and had provided her with a refuge from vulturine reporters eager to quiz her about the scandalous stories concerning the evening she had recently spent at Ciro's in the company of the Russian-born director Anatole Litvak, familiarly known as Tola.

The Romanian-born director Jean Negulesco and a cigarette model, Alice Eyland—"Miss Chesterfield"—were at the next table that night. In his memoir, *Things I Did and Things I Think I Did* (1984), Negulesco left an account of what he thinks happened.

> Returning to the table from the dance floor, Paulette dropped one of her earrings under the table. Tola—quite drunk by now (as was Paulette), but still the perfect gentleman—disappeared under the table to find it. But how long does it take to look for an earring? The silly joke grew to be phony acting. Tola's disappearance under the table lasted beyond the time limit of a prank. Paulette began to moan convincingly. Friends, waiters and photographers became voyeurs. They laughed and whistled encouragement to Tola. They felt they were witnessing a free and bold Hollywood scandal. When finally, fifteen minutes later, Tola appeared from under the table to the applause of the amused audience, he straightened his hair with just the right amount of embarrassment.[39]

According to another version of the incident, Paulette and Litvak both disappeared from view. But in the most widely believed version of all, it was Paulette who slipped under the table, while Litvak remained seated. Years later, the scandal was recycled in an intimacy between Warren Beatty and Julie Christie in an unrelievedly tawdry satire of modern-day movieland called *Shampoo* (1975).

Back in Hollywood following obligatory appearances at *The Great Dictator* openings, Paulette stayed on alone at Summit Drive—Chaplin having elected to remain in the East—until December, when Myron Selznick lent her his beach house in Santa Monica. A year and a half later in Juarez, Mexico, she and Chaplin were granted a divorce. The overwhelming likelihood is that they had never been married, and that the divorce proceeding was undertaken at Goddard's insistence in order to provide her with a career-protecting cloak of moral respectability. As for the settlement she received, it included Chaplin's yacht and—the rumors varied—between $300,000 and $1 million.[40]

9

Because of the peace speech in *The Great Dictator*, the isolationist Daughters of the American Revolution invited Chaplin to address them during the presidential inaugural festivities in Washington in January 1941. On the morning of the 19th, he left New York, where he had been disporting himself ever since the opening of his picture. In the late afternoon, he met privately with the President in the White House. At first, the conversation was serious. "Sit down, Charlie," Roosevelt said. "[*The Great Dictator*] is giving us a lot of trouble in the Argentine." Because of the sizable German-immigrant population there, the picture had aroused resentment that, in turn, had stirred up historic resentments of the United States. Mercifully, Roosevelt did not pursue the matter for long. Instead, he offered Chaplin light talk and a succession of warm martinis, which Chaplin, a modest drinker, did not refuse. When it became time for him to leave the White House, he had difficulty in walking without stumbling.

That evening he was scheduled to appear, along with Nelson Eddy, Raymond Massey, Ethel Barrymore, and several other notables from the entertainment world, before a capacity crowd of D.A.R. members and their guests in Constitution Hall and in front of microphones connected to a nationwide radio hookup. Chaplin intended to read the peace speech. In the free time remaining to him before the performance, he returned to his hotel, took several cold showers, drank quantities of black coffee, and more or less pulled himself together. But as he began speaking in the hall, he was very nervous, as he always was in public appearances. His mouth became dry. His tongue stuck to the roof of his mouth. Finally, he could not speak any longer. An usher went off to get him a drink of water. As the audience in front of him—and sixty million listeners across the country—waited, the usher took two interminable minutes to return to the stage with a brimming paper cup. At last, he was able to complete the speech, and the audience gave him a prolonged ovation. Charles Chaplin, Jr., would later remark that "my father's appearance at [that] gathering, the heartfelt applause at his earnest words, might be called the pinnacle of his public success in this country. From then on the path led downward by subtle degrees until it ended in self-imposed exile."[41]

10

During 1941 Chaplin spent more time in the company of his two teenage sons than he ever had before. "Sometimes," he told them one day in a burst of emotion, "I think you two . . . are the only ones in the whole world who have ever really loved me." Charles Jr. interpreted this remark as a revelation of "inward loneliness and dependence on us."[42]

At the same time, he seemed to resent the fact that these "Mexican" sons of his had been raised in far more comfortable circumstances than he had. On Christmas mornings, as they were opening their presents, he would invariably remind them that at Christmastime in his London childhood he had never received anything more than an orange. He also set quite arbitrary limits on their freedom of choice. Their boyhood friend Lionel Krisel would remember that he was "even more of a disciplinarian than the masters at the military school that the boys attended." Behind his back, the boys found ways to flout his authority. Thus they set up a drink stand at the end of the driveway and, at rock-bottom prices, sold the crates of expensive beer they had found in the basement to passing motorists, including their neighbor, David O. Selznick. In the producer's house one afternoon, Chaplin commented appreciatively on the quality of the beer he was offered. Selznick took pleasure in telling him where he had bought it and for how much.

When Sydney, at fifteen, wanted to take up golf, Chaplin declared that it was an old man's game and vetoed the idea. To sweeten the pill, he offered his son one hundred dollars if he could beat him in tennis. Observing that his father liked to hit ground strokes from the base line, Sydney worked on other aspects of his own game and eventually overcame his old man with drop shots and lobs. Chaplin refused to hand over the hundred dollars. Instead, he gave the money to Bill Tilden for a tennis lesson for Sydney.

As he did with other people, Chaplin blew hot and cold with his sons. Often he was supportive when things were going well for them, but when they were not, he was apt to turn against them. As the years passed and it became apparent that Sydney was a talented actor who was headed for a significant career, whereas young Charlie was floundering, he treated his namesake cruelly, inviting Sydney to attend parties and leaving Charlie out. Charlie was deeply wounded by these exclusions, Sydney knew, but there was nothing he could do to ease his brother's pain. During army service in World War II, Charlie picked up the drinking problem that would contribute to the failure of his two marriages. By the late 1960s he may have wanted to die. Be that as it may, the thrombosis that killed him at age forty-three resulted from his neglect of an injury received in a fall.[43]

The first of Chaplin's romantic conquests in 1941 was twenty-two-year-old Carole Landis, a favorite afternoon partner of her lascivious boss at Twentieth-Century Fox, Darryl F. Zanuck. Landis prided herself on the fabulous figure that had inspired a Hollywood publicist to label her "the Ping Girl." Yet there was an out-of-kilter intensity in her emotional makeup that could also have been one of the reasons the son of Hannah Chaplin was drawn to her. During her much-discussed love affair with Rex Harrison half a decade later, Landis became, in the words of the producer Ross Hunter, "absolutely insane over him." When Harrison finally told her he was leaving Hollywood for New York—where his estranged wife, Lilli Palmer, was living and where he had been offered the part of Henry the Eighth in Maxwell Anderson's new play, *Anne of the Thousand Days*—the Ping Girl committed suicide.[44]

Chaplin also dated Hedy Lamarr in early 1941. In repose, her Madonna-like face could capture the heart of any man in the world, the comedian remarked to his son Charlie, but its serene quality, he insisted, was marred whenever she smiled. The amount of time his father spent in thinking about young women amazed young Charlie. Still, the boy was convinced that tennis occupied "the most important place in my father's life after Paulette left." His white-haired head was visible in the stands at every match at the tennis club to which he belonged. World-famous players—Helen Wills, Pauline Betz, Don Budge, and Fred Perry among them—were his frequent guests on Summit Drive. Whether or not they could keep up with him on the court, his open-house tennis parties also attracted such movieland luminaries as Katha-rine Hepburn, Ronald Colman, Gary Cooper, John Garfield, Greta Garbo, David Niven, and John McCormack, as well as bevies of un-known beauties who came as the friends of friends.[45]

At the conclusion of a match between Chaplin and his young socialite friend Tim Durant on a Sunday afternoon in May 1941, Durant told Chaplin that he was planning to have dinner with two young women that evening at Perino's restaurant. One of the women, Joan Barry, who had just returned from Mexico City, had expressed a desire to be introduced to Chaplin. Why don't you join us? Durant asked. Chaplin said he would be delighted to do so. In addition to being "pleasant and cheerful enough," Barry turned out to be "a big handsome young woman of twenty-two, well-built, with upper regional domes immensely expansive." Nevertheless, Chaplin claimed in *My Autobiography*, at the end of an "innocuous" evening together "I never thought of seeing her again." Had he stuck to that resolve, he would have saved himself a lot of trouble. Barry, like Carole Landis, had a history of easy availability to men, but in her case it was an even clearer indication of psychological disequilibrium. According to FBI documentation, her father, Jim Grib-ble, a World War I victim of shell shock, committed suicide shortly before her birth, in Detroit, on May 24, 1919. The widowed mother of Mary Louise, as the baby was named, then married a man named Berry and moved to New York. Among the names that the voluptuous Mary Louise assumed in quick succession upon arriving in Los Angeles in 1938 in quest of a movie career were Mary Louise Barry, Mary L. Barratt, Joan Barratt, Joanne Berry, Joan Berry, and, finally, Joan Barry.[46]

During her first year in Los Angeles, the FBI summary continues, she was twice apprehended for shoplifting, and for the second of these offenses she received a suspended ninety-day jail sentence and a year's probation. Only by taking up with a local businessman was she able to remain in town. He established her in an apartment-hotel and main-tained her there for the better part of two years. During this period her mother also settled in Los Angeles.[47]

In 1940, while working as a waitress, Barry met one of the world's richest men, J. Paul Getty. Although the oilman had recently married for the fifth time and was involved as well with the full-bodied German actress Hilde Kruger, whom the FBI had been tailing ever since her arrival in the United States in 1939 (for the simple reason that in Germany she had been seen at parties attended by Hitler and Goebbels), he still had a penchant for picking up waitresses. At the end, as he believed, of his interlude with Barry, Getty moved on to business appointments in Mexico City—where a cable from Barry caught up with him. "Need $200. Would you please send it to me." A few days later, she surprised him in the same way that she would surprise Chaplin—by unexpectedly showing up. She professed "admiration and affection for me," Getty later told FBI interviewers. He began paying her $150 a month, he explained, in an inadvertent *double entendre*, because he was "impressed at the enthusiasm and energy she put into her work." By which he meant, he hastened to add, that she was "a girl who was on the threshold of having a movie career." [48]

To help her gain entrée into Hollywood circles, Getty passed her on to the movie-industry financier A. C. Blumenthal. Blumenthal vividly remembered the sex orgy in his New York penthouse in 1925, during which Chaplin and Louise Brooks had gone at it day and night. It made sense, Blumenthal decided, to send Barry to Chaplin, via a letter of introduction from him to Tim Durant. [49]

My Autobiography would once again present its author as the weak-willed victim of a brazen hussy. On the Sunday following the dinner at Perino's, Tim Durant brought Barry to Summit Drive for tennis. That evening, she and Durant dined with him, at his invitation, at Romanoff's. The very next morning, she phoned him and asked if he would take her to lunch. He told her that he was attending an auction in Santa Barbara and that she could come along if she wished, which she did. On the way home, she told him that she had quarreled with Paul Getty and was planning to return to New York the following night, but that if he, Charlie, wanted her to stay in Los Angeles, she would. In response to this astonishingly sudden proposition, "I reared away in suspicion. . . . I told her quite frankly not to remain on my account, and with that I dropped her off outside her apartment and bade her goodbye." But to his further astonishment, she phoned him a day or so later to say that she was staying on and asked if he would see her that evening. "Persistence is the road to accomplishment," he would write in *My Autobiography*, by way of a preface to the laconic admission that he then began to see Barry often. [50]

At lunch one day with Sinclair Lewis and Sir Cedric Hardwicke, he took the opportunity to quiz them about the Irish playwright Paul Vincent Carroll's international hit, *Shadow and Substance* (1937). Hardwicke had played the leading role of Canon Thomas Skerritt in the Broadway production. Lewis had played it, too, in summer stock in 1940, opposite his newest mistress, Marcella Powers, as the canon's simple servant girl, Brigid, who believes herself to be in touch with Saint Brigid. When Chaplin displayed a keen interest in the play, Hardwicke offered to send him a copy.[51]

At Summit Drive a few nights later, he mentioned *Shadow and Substance* to Joan Barry. She told him she had seen it and wanted to play the girl. In *My Autobiography*, the claim is made that she then read the part with breathtaking effectiveness. Even her Irish accent was good. Whereupon Chaplin put her under contract at $250 a week and sent her to Max Reinhardt's acting school. Inasmuch as she was busy at the school, and since he himself became absorbed—after acquiring the film rights to the Carroll play for $20,000—in writing the film script, he "seldom saw her."

> Then strange and eerie things began to happen. Barry began driving up [to Summit Drive] in her Cadillac [a gift from Paul Getty] at all hours of the night, very drunk, and I would have to awaken my chauffeur to drive her home. One time she smashed up her car in the driveway and had to leave it there. . . . Finally she got so obstreperous that when she called in the small hours I would neither answer the phone nor open the door to her. Then she began smashing in the windows. Overnight, my existence became a nightmare.[52]

For a payoff of $5,000, she finally consented to a termination of her contract with the Chaplin Studio. The formal severance was signed on May 22, 1942. Exactly a year had elapsed since the dinner at Perino's.

A brazenness born of—or at least amplified by—craziness was surely one of the prime characteristics of Joan Barry's personality. No less true, however, is the fact that Chaplin never acknowledged either the methodical exploitativeness that marked his treatment of her. As for the "eerie" conduct of a woman scorned that he evoked so vividly in *My Autobiography*, it did not occur until the final days of 1942 and the early months of 1943. For an appreciation of the events of the first year of the Chaplin-Barry drama that Chaplin had no wish to remember, it is necessary to turn to the detailed recital that Barry poured out to an FBI interviewer in January 1944. The story she told was no less self-serving than Chaplin's. By and large, however, it compels belief, if only because so much of it meshed with the patterns of earlier episodes in Chaplin's life.

II

On the phone, Tim Durant asked Barry, upon her return from Mexico City, whether she would like to meet Chaplin or Spencer Tracy. She picked Tracy. Whereupon Durant invited her to a party on Errol Flynn's yacht. In a later phone talk with Durant, however, she said she would like to meet Chaplin, and Durant agreed to set up a dinner engagement.

Chaplin's limousine pulled up in front of her apartment. Durant came up to the door to get her. The fifty-two-year-old comedian was standing beside the car as she walked out. The Japanese chauffeur drove them to Perino's. After dinner, Durant left with the date he had brought. Barry and Chaplin remained talking until closing time. She complained that it was almost impossible for a girl to break into the movies without some type of connection or influence. Chaplin replied, "I could tell that you have a great deal of talent just by speaking with you." She was "fresh and alive," he told her. He would like to place her under contract, he avowed. As the FBI interviewer summed up her reaction, "she could scarcely believe this offer and thought that he would promptly forget it, but later in the evening CHAPLIN gave her his phone number and asked her to contact him." At some point in the evening, curiosity prompted her to ask him "how many times he had been married and he said, 'Twice.' I said, 'What about PAULETTE GODDARD?' He said, 'Well, I mean three times.'" Later in their acquaintance, however, "he admitted that he and GODDARD had never been married." [53]

In the weeks following their talk in the restaurant, they saw one another a number of times. Then Chaplin invited her to attend an auction in Santa Barbara. He spent most of the trip "pawing and mauling me," but "I resisted him at all times." Not long after their return, she signed a contract with the Chaplin Studio—for seventy-five dollars a week—"and it was not until after the signing" that "I had sexual relations with [him]."

This took place in CHAPLIN's house. I might add here that CHAPLIN's success in this regard was due to his verbal persuasiveness. I have been told, and from my personal experience with him I know it to be true, that he is very proud of his success with women along these lines. This verbal persuasivesness of CHAPLIN's was his violent insistence that he was madly in love with me. He began calling me his favorite name for his lady loves, "Hunchy."

A high point of their romance was a weeklong yacht trip in the waters around Catalina Island. Every morning Chaplin gave her lessons in voice training. For two hours at a stretch, she was required to scream at the seagulls, on the theory that the exercise would strengthen her vocal cords. The main event of the trip, however, was her realization that she had fallen in love with Chaplin. "He, of course, continued his protestations of love."

Soon enough, she concluded that she was pregnant, even though "I remembered that the first time I was ever intimate with CHAPLIN he told me he couldn't have children. As a matter of fact, this was one of the devices which he used to persuade me to be intimate with him." At the time that she broke the news to him about her condition, she was planning a trip to New York. He told her that if she knew someone there who would perform an abortion—a criminal abortion, that is, for this was the 1940s—he would give her $800 to make the trip. Shortly thereafter he did give her the money. But while she was in New York she did not have an operation. As soon as she and Chaplin were reunited, he asked how she was, and she confessed that she was still pregnant. "For God's sake," she remembered him shouting, "you've got to do something about it." She said no, she would not. A "big argument" ensued, which was made even more upsetting for her by Chaplin's determination to ask Tim Durant for help in arranging for an abortion in Los Angeles. Despite her vehement opposition to involving the young socialite, Chaplin did so anyway. Durant proceeded to harass her as well. "I really wanted to go ahead and have the baby," Barry exclaimed to the interviewer in piteous tones, "and here were CHAPLIN and DURANT trying to high-pressure me into having an operation."

To get away from them, she fled to the St. Francis Hotel in San Francisco. Durant tracked her down there by phone. After admonishing her to be "calm and not . . . emotional," he succeeded in persuading her to return to Los Angeles, where he had made arrangements to "have the whole thing taken care of." Durant and a woman who owned a sanitarium "near the corner of Sunset and Alvarado" met her plane. They took her to the sanitarium. The next day the woman took her to see a certain Dr. Immerman, "whose offices as I recall were located in the Taft Building at the corner of Hollywood and Vine." Immerman sent them to the establishment of a certain Dr. Tweedie on Crenshaw Boulevard. But while waiting in Tweedie's office, "I changed my mind and decided not to go through with it."

In a long talk that night on Summit Drive with Chaplin and Durant, Durant again convinced her that it was in her best interest to terminate her pregnancy. The next morning Durant escorted her to Tweedie's office, where Durant made an appointment for the operation. On the way back to Chaplin's house, Durant's "remarks to the effect that I should be sensible about these things, etc., so aroused me that I remember I called him a beast and slapped his face." The following morning, Durant handed her over to Tweedie's ministrations. She remained in his establishment for five days. During this period, Chaplin phoned her several times, but did not come to see her. Upon her release, she at once went to Summit Drive. The Japanese houseman said that Chaplin was over on Catalina. So she took the ferry to the island. She looked around for Chaplin's yacht, but it was nowhere to be found. By telephone she reached Tim Durant. "I was probably hysterical when I was talking to him." Durant told her that Chaplin was at home again and that she could see him in the morning.

Months passed. During this period, Barry went to a doctor and was fitted with a diaphragm. Unfortunately, Chaplin "did not want me to use it and so I didn't whenever we had intercourse. He made no mention of being sure that nothing like that [pregnancy] happened again and showed no concern. I myself took ordinary precautions, but same was not effective, because by the end of December I believed I was again pregnant." She told Chaplin about this "and he laughed and thought it was a big joke. He said, 'We have got to get ahold of [Tim] again.' " Although she asked whether Tim had to be told, Chaplin as usual did as he pleased. The next time she saw Durant, he took her by the arm in a friendly manner and said, "Well, Joan, this time it won't be quite as bad." Again he took her to Tweedie's office. This time, however, she convalesced on Summit Drive, "in the room that has been variously known as PAULETTE'S room and my room."

Although Charles, as she called the comedian, was "very solicitous during this period," she was very upset and needed the sleeping tablets she had obtained from a doctor. "I . . . told CHARLES I was sick and I would not go through one of these things again, and he called TIM who came over and said he was sick and tired of my antics and slapped me and CHARLES held my hands and would not let me strike him." Durant phoned a lady friend of his, the actors' agent Minna Wallis, and asked her to take Joan home. In the car, Wallis

> made some comment about my bruised face, but said she did not want to know anything about it. I told her that of course she did not want to know anything bad about DURANT. She had always closed her eyes to such things about him, thinking he was perfect. She said that whatever caused it, I had brought it on myself.

This slapping incident, Barry emphasized to the FBI interviewer, was "only one of many times" when Durant hit her.

By the following May she and Chaplin had both concluded that her contract with the Chaplin Studio ought to be voided, and "on an amicable basis" it was. Barry's newest career hope was that a screen test at MGM would lead to a film assignment. She also went to Tulsa to see J. Paul Getty. But while she dated other men upon her return to Hollywood, the fires of her obsession with Chaplin had only been banked.

12

May 1942 had a further significance for the comedian. It was the month in which he received a phone call from the head of the American Committee for Russian War Relief in San Francisco, asking if he would speak at the Civic Center in lieu of the former ambassador to the Soviet Union, the passionately pro-Soviet Joseph E. Davies. Davies, it seemed, was suffering from laryngitis. That the moving forces within the committee had come up with the idea of Chaplin as a replacement was no accident. For the peace preacher of yesterday now shared with Davies and many other Americans—political centrists and leftists for the most part, according to Ralph Levering's *American Opinion and the Russian Alliance, 1939–1945* (1976)—a military impatience. America and Britain must abandon their stalling and heed Stalin's call for the immediate establishment of a second front in Western Europe. Such a move would have resulted in hideously high Allied casualties and might well have failed. Forecasts of this sort had little effect, however, on the fervor of the second fronters.[54]

Chaplin caught the night train and reached San Francsico in the morning. The committee, he discovered, had scheduled him to appear as well at a luncheon and a dinner, so that he had next to no time to prepare his Civic Center speech. On arriving onstage, he looked across a sea of ten thousand faces. Ham acting rescued him from the fright he felt. "Comrades!" he began. Before he could say anything further, he recalled, "the house went up in a roar of laughter." When it subsided, he went after the same effect again. "And I mean comrades." At this, there was more laughter, and some applause as well. "I assume there are many Russians here tonight," he continued, "and the way your countrymen are fighting and dying at this very moment, it is an honor and a privilege to call you comrades." After urging the crowd to open its wallets to the heroic Soviet fighters, he implied that the Allied chiefs of staff in Washington and London lacked guts. "I am told," he declared, "that the Allies have two million soldiers languishing in the North of Ireland, while the Russians alone are facing about two hundred divisions of Nazis."[55]

At supper afterwards, the leftist actor John Garfield told him that he had a lot of courage. Chaplin was dismayed by the remark, he would unconvincingly claim in *My Autobiography*, "for I did not wish to be valorous or caught up in a political *cause célèbre.*" In any event, the wishes that counted were those of the unseen marionette-pullers who had taken the measure of his success and his vanity. On May 25 he spoke at a Russian War Relief rally at the Shrine Auditorium in Los Angeles and again wowed his listeners by addressing them as "Comrades—and I do mean comrades." It was a "superb speech," that unwavering Hollywood Stalinist Donald Ogden Stewart recalled, and after Chaplin left the mike "we . . . followed the lead of Walter Huston in singing our tribute to 'the victorious banners of the glorious Soviet Army.'" Two months later, Chaplin communicated his views by telephone to a crowd of sixty thousand at a CIO-sponsored outdoor rally in New York City. A booklet describing the event—and couched in the kind of rhetoric to which leftist writers of the day automatically resorted—was subsequently published by the CIO. "The great crowd, previously warned not to interrupt with applause, hushed and strained for every word. Thus they listened for fourteen minutes to Charles Chaplin, the great people's artist of America, as he spoke to them by telephone from Hollywood." Similar harangues were offered by the farthest-left figures in the U.S. Congress, Representative Vito Marcantonio and Senator Claude ("Red") Pepper, as well as by such labor union militants as Michael ("Red Mike") Quill and Joseph Curran. But New York mayor Fiorello H. La Guardia and U.S. senator James M. Mead also spoke, while other mainstream Americans, including the Republican candidate for President in 1940, Wendell L. Willkie, and the labor leaders Philip Murray and Sidney Hillman, sent enthusiastic messages. "Give us a second front now," Chaplin managed to say in several ways. "Let us aim for victory in the spring," he pleaded.[56]

In the fall he gave three more speeches. At a dinner in Carnegie Hall in New York on October 16, to which the Communist-front organization Artists' Front to Win the War had sold three thousand tickets, Sam Jaffe, I. F. Stone, Joris Ivens, Lillian Hellman, and other hard leftists kept the crowd whipped up until Orson Welles finally arose and introduced Chaplin as the featured speaker of the evening. "Dear comrades," Chaplin said, as the applause died away. "Yes, I mean comrades. When one sees the magnificent fight the Russian people are putting up, it is a pleasure and a privilege to use the word 'comrade.'" He went on to speak of the need for "a second front now," to salute Franklin Roosevelt for having done more for the "little people" than any other American President except Lincoln, and to praise FDR in equally warm terms for granting the veteran Communist leader Earl Browder an early release from federal prison. In a crowd-pleasing confession, he then made clear his lack of concern about various prophecies that after the war Communism might spread across the entire world, because "I can live on $25,000 a year."[57]

At a "Salute to Our Russian Ally" rally at Orchestra Hall in Chicago on November 25, he denounced the Boston branches of the American

Legion for having objected to the appearance of Harry Bridges on a podium at Harvard University. "No longer is the world shocked at the word 'communism,' " Chaplin declared.[58]

The occasion for his final speech was a dinner on December 3 at the Hotel Pennsylvania in New York City, sponsored by the "Arts to Russia" committee of Russian War Relief. In an extremely excited statement, he told the seven hundred guests that the American people were finally beginning

> to understand the Russian purges, and what a wonderful thing they were. Yes, in those purges the Communists did away with their Quislings and Lavals and if other nations had done the same there would not be the original Quislings and Lavals today. The only people who object to Communism and who use it as a bugaboo are the Nazi agents in this country, the open ones and the secret ones and the pro-axis and appeaser press and columnists. I am not a Communist but I am proud to say that I feel pretty pro-Communist.[59]

Today, the breathtaking naïveté of that argument makes Chaplin seem very foolish. But 1942 was a different time. As Richard Gid Powers has observed in his judicious study of American anti-Communism, on the day that Hitler's armies crossed the Russian border it became "almost un-American" for critics in the United States to attack the Soviet Union in any way, and it "also seemed almost unpatriotic to attack the Soviet Union's American comrades."[60] Only exceedingly combative right-wingers—for example, columnist Westbrook Pegler of the Scripps-Howard newspaper chain—were willing to take on Chaplin's politics. "Chaplin lately has said that he is pro-Communist, which means only that he is anti-American," Pegler cuttingly wrote. His further opinion was that the success of *The Great Dictator* was a fluke, that Chaplin's career was, in fact, on the skids, and that his awareness of this lay behind his new willingness to make "an open profession of his political faith. . . . Now that he has all the money he needs and has lost his way with the public, [he] has frankly allied himself with the pro-Communist actors and writers of the theater and the movies who call themselves artists, but who are mostly hams and hacks."[61]

Such potshots were scorned by the comedian. He was riding high in his new role as a nationally sought-after speaker on world events, and the praise of Communists and fellow travelers who had regained their standing as leaders of the antifascist left in America rang loudly in his ears. Those wonderful people took him seriously. Pegler's column, however, was a marker on the road to political calamity for Chaplin.

13

Shortly before his departure from Hollywood on October 12 for his Carnegie Hall speech, Chaplin contacted Joan Barry "out of a clear blue sky," according to Barry's FBI testimony, and offered her and her mother round-trip train fares to New York. Clearly, he wanted to see her there. To hear Chaplin tell it—and the world eventually would—he had no interest in seeing her in New York or anywhere else. The train money—for one-way tickets, he insisted—was a part of the payoff to her for tearing up her contact with the Chaplin Studio. The cost of getting her back to New York had been included in the deal because she had decided that "she did not want to be an actress." [62]

On leaving Carnegie Hall, Chaplin recalled in *My Autobiography*, he and Tim Durant returned to their suite at the Waldorf-Astoria. The discovery that he had several telephone messages from Barry made his flesh creep, Chaplin swore. His impulse was to tell the telephone operator not to put through any calls, but Durant told him, "You'd better not, you'd better answer or she'll be up here to create a scene." Thus when the phone rang, Chaplin answered. "She seemed quite normal and pleasant," so when she asked if she could come up and say hello, he said she could. But he also instructed Durant to stay with him. At the end of a half-hour visit, Chaplin took her to the Hotel Pierre, where she and her mother were staying rent-free, presumably, because the Pierre at this time was owned and operated by a realty company controlled by Paul Getty. To gossip columnists and law-enforcement officials Barry would before too long be telling a different story about their get-together at the Waldorf: she and Chaplin had had sexual intercourse. Why else would he have paid her way to New York? [63]

On her way back to Los Angeles—for she was still paying rent on an apartment there, despite a desperate shortage of funds—Barry spent a week to ten days in Tulsa. In the scenes she staged in front of Paul

Getty, she alternately threatened to commit suicide and demanded money. Through Getty's attorney, Claude Rosenstein, a loan of approximately $1,700 was arranged, against a collateral consisting of her Cadillac and the silver-fox coat that Chaplin had given her.[64]

14

Chaplin, meanwhile, was thinking intensely about a new film project. In July 1941, Orson Welles had showed him a movie script he had written about the wife-murderer Landru, and after reading it Chaplin bought it from him.* In an interview with Peter Bogdanovich long afterwards, Welles recalled how he came to write the script and why he sold it.

> *OW:* I had an inspiration in the subway—one of those real "Eureka" kind of things. I saw an advertisement for an antidandruff remedy which had a picture of a bright-faced little hairdresser type making that gesture of the stage Frenchman which indicates that something or other is simply too exquisite for human speech. *"Avez-vous Scurf?"* he was asking us.
> *PB:* It made you think of Chaplin?
> *OW:* Chaplin *as* Landru. I'd gotten to know him by then, through Aldous Huxley and King [Vidor], so I . . . told him about it. He said, "Wonderful." I went away, wrote a script and showed it to him. He said, "Wonderful!—I'm going to act it for you!" But then, at the last moment, he said, "No. I can't—I've never had anybody else direct me. Let me buy it." So I did, and he made it as *Monsieur Verdoux.* My title was *The Ladykiller.*[65]

Sometime during the fall of 1942, *The Ladykiller* overtook *Shadow and Substance* in Chaplin's cinematic imagination. The actors' agent Minna Wallis—whom Joan Barry despised for having taken no interest in her bruised face—was unaware of this, however, as illustrated by the fact that she phoned Chaplin in early November to say that she had a new client who she believed might be right for the role of Brigid. The client was Oona O'Neill, the daughter of Chaplin's all but exact

---

* Chaplin would insist that he paid Welles $5,000 merely for "an idea for a comedy," and this indeed may be the truth of the matter. Welles, like Chaplin, was much given to embroideries of his personal history. *My Autobiography*, p. 418.

contemporary, Eugene O'Neill. Since arriving in southern California, following her graduation from the Brearley School in New York, Oona had been having a marvelous time. To her schoolgirl friend and fellow debutante Carol Marcus, she sent reports about Orson Welles and the other male movie stars she had been meeting, all of whom wanted to take her out, fix her up with jobs, and, she tensely added, "sleep with me. It makes me nervous." Agent Wallis, sensing Chaplin's interest in meeting this interesting addition to the Hollywood scene, said that Oona was coming to dinner at her house that very evening and that it would be nice if he and Tim Durant were to join them. Nice it proved to be. Here was a startlingly lovely, deliciously witty girl of seventeen whose father had received the Nobel Prize for Literature. In short order, Hollywood gossip columnists were putting out the word that Chaplin had a brand-new protégée.[66] But if he believed that he could cast Joan Barry aside without further ado, he was very much mistaken.

13

TWO DISTINCT PERSONALITIES

As the wife-killer in Monsieur Verdoux *(1947) with Marilyn Nash.*

On the night of December 23, 1942, Chaplin had just gone up to his bedroom when someone knocked on the front door. Because he sensed who it was, he did not go back downstairs. Barry found a ladder and propped it against the sill of an open window on the second floor, but changed her mind and broke through the glass door to the ground-floor study. On reaching Chaplin's bedroom, she pulled out a gun. Even though she kept it pointed at him, she spoke of suicide. With a good deal of sweet talk, Chaplin calmed her down. In the words of the FBI interviewer who summarized her account of what happened, he "finally convinced her that she should spend the night and remarked that she should not kill herself until morning." They then had sexual intercourse, she claimed, "with the gun which she had brought with her resting on the night stand between the twin beds, where she could reach it with her right hand." Chaplin joked that having sex with a gun nearby was a "new twist." Having satisfied himself, he dropped off to sleep. His snoring kept her awake, however, so at last she retreated into another bedroom.

When Charlie Jr. and Sydney arrived home from a Christmas party sometime after two, their father appeared in the upstairs hall. He was fully dressed, they noticed. He told them to go to bed at once and not to ask any questions. The next morning, said Barry, Chaplin came into her bedroom and promised to pay her twenty-five dollars a week. Then he took off his pajamas. But before climbing into bed with her, "he walked back and forth in front of the mirror flexing his muscles and said: 'You know, Joan, I look something like Peter Pan, don't you think?'" After a while, her narrative concluded, "we . . . lay there together talking over my career and my bills."[1]

Undeterred by the weekly bribe he had offered her, she continued to pay unannounced visits to Summit Drive in succeeding days, bathing fully clothed in the sprinklers and driving around the circular drive so fast that her car almost turned over. At times, her speech was so incoherent as to be unintelligible. About the events of the night of December 30 she was "vague," she admitted to the FBI. But she seemed to remember that she arrived by taxi at Summit Drive, that Chaplin admitted her to the house by the back door, that they sat by the fireplace in the living room talking, and that after having sexual intercourse they "got into their usual arguments." Chaplin tried to persuade her to live within her means. "Go to live at the Studio Club," he urged.

Having given her advice that cost him nothing in lieu of financial assistance for psychiatric care, he offered to take her home. But as they were driving down the street, she confessed that she had no place to sleep. Chaplin braked the car outside the Beverly Hills police station and brutally asked why she did not go in there. Barry declared to the FBI that she did, and that she told her story to the man at the desk. Official records did not confirm this, however. What they showed, rather, was that a day and a half later, on New Year's morning, 1943, Barry was arrested on a sidewalk in Beverly Hills in a state of bewilderment from a heavy dose of barbiturates. It was further established that she had no money on her and that she had been evicted from the hotel to which she had recently moved for nonpayment of the rent on her apartment.

At a hearing on January 2, she was represented by a certain Cecil Holland, whose services had been recommended to her by Minna Wallis. (Five months later, the *Los Angeles Times* would report that investigators were questioning Wallis in order to determine whether Barry's civil rights had been violated in consequence of a deception. For it made sense to believe that Chaplin had covertly urged Wallis to intervene in the case, inasmuch as she was close to him and to Oona O'Neill and kept "company with Tim Durant" as well.) The presiding judge gave Barry a suspended sentence and placed her on probation, the cardinal condition of which was that she was to stay out of Beverly Hills. On January 5, she left for New York by train, stopping en route in Tulsa.[2]

2

Chaplin devoted long hours in the early months of 1943 to composing a movie script of his own about a wife-killer. That the harassments of Joan Barry colored his murderous fantasies was more than likely. But before a Bluebeard kills, he must beguile, and in this respect, too, the wife-killer script was an imitation of life. For all of the comedian's seductive wiles were focused in these months on the beguilement of Oona O'Neill. In *My Father, Charlie Chaplin*, Charlie Jr. would make clear how successful his father's efforts were.

> Whenever Oona was with our father a rapt expression would come into her eyes. She would sit quietly, hanging on his every word. Most women are charmed by Dad, but in Oona's case it was different. She worshipped him, drinking in every word he spoke, whether it was about his latest script, the weather or some bit of philosophy.[3]

At Brearley, she had been an academically indifferent student and, unlike almost all her schoolmates, had had no interest in going to college. One of her chums in that period remembers her as a sunny, fun-to-be-with, good-time girl who may have had a good mind but was uninterested in anything serious. With her long black hair, high cheek bones, generous mouth, and lovely coloring, Oona had flocks of male admirers, some of whom took her to the Stork Club with such frequency that the headmistress of Brearley, Millicent Carey McIntosh, was prompted to write a letter to the nightclub's proprietor, Sherman Billingsley, protesting that Oona was not yet of age and was spending entirely too much time in his establishment. The visits continued, however, and in her senior year the celebrities and glamour girls of past years who were habitués of the place voted her Debutante Number One of 1942, a triumph to which the "saloon editor" of the *New York Post*, Earl Wilson, devoted an entire column.

One of her former schoolmates would recall having become aware, while riding beside Oona in the bus to Brearley every morning, of a barely controlled rebelliousness in her, a constant impulse to kick against the traces, that bespoke something more than a mere determination to have a good time. Two other friends also discerned a darkness within her sunniness, a core of isolation at the heart of her sociable manner, that was related in their judgment to the tension between her and her mother, Agnes Boulton. At the beginning of her junior year, she and her mother—whom one of Oona's prep-school escorts regarded as "mad in an eccentric way"—were living in a hotel suite, oppressively decorated with heavy, dark hangings, on Madison Avenue. Her mother, however, was engaged in one of her numerous romantic affairs and was rarely at home in the evenings. Out of a concern about Oona's lack of maternal care, the Brearley administration arranged for her to live during the spring semester with a few girls from out of town in the brownstone home of Dr. and Mrs. Wallace Hamilton on East Sixty-fifth Street, and in her senior year she continued to live there. Oona and the Hamiltons' daughter, Kitty, who was also a Brearley student, were roommates. In contrast to Kitty and the other girls in the house, Oona had "bottles of nail polish and lipsticks galore." And because the girls had keys to the front door, it was easy enough for Oona to slip out at night whenever she wished. When stories about her appeared in the papers, she proudly showed them to her housemates. The girls were impressed, too, by the fact that she seemed to know a number of men

—press agents, perhaps—whom they thought of as "unsavory." Yet while it was her announced ambition to become famous, her manner was never haughty. Indeed, she was clearly grateful for the friendly atmosphere of the Hamiltons' home and for the motherliness of "Lady Hamilton," as Mrs. Hamilton was called.[4]

Above and beyond her tense relations with her mother lay her grief about her absent father's seeming indifference to her. She was fixated on him, one of her friends would remember, and talked about him constantly. Oona had been so young when O'Neill had jettisoned Agnes in favor of Carlotta Monterey that she retained virtually no childhood memories of him. But the crusher was that while he had been granted visitation rights at the time of the divorce, he almost never exercised them. The result was that "Oona did not think her father loved her," according to Carol (Marcus) Matthau in *Among the Porcupines.* Therefore, when he suddenly consented to a visit from her in the summer of 1941, she was thrilled. At the San Francisco airport a chauffeur met her and drove her to the mansion in the San Ramon Valley that O'Neill and Carlotta had named Tao House. "I . . . found her a most delightful and charming young lady," O'Neill subsequently wrote to a friend. He gave no indication, however, of a wish to see her again anytime soon. Carlotta, for her part, considered their houseguest "a snippy little girl" with appalling values. One day, she recalled, Oona "saw me darning a pair of her father's socks . . . and asked me "what on earth" I was doing. "What do you think I'm doing? I'm darning your father's socks, of course!" Oona curled her lip and said, 'You'd never catch me dead doing a thing like that. I'm going to marry a rich man.' "

Marry a rich man, that is, who was old enough to be her father. In Carol Matthau's words, "Oona felt something [with Charlie] she had always wanted to feel, but had never felt before now—safe. Not only was he older and a great man, he protected her and she knew he would for the rest of their lives." Unfortunately, that guarantee of protection came at a price, Matthau conceded. In exchange for it, Oona "was to allow parts of herself to go dormant. . . . Part of her always had to be a little girl. Charlie's little girl. He always had to be The One. He had had that from the public for a long time, but then the public turned on him. He still had to get that, all of it, but from one person, Oona."

Another of Oona's old New York friends, Nuala Pell, concurred in the judgment that in the country of her marriage her husband was an absolute monarch. At a luncheon on Long Island in honor of the Chaplins in 1947, Mrs. Pell was struck by the "strict hold" that Chaplin maintained on his wife. That they delighted in each other's company, that they became indispensable to each other, was certain. But never was it a partnership of equals.

Besides a need for the sheltering presence of an older male authority figure, a defiant, rebellious payback may also have figured in the psychology of Oona's shocking decision to marry Chaplin. In the summer of 1941, her hopes of arousing her father's interest in regular visits had been crushed but not quite killed. En route to Hollywood in 1942, she stopped in Sacramento and phoned Tao House. Carlotta answered the phone. Oona asked her if she could come to see her father. After consulting with him, Carlotta returned to the phone and told her that he preferred not to see her and that she was not to phone him any more. He did, however, send her a letter:

> All the publicity you have had is the wrong kind, unless your ambition is to be a second-rate movie actress of the floosie variety—the sort who have their pictures in the papers for a couple of years and then sink back into the obscurity of their naturally silly, talentless lives. . . .
>
> I hoped there was the making of a fine intelligent woman in you, who would remain fine in whatever she did. I still hope so. If I am wrong, goodbye. If I am right, you will sometime see the point in this letter and be grateful—in which case, *au revoir.*

By becoming the wife of a scandal-scarred entertainer only one year younger than he was, Oona could wound her father as deeply as he had wounded her. Following O'Neill's death, Carlotta spoke of the effect on him of what his daughter had done. "Oona broke Gene's heart," she said. "He never mentioned her name after her marriage. Friends would ask him about her, and he simply wouldn't answer." In the playwright's dark mind, Oona's marriage represented yet another degrading chapter in the fate-haunted story of the O'Neills.[5]

All this lay in the future, however. In the late spring of 1943, an informant told the FBI, Chaplin's attorney advised him not to marry Oona because of his "Barry predicament."[6]

3

Barry returned to Los Angeles in the first week of May. On the 7th she appeared on Summit Drive and informed Chaplin that she was pregnant again, thanks to him. In response to a complaint that he immediately filed, the Beverly Hills police arrested and jailed her for violating her probation rules. At a hearing on the 12th, a judge ordered her removed to a sanitarium because of her pregnancy. Later in the month, her mother, who by this time had also returned from New York, took her into the apartment she had rented.[7]

On or about June 1, Barry told the FBI, she again went to Summit Drive to see Chaplin, because "she believed she was still in love with him."

I came in the front way and he was in the sun room. When he saw me come in he said, "Don't talk here—come out by the pool." No one else was down there. I remember saying, "How could you have ever let me stay there [in jail]?" He said he was doing it so he could teach me a lesson. I said, "Teach me a lesson?" and he said, "Yes, you were getting very, very annoying. You were annoying me and after all, good G—, I've got to have peace." We didn't talk about the baby at first at all. Then I said, "Well, CHARLES, what are we going to do about it?" He said, "Well, this is what I suggest. People have gotten over things like that. You're a fine actress. I suggest that you go back to New York and have the baby and then continue on the stage." He said, "JOAN, I'll always take care of that baby, you know that. I would take care of that baby even if it wasn't my own." Then I said, "Well, CHARLES, why can't you marry me?" He said, "I'm not marrying you—I'm not marrying anybody. Nobody's forcing me to get married to anybody." Then I thought perhaps there was somebody else.

She demanded to know if he was in love with another woman. He vehemently denied that he was. She began to cry and ran in the house and up the stairs to Paulette's room,

and I saw OONA's clothes there. I ran down by the pool and said, "Whose clothes are up there? OONA O'NEILL's? Is she living here?" and he said, "No." I said, "She is living here." He said, "It's your unsubstantiated word against mine."

Then he pleaded for her cooperation:

> "You've got to protect me, JOAN. I've got to have peace. I would rather go to jail for twenty years and have peace. JOAN, if you bring this into court, you know what it will be. The newspapers will be after you, your picture will be taken—oh, it will be grand for a couple of months."

Then he threatened her. He told her that he would spend his whole fortune on defending himself if necessary, and that even if it was proved that he was the father he would blacken her name and drag it through the mud. He said he would cite Paul Getty and the screenwriter Sam Marx and another writer named Hans Reusch with whom she had also been seen.

As he was carrying on in this vein, the butler, Edward Chaney, brought down lunch. While they were eating, she told him again that he was responsible for her pregnancy. He said, "JOAN, if you say so, I believe you completely." She accused him of thinking only of himself. "Don't talk to me like that," he warned her, "because if I have any sympathy for you or feel sorry for anything that's happened, that's not the way to talk to me, because [I'll] just turn around the other way. I don't like it at all."[8]

It is very far from certain that he actually acknowledged that he was the father, and even if he did he may not have believed that he was; rather, he may only have been trying to placate Barry and calm her down, in order to head off a public relations disaster. Once she realized that Oona was living with him, however, the disaster became inevitable. At the end of lunch, she reentered the house and "called home and [was told] that my mother had gone up to Hedda Hopper's . . . and I called her there and Florabel [Muir] was there." Edward the butler thereupon drove her to Hopper's home, where she proceeded to tell both Hopper and Muir—with whom she and her mother had been in touch ever since her emergence from jail—about the emotionally wrenching experience she had just had. Hopper and Muir were nationally syndicated gossip columnists, for the *Los Angeles Times* and the *New York Daily News* respectively. Hopper, in particular, already had a well-developed dislike of Chaplin, for political reasons. While she may have been famous for her crazy hats, no other conservative in Hollywood was more concerned than she was about Communist infiltration of the movie industry, and in her opinion Chaplin was either a card-carrying Red or the next thing to it.[9]

Muir's reference in her column of June 2 to Barry's luncheon with Chaplin and her insidious declaration that "Joan's momma is saying it would be nice—with a baby on the way—if Joan and Chaplin would wed" launched Chaplin's ordeal by newspaper. The following day, Hopper denounced him in print for never having become a U.S. citizen, for having refused to contribute to the Motion Picture Relief Fund Home, for having given only $100 to the American Red Cross in its recent appeal for funds, and for denying that he was Jewish (!), as well as for his exploitation of Barry and his caddish attitude toward her during the "cozy little luncheon" beside his swimming pool. "Will her child have a name?" Hopper asked in conclusion. "What is to become of that child and its mother, Joan Barry? Those are the questions Hollywood is asking today. Those are the questions Hollywood has a right to ask and not only hope for an answer but to demand one." [10]

Only hours after greater Los Angeles had ingested the Hopper column with its morning coffee, Barry's lawyer, John Irwin, filed a paternity suit against Chaplin. Inasmuch as the baby was due at the end of September, conception must have occurred during one of Barry's nighttime descents upon Summit Drive the previous December. Over the phone with his own lawyer, Loyd Wright, a past president of the California Bar Association, Chaplin proclaimed that he had "had nothing to do with the Barry woman for two years." [11]*

An informant told the FBI that a maid on Summit Drive had been threatening for some time to announce to the newspapers that Oona was living with Chaplin unless he paid her several thousand dollars in hush money. The informant further stated that the comedian had finally decided to "get out from under" the blackmail by making Oona his wife right away. Whatever the truth of this tale, they were married on June 16, 1943, in Carpinteria, California, by a justice of the peace. The ceremony was mercifully tranquil, thanks to the daring and resourcefulness of Frank, the chauffeur, in outracing and evading pursuing reporters. The following day, Chaplin appeared in court and denied responsibility for his accuser's pregnancy. The judge then approved a postponement of the trial until early 1944, at which time Chaplin, Barry,

---

* Two years before, however, Chaplin had been acquainted with Barry for exactly one month.

and the baby would be given blood tests. John Irwin, representing Barry, agreed to drop the suit if the tests vindicated Chaplin's claim that he was not the father. In exchange, Loyd Wright committed his client to paying Barry $2,500, plus $100 a week to support her, $500 a month to support the baby until the time of the trial, $1,000 to cover the blood-test costs, and $5,500 in lawyers' fees and court costs.[12]

4

For two months following their wedding, Chaplin and Oona led a secluded life on the outskirts of Santa Barbara, while the ladies and gentlemen of the press looked high and low for them. Every now and again, waves of sickening depression broke upon him with the regularity of the evening rollers washing in from the Pacific. He felt that the "acrimony and hate of a whole nation" were being directed at him. Yet whenever his black moods threatened to crush his spirit, Oona would lift him out of them "by reading *Trilby* to me." The story was "very Victorian and laughable," he would dissemblingly write in *My Autobiography*, as if he sincerely believed that his readers would not remark upon the oddness of the choice of a novel—did Oona make it, or did he?—about the total domination of a man over a woman as a means of cheering him up.[13]

Meantime, his lawyers were busy. As an FBI assessment of Loyd Wright put it, this prominent attorney was "not beyond engaging in sharp practices." Furthermore, the probity level of the comedian's legal representation did not improve when, in midsummer, he acquired the services of the slick-talking Jerry Giesler, who had recently saved Errol Flynn from conviction on statutory-rape charges. On August 25 an FBI memo from Special Agent R. B. Hood to the director in Washington duly reported that Chaplin's attorneys were "buying up witnesses who will testify that they were intimate with Berry [*sic*] at the time instant [the] child was conceived." On September 2, another report to FBI headquarters from an agent in Los Angeles asserted that one of Giesler's employees, George Wood, "had been going about Hollywood trying to manufacture witnesses for Chaplin's side of the case." An FBI teletype to the director informed him that Chaplin's butler, Edward Chaney, had implicated Wright and Giesler "in witness fixing." A second teletype spoke of "unlimited funds being expended by Chaplin attorneys." And a third implied that Edward Chaney's silence had been purchased by Chaplin.[14]

Hollywood, not surprisingly, was awash in rumors about Chaplin and his love troubles, some of which an aspiring actress, Katharine Marlowe, relayed to the FBI. One was that Oona had had an abortion performed on her on the day of her marriage. Another was that the comedian was taking some kind of shots in order to change his blood type. The idea that he could effect such an alteration was crazy, of course, but this did not necessarily mean that he was not trying to, or that the rumor did not spread beyond the borders of movieland into the suggestible thinking of ordinary Angelenos, including potential jurors.[15]

In addition to dispatching a steady stream of reports to Washington concerning the paternity suit, the FBI's Los Angeles office undertook an investigation of Chaplin's October 1942 trip to New York for evidence of a violation of the Mann Act. If he had indeed paid for Barry's transcontinental transportation for the intent and purpose of having illicit sexual relations with her, then the U.S. Attorney in Los Angeles might decide to prosecute him. The investigation lasted through the summer and continued into the fall. In November, the Bureau broadened the scope of its inquiry in order to help the U.S. Attorney in Los Angeles, Charles Carr, determine whether Barry's civil rights had been violated at the time of her January and May arrests. In pursuing this question, Carr was encouraged by FDR's patrician attorney general, Francis Biddle, and Assistant Attorney General Tom Clark.[16]

Carr presented his multifarious materials on Chaplin to a federal grand jury in mid-January 1944. On February 10, the jury handed down four indictments against him. The first alleged violation of the Mann Act. The second charged that he and two public officials, Beverly Hills police detective W. W. White and municipal judge Charles Griffin, had violated Barry's civil rights by persuading her to plead guilty to vagrancy and leave Los Angeles following her arrest in January. The third accused Chaplin and a left-wing radio broadcaster, Robert Arden, who was one of his hangers-on, of having conspired with Detective White in the task of persuasion. The final indictment charged that Chaplin, Tim Durant, Robert Arden, Detective White, Judge Griffin, police sergeant Claude Marple, and police matron Jessie Billie Reno had conspired to deny

Barry her civil rights in the May as well as the January arrest. Conviction on all counts would make Chaplin liable to a sentence of twenty-three years in prison and to fines up to $26,000.[17]

To his intense humiliation—which he would scornfully and bitterly reenact in *A King in New York*—Chaplin was fingerprinted and photographed while being booked, and on March 21 he went to trial on the Mann Act charge. As a longtime student of courtroom masquerades, Jerry Giesler was so full of admiration for Chaplin's performance that in *The Jerry Giesler Story* (1960) he called him "the best witness I've ever seen in a courtroom." Even when he was not on the stand "he looked helpless, friendless and wistful, as he sat there with the weight of the whole United States Government against him." Called as a witness by the defense, Paul Getty badly damaged the government's case by admitting that he not only knew Barry, but that she had visited Tulsa after leaving New York. For while the jury was not supposed to think about the young lady's involvements with other men, undoubtedly it did. On April 4, Chaplin was acquitted.[18]

Shortly thereafter, attorney Carr dropped the three other federal indictments, on orders from Assistant Attorney General Tom Clark. From the beginning, an FBI agent in Los Angeles subsequently acknowledged, Clark had had concerns that "the case against Subject [Chaplin] was weak, but had deferred his judgment until the Department [of Justice] had a chance to go over all the evidence." Once the department had done so, Clark concluded that there was "no case."[19]

5

Meanwhile, Joan Barry had given birth to a baby girl, whom she named Carol Ann (did "Carol" equate with "Charles" in her dreaming mind?) on October 2, 1943. Chaplin received the news at his studio office, where he had resumed work on his wife-killer script. Oona heard about it at home. In deference to her husband's wishes, she had abandoned thoughts of a career. His startling intention to have a large family had become her intention as well.

Blood samples were taken from him, from Barry, and from Carol Ann on February 15, 1944. The following day, a panel of three doctors announced their findings. Chaplin was blood type O, Barry blood type

A, and Carol Ann blood type B. Chaplin was not the baby's father. Accordingly, Loyd Wright filed a motion for dismissal of the paternity suit. Unfortunately, blood-test results were not yet admissible as evidence in California state courts. "The ends of justice will best be served," Superior Court Judge Stanley Mosk intoned, "by a full and fair trial of the issues." Barry needed no further encouragement to press forward, whereupon John Irwin refused to represent her any longer, on the grounds that she was reneging on the agreement he had worked out with Wright that she would abide by the blood-work findings. Undeterred, the monomaniacal Barry immediately hired another lawyer, Joseph Scott. A decade earlier, Scott had converted a moral message from Bishop Cantwell to the Hollywood moguls into an anti-Semitic tirade. Now seventy-seven years old, he looked like an Old Testament prophet and had lost none of his flamboyant mannerisms.[20]

The case came to trial on December 19, 1944. As his representative, Chaplin chose Charles A. (Pat) Millikan, whose low-keyed manner was at the opposite end of the dramatic scale from Scott's. The rhetorical thunderbolts that Scott hurled at Chaplin ranged from "pestiferous, lecherous hound" to "cheap Cockney cad" to "little runt of a Svengali." Pulled one way by Scott's purple indignation (and possibly by the rumor that Chaplin had taken shots to change his blood type) and yanked back the other way by Millikan's matter-of-factness and Chaplin's air of helpless innocence, the jurors could not make up their minds. In their final ballot on January 4, 1945, there were seven votes for acquittal and five for conviction. That Barry and Scott would try again for conviction was a foregone conclusion. The second trial began on April 12, 1945. In the end, the jury foreman announced a deadlock, with nine votes for conviction and three for acquittal. Judge Clarence L. Kincaid thereupon ordered Chaplin to pay Barry $5,000, plus $75 a month in child support for Carol Ann until she was twenty-one.[21]

Barry subsequently married a businessman and settled in Pittsburgh. But she could not escape the Hannah Chaplinesque tragedy that swallowed up any chance she had to be either a good wife or a good mother. Following her return to California in the early 1950s, doctors diagnosed her as a schizophrenic and consigned her to a state mental hospital. Carol Ann—whom she still regarded as Charlie Chaplin's daughter— was sent to live with relatives.

6

Throughout his ordeal, Chaplin would write, he and Oona "had been surrounded by very dear friends—all of them loyal and sympathetic." And all of them hard-leftists, he might have added. Presumably, they supported his sense of himself as a victim, a political victim, of right-wing gossip mongers in the press, of harassment by the FBI, and of a system of justice in the courts that had proved to be unjust. But while Chaplin drew closer to every one of these friends—to Salka Viertel, the Clifford Odetses, the Hanns Eislers, the Lion Feuchtwangers[22]—he was especially fond of Eisler. A brilliant and witty conversationalist on a wide variety of topics, this German refugee composer had been one of Arnold Schönberg's most promising students. In addition to symphonic works, his oeuvre included a number of the workers' songs of struggle and liberation that were sung in the 1930s by left-wing labor militants in Western Europe and by Loyalist troops in the Spanish Civil War.

For a period beginning in 1935, he worked as the head of the Comintern-connected International Music Bureau in Moscow, the purpose of which was to foster allegiance to the Soviet Union among musicians, music critics, and composers all over the world. When Eisler came to Hollywood, it was not because of the remunerative assignments in the movie industry that he quickly obtained, but because the Kremlin believed in his aptitude for orchestrating cultural infiltration. Among other achievements of this nature, Eisler became the driving force, once Hitler invaded the USSR, behind Artists' Front to Win the War, which drew Chaplin, Rockwell Kent, Paul Robeson, Larry Adler, Muriel Draper, and three members of the future Hollywood Ten—Albert Maltz, John Howard Lawson, and Dalton Trumbo—into its fold. With the division of Germany at the end of World War II, the Communist rulers of East Germany picked Eisler to compose the national anthem of the German Democratic Republic.[23]

Gerhart Eisler, Hanns's brother, who had entered the United States from China in 1933 in the guise of an antifascist refugee, was recognized within the CPUSA as the voice of official Moscow. At the same time, he engaged in espionage activities. Hanns and Gerhart's sister, Ruth Fischer, on the other hand, turned against the faith that had once earned her the sobriquet of *die rote Ruth* (Red Ruth). In testimony before the

House Committee on Un-American Activities, she would emphatically declare that members of the Soviet secret police had systematically insinuated themselves into key institutions of American life and that her brother Gerhart was at the center of the web. "The perfect terrorist type," she called him, a man who without a particle of remorse would turn over to Stalin "his child, his sister, his closest friend." She also regarded both her brothers as capable of murder.[24]

Looking back on his years of residence in the United States, Hanns declared that it was then that he got to know capitalism in its "most naked, most savage and most brutal form." Furthermore, the United States was a country where "a dictatorship could be practiced without a superstructure and where your creations go to wrack and ruin." Nevertheless, he had accomplished things there, and one of them was that he and his fellow Communist Bertolt Brecht, whom he and his wife had often entertained with the Chaplins, had "radicalized" the comedian. They had also done their best to show him that his destiny lay in making his humor more consistently radical. For although Chaplin had told Brecht and Eisler many jokes, they had mainly laughed at those that had "a strong political thrust." The success of Brecht and Eisler's effort would be seen in *Monsieur Verdoux*.[25]

7

On February 12, 1946, six months after the bombing of Hiroshima and Nagasaki stunned the world with the revelation that the United States possessed atomic weapons, Chaplin completed his work on the script of *Comedy of Murders*, *Monsieur Verdoux*'s working title, and turned it into the PCA office for preliminary approval. Joe Breen's response on the 20th had the shock of an ice-cold shower. A screenplay prepared from this material, he announced, "WOULD BE UNACCEPTABLE under the provisions of the Production Code."[26] His explanation of why began with the contention that "the story contains a false enunciation of moral values, which seems to be in fundamental conflict with the theory of sound ethics as set forth in the Industry's Production Code."

> Specifically, it seems to us that the closing pages of the script attempt to present an *evaluation* of the moral heinousness or lack of heinousness . . .

of Verdoux's Bluebeard career. As we read . . . it seems to us that the burden of the argument comes inevitably down to this conclusion . . . that Verdoux's "comedy of murders" is not such an outrageous transgression against the moral order as the court [of law] would make it seem.

It offended Breen—it nauseated him—that in his speech in the courtroom and follow-up remarks in his cell Chaplin's bloody-handed killer would sneer at the "sham exhibitionism" of the prosecuting attorney for having called his cynical murders "monstrous," that he would minimize his own crimes by asking the world to look at the vast loss of human lives incurred in war, that he would consider it ridiculous, in fact, for anyone to be shocked by his actions when they were simply a "comedy of murders" in comparison with "the legalized mass murders of war which are embellished with gold braid by the 'system.' " Beneath the generalized assault on the "system" lay Chaplin's real target, the United States. But Breen chose not to mention this obvious fact.

The censor's second reason for rejecting the manuscript was that it dealt with "a type of confidence man" who induces a number of women to turn over their finances to him by beguiling them into a series of mock marriages. As told, the story was pervaded by a "distasteful flavor of illicit sex" which was "not good."

The characterization of "The Girl" in the picture as a prostitute, clearly, who in due course "flourishes materially" was also a violation of Code regulations, said Breen, and would have to be "substantially revised and qualified."

Lastly, there was the question of Verdoux's attitude toward God, as manifested in his exchange with the priest who visits him just before his execution. In Breen's tentative opinion, the killer's remarks were "possibly blasphemous in flavor, if not in fact."

Because of the "serious character" of these objections, the movie industry's arbiter concluded, "we will place ourselves at your disposal to discuss [them] should you desire." Although the script was unacceptable in its present form, he was optimistic that it could be brought within the requirements of the Code without seriously "impairing entertainment values."

Chaplin's clearly furious reply on the 25th declared that the Code was close to "encroaching on Constitutional rights of free speech." He then huffily asserted that he had "tried hard to understand" Breen's letter, but had found it confusing because of its "generalities, suppositions and misnomers." Please elucidate further, he said, so that "I shall be more competent to discuss [your] imputations."

Patiently, politely, and promptly, Breen sent him a second letter. "Let us endeavor to restate the reasons for the basic unacceptability of your story," he wrote. The most important reason was the first. "This story violates the provisions of the Production Code, in that it sets forth a false evaluation of the evil of Verdoux's crimes. The final pages of this story, in effect, enunciate the thesis that individual crimes are of little import, when one considers the crimes committed by nations on a wholesale scale."

Chaplin came back at him on March 3, with an argument that had two salient features. It asserted that *Comedy of Murders* was a work of art, not a political editorial, and it enveloped the hero in victimism. Verdoux's statements at the end were "within his characterization," the comedian insisted. "They do not connote the message of the story, but are an adjunct of the plot." This, he declaimed, is "the story of a man— a weak character with latent criminal tendencies." ("It might be the head of a criminal, mightn't it?" Chaplin had mused aloud while contemplating Clare Sheridan's bust of him.) These tendencies, he continued, have been "aggravated by conditions of the time. Depressions, wars, economic insecurity and frustration bring [them] out ... and set him on a path of crime." Consequently, "such phrases [in your letters] as 'anti-social,' 'indite [*sic*] the system,' 'impugn the present-day social structure,' 'evaluation of moral heinousness or lack of heinousness,' 'attempts to minimize the heinousness of his crime,' are false interpretations of COMEDY OF MURDERS, and have nothing to do with the theme." He concluded by accusing Breen's people of not having read his script with sufficient care. If they would do so now, they "will not see any 'indictment' or 'impugning of a system,' but they WILL see, in part, a criticism of it, and surely no system is above criticism."

Before criticizing Breen's performance in this correspondence, it must be acknowledged that it was not simply an accident that his years in office were a golden time in the history of Hollywood moviemaking. There is merit, for instance, in the argument that the constraints that the Code imposed on sexual conduct were actually beneficial, dramatically speaking, in that they enhanced the agony of Bergman and Bogart in *Casablanca* (1942) and the evil manipulativeness of Jane Greer in *Out of the Past* (1947) and of Barbara Stanwyck in *Double Indemnity* (1944). Ingenious producers, directors, and writers were spurred, too, into making a slew of charming comedies centered on romantic postponement and conflict, such as *Swing Time* (1936), with Fred Astaire and Ginger Rogers; *Bringing Up Baby* (1938), with Cary Grant and Katharine Hepburn; and *His Girl Friday* (1940), with Grant and Rosalind Russell. ("A fine romance, with no kisses," Fred and Ginger complainingly warble.) What was inexcusable about Breen, however, was that in rejecting Chaplin's script—among others—on the grounds of its political ideas, he was exerting a thought-control power that his office should never have been vested with in the first place. On the other hand, Chaplin's elaborate protest that Breen had misunderstood his script was a model of disingenuousness. For there can be no doubt that he was intent on "impugning a system," in terms every bit as bitter as his friend Hanns Eisler's characterization of American capitalism as savage and brutal.

Chaplin met with Breen and two members of his staff in the PCA director's office on March 12. In a voluminous follow-up letter to the comedian on the 15th, Breen summarized the lengthy agreement they had reached. The following excerpts will convey the flavor of the whole.

Revisions must be made to Verdoux's final speeches to avoid confusing the issue of [his] guilt as well as to avoid what might be construed as an unjust attack on society.

An added scene is to be developed between newspaper reporters, in which it will be clearly and forcefully pointed out that despite what Verdoux says, there is no minimizing the feeling that he is a scoundrel.

"The Girl" will be changed from a streetwalker to a derelict.

We advise you that censor boards would delete any references to specific chemical poisonings, such as cyanide.

Verdoux may *not* give Mme. G's [Grosnay's] rear view the once over.

There is to be no vulgar emphasis on the outlandish curves, both in front and behind, of the middle-aged woman.

Please rephrase Lydia's line, "Well forget about him and *come* to bed," to read ". . . and *go* to bed." We presume that this whole action will be played in such a way as to avoid any feeling that Verdoux and Lydia [a particularly homely but well-heeled older woman whom he has gulled into marrying him] are about to indulge in marital privileges [prior to his murder of her].

The business on the bottom of this page, and all similar action throughout the story, will have to be masked, or suggested, or presented in such a manner that it could not easily be construed as *details of crime which are easily imitable.*

Breen wound up the letter with an expression of confidence that "we can arrive at a conclusion satisfactory to all in each specific instance. In any event, as you know, our final judgment will be based upon the finished picture."

Upon a *fait accompli*, that is to say. While the picture that finally received a PCA certificate of approval bore marks of Breenian censorship, what is striking was the degree to which Chaplin prevailed. When Breen sat down to review the first finished film in more than half a decade by the man whom he revered as Hollywood's premier artist, he flinched from enforcing the political guidelines that he himself had established.*

8

On an early spring evening in 1946, just as the production of *Monsieur Verdoux* was getting under way, the French-born film director Robert Florey and his wife arrived on Summit Drive to have dinner with the Chaplins. Florey expected that their host would enliven the occasion with the same sort of mimetic anecdotes that he, Florey, had first been amused by in 1921, when as a newcomer to Hollywood who was trying

---

* A year after *Monsieur Verdoux*, he also gave a seal of approval to *Force of Evil*, directed and written by the soon-to-be-blacklisted Abraham Polonsky and starring John Garfield. Like *Monsieur Verdoux*'s political meanings, *Force of Evil*'s were encased in a crime story. Quite explicitly, the movie makes clear that the numbers-game racket on which it focuses is a metaphor for the corruption of *all* of American business. Similarly, Polonsky's portrayal of wiretaps as an evil reflected his feelings about FBI monitorings of phone conversations. Perhaps Breen's judgment was influenced by the fact that *Force of Evil* was made by a fledgling independent company that was in financial trouble, or perhaps it was the picture's outstanding cinematography that swayed him.

to live by his journalistic wits he had interviewed Chaplin for the French film weekly *Cinémagazine*. Instead, Chaplin spent the first part of the evening outlining the scenario of *Monsieur Verdoux*, and after dinner he acted out several scenes, in between darts to the piano to play some of the music he had composed for the picture. Florey had a macabre imagination, and a comedy about a wife murderer fired him up. Thus when Chaplin told him that he would be grateful for any suggestions he might have and offered to lend him a copy of the script to take home with him, he was delighted. A few days later, Florey appeared at the Chaplin Studio with twenty pages of notes. After perusing them, Chaplin proposed that he become the director of *Monsieur Verdoux*.[27]

Behind this startling proposal lay the fact that Chaplin had suffered a painful loss the week before. Alf Reeves, his seventy-year-old studio manager, had died after a long illness. Although Chaplin immediately replaced him with a man whom his lawyer recommended, he still felt the need of having an old friend around who also was wise in the ways of moviemaking. Florey seemed like the perfect choice.

In 1923, the young Florey had astounded film buffs on both sides of the Atlantic by publishing a book called *Filmland*, based on the detailed information he had accumulated as a Hollywood reporter about the structure of the movie industry and the various functions of its employees. Four years later, he produced a four-volume series of star biographies, the most perceptive of which dealt with Chaplin, whose movies he had adored since childhood. But while this exuberant, gregarious Frenchman would later write other informed books about the movie business, his premier ambition was to be directly engaged in it.[28]

After apprenticing himself to such gifted directors as Josef von Sternberg, King Vidor, and Edmund Goulding, he began writing and/or directing feature films for some of the smaller studios in the Los Angeles area, while on his own time he somehow found the money to make several avant-garde shorts. Chaplin was so impressed by his semiexpressionist fantasy, *The Life and Death of 9413—A Hollywood Extra* (1927), that he saw it five times and then screened it himself at a big party on Summit Drive. The enthusiastic notices that Florey received for his work as codirector of the Marx Brothers' crazy carryings-on in *The Cocoanuts* (1929) led to an invitation from Universal Studios to write the screenplay and direct the original *Frankenstein* (1931). Unfortunately,

Universal's incompetent boss, Carl Laemmle, Jr., became uneasy about Florey's "Continental" ideas about cinematography and other matters, and replaced him in the director's chair with James Whale. As for Florey's screenplay, elements of it were retained—including the memorable detail of the bolt in the monster's neck—but by and large the final script was the product of other hands. Had he been allowed to make this picture and attach his name to it, its development into a cult classic would in all probability have transformed him into a major Hollywood figure.

In the wake of the *Frankenstein* disappointment, he went on to direct scores of other feature films, including such stylish exercises in horror as *Murders in the Rue Morgue* (1932), starring Bela Lugosi. Nevertheless, he was never given the opportunity to fulfill the grand expectations of his admirers, and his connection with *Monsieur Verdoux* proved to be another case of what-might-have-been. For when Chaplin got down to the particulars of his offer to Florey, he elected to keep the title of director for himself, while making it clear in the fine print of Florey's contract that his position as associate director entailed all the responsibility of a codirector. As Florey's biographer, Brian Taves, has pointed out, this arrangement not only robbed Florey of ultimate creative control, but deprived him of a proper acknowledgment in the screen credits of the extent of his work for Chaplin.[29]

9

Something that augured well in Florey's opinion, as he contemplated the situation he had gotten himself into, was that Chaplin had already recruited Martha Raye for the role of Verdoux's indestructible foil, Annabella Bonheur. The experience of directing her in *Mountain Music* (1937) had led Florey to exactly the same conclusion that Chaplin had reached after seeing her and Carole Landis in a film about entertaining GIs overseas called *Four Jills in a Jeep* (1944): Raye's knockabout vitality and brassy vulgarity recaptured the old-time spirit of silent-screen slapstick.

On the other hand, Florey was distressed by the clumsiness with which Chaplin raised and then dashed Edna Purviance's hopes that she might be awarded the part of the matronly Madame Grosnay, whom

Verdoux woos and finally wins but is thwarted from marrying. When Edna arrived at the studio for her film test, Florey, who had known her in the 1920s, was amazed by how little she had changed. "The same pretty smile lit up her features, and she had lost none of her charm and sweetness." Chaplin rehearsed her, Florey said, and then bluntly informed her that she was not right for the part. "Afterward," Florey went on to say, "I walked across the studio yard with her. There were tears in her eyes, knowing that she would never come back. I kissed her and promised to call her soon."[30]

Florey was likewise distressed by Chaplin's treatment of Henry Bergman. Bergman was seventy-eight years old and in poor health. Nevertheless, when he came to Florey and asked if there might be something in the picture that he could do, Florey decided that he certainly would be capable of handling the part of one of the judges who listen in silence to Verdoux's speech after convicting him. For thirty years, Chaplin had benefited off the set as well as on from Bergman's eagerness to please him. In 1946, unfortunately, he retained no sense of obligation. With icy disdain, he informed Florey that he preferred "to send Bergman to rest." Before the year was out Bergman was dead.[31]

10

Forebodings of difficulty ahead in his own dealings with Chaplin were never far from Florey's mind during their lengthy story conferences prior to the commencement of the shooting. Time and again, as they were tossing ideas back and forth, Chaplin's great show of enthusiasm about the script would suddenly flag, and whenever it did the thought struck Florey that here was a man whose heart was no longer in his work and who was forcing himself to create situations at which people might laugh. "All this is felt," Florey later remarked, "in the cynical and disillusioned character of M. Verdoux."[32]

The shooting started on June 3, at which point the full truth about his old friend became apparent to Florey. Charlie Chaplin, he wrote, "the greatest comic revelation of the twentieth century, [had] two distinct personalities." On the one hand, there was "the amiable Charlie, the cajoler, the charmer, the Charlie whom the whole world adores, the Charlie who wants to please, to amuse, to seduce." And on the other hand, there was "the tyrannical, wounding, authoritarian, mean, despotic man imbued with himself. One could attribute to him by masculinizing it, the verse of Corneille, in the tragedy of *Medea*. 'Me, me alone, and that's enough.' "[33]

Chaplin's primitive command of the mechanics of telling a story on film and his egotistical refusal to acknowledge his limitations in this respect lay at the heart of the worst of the problems that Florey had with him. For years, the comedian had expressed admiration for Florey's knowledge of the camera. While sitting beside him on the set of *Monsieur Verdoux*, however, Chaplin proved to be "the irreconcilable enemy of all that is photographic composition," especially when it involved "daring camera shots." Only shots from a certain distance from an immobile camera consistently met with his approval, and the ones he liked best were those that focused head to foot on himself; everything else he was apt to dismiss as "Hollywood chi-chi."

In a re-creation of a typical series of takes, Florey showed that Chaplin did not think of him and the chief cameraman, Wallace Chewning, as collaborators in a collective enterprise; rather, he looked down upon them as mere facilitators, whose function was to enable him to do whatever he wanted—no matter how many times he changed his mind.

He knows what he's trying to obtain without however knowing how to express it; he doesn't see with a photographic eye. . . . "I would like now to have a foreground close-up of my head, very close." And Wallace Chewning would furnish his objective with a lens of three inches. We repeat: Charlie notices that the camera is now very close to him, he continues to say his lines, but he doesn't seem at ease; suddenly he stops and asks: "How can you see my feet, if you are so close?" I explain to him that I had asked Chewning to photograph with a 35 mm lens, but that he himself countermanded my order. He explodes. He knows he is wrong, but that makes no difference, he bounds in the other direction, he also wants to show the little cat on the ground and the female actress in the back, and the table at the left. His close-up becomes an angle of 25 mm. He is not pleased. We film, we begin again, and between two takes, approaching the operator, he asks him: "You have my head in the foreground in the whole scene, don't you?" Chewning tears his hair and consults me; he is afraid of the "bawling out" tomorrow, after the rushes. Knowing that we are going to reshoot this scene many times, I give him the best advice under the circumstances: "Film twice more with the 25 mm, then the next time with the 35 mm, then with the 40 mm, and finally, follow him everywhere he goes with the two inch. That way, he'll have his choice!"[34]

Close-up shots of other performers were of little interest to a movie-maker who operated on the principle that "people come to see me." If from time to time Florey succeeded in convincing him of the dramatic necessity of including one or more shots of this nature, he always paid a price for victory.

I pointed out to him that . . . he would only have, for his editing, an establishing shot and a close-up of himself and nothing of the actress to cut in with his close-up. He gets excited and angry. What is the use of this cutting in, etc., etc. We pass on then to the next scene. Around five o'clock, he has finished and is getting ready to go home but, as if he wanted to do me a favor or do something gracious for me, he says: "Robert, since that seems to mean so much to you, take, if you wish, this close-up of my partner after I leave." And then he gave me his fawn-like and malicious smile."[35]

The lighting supervisor, Curt Courant, likewise found it a thankless task to offer technical advice that cut across the grain of the master's desires, Florey recalled.

[There was] some light to adjust, but Charlie doesn't allow [Courant] any more time; "You will have a shadow on your face when you step near the door," Courant murmurs. "I laugh at your shadow," Charlie answers. "It's natural to have some shadow, after all. Let's go, let's start. Hurry! Hurry!" But he has changed his movement and now the silhouette of the microphone stands out clearly for several seconds on the wall of the background. It is pointed out to him. "It doesn't matter to me," he says. "They will think that it's a bird, let's go, hurry up, film!" And confusion reigns because Courant is changing one of the "spots" to avoid the shadow of the microphone. "Why are you changing again?" [Chaplin] asks, more nervous. "You annoy me with all your technical tricks. Come on, hurry up!"[36]

As Florey's resentment of his ill treatment mounted, Chaplin added insult to injury by appointing a second associate director, his mild-mannered half-brother Wheeler Dryden. Since 1939, Dryden had been variously employed at the Chaplin Studio as a wardrobe keeper, secretary, assistant director, glorified gofer, and ready-to-hand whipping boy. Examples of Chaplin's abuse of Dryden during the filming of the greenhouse scene in *Monsieur Verdoux* were jotted down by the seething Florey.

"No, no, no, shut up, you silly bastard, for Christ's sake, we cut to Annabella, you don't understand anything about motion pictures. I know what I am doing, yeah, that's what I cut to, I have been in this business for 20—for 30 years, you don't think I am gaga? Oh, shut up. . . . Christ. . . . We cut to Annabella, I know goddamn well what I am doing. . . . For Christ's sake, I have been cutting this scene in my mind for the past three years. . . . I know exactly . . . then the music starts. . . . Don't talk to me."[37]

Chaplin's elevation of Dryden to a position equal to Florey's violated the spirit if not the letter of his contract with the Frenchman. In a further attempt to make Florey's contribution to the picture look unimportant, he placed his name alongside Dryden's on a screen-credit card. Only after the Screen Directors' Guild complained to him about this did he place them on separate cards. Even so, he managed to add a final drop of retributive malice by running Dryden's card first.[38]

Florey could have sued Chaplin. Instead, he elected to memorialize his experiences on *Monsieur Verdoux* in a couple of books, *Hollywood d'Hier et d'Aujourd'hui* (1948) and *Monsieur Chaplin ou Le Rire dans la Nuit* (1952), which was written in collaboration with another French writer on the cinema, Maurice Bessy.* Among his grateful readers was another ex-friend of Chaplin's, Harry d'Arrast, who had worked as a research assistant on *A Woman of Paris* and as an assistant director of *The Gold Rush*. If ever there was anyone who wished Chaplin ill, it was d'Arrast. Thus in 1967, the year before his death, he wrote a letter to

---

* Although Florey's command of English was grammatically flawless, his expression lacked style, in his discriminating opinion. He therefore preferred to write his books in French.

Florey in which he gave vent to his glee about the all-encompassing disaster that Chaplin had wrought in *A Countess from Hong Kong*. "I have never gloated over the defeat of an enemy," he asserted, "but in this case he has been so miserable with all of us that it is 'shit' cast upon the waters which is returning a hundredfold. . . . To add to my delight he has threatened to make another picture but I can't believe God can be that kind to me!" [39]

II

In the first of the scenes in which Verdoux returns to his wife—his real wife—and little boy, the boy pulls the tail of the family cat. Verdoux is shocked. "Peter," he exclaims, *"don't* pull the cat's tail. You have a cruel streak in you. I don't know where you get it." That speech was probably sarcastically echoed more than once in the private comments of Chaplin's fellow actors and staff following the cat atrocity. Later in the filming, as the comedian was holding the cat that "The Girl" brought with her to Verdoux's apartment in Paris, the creature "scratched him," Robert Florey related, "and he threw it violently. The company was dismissed, and on reassembling after the weekend, everyone was shocked and disgusted to see that the cat, rather than being replaced, had been killed and stuffed—the easier to rest in [Chaplin's] arm." [40]

Chaplin the charmer versus Chaplin the monster. A far greater contrast divides Verdoux the coldly efficient killer from Verdoux the accident-prone clown whose bungling foreshadows the law-enforcement clumsiness of Peter Sellers's Inspector Clouseau. In part, the failure of *Monsieur Verdoux* to hold together dramatically can be blamed on the helter-skelter nature of its narrative organization. The fatal reason, however, was Chaplin's inability to reconcile the violently opposing selves in his hero's personality.*

---

* Aldous Huxley, who frequently saw Chaplin socially in the 1930s and 1940s, summed up the *Monsieur Verdoux* problem as follows: "What an aesthetic mess! [Chaplin] passes from a mime about murder, which depends on *not* being taken seriously, to attempts at serious psychology . . . not conceivably a subject for comedy. One feels terribly sorry for Charlie—such talents, such a mess—in art no less than in life." David King Dunaway, *Huxley in Hollywood* (New York, 1989), pp. 227–28.

The ascription of Verdoux's murderous career to his experience of being fired as a bank clerk three years before the picture begins is the takeoff point of its political parable. Thirty-five years of loyal service to the bank had not been sufficient to protect him from being let go.* He was worried, moreover, about his young wife, Mona (Oona?), and his little boy. Like Hannah Chaplin, Mona has been disabled for years by illness, as her confinement to a wheelchair and the steel braces on her legs attest. Hence his decision to enter the "business" of "liquidating" wealthy women. As is so often the case in Chaplin's pictures, it is the trapped or crippled innocent who engages his imagination and arouses his sympathy. But what makes *Monsieur Verdoux* different, as Robert Warshow was the first to point out, is that "the crippled wife and the helpless child . . . have become formal symbols without content, expressing only an abstract belief in the moral importance of helplessness."[41] Mona is a dull and lifeless character and the boy is a mildly annoying nonentity—and when Verdoux is with them, he becomes as stuffy as the most conventional suburban husband. Only when he is on the hunt for victims does his sparkling charm emerge. As his fashion-plate clothes, impeccable homburg, and frequent telephone calls to his broker indicate, he has made a stunning success in his "business."

The camera discovers the killer clipping roses† in the garden of a villa in the south of France. He is wearing a garden smock and a jaunty beret. His mouth is pursed, his mustache is freshly waxed, and his gestures are finicky. Here is a man of exquisite sensibility. At the back of the garden is a kiln belching smoke from the fiery remains of his latest victim. Once he has finished his garden work, he will phone a series of buy orders to his broker in Paris. Presumably the funds for these purchases have come from the wife he has just disposed of.

His next excursion into evil is gripping. One afternoon, he appears at the door of another of his wives, the horse-faced, late-fiftyish Lydia Floray (Margaret Hoffman). She has not seen him for three months, she sourly reminds him. He has been in Indo-China on business, he

---

* That his own indifference to Henry Bergman's years of loyal service paralleled the bank's indifference to Verdoux's was an irony that Chaplin did not perceive.
† Only in *City Lights* does Chaplin give flowers greater prominence than he does in *Monsieur Verdoux*.

explains. "The only time I see you is when you want something," she says. With a flood of palaver and an ardent seizure of her hand, he begins to soften her. "I'm too old for that nonsense," she murmurs, coyly patting her hair and smiling. The "financial crisis" has compelled his return to France, Verdoux remarks. Taking the bait, she asks, "What crisis?" Tomorrow, he assures her, there will be a run on every bank in the country. "Fiddlesticks!" Lydia exclaims. With cynical skill, he stampedes her. Even while saying that "I must be out of my mind to do this," she allows him to hustle her off to her bank to withdraw all her money.

That night they sit in the parlor, Verdoux at the piano and Lydia in front of her strongbox and all the cash it contains. Her conviction that she has done something very foolish is lividly apparent in her staring eyes. At bedtime, they start up the stairs. Her compulsive questions about whether he has put out all the lights and locked up and the deadly quiet way in which he answers "Yes, my dear" create an atmosphere of dread. She disappears into her bedroom. Verdoux remains in the dark hallway, gazing at the full moon through an open window. "This pale Endymion hour," he says softly. Her call to him to go to bed rouses him from his poetizing. With his arms held close to his sides and his hands flat out as if they were miniature wings, he glides into her bedroom as silently as a shadow, either to stab her to death or to suffocate her. The next morning, looking as fresh as paint, he bounces down the stairs with the strongbox under his arm and phones his broker.

None of the schemes of Verdoux the clown work out properly. Within minutes of meeting the shapely matron Madame Grosnay (Isobel Elsom), who has come to his villa with the thought of renting it, he boldly comes on to her. But when the friend who has accompanied her suddenly reenters the room, he is so discomfited that he tumbles backwards out of a window. Since they are on the second floor, he might have broken his neck, had he not landed on a section of roof. Later, in Paris, Madame Grosnay refuses to see him, so he bombards her with flowers. Finally, she consents to see him. In a preliminary phone call, he protests that he is madly in love with her with a vehemence that calls to mind Joan Barry's description of Chaplin's seduction technique. Luck, however, is not with him. His wedding to this fancy lady turns into a fiasco from which he is forced to flee, thanks to the unexpected appearance of the vulgarian with the braying laugh, Annabella Bonheur (Martha Raye), to whom he has been married for quite some time.

Earlier attempts on his part to murder Annabella had ended miserably. In a parody of the drowning scene in Dreiser's *An American Tragedy*,* he had taken her out in a rowboat on a remote lake with malice aforethought, only to end up in the water himself. A plan to add poison to the wine he selects to serve Annabella one evening goes completely awry when the maid finds the bottle of poison he has placed on the washbowl in the bathroom and, on the assumption that the liquid in it is peroxide, uses it to lighten her hair. After accidentally breaking the bottle, she replaces it with a fresh bottle of peroxide. Verdoux, in his ignorance of the switch, pours virtually the entire bottle into Annabella's wine. The upshot is that the maid's hair falls out and dumbbell Annabella finds the wine tasty. But when Verdoux realizes that he himself has inadvertently drunk a glass, he imagines that he is dying and goes into spasms that continue until a doctor pumps out his stomach.

The sad truth about Verdoux the clown is that he is rarely more than mildly amusing and sometimes downright boring. Robert Florey's sense of Chaplin as a man who was forcing himself to create situations at which people might laugh is supported time and again by the forced quality of the picture. By a very wide margin, then, the best moments in this "comedy of murders" are the scant handful of unfunny scenes in which suavely self-controlled killer Verdoux is at the center of the action. Each of them is suspenseful in its own way, but the most suspenseful of the lot takes place on the night when he leads "The Girl" back to his apartment.

Joe Breen had warned Chaplin against making The Girl a prostitute. The task of obfuscating this obvious fact about her compelled him to make a number of dialogue changes and may also have inspired him to hire Marilyn Nash for the part. An intelligent, conventionally good-looking young woman who had originally planned to study medicine,

---

* In the years preceding Dreiser's formal request to join the Communist Party, he and Chaplin often attended the same parties (including at least one function at the Soviet consulate in Los Angeles) and a fellow feeling developed between the two men. At the novelist's funeral at Forest Lawn's Church of the Recessional on January 3, 1946, Chaplin read one of Dreiser's poems, "The Road I Came."

Nash had a wholesome, college-girl personality far removed from standard images of streetwalkers. The downside of her candidacy was that she was an awkward and self-conscious actress. To make her faults less glaring, Chaplin spent many hours with her in special rehearsal.

Verdoux has concocted the poison with which he hopes to kill Annabella Bonheur. Before making the attempt, however, he wants to try out the potion on a stranger. While walking through Paris streets on a rainy night, he spots The Girl standing out of the downpour in a doorway. After passing her, he pauses. A mad gleam comes into his eye. Perhaps he can involve this young woman in his lethal experiment. He turns back to the doorway and engages her in conversation. Persuading her to accompany him to his apartment is but the work of a minute.

On helping her out of her coat, Verdoux discovers that she has been sheltering a kitten inside it. She had found the poor little thing, all cold and wet, in the doorway, she explains, and then impulsively asks, "I don't suppose you have a little milk you could give it?" The incident testifies to Chaplin's lasting admiration of the passage in "Chaplinesque" in which Hart Crane had spoken of loneliness and deprivation and love:

> For we can still love the world, who find
> A famished kitten on the step, and know
> Recesses for it from the fury of the street . . .

As Verdoux is pouring milk into a saucer and putting it on the floor for the kitten, he brings up the subject of The Girl's own predicament. While the ambiguity of his comments managed to quiet Joe Breen's objections to the scene, it is nonetheless clear what Verdoux thinks his guest has become. "To be out on a night like this, you're an optimist," he remarks. That she is "up against it" he has no doubt. "Your faculties of observation are remarkable," says The Girl. "Indeed," he says sardonically.

His guess is that she is just out of a hospital or a jail, but she refuses to give him a straight answer. "What do you want to know for?" she asks. To her surprise, Verdoux tells her that he wants to help her and that he asks nothing in return. She breaks down and admits that this has been her first day out of jail, after serving three months for petty larceny. He responds by inviting her to stay for a bite of supper, and she accepts.

He also declares that he wants to adopt the kitten she has brought with her.

Apparently, his show of concern has been a part of his plan to kill her. After serving her scrambled eggs on the table in the sitting room and pouring her a glass of wine laced with poison, he returns to the kitchen with the bottle in hand, saying that he has forgotten the toast. Out of her sight, he puts away the poisoned bottle, picks up another, unadulterated bottle, and, on returning to the table, fills his own glass with wine. "*Voilà*," he says, and urges her to begin. Beneath his smooth-as-silk cordiality, she detects something phony. "You're funny," she says. "Why?" he asks. "I don't know," she says. As she begins eating—but not drinking—he stares at her wineglass and drums his fingers on the table. To encourage her to drink, he takes a sip from his own glass. While this causes her to pick up her glass, she merely transfers it to the other hand and puts it down again. She continues to eat, and he continues to stare in silence at her glass.

Finally, he asks about the book she has brought with her. It's by Schopenhauer, she tells him—the philosopher whom Chaplin had been reading off and on for more than thirty years. "Have you read his treatise on suicide?" Verdoux asks. The question kicks off an animated if cloudy discussion of life, death, women, and love. The misogyny in the killer's heart—and in Chaplin's—emerges in his confession that he loves women but does not admire them, because of their habit of betrayal. Furthermore, he says, "Once a woman betrays a man, she despises him. In spite of his goodness and position, she will give him up for someone inferior, if that someone is, shall we say, more attractive." (Was Chaplin thinking specifically here of Paulette Goddard's unfaithfulness to him?) The Girl refutes his cynicism by citing the example of her own devotion. She herself had been married, but her husband had died while she was in jail. Due to wounds suffered in the war, he had been a hopeless invalid. But that was precisely why she had married him. He needed her, she says, as a child might have. This man, she fiercely adds, had been like a "religion" to her. "I'd have killed for him!" So saying, she at last lifts her wineglass toward her lips.

Verdoux's reaction is lightning quick. "Pardon me, I believe there's a little cork in that wine. Let me get you another glass." He takes the deadly potion from her hand, places it on the sideboard, and pours her a fresh glass from the unadulterated bottle. While she is finishing her meal, he sits pensively, completely enveloped in a private world. Suddenly he bursts out laughing. "A penny for your thoughts," says The Girl. "Oh, no," says the killer.

In *City Lights* and other Chaplin pictures, the moral center is located in the helpless figure. In *Monsieur Verdoux*, it resides in the person who loves the helpless figure—which is to say, in Chaplin himself. But if Verdoux is a projection of Chaplin, so is the Schopenhauer-fancying young woman whose life the killer has spared. She, too, has been devoted to an invalid; she, too, would kill for love; and she, too, will achieve wealth—as the mistress of a munitions manufacturer. And as her attendance at Verdoux's trial implies, she shares his belief that business is murder.

12

In *Monsieur Verdoux*'s recapitulation of history, modern-day capitalism crashes again in the mid-1930s. Sweeping through a kaleidoscope of disasters, the camera moves from a stock-exchange floor in pandemonium to a banner headline in the French Communist newspaper *L'Humanité* about bank failures and riots in the streets, to an investor jumping out of a tall building, and to another investor aiming a pistol at his head. Verdoux desperately tries to prevent foreclosure of the mortgage he has been forced to take out on his wife and son's home by phoning his broker and instructing him to sell every stock he owns—only to be told that his holdings have been wiped out. Verdoux is horror-stricken. Newsreel clips follow, rerecalling the drunk-with-power exultation of Hitler and Mussolini and the battle-readiness of awesomely long files of German troops.

The camera picks up Verdoux once again. He is seated in a sidewalk café in Paris, reading a newspaper with a headline story about Nazi bombardments of Spanish Loyalists. Like Charlie after his release from jail in *City Lights*, he looks old and broken, although he is still nattily dressed. For reasons that are not explained, his wife and son are both dead. When the police who are looking for him finally show up in the right place at the right time, he deliberately allows himself to be captured. Having nothing left to live for, he is ready to die.

Before being sentenced, he arises in the courtroom and, instead of speaking in anguish about the monstrous criminality for which he has been convicted, he arraigns atomic America, although not by name, as a criminal nation. The equivalent of his point of view could be read every day in the postwar 1940s in the editorial columns of the Communist press worldwide. For thirty-five years, he begins in his most mincing tones, he had loyally served his employer, but had then been forced "to go into business for myself." "As for being a mass killer," he rhetorically asks, "does not the world encourage it? Is it not building weapons of mass destruction for the sole purpose of mass killing? Has it not blown unsuspecting women and little children to pieces? And done it very scientifically. As a mass killer, I am an amateur by comparison."

Back in his cell, he enlarges upon his anti-American innuendos for the benefit of a newspaperman who visits him. "You'll have to admit," the newsman says, "crime doesn't pay." "No, sir, not in a small way," Verdoux says. "To be successful in anything, one must be well organized." The reporter asks him for a story about himself as a "tragic example of a life of crime." "I don't see how anyone can be an example in these criminal times," Verdoux replies. "Well, you certainly are," says the reporter, "robbing and murdering people." "That's business," says Verdoux. "Well, other people don't do 'business' that way," the reporter protests. "That's the history of many a big business," Verdoux insists, "—wars, conflict, it's all business. One murder makes a villain; millions a hero. Numbers sanctify."

13

Leftist reviewers loved it. This film, James Agee gushed in *The Nation*, is "one of the few indispensable works" of a time in which "the bare problem of survival" has become paramount. In an editorial in left-liberal *PM*, the New York daily newspaper edited by Ralph Ingersoll, Max Lerner called on moviegoers to forget about the political beliefs of Chaplin the man and simply judge his art. "As for myself, I am content to take him as an artist and to face the criticisms of our institutions that his art implies," Lerner wrote, in sublime disregard of the fact that the "art" of *Monsieur Verdoux* was grounded in the politics of Chaplin the man. "What he did or did not do about the war, what he thinks of

Russia or Communism: these are his affairs, not ours," said Lerner. Writing in a new Communist magazine called *Mainstream*, Arnaud d'Usseau argued that Chaplin's placement of the "moral burden" of Verdoux's crimes "entirely on society" was brilliantly appropriate, for his killings are "a comment on those values our society celebrates."[42]

These voices, however, were overwhelmed by the negative commentaries. "In *Monsieur Verdoux*," Howard Barnes wrote in the *New York Herald-Tribune*, "Charles Chaplin has composed what he likes to term a 'comedy of murders' with a woeful lack of humor, melodrama, or dramatic taste." John McCarten, writing in *The New Yorker*, declared that Chaplin had filled *Monsieur Verdoux*

full of cloudy observations, . . . apparently in an effort to prove, among other things, that a man who kills women for money is more sinned against than sinning. . . . It would take a psychologist to figure out why Mr. Chaplin considered the career of M. Landru, the famous French Bluebeard, the proper theme for a comedy, or why he tried to justify that lethal gentleman's activities on the ground that they were inspired by the twisted economic state of the modern world. It takes no particular insight, however, to determine that in *Monsieur Verdoux* Mr. Chaplin has succeeded only along sartorial lines, cutting quite a figure in a variety of elegant get-ups.

Chaplin's "broadsides of indictment against society (particularly the ruthlessness of business)," said the *Christian Science Monitor*'s reviewer, "become merely petty and meaningless expressions of hatred, contempt, and personal bitterness."[43]

The response of the public was commensurately harsh, beginning with the scattered hissing by the audience that attended the premiere at the Broadway Theater in New York on April 11, 1947. In its third week at the Broadway, the picture took in a mere $18,000; the following week the take slipped to $15,000; and when it sank to $12,000 in the fifth week, the theater manager closed out the run. Chaplin thereupon withdrew the picture from circulation and rereleased it the following September, accompanied by a drumfire of challenging ads ("Chaplin changes! Can you?"). Yet when he resignedly took it off the market again in mid-1949, the grand total of its domestic earnings came to a paltry $325,000. Abroad, the picture fared considerably better. Only in Paris, however, where an anti-American intelligentsia exercised a potent influence on public taste, did *Monsieur Verdoux* set box-office records.[44]

14

On February 4, 1947, two months before the release of *Monsieur Verdoux*, the FBI arrested Gerhart Eisler on charges of passport fraud and incarcerated him on Ellis Island. Two days later, Chairman J. Parnell Thomas, Republican of New Jersey, gaveled to order the first meeting of the House Committee on Un-American Activities (HUAC) of the new session of Congress. The committee's chief investigator, Robert Stripling, immediately called Eisler to the stand. Like Verdoux in the courtroom, the veteran conspirator was defiant and unrepentant. "I am not going to take the stand," he told Stripling. In response to his demand that he be permitted to deliver a three-minute speech, Chairman Thomas promised him this courtesy, but insisted that prior to his remarks he would have to be sworn and questioned. "That is where you are mistaken," Eisler cried. "I have to do nothing. A political prisoner has to do nothing." A shouting match with Thomas ensued, at the end of which the committee cited Eisler for contempt and returned him to Ellis Island.

Eleven days later, a freshman member of the committee, Richard M. Nixon, devoted his maiden speech in Congress to a demand that the full House find Eisler guilty of contempt. Eisler is "a seasoned agent of the Communist International," Nixon began, "who [has] been shuttling back and forth between Moscow and the United States from as early as 1933, to direct and mastermind the political and espionage activities of the Communist Party in the United States." Far from being a grateful refugee, said Nixon, Eisler was "an arrogant and defiant enemy of our government" whose "criminal acts" included the forging of official documents, perjury, and failure to register as an enemy alien. Except for New York's overtly pro-Communist congressman, Vito Marcantonio, the entire House voted in favor of the contempt citation.

Eventually, Eisler wound up in federal court, along with two other Communists who had incurred contempt citations, Eugene Dennis and

Leon Josephson. Chaplin and other notables urged that their trials be postponed, "in order," as the *Daily Worker* reported, "that they may have proper time to prepare their case and in order to avoid undue prejudice against them at a time when red-baiting hysteria is so violent." Their pleas went unheeded, and Dennis and Josephson went to prison for a year. Eisler was wilier. He stowed away on the Polish freighter *Batory*. Upon arriving in East Germany, he was promptly awarded a professorship at the University of Leipzig.[45]

His brother Hanns's hour of reckoning with American authorities came around in September 1947. HUAC accused him of perjury and asked the Immigration and Naturalization Service to deport him. An INS hearing was duly held and a deportation warrant against Eisler and his wife was issued in February 1948. Chaplin fought these proceedings every step of the way. In November 1947, he and Oona sent a cablegram to Pablo Picasso, asking him to lead a group of artists to the American embassy in Paris in a protest demonstration against the "outrageous deportation proceedings against Hanns Eisler." Chaplin also requested Picasso to send him a copy of their protest statement so that he could publicize it in Los Angeles. A month later, he joined Albert Einstein, Thomas Mann, and eleven other prominent artists and scientists in petitioning President Truman's attorney general, Tom Clark, to drop the effort to deport the Eislers. Once the deportation warrant was issued, Chaplin promised to provide the Eislers with financial support if the U.S. government would allow them to leave the country voluntarily, rather than under the stigma of a warrant. The government agreed to do so—in exchange for the Eislers' written promise never to attempt to return to the United States. Once this stipulation was fulfilled, the couple left the country for Czechoslovakia.[46]

The question of deporting Chaplin was raised on the floor of the U.S. Senate on March 7, 1947. Why is it, asked Senator William Langer, that "a man like Charlie Chaplin, with his communistic leanings, with his unsavory record of law-breaking, or rape, or the debauchery of American girls 16 and 17 years of age, remains [in this country]?" Six months later, Parnell Thomas did not forget Chaplin when he sent out subpoenas to more than three dozen Hollywood figures whom he wanted to testify before his committee. In the expectation of receiving the subpoena, Chaplin had already sent Chairman Thomas a sarcastic telegram, suggesting that in order for him to be completely *au courant* with his—Chaplin's—way of thinking, he should "view carefully my latest production *Monsieur Verdoux*. It is against war and the futile slaughter of our youth. I trust you will find its humane message distasteful. While you are preparing your engraved subpoena I will give you a hint on where I stand. I am not a Communist. I am a peace-monger." In addition to reflecting Chaplin's arrogance, the telegram was a classic example of the sort of propaganda that the Soviets wanted fellow travelers and covert Communists to manufacture. Thomas and his confreres, however, did not in the end call him to Washington, for reasons they did not explain.[47]

15

The opportunity to grill Chaplin that HUAC passed by had already been seized by newspapermen, at the press conference he held in the Grand Ballroom of the Hotel Gotham in New York on April 14, three days after the stunningly hostile reaction of the audience at the premiere of *Monsieur Verdoux*.

United Artists officials were wary about the comedian's decision not to restrict the conference to three reporters, as originally planned. In the words of *Motion Picture Daily*'s well-informed columnist Red Kann, the fear at United Artists was that in an "en masse cross-fire" Chaplin would "have to take on all comers including those who might be after answers as to why he never became an American citizen and his version of his alleged lack of cooperation in the war effort [*i.e.*, his refusal to entertain troops overseas or to help sell war bonds]." But Chaplin, said Kann, had assured the worrywarts that he could "handle it."[48]

When he entered the Grand Ballroom, every seat was taken and people were standing in doorways and on the seats encircling the balcony. Apparently, every major newspaper and magazine in the country had a representative on hand. Except for the moment when James Agee of *Time* lashed out in an angry, barely coherent attack on his fellow reporters and on "a . . . country where those people are thought well of," the next hour offered Chaplin unmitigated discomfiture. Inflamed by what seemed to them to be prevaricating answers, his inquisitors kept coming at him with loaded questions.

Chaplin: Thank you, ladies and gentlemen of the press. I am not going to waste your time. I should say—proceed with the butchery. If there's any question anybody wants to ask, I'm here, fire away at this old gray head.

Question: There have been several stories in the past accusing you more or less of being a fellow traveler, a Communist sympathizer. Could you define your present political beliefs, sir?

Chaplin: Well, I think that is very difficult to do these days to define anything politically. There are so many generalities, and life is becoming so technical that if you step off the curb with your left foot, they accuse you of being a Communist. But, I have no political persuasions whatsoever. I've never belonged to any political party in my life, and I have never voted in my life! Does that answer your question?

Question: Not precisely. Could you answer a direct question? Are you a Communist—

Chaplin: I am not a Communist!

Question: A Communist sympathizer was the question.

Chaplin: A Communist sympathizer? That has to be qualified again. I don't know what you mean by a "Communist sympathizer." I'd say this —that during the war, I sympathized very much with Russia because I believe that she was holding the front, and for that I have a memory and I feel that I owe her thanks. I think that she helped contribute a considerable amount of fighting and dying to bring victory to the Allies. In that sense I am sympathetic.

Question: Mr. Chaplin, did you intend to create sympathy for the character of Monsieur Verdoux?

Chaplin: No, I intended to create a pity for all humanity under certain drastic circumstances—in times of stress, I think—in catastrophe— conditions bring out the worst in humanity and I've been intensifying that in this picture, and I wanted to show that any time we have a depression or any time that we have a natural catastrophe, that it brings out these cancerous conditions—like the figure of Verdoux, which to me is not—is a figure of pity and tragic from the point that you ask me now.

Question: Shouldn't there be somebody in a vehicle of entertainment for whom the public has sympathy?

Chaplin: As for sympathy, I think—unless I'm mistaken—I intended that the feeling should be that you have a sympathy for the whole human race. I think that's the doctrine of Christianity. My motive—if there is any sympathy for Verdoux, it is to understand crime and the nature of crime. I'd sooner understand it and the nature of it than condemn it.

. . .

Question: Mr. Chaplin, according to a report from Hollywood, you are a personal friend of Hanns Eisler, the composer?

Chaplin: I am. I am very proud of the fact.

Question: Are you aware of the fact that his brother is a Soviet agent, so attested by—

Chaplin: I know nothing about his brother!

Question: Do you think Mr. Eisler is a Communist?

Chaplin: I don't know anything about that. I don't know whether he is a Communist or not. I know he is a fine artist and a great musician and a very sympathetic friend.

Question: Would it make any difference to you if he were a Communist?

Chaplin: No, it wouldn't.

Question: A Soviet agent, as he's been accused of being—

Chaplin: I don't know what you know of—a Soviet agent? I don't know —I don't—amplify that. Do you mean a spy?

Question: Yes.

Chaplin: It certainly would—if he were a spy, that would make a great deal of difference.

Question: If that were proven to you.

Chaplin: Of course. If anybody treacherous to the country you are living in—of course, naturally.

[Questioner asks Chaplin to compare Russian expansionism following World War II to German expansionism before it.]

Chaplin: Now, when we're getting my opinion on political matters, and on military matters, I'm not going to be embroiled, I'm not touting for any ideology or any schism that exists. I don't think it is polite of me to do so, and I'm not going to do so. My status is that of a motion picture comedian, artist and producer of motion pictures, and I'm not going any further than that. If you are talking about the war effort and whether I am a Communist or not, that's something else. But now, you want my opinion—my political opinion—that, I think, I keep to myself whatever they are.

. . .

Question: Mr. Chaplin, I disagree with what you said a few minutes ago that President Roosevelt or General Marshall ever believed in a second front in 1942. Just where did you find that information? Eisenhower's diary, or none of those—no documents yet have shown that they were in agreement with you.

Chaplin: Well, if you disagree, then you disagree.

Question: Not me, I say you said that General Marshall and—

Chaplin: I know. I'm not going to amplify it any more. I've read it somewhere.

Question: Mr. Chaplin, do you share M. Verdoux's conviction that our contemporary civilization is making mass murderers of us?

Chaplin: Yes.

Question: Would you enlarge on that a little bit? I felt in the picture that that was the most striking line and I would like to have you enlarge on that.

Chaplin: Well, all my life I have always loathed and abhorred violence. Now I think these weapons of destruction—I don't think I'm alone in saying this, it's a cliché by now—that the atomic bomb is the most horrible invention of mankind, and I think it is being proven so every moment.

. . .

Question: Mr. Chaplin, your pictures carry a message—are you going to continue to do pictures with a message?

Chaplin: Yes. They have always been for the underdog and with great pity and understanding—I've always been cognizant of that. I think pity is a great attribute. Civilization—without it—we would have no civilization.

Question: Mr. Chaplin, have you ever used the proceeds of your films overseas, abroad, for resistance work and for the alleviation of poverty and for—well, the alleviation of poverty of the people abroad. For example, in France—did the proceeds of *The Great Dictator*, were the proceeds of *The Great Dictator* used for the salvation of the people in D.P. camps, political refugees?

Chaplin: That I don't know. I know that we contribute to foreign uh-uh-uh charities.

Question: Oh, I didn't mean in that sense, sir. I mean, for example, *The Great Dictator* had a definite political *leit motif.* I mean—I think you will agree to that—and it certainly wanted to lift the human being a little higher on the pedestal than he is right now, but I know you made some reference that seventy per cent of the proceeds of your films have been received from abroad. Now what I wanted to know, sir, was whether or not any of these proceeds were used for humanitarian work, right there in the countries where they were shown and where they were so sorely needed.

Chaplin: I don't know. . . . Uh-uh-uh we loaned the picture to the military staff when they wanted it. What they did about it I don't know. In Germany and other places: oh yes, the picture was loaned out—when the American Army wanted it, they got it.[49]

In believing that he could "handle" the press Chaplin had badly miscalculated. His dancing around the word "sympathizer," his denial of any knowledge that Hanns Eisler was a Communist, and his unwillingness to admit that he was mistaken in saying that President Roosevelt and General Marshall had favored a second front created an image of mendacity. The Gotham confrontation was a public relations disaster for him.

16

As the 1940s wound down and the Cold War grew colder, Chaplin refused to lower his politically radical profile. A *Los Angeles Times* photo of him writing a check for $1,000 for Henry Wallace's peace-mongering, Communist-infiltrated campaign for the presidency in 1948, the public statement he made in April 1949 in support of the Paris meeting of the Communist-front World Congress for Peace, and his endorsement of the Mexico City meeting the following September of the Communist-front American Continental Congress on World Peace were gestures that gave the lie to his press-conference statement that "I'm not touting for any ideology of any schism that exists." They also provided further ammunition to the newspaper columnists and congressmen who wanted him deported.

As a moviemaker, however, he temporarily forswore his promise that he would go on putting out pictures with a message. Instead, he fastened on the idea of a memory picture about the life of a faded star of the English music halls on the eve of World War I. A crisis in the affairs of United Artists heavily influenced this switch in plans.

Whenever he and Mary Pickford got together for the purpose of reaching an agreement as to what to do about the company, they usually fought. While they both insisted that their antagonism was purely a matter of differing business judgments, it was in fact *"very* personal," in the informed opinion of Vitalis Chalif, one of Pickford's lawyers and her representative on the United Artists board.

> They were both strong-willed, spoiled, physically little people. And when they became angry, they became actors. They would storm, rave and rant, although no matter how heated the argument might become, [Pickford] never used vulgar language. [Did Chalif mean to imply that Chaplin did?] She was Irish and very emotional and, like Chaplin, never could forget her early poverty.

Out of Pickford's hearing, Chaplin referred to her as "the Iron Butterfly," while she privately called him "the dirty old man." Even compatible partners, however, would have had their tempers tried by the economic squeeze that the company found itself in in the late 1940s.[50]

The amount of money earned by Hollywood pictures in foreign markets was declining. The revival of the European film industry, the imposition of import quotas, and high taxes all figured in this phenomenon. Meanwhile, movie attendance in the United States was shrinking at an alarming rate, as more and more Americans moved away from the central cities and their concentrations of movie theaters and took up other forms of leisure-time activity. For United Artists, these developments raised the specter of bankruptcy. At the end of 1947, the company was half a million dollars in debt, and its indebtedness in 1948 was projected to double. Chaplin and Pickford quarreled bitterly about what they should do. Arrangements that would have enabled one or the other to be bought out of the company failed to win their common consent, and takeover offers by outsiders died on the vine in the heat of their bickering. Perhaps the only thing about which there was no disagreement between the warring stars was that it would certainly help if Chaplin came up with a winner in his next picture.[51]

One of Chaplin's early thoughts about *Footlights,* as *Limelight* was originally called, was that he might film at least a portion of it in London. So that he could scout out this possibility and at the same time show Oona the scenes of his youth, he made plans in February 1948 for a visit to England in the spring. He and Oona would sail on the *Queen*

Elizabeth and stay at the Savoy. That the Immigration and Naturalization Service did not respond as readily as it had in the past to his application for a reentry permit was an indication of trouble ahead.

17

In April an INS officer finally telephoned him and requested that he come to the Federal Building for an interview. The date proposed was inconvenient for Chaplin, so he in turn proposed another. The officer accepted the alternative date—and as a further courtesy to the comedian offered to send the interviewer to his home. John Boyd, the executive assistant to the INS commissioner, appeared on Summit Drive shortly thereafter, accompanied by an FBI man and a stenographer. The three of them were conducted to the sun porch, where Chaplin and his lawyer, Pat Millikan, were awaiting them.

Boyd raised—and after a fashion Chaplin answered—a series of questions about the comedian's association with various groups that the FBI had reason to believe were Communist fronts, including the New Workers Party ("I am sure I am not a member of anything," said Chaplin), the Russian-American Society for Medical Aid to Russia, the National Council of American-Soviet Friendship ("I think, yes, maybe, yes . . . it was one of those things that perhaps went on during the war"), the Artists' Front to Win the War, and the Screen Actors Guild ("I think I have to belong to an Actors Guild in order to work"). In regard to Chaplin's friendships, his interrogator asked him about Harry Bridges ("I think I met him once," he replied with disingenuous vagueness),* Hanns Eisler ("I met him socially, through other people"), and officials

---

* Later on in life, his recollection of this friendship would become miraculously clearer. In the late fall of 1940, the news that *The Great Dictator* was about to be released brought a surge of pro-Nazi crank letters to the Chaplin Studio that spoke of stink bombs in the seats, revolver shots at the screen, and riots in front of the theater where the picture would open. Chaplin at first thought of going to the police, but decided instead to invite Harry Bridges to dinner. "I told him frankly my reason for wanting to see him," Chaplin related. "I said: 'If I could invite, say, twenty or thirty of your longshoremen to my opening, and have them scattered amongst the audience, then if any of these pro-Nazi fellows started a rumpus, your folks might gently stamp on their toes before anything got seriously going.'" Bridges laughed and told him in effect to relax. "I don't think it will come to that, Charlie," he said. *My Autobiography*, pp. 396–97.

at the Soviet consulate in Los Angeles ("I think I have been one time. I remember practically the whole of Hollywood there"). When asked whether officers of the Soviet consulate had ever been his guests on Summit Drive, he took refuge in amnesia ("I don't recall. You see, we get a lot of people. I entertain lots of these consulates [*sic*], ambassadors, and Chinese and so forth. They all come up here, you know, because I am pretty much of an international figure, but not much").

Questions about his benefactions were also on Boyd's agenda.

Q: Have you ever made any donations to the Communist Party?
A: I am sure, never, not to my—I am sure.
Q: Hedda Hopper, Hollywood columnist, in her column December 27, 1943, stated, "From things I have learned, Charlie Chaplin contributed $25,000 to the Communist cause and $100 to the Red Cross." What have you to say about that, Mr. Chaplin?
A: That is a complete lie. . . . We make our yearly thing to the Red Cross and have done so throughout the years. Same thing with the buying of war bonds and everything. I bought half a million dollars' worth of war bonds.

When asked for his views about Communism as a way of life, Chaplin talked of peace, and implied that the United States was obstructing it:

Frankly, I don't know anything about the Communist way of life. I must say that, but I must say this, I don't see why we can't have peace with Russia. Their way of life—I am not interested in their ideology, I assure you. I assure you. I don't know whether you believe me or not, but I am not. I am interested to the point where—they say they want peace. I don't see why we can't have peace here. I don't see why we can't have trade relationships and [other] ameliorated matters and so forth and avoid a world war.

Yet when asked for his "reaction to the way Czechoslovakia was taken over by the Soviets," the peace-monger somehow failed to perceive brutal aggression:

Frankly, I don't know very much about the situation. I am very ignorant on the subject. From what I read in the papers, I still maintain I don't think Russia has done a damn thing. That is my personal belief. What is it they have done in handling the thing? No soldiers were there. There was no bloodshed. . . . I frankly believe the press is trying to start and create a war with Russia, and I wholeheartedly disapprove of it.[52]

At the conclusion of the interview, Boyd indicated to Chaplin that his reentry permit would be granted—but that before it was issued, he would have to sign the stenographer's transcript of the interrogation. Interestingly enough, Chaplin's lawyer advised him not to comply with this stipulation unless he was absolutely determined to go to England. Upon reconsideration, the comedian decided against making the trip. Did Millikan fear that by signing the transcript Chaplin would have exposed himself to the risk of perjury charges? It would seem likely that he did. For in listening to the questions put to his client, Millikan could only have concluded that the FBI had accumulated a rather large file on Chaplin, against which the INS could measure the truthfulness of a good many of his answers. Millikan may also have assumed that the FBI's investigation of Chaplin was ongoing.

This assumption was correct. The Bureau's Los Angeles office continued to investigate Chaplin for another year and a half. On October 7, 1949, however, an agent informed J. Edgar Hoover that "no new information of value has been obtained," and he recommended that the Chaplin internal security issue be closed. One month later, a Truman appointee at the Justice Department intervened in the matter. Assistant Attorney General Alexander M. Campbell requested that the Bureau "check its file to see if there is any information therein which could be used in a trial to establish that Chaplin was a member of the Communist Party or had donated funds to the Communist Party itself." Hoover bucked this request westward to Los Angeles on December 22. On the basis of the negative report he received five days later, the director informed the attorney general's office that "there are no witnesses available who could offer testimony that Chaplin had been a member of the Communist Party in the past, is now a member, or that he has contributed funds to the Communist Party."*

---

* Paul Crouch, it should be borne in mind, did not offer the INS his lengthy testimony about Chaplin's affiliation with CPUSA until October 1952.

There matters stood until the summer of 1950, when the former managing editor of the *Daily Worker*, Louis Budenz, told an FBI interviewer in New York that Chaplin was a "concealed Communist." Budenz further accused him of belonging to a host of Communist-front organizations and of contributing money to a number of them. After six months of hesitation about acting on this testimony, Hoover ordered Los Angeles to reopen its investigation of Chaplin once again. Doubtless to his disappointment but probably not to his surprise, nothing came of his order, except a ludicrously weak report in April 1951 that made no attempt to conceal the investigating agents' profound disbelief in the usefulness of pursuing the Chaplin case any further.[53]

By that time, too, Chaplin had muffled his political voice. The sneering anti-Americanism of *Monsieur Verdoux* had cost him dearly in revenues and goodwill. Nevertheless, he had defiantly persisted in expressing his views, thereby abetting the Soviets' propaganda game. What finally gave him pause was the cumulative effect on the American mind of the back-to-back nightmares of 1949–50, in which Mao's Red Army conquered the whole of mainland China, the Soviets exploded an atomic bomb, Alger Hiss was convicted of perjury, Klaus Fuchs confessed to having passed top secret atomic information to the Soviets, and Julius and Ethel Rosenberg and other Americans in their atom spy ring—FELLOW COUNTRYMEN was the KGB code for them— were arrested. Half a decade after total victory in a global war, the United States found itself facing "an unprecedented threat to its continuance," as Edward A. Shils of the University of Chicago would observe in *The Torment of Secrecy* (1956). And while real enemies were endangering the nation, waves of paranoia were agitating it. Some Americans saw conspiracy everywhere. Blacklisting, illegal snooping, and other deplorable practices arose and demagogues prospered. The crude formulations that obsessed Senator Joseph McCarthy, Senator Patrick McCarran, *et al.*, were "mirror images," in Professor Shils's words, of the polemics of Communist spokesmen in the 1930s and 1940s—or of Monsieur Verdoux, for that matter. In an atmosphere of mounting ugliness, Chaplin prudently decided to refrain—temporarily—from further "peacemongering."[54]

I 4

A KING, CONDEMNED TO EXILE

As Calvero, the washed-up clown, with Claire Bloom in Limelight *(1952).*

LIMELIGHT possessed him with a special intensity. For the first and only time in his career, his advance preparations included the composition of a two-part "novel" about the backgrounds of the two main characters.

In the midst of these labors, he described the picture that had taken shape in his mind to a steadfast admirer, Richard Lauterbach, who was writing a hero-worshipping piece on "The Whys of Chaplin's Appeal" for the *New York Times Magazine.** "It will have music, dancing, humor, pity—everything but the tramp," Lauterbach reported. "The story concerns the attempted comeback of an aging English music-hall comic who falls in love with a young dancer. He has been on the top, but feels he is losing his touch and is afraid he can no longer make audiences laugh." While the piece was reasonably accurate, Lauterbach might have been able to make it more interesting had Chaplin been willing to respond candidly to questions about his autobiographical intentions, instead of deflecting them with the remark that "everything is autobiographical, but don't make too much of that." Not until the triple premiere of *Limelight* on October 23, 1952, at the Odeon Theater in Leicester Square, London, and the Astor and Trans-Lux theaters in New York would audiences realize that the picture was strewn with references to Charlie Chaplin.[1]

Thus a photograph of Chaplin hangs above the mantel in the aging comic's rooming-house parlor. From the faded posters in his possession that date from the days of his top billing, it can be seen that he used to be known as "the tramp comedian." And his very name, Calvero, with its combination of "vero" with three of the letters in "Chaplin," proclaims him to be the true Chaplin. The proposition that Calvero is indeed Chaplin is underscored by such further details as his old-fashioned button shoes, his left-handed violin playing, and his gently mocking description of himself to the young dancer, Terry Ambrose, as an "old sinner" who has had five wives.

In a clever public relations maneuver aimed at demonstrating to the world that in spite of all the scandalous stories in the press about his lack of morals he was actually a family man, Chaplin bestowed parts in the picture on five of his children and one of his half brothers. This move, too, had the effect of thickening its autobiographical texture. Handsome, twenty-six-year-old Sydney appears as the young composer, Neville, who falls in love with Terry and tries to woo her away from Calvero. Twenty-seven-year-old Charles Chaplin, Jr., is the policeman in the "Death of Columbine" ballet in which Terry makes her come-

---

* Lauterbach was an editor of *Life* and, if Louis Budenz can be believed, a Communist. At the time of his unexpected death from polio, he was at work on a biography of Chaplin.

back. Wheeler Dryden is the doctor who attends Terry after her suicide attempt and surfaces again as one of the clowns in the "Columbine" ballet. Three of Chaplin's children by Oona—seven-year-old Geraldine, five-year-old Michael, and two-year-old Josephine—figure in the street scene at the start of the picture. Even Oona makes an appearance, as a stand-in for Terry in carefully contrived long shots.

For the vitally important role of Terry, Chaplin recruited an outsider. Yet the twenty-year-old English actress he selected would cause many Chaplin fans to think at once of Oona. For "at that period of my life," Claire Bloom would later affirm, "I bore . . . an extraordinary resemblance to [Chaplin's] wife." [2]

2

As the child of a suburban London family whose life together was severely disrupted by World War II and then broken beyond repair by her disenchanted father, Bloom still cherished a girlhood dream of deliverance from unhappiness through the intervention of a fairy godfather. In *Limelight*, she realized in the course of the filming, she was acting out that dream. "Inherent" in the film, she later wrote, was "the dream of the fairy godfather who comes to look after the ailing girl, who heals her with his loving presence, then steps aside for her to assume her glorious role in the world." This dream "was so rooted in my real life," Bloom averred, that "the youthful crudities of my performance seemed to me overshadowed by my fervor and conviction in the role." Speaking even more personally, she confessed that upon meeting Chaplin she abandoned the "little loyalty I had left for the natural father who had disappointed me, and adopted, on the spot, the father I felt I'd had every right to expect: a father brilliant, worldly, charming, handsome, rich, and strong." [3]

The number of superlatively fine actors and actresses on the English stage in the late 1940s was remarkable. Nevertheless, Bloom's emergence from dramatic obscurity was swift. At Stratford she played Perdita in *The Winter's Tale* and Ophelia opposite Paul Scofield's Hamlet. John Gielgud, the director and star of Christopher Fry's *The Lady's Not for Burning*, made a place in the company for this shy, intelligent, strikingly lovely newcomer, as he likewise did for a much more self-assured young actor, Richard Burton. With her acclaimed performance in a production by Peter Brook of *Ring Round the Moon* (Christopher Fry's adaptation of Anouilh's *L'Invitation au Château*), starring Margaret Rutherford and Paul Scofield, there was a sharp rise in press attention to her. She also impressed the American playwright Arthur Laurents. When he heard in the winter of 1951 that Chaplin was having difficulty finding a leading lady for *Limelight* who was under five feet five, dark-haired, very young, and talented, Laurents gave him Bloom's name.[4]

At the cabled request of the Chaplin Studio, she mailed photos of herself to Hollywood. Subsequent phone calls from Harry Crocker indicated that Chaplin had seen them and wished to give her a screen test as soon as possible. Finally, it was agreed that he would go to New York to meet her and her mother—who would be accompanying her to the United States at his stipulation, since he "didn't want any gossip in the press about him and still another young actress"—and that the test would take place there.[5]

During the rehearsals in a rented studio, Bloom was startled to discover that "Chaplin was the most exacting director, not because he expected you to produce wonders on your own, but because he expected you to follow unquestioningly his every instruction." She was surprised, too, at how old-fashioned his aims were—"rather theatrical effects that I didn't associate with the modern cinema." Once the work of the day was done, the drillmaster of acting technique became the great dictator of conversation. At Le Pavillon, "21," and the other elegant restaurants to which he took Bloom and her mother, "he spoke endlessly of his early poverty; the atmosphere he was creating for *Limelight* brought him back night after night to the melancholy of those years at home with his mother and brother." Yet on an evening when "people dining at other tables couldn't stop looking his way and expressing their opinions of him, ranging from adulation to loathing," he switched from talk of the painful past to a confession that in recent years he had become "deeply homesick" for his birthplace, but that he did not dare leave the United States for fear that the government would not permit him to reenter the country.[6]

The results of the screen test did not immediately convince Chaplin that Bloom was the actress he wanted. On his return to Hollywood, he seriously considered a young hopeful named Joan Winslow, among other candidates. Not until early September, a mere two and a half months before the shooting was slated to begin, did he instruct Harry Crocker to phone London and offer Bloom a contract for three months work at $15,000, plus a living allowance for herself and her mother and reimbursement for travel expenses.[7]

Bloom had been made to feel at the time of her screen test "like a monkey in the zoo being put through . . . paces," but the discipline to which she was subjected in Hollywood was considerably stricter. Her Chaplin-devised schedule required her to begin each day with a strenuous gymnasium workout before proceeding on, without any break for lunch, to a punishing five hours of rehearsals at the studio, followed by an hourlong ballet class. During evening meetings with Chaplin, he "again and again" spoke to her of his London childhood. "He described the London parks that I enjoyed as places of the lonely and the destitute." (Was he thinking of the day he and Sydney had spent with Hannah in Kennington Park prior to their renewed separation from her?) "Oddly," she continued, "he seemed to be longing for a London that hurt and horrified him, a London that from his description I hadn't known at all."

Limelight reflects, to be sure, other experiences in other places and with other women besides the mother whose illness had been the radiating center of the hurt and the horror of his childhood. Several aspects of Oona, for instance, can be discerned in Terry, including her manifest gratitude at finding a father figure to take care of her, her habit of listening in rapt silence to Chaplin's windy philosophizings about the meaning of life or whatever, and her black, self-destructive moods which marked her as an O'Neill.* Dipping into his fund of memories of other young women, Chaplin lifted the details of Terry's frustrated attempt to commit suicide by gas-pipe asphyxiation from the tragically successful attempt of his and Max Eastman's shared mistress, Florence Deshon. And the montage shot of Terry dancing in Moscow during her rise to fame as a ballerina was inspired by his recollection of being told in Paris

---

* When she was in her eighties, the no-nonsense Englishwoman Rachel Ford, who went to work as a secretary for Chaplin in Vevey, Switzerland, in 1953 but quickly became the manager of his business affairs, would conclude a description of Oona's self-destructiveness by remarking, *"Limelight* was about Oona." Patrice Chaplin, *Hidden Star: Oona O'Neill Chaplin* (London, 1995), p. 127.

in the autumn of 1909 by young Mabelle Fournier that his first love, Hetty Kelly, was currently dancing in Moscow. Yet the basic model for Terry, the psychologically troubled dancer, was Hannah Chaplin. On a visit with Claire Bloom to the workrooms of Brooks the costumer, Chaplin's purpose beyond all other purposes was to make sure that in certain scenes Terry would be dressed in a way that recalled Hannah. "My mother," he told Brooks, "used to wear a loose knitted cardigan, a blouse with a high neck and a little bow, and a worn velvet jacket."[8]

3

At their very first meeting in New York, Bloom recalled, Chaplin informed her that the opening scenes of *Limelight* were set "in the Kennington slums where he was born." Strikingly enough, she never saw anything wrong with this statement. Yet how could she not have realized, as soon as the shooting began, that there was nothing slumlike about those scenes?* The picture opens on a vista of a tidy street lined on the side that we can see with a solidly built row of brownstones fronted by stone stoops and white-pillared columns. The passers-by are uniformly well dressed. As for the three little children (played by Chaplin's children) who are listening to a hurdy-gurdy player, their demeanor and their accents as well as their clothes bespeak a background of comfort, not Cockney squalor. When Calvero comes into view, his staggering walk and the difficulty he experiences in fitting a key into the front door establish the fact that he is shamefully drunk. His fashionable light-gray homburg, natty suit, and ascot are not the marks, however, of destitution.

In the course of the next several minutes, further signs of his situation in life emerge. The two flights of stairs he has to climb to his quarters are well carpeted. The two-room suite he occupies is ample-sized if simply furnished and boasts a fireplace. His finances, on the other hand, are obviously in decline. Thus the trousers of another handsome suit lie

---

* Nor were the exterior shots London-like inasmuch as they were filmed on the back lot at Paramount, which Chaplin rented for three days so that he could make use of the Washington Square set from William Wyler's *The Heiress* (1949). Jerry Epstein, *Remembering Charlie* (New York, 1989), p. 92.

under the mattress on his bed to keep them well pressed. And when in obedience to the doctor's instructions he goes to buy some oranges and pick up a prescription for the suicidal Terry, he has to pawn his fiddle in order to pay for these out-of-the-ordinary purchases. In sum, the aging Calvero is living in reduced but not impoverished circumstances.[9]

The mesmerizing power of the opening of the picture does not stem from any sociological grimness but from the drastic, life-and-death drama in which Chaplin put into play his everlasting fantasy of rescuing his mother. Bloom's guesswork about the picture's governing dynamic was inspired. "Recounting the story of *Limelight* to his dinner guests Saturday after Saturday," she would write in *Limelight and After* (1982), "seemed to provide Chaplin not just with the thrilling expectation of a new film achievement, but with something almost like the satisfaction of reaching back to the London of 1914 to rescue his mother once and for all from the blight of mental disease."[10]

To the portrayal of a drunken has-been blundering into his rooming house and starting to weave up the stairs Chaplin brought old-time, Karno-trained skills. As an American columnist had exclaimed in 1911, after witnessing his performance as the falling-down drunk in "*A Night in an English Music Hall*," Chaplin was "the world's greatest impersonator of inebriates and the biggest laughmaker on the vaudeville stage."[11] In *Limelight*, the scene is comic up to the point at which Calvero ascertains that the strange odor he has sniffed is coming neither from the cigar in his mouth nor from something foul on the bottom of his shoe. Despite his befuddlement, he decides to peer through a peephole in the door of the room next to the staircase. Inside is the horror that the camera has already disclosed. An exquisitely beautiful young woman is lying on her back on the edge of her bed. Her eyes are closed, her right arm is flung back, and her clinging nightgown outlines the swell of her breasts. While her attitude is suggestive of sexual surrender, she is actually giving herself to death. A small bottle of poison is clutched in her hand; the door of the gas oven beside the bed is open, and a towel has been jammed into the crack beneath the door leading into the hall. Calvero smashes the door open, slings the unconscious girl over his shoulder, and carries her into the hall. After depositing her on the stairway, he stumbles off in search of a doctor. When she finally wakes up, she finds that she is in Calvero's bed. "Why didn't you let me die?" she cries. "What's your hurry?" he drunkenly asks.

Calvero's initial assumption about Terry is that she is a prostitute who has fallen into despondency because of her infection with a venereal disease. His cynicism is mistaken. At one time, she tells him, she had been a member of the ballet company at London's famed Empire Theater, but had lost her position when fever-related trouble with her legs compelled her to quit. With the failure of her career dreams, life has lost all its meaning for her. Again she cries, "Why didn't you let me die?" Calvero replies with an apostrophe to the miracle of existence.

As he cares for her during the days of enforced bed rest that follow, tucking in the blanket around her feet and making breakfast for her, he continues to speechify, with deadly effect on the picture's dramatic momentum. It is as if Chaplin had filmed a particularly static stage play. At times, the old entertainer's monologues center on the wreckage of his own career. Verdoux's line about loving women but not admiring them is recycled into a confession that while Calvero may love the public he does not admire it. The public, he declares, in a sentence dripping with Chaplin's own bitterness about his terrible loss of pulling power in American movie houses, is "a monster without a head that never knows which way it's going to turn—and [that] can be prodded in any direction." At other times, he indulges in pseudopoetic flights about the nature of the cosmos. At still others, he gives Terry pep talks about the need for her to believe in herself and to fight back against feelings of discouragement. Only in the old boy's sleep-disturbing dreams of music hall performances is there any action worthy of the name in this part of the picture.

The first of them might be called his circus-master dream. Clad in a top hat, riding breeches, and boots, and wielding a whip, Calvero presents an act with a pair of trained fleas who keep misbehaving, in spite of his stern commands and the pistol-like cracks of his whip. In a second and infinitely more charming dream, he prances onstage dressed as a tramp and twirling a cane. His chapeau, however, is a straw hat—and his shoes are normal-sized. After plucking and eating a flower, he launches into a song of celebration—accompanied by the niftiest dance steps that Chaplin ever filmed—of the renewals of springtime ("Birds are calling/Skunks are crawling") and of the itches within them of eroticism ("Oh, it's love, it's love, it's love-love-love-love-love").

A pretty woman appears, carrying a fancy parasol and dressed like a dance hall version of Little Bo-Peep in a fashionable bonnet, bare-shouldered top, flouncy, tutu-like skirt, and high heels. It is Terry. The tramp engages her in joyously incoherent banter, full of mock takings-of-umbrage on her part and sly digs at her on his. Out of nowhere he produces a feather duster and dusts her off. As a veritable cloud of powder arises from her shoulders and arms, he asks her whether "they" (whoever "they" are) have been keeping her on the top shelf. Using the handle of the duster as an eating utensil, he removes an imaginary spot of powder from her arm and eats it. "Cornstarch," he declares. "Just think," she replies in non-sequitur wonderment, "all life motivated by love! How beautiful! . . . I like you," she continues. "You're sensitive. You feel things." "Now, don't encourage me," he warns, prancing toward her. "So few people have the capacity to feel," she adds. "Or the opportunity," he giggles, adding a goat step for priapic emphasis. With a deep, formal bow, he presents the feather duster to her as though it were a corsage. With an equally deep curtsy she accepts it. He takes her hand. They go skipping offstage. To this day this remains, Claire Bloom has declared, "my favorite scene in the film." "I was strangely moved to think," she explained,

> that this must reach back to [Chaplin's] earliest memories of the Edwardian music hall—moved too by the connection between my role in the scene and those young and unobtainable girls he adored while still a young performer on the London stage. It seemed to me, even while playing [it], that more was crystallized for him in this scene than any audience would ever realize, including even the feelings of incredulity and loss he had suffered when his pretty, young mother had become insane and disappeared in an asylum. This was the sweet and easy way it was supposed to have been, but alas, could only be in a sketch with a bonneted young innocent on a music hall stage.[12]

Terry's free movements in the dream are mocked by her tearful announcement from her bed in Calvero's flat that her legs have suddenly become paralyzed. In a confidential conversation with the doctor, Calvero learns that her affliction is a case of hysterical paralysis. Although Calvero mentions "Dr. Freud-uh" in an ironic tone of voice, he indicates to the doctor that he himself will act as Terry's psychiatrist. During his next marathon talk session with her, he zeros in on the fact that at the age of eight she and a few of her ballet school chums had discovered that Terry's sister, Louise, who had been paying for her ballet lessons, was a streetwalker. Calvero perceives that this information is the key to Terry's problem. A life of shame had paid for the dance lessons she had received; ever since being reminded of this by a new recruit in the Empire ballet who had been one of her companions on the night she found out the truth about Louise, she has been ashamed to dance. Q.E.D.: paralysis. Having accomplished his psychodetective work in well under an analytic hour, Calvero turns to lecturing Terry on the power of the will. Holding on to his outstretched hands with hers, she takes a few trembling steps. Her improbable rise to the position of prima ballerina at the Empire has begun.*

As in *The Circus* and *City Lights*, the redemption of a young woman from despair is counterpointed by her redeemer's descent into its depths. Calvero's own attempt at a comeback earns him nothing except humiliation, while in his personal life he deliberately courts heartbreak. Terry proclaims that she loves him and wants to marry him, yet he is sure that she does not know her own mind. The man whom she really wants and will someday find, he prophesies, is a young man. By dropping out of her life without warning, he enables her to become involved with the young composer Neville.†

Near the close of the benefit performance that old friends in the theater finally arrange in his honor, Calvero and another old-time entertainer (played by Buster Keaton) do an encore that brings down the house—and precipitates Calvero's death. As he finishes the skit with an alarmingly hard backward tumble into a drum in the orchestra pit, he suffers a serious heart attack and has to be carried off. In the property room, he is placed on a couch. Was Chaplin envisioning his own death in this scene? Rather, he was offering a defense of his history of taking control of the lives of young women.

Terry rushes to Calvero's side. She is wearing a ballet costume and elaborate eyeliner makeup, for her own performance in front of the benefit audience is about to begin. Once she leaves the room, Calvero

---

* To perform Terry's ballet routines, Chaplin brought in Melissa Hayden from New York, along with her dance partner, André Eglevsky.
† The tentatively serious offscreen attachment that developed between Bloom and Sydney Chaplin added to the profusion of parallels between *Limelight* and real life. Bloom, indeed, raised the possibility that her own heart, like Terry's, was divided: "Here was I: young, pretty, slightly in love with Sydney—or was it Charlie?—Chaplin."

will reveal his awareness that he is dying. But while she is with him he pretends he is all right. Did you notice how the audience applauded me? he asks her. "That's how it used to be," he says softly, "that's how it's going to be from now on." He has plans for the two of them to tour the world together, he explains, "you doing ballet, me comedy." By this time, other people have clustered around the couch, young Neville among them. Glancing up at him, the old entertainer repeats the sentence in which he had long ago prophesied to Terry, as she lay in bed in his rooming-house digs, what would happen when the right young man came along. "And in the elegant melancholy of twilight," Calvero murmurs, "he will tell you that he loves you."

Quite deliberately, he is attempting to evoke a certain response from Terry, and she does not disappoint him. "It doesn't matter," she says, clasping his hand to her cheek, "it's you I love." She loves him because he saved her from death, nursed her while she was confined to bed, infused her with a will to live, coaxed her into walking again and then into dancing. In the wings of a theater on the very brink of her comeback, she had panicked again about her legs and cried that she couldn't go on, and he had slapped her face and compelled her to. As well as her life, she owes her career to Calvero's interventions.

An assistant stage manager whispers to Terry that she is due onstage. She leans forward and embraces Calvero. "I won't be long, my darling," she promises, as she rises and departs. When Calvero indicates that he wishes to see her dance, his couch is carried to the wings. He has time, alas, for only one glimpse of her, if that, before death claims him. A sheet is pulled over his face. The camera shifts to a medium-distance shot of a breathtakingly graceful ballerina—a twentieth-century Trilby, but not doomed, as du Maurier's heroine was, to insanity and early death—twirling and twirling about in a perfectly executed solo on a huge stage.

4

Chaplin spent the first half of the summer of 1952 editing *Limelight* and dubbing in its beautiful music. On August 2, his work complete, he held a screening at the Paramount Studios Theater for two hundred guests. Like the white-tie, formal-gown crowd at the Calvero benefit, the *Limelight* previewers were predisposed to love the show. When the lights came up at the end, everyone present, "from Ronald Colman to David Selznick to Judge Pecora to Sylvia Gable, stood up and applauded and shouted 'Bravo,' " the columnist Sidney Skolsky declared in *Variety*.[13]

To a degree, their response calmed Chaplin's nerves about the New York openings in October. Nevertheless, he had no intention of being on hand for that acid test. For months he had been talking about taking Oona and the children and Harry Crocker, whom he had not only rehired but who was once again a bosom friend, on a trip to Europe. Being hailed by a predictably friendly crowd at the opening of his picture at the Odeon Theater in Leicester Square was an experience that he was particularly looking forward to.

The Immigration and Naturalization Service had issued him a reentry permit in mid-July. Yet why was he risking the trip? He had told Claire Bloom of his fear that if he went abroad his return would be barred. To Harry Crocker he had expressed the same premonition. In retrospect, Crocker wondered if, in going ahead with his travel plans, he was acting through "a subconscious desire to suffer martyrdom." Or was it merely that "his ingrained obstinacy, his well-known stubbornness" made it "impossible for him to act otherwise"? Crocker's most arresting idea, however, was that Chaplin wanted to move to Switzerland, for tax reasons. "If he established his residence in Switzerland," Crocker would write in his unpublished Chaplin biography, "all international monies he received from his films would flow into Swiss banks, and Switzerland, being a rich little nation, [had] hardly any income tax."[14] He might also have had thoughts about revenge. Take away his magical popularity, dim it even for an hour, Waldo Frank had long ago observed, and Chaplin's latent melancholy "flames into hysteric rage." It is possible that he had come to hate America for rejecting *Monsieur Verdoux* and had made a vow to get out and maybe get even as well.* For if the government

---

* On December 7, 1947, Chaplin published a piece in a British newspaper, *Reynolds News*, in which he made bitter reference to "the reception that was given in certain American picture-houses, and more especially in New York, to my latest film, *Monsieur Verdoux*," and to the "cranks" who "began calling me communist and anti-American." In conclusion, he declared that "before long, I shall perhaps leave the United States, although it has given me so many moral and material satisfactions. And in the land where I go to end my days, I shall try to remember that I am a man like other men, and that consequently I have a right to the same respect as other men." Reprinted in Peter Haining, ed., *The Legend of Charlie Chaplin* (Secaucus, N. J., 1982), pp. 163, 166.

decided to revoke his reentry permit after he left American shores, he would be able to dramatize himself as a victim of political persecution, and anti-American commentators around the world would have a field day with the story.

One thing was certain. He was not deterred as he got ready to leave by any thoughts of how his young American wife might feel if they were forced into a life elsewhere. On September 9, he and Crocker escorted Oona and the children aboard the Santa Fe Chief for the first leg of their trip to New York.*

On the same day, the fact that Chaplin was going abroad came up in a meeting at the Department of Justice between President Truman's final appointee as attorney general, James P. McGranery, and J. Edgar Hoover. McGranery informed Hoover that he was considering "taking steps which would prevent [Chaplin's] re-entry . . . because of moral turpitude." The statement betokened the attorney general's strong religious convictions, as well as his lawyerly views, about the crime of arranging and paying for illegal abortions. Before making his decision, McGranery told Hoover, he wished to review all of the FBI's files on the comedian. On the morning of the 18th, only hours before the Chaplin party was due to board the *Queen Elizabeth*, a courier delivered a freshly prepared summary of the seven volumes of moral-conduct files and the six volumes of files on the subject of Chaplin's politics to the attorney general's office.[15]

5

Five months before, Truman had reached Judge McGranery by phone in his chambers in Philadelphia. "Jim, I've got a job for you, and I expect you to take it," he said bluntly. When he told him what the job was, the judge said that he would like to discuss it with his wife, who was also a lawyer. Do that by all means, the President replied, "but let me tell you that I'm announcing your appointment to the press in twenty minutes."[16]

---

* While in New York, Chaplin sat for a series of photographs by Richard Avedon. In one of them, he posed as the devil by assuming a cunning look and framing his brow with his index fingers.

Truman's words were a measure of the desperate political trouble he was in. Voter frustration about the bloody stalemate of the Korean War was the first reason. Furthermore, to portions of the electorate, including many traditional Democrats, the relentless and reckless charges by the McCarthyites that the Truman administration was soft on the issue of Communists in government sounded like the truth, even though the president had approved—to the unmitigated horror of civil libertarians—a new standard for the dismissal of federal employees based on nothing more substantial than a "reasonable doubt" of the person's loyalty. No matter what he did or said, people still remembered that in August 1948, when Whittaker Chambers had identified Alger Hiss as a Communist at a HUAC hearing, Harry Truman had allowed a reporter to put the words in his mouth that the committee's probe was a "red herring." The President's prestige had also been undermined by a two-year stream of revelations of wrongdoing in the Bureau of Internal Revenue and the Tax Division of the Justice Department. An ominously wide spectrum of Americans had concluded that neither he nor his attorney general, J. Howard McGrath, had the will to root out this corruption.

Given one last chance by Truman to demonstrate to the administration's critics that he was serious about cleaning out the influence peddlers and the bribe takers, McGrath brought in a reform Republican from New York City, Newbold Morris, as a special investigator. Morris immediately announced with great fanfare that he intended to make every federal employee, beginning with Attorney General McGrath and the Justice Department staff, fill out a financial questionnaire about outside income sources. McGrath, a hard-drinking, glad-handing pol who had managed to amass a fortune of $4 million while spending his entire career on public payrolls, detested the questionnaire idea. Indeed, he found that he detested Morris, for reasons that appeared to include anti-Semitism, and on April 3, 1952, he summarily fired him. Upon hearing of his action, Truman phoned McGrath and in steely tones informed him that he was finished as attorney general. Then he instructed the White House operator to get Judge McGranery on the line.[17]

McGranery was a man of impeccable rectitude. In the early 1930s he had been chairman of the Registration Commission of the city of

Philadelphia and had cleaned up voter lists, getting rid of thousands of tombstone voters. During his three terms as a congressman, from 1937 to 1943, he had been greatly respected by his colleagues, as his early appointment to the powerful Ways and Means Committee attested. An ardent New Dealer whose moral conscience impelled his interest in civil rights causes and racial integration, he and his wife worked with Eleanor Roosevelt to find a place for Marian Anderson, a fellow Philadelphian, to sing when the D.A.R. barred her from Constitution Hall. On leaving Congress, he served as the assistant to the attorney general under Francis Biddle and then Tom Clark until 1946, at which point Truman appointed him to the U.S. District Court for the Eastern District of Pennsylvania.

Four years later, McGranery presided over the trial of Harry Gold, a CPUSA member and a key agent in the effort headed by Julius and Ethel Rosenberg to transmit the secrets of ENORMOUS, as the KGB called the U.S. project to build an atomic bomb, to the Soviet Union. Gold was arrested in 1950 after the British arrested the nuclear physicist Klaus Fuchs. Gold then implicated Ethel Rosenberg's brother, David Greenglass, an employee of the atom bomb project. Greenglass in turn named the Rosenbergs. The Rosenbergs thereupon became a rallying point for the left both at home and abroad, in the most fervent propaganda campaign of its kind since the Sacco-Vanzetti case. These humble people were not spies, their advocates maintained, but victims of the Cold War politics of false accusation known as McCarthyism.[18]

This myth would be kept alive by true believers until the summer of 1995, when the National Security Agency released U.S. intelligence documents dating from 1943 through 1945 which demonstrated that the NSA's code-breaking program called Venona had intercepted and cracked Soviet diplomatic ciphers. The ciphers revealed to the NSA that the ring headed by the methodical man known as LIBERAL or ANTENNA, *i.e.*, Julius Rosenberg in KGB lingo, was a part of the "massive" Soviet effort involving approximately two hundred agents to acquire the technology for constructing atomic bombs. Many of the agents were members of the CPUSA, while others would never be successfully identified by U.S. counterspies. Because the NSA did not wish to tip off the Soviets about Venona's code-breaking achievements, it did not share what it knew about the Rosenbergs with the American people. Judge McGranery, however, came face-to-face in his courtroom with the seriousness of the Rosenbergs' crimes because Harry Gold proved to be a most cooperative witness. Upon his conviction in December 1950, the prosecuting attorney took his cooperativeness into consideration and asked McGranery for a sentence of twenty-five years. That the judge gave him thirty said something once again about his moral implacability.[19]

No other aspect of McGranery's life was more vital to an understanding of him than his Catholicism. He sent his two sons and his daughter to Catholic schools from the elementary grades onward. Both boys then went on to Notre Dame and his daughter to Trinity College in Washington, D.C. In 1950 a decoration from Pope Pius XII signified his election as Knight Commander of the Order of Saint Gregory the Great. The following year, His Holiness named him Private Chamberlain of the Cape and Sword, and in 1952 he made him a Knight of the Holy Sepulchre of Jerusalem. Needless to say, this dedicated Catholic abhorred abortion as the taking of life. He also hated Communism with every fiber of his being. As attorney general he redoubled the efforts of the Department of Justice to indict and convict Communist subversives. To this end, he expanded the internal security section of the department's criminal division and appointed a young zealot, Roy Cohn, as a special assistant.

In reading through the summary of the FBI's Chaplin materials, McGranery was deeply offended by what he later referred to as the comedian's "leering, sneering attitude" toward the nation whose hospitality had made his career possible. As a lawyer, however, he could only have agreed with the FBI that on the issue of affiliation with the Communist Party the government had no case against Chaplin. In regard to the moral-turpitude issue, McGranery was revolted, it would seem certain, by Joan Barry's account of how she had been hassled by Chaplin and Tim Durant. For at a press conference ten days after his ruling, he would disdainfully refer to Chaplin as "in my judgment an unsavory character." At the same time, he was aware that Barry's claim that her famous lover had paid for two illegal abortions had never been supported by collateral testimony, although the possibility that it might be may very well have struck him as strong.[20]

Finally, he made his decision, and it could not have been an easy call.

On September 19, two days out into the Atlantic, Chaplin received word that McGranery had canceled his permit. The regulation that the attorney general invoked permitted the barring of aliens on grounds of "morals, health or insanity, or for advocating Communism or associating with Communists or pro-Communist organizations." Thus Chaplin would have to satisfy INS questioners on political as well as moral grounds before they would sanction his reentry. Nevertheless, the morals charges were the governing consideration for the attorney general, as the solicitor general would subsequently make clear.

The atmosphere of a meeting on September 29 of an FBI supervisor with three INS commissioners was heavy with pessimism. One of the commissioners bluntly stated that "at the present time the INS does not have sufficient information to exclude Chaplin from the United States if he attempts to re-enter." Another commissioner affirmed that while the INS could make it difficult for him, "in the end, there is no doubt Chaplin would be readmitted." He also stressed that any effort on the part of INS to delay action on a Chaplin petition to reenter "might well rock INS . . . to its foundations." The meeting ended with a discussion of plans to interrogate Chaplin's maid or butler with a view to obtaining confirmation of the story that he "conspired to cause one of his girl friends [Joan Barry] to abort." As in the meeting between McGranery and Hoover on September 9, so in the concluding conversation of the INS commissioners on the 29th: the charges of morally turpitudinous conduct were paramount. Two years later, the highly competent, politically moderate Philip Perlman, who had been Truman's solicitor general at the time, told Alistair Cooke that "Chaplin's politics had nothing to do with the excluding order."[21]

In the early 1950s, Communism was the most salient issue in the Western world. When the Chaplin story broke, most editors of American newspapers—and of leading newspapers abroad—were not disposed to have their reporters make inquiries as to whether morals or Communism would be the operative issue in the INS questioning of Chaplin. McGranery, they were dead certain, had revoked the comedian's reentry permit for political reasons. Which is why they played the story that way, and why the pundits whom they published took the same line. Only rarely was the excluding order interpreted properly.

In New York, the *Daily Worker* labeled the government's decision "fascist." Hitler and Mussolini banned Chaplin's films, but "Truman and

McGranery had gone one step further. They want to ban Chaplin." That he is "now being barred from the U.S. because of his anti-fascist convictions shows how badly conditions have deteriorated in our country since the defeat of the fascist dictators." A *New York Times* editorial not only emphasized the politics of the case, but reduced Chaplin's record of cooperation with Communist causes to nothing more than the possibility that it "will be shown that he has in some way been connected with or deceived by what have been described as Communist fronts." In the *New York Herald-Tribune* Dorothy Thompson argued that Chaplin was one of the "most effective anti-Communists alive," for his tramp was "the eternal nonconformist," whereas communism exalted "the mass against the individual." [22]

The right-wing *Chicago Tribune* played up the fact that Chaplin had always "scorned citizenship in this country" and had supported Communist-organized peace conferences. Hedda Hopper fancifully assured her readers that "there are hundreds of people in Hollywood, perhaps thousands—stars, directors, producers and all those wonderful people we call little people, workers behind the camera, electricians, cameramen, props—who are dancing in the street for joy over Attorney General McGranery's statement that before Charlie Chaplin can return to the United States he will have to pass the board of immigration." Westbrook Pegler, now a columnist for Hearst newspapers, having become too bitter for Scripps-Howard's taste, dismissed Chaplin as "never more than a custard-pie comedian" and hailed McGranery's decision as "the first honest show of initiative against the Red Front of Hollywood by the Department of Justice." [23]

Unlike the reaction of the Communists and the liberals, the reaction of the right was not limited to rhetoric. The American Legion, boasting a membership of 2.5 million in the early 1950s, passed a resolution at its convention in October 1952 calling on theater owners to refuse to show any of Chaplin's pictures until and unless he submitted to INS questioning and the INS pronounced itself satisfied with his answers. The following January, the president of the West Coast's largest movie house chain, Charles Skouras, responded to the Legion's resolution by barring *Limelight* from his theaters. Two days later, Loew's put out a pressure-dictated statement to the effect that contrary to its usual practice of distributing United Artists pictures, it would not handle *Limelight*.

Although RKO quickly stepped into the breach, Chaplin's difficulties in getting his picture exhibited were far from over. The board chairman of RKO Pictures, and the biggest investor in RKO Theaters Corporation, was Howard Hughes, who abhorred Chaplin's politics. In a letter to a Hollywood American Legion post, Hughes acknowledged that he had no control over the policies of RKO Theaters. Nevertheless, he pledged that he would try to persuade the officers in charge to "take the necessary legal measures to cancel all bookings of *Limelight*." Meantime, independent exhibitors and in some cases local-chain owners in New York City, Philadelphia, Washington, D.C., Columbus, Ohio, New Orleans, and other cities were pulling *Limelight* off their screens, either because of their own anti-Chaplin feelings or out of fear of boycott threats and picket lines. As for those theaters where it was shown without incident, slim attendance led to short runs. Domestic box-office returns from *Limelight* would not exceed $1 million, *Variety* predicted— correctly—in February 1953.[24]

6

At the gala premiere on a crisp autumn night in London, two hundred bobbies were needed to hold back a throng of ten thousand onlookers. The BBC televised the arrival by Rolls-Royce or Bentley of Princess Margaret, Lady Mountbatten, the Marquess of Milford Haven, the Duke of Alba, Lord Inchape, Lord Inverclyde, Vivien Leigh, and Douglas Fairbanks, Jr. In every respect, the evening gratified Chaplin. While the reviews the next day were mixed, they did not matter. From the moment that the Odeon opened its doors to the general public, every performance was jammed. Ultimately *Limelight* grossed more money, not only in Britain but in all foreign markets, than any other Chaplin picture. In the thunderous aftermath of the Wehrmacht's triumphs in the West, the comedian had come before the world as a comic Hitler, and *The Great Dictator* had set box-office records; in the celebrity-conscious culture of the postwar world, he played himself and made even more millions.[25]

Before leaving London for comparably exciting premieres in Paris and Rome, Chaplin and Oona attended a Toscanini concert, heard Emlyn Williams read Dickens, went to the Old Vic to see Claire Bloom and Alan Badel in *Romeo and Juliet*, and as guests of Lord Strabolgi had dinner at the House of Lords, where Chaplin sat next to the Labour Party's Herbert Morrison and tried to convince him that the soundest defense strategy for England in the atomic age was to cut loose from U.S. foreign policy and adopt a stance of absolute neutrality. That Morrison, a socialist, emphatically disagreed with this recommendation came as a surprise to him, Chaplin would confess in *My Autobiography*.[26]

One morning he and Claire Bloom went for a walk around Covent Garden market. The news of his presence quickly spread among the fruit and vegetable sellers. Instead of crowding around him and asking for his autograph, American-style, they stood in front of their stalls and patiently waited for him to pass. As he did, Bloom remembered, each man "put his hand to his forehead in an informal salute and . . . [said] 'Hello Guv'nor.' " It was a display of affection, Bloom added, "that touched him to the heart. It was a royal progress." *A royal progress*. From the moment of the McGranery announcement, Chaplin had adopted a new persona, to which he would cling until his death. He was a king, condemned to exile by the fact, as he saw it, that "in an atmosphere of powerful cliques and invisible governments [he] had engendered a nation's antagonism and unfortunately lost the affection of the American public." Is it any wonder that in December 1952, while looking for a permanent residence in Switzerland, he temporarily established himself and his family in that famous haunt of deposed monarchs, the Hotel Beau Rivage in Lausanne?[27]

7

The Manoir de Ban at Corsier-sur-Vevey, which Chaplin rented in January 1953 and purchased a month later, was likewise fit for an exiled king.* A handsome, fifteen-room villa set in thirty-seven acres of green-

---

* The rumored sale price of the Manoir was $300,000, although it may, in fact, have been a third of that amount. In any event, Chaplin was able to pay it without difficulty. For on November 17, 1952, Oona had quietly flown back to New York and then to Los Angeles, where many of Chaplin's personal assets were stashed in safety deposit boxes to which she had access. The paperwork giving her the right to invade those boxes had been executed just before the Chaplins' departure for Europe, another indication that the comedian had been counting on not coming back. While in Los Angeles, Oona also transferred more than $4 million to accounts abroad, closed up the house on Summit Drive, and arranged to have the furniture shipped to Switzerland.

sward, orchards, and gardens, and fronted by a lengthy colonnaded terrace, an endless lawn, and cedar trees framing a spectacular view of Lake Geneva and the Alps of Savoy in the distance, the Manoir required, at minimum, a staff of twelve for proper maintenance. Once the family was settled there, Chaplin turned in his reentry permit at the U.S. consulate in Geneva and later in London issued a statement of farewell to America that asserted his belief that he was a political martyr:

> It is not easy to uproot myself and my family from a country where I have lived for 40 years without a feeling of sadness. But since the end of the last war, I have been the object of vicious propaganda by powerful reactionary groups who by their influence and by the aid of America's yellow press have created an unhealthy atmosphere in which liberal-minded individuals can be singled out and persecuted. I have therefore given up my residence in the United States.[28]

In addition to hiring a butler, a cook, a chauffeur, and various maids and gardeners, Chaplin retained the services of Nurse Edith "Kay-Kay" Mackenzie, who had taken care of the Chaplin children in Hollywood, and brought in Mabel Rose "Pinnie" Pinnegar from Canada to relieve "Kay-Kay" of nursery responsibilities—for Oona was expecting again and her fifth baby would not be her last. Furthermore, on the cook's night off Oona liked to take over at the stove, with a repertoire mainly consisting of her husband's favorites from his past—tripe and onions, steak and kidney pies, and stew with dumplings.[29]

Rachel Ford became Chaplin's secretary, and Isobel Deluz and, later, Eileen Burnier were engaged as stenographers. In contrast to Miss Ford, for whom Chaplin's every whim was a serious command, Madame Deluz was alternately amused and exasperated by her work with him. Unfortunately, as the months passed it became less and less amusing, and in the summer of 1954 it turned ugly. A pert, bright, thirty-three-year-old Englishwoman married to a Swiss professor and fluent in four languages, Madame Deluz had already had more than a decade and a half of secretarial experience, including two years of script work in Alexander Korda's office in London, on the day she found Chaplin's help-wanted ad in the *Gazette de Lausanne*.

The experience of being interviewed by him was breathtaking. A darting, dancing-eyed bundle of energy in his mid-sixties came dashing into the library of the Manoir, where she had been asked to wait for him. He could not sit still and he could not stop talking about all the "typing, typing, typing" he needed to have done for him on everything, from his business affairs to his renewed interest in filming *Shadow and Substance* to his bursting ideas for a movie script about an exiled king's visit to New York. Eventually she was able to ascertain that he was offering her only forty dollars a week. In Switzerland that was a beginning stenographer's wage. Nevertheless, she took the job. The chance to work for Charlie Chaplin did not come along every day.

"I worked for a year for that aggressive little genius," she recalled a few years later, "and all it cost me was a fortnight's nervous collapse and a miserable suit for my back pay. When Charlie was actually working, which wasn't often, he could be delightful. Most of the time he was just brooding and mooching about, and then he was a neurotic terror. I was just beaten down by his tantrums—his first-rate clowning, his second-rate manners and his sixth-rate philosophy." He ordered her to arm herself with notepads and pencils and take down every word he uttered, as he wandered about, often barefoot, from the sun lounge to the terrace to the rose garden and the grove of cedars beyond. "My fantastic, whirlwind boss was never offstage. He never just dictated a letter to me. With his snowy-white hair shaking all over his handsome head, he acted every word. Even a four-line letter to his Swiss banker about a thirty pound check made him tender and angry, relaxed and then raging." [30]

One day she rejoined him on the terrace after being made to retype an entire scene in which he had changed only two words and found him rehearsing a love scene. His face wore an expression that he himself described as his "passionate young girl look," and he was wringing his hands and gazing amorously at an ant crawling up a pillar of the colonnade. Madame Deluz, who had a sense of humor, chose to record his declamation in script fashion: "Chaplin: I love you. (The ant looks startled.) I—I love you. No, no. I love you so—I love you—so much! No, no, no!" At least she knew that the scene was intended for *Shadow and Substance*. Sometimes, though, she could not be sure what the context was of the lines he came out with. "Is that an El Greco? No, I think it's a Filipino. Write that down." (As it turned out, the joke was destined for *A King in New York*.)

Much more bewildering were the times when she simply could not catch his words. As the Muse of the Seventh Art took over, she wryly remembered,

> he would begin to prance around, talking at the top of his voice, re-peating the same sentence over and over again, and then, when he was at the farthest corner of the room, with his back to me, he would whisper something I could not hear, and bounce round with a "That's it—that's it. Fine. Got it at last." But I had not! Then he would fall into silent brooding, sometimes for half an hour on end, with a faraway look in his eyes. Or he would gesticulate madly, his mouth forming noiseless words. Every possible expression would cross his moving face—joy, sadness, courage, irony, tragedy, contempt.

Yet he also was capable of snapping out of these moods with startling abruptness and making some sort of wisecrack, such as "That's the tear-jerker stuff that really wows them at the box office."[31]

His moods took on a malevolent cast in the spring of 1954, when problems with the *King in New York* script cut the power lines of his inspirational energies. It was an old story. In periods of creative paralysis —*e.g.*, the early 1940s—he generally got into trouble, one way or an-other. This time he did so by picking quarrels with the architect and the contractor whom he had hired to design and build a servants' lodge, a summer pavilion, a tennis court, a swimming pool, and otherwise re-create Beverly Hills in the Alps. His basic attitude was that he knew more about how to carry out these projects than any Swiss provincial possibly could. "I've been building swimming pools for thirty years," he would cry. Furthermore, he was convinced that these French-speaking thieves were overcharging him. "And tell them I won't pay for it," he furiously instructed his trapped-in-the-middle translator, Madame Deluz. Challenges to the architect's competency and the contractor's honesty mounted into daily rituals. And "as a chorus to these flaps, which went on for weeks," according to Madame Deluz, "the workmen, their picks and shovels at their feet, would stand behind Chaplin, grin and wink at each other, point a finger to their foreheads, raise their eyes to the heavens and repeat his refrain: 'I've been building—for thirty years.' They called him Old Windbags."[32]

He ruined the red-asphalt surface of the tennis court by playing on it before it had set properly. In a rage, he refused to replace the asphalt and had the court covered with concrete. But it was the swimming pool that aroused his climactic tantrum. Having admired another pool in the Vevey environs with a deck made of granite slabs, he ordered similar slabs for his own deck. They were delivered on a rainy day, and their rain-darkened surfaces made them appalling to Chaplin. "Tombstones!" he cried. "They're ghastly. I won't have them. Must put in green-slate ones. Awful, depressing, like a funeral. I don't want to feel I'm going to a funeral when I walk around my pool. I've been building swimming pools for thirty years. . . . I won't have my children swimming in a graveyard."

Paranoia now swept away every vestige of rationality. The slabs must be changed, he shouted at Madame Deluz, who was on the phone trying to reach the contractor, and she herself would have to pay for them. He knew full well, he screamed, that she had "fiddled" the bill with the contractor. She dropped the phone, ripped Chaplin with her scorn, and then, overcome by emotion, fled down the hill from the Manoir, never to return. Some months later she encountered Chaplin in a courtroom in Vevey, where she was suing him for three months' back salary and vacation pay.[33]

8

In the opinion of a shrewdly observant *Saturday Evening Post* writer, James P. O'Donnell, who spent time at the Manoir in 1957, Chaplin and Oona were as Californian as two avocados, and so were their children. "He calls her 'Honey,' " O'Donnell reported, "she calls him 'Charlie My Boy' and the kids call him 'Fatcheeks.' " While the famous couple had continuing difficulties with the French language, the metric system, and the rituals of European servants, they remained steadfastly fond of California-casual clothes, barbecued steaks, corn on the cob, pineapple-on-ham, and old-fashioneds before supper.[34]

Yet for all his Americanisms, Chaplin continued to show his contempt for the U.S. government. Since turning in his reentry permit, he had acquired the status for tax purposes of a nonresident alien. For such a person the government's tax rate was 30 percent. The amount Chaplin owed on his American earnings in 1953 was $516,167, the Treasury Department duly informed him. He refused, flat out, to pony up the money. A year later, accordingly, the Treasury invoked a penalty double, in addition to sending him a tax bill on new earnings. All told, he now owed $1.4 million. From his Swiss fastness, Chaplin ordered his American lawyers into action. Three years later, the Treasury grew tired of the battle and reduced his tax liability to $542,000. With interest, the total came to $700,000. Eventually, the claim was settled for $425,000.[35]

With the citizens of Vevey, by contrast, Chaplin went out of his way to prove that he was a good fellow. Thus on a bright October day in 1953 he accepted the invitation of the town councillors and their wives to accompany them on their harvest-celebration tour of local vineyards. All the ceremonial speeches were in French, of course, but he nodded and smiled as if he understood them and appreciatively sampled the ripe grapes. That evening there was a candlelight dinner in his honor at a lakeside château. The leading dignitaries of the town presented him with a splendid gold watch, and Chaplin responded by singing a song in Charlie Chaplin Chinese. Later that fall he also arranged a Charlie Chaplin Film Festival at the Rex Cinema in Vevey. *Tillie's Punctured Romance*, *One A.M.*, *The Pawnshop*, *The Kid*, *The Pilgrim*, *The Circus*, *City Lights*, and *Modern Times* were among the selections he made available from his film archive. His stock in the community was so high by this time that the local paper, the *Feuille d'Avis*, prefaced a profile of him by admitting that his prior approval of it had been sought. "Since we desire to conserve the good opinion which our guest has of our country and its people, we have asked Monsieur Chaplin to read this article before publication, so that it contains nothing that could injure the quality of [his] sojourn, which we hope will be as pleasant and fecund as possible."[36]

Mocking echoes of that remark about "the good opinion which our guest has of our country and its people" started circulating around town in early 1955, when Isobel Deluz's suit for back pay came up in court. With practiced ruthlessness, Chaplin had assembled a battery of smart lawyers from Lausanne, along with a parade of witnesses from the staff at the Manoir, all of whom understood that the price of not being fired from their jobs was a willingness to affirm the magnanimity of their employer. Their testimony, however, created the counterproductive impression that Madame Deluz had been working for a tyrant. Further-more, she found supporting witnesses for her tales of Chaplin's sneering comments about Swiss workmanship and Swiss honesty. His refusal to pay Madame Deluz ended with his being forced to.

Between fitful bursts of work on the *King in New York* script, he brooded about the injustice of Vevey justice. Finally, he struck back at the town. In a formally worded paper hand-carried to the town hall by his secretary in September 1955, he protested against the sound of rifle fire coming from the ravine next to his estate. The noise was making it impossible for him to work, he claimed.

On a rifle range built in the ravine in 1874, the able-bodied men of Vevey had engaged ever since in marksmanship exercises, with the rifles that by law they kept at home, as a part of their duties as citizen-soldiers in the Swiss army. Yet in spite of the social sacredness of this tradition, the Vevey authorities wished to be reasonable. They offered to ban firing on Mondays and Thursdays and on Tuesday and Friday mornings. They further promised to "do all in the realm of the possible to diminish the noise due to the proximity of [the] shooting range." At the same time, they stressed that "under the terms of the Federal ordinance on militia shooting, we must furnish freely a range, and we intend to con-tinue to do so." Despite Chaplin's longtime dramatization of himself as a pacifist, he followed an attack strategy whenever his interests were somehow threatened, and this contretemps was no exception to the rule. Having discovered that riflemen from other communes were also being permitted to use the range, he not only made this information public but coupled it with an insinuation that bribery was involved. The town council immediately put out an irate denial: "The Commune of Vevey makes no profit in putting the range at the disposal of other communes. On the contrary, it costs us money."

In the spring of 1956—by which time Chaplin had gone to London to film *A King in New York*—Vevey's political leadership authorized the expenditure of several thousand dollars for the construction of a con-crete wall along the line of fire in the ravine, the purchase of plastic mats as soundproofing for the inner lining of the shooting stand, and the installation of dampers around the bull's-eyes. At Chaplin's undeterred insistence, his lawyers thereupon filed suit against Vevey, in which an indemnity of $125 a day was demanded for failure to comply with his original request for absolute cessation of the firing. His publicist swung into action as well, with a bombardment of press releases aimed at public opinion. "Can one deprive us, entirely and every day," the most fanciful of these purported statements by the master of the Manoir demanded to know, "of the beauty of the spring, of summer and autumn, in this admirable setting facing Lac Leman and the Alps? Must we rest immured, sealed up in our house, windows jammed shut during the most beautiful months of the year—so as not to succumb to these terrible detonations?"

The hyperbole was more than an editorial writer for *Die Weltwoche* in Zurich could bear. "Why does the noise of Swiss militia soldiers disturb *Charlot* more than the noise coming from Budapest?" he asked in October 1956, just after the Soviet troops had moved into the city to crush the mass revolution against Communist rule.

Why are rifle shots from a Swiss Army service weapon so much worse than the cannon of Russian panzers? Only because Vevey is closer? Perhaps we deceive ourselves, but a truly great pacifist should have sharper ears. . . . M. Chaplin has, it seems, been in our country too long not to pass over certain Swiss customs that may not please him. But not long enough to understand their reason, and what they mean for the Swiss.

At the time of the *Weltwoche* editorial, Chaplin had another twenty-one years to live. In all that time, he would never come to understand what the training of its citizen-soldiers meant to the Swiss, and he would die with his dispute with Vevey still festering.[37]

9

Chaplin's silence about events in Hungary in 1956 complemented his shameless acceptance of a peace prize in 1954 from the Soviet-financed World Peace Council. "To promulgate a demand for peace, whether from East or West, I firmly believe is a step in the right direction," he silkily explained. Among the many newspapers that gagged on this remark was the *New York Times*. If Chaplin "knew more about Russia, or if he were perhaps less bitter," the *Times* asserted in an editorial on

June 5 entitled "Little Man, Farewell," "he would be well aware that the 'peace prize' is not a peace prize at all but a prize offered to those in Russia or outside of Russia who serve the purposes of a brutal and tyrannical imperialism." In a fusion of fact and fiction, the *Times* imagined *The Tramp* with a different ending: "He shuffles off leftward, toward Moscow, perhaps not calling himself a Communist or a fellow-traveler —but there he goes and the sag of his back, the flap of his coattails, the set of his little derby hat over the ears and the sadly reminiscent twirling of his cane can move us almost to tears."[38]

The editorial was poignant. Still, it did not keep him from accepting an invitation from Chou En-lai, newly arrived in Switzerland for the Geneva Conference, to have dinner with him at his temporary residence. On a warm July evening, toasts were exchanged, camera bulbs flashed, and pictures of the host and his guest standing side by side and smiling went out to newspapers around the world. Before too long, Chaplin also made the acquaintance of the two leaders of the Soviet Union. In London, on April 24, 1956, two weeks before the filming of *A King in New York* commenced at the Shepperton Studios, he attended a Soviet embassy–sponsored reception for Nikita Khrushchev and Nikolai Bulganin at Claridge's Hotel. "In the surging and eddying of the crowd," Chaplin would write in *My Autobiography*, "we were introduced." But it was not until he and Khrushchev and four unidentified men (Soviet security agents?) were apparently pushed into a private room (by other security agents?) that he was able to salute the chairman in a fashion that he deemed appropriate. "Khrushchev had just made a wonderful speech of good will on his arrival in London," Chaplin remembered, "and I told him so, saying that it had given hope for peace to millions throughout the world."[39]

IO

Young Sydney Chaplin's good friend and theatrical associate Jerome Epstein, of the Circle Theater in Hollywood, had been thrilled to serve as one of the assistant producers of *Limelight*. On assuming the position of coproducer of *A King in New York*, he faced more challenging tasks, the first of which was to assemble a technical staff from scratch. Of the choices he made, the photographer Georges Périnal was the most highly regarded. Unfortunately, Périnal's work on the film did not enhance his reputation. The Manhattan of his London-made evocations, for instance, is neither grounded in tellingly realistic details nor uplifted by poetry, as the representation of the high-skyline city at the outset of *City Lights* had been.[40]

Taking charge himself of recruiting the other members of the cast, Chaplin deliberately went after B-picture performers and veterans of the legitimate stage who were likewise used to small salaries. For he had no plans to distribute his picture in any systematic way in the United States, and with the cutoff of this market he felt impelled to hold down production costs wherever possible. As his costar he first thought of making an exception to his economy rule for the sake of obtaining his son Sydney's ex-girlfriend Kay Kendall. But after seeing Kendall in *Genevieve*, he proclaimed that the picture was so bad that it had soured him on the idea of an association with her. What is more likely, however, is that he suddenly realized that Dawn Addams was available for less money.

He had first met the English-born Addams in Hollywood, where she won a bit part in *Singin' in the Rain* (1952) and thereafter played a small part in *The Moon Is Blue* (1953). Her saucy haircut, trim figure, and good-sport personality made her well suited for the role in *A King in New York* of the TV performer-*cum*-director Ann Kay, who fends off the sexual advances of the aging King Shahdov (*i.e.*, Chaplin) without losing him as a friend. The rest of Chaplin's on-the-cheap choices turned out well. Thus a forgotten old-timer named Oliver Johnston emerged from the shadows with a winning performance as the King's faithful ambassador and solemn-serious straight man. In her brief appearance as the King's divorce-minded Queen, the Shakespearean actress Maxine Audley was appropriately regal. And while ten-year-old Michael Chaplin lacked the charm of Jackie Coogan, he brought a declamatory verve to the political speechifying of the boy Communist Rupert Macabee.

"Shahdov." In a name coinage almost as clever as "Calvero," Chaplin combined the Persian equivalent of "king" with a shorthand allusion to his potentate-hero's peacemongering proclivities. In a hawkish world, Shahdov is a dove. Whereas his nefarious ministers and the "revolutionary" populace in his kingdom hunger in the American style for stockpiles of atomic bombs, he dreams of using atomic energy to create a social utopia. The division between the people's wishes and his own leads to his overthrow and flight from the country. The fact that he seeks, and is granted, refuge in the United States might have evoked a sincerely meant salute to American liberty. But there is no room for anything but sarcasm on that subject in this relentlessly anti-American tale. While making his way through customs, Shahdov is informed that he has to be fingerprinted. Through this scene Chaplin expressed at least a measure of his fury at U.S. officialdom for an unforgettable humiliation: the fingerprinting procedure that his indictment on Mann Act and civil rights charges had entailed.

Similarly, his enduring grudge against the American media lies behind the violent gesture with which Shahdov thrusts aside the microphone that a TV reporter plants in his face. The next trial of the royal nerves is the noise level of the popular music that assaults his ears. An overly zealous drummer in a restaurant orchestra is bad enough, but the blasts of sound from a rock-and-roll band in a theater and the accompanying frenzies of the teenage audience are symptomatic in his view of cultural madness. When a pretty girl collapses in the central aisle after rock-and-rolling her head off, Shahdov has to step over her on his way to his seat, and as he does so she bites his ankle. "Completely insane," the King exclaims to his horrified ambassador.

While the mass hysteria that Elvis Presley unleashed was an undeniable fact of life in mid-1950s America, the sour-tempered Chaplin had conveniently forgotten the madness that he himself had once stirred up in crowds. But the larger point about the scene in the theater is the absence of anything about it that could possibly be construed as funny. Indeed, the only really amusing scene in the entire picture—and it is amusing for no more than a few minutes—takes place at a formal dinner party that Shahdov attends. Without his knowledge, the occasion is being broadcast nationwide on a TV program called "Ann Kay's Real-Life Surprise Party." Inasmuch as Ann Kay has been targeted by Shahdov for sexual conquest, he is delighted to find himself seated beside her. Yet he is puzzled by her conversational non sequiturs—which, in fact, are pitches to her unseen audience on behalf of a deodorant and a dentifrice. Finally he asks her whether she usually goes off "the deep end" this way. "You think I'm crazy" is her parrying answer. "I know so," Shahdov declares emphatically. The exchange rams home another indictment of modern America as a society gone mad.

But finally Chaplin preferred political commentary to cultural satire as a vent for his rage. In the course of the King's inspection of a progressive school for boys, he comes across the boy Communist Rupert Macabee and is transfixed by his rhetorical assaults on the menace of free enterprise, the crime of atomic weaponry, and the threat posed by "too much power"—in the hands, of course, of the United States—to the peace and safety of the world.

At a hearing staged by the villainous members of HUAC, Rupert's father acknowledges that he had once been a Communist, but refuses to furnish the committee with the names of former comrades. As a result, he and his wife as well (there is an echo here of the linkage of Ethel Rosenberg's fate to Julius's) are cited for contempt. The nature of Shahdov's own remarks when he, too, is summoned before the committee is never spelled out. Instead there is a painfully unfunny sequence prior to his testimony in which he appears in the committee room with his finger stuck in a fire hose and proceeds to get every one of his inquisitors soaking wet. In the aftermath of his testimony, newspaper headlines announce that all charges against him have been dropped and that he is slated to receive a Congressional Medal of Merit. In the teeth of his anti-American paroxysms, Chaplin still dreamed, paradoxically, of being honored by America.

Even so, the picture ends on a note of unmitigated bitterness. Shahdov discovers that Rupert has purchased his parents' release from the threat of a jail sentence by furnishing the committee with the names of their Red friends. The boy's betrayal of the cause comes as a shock to Shahdov, while Rupert's tears and bowed head indicate the depth of his feelings of shame. As Shahdov's plane takes off for Europe, where he has decided to live, he leaves behind him a corrosive image of the agony of life in McCarthyist America: a sobbing child.

II

"Fathers can be fun, I'm told," Michael Chaplin sarcastically declared in his ghostwritten memoir, *I Couldn't Smoke the Grass on My Father's Lawn* (1966). But fun for the children of Charlie Chaplin sooner or later collided with his "inflexible belief in the absolute rightness of his own convictions," his "terrible temper," and his "tyrannical side." Geraldine's childhood impression was that her father worked every day of the year.

"The house was big enough, but downstairs you could not make *any* noise, ever. Tiptoe past, tiptoe out in the garden, tiptoe in. If Daddy heard us, he'd come out screaming. But he hardly ever did. That was the law. That was just the way it was." Frequent wallopings of all the kids were also a feature of his rule. "We got the full routine," Geraldine recalled in her forties, "—on the bum, over your father's knee, and bang-o. I used to throw myself on the floor screaming when I got summoned, and I didn't get hurt. But Michael was stupid and wouldn't cry. 'That didn't hurt,' he'd say. So he'd get another one." Occasionally the children were permitted to see films—Charlie Chaplin films, that is. "Those were the only films allowed," according to Geraldine.

> I don't think I realized other people made films. Films! That was Charlie Chaplin. The first other film Michael and I saw was *Quo Vadis*. It was in color and there was no Charlie Chaplin in it—can you imagine? We were thrilled. It didn't go down very well when we came home and said we'd seen this wonderful movie with *lions!*[41]

More conscious of his own lack of schooling than of his children's individual needs, Chaplin enrolled them in proper boarding schools whether or not they were suited for that kind of education. Michael, not surprisingly, was the first to rebel, for the tension between them had begun in Michael's babyhood, as the remembrances of Betty Chaplin Tetrick* have made clear. "The baby Oona loved most was Michael. She used to cuddle him against her face. And that made Charlie jealous. He wasn't very nice to Michael and often he was a sad little boy." When Michael disappeared from his school at age fourteen, his father hired a detective, who traced him through Michael's girlfriend of the moment. Upon being reunited with his son, Chaplin socked him in the eye.[42]

In 1961 Geraldine left home to study at the Royal Ballet School in London. In spite of her father's own love of ballet, her decision angered him, she later affirmed in a magazine interview. "Eldest daughter, you

---

* Betty Chaplin, a descendant of Charles Chaplin Senior's pub-owning brother, Spencer Chaplin, arrived in Hollywood in November 1939 and subsequently married the Chaplin Studio's wardrobe chieftain, Ted Tetrick. Although Chaplin was fond of Mrs. Tetrick, she developed a much closer relationship with Oona, which was sustained throughout the Vevey years.

know, the whole thing. The fact that I was wearing make-up made him angry. The fact that I was growing up, that I was interested in boys, that I wanted to be a ballet dancer made him angry. Everything made him angry." Underneath the anger lay a terror. Geraldine recalled that at a Matisse exhibition in Paris at which the crowd had been far more interested in art than in the white-haired entertainer in its midst, "my father turned to my mother and said, 'I used to be very famous, you know.' . . . He was terrified of being forgotten." (Perhaps it was that passage in the interview—which also included criticisms from Geraldine's siblings, Michael and Annie—that caused Oona to throw down the magazine and bitterly exclaim to her ex-daughter-in-law, Patrice Chaplin—Michael's ex-wife—who was visiting Vevey at the time, "Can't they say something else? Is that all they've got to say about their fucking childhood?"[43])

A year after Geraldine's departure, Michael again dropped out of school, this time for good, and followed his sister to the swinging London of the 1960s. During a talk years later with Patrice Chaplin, who, Oona knew, was writing a memoir about her, Oona relived Michael's leaving: "the shock of the empty room; his not coming back." Yet she could not see that "it had anything to do with his father," whereas Patrice knew from Michael that he saw his departure as an escape from "a madhouse of discipline, inequality, brilliance, egocentricity, nanny order and control. He took off from the clean grass of Switzerland and leapt into chaos and disorder—his life was night-time. He gulped it as though he'd been crossing a desert and was dying of thirst."

As a long-haired, pot-smoking, guitar-playing hippie who took a few courses at the Royal Academy of Dramatic Art, cut a few records, and acted in a few pictures, Michael affronted his father several times over. And there was worse to come. In 1965 he claimed and received National Assistance, to the wisecracking delight of the press. The son of multimillionaire Charlie preferred government handouts to help from his father! The uproar stung Oona into making a public statement: "Concerning my son Michael Chaplin: the young man is a problem, and I am sorry he was given National Assistance. He has stubbornly refused an education for three years and therefore he should get a job and go to work. If I do not wish to indulge him as a beatnik, that is my privilege —sincerely, Oona Chaplin."[44]

Her assertion of her autonomous rights in that final sentence fooled no one who knew her. Oona's "privilege," as she and her husband both construed it, was the privilege of bonding with him. Her parents' relationship was "so perfect," their daughter Annie confessed, "that for me it's nearly a problem." It was a problem for all the children. Their father and mother's airtight closeness left no emotional room between them for anyone else. In *Irving Berlin: A Daughter's Memoir* (1994), Mary Ellin Barrett recalled her surprise at a dinner party one evening in 1945 at seeing Chaplin and Oona (who had been two years ahead of Mary Ellin at Brearley) holding hands and snuggling during the after-dinner movie. Likewise at Vevey, Patrice Chaplin reported, their children saw them sitting together for hours and holding each other and kissing. In Oona's universe, according to Betty Tetrick,

> Charlie came first. The children had to understand that. She tried to make his exile pleasant. She entertained him at dinner—she was always a witty conversationalist. And she always made sure she looked her best —wore lovely wraps. She favored those. And kimonos in silk and crepe de Chine, informal but beautifully made and embroidered. He liked her in those. And she'd put on her jewelry. She'd get his friends over from the States. And she encouraged him to work. She knew what he needed. And he had that terrible temper and she had to defuse that.

By the early 1960s, her elegance as a hostess had caught up with the sophistication of her clothes. The flowers, the food, the wines at the Manoir were perfect, in the opinion of her longtime American friend the Countess Vivian Crespi, who had a house at Gstaad and was often a guest at the parties Oona gave for Noël Coward, Graham Greene, Ian Fleming, Ivor Montagu (he of the possible Soviet secret service connection), and a stream of other visitors. Christmas dinner at the Manoir was an especially wonderful occasion, Crespi affirmed.[45]

That is not the way the Chaplin children remembered the day. His father hated Christmas, said Michael, and Geraldine agreed. Christmas "depressed him," she said. "It brought back memories that he wasn't fond of. . . . He used to try to spoil the day for every one, and he finally did. He [even] died on Christmas morning."[46]

12

As Oona knew better than anyone else, waiting for the critical reaction to *A King in New York* was a trying time for Chaplin. To his politically simpatico friend Ella Winter, who interviewed him in Vevey just before the release of the picture in September 1957, he half-boastfully, half-pleadingly declared, "It's good, my best picture, it's entertainment, don't you think?" But with the conspicuous exception of Dilys Powell, who boldly asserted in the *London Times* that the picture enabled the cinema "to take its place without question among the seats reserved for the major arts," the influential English reviewers failed to give him the caliber of praise that he craved. While Kenneth Tynan, for example, emphasized in the *Observer* that the picture was never boring, he felt it necessary to add that "many of the slapstick interludes are both ill-judged and perfunctory; and none of the backgrounds conveys the remotest feeling of America. When it aspires to epigram, the dialogue falls into a quaint, soggy prissiness; when it attempts 'real feeling,' we find ourselves in the dread company of lines like: 'To part is to die a little.' " As for the American estimates, the bulk of them resembled *Time*'s: "Intended as satire, *King*'s few funny spots are outweighed by its shrill invective and heavy-footed propaganda." *Time* also chose to remind its readers that, unlike the king whom he had portrayed in the movie, Chaplin was a "self exile" who "decided to deprive the U.S. of one of the few authentic geniuses produced by the movies." [47]

After three years of licking his wounds and brooding, during which his most significant accomplishment was the settlement of tax differences with the U.S. government, Chaplin finally fastened on a project that fully engaged him. Backed by Oona's encouragement, he began writing *My Autobiography.*

As he was completing it in 1964, Truman Capote—a Swiss neighbor at the time—made the mistake of trying to help him. The gossipy writer later gave his gossipy pal and reputed model for Holly Golightly, Carol Matthau, a full account of what happened. Chaplin phoned him one day and announced that he had just finished the manuscript of his life story. Come to lunch tomorrow, he proposed, "and then, if you will, I'd love to have you take the book with you and tell me everything you feel and think. It would be a great help." Capote did not wish to do this, he assured Matthau, because he was in the middle of writing something himself. But out of love for Oona—born of enchantment with her dry wit and discerning judgments of people—he agreed to. "I started to read," Matthau remembered Capote saying, and it broke my heart. I wanted Chaplin to have a great autobiography. Instead, he was writing about the people he'd met, and they're all lesser people, none of them could take a reader's interest the way he could. It was the book of a poor little English boy who will never be part of the royal family. So I went to work on it. In pencil. And I took it down to him. We started to talk about it and Charlie threw me out. "Get the fuck out of here," he said. "I wanted you to read it. I wanted you to enjoy it. I don't need your opinion." And he never spoke to Truman again.[48]*

13

Coincident with the commencement of his autobiographical labors, favorable images of him began to accumulate in the American press. The new presentations were spearheaded by the *New York Times*. In November 1960, Bosley Crowther reported on his interview with Chaplin in an article that appeared in the Sunday *Times Magazine*. The man who had had nothing but scorn for the United States in *A King in New York* only four years before did not appear in the piece; only a "mellower" figure was in evidence. "I cannot help but be bitter about many things that happened to me," Crowther quoted Chaplin as saying, "but the country and the American people—they are great, of course." The reference to bitterness did not prompt Crowther to press Chaplin about whether, before leaving the United States, he had already made up his mind not to return. Nor did the critic make mention of the extremely high probability that Chaplin could have achieved reentry in 1952 had he elected to confront the INS. From first to last, Crowther's implicit message to his readers was that here was a great artist whom America had victimized for no good reason in an irrationally repressive time.[49]

In 1962 the *Times* resumed its attentions to the Chaplin case. The

---

* *Cf.* Betty Chaplin Tetrick's story, as related to Patrice Chaplin, about the time that she and Oona accompanied Chaplin to a dentist's office in Lausanne. The dental technician, a young woman, "was so nice and gentle and she examined his mouth and said, "Oh dear, your teeth are packed with tartar." And she gave a prod and he'd had enough. He got the girl's prong, threw it on the floor, and said, 'My teeth are *perfectly* packed with tartar and they're going to stay that way.' And he never went back." Patrice Chaplin, *Hidden Star*, p. 154.

occasion was provided by the news that on June 27 Oxford University had awarded the seventy-three-year-old entertainer a degree of Doctor of Letters, in a ceremony in which the U.S. Secretary of State, Dean Rusk, was also honored. The *Times* played the story on page one and four days later published an editorial entitled "Re-enter the 'Little Tramp.' " The Communists, said the *Times*, had "tried to use [Chaplin] for their purposes," but "he insisted that he never had belonged and never would belong to their humorless fraternity of the Left." Red schemers—that is to say, not the comedian himself—were to blame for his excursions into political commentary. The phrase "tried to use" also suggested that the schemers had not really been successful in their efforts to exploit him.[50]

Along with exasperating obscurantism, "Re-enter the 'Little Tramp' " offered two propositions worth pondering. Chaplin's tramp pictures were one of the glories of American culture, and the *Times* came close to saying that. The little tramp "lives," the editorial proclaimed, "and will live until the last of the films that show him in action have turned to dust." The editorial then called on the Kennedy administration to remove the impediments to the comedian's free return to the United States, and the language of its appeal for magnanimity and reconciliation was stirring: "We do not believe the Republic would be in danger if yesterday's unforgotten little tramp were allowed to amble down the gangplank of a steamer or plane in an American port."[51]

Word of the editorial reached Chaplin at the beginning of a busy week. On July 6 he received another honorary degree, a Doctor of Letters from the University of Durham, and two days later, having hurried back to Switzerland, he accompanied Oona to a clinic in Lausanne for the birth of their eighth and last child, Christopher. These happy events, however, did not distract him from mulling over the significance of the *Times*'s kind words. Neither Dean Rusk's State Department nor Robert Kennedy's Justice Department had responded to them. Nevertheless, the climate of opinion in the United States seemed to be changing. Perhaps it was time for his business representatives to arrange a limited rerelease in New York of a selection of his pictures.

Eventually the manager of the Plaza Theater agreed to cooperate, and in the last week of November 1963, amidst the aftershock from President Kennedy's assassination, the theater inaugurated a yearlong series of Chaplin programs with *City Lights*. The next presentation was a so-called Chaplin Revue, consisting of *Shoulder Arms*, *A Dog's Life*, and *The Pilgrim*. Only feature-length pictures were shown thereafter— *The Gold Rush, Modern Times, The Great Dictator, Monsieur Verdoux*, and *Limelight*. While the entire program fared well at the box office and in the reviews, the highest number of sellouts was racked up by *Monsieur Verdoux*, and glowing tributes were lavished upon it by the *Herald-Tribune's* Judith Crist ("fantastic comedy," "biting ironies," "crushing social satire") and the *Times's* Bosley Crowther ("an engrossingly wry and paradoxical film" that is "screamingly funny in places" without ever losing the thread of an "unusually serious and sobering argument"). In a piece in the Sunday *Times* eight days later, Crowther went even further. The current availability of the picture at the Plaza is "a rare and rousing privilege that no one should miss." His own visit to the theater, he averred, had also served to bring back "melancholy memories" of the "outrage and abuse so cruelly heaped on Mr. Chaplin" at the time of *Monsieur Verdoux's* original release.[52]

That *Monsieur Verdoux* repeatedly played to all but full houses at the Plaza for seven straight weeks following its record-setting opening on the Fourth of July 1964 weekend was phenomenal. "Chaplin is no longer a villain," said *Newsweek*, by way of explaining the film's success.[53] Yet it also was related, ironically enough, to the risingly influential youth culture that Chaplin had deplored in *A King in New York*. Verdoux may have been middle-aged and decked out in fashion-plate attire, but his disaffection from society and his revolt against it linked him in spirit to the gathering rebelliousness of the postwar young.

That rebelliousness was reflected in a line of movies about ill-mannered misfits that began with a piece of trash called *The Wild One* (1954), starring Marlon Brando as the sullen, brooding Johnny ("What are you rebelling against?" a girl asks Johnny, and Johnny says, "Whaddaya got?") and attained a certain force with the doomed James Dean's performance as the sullen, brooding Jim in *Rebel Without a Cause* (1955). "When you first see Jimmy in his red jacket against his black Merc," said director Nicholas Ray, "it's not a pose. It's a warning. It's a sign."[54] Twelve years later, on the very eve of apocalyptic 1968, when student protesters against the Vietnam War would stage 221 major demonstrations on university and college campuses and Abbie Hoffman would publish a much-talked-about primer called *Revolution for the Hell of It*, the egotism, incivility, and contempt for authority on display in *The Wild One* and *Rebel Without a Cause* reached new levels of intensity in the bloody odyssey of Bonnie and Clyde and the acts of defiance of Cool Hand Luke.[55]

And speaking of Cool Hand Luke, the 1960s loved cool. Verdoux possessed it, too, in all his serious moments in the picture, even in the shadow of the guillotine. With his head held high and his wrists bound behind him, he was Cool Hand Verdoux. A taste for black humor aimed at America's armed might was still another of the decade's attributes— and another explanation of why *Monsieur Verdoux* caught on. A good many of the people standing in line to get into the Plaza, it is fair to suppose, had read Joseph Heller's *Catch-22* (1961) and had seen Stanley Kubrick's *Dr. Strangelove* during its New York run the preceding January. Moviegoers who cottoned to the grotesqueries of Kubrick's portrait of a crazy anti-Communist general who wants to launch a nuclear strike of his own against the Soviets were apt to find the atom bomb invective of Chaplin's wife killer to their taste as well.*

14

As the Chaplin series at the Plaza entered its final weeks in the fall of 1964, editions of *My Autobiography* simultaneously appeared all over the world. In the United States, an advance sale of forty-seven thousand copies and selection by the Book-of-the-Month Club presaged the book's rise to a top-ten position on the nonfiction best-seller list, where it remained for six months.[56]

In the final stages of his compositional labors, the author had sent a message to the American people. One of the intermediaries he picked to convey it was the distinguished theater critic Harold Clurman, his first guest at the Manoir following the appearance of the *New York Time*'s "Re-enter the 'Little Tramp'" editorial. While bombarding Clurman one evening with readings from various chapters, Chaplin

---

* *Cf.* another film of 1964, John Frankenheimer's *Seven Days in May*, about an anti-Communist Air Force general who makes a maniacal effort to prevent a liberal President from signing a nuclear arms treaty with the Soviet Union.

suddenly exclaimed, "On reading my book I'm really surprised how well America comes off!" Four months later, Clurman not only quoted those words in an article in *Esquire*, but added that he had no doubts about their sincerity.[57] Before arriving at the Manoir, it seemed, Clurman had come across press reports that in his forthcoming autobiography Chaplin had adopted a "benign attitude" toward America. This information had caused Clurman to wonder whether the attitude was "a matter of tactics." But on meeting him face-to-face, "I felt sure his moderation was genuine." Yet in a very real sense the entire tale that Chaplin had concocted was "a matter of tactics."

He had always taken enormous liberties with the truth in his accounts of his life. With his appetite for acclaim made even keener by the fear that he was being forgotten, he did not lack for motives for further prevarications. Through the British edition of a sufficiently appealing autobiography, he might firm up his chances for a knighthood from the Queen. By means of the U.S. edition, he might make further strides in fostering a renewed American attention to his work.

The reaction of American reviewers to *My Autobiography* was by no means devoid of criticism. Many raised the Truman Capote objection: once the narrative reached the point at which famous and fashionable people began to seek Chaplin out, lists of their names started to appear in the text, and in the second half of the book the proliferation of these roll calls became ridiculous. (Who cared that the Chaplin home in Vevey was "relatively near" the residences of the Queen of Spain and the Count and Countess Chevreau d'Antraigues?) There were expressions of disappointment as well about the comedian's limited insight into his movies and about his failure even to mention such classics as *The Tramp* and *The Circus*, while his fondness for pompous phrases adorned with five-dollar words obviously culled from a thesaurus ("the subject was a glib braggart in an esurient state of libido") aroused amusement.

Time magazine, a persistent Chaplin critic, complained that the book was "uneven and uncommunicative about [the author's] many loves and his vociferous left-wing politics," as did Francis Russell in William F. Buckley, Jr.'s *National Review*. Chaplin's earlier marriages and alleged promiscuity "are passed over, almost pushed aside," Russell observed, but what really bothered him was Chaplin's failure to offer any explanation for his second-front speeches in 1942 other than to say that he just happened to be asked to substitute for the ailing Ambassador Davies at a Russian War Relief rally.* (In Russell's mordant opinion, his pro-Soviet activism was born of "the desire of a man of thin education and little reading to get himself accepted as an intellectual. He, whose normal level was Marion Davies, thereby found himself the peer of Hanns Eisler and ... Brecht." [58])

Actually, he had pruned his political record in more ways than Francis Russell indicated. Conspicuously absent from the several pages of quotes that he reproduced from his second-front speeches was his celebration of the Moscow purges as a "wonderful thing" in which "the Communists did away with their Quislings and Lavals." The eight pages of dialogue from *Monsieur Verdoux* that precede a series of anecdotes about "the cleverest and most brilliant film I have yet made" did not include the transparently veiled condemnation of atomic America as a mass-scale murderer. His defense of the Soviet Union's destruction of Czechoslovakian democracy ("No soldiers were there. There was no bloodshed. . . .") was not to be found in the two pages of answers that he reproduced from the INS interview conducted in his home, nor did he choose to mention the Communist-front peace conferences to which he lent his name in 1949 and 1950.

Much else in Chaplin's book ought to have warned alert readers not to trust it: The lack of hard facts and dates in the early chapters. The suspiciously Dickensian sound of his evocations of the poverty of his childhood and of the disciplinary horrors of the Hanwell School. The romantic tale that his half brother Sydney was the son of an English lord and had been born in Africa, following Hannah's elopement to a life of luxury there. The failure to acknowledge the existence of his other illegitimate half brother, Wheeler Dryden. The paucity of information about Hannah's disturbed behavior in the years leading up to her institutionalizations and in the periods in between. The prima facie dubiousness of his claim that at the age of five he had taken the place of

---

* What Chaplin should have done during the war, Irving Berlin had sternly insisted at the time, was to entertain British and American troops in Britain. "All he'd have to do," said Berlin, "was stand in the middle of Piccadilly Circus and say, 'I'm here.' " Mary Ellin Barrett, *Irving Berlin: A Daughter's Memoir* (New York, 1994), p. 236.

a star on a music hall stage. The absence of reflective discussion of the possible connections between the psychological disorder of his early years and the compulsions of his later conduct. The brutally inadequate recollections of the author's professional associates.

Perhaps that last fault is the least forgivable of them all. *My Autobiography* either completely ignored or made but a single passing mention of Rollie Totheroh, Mack Swain, Henry Bergman, Eric Campbell, Georgia Hale, Chuck Riesner, Robert Florey, Harry d'Abbadie d'Arrast, David Raksin, Eddie Sutherland, Carlyle Robinson, Merna Kennedy, and half a dozen other studio people who had once been important to him. As for his old friend from music hall days Stan Laurel, he appeared in a group photograph of the Karno hockey team but not in the narrative. Nor was mention made of Max Linder, or Buster Keaton.

Never underestimate the inattentiveness of reviewers. *"My Autobiography* by Charles Chaplin is the most original, virile book about the theater that has been written in a long, long time," glowed the *Atlantic Monthly*'s Edward Weeks. No less striking than the prevalence of such effusions was the eagerness of many reviewers to side with Chaplin in his post–World War II political tribulations. In their view, the anti-Communism of the day had been nothing more than a phobia. That an impressive array of liberal and conservative anti-Communists had deplored the activities of Joseph McCarthy was forgotten. As for the achievements of James McGranery as a New Deal liberal, a fighter for civil rights, an opponent of corruption, and a papally decorated Catholic layman, they were erased from history by the 1960s revisionists, and over the blankness a portrait of a witch hunter was hung. His revocation of Chaplin's reentry permit under the provisions of immigration law was a "cowardly act" (Brooks Atkinson in the *New York Times*) that had been "disgracefully, sneakily perpetrated" (*Newsweek*).

Where Chaplin had suffered an undeniable injustice was in the barring of *Limelight* from many theaters and the hasty withdrawal of it from many others. But for the revisionists, that criticism of America's treatment of him was not enough. Speaking for the Hollywood left, John Houseman depicted the comedian in the pages of the *Nation* as one of the targets of the "Red purge" that had "reached a virulent and spiteful climax in Hollywood during the late forties"—even though Chaplin as the owner of his own studio had obviously never been in danger of being "purged" (*i.e.*, blacklisted). With overkill rhetoric, Robert Hatch declared in *Harper's* that "the persecution of Chaplin in the name of American patriotism is a scandal this era is saddled with forever."[59]

Alone of all the reviewers of *My Autobiography*, Harry Feldman, writing in *Film Comment* two years after the book's appearance, fully understood that the facts of the Chaplin case had "become hopelessly garbled." The distortion and innuendo, the mixture of truth and error, in accounts of his exile, Feldman continued, "are worthy of an editorial in *Pravda*."

> Chaplin left this country voluntarily. He was not an American citizen because, for reasons of his own, he chose to remain a British subject. . . . [Subsequently,] he was informed that his right to re-enter the United States would be challenged because of a morals charge. Chaplin, again for reasons of his own, chose not to contest this charge. Martyrs should be made of sterner stuff.[60]

Feldman's straight talk, however bracing, had no effect on public opinion. By the mid-1960s, Chaplin had been happily married for more than twenty years. Newspaper photos of him and Oona walking together in London, or on vacation with their children in the south of France, had replaced the headlines of yesteryear about paternity suits and declarations of support for Communist-dominated peace conferences. In common with many other peoples, moreover, the American people were inclined to forgive the moral and political failings of artists whose work they cherished. More than any other solvent, it was fond memories of the Tramp that washed away American bitterness about his creator.

15

"STAY WARM, GROUCHO,
YOU'RE NEXT"

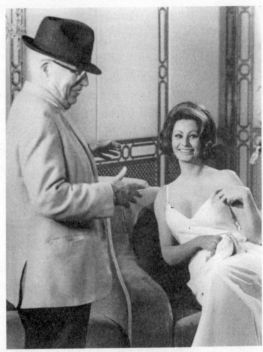

Joking with Sophia Loren on the set of A Countess
from Hong Kong *(1967).*

A COUNTESS *from Hong Kong* (1967), Chaplin's final film although not the last that he thought of making, was his first in color, his
first in more than forty years to be backed by the financial resources of
an outside company (in this case, Universal), and the first since *A Woman
of Paris* in which he cast himself in a bit part.* The stars of the picture,

* The part was that of a ship's steward. In playing it, Chaplin paid silent tribute to his
brother Sydney, who had died in April 1965. As a youth, Sydney had shipped out as a
steward on a number of ocean voyages.

Sophia Loren and Marlon Brando, had committed themselves to it without knowing much more about the script than its comedy situation: an impoverished White Russian countess named Natascha, living in exile in Hong Kong, decides to stow away on a luxury liner bound for Honolulu; an American millionaire, Ogden Mears, finds the voluptuous Natascha in his stateroom; as a comedy of hide and seek with the authorities unfolds, love blossoms.[1]

The filming, at the Pinewood Studios near London, got under way on January 25, 1966, in an atmosphere of mounting tension. Soon enough, Brando and Loren were not speaking to each other. The prime source of the tension, however, was Chaplin, and it took its toll on him as well as on others. By quitting time each day, he usually looked exhausted and the sweatband of his hat was apt to be wet. Yet he astounded everyone with his energy, as he always had on every picture he had ever made. During a visit to the set, the historian of the silent screen Kevin Brownlow asked a young publicity woman who was standing near him, "Is he always as energetic as this?" "Oh, yes," she said, "he's extraordinary. Really wonderful."[2] It was not a part of her job, of course, to say anything about how unwonderful he could be.

Chaplin was "a fearsomely cruel man," Brando discovered. Indeed, he was "probably the most sadistic man I'd ever met," an "egotistical tyrant" and "a penny-pincher."

> He harassed people when they were late, and scolded them unmercifully to work faster. Worst of all, he treated his son Sydney, who played my sidekick, cruelly. In front of everybody, he humiliated him constantly: "Sydney, you're so stupid! Don't you have enough brains to know how to place your hand on a doorknob? *You know what a doorknob is, don't you?* All you do is turn the knob, open and enter. *Isn't that easy, Sydney?*

Chaplin repeatedly spoke to Sydney this way, according to Brando, and for no perceptible reason reshot his scenes again and again, assaulting him all the while with further sarcasms. Oona, said Brando, witnessed many of these degradations, but never defended her stepson. In private, Sydney assured Brando that this was the way his father treated all his children. Furthermore, said Sydney, the old man never gave his children any money to speak of, citing as an example his refusal to lend Sydney the money to fulfill his dream of opening a restaurant.

One day Brando arrived on the set fifteen minutes late. "I was in the wrong," he realized, but his contrition vanished in the face of Chaplin's brutally vindictive reaction. "In front of the whole cast [he] berated me, embarrassing me, telling me that I had no sense of professional ethics and that I was a disgrace to my profession." Brando took this as long as he could and then said, "Mr. Chaplin, I'll be in my dressing room for twenty minutes. If you give me an apology within that time, I will consider not getting on a plane and returning to the United States. But I'll be there only twenty minutes." A few minutes later, a humbled Chaplin showed up and apologized.*

"I still looked up to him," Brando emphasized, "as perhaps the greatest genius that the medium has ever produced. I don't think anyone has ever had the talent he did; he made everybody else look Lilliputian. But as a human being he was a mixed bag, just like all of us."[3]

If Oona was sometimes upset, it was not because of the humiliations visited upon Sydney, but because Sophia Loren was "perhaps too Italian with Charlie," as Patrice Chaplin would put it in her Oona memoir, *Hidden Star*. Although she had no reason to believe that her husband was unfaithful to her, she was susceptible nevertheless to jealousy. Whenever she felt she could safely leave the set, she went shopping. As her friend and frequent companion Betty Tetrick well knew, shopping was Oona's passion. In California, Rodeo Drive had been her haunt; in Paris she habitually chose her clothes from the famous designers, especially Balenciaga, and then had fittings in Switzerland; in London she was a familiar sight on Bond Street with her shopping missions for the whole family as well as herself.[4]

---

* Jerry Epstein, the producer of *A Countess from Hong Kong* and Chaplin's close associate since *Limelight*, presented a radically different version of this story in his memoir of Chaplin. "Two hundred extras were hired. Charlie and Sophia were there at eight-thirty in the morning, ready for rehearsals. Two hours went by. No Marlon. Charlie was fit to be tied. . . . Marlon came on the set like an innocent little boy. Charlie stormed towards him like a tornado. I tried to hold him back, but it was futile. He grabbed Marlon by the arm: 'Listen, you son-of-a-bitch, you're working for Charlie Chaplin now. If you think you're slumming, take the next plane back to Hollywood. We don't need you.' . . . Marlon was like a small child in front of Big Daddy, sweet and apologetic. 'Gee, Charlie, I was sick and . . .' Charlie continued: 'Listen—I'm an old man and I manage to be here on time. Now you're to be on the set every day, ready to shoot by eight-thirty, just like me.' Marlon, the little boy, nodded, wide-eyed: 'Yes, Charlie.' " Jerry Epstein, *Remembering Charlie* (New York, 1989), pp. 177–79.

On the weekends, the Chaplins were apt to see their politically com-patible friends Donald Ogden Stewart and Ella Winter, who were living in a mansion in Hampstead amidst a huge collection of Klees, and on a few occasions they got together with Harry Cushing, who had been one of Oona's escorts in her Brearley days. Cushing noted that as a result of drinking the perfect wines and eating the perfect food at the Manoir de Ban, Chaplin's body had thickened considerably. Cushing was struck, too, by the intensity of his emotional investment in *A Countess from Hong Kong*. "It's my best film," the comedian assured him.[5]

At the London premiere in January 1967, the house was crowded—and the boredom palpable. There was no doubt that the critics were sharpening their knives. Oona phoned her son Michael. "The film's gone down. They hate it. We've just got to be—" "Cool?" "That'll do, yes." But Chaplin was not at all cool. In a public statement he lashed out at his British detractors as "bloody idiots." That the French critics were kind to the picture (in Paris Charlot could do no wrong) helped a little—until the crushing American returns came in. The plaintive ques-tion raised by Hugh Kenner defined the attitude of other reviewers from coast to coast: "How did Charlie get trapped inside this turkey?" The broad American public heard nothing by word of mouth to the contrary. Despite the pulling power of Brando and Loren, *A Countess from Hong Kong* failed to do one weekend of good business. At the close of 1967, it ranked a dismal sixty-second on *Variety*'s list of the year's box-office attractions.[6]

2

Oona tried to explain away the catastrophe of the film's British recep-tion by telling herself that "of course the Beaverbrook papers would turn against Charlie. Beaverbrook always disliked him because he didn't pay English taxes. He used to say he has his cake and eats it too." Because she refused to believe that her husband's muse had deserted him, and because he was always happier when a project was preoccu-pying him, she urged him to make another film.[7]

By the end of 1967, he was full of plans for *The Freak*, a story about a girl who suddenly sprouts a pair of wings. His and Oona's third daugh-ter, sixteen-year-old Victoria, had a flair for comedy and a large-eyed, waiflike beauty. Writing the story with her in mind as the lead made it infinitely more interesting to him. For well over a year he coached her, while laboring over the script and talking and talking about how enchanting the picture was going to be. Then Victoria fell in love with a young French actor, Jean-Baptiste Thierrée, who yearned to create his own circus. Chaplin was furious and confined Victoria to the grounds of the Manoir. Like Michael before her, she ran away. Shortly afterwards, she and Thierrée were married.* Never, according to Patrice Chaplin, had Oona seen her husband so hurt; attempting to soften his raging vow that he would deny the couple entrance to the Manoir should they ever appear at the door enmeshed her in anguishing scenes with him.[8]

In *Limelight*, Terry receives the vitally needed support of a father figure, who then sets her free to find a lover and to soar as a ballerina. In life Oona received the vitally needed support of a father figure who was also her lover—and who confined her in a gilded cage. As the wife of a man three times her age, she abandoned whatever career dreams she might have had and started having children. In her schoolmate Joan Ridder Challinor's opinion, no other girl at Brearley had seemed less likely to become the mother of a large family. The traditional recourse for the alleviation of unbearable pain in the haunted house of O'Neill had been drink and/or drugs. Oona chose drink. "She always drank," Rachel Ford declared after Oona's death. "Secretly. Charlie knew. She tried to shut herself away when they had a row—locked herself in for days at a time and drank." Ford insisted—not very convincingly—that the children did not know. "They were upstairs with their nannies. I used to come in to sort out some business and he was in a terrible rage and she'd run into her room and lock the door. And he'd try to get her out, and it was all hell."[9]

3

In June 1969, a jet-setter playboy, Taki Theodoracopulos, spent three days at Vevey. Taki—as he is known professionally—is now a gossip columnist for the *Spectator* of London, but in those days he was a pho-

---

* The Cirque Imaginaire that they set up would acquire a reputation as a fey, whimsical, but finally rather precious entertainment.

tographer. Through his acquaintance with a fellow Greek, Nico Sisto-
zaris, who was marrying the brightest of the Chaplin children,
Josephine, he was given the sole right to photograph the wedding and
attendant festivities. On the strength of this exclusive, he received press
credentials from the editors of *Paris-Match*, to whom he sold his work.

Taki's primary impression was that an enormous tension existed between Chaplin and his children. The children were "scared shitless" of
him, in his opinion. Chaplin corrected them all the time. Hence they
gave him a wide berth, and did not speak to him if they could help it.
Oona was gracious, but also very nervous, he remembered. So Taki
ended up talking to Chaplin one-on-one at great length. Having heard
terrible stories about him, he expected the worst. But in fact he found
him charming, and interested in Taki as a person. The great surprise,
however, was his conservatism. He said "terrible things about the world
and the way it had turned out." He was outraged by the spectacle of the
youth of "the West." Spoiled rotten by too many material possessions,
he declared. That these rich kids were rebelling was outrageous. The
student rebellion in Paris in 1968 should have been put down at once.
It was disgusting that these rich kids had risen up. He compared them
—to their distinct disadvantage—to the poor youngsters he had known
in England when he was growing up. He was appalled by their habit of
wearing blue jeans, he said, and by their abominable lack of manners.
His animadversions reminded Taki of Solzhenitsyn's. Yet if he was contemptuous of youth it pained him to be old, Taki realized. He asked to
be warned before any pictures were taken of him, and he made it clear
that he wanted to be shot from above, so that he would appear less
jowly. His vanity was breathtaking.

The children were all left-wingers, Taki felt, especially Victoria,
whose presence at the wedding had apparently been negotiated by
Oona. Six or seven years later, he ran into Victoria in the train station
in Florence. She was still married to the clown she had run away with
and looked very scruffy. Taki asked her if she was still a lefty. "More
than ever," Victoria replied.

Oona and Chaplin led a *secluded* life, Taki emphasized. The only
celebrity on hand for the wedding was Noël Coward, who came on to
the dashing photographer by accusing him of being a *paparazzo*. "I can
see the Via Veneto rising behind you," Coward said.

Once again, Taki spoke of how extremely nervous Oona was. There was definitely a tension between her and Chaplin. As a vastly experienced connoisseur of the feminine face and form, Taki was of the opinion that when it came to ageless beauty Oona was no C. Z. Guest or Gloria Guinness. And she drank, he was sure. Even though he never came across her drinking alone, he got the impression that that was her habit.[10]

4

There was money to be made out of a worldwide redistribution of a judicious selection of his father's films, Sydney Chaplin believed. Toward the close of a convivial lunch one afternoon at the Manoir, Sydney and a Hollywood producer pal and potential partner, Sandy Lieberson, broached the proposition they had in mind. To their stunned surprise, Chaplin responded with a barrage of insults—mainly aimed at Sydney. As the storm continued without any signs of letting up, the petitioners fled the premises.[11]

Moses "Mighty Mo" Rothman, on the other hand, was treated with respect for his business acumen. The idea for a deal with Chaplin had first occurred to Rothman in 1970, when he was living in Paris and working for United Artists. Although he and Chaplin were not friends, they had known each other for years. Because the deal would involve a lot of money up front, he brought in a highly successful young Hollywood producer, Bert Schneider, as his junior partner. According to Rothman, Schneider promised to invest in the company—hopefully entitled Black, Inc.—that the two of them formed, but in the end he never did.[12]

The deal with Black, Inc., that Chaplin finally agreed to in 1971 called for a $6 million advance against 50 percent of the profits, which would go to Chaplin's Roy Export Company, for global distribution rights to ten feature films and the three shorts in the *Chaplin Revue*. The rights would last until 2001. Chaplin also agreed to help publicize the rerelease of his pictures by making so-called balcony appearances at appropriate times in appropriate places.[13]

A showing of *Modern Times* in Paris in November 1971 launched the enterprise. Chaplin and Oona went over from Vevey a few days in advance of the press conference and reception that were to precede the premiere. One evening they were joined in their suite at the Ritz, before going on to dinner *à quatre* amidst the eighteenth-century splendors of the Grand Véfour, by Bert Schneider and his twenty-five-year-old girlfriend, Candice Bergen. The idea of spending an evening with the Chaplins had overwhelmed Bergen, but in the flesh she found them to be as "uncomfortable and timid" as she herself was. "At once courteous and shy," she would later write in her memoir, *Knock Wood* (1984), "neither had acquired the protective finish of social shellac. Their love for each other was palpable: it was good to see them together, impossible to imagine them otherwise. Oona walked by Charlie's chair, gently smoothing his hair, and Charlie smiled wistfully, clasping her hand." Perhaps their devotion to each other caused Bergen to wonder about the future of her relationship with Schneider.[14]

Very tall, very thin, very handsome, and very self-assured, Schneider had been used to the privileges of wealth since childhood. His father, Abraham Schneider, was a top executive at Columbia Pictures. In his rebellious youth, Schneider had been thrown out of college because of gambling and girls and then rejected by the U.S. Army because of his extremist politics. Yet this black-sheep, rich-boy radical proceeded to show Hollywood that he had the Midas touch. In 1966 he and a boy-hood friend, Bob Rafelson, who had become a successful TV executive after dropping out of Dartmouth, working as a jazz musician in Mexico, and questing for philosophical enlightenment in Japan and India, cre-ated the popular series "The Monkees," featuring a pop group manufac-tured especially for the show. The partners' profits from the series enabled them to form their own company, Raybert Productions (subse-quently reorganized as B.B.S. Incorporated). In short order Schneider emerged as Hollywood's first significant countercultural filmmaker. Be-ginning with a quasisurrealistic satire called *Head* (1968), starring the Monkees, directed by Rafelson and cowritten by Jack Nicholson, Schneider was deeply involved in a string of notable movies—*Easy Rider* (1969), which made $35 million and propelled Jack Nicholson toward stardom, *Five Easy Pieces* (1970), *Drive He Said* (1970), and *The Last Picture Show* (1971).[15]

Bergen was acting in a film in Los Angeles for Columbia Pictures when she began to catch glimpses of Schneider sitting at a table in the studio dining room with Dennis Hopper, Peter Fonda, and Jack

Nicholson. Although Schneider and his tablemates thought alike about many things, he was smarter than they were. Indeed, he was "extremely smart," in Bergen's opinion. On her first visit to his house in Beverly Hills, she could not get over the "sea of papers and periodicals," ranging from the *New York Review of Books* to the *Black Panther Paper* to *Screw*, that was spilling out of shelves and off tables, along with a flood of books by Erikson, Reich, Gurdjieff, Mao, Hegel, Marx, Jung, Castañeda, and the provisional head of the spiritual movement in America, Baba Ram Dass, formerly Professor Richard Alpert of Harvard.

Schneider's range of friends impressed the impressionable actress even more. A few weeks into his whirlwind courtship of her in early 1971, he took her up to Oakland to the penthouse apartment—guarded by a black giant called "Big Man"—of his revolutionary comrade Huey P. Newton, the Black Panther minister of defense. The next day, he introduced her to Ram Dass, who sucked serenely on a Sugar Daddy while reciting anecdotes about recent miracles in India, and in the evening he drove her to Joan Baez's house for dinner, where they discussed her Institute for the Study of Nonviolence. Once she was firmly established as Schneider's girl, a steady stream of radicals, political outlaws, and followers of the Spiritual Path entered Bergen's life. There were Rolfing sessions with a sad-eyed poet with hands like meat hooks, who took before-and-after snapshots of her naked body; there were Esalen Institute hot baths at Big Sur; and on one occasion there was a new drug known as MDA that turned low plaster ceilings into jeweled Byzantine domes.[16]

At the Grand Véfour in November 1971, Schneider broached an idea to Chaplin on behalf of the president of the Academy of Motion Picture Arts and Sciences, Daniel Taradash. If the Academy were to vote to give Chaplin an honorary award at the Oscar ceremonies in the spring of 1972, would he be willing to accept it? His reaction, as Taradash summarized Schneider's report, was "one of interest but tempered by fear of the long trip and even more by the possibility of outraged editorials, pickets at the airport, even catcalls at the Awards ceremonies." There was also the question of whether the State Department would grant Chaplin and Oona—who had long since renounced her American citizenship—nonimmigrant visas. Schneider assured Chaplin that the United States had changed in twenty years. And there the matter rested.[17]

5

Taradash, a Harvard graduate and a gifted screenwriter (*From Here to Eternity* and *Picnic* were among his credits), passionately believed that the revocation of Chaplin's reentry permit was a "contemptible edict" that represented "McCarthyism at its height." In 1970 he became the president of the Academy. By the time he was reelected a year later, he had only one objective, a noble one in spite of its being encircled in his mind by the false piety of undoing a political crime: to have the Academy honor Chaplin. Some years before, a proposal to give him the Academy's Irving Thalberg award as a "creative producer" had been soundly rejected by the board of governors. Taradash's disappointment about this defeat was tempered by his feeling that the terms of the Thalberg award did not really suit the far broader achievement of Charlie Chaplin. In the summer of 1971, he presented a different idea at a confidential meeting of the board of governors but avoided taking a vote. Suppose, he said, that we give only one honorary award in the spring of 1972 instead of the customary four or five and that we make Chaplin the recipient, provided that he agrees to be on hand to accept it? The governors for the most part were political conservatives. Yet while they thought the idea was farfetched, they recognized the justice of it and allowed Taradash to proceed. Taradash thereupon asked Bert Schneider to serve as his emissary to the comedian.[18]

Meantime, Mo Rothman had entered into negotiations with Martin Segal, president of the Lincoln Center Film Society in New York, about the possibility of a Chaplin appearance at a Film Society celebration in his honor. For Rothman knew that the publicity generated by such a nostalgic occasion would provide a tremendous promotional boost to Black, Inc.'s distribution of Chaplin films in the United States. A convergence of forces was developing.[19]

In January 1972, Taradash decided that the time had come to go for broke. He assembled another confidential meeting of the board of governors and obtained a unanimous vote in favor of a motion to honor Chaplin. Taradash then asked Bert Schneider to hand-carry a formal letter from him to Vevey. "It is a privilege and a joy to inform you," it began, and it went on to say that "Chaplin" was an immortal word in the vocabulary of the cinema. It ended by asking if the comedian would accept the Academy's award and whether he would be willing to be present to accept it. Schneider reported that "the old gentleman almost swooned as he read the letter. And he murmured 'Yes.' " At about the same time, Chaplin also responded in the affirmative to a formal letter of invitation to attend the Lincoln Center celebration.[20]

Some months earlier, Chaplin had thought to smooth his way with the State Department by making a conciliatory political statement. Now he made another, telling an interviewer in February that the press had always exaggerated his anger about the criticisms that Americans had leveled at him in days gone by and that he and his wife were looking forward to their visit. There is no indication, however, that these gestures were necessary. For no one in the Nixon administration had shown the slightest inclination to oppose his return.[21]

Bert Schneider was exultant at the way things were turning out. Although the Nixon administration was not creating any difficulties for Chaplin, he nevertheless saw Chaplin's return as a rebuke to Nixon. In a 1995 interview, Schneider avowed that the sight of Chaplin onstage at the Academy Awards ceremony was the most personally rewarding moment of his entire life, far exceeding the Academy Award that he himself had received in 1975. Chaplin was a hero to him, he said fervently, even more so politically than artistically.[22]

Yet if Schneider was a far-left fantasist, there was a shrewd practicality in him as well. At some point he thought to propose that Bergen, a talented photographer, be granted exclusive photo rights to the high moments of the Chaplin visit. Having obtained Chaplin's permission, he presold the photos to *Life*, which further commissioned Bergen to record her impressions of Chaplin in print. Bergen was "half paralyzed by the pressure" of all this, but her feelings merely made Schneider impatient. "*Life* has agreed and the deal is made," he sternly told her. "Oona and Charlie like you and trust you; these ten days will be a . . . strain on them and you're someone whose presence they accept." Because Schneider was also aware of the Motion Picture Academy regulation that pictures had to be exhibited in Los Angeles for a minimum of a week before they could qualify for Academy Award nomination, he quietly helped to set up a showing of *Limelight*, which had been seen for only a few days in L. A. in 1952.[23] Perhaps *Limelight* would win an award or two in 1973.

6

Following a brief stopover in Bermuda, where Oona had been born, the Chaplins flew to New York on the morning of April 3, 1972. On the flight he was tense. Furthermore, most of the people awaiting his arrival at Kennedy Airport, he noted uneasily as he cleared through customs, were from the media, and their shouting and jostling unnerved him. He need not have fretted. With very few exceptions, the press reporters and their radio and TV counterparts were in his corner. In some cases, indeed, their stories about him were not only slanted in his favor but drastically at variance with historical fact.

Three months before his arrival, the *New York Times*'s Judith Kinnard had asserted in a piece called "Chaplin May Attend Oscar Ceremony" that "Mr. Chaplin left the United States after allegations of moral turpitude were made by United States authorities." The nasty implication was clear: Chaplin had not voluntarily gone abroad with his family, he had been hounded out of the country by governmental bluenoses. But it remained for the *Times*'s Alden Whitman, in "Re-enter Charlie, Smiling," written during the comedian's stay in America, to set a new standard of *Times*ian inaccuracy in Chaplin reporting. "He was hurt, deeply hurt when he was booted out [of the country] in the frenzy of the Cold War." *Booted out*. The assertion was aimed not only at heightening the portrait of Chaplin as a victim but at demonizing the U.S. government —which in the early 1970s was a very fashionable thing to do.[24]

On the Chaplins' first evening in New York, Gloria Vanderbilt, whose acquaintance with Oona went back a long way, gave a black-tie dinner for them in her Manhattan town house. To Candice Bergen's artistic eye, the bejeweled hostess looked like a white swan in a rhinestone bib. Standing shyly beside her in the receiving line, Chaplin greeted the sixty-two other guests, who included Lillian Gish, Geraldine Fitzgerald, Kitty Carlisle, Senator and Mrs. Jacob Javits, George Plimpton, Johnny Carson (of whom Chaplin had never heard), Truman Capote (dressed in a pastel sweater set and presumably wary about shaking the hand of the author of *My Autobiography*), and Adolph Green, who would later persuade everyone present to hum along with him as he charmingly demonstrated his amazing recall of the themes from Chaplin's film scores. As the handshakes continued, Chaplin began operating on conditioned reflexes, much as the Tramp had in the assembly-line sequence in *Modern Times*. Once the last guest had passed him, he turned to Oona and shook hands with her as well, and with the waiter who had served him a drink. His eyes were wide, he looked exhausted, and he kept murmuring about the presence of "so many famous people."[25]

At a cocktail party limited to fifty notables the next afternoon, Chaplin was again quite tense. He arrived late, holding on to Oona's arm, sat down at once, and vaguely said how-do-you-do and very little else to the stream of well-wishers who came up to him. He was husbanding such strength as he had at eighty-three for the evening ahead.

Strung across the front of Philharmonic Hall was a huge banner adorned with a sketch of the Tramp spiffed up in black-tie finery and a soft black hat and bearing the words "Hello, Charlie." As if on cue, the fifteen hundred people who had paid either ten or twenty-five dollars for admission to a screening of *The Idle Class* and the twelve hundred people who had paid one hundred dollars or two hundred and fifty dollars for the additional privilege of attending a black-tie champagne reception afterwards rose in unison and cheered their heads off when Chaplin and Oona came to the front of the first tier of the balcony. From the moment that the picture began the crowd responded to Chaplin's antics "with such delighted empathy," *Time* magazine's reporter would relate, "that the big concert hall all but glowed in the dark."

As the lights came on again, it became evident that many people had tears in their eyes. Another standing ovation followed, punctuated by shouts of "Charlie! Charlie!" A microphone was placed in front of Chaplin. He waved at the crowd and delighted it anew with a bit of miming. Finally, the hall fell silent. "This is my renaissance," he began in an emotion-choked voice. After a moment's pause, he revealed that he was struggling to affirm a birthright kinship with the nation that had given him his great chance in life and was telling him now that it had always thought of him as one of its own. "I'm being born again," he said. "It's easy for you, but it's very difficult for me to speak tonight, because I feel very emotional." At this point, self-control failed him and he finished in a rush. "However, I'm glad to be amongst so many friends. Thank you."[26]

The champagne reception immediately degenerated into chaos, as glitterati by the hundreds closed in on Chaplin's table. Someone gave him a derby, which he put on with his left hand while improvising a mustache with the index finger of his right hand. Paulette Goddard appeared out of the swirl, her still-beautiful face set off by an eye-popping necklace of rubies linked by clasps of gold. Shouldering through the crowd like a fullback bulling for a short-yardage touchdown came Congresswoman Bella Abzug, wearing a floppy pink hat. "The audience, the audience!" Chaplin squealed at her. "*Everybody* was in the audience!" Claire Bloom managed to kiss him; so did Zero Mostel, through a thick growth of beard. Finally, a phalanx of policemen escorted him and Oona around the edge of the crowd and through the masses of fans in the darkness outside to a waiting limousine at the curb.[27]

On entering "21" the next day for a luncheon party hosted by Manhattan councilman and Vanderbilt heir Carter Burden, Chaplin was greeted by warm applause from the other patrons. As he was being seated, the comedian George Jessel crossed the room and fervently embraced him, according to the ever-present Candice Bergen, even though Jessel was a "pillar" of the "right wing." The next man who approached the table came from the opposite end of the political spectrum. "Mr. Chaplin," he said timidly, his hands trembling, "my name is Jack Gilford and I'm an actor and I just wanted to thank you for all you've given us. I was blacklisted, and now I'm alive and well in New York [and prospering, one might conclude from the fact that he was lunching at "21"] and we've all lived for the day when you'd come back." Chaplin's reply indicated either that he wasn't "all there" at that moment, or that he was swerving to avoid a controversial conversation. "Thank you," he said sweetly. "Someone once wrote me a letter telling me that when I was eighty I should keep warm, so I'm keeping warm." [28]

Even when his remarks made sense, his mind seemed to be floating on a faraway sea of remembrance. Somehow the subject of penal systems came up among the other guests. "It's horrible the way they put men in cages," Chaplin suddenly interjected. "Put men in prison and you make them abnormal." From these pronouncements he drifted into talking—somewhat incoherently—about his trial on Mann Act charges. The trial had ended with his acquittal, but one of the women on the jury had had a look of hatred on her face as he came up to thank the panel. "All the jurors were for me but one," he said, "—a musician, a pianist, a girl with a very pretty face, but she was against me." He looked down and fondled the napkin tucked in his shirt like a bib, smoothing it over the dinner jacket he had worn by mistake. "She said . . ." He couldn't finish the sentence. His eyes filled. "I can't talk about it," he whispered.[29]

The conversation took a happier turn. Chaplin gave a killing imitation of Truman Capote, and when he was asked, amid roars of laughter, to do it again, he did. His recovered loquacity and his slow, precise way of cutting his food—"like a child who has just mastered a knife and fork," Bergen observed—made him the last to finish eating. The waiter who finally assisted him from his chair had something he wanted to say. "Mr. Chaplin, I was your waiter in '52 when you were here the last time —it's wonderful to have you back, you know." "They all love you, Charlie," someone said. "Yes," he said softly in another off-the-wall remark, "but they loved Kennedy too."[30]

Back at the Plaza Hotel, where he and Oona were staying, he spent the middle of the afternoon sitting for some photographs by Richard Avedon, just as he had twenty years earlier, before his departure for Europe. Later he went to Gracie Mansion, where Mayor John V. Lindsay presented him with the city's highest cultural award, the Handel Medallion. "Smile," a photographer yelled. "I'm afraid my teeth would fall out," Chaplin shot back, cupping a hand beneath his chin with the storied quickness of a music hall trouper.[31]

Before leaving the Plaza for another gala dinner party, he talked in the privacy of his bedroom with Richard Meryman of *Life*. Speaking softly, sitting in a straight-backed chair, Chaplin confessed to being emotionally wrung out as well as physically exhausted. "I hear the applause and I tighten up. Last night at Lincoln Center was a terrific thing. My God, the affection of the people. So sweet." Suddenly, a savage mood overtook him. "Like children," he burst out, "after they've been slapped down and they're sorry they've done something." (Was he thinking, as he said that, of his own children?) The mood passed. "The kindness that came through," he continued. "Thought I was going to blubber like a big kid. I cannot cope with emotions any more. It's very hard to respond to affection. I can respond to antagonism. But love and affection . . ."[32]

Not even on his first triumphal visit to New York in 1916, following his big success with Essanay, he averred, had he experienced such an outpouring of feeling. "Lincoln Center . . . everything was like a dream." His next remark recalled Thomas Burke's observation about his need to assume roles in order to feel authentic: "What was real was afterwards, here in the hotel, after everybody had left and gone home and I felt as Hamlet felt. 'So now I am alone.' It sort of jumped me back into the beginning of my career. Very vivid. I had the same sort of depression inside me."

After a few more reminiscences he fell silent. Finally, he said that he wished his children were with him. Self-pity was evident in the reason he offered: "Because they look on me as somebody rather commonplace and they could see what an important guy I am. You're not a hero to your own children. There's always a little restraint, a reserve they feel —which is rather sad. I'm an austere person; I'm not . . . exactly friendly. I think that's been due to the fact that all my life I've been on the defensive—with the exception of politics. I gave that up long ago. I don't think it matters how the world progresses." Meryman interpreted the reference to politics as an oblique allusion to the "ugliness of those last years in America." With a rush of sympathy in his voice, he asked Chaplin if he felt any bitterness or sadness in looking back at those times. "No, no," Chaplin replied. "I don't feel anything at all."[33]

7

Candice Bergen was on the Chaplins' flight to the West Coast. As she watched the comedian boarding the plane, she sensed that he was experiencing "great ambivalence." The thought of returning to the scene of so many triumphs and humiliations obviously "terrified him." As the hour for landing drew near, "he looked fearful and trapped, but made a brave attempt to fight it." "Oh well," he finally sighed, "it wasn't so bad. After all, I met Oona there."[34]

Daniel Taradash, Bert Schneider, and Howard Koch, the coauthor of *Casablanca*, a Hollywood blacklistee in the 1950s, and the producer of the upcoming awards show, were on hand at the airport to greet him. "He was—what's the word—chubby," Taradash recalled. "He shook our hands and said, 'It's so good to be back in New York.' " Taradash was stunned, having not yet learned that the Academy's honored guest "was apt to go in and out of focus mentally, now lucid and charming, now hazy and remote."[35]

On the Sunday afternoon just prior to the Monday evening Oscar ceremonies, Carol and Walter Matthau held a luncheon for the Chaplins. Although the weather was superb, Chaplin wore a cloth coat over his shoulders and ate at a special table inside the house to protect him from the sea breezes. "Reminiscences abounded during lunch," wrote reporter Joyce Haber, who covered the event for the *Los Angeles Times*. George Burns started talking about "the three greatest entertainers of all time." They were "Chaplin, of course, and Al Jolson and Sinatra." Before and after lunch Chaplin sat in his chair and talked rather aimlessly to Cary Grant, Greer Garson, Mrs. Sam Goldwyn, Rosalind Russell, and other well-worn Hollywood figures who appeared before him. One observer was of the opinion that he recognized very few of these people, but that he got away with it by calling each of them "dear old friend." As Bergen circulated among the guests, she came upon Oscar Levant.

At age sixty-five, Levant had been living within the Proustian confines of his bedroom for years, surrounded by bottles of pills. Except for Howard Hughes, he was movieland's most resolute recluse. But he had known Chaplin since 1929 and had enormous respect for his comic genius, albeit finding him rather tedious off camera. After much debate with himself, he accepted the Matthaus' invitation. Bergen was astounded to see him. "Sulking in the shadows, a spectral silhouette, loomed the face that had launched a thousand analysts," she wrote. "Was I seeing a ghost? I thought Oscar Levant had been dead for years." Yet he was one of the few guests whom Chaplin greeted with genuine warmth. Four months later he was dead.[36]

On the big night, the Chaplin party was let out at the underground entrance of the Dorothy Chandler Pavilion to avoid the possibility of an anti-Chaplin demonstration in front of the main entrance. (In fact, a demonstration never materialized.) On a TV set backstage, Chaplin saw that the auditorium was packed, contrary to his *idée fixe* that hardly anybody would be there. For the first time in the Academy's forty-four years, the event did not end with the Best Picture award (which went to *The French Connection*). The Chaplin ceremony had been given that place of honor. A compilation of clips from his pictures was shown on a giant screen. Assembled by Peter Bogdanovich with the assistance of a promising young graduate of the American Film Institute, Richard Patterson, the clips were poignantly arranged. For the ending, Bogdanovich and Patterson selected the closing frames of *The Circus*, showing the Tramp shuffling off the deserted grounds toward far-distant trees.

The screen disappeared into the Chandler Pavilion heavens, revealing Chaplin standing alone on the vast stage. The greatest ovation in Academy history ensued. Taradash joined him at the lectern, and after announcing that the Oscar was "for the incalculable effect he has had in making motion pictures the art form of this century," he handed it to him. As another ovation burst upon him, Chaplin kept shaking his head back and forth. His mouth worked strangely, as if he were close to breaking down. A look of wonderment, edged with infinite regret, was in his eyes. Tentatively, he waved his hand and blew the crowd a kiss. He could barely find any words at all. Uncannily and inadvertently, he proclaimed the superiority of the silent-film aesthetic. "Words are so futile, so feeble," he began. Less than sixty seconds later, he thanked the members of the audience for honoring him, called them "sweet people," and abruptly stopped talking.

Jack Lemmon came onstage and handed Chaplin a derby and a cane. After fumbling with the cane, he finally laid it on the lectern. But he put on the derby and then made it fly off, as he so often had done in his silent comedies. Oona emerged from the wings, trailed by all of the evening's winners, presenters, and entertainers. The anti–Vietnam War politics of the group that clustered around Chaplin were defined most clearly by three figures: Jane Fonda, winner of the Best Actress award for her role in *Klute* (and eventual recipient of her absent father's profound gratitude for heeding his plea not to turn her acceptance remarks into a pro-Hanoi harangue); Bert Schneider's buddy, Jack Nicholson, wearing a print shirt and a McGovern button; and emcee Sammy Davis, Jr., who had pleased the crowd a few hours earlier by flashing a peace sign and whose main item of jewelry was a peace-symbol necklace.

The Puccini-like strains of "Smile" (from *Modern Times*) filled the hall. Jack Lemmon grabbed the mike and invited everyone to sing along. ("Smile though your heart is breaking . . .") Chaplin seemed unaware of the music. To the viewers in America's family rooms and bedrooms, the end of the telecast was signaled by the superimposition upon the old comedian's face of a Shell gasoline logo.

Taradash, who had been less than confident that Chaplin would feel up to attending the Governors' Ball at the Beverly Hilton, was astounded that he not only appeared promptly but stayed until 1:30 A.M., partook of the lavish spread that had been laid on, and drank at least two Zombies without visible effect. After supper he exchanged a few remarks with bald, stout, fifty-seven-year-old Jackie Coogan. Groucho Marx also snagged him before he and Oona departed and offered congratulations on his gold statuette. "Stay warm, Groucho, you're next," Chaplin whispered. Inevitably, he also had to deal with a reporter who was hoping for some sort of comment about world politics. "I've retired from all that political sort of thing," the weary honoree replied.[37]

8

At the 1973 Academy Awards ceremony, Marlon Brando won the Oscar for Best Actor (as the brooding Mafia don in *The Godfather*) and Chaplin won the award for the best original musical score (in *Limelight*).* Neither winner was on hand for the occasion. Brando's Oscar was presented by Roger Moore to a twenty-six-year-old Apache named Sacheen Littlefeather, dressed in beaded buckskin. She rejected the award and began to read but was not allowed to finish a statement to the effect that Brando was taking this means to protest the treatment of American Indians by the film industry and American racism in general. A mixed chorus of shouts and boos arose from the audience. Roger Moore was left holding the Oscar. Indeed, he carried it around with him all evening, to the Board of Governors' Ball and then home. The next day he returned it to Academy headquarters. Chaplin's Oscar, meantime, was mailed to him in Vevey but arrived damaged. When he returned it, Academy officials sent him Brando's statuette as a replacement.[38]†

* Raymond Rasch and Larry Russell were Chaplin's collaborators, but by 1973 they were both dead.
† As late as 1994, Brando was vague about the fate of his Oscar. "I don't know what happened to [it]. The Motion Picture Academy may have sent it to me, but if it did I don't know where it is now." Marlon Brando, *Songs My Mother Never Taught Me* (New York, 1994), p. 404.

Buoyed up by the key contributions he had made to Chaplin's back-to-back Oscar triumphs, Bert Schneider was on a roll and brimming with creative energy. America's involvement in the Vietnam War, which had been an invisible presence in his most important accomplishments as a filmmaker, now demanded, he felt, his explicit attention. The amazing life of Charlie Chaplin was another topic in which he saw ideological possibilities. Out of the first of these interests came a dramatically powerful and blisteringly anti-American documentary, *Hearts and Minds* (1974), that won him an Academy Award in the spring of 1975.

For his Chaplin documentary, *The Gentleman Tramp*, Schneider assembled a cluster of talented people who with one conspicuous exception shared his enthusiasm for everything in it that was slanted to the left, from its presentation of Chaplin's childhood to its shot of Nixon. (Not for nothing would Schneider hang a poster of *The Gentleman Tramp* on a wall in his office alongside a poster of a *guerrillero* with a rifle at the ready and around him the words "Guatemala—9 AÑOS DE LA LUCHA ARMADA.") To write and direct, he picked Richard Patterson, who had worked so effectively with Peter Bogdanovich on the Chaplin film clips for the Oscar show. To handle the narration, Walter Matthau was the choice. But for the cinematography, he turned to the gifted, politically conservative Nestor Almendros. Born in Spain, raised in Cuba, and educated at CCNY, Almendros had gotten his professional start making propaganda films for Fidel Castro. The experience alienated him from Communism forever after. Admiration for the directional techniques of François Truffaut and Eric Rohmer led him to Paris, where he acquired a reputation for visual care with his work on *Claire's Knee* (1970). Following *The Gentleman Tramp*, Almendros would shoot *Days of Heaven* (1978), which would earn him an Oscar, and *Kramer vs. Kramer* (1979).[39]

Schneider's documentary was seen for the first time in America in March 1975, the same month in which Chaplin was knighted by Queen Elizabeth II. The circulation problems that had interfered with his thought processes for years had now so disabled him physically that when he was requested to approach the Queen he had to be wheeled forward by a palace steward. After the ceremony he also needed assistance to get into the backseat of his car. In response to his plea, the TV cameramen refrained from recording this further instance of his feebleness.[40]

The Gentleman Tramp is a rags-to-riches saga, with an emphasis on rags that recalls the tall tales that Chaplin had fed to Rose Wilder Lane in 1915. "His childhood was like something in a Dickens novel," Walter Matthau's wise-guy voice proclaims. Historical stills of barefoot street urchins with dirty faces suddenly materialize on the screen. There is no indication of where, or when, these photos were taken. Nevertheless, their meaning as emblems of the unalloyed degradation of little Charlie's early days is unmistakable.

At the age of twelve, Matthau continues, Charlie returned to find that "his mother had finally succumbed to the strain of poverty and malnutrition." This sociological explanation of Hannah's mental illness —accompanied by a subtraction of two years from Charlie's actual age at the time—is then followed by the assertion that "for a while Charlie lived alone, virtually on the streets, taking whatever odd jobs he could find, stealing food and waiting for Sydney to come home [from sea]."*

Like most of his colleagues in daily newspapers, *Variety*'s reviewer of *The Gentleman Tramp* put up no resistance to its mythmaking about little Charlie, the dirty-faced, barefooted urchin. To his credit, however, he was slightly wary of the Schneider team's "acid picture of Chaplin's treatment at the hands of rightist politicians and puritanical moralists" and its shadow-free characterization of him as "an innocent nonconformist dogged by Mrs. Grundy." "While it's hard to quarrel with any specific points made in the film," said the reviewer, "the overall portrait of Chaplin will strike many as too saintly to be entirely convincing."[41] His cautious phrasing and diffident tone of voice were understandable. By the mid-1970s, the victimization interpretation of Chaplin's tribulations reigned supreme, and vigorous dissent from it could get a writer in trouble. Better, then, not to mention the documentary's contemptuous

---

* "For a while" and "virtually on the streets" create an exceedingly false impression. Charlie handed his mother over to the authorities in the Lambeth Infirmary on May 5, 1903. A doctor asked him what he was going to do, now that he had lost her. He said that he would be living with his aunt Kate. That seemed like a sensible solution. Nevertheless, he returned to Pownall Terrace, and was pleased when "the landlady came up and said that I could stay on there until she let the room. . . . I thanked her and said that Sydney would pay all our debts when he returned." He also seems to have found work as an assistant to some woodchoppers who worked in a mews at the back of Kennington Road. But this arrangement probably did not last for more than a few days, inasmuch as Sydney's ship docked in England on May 9. *My Autobiography*, pp. 72–73.

treatment of Joan Barry as a dog who ought not to have whimpered when she was abandoned, or the whitewash it offered in lieu of a serious formulation of Chaplin's political record. "He was not a Communist," the documentary's mouthpiece, Walter Matthau, asserts with unearned authority. He was, rather, "a humanitarian and an idealist in a way that few of us have the strength, or courage, to be."

One of the virtues of *The Gentleman Tramp* is its newsreel footage of such events as the tumultuous greeting that Chaplin received from a crowd of mind-boggling size upon his arrival in London in 1921. Another is its excerpts from the Tramp movies, which include the delightful street scene in *The Kid* involving a policeman, the Kid, and a discomfited Charlie; the dance of the rolls from *The Gold Rush;* the sexy nonsense song and butt-twitching dance from *Modern Times;* the famous recognition scene at the close of *City Lights;* and the hilarious cat-and-mouse game that Charlie plays with the lunch-stand proprietor (Sydney Chaplin) in *A Dog's Life*, in which the proprietor repeatedly tries and fails to catch Charlie in the act of stealing goodies off the counter and stuffing his face with them. Unfortunately, room was also made for the courtroom speech of the convicted hero in *Monsieur Verdoux* and the fingerprinting of the King by officious customs men in *A King in New York*, rather than for "Elizabethan" tidbits from the Keystone and Essanay comedies, or for any of the truly exquisite moments in the Mutual two-reelers, such as the eviscerating appraisal of the alarm clock in *The Pawnshop*.

The final episodes in *The Gentleman Tramp* were filmed at the Manoir de Ban. Nestor Almendros's camera tenderly discloses the dependence of Chaplin and Oona upon each other. With a greater degree of understatement, the powerful connection between Chaplin and another woman is also revealed. The scene is a luxuriously furnished room. Chaplin is seated in an armchair a few feet from a fireplace in which a fire is burning briskly. At eighty-five, he looks overweight and weak. Three years hence he will die in his sleep, in the pre-dawn hours of Christmas Day 1977. On the floor in front of the fireplace a tape recorder is playing an old music hall tune, "I'm a Little Bit Faint." Chaplin is singing along with the music. "My mother used to sing this to me," he says by way of explanation.

The staging of the closing sequence might have been anyone's idea, it was so obvious. Yet its sentimentality "works." Chaplin and Oona are standing outdoors. Although the sun is shining, they are wearing coats against the chill of the mountain air. Behind them a greensward stretches, ending in a stand of trees. Chaplin is carrying a cane. He takes Oona's arm. They move off toward the trees. Chaplin's walk is a shuffle —an old man's shuffle. He gestures at something with his cane. Through the eye of Almendros's camera, we watch him and the girl of his dreams move farther and farther away. Hail and farewell.

EPILOGUE

Oona O'Neill Chaplin, far right, and other mourners at Chaplin's funeral service, December 27, 1977.

T H E body-snatch caper moved into high gear on the rainy night of March 1, 1978, nine weeks after Chaplin's body was laid to rest in the Vevey cemetery. On the morning of the 2nd, the superintendent of the cemetery discovered that the coffin had been unearthed and taken. Conspiracy theories sprang up overnight. Neo-Nazis were responsible, or anti-Semites at the very least. That money was the actual motive became clear with the first phoned-in demand for a ransom of 600,000 Swiss francs. The so-called brains of the operation, an unemployed auto mechanic of Polish birth, and his tagalong accomplice, a Bulgarian auto mechanic working in Lausanne, both of whom were as feckless as some of the petty crooks in Chaplin's pictures, placed twenty-six additional phone calls before the police closed in and arrested them. Confessions followed, from which it was learned that the coffin had been hidden in a wheat field near the nearby village of Noville. The Pole got four and a half years in jail; the Bulgarian received a suspended sentence of eighteen months. The farmer who owned the wheat field erected a simple wooden cross adorned with a cane as a marker of where the coffin had been found. For years thereafter, someone regularly placed a bouquet of flowers beside the cross. Oona also liked visiting the site. "In some ways," she said, "it's lovelier than the official grave."[1]

On the whole, Oona's Hollywood years had been quite happy. During exile, on the other hand, shadows had gathered. She had missed America more keenly than her husband did, and if the children often angered him they eventually disappointed her as well.* In Chaplin's wheelchair years, furthermore, she had to wait on him hand and foot, inasmuch as he rejected every nurse who was hired to care for him. He wanted Oona, he said firmly, and it was Oona he got, at all hours of the day and night. In helping him to the toilet one day, she hurt her back.[2]

The woman whose fate made her uneasy about her own was Georges Simenon's wife. For tax reasons, Simenon took up permanent residence in Switzerland in 1957. A castle outside of Lausanne, the Château d'Echandens, was the home address of his family for six years, after which he and his French-Canadian second wife, Denise, moved their menage to a vast new house built to their design on the opposite side of Lausanne. Chaplin and Simenon had spent time together during the latter's visits to Hollywood and had discovered that they were kindred

---

* The journalist James Bradley, to whom Oona drew close during her widowhood, told Patrice Chaplin that "Oona's disappointed in her children. Not one has really done anything in a major way. Vicky with her circus—she's getting there. Geraldine had promise . . . but thirty movies later? Christopher was her last hope. She put all her frustrated ambition on to Christopher. She wanted him to be a concert pianist. . . . He practiced for hours a day. Then she got a world-famous pianist to Vevey to hear him play. He said it was good enough for the drawing room. So Christopher slammed the piano lid shut and never played again." In Rachel Ford's opinion, the children were "a lifeless lot . . . except Vicky." Patrice Chaplin, *Hidden Star* (London, 1995), pp. 122, 133.

spirits. "Like Maigret, Simenon could very easily have become a criminal," the novelist's biographer, Patrick Marnham, has written, in a sentence that calls to mind Chaplin's musings about criminal resemblance while contemplating Clare Sheridan's sculpture of his head. In Switzerland the two men renewed their friendship. Thus Chaplin penned a note to Simenon in 1965, thanking him for a "superb lunch, superb wine [in] your beautiful house. . . . The overcast weather had left me depressed and pessimistic, until I had that charming visit with you." Denise served her lord and master as wife, companion, mother to his children, business agent, and daily sex target, rain or shine. In addition, she put up with the presence of a live-in mistress, who received Simenon in her bedroom every night.

Then there were the maids, whom Denise recruited and whom Simenon "honored" with relentless regularity. Denise later wrote that one new maid asked a backstairs chum, *"On passe toutes à la casserole?"* (Do we all get laid?), and was told that while she had no obligation to submit she would certainly be asked to. Finally, Denise was unable to tolerate the situation any longer. In Oona's words, "A woman there did everything to smooth [Simenon's] day. We thought it was his secretary at first. It was his wife. She'd been doing the routine for twenty years or something, and one day she just snapped. They couldn't get her better. . . . She was worn away bit by bit, like water dripping on a stone. Bit by bit slowly."[3]

Oona's solitary bouts with booze behind the locked doors of her bedroom suite were indications that she, too, was being worn away. Chaplin's poundings on the door and shouted insistences that she come out, and her everlasting sense of indebtedness to him, had always served, however, to delimit the length of these alcoholic withdrawals. It was not until after he died that she snapped.

She began wearing clothes intended for twenty-year-olds. She fantasized about meeting Mel Gibson and other movie star hunks. She purchased a penthouse in New York and spent as much time there as her tax situation would permit. For one of the men who entered her life she bought a New York apartment, while for another she wrote out checks for staggering amounts of money. And with a truly O'Neillian compulsion, she drank. On more than one alcoholic occasion, she danced around the ledge on her penthouse roof, as if debating whether to jump. Her older brother Shane, after all, had flung himself from an upper-story window in a police station. She appeared drunk in the streets of Veyey, wearing her dressing gown and no shoes and shouting at people. Her hands sometimes shook, as her father's had.

Finally, she stopped going out and spent most of her time in bed. DT attacks and vomiting episodes overcame her, and apparitions of her late husband loomed before her. Her children's efforts to cut off her supplies by hiding the bottles in her liquor closet came to naught, for she had secreted emergency supplies in bath-essence containers and shampoo bottles. One night, she watched a videotape of *Zelig* four times, in the drunken belief that each showing was the first. (But in all probability, she was still sufficiently alert to catch not only the actual shots of Chaplin in the movie but the various echoes of his life in Zelig's. She later asked daughter Annie to send a telegram to Woody Allen. "Say he's incredible," she instructed Annie.[4])

In Patrice Chaplin's *Hidden Star*, Josie Chaplin is quoted as saying that "I loved my mother but I also hated her. She had a good side but she was also bad." The implication appeared to be that in her drunken, spendthrift widowhood she had been bad. Son Michael—Patrice Chaplin assures us—had a very different reaction. "I liked her better during those years, strangely enough. She was more herself." At age eighteen, he emphasized,

> she went straight into marriage with my father. After his death she had her teenage years. . . . She stopped being the good person and became bad, and I think she really enjoyed it. She enjoyed the drinking because it fucked us all up. . . . But she was not the helpless drunk victim. She loved it because she was getting her own back on all of us for having had to be good. I thought she was a lot of fun, although the physical side of the drinking and the after-effects were hell. She'd get right up on a high, but coming down was terrible.[5]

She was buried in Vevey in September 1991. The cause of death was cancer of the pancreas. At her request, her coffin was covered with concrete to thwart grave robbers. She was sixty-six years old, not seventy, as the obituary by Alessandra Stanley in the *New York Times* asserted.[6]

2

Eight months after Oona's funeral, a woman freshly arrived from Washington, D.C., was admitted to the Manoir and guided down a narrow, dark stone stairway into the cavernous gloom of the basement. The visitor was Gillian Anderson, a music specialist in the Library of Congress Music Division. Her guide ushered her past a film-storage room and a capacious wine cellar and then left her to her own devices in a room containing all of Chaplin's materials pertaining to his films: business correspondence and contracts, photographs, newspaper clippings, scripts—and music. "I began to examine and inventory the music in the archives," Anderson later wrote, "and over the next several hours I discovered the scores and orchestral parts that had been used to accompany *The Gold Rush, The Circus* and *A Woman of Paris* when they were first conceived or premiered during the [silent-era] 1920s." That these musical documents had survived was an utter surprise to her. "To put it mildly," Anderson later wrote, "I was pretty excited."[7]

At dinner that evening with four of Chaplin and Oona's children, the musicologist was delighted when Jane and Victoria expressed the hope that she might someday conduct the original musical accompaniment to one or more of their father's films. Photocopies of the orchestral parts of *The Circus* were mailed to her following her return to the United States, and Roy Export, the Chaplin business office in Paris, supplied her with a mint-condition print of the picture.[8]

The illegibility of some of the parts was only one of the problems that made the task of making the music playable once again a painstaking task. And when Anderson finally started to synchronize the film with the music, she discovered with the help of the head of the Library of Congress's motion picture division, David Francis, that the Chaplin estate's instruction that the film should be screened at twenty-four frames per second (fps) was mistaken. In fact, it was geared to run, the musical cues made clear, at 20 fps, which was "18 percent slower than it [had] been run for 30 or 40 or even 60-some years." The benefit of this discovery of the proper speed, Anderson came to realize, was that audiences would now have even more time in which to savor the development of Chaplin's gags. The music, of course, also enhanced the picture, just as she was sure it would. Thus the emphatic accents of

"Speed" added a percussive beat to Charlie's pell-mell flight from the cops, while the plaintive strains of Irving Berlin's "Blue Skies" underscored his desperate loneliness in the deserted field at the end of the story.[9]

With the completion of her work on *The Circus*, Anderson took on the challenge of reconstructing the accompaniment to the original version of *The Gold Rush*. But it was only when she brought the results of her scholarship to the conductor's platform at Wolf Trap Farm State Park in Virginia, in the Terrace Theater of the Kennedy Center in Washington, and in other locales that she was able to fulfill her dream of re-creating the experience that silent-era moviegoers had had when they went to a theater to see Chaplin. I was privileged to be on hand for one of her presentations, at the Metropolitan Museum of Art in New York on Friday evening, February 25, 1994.

A crowd ranging in age from eight to eighty filled the museum's nine-hundred-seat auditorium to capacity. Anderson and the ten members of the Manhattan School of Music Chamber Sinfonia were gathered on one side of the stage. At last the lights went down. Roy Export's beautiful print of *The Circus* quickened into life on the screen.

The sight of Charlie's baffled, almost fearful reaction to the reflections of his face and figure in the surrounding mirrors of the funhouse suddenly reminded me of a comment by Sergei Eisenstein: "In thinking about Chaplin, one wants above all to delve into that strange structure of thought which sees Phenomena in such a strange fashion and replies to it with images of equal strangeness."[10] Did the disorienting reflections in the funhouse mirrors simply represent a marvelously comic variation on a cinematic trick that Chaplin had borrowed from other directors? Or had those images originated long before, in a structure of thought that had been shaped by a boy's awareness of his mother's terrible sensations of personal fragmentation? Whatever the truth of this matter, the cascading laughter of the audience on that February night at the Metropolitan left no doubt in my mind about one thing: the magic of *The Circus* was still potent.

In the two decades since Chaplin's death, the amazing appeal of his Charlie persona has continued to be evident in the sale of dolls, postcards, and other knickknacks; in IBM's employment of an actor to imitate him in its television and magazine marketing campaigns during the

1980s; and in the current availability on videocassettes of all the feature pictures in which he appears, as well as a number of the shorts. "[Chaplin] lives in the subconscious of everyone who loves movies," the *Guardian* of Great Britain declared on March 10, 1995, in announcing the results of a poll of sixty-two top movie critics worldwide in which he won the vote for the greatest actor of all time. "You can't get away from him," the *Guardian* added.[11]

NOTES

-∂-

CHAPTER I. A WOMAN OF SORROWS

1. Charles J. McGuirk, "Chaplinitis," *Motion Picture Magazine*, July 1915, p. 121; Charles J. McGuirk, "Chaplinitis," *Motion Picture Magazine*, August 1915, p. 85; David Robinson, *Chaplin: His Life and Art* (New York, 1985), p. 136.

2. Charles Chaplin, *My Autobiography* (New York, 1964), p. 173; Charles J. Maland, *Chaplin and American Culture* (Princeton, N.J., 1989), pp. 10–11; Wes Gehring, *Charlie Chaplin: A Bio-Bibliography* (Westport, Conn., 1983), pp. 61–62; Raoul Sobel and David Francis, *Chaplin: Genesis of a Clown* (London, 1977), p. 144; *Cleveland Plain Dealer*, June 9, 1915 (Robinson Locke Collection, vol. 110, Lincoln Center Branch, New York Public Library); *Moving Picture World*, July 17, 1915, p. 505; *Moving Picture World*, July 24, 1915, p. 707; William Robert Faith, *Bob Hope: A Life in Comedy* (New York, 1982), p. 39.

3. McGuirk, "Chaplinitis," August 1915, p. 87.

4. Jane Addams, *The Spirit of Youth and the City Streets* (New York, 1909), pp. 75 *et seq.*

5. Richard De Cordova, *Picture Personalities* (Urbana and Chicago, 1990), pp. 103, 106–109; Robert Giroux, *A Deed of Death* (New York, 1990), pp. 40–41; *Motion Picture Magazine*, February 1917, p. 192; Neal Gabler, *An Empire of Their Own* (New York, 1988), p. 259.

6. Richard Koszarski, *The Man You Loved to Hate* (New York, 1983), pp. 4–5; Kevin Brownlow, *The War, the West and the Wilderness* (New York, 1979), p. 143; Roger Manvell, "Theda Bara," in James Vinson, ed., *Actors and Actresses* (Chicago and London, 1986), pp. 46–47; Donald Kagan, *On the Origins of War and the Preservation of Peace* (New York, 1995), p. 167.

7. E. V. Whitcomb, "Charlie Chaplin," *Photoplay*, February 1915, pp. 35–36.

8. Edward Sutherland transcript, Columbia University Oral History Project.

9. Chaplin, *My Autobiography*, pp. 57–58.

10. William Holtz, *The Ghost in the Little House* (Columbia, Mo., 1993), p. 380.

11. *Ibid.*, p. 67; Robinson, *Chaplin: His Life and Art*, pp. 180–82.

12. Quoted in Robinson, *Chaplin: His Life and Art*, p. 183.

13. Harry M. Geduld, ed., *Charlie Chaplin's Own Story* (Bloomington, Ind., 1985), pp. 1, 2.

14. Édouard Ramond, *La Passion de Charlie Chaplin* (Paris, 1927), p. 253.

15. Geduld, ed., *Charlie Chaplin's Own Story*, p. 3.

16. *Ibid.*, pp. 4, 5, 6, 7.

17. Chaplin, *My Autobiography*, pp. 21–22.

18. Microfilms of *The Era* are on file in the Billy Rose Theater Collection of the New York Public Library for the Performing Arts at Lincoln Center. See, too,

David Robinson's accurate but uncomprehending summary of *The Era* data on Hannah Chaplin's career in *Chaplin: His Life and Art,* pp. 5–7—uncomprehending because of Robinson's blind faith in Chaplin's assertions about the length of his mother's career. In regard to the whole sweep, indeed, of Chaplin's account of his childhood in *My Autobiography,* Robinson rashly declares that the book offers "a strikingly truthful record of things witnessed" (xii).

19. T. S. Eliot, *Selected Essays 1917–1932* (New York, 1932), p. 369; Shaw Desmond, *The Edwardian Story* (London, 1949), p. 327.

20. "Families in the Treatment of Schizophrenia—Part I," *Harvard Medical School Mental Health Letter,* June 1989, p. 1; Louis A. Sass, *Madness and Modernism* (New York, 1992), pp. 13, 14, and *passim;* Karl Jaspers, *General Psychopathology* (Chicago, 1963), p. 447; Manfred Bleuler, *The Schizophrenic Disorders* (New Haven, 1978), p. 15; Otto Fenichel, *The Psychoanalytic Theory of Neurosis* (New York, 1945), pp. 418, 436.

21. Patrice Chaplin, *Hidden Star: Oona O'Neill Chaplin. A Memoir* (London, 1995), p. 144.

22. Quoted in Harry Crocker, unpublished biography of Chaplin, Margaret Herrick Library, Center for Motion Picture Studies, Beverly Hills, California.

CHAPTER 2. "THAT BOY IS A BORN ACTOR"

1. Thomas Burke, *City of Encounters* (London, 1932), pp. 153–54.

2. Charles Chaplin, *My Autobiography* (New York, 1964), p. 19; Gerith von Ulm, *Charlie Chaplin: King of Tragedy* (Caldwell, Idaho, 1940), p. 31.

3. Charles Chaplin, Jr., *My Father, Charlie Chaplin* (New York, 1960), p. 8.

4. David Robinson, *Chaplin: His Life and Art* (New York, 1985), p. 3.

5. *Ibid.,* pp. 3–4, 15–16; letter from Nicola Smith, Local Studies Librarian of the Southwark Council, to the author, December 10, 1990; census of 1891 for St. Peter, Walworth, p. 5; Lambeth Board of Guardians, Lunacy Examinations Book, 1893, p. 196; St. Saviour Union, Southwark, Lunatic Report Book.

6. Quoted in Steven Marcus, *The Other Victorians* (New York, 1985), p. 6. For a general study of prostitution in this period, see Judith Walkowitz, *Prostitution and Victorian Society* (New York, 1980).

7. G. J. Mellor, *The Northern Music Hall* (Newcastle upon Tyne, 1970), pp. 49, 58–59. Chaplin estimated that in his peak years Charles Senior earned forty pounds a week. Chaplin, *My Autobiography,* p. 18. Gordon Craig's words are quoted in John Russell, *London* (New York, 1994), p. 227.

8. Chaplin, *My Autobiography,* p. 18.

9. Robinson, *Chaplin: His Life and Art,* pp. 554–55.

10. Chaplin, *My Autobiography,* p. 14; Harold L. Geduld, ed., *Charlie Chaplin's Own Story* (Bloomington, Ind., 1985), p. 173.

11. Robinson, *Chaplin: His Life and Art,* p. 10.

12. Register of King and Queen Street School Walworth, 1890; register of Addington Street School Lambeth, 1890; register of Flint Street, East Street School Walworth, 1890; census of 1891 for St. Peter.

13. Raoul Sobel and David Francis, *Chaplin: Genesis of a Clown* (London, 1977), p. 50; Mellor, *The Northern Music Hall,* p. 38; Charles Chaplin, *My Life in Pictures* (New York, 1975), pp. 290–91; Robinson, *Chaplin: His Life and Art,* pp. 217, 272; interview with Wyn Ray Evans, winter 1994.

14. All of the quotations in this section are drawn from Chaplin, *My Autobiography,* Chapter 1.

15. Chaplin, *My Autobiography*, pp. 22–23.

16. Andrew Mearns, *The Bitter Cry of Outcast London*, edited and with an introduction by Anthony S. Wohl (New York, 1970), title page, pp. 58–59, 63, 67.

17. The English newspaper is quoted in Anthony Wohl, "The Bitter Cry of Outcast London," *International Journal of Social History*, 1968, p. 189; Mearns, *The Bitter Cry*, p. 61; Gertrude Himmelfarb, *Poverty and Compassion: The Moral Imagination of the Late Victorians* (New York, 1991), p. 62. The Tennyson and Beatrice Webb quotes may also be found in Himmelfarb, *Poverty*, pp. 62, 62n–63n.

18. Harold W. Pfautz, ed., *Charles Booth on the City* (Chicago, 1967), p. 6; Helen M. Lynd, *England in the Eighteen-eighties* (New York, 1945), p. 426.

19. Charles Booth, *Life and Labour of the People in London*, vol. I (London, 1892), p. 33; Charles Booth, *Life and Labour of the People in London*, vol. II (London, 1892–1897), pp. 20–21, 40–41.

20. Chaplin, *My Autobiography*, pp. 11, 24, 34, 40, 62; Booth, *Life and Labour* II, p. 39; interview with Colin Sorensen, October 21, 1992.

21. Robinson, *Chaplin: His Life and Art*, p. 38.

22. Chaplin, *My Autobiography*, pp. 22–25.

23. *Ibid.*, p. 25.

24. Robinson, *Chaplin: His Life and Art*, pp. 18–19; Chaplin, *My Autobiography*, p. 26.

25. Robinson, *Chaplin: His Life and Art*, p. 19.

26. Charles Chaplin, Jr., *My Father*, p. 10; Pola Negri, *Memoirs of a Star* (New York, 1970), pp. 214–15.

27. Chaplin, *My Autobiography*, pp. 29, 30, 31.

28. Aunt Kate's remarks are quoted in Robinson, *Chaplin: His Life and Art*, p. 22; Chaplin, *My Autobiography*, p. 33.

29. Harry Crocker, unpublished biography of Chaplin, Margaret Herrick Library, Center for Motion Picture Studies, Beverly Hills, California.

30. St. Saviour's Union Minute Book, Southwark Board of Guardians, folio 80, pp. 139, 249, 259, 314, 351.

31. Chaplin, *My Autobiography*, pp. 24, 34.

32. Lunacy Examinations Book, September 12, 1898, Lambeth Board of Guardians; Robinson, *Chaplin: His Life and Art*, pp. 25–26.

33. Chaplin, *My Autobiography*, p. 34.

34. Booth, *Life and Labour of the People in London*, II, p. 41.

35. Chaplin, *My Autobiography*, p. 40.

36. Charles Chaplin, *My Trip Abroad* (New York, 1922), p. 62; Chaplin, *My Autobiography*, p. 36.

37. Henry Mayhew, *London Labour and the London Poor, 1861–62* (London, 1985), pp. 295–335.

38. The *Glasgow Weekly Herald* quote is in Robinson, *Chaplin: His Life and Art*, p. 28; Chaplin, *My Autobiography*, p. 44.

39. Chaplin, *My Autobiography*, *op. cit.* Charles Booth's words about landladies are quoted in Judith R. Walkowitz, *City of Dreadful Delight: Narratives of Sexual Danger in Late-Victorian London* (Chicago, 1992), pp. 257–58.

CHAPTER 3. THE POISONOUS WOUND

1. Christopher Pulling, *They Were Singing* (London, 1952), p. 197.

2. Raoul Sobel and David Francis, *Chaplin: Genesis of a Clown* (London, 1977), pp. 56–57; Pulling, *They Were Singing*, pp. 198–201.

3. G. J. Mellor, *The Northern Music Hall* (Newcastle upon Tyne, 1970), pp. 38, 58, 69, 73–74; A. E. Wilson, *The Story of Pantomime* (London, 1949), pp. 3, 14, 15, 107; David Madden, *Harlequin's Stick, Charlie's Cane* (Bowling Green, Ohio, 1975), *passim.*

4. Harold Scott, *The Early Doors: Origins of the Music Hall* (London, 1946), p. 175; Gyles Brandreth, *The Funniest Man on Earth* (London, 1977), *passim;* Max Beerbohm, *Around Theaters* (New York, 1968), p. 350; Charles Chaplin, *My Autobiography* (New York, 1964), p. 48.

5. Chaplin, *My Autobiography*, pp. 46–47.

6. *Ibid.*, pp. 48–49; Francis Wyndham, "Chaplin, the Critics, the Beatles and the Mood of London," *Sunday Times* (London), March 26, 1967, p. 10. The Henry James quote is taken from Gertrude Himmelfarb, *Poverty and Compassion: The Moral Imagination of the Late Victorians* (New York, 1991), p. 418.

7. Chaplin, *My Autobiography*, pp. 45, 46.

8. *Ibid.*, p. 50. For a horrific account of Jackson's disciplinary conduct, see Chapter 3 of Harry M. Geduld, ed., *Charlie Chaplin's Own Story* (Bloomington, Ind., 1955).

9. Chaplin, *My Autobiography*, p. 58.

10. *Ibid.*, pp. 59–60; Harry Crocker, unpublished biography of Chaplin, Margaret Herrick Library, Center for Motion Picture Studies, Beverly Hills, California.

11. Chaplin, *My Autobiography*, p. 60; Peter Ackroyd, *Dickens* (New York, 1990), pp. 23–24; David Robinson, *Chaplin: His Life and Art* (New York, 1985), pp. 39–40.

12. Chaplin, *My Autobiography*, pp. 11–13.

13. Thomas Burke, *City of Encounters* (London, 1932), pp. 133–34, 166–67.

14. May Eastman, *Love and Revolution: My Journey Through an Epoch* (New York, 1964), pp. 173–74.

15. Burke, *City of Encounters*, pp. 129–30.

16. Chaplin, *My Autobiography*, pp. 69–71.

17. Order for the Reception of a Pauper Lunatic, Lambeth Board of Guardians, folio 80, May 9, 1903.

18. Charles Chaplin, Jr., *My Father, Charlie Chaplin* (New York, 1960), p. 10; Timothy J. Lyons, ed., "Roland H. Totheroh Interviewed," *Film Culture*, Spring 1972, p. 261.

19. Chaplin, *My Autobiography*, pp. 73–75.

20. Theodore Huff, *Charlie Chaplin* (New York, 1951), p. 86; John McCabe, *Charlie Chaplin* (Garden City, N.Y., 1978), pp. 128, 235–36.

21. Alistair Cooke, *Six Men* (New York, 1977), p. 23; Thomas Burke, "Why Is 'Charlie' So Funny When He Is So Sad?" *Literary Digest*, January 28, 1922, p. 48.

22. Chaplin, *My Autobiography*, p. 77.

23. Jim Tully, *A Dozen and One* (Hollywood, 1943), p. 31.

24. Chaplin, *My Autobiography*, p. 81.

25. *Ibid.*, p. 82.

26. William Gillette, *The Painful Predicament of Sherlock Holmes* (Chicago, 1955), p. 24.

27. Harry M. Geduld, ed., *Charlie Chaplin's Own Story* (Bloomington, Ind., 1985), p. 98.

28. Ricky Jay, *Learned Pigs and Fireproof Women* (New York, 1986), pp. 127, 131; Geduld, ed., *Charlie Chaplin's Own Story*, pp. 100–103.

29. Avis Berman, "George du Maurier's *Trilby* Whipped Up a Worldwide Storm," *Smithsonian Magazine*, December 1993, pp. 110–26 *passim.*

30. Quoted in Peter Cotes and Thelma Niklaus, *The Little Fellow* (New York, 1965), p. 26.

31. Chaplin, *My Autobiography*, pp. 96–97.

32. *Ibid.*, p. 99.

33. Paul Thompson, *The Edwardians: The Remaking of British Society* (Bloomington, Ind., and London, 1975), *passim*.

34. Samuel Hynes, *The Edwardian Turn of Mind* (Princeton, N.J., 1968), p. 339; H. E. Meller, *Leisure and the Changing City* (London, 1975), p. 212.

35. H. G. Wells, *Tono-Bungay* (New York, 1935), p. 10; C. F. G. Masterman, *The Condition of England* (London, 1909), pp. 120–21; Thompson, *The Edwardians*, *passim*.

36. Thompson, *The Edwardians*, pp. 266–75; George Dangerfield, *The Strange Death of Liberal England* (New York, 1961), pp. viii, 215, 217, 230, 231, 233.

37. Dangerfield, *Strange Death of Liberal England*, p. 145; Thompson, *The Edwardians*, pp. 252, 271–73.

38. Wells, *Tono-Bungay*, p. 10.

39. J. P. Gallagher, *Fred Karno: Master of Mirth and Tears* (London, 1971), p. 17; Eric Partridge, *A Dictionary of Slang* (London, 1961), p. 300.

40. Gallagher, *Karno*, pp. 83–86; McCabe, *Charlie Chaplin*, pp. 31–34.

41. Gallagher, *Karno*, p. 86.

42. Quoted in Robinson, *Chaplin: His Life and Art*, p. 95.

43. Sobel and Francis, *Chaplin: Genesis of a Clown*, p. 92; McCabe, *Charlie Chaplin*, pp. 27, 28–29.

44. Robinson, *Chaplin: His Life and Art*, pp. 147, 198.

45. Sobel and Francis, *Chaplin: Genesis of a Clown*, pp. 134–36.

46. Cotes and Niklaus, *The Little Fellow*, p. 27.

47. Chaplin, *My Autobiography*, p. 103; interview with Lionel Krisel, January 30, 1995.

48. McCabe, *Charlie Chaplin*, p. 41.

49. Chaplin, *My Autobiography*, p. 123.

50. Jim Tully, "Charlie Chaplin: The Real-Life Story," *Pictorial Review*, February 1927, p. 72.

51. Charles Chaplin, "A Comedian Sees the World," *Woman's Home Companion*, September 1933, p. 8; Chaplin, *My Autobiography*, p. 104.

52. Chaplin, "A Comedian Sees the World," p. 8.

53. Chaplin, *My Autobiography*, p. 104; Vladimir Nabokov, *Lolita*, vol. I (Paris, 1955), p. 30.

54. Chaplin, *My Autobiography*, pp. 106–107.

55. *Ibid.*, pp. 107–108, 116.

56. *Ibid.*, pp. 111–14.

57. The Mabelle Fournier story is related in Chapter 4 of Harry Crocker's manuscript in the Margaret Herrick Library, Center for Motion Picture Studies, Beverly Hills, California.

CHAPTER 4. "THIS IS WHERE I BELONG!"

1. Charles Chaplin, *My Autobiography* (New York, 1964), pp. 114–15.

2. *Ibid.*, pp. 116–18.

3. *Ibid.*, pp. 117–18; Thomas Burke, "The Tragic Comedian: A Close-up of Charles Chaplin," *The Outlook*, January 18, 1922, p. 100.

4. Chaplin, *My Autobiography*, pp. 120–21.

5. Quoted in John McCabe, *Charlie Chaplin* (New York, 1978), p. 40.

6. Chaplin, *My Autobiography*, p. 123.

7. McCabe, *Charlie Chaplin*, p. 44.

8. J. Clarke, C. Critcher, and R. Johnson, eds., *Working-Class Culture* (New York, 1979), pp. 152–54.

9. David Thomson, *A Biographical Dictionary of the Cinema* (London, 1975), p. 350; Jack Spears, *Hollywood: The Golden Era* (South Brunswick, N.J., and New York, 1971), pp. 77, 79, 81.

10. The Védrès quotation is taken from Raymond Durgnat, *The Crazy Mirror* (London, 1969), p. 67. See also André Bazin, *What Is Cinema?* (Berkeley and Los Angeles, 1967), p. 81.

11. McCabe, *Charlie Chaplin*, p. 117. *Cf.* the biographical materials cited in the film compilation *En Compagnie de Max Linder* (Paris, 1963).

12. Chaplin, *My Autobiography*, pp. 126–28.

13. *Ibid.*, pp. 128–29.

14. Harry Crocker, unpublished biography of Chaplin, Margaret Herrick Library, Center for Motion Picture Studies, Beverly Hills, California.

15. Chaplin, *My Autobiography*, p. 132.

16. *Ibid.*

17. Quoted in McCabe, *Charlie Chaplin*, p. 45.

18. Harry Crocker, unpublished biography of Chaplin, Margaret Herrick Library; Chaplin, *My Autobiography*, p. 134; David Naylor, *Great American Movie Theaters* (Washington, D.C., 1955) pp. 203, 208; "Broadway Historic Theater District" (Los Angeles Conservancy, 1992), p. 1.

19. Chaplin, *My Autobiography*, p. 134.

20. Joachim C. Fest, *Hitler* (New York, 1973), p. 200.

21. Arthur Schopenhauer, *The World as Will and Representation*, tr. E. F. J. Payne, vol. 1 (New York, 1966), pp. 533–35.

22. Mack Sennett, *King of Comedy* (as told to Cameron Shipp) (New York, 1954), p. 148; Chaplin, *My Autobiography*, p. 138; David Robinson, *Chaplin: His Life and Art* (New York, 1985), pp. 98, 101.

23. Robinson, *Chaplin: His Life and Art*, p. 102.

24. *Ibid.*, p. 103.

25. Chaplin, *My Autobiography*, pp. 138–39.

26. Sennett, *King of Comedy*, pp. 11–44 *passim*; Kalton C. Lahue and Terry Brewer, *Kops and Custards* (Norman, Okla., 1968), pp. 3–11; Richard Schickel, *D. W. Griffith: An American Life* (New York, 1984), pp. 15–105 *passim*.

27. Bebe Bergsten, ed., *Biograph Bulletins 1896–1908* (Los Angeles, 1971), p. 350; Eileen Bowser, *Biograph Bulletins 1908–1912* (New York, 1973), pp. ix–x; Patrick George Loughney, "A Descriptive Analysis of the Library of Congress Paper Print Collection," Ph.D. diss., George Washington University, 1988, pp. 128, 174–75, 177, 198.

28. Terry Ramsaye, *A Million and One Nights: A History of Motion Pictures Through 1925* (New York, 1954), pp. 469, 474, 475, 476.

29. Eileen Bowser, *The Transformation of the Cinema, 1907–1915* (New York, 1990), p. 39.

30. Patrick Loughney, "Leave 'Em Laughing: The Last Years of the Biograph Company," in Eileen Bowser, ed., *The Slapstick Symposium* (Brussels, 1988), pp. 19, 20, 21; Russell Merritt, "D. W. Griffith," *International Dictionary of Films and Film-Makers* (Chicago, 1991), p. 352.

31. Sennett, *King of Comedy*, p. 60; Kemp R. Niver, *Early Motion Pictures* (Washington, D.C., 1985), p. 188.

32. A. Nicholas Vardac, *Stage to Screen: Theatrical Method from Garrick to Griffith* (Cambridge, Mass., 1949), pp. 20–67, 194–210; Schickel, *Griffith*, pp. 138–39.

33. Sennett, *King of Comedy*, p. 51.

34. Loughney, "Leave 'Em Laughing," p. 23.

35. *Cf.* the comments on Sennett's achievements in Durgnat, *The Crazy Mirror*, pp. 69–71.

36. Richard V. Spencer, "Los Angeles as Producing Center," *Moving Picture World*, April 8, 1911, p. 768.

37. Kevin Starr, *Inventing the Dream: California Through the Progressive Era* (New York, 1985), p. 294.

38. Kalton C. Lahue, *Mack Sennett's Keystone: The Man, the Myth and the Comedies* (South Brunswick, N.J., and New York, 1971), *passim*; Sennett, *King of Comedy*, p. 160.

39. David A. Yallop, *The Day the Laughter Stopped* (New York, 1976), pp. 3–10, 255, 267, 270, 274; Robert Giroux, *A Deed of Death* (New York, 1990), pp. 37–40.

40. Betty Harper Fussell, *Mabel* (New Haven and New York, 1982), p. 6.

41. *Ibid.*, p. 44.

42. *Ibid.*, p. 113.

43. Samuel Goldwyn, *Behind the Screen* (New York, 1923), pp. 110–18 *passim*.

44. Robert Giroux, *A Deed of Death*, pp. 202, 203, 207.

45. Benjamin B. Hampton, *A History of the Movies* (New York, 1931), p. 286.

46. Quoted in Giroux, *A Deed of Death*, pp. 219–20.

47. Theodore Dreiser, "The Best Motion Picture Interview Ever Written," *Photoplay*, August 1928, p. 32.

48. Quoted in Sennett, *King of Comedy*, p. 153.

49. Quoted in Fussell, *Mabel*, p. 70.

50. Chaplin, *My Autobiography*, pp. 141–42.

51. *Ibid.*, pp. 140–42.

52. Lahue and Brewer, *Kops and Custards*, pp. 22–23.

53. Interview with Wyn Ray Evans, February 14, 1994.

54. Chaplin, *My Autobiography*, p. 144; Sennett, *King of Comedy*, p. 153.

55. Sennett, *King of Comedy*, pp. 153–54.

56. *Ibid.*, p. 154; Fussell, *Mabel*, p. 71.

57. Starr, *Inventing the Dream*, p. 80.

58. Quoted in Maurice Bessy, *Charlie Chaplin* (London, 1985), p. 54.

59. My discussion of the camera in modern culture is heavily indebted to Miles Orvell's article "Weegee's Voyeurism and the Mastery of Urban Disorder," *American Art*, Winter 1992, pp. 19–41.

60. Dan Kamin, *Charlie Chaplin's One-Man Show*. Foreword by Marcel Marceau (Metuchen, N.J., and London, 1984), xiii; Kevin Brownlow, *The Parade's Gone By* (New York, 1968), p. 498; Theodore Huff, *Charlie Chaplin* (New York, 1951), pp. 31–32.

61. Chaplin, *My Autobiography*, pp. 147–48.

62. Gerald D. McDonald, Michael Conway, and Mark Ricci, *The Complete Films of Charlie Chaplin* (Secaucus, N.J., 1988), p. 34.

63. Sennett, *King of Comedy*, p. 163.

64. Theodore Dreiser, "The Best Motion Picture Interview Ever Written," *Photoplay*, August 1928, reprinted in Anthony Slide, ed., *They Also Wrote for the Fan Magazines* (Jefferson, N.C., and London, 1992), pp. 50, 51.

65. Sennett, *King of Comedy*, p. 163.

66. *Ibid.*, p. 160.

67. Chaplin, *My Autobiography*, pp. 149–52.

68. James Agee, *A Death in the Family* (New York, 1957), p. 11.

69. Genevieve Moreau, *The Restless Journey of James Agee* (New York, 1977), p. 33.

70. Agee, *A Death*, pp. 12–13.

71. John Fuegi, *Brecht and Company: Sex, Politics and the Making of the Modern Drama* (New York, 1994), p. 86.

72. Charles J. Maland, *Chaplin and American Culture: The Evolution of a Star Image* (Princeton, 1989), pp. 15–17.

73. Schickel, *D. W. Griffith*, pp. 267–302, *passim*; Kenneth S. Lynn, "The Torment of D. W. Griffith," *American Scholar,* Spring 1990, pp. 259–62.

74. Norman Lloyd, *Stages: Norman Lloyd* (Metuchen, N.J., and London, 1990), p. 131; Carol Matthau, *Among the Porcupines* (New York, 1992), p. 252; "Small Talk of Great People," collected by Harry Crocker, unpublished, Margaret Herrick Library; Clare Sheridan, *Naked Truth* (New York, 1928), pp. 269–70.

75. Walter Lippmann, *Drift and Mastery* (Englewood Cliffs, N.J., 1961), p. 100.

76. Chaplin, *My Autobiography*, p. 157.

77. *Ibid.*, p. 156.

CHAPTER 5. THE MOB-GOD

1. Charles Chaplin, *My Autobiography* (New York, 1964), p. 159; Mack Sennett, *King of Comedy* (as told to Cameron Shipp) (New York, 1954), p. 157.

2. Quoted from the full text of the letter in David Robinson, *Chaplin: His Life and Art* (New York, 1985), pp. 131–33.

3. Theodore Huff, *Charlie Chaplin* (New York, 1951), pp. 40–41; Alexa L. Foreman, "Marie Dressler," in James Vinson, ed., *The International Dictionary of Films and Filmmakers* (Chicago, 1990), vol. 3, pp. 201–202.

4. Chaplin, *My Autobiography*, pp. 159–60.

5. Terry Ramsaye, *A Million and One Nights: A History of Motion Pictures Through 1926* (New York, 1954), pp. 300–301, 417, 443–44.

6. Chaplin, *My Autobiography*, pp. 162–63.

7. *Ibid.*, p. 165.

8. Gloria Swanson, *Swanson on Swanson* (New York, 1980), p. 40.

9. John Baxter, "Gloria Swanson," in Vinson, *The International Dictionary*, p. 598; Lawrence J. Quirk, *The Films of Gloria Swanson* (Secaucus, N.J., 1984), p. 21.

10. Chaplin, *My Autobiography*, p. 169.

11. *Ibid.*

12. Timothy J. Lyons, ed., "Roland H. Totheroh Interviewed: Chaplin Films," *Film Culture*, Spring 1972, pp. 225–36; Chaplin, *My Autobiography*, p. 169.

13. Anthony Slide, *The Vaudevillians* (Westport, Ct., 1981), p. 136; Huff, *Charlie Chaplin*, p. 56; Kalton C. Lahue, *Mack Sennett's Keystone: The Man, the Myth, and the Comedies* (South Brunswick, N.J., and New York, 1982), pp. 153–54.

14. Lyons, "Roland H. Totheroh Interviewed," p. 270.

15. Chaplin, *My Autobiography*, p. 170.

16. *Ibid.*, pp. 170–71; interview with Robert Hoover, June 4, 1995.

17. Jean Renoir, *Renoir on Renoir* (New York, 1989), p. 251.

18. Chaplin, *My Autobiography*, p. 159.

19. Robinson, *Chaplin: His Life and Art*, pp. 141–42.

20. Peter Stallybrass and Allon White, *The Politics and Poetics of Transgression* (Ithaca, N.Y., 1986), p. 191.

21. Henry James, "London at Midsummer" in *Collected Travel Writings: Great Britain and America* (New York, 1993), pp. 133–34, 137–38.

22. Paul Ringenbach, *Tramps and Reformers, 1873–1916* (Westport, Ct., 1973), pp. xiv, 3, 5; Allan Nevins, *The Emergence of Modern America, 1865–1878* (New York, 1927), p. 301.

23. Ringenbach, *Tramps and Reformers*, p. 10; Francis Wayland, "The Tramp Question," in *Proceedings of the Conference of Charities Held in Connection with the General Meeting of the American Social Science Association in Saratoga, September, 1877* (Boston, 1877), p. 112; Agile Penne, "Jimmy, the Tramp," *Saturday Journal*, 1, no. 25 (September 3, 1870), pp. 4–5. For the Francis Wayland and "Agile Penne" quotations, I am indebted to an unpublished paper by Jim Deutsch.

24. Schickel, *D. W. Griffith*, p. 53; Kenneth S. Lynn, "The Torment of D. W. Griffith," *American Scholar*, Spring 1990, p. 256.

25. Ringenbach, *Tramps and Reformers*, xiv.

26. Jack London, "The Road," in *Novels and Social Writings* (New York, 1982), pp. 218, 274.

27. *Ibid.*, p. 289.

28. Robert H. Ferrell, ed., *Dear Bess: The Letters of Harry to Bess Truman, 1910–1959* (New York, 1983), pp. 84–85.

29. Ringenbach, *Tramps and Reformers*, pp. 162–63.

30. *Ibid.*, pp. 164–65.

31. *Ibid.*, pp. 166–67, 183.

32. Wilfred M. McClay, *The Masterless: Self and Society in Modern America* (Chapel Hill, N.C., 1994), p. 218; Robert Nisbet, *Sociology as an Art Form* (New York, 1976), pp. 44–49.

33. Joachim C. Fest, *Hitler*, tr. by Richard and Clara Winston (New York, 1973), pp. 32–33.

34. *Ibid.*, pp. 45–46.

35. *Ibid.*, p. 53.

36. *Ibid.*, p. 46.

37. *Ibid.*, p. 113.

38. *Ibid.*, pp. 117–18, 119–20.

39. David Thomson, *A Biographical Dictionary of the Cinema* (London, 1980), p. 96.

40. David Magarshack, Introduction to Nicolai V. Gogol, *The Overcoat and Other Tales of Good and Evil* (New York, 1957), p. 8.

41. Charles J. McGuirk, "Chaplinitis," *Motion Picture Magazine*, July 1915, p. 89.

42. "The Scavanger [*sic*]," "The Mob-God," *The Little Review*, April 1915, pp. 45–46.

43. Tom Dardis, *Harold Lloyd: The Man on the Clock* (New York, 1983), pp. 30, 38, 48–52.

44. Charles Chaplin, "How I Made My Success," *The Theatre*, September 1915, pp. 121, 142.

45. Robinson, *Chaplin: His Life and Art*, pp. 147–51; Uno Asplund, *Chaplin's Films*, tr. by Paul Britten Austin (Cranbury, N.J., 1976), pp. 81, 82–84. See, too, Jazzmedia's two-part film presentation, *The Chaplin Puzzle*, written by Joe Adamson and produced, edited, and directed by Don McGlynn.

46. Chaplin, *My Autobiography*, p. 25.

47. Slide, *The Vaudevillians*, p. 63; Chaplin, *My Autobiography*, pp. 174–75.
48. Chaplin, *My Autobiography*, pp. 180–83, 188.
49. Thomas Burke, *City of Encounters* (London, 1932), pp. 129, 139.

CHAPTER 6. "SHEER PERSEVERANCE TO THE POINT OF MADNESS"
1. Charles Chaplin, *My Autobiography* (New York, 1964), pp. 174–77.
2. Terry Ramsaye, *A Million and One Nights: A History of Motion Pictures Through 1926* (New York, 1954), pp. 733–34.
3. *Ibid.*, pp. 731–32.
4. David Robinson, *Chaplin: His Life and Art* (New York, 1985), p. 159: Ramsaye, *A Million and One Nights*, p. 734, Chaplin, *My Autobiography*, pp. 177, 179.
5. Quoted and discussed in Raoul Sobel and David Francis, *Chaplin: Genius of a Clown* (London, 1977), pp. 151–52, and in Charles J. Maland, *Chaplin and American Culture* (Princeton, N.J., 1989), pp. 26–27.
6. Quoted and discussed in Sobel and Francis, *Chaplin: Genius of a Clown.*
7. *Ibid.*, pp. 150, 151.
8. Maland, *Chaplin and American Culture*, p. 36; Kevin Brownlow, *The War, the West and the Wilderness* (New York, 1979), pp. 39, 40; Alistair Cooke, "Charles Chaplin: The One and Only," in *Six Men* (New York, 1977), p. 19.
9. Brownlow, *The War, the West*, p. 40; R. J. Minney, *Chaplin: The Immortal Tramp* (London, 1954), p. 53; Donald Spoto, *Laurence Olivier: A Biography* (New York, 1992), p. 17.
10. Chaplin, *My Autobiography*, p. 178.
11. Robinson, *Chaplin: His Life and Art*, p. 162.
12. Chaplin, *My Autobiography*, pp. 183, 208–209.
13. Edward Sutherland tape, Columbia University Oral History Project; Chaplin, *My Autobiography*, p. 208.
14. Chaplin, *My Autobiography*, pp. 204, 206–207.
15. *Ibid.*, p. 476; interview with Robert Hoover, June 4, 1995; Robinson, *Chaplin: His Life and Art*, pp. 441–43.
16. Chaplin, *My Autobiography*, p. 189.
17. *Ibid.*, pp. 226–27.
18. Gerith von Ulm, *Charlie Chaplin: King of Tragedy* (Caldwell, Idaho, 1940), pp. 19–28, 87–88.
19. *Ibid.*, pp. 83–84.
20. Joe Laurie, Jr., *Vaudeville: From the Honky-Tonks to the Palace* (Port Washington, N. Y., 1952), pp. 87–88; Anthony Slide, *The Vaudevillians* (Westport, Ct., 1981), pp. 51, 134–35; Walter Lippmann, *Drift and Mastery* (Englewood Cliffs, N.J., 1961), p. 118; Mae West, *Goodness Had Nothing to Do with It* (Englewood Cliffs, N.J., 1959), pp. 41–43.
21. Laurie, *Vaudeville*, p. 92; Slide, *The Vaudevillians*, p. 46.
22. Uno Asplund, *Chaplin's Films*, tr. by Paul Britten Austin (Cranbury, N.J., 1976), pp. 74–75; Sime Silverman, "Charlie Chaplin in 'Work,' " *Variety*, June 25, 1915, p. 20.
23. Chaplin, *My Autobiography*, p. 192.
24. Timothy Lyons, ed., "Roland H. Totheroh Interviewed," *Film Culture*, Spring 1972, pp. 283–84.
25. Chaplin, *My Autobiography*, pp. 197–99.
26. *Ibid.*, p. 199.
27. Scott Eyman, *Mary Pickford: America's Sweetheart* (New York, 1990), p. 109.

28. Frank Case, *Tales of a Wayward Inn Keeper* (New York, 1938), p. 100.

29. Chaplin, *My Autobiography*, pp. 200–201; Booton Herndon, *Mary Pickford and Douglas Fairbanks* (New York, 1977), p. 144.

30. Eyman, *Mary Pickford*, p. 110; Douglas Fairbanks, Jr., *The Salad Days* (New York, 1988), p. 23.

31. Herndon, *Mary Pickford*, pp. 12–13.

32. *Ibid.*, p. 45; David Niven, *Bring On the Empty Horses* (New York, 1975), p. 193.

33. Quoted in John C. Tibbetts and James M. Welsh, *His Majesty the American: The Cinema of Douglas Fairbanks, Sr.* (South Brunswick, N.J., and New York, 1977), p. 9.

34. Chaplin, *My Autobiography*, pp. 200–201.

35. Eyman, *Mary Pickford*, p. 114.

36. *Ibid.*, p. 113.

37. *Ibid.*, p. 83.

38. *Ibid.*

39. *Ibid.*, p. 104.

40. Chaplin, *My Autobiography*, p. 201.

41. Eyman, *Mary Pickford*, p. 116.

42. *Ibid.*, p. 123; Richard DeCordova, *Picture Personalities* (Urbana and Chicago, 1990), p. 122.

43. DeCordova, *Picture Personalities*, pp. 123–24.

44. Terry Ramsaye, "Chaplin—and How He Does It," *Photoplay*, vol. XXII, no. 4 (September 1917), p. 20.

45. Lyons, "Roland H. Totheroh Interviewed," p. 239; Ramsaye, "Chaplin—and How He Does It," p. 20.

46. Lyons, "Roland H. Totheroh," p. 240.

47. Ramsaye, "Chaplin—and How He Does It," pp. 22–23.

48. Lyons, "Roland H. Totheroh," pp. 240, 245.

49. *Ibid.*, p. 259.

50. *Ibid.*, pp. 260–62.

51. Chaplin, *My Autobiography*, p. 252.

52. *Ibid.*, pp. 188, 207, 211.

53. Dan Kamin, *Charlie Chaplin's One-Man Show* (Metuchen, N.J., and London, 1984), xiv.

54. Harvey O'Higgins, "Charlie Chaplin's Art," *New Republic*, February 3, 1917, pp. 16–18.

55. Quoted in J. B. Hirsch, "The New Charlie Chaplin," *Motion Picture Magazine*, January 1916, pp. 115–17.

56. Bruce LaBruce, "Picking a Bone," *Sight and Sound*, March 1995, p. 31.

57. Kevin Brownlow, *Behind the Mask of Innocence* (New York, 1990), p. 308.

58. *Ibid.*, p. 307.

59. Chaplin, *My Autobiography*, p. 210.

60. *Ibid.*

61. Oscar and Lilian Handlin, *Liberty in Peril, 1850–1920* (New York, 1992), p. 3.

62. David M. Kennedy, *Over Here: The First World War and American Society* (New York, 1982), p. 24.

63. *Ibid.*, p. 25.

64. Oscar Handlin, *The American People in the Twentieth Century* (Cambridge, Mass., 1954), p. 122.

65. Handlin and Handlin, *Liberty in Peril*, p. 23; Kennedy, *Over Here*, pp. 73–74.

66. Charles Chaplin, "In Defense of Myself," reprinted in Wes Gehring, *Charlie Chaplin: A Bio-Bibliography* (Westport, Ct., 1968), p. 113.

CHAPTER 7. "A PICTURE WITH A SMILE—AND PERHAPS A TEAR"

1. Carol Matthau, *Among the Porcupines* (New York, 1992), pp. 60–61.

2. Charles Chaplin, *My Autobiography* (New York, 1964), pp. 119–20.

3. *Ibid.*, p. 227.

4. Jean Darnell, "Mildred Harris—of the Broncho Company," *Photoplay*, February 1914, p. 54; " 'Stage Experience? No!' " *Photoplay*, October 1918, p. 43; Marguerite Sheridan, "The Girl from Wyoming," *Motion Picture*, November 1918, p. 51; Anthony Slide, "Lois Weber," in *Early Women Directors* (South Brunswick, N.J., and New York, 1977), *passim*.

5. Darnell, "Mildred Harris," p. 54.

6. Thomas P. Riggio, ed., *Theodore Dreiser: American Diaries 1902–1926* (Philadelphia, 1982), p. 350.

7. Chaplin, *My Autobiography*, pp. 227–28; Theodore Huff, *Charlie Chaplin* (New York, 1951), p. 88.

8. Huff, *Charlie Chaplin*, pp. 88–89.

9. Quoted in Kenneth S. Lynn, "The Torment of D. W. Griffith," *American Scholar*, Spring 1990, p. 260.

10. *Ibid.*

11. *Ibid.*, p. 261.

12. Quoted in Huff, *Charlie Chaplin*, p. 89.

13. Riggio, *Theodore Dreiser: American Diaries*.

14. Chaplin, *My Autobiography*, p. 230.

15. *Ibid.*

16. Quoted in Huff, *Charlie Chaplin*, p. 89; Robert Florey, "The Forgotten Friends," reprinted in Peter Haining, ed., *Charlie Chaplin: A Centenary Celebration* (London, 1989), p. 130.

17. Phyllis Greenacre, "Child Wife as Ideal: Sociological Considerations," in *Emotional Growth*, vol. 1 (New York, 1947), p. 4.

18. Quoted in David Robinson, *Chaplin: His Life and Art* (New York, 1985), p. 221.

19. Neal Gabler, *An Empire of Their Own* (New York, 1988), pp. 37–38; Ramsaye, *A Million and One Nights*, pp. 749–50; "United States of America v. Paramount Pictures, Inc., et al. Equity No. 87–273," *Film History*, vol. 4, no. 1 (1990), p. 8.

20. Ramsaye, *A Million and One Nights*, pp. 790–91; Robinson, *Chaplin: His Life and Art*, p. 223.

21. Alistair Cooke, "Charles Chaplin: The One and Only," in *Six Men* (New York, 1977), pp. 21–22.

22. Harry Crocker, unpublished biography of Chaplin, Margaret Herrick Library; Cooke, "Charles Chaplin," pp. 21, 33.

23. Julian Johnson, "Charles Not Charlie," *Photoplay*, September 1918, pp. 81, 83, 117.

24. Chaplin, *My Autobiography*, pp. 209–10.

25. *Ibid.*

26. *Ibid.*, p. 220.

27. *Ibid.*, pp. 220–21.
28. Walter Kerr, *The Silent Clowns* (New York, 1975), p. 182.
29. Chaplin, *My Autobiography*, p. 231.
30. Joseph McBride, *Frank Capra: The Catastrophe of Success* (New York, 1992), pp. 60–64.
31. Max Eastman, *Love and Revolution: My Journey Through an Epoch* (New York, 1964), p. 146.
32. Max Eastman, *Great Companions* (New York, 1943), pp. 244–45. Chaplin's statement about the Russian Revolution is taken from *Rob Wagner's Script*, November 20, 1943, as quoted in Joyce Milton, *Tramp: The Life of Charlie Chaplin* (New York, 1996), p. 404.
33. Richard Gid Powers, *Not Without Honor: The History of American Anticommunism* (New York, 1995), pp.7–9.
34. William E. Leuchtenberg, *The Perils of Prosperity* (Chicago, 1958), pp. 68 *et seq.*; Arthur M. Schlesinger, Jr., *The Crisis of the Old Order, 1919–1933* (Boston, 1957), pp. 41–43; Eastman, *Love and Revolution*, p. 145.
35. Leuchtenberg, *The Perils of Prosperity*; Harvey Klehr, John Earl Haynes, and Fridrikh Igorevich Firsov, *The Secret World of American Communism* (New Haven, 1995), pp. 5–6.
36. Schlesinger, *The Crisis of the Old Order*; John Dos Passos, Introduction, *Three Soldiers* (New York, 1932), v.
37. Tom Dardis, *Harold Lloyd: The Man on the Clock* (New York, 1957), pp. 74, 78.
38. Chaplin, *My Autobiography*, p. 193.
39. Robinson, *Chaplin: His Life and Art*, p. 251.
40. Huff, *Charlie Chaplin*, pp. 89–90.
41. Lita Grey Chaplin, *My Life with Chaplin: An Intimate Memoir* (New York, 1966), p. 170.
42. Chaplin, *My Autobiography*, pp. 231, 233.
43. *Ibid.*, p. 234.
44. *Ibid.*
45. *Ibid.*, p. 239.
46. *Ibid.*, p. 240.
47. Eastman, *Great Companions*, p. 216.
48. Eastman, *Love and Revolution*, pp. 7, 9.
49. *Ibid.*, p. 101.
50. *Ibid.*, p. 172.
51. *Ibid.*
52. *Ibid.*, p. 183.
53. *Ibid.*, pp. 184–85.
54. *Ibid.*, p. 206.
55. *Ibid.*, p. 186.
56. Samuel Marx, *Mayer and Thalberg: The Make-Believe Saints* (Hollywood, 1975), p. 24; Robinson, *Chaplin: His Life and Art*, p. 260.
57. Eastman, *Love and Revolution*, pp. 184–85.
58. *Ibid.*
59. Robinson, *Chaplin: His Life and Art*, pp. 262–63.
60. Eastman, *Love and Revolution*, p. 206.
61. *Ibid.*
62. *Ibid.*, p. 207.

63. *Ibid.*, p. 208.

64. *Ibid.*, pp. 210–11.

65. *Ibid.*, pp. 231–32, 243.

66. *Ibid.*, p. 245.

67. *Ibid.*, p. 277–79.

68. Huff, *Charlie Chaplin*, pp. 125–26; Robinson, *Chaplin: His Life and Art*, p. 265.

69. Harcourt Farmer's review is reprinted in Stanley Hochman, *A Century of Film Criticism* (New York, 1974), p. 44.

70. Thomas Burke, "The Tragic Comedian: A Close-up of Charles Chaplin," *The Outlook*, January 18, 1922, p. 102.

71. Konrad Bercovici, "A Day with Charlie Chaplin," *Harper's Magazine*, December 1928, p. 45.

72. Chaplin, *My Autobiography*, pp. 234–35.

73. *Ibid.*, p. 10.

CHAPTER 8. "STICK TO ME! FOR GOD'S SAKE, STICK TO ME!"

1. Interviews in April 1993 with Jackie Farber, Don Preston, and Morton Cooper; interview with Lita Grey Chaplin, February 1994.

2. Lita Grey Chaplin, with Morton Cooper, *My Life with Chaplin: An Intimate Memoir* (New York, 1966), pp. 28, 30, 31, 32–33.

3. *Ibid.*, pp. 35–36, 37.

4. *Ibid.*, pp. 40, 41.

5. Theodore Huff, *Charlie Chaplin* (New York, 1951), p. 162.

6. Tina Balio, *United Artists: The Company Built by Stars* (Madison, Wis., 1976), pp. 3–12; Charles Chaplin, *My Autobiography* (New York, 1964), p. 222.

7. Russel Nye, *The Unembarrassed Muse: The Popular Arts in America* (New York, 1970), pp. 373–74.

8. Balio, *United Artists*, pp. 3–12.

9. *Ibid.*, pp. 13–14.

10. Scott Eyman, *Mary Pickford: America's Sweetheart* (New York, 1990), p. 131.

11. Charlie Chaplin, *My Trip Abroad* (New York, 1922), pp. 2–3.

12. Chaplin, *My Trip*, pp. 7–8, 11.

13. Max Eastman, *Great Companions* (New York, 1959), pp. 211–12.

14. Edmund Wilson, *The Twenties* (New York, 1975), p. 158; Chaplin, *My Autobiography*, pp. 247–48; Charles J. Maland, *Chaplin and American Culture* (Princeton, N.J., 1989), p. 85; Chaplin, *My Trip*, p. 19.

15. Edward Knoblock, *Round the Room* (London, 1939), pp. 310–11.

16. David Robinson, *Chaplin: His Life and Art* (New York, 1985), pp. 283–84.

17. Chaplin, *My Trip*, p. 74.

18. Knoblock, *Round the Room*, p. 311.

19. Norman and Jeanne Mackenzie, *H. G. Wells* (New York, 1973), p. 327.

20. Chaplin, *My Trip*, p. 99.

21. *Ibid.*, p. 89.

22. *Ibid.*, p. 90.

23. Thomas Burke, *City of Encounters* (London, 1932), pp. 131–67.

24. Gorham Munson, *The Awakening Twenties* (Baton Rouge, La., 1985), pp. 68–69.

25. Chaplin, *My Autobiography*, p. 248.

26. Waldo Frank, *Time Exposures by Search-Light*, 1926 (New York, 1976), pp. 87–88.

27. Waldo Frank, *Memoirs of Waldo Frank* (Amherst, Mass., 1973), p. 120.

28. Frank, *Time Exposures*, p. 88.

29. Chaplin, *My Trip Abroad*, p. 143.

30. Pola Negri, *Memoirs of a Star* (New York, 1970), pp. 179–80.

31. *Ibid.*, p. 180.

32. Chaplin, *My Trip Abroad*, p. 143.

33. *Ibid.*, p. 146.

34. *Ibid.*, pp. 147 ff.

35. Anita Leslie, *Clare Sheridan* (New York, 1977), p. 175; Clare Sheridan, *My American Diary* (New York, 1922), pp. 332–50.

36. Leslie, *Clare Sheridan*, pp. 175–76.

37. Clare Sheridan, *Naked Truth* (New York, 1928), p. 274.

38. Benjamin De Casseres, "The Hamlet-Like Nature of Charlie Chaplin," *New York Times*, December 12, 1920, sec. 3., p. 5.

39. Negri, *Memoirs*, p. 216.

40. Chaplin, *My Autobiography*, p. 298.

41. Quoted in Carlos Baker, *Ernest Hemingway: A Life Story* (New York, 1969), p. 91.

42. Adolphe Menjou and M. M. Musselman, *It Took Nine Tailors* (New York, 1948), pp. 110–11.

43. Chaplin, *My Autobiography*, p. 300; Roger Manvell, *Chaplin* (London, 1975), p. 127.

44. Stephen Vaughn, "Morality and Entertainment: The Origins of the Motion Picture Production Code," *Journal of American History*, June 1990, pp. 39–65; Gregory D. Black, *Hollywood Censored: Morality Codes, Catholics and the Movies* (New York, 1994), pp. 31–33.

45. Menjou and Musselman, *It Took Nine Tailors*, p. 117.

46. Eric Bentley, "Charlie Chaplin and Peggy Hopkins Joyce: A Comment on *A Woman of Paris*," *Moviegoer*, Summer 1966, pp. 10–18.

47. Robinson, *Chaplin: His Life and Art*, pp. 325–27, 329.

48. *Ibid.*, p. 320.

49. Quoted in Gorham Munson, *The Awakening Twenties* (Baton Rouge, La., 1985), pp. 235–36.

50. *Ibid.*, pp. 233–34.

51. *Ibid.*, p. 237.

CHAPTER 9. "WHY DON'T YOU JUMP?"

1. David Robinson, *"A Woman of Paris,"* *Sight and Sound*, Autumn 1980, p. 223.

2. Charles Chaplin, *My Autobiography* (New York, 1964), p. 303.

3. Bernard De Voto, *The Year of Decision 1846* (Boston, 1943), pp. 353–444 *passim*.

4. Edwin Schallert, "Stark Realism—At Last!" *Picture Play*, October 1923, pp. 47, 104.

5. "Screen Needs Realism," *New York Times*, August 5, 1923, sec. 6, p. 2.

6. David Robinson, *Chaplin: His Life and Art* (New York, 1985), p. 343.

7. Edmund Wilson, *The American Earthquake: A Documentary of the Twenties and Thirties* (New York, 1958), p. 72.

8. Chaplin, *My Autobiography*, pp. 209–10.

9. John Peale Bishop, "Sex Appeal in the Movies," in *The Collected Essays of John Peale Bishop*, ed. Edmund Wilson (New York, 1948), pp. 218–19; Chaplin, *My Autobiography*, p. 69.

10. Chaplin, *My Autobiography*, p. 210.

11. *Cf.* the discussions of this episode in Charles J. Maland, *Chaplin and American Culture* (Princeton, N.J., 1989), p. 80, and Dennis De Nitto and William Herman, *Film and the Critical Eye* (New York, 1975), p. 101.

12. Lita Grey Chaplin, with Morton Cooper, *My Life with Chaplin: An Intimate Memoir* (New York, 1966), pp. 43–57 *passim*.

13. *Ibid.*, pp. 63, 65, 67–68; interview with Morton Cooper, April 22, 1993.

14. Lita Grey Chaplin, *My Life with Chaplin*, pp. 79–82, 84.

15. *Ibid.*, p. 84.

16. *Ibid.*, p. 89.

17. *Ibid.*, p. 90.

18. *Ibid.*, pp. 91–93, 94; William de Mille is quoted in Arthur Knight, *The Liveliest Art* (New York, 1957), p. 118; interview with Don Preston, April 13, 1993.

19. Victoria Glendinning, *Rebecca West: A Life* (London, 1987), p. 94.

20. Lita Grey Chaplin, *My Life with Chaplin*, pp. 104, 105.

21. *Ibid.*, p. 127.

22. *Ibid.*, pp. 127–32.

23. Fred Lawrence Guiles, *Marion Davies* (New York, 1972), pp. 151, 153, 154.

24. Lita Grey Chaplin, *My Life with Chaplin*, pp. 135, 136.

25. *Ibid.*, pp. 137–39.

26. *Ibid.*, pp. 3–4.

27. Georgia Hale, *Charlie Chaplin: Intimate Close-Ups*, ed. Heather Kiernan (Metuchen, N.J., 1995), p. x.

28. *Ibid.*, pp. 3, 12.

29. *Ibid.*, pp. 12–13.

30. *Ibid.*, pp. viii, 119 and *passim*.

31. Lita Grey Chaplin, *My Life with Chaplin*, pp. 115, 149, 154, 173.

32. Clare Sheridan, *Naked Truth* (New York, 1928), p. 271.

33. Lita Grey Chaplin, *My Life with Chaplin*, pp. 180, 182–86, 188–95.

34. Robinson, *Chaplin: His Life and Art*, pp. 356–57; Maland, *Chaplin and American Culture*, p. 81; David Naylor, *Great American Movie Theaters* (Washington, D.C., 1987), p. 209.

35. Chaplin, *My Autobiography*, p. 305.

36. *Ibid.*

37. Bruce Kellner, *The Last Dandy: Ralph Barton, American Artist, 1891–1931* (Columbia, Mo., 1991), pp. vii, 1, 79.

38. *Ibid.*, pp. 79, 110, 120.

39. *Ibid.*, pp. 90, 91.

40. *Ibid.*, pp. 129–31.

41. Edmund Wilson, "The Finale at the Follies," *The American Earthquake* (New York, 1964), p. 45.

42. Barry Paris, *Louise Brooks* (New York, 1989), pp. 83, 84, 107, 250.

43. Paris, *Louise Brooks*, pp. 71, 89, 99, 101, 105; Louise Brooks, "Charlie Chaplin Remembered," *Film Culture*, Spring 1966, p. 5.

44. Brooks, "Charlie Chaplin Remembered"; Paris, *Louise Brooks*, p. 107.

45. Paris, *Louise Brooks*, pp. 107–108.

46. Brooks, "Charlie Chaplin Remembered," p. 6.

47. Paris, *Louise Brooks*, p. 109.

48. *Ibid.*, p. 110.

49. Louise Brooks, *Lulu in Hollywood* (New York, 1982), pp. 98, 104.

50. Lita Grey Chaplin, *My Life with Chaplin*, pp. 211, 219, 226.

51. V. S. Naipaul interview with Mel Gussow, *New York Times Book Review*, April 23, 1994, p. 30.

52. Interview with Henry Bergman by an unidentified source, quoted in Robinson, *Chaplin: His Life and Art*, pp. 360–61.

53. Robinson, *Chaplin: His Life and Art*, p. 362.

54. Lita Grey Chaplin, *My Life with Chaplin*, pp. 211, 219, 226.

55. Robinson, *Chaplin: His Life and Art*, p. 370.

56. Lita Grey Chaplin, *My Life with Chaplin*, p. 235; Maland, *Chaplin and American Culture*, p. 96; *New York Times*, December 2, 1926, p. 1, and December 3, 1926, p. 1.

57. Lita Grey Chaplin, *My Life with Chaplin*, pp. 195, 230–31, 252–53.

58. *New York Times*, January 16, 1927, p. 5, and January 28, 1927, p. 7; Maland, *Chaplin and American Culture*, pp. 97–98.

59. *New York Times*, January 12, 1927, p. 1, and January 13, 1927, p. 27; Lita Grey Chaplin, *My Life with Chaplin*, p. 260; Maland, *Chaplin and American Culture*, p. 99.

60. *New York Times*, January 15, 1927, p. 1, and January 26, 1927, p. 9; *New York Herald-Tribune*, January 23, 1927, sec. 6, p. 3, and January 30, 1927, sec. 6, p. 3; Theodore Huff, *Charlie Chaplin* (New York, 1951), p. 205; Lita Grey Chaplin, *My Life with Chaplin*, p. 260; Ralph Barton, "Picking on Charlie Chaplin," *New Yorker*, January 23, 1927, pp. 17–18; Maland, *Chaplin and American Culture*, pp. 99–101.

61. Lita Grey Chaplin, *My Life with Chaplin*, pp. 268–69. *New York Times*, August 23, 1927, pp. 1, 8; Robinson, *Chaplin: His Life and Art*, pp. 377–78; Barbara Goldsmith, *Little Gloria . . . Happy at Last* (New York, 1980), p. 262.

62. Quoted in Robinson, *Chaplin: His Life and Art*, p. 380.

63. Stark Young's review is reprinted in Stanley Kauffmann, ed., *American Film Criticism* (New York, 1972), pp. 200–204; "Bonnie Prince Charlie of the Custard Pies," *Literary Digest*, March 24, 1928, p. 36; Maland, *Chaplin and American Culture*, pp. 106, 110.

64. Anna Mazzarelli, "Fellini in Conversation," *Sight and Sound*, April 1993, p. 15; Robinson, *Chaplin: His Life and Art*, p. 632.

CHAPTER 10. "YOU WANNA HEAR 'TOOT-TOOT-TOOTSIE'?"

1. Sources for section 1 of this chapter are as follows: Harry M. Geduld, *The Birth of the Talkies: From Edison to Jolson* (Bloomington, Ind., 1975), pp. 108–201; Herbert G. Goldman, *Jolson: The Legend Come to Life* (New York, 1988), pp. 145, 146, 150, 151, 152; Mary Lea Bondy, ed., *The Dawn of Sound* (New York, 1989), p. 7; Alexander Walker, *The Shattered Silents* (London, 1978), pp. 36, 37, 38, 41, 70, 132, 133.

2. Walker, *The Shattered Silents*, p. 132; Gladys Hall, "Charlie Chaplin Attacks the Talkies," *Motion Picture*, May 1929, p. 29.

3. Walker, *The Shattered Silents*, p. 132.

4. David Robinson, *Chaplin: His Life and Art* (New York, 1985), p. 396; Theodore Huff, *Charlie Chaplin* (New York, 1951), p. 221.

5. *New York Times*, February 10, 1928, p. 26.

6. *The Letters of Evelyn Waugh and Diana Cooper*, ed. Artemis Cooper (New York, 1992), p. 129.

7. Charles Chaplin, *My Autobiography* (New York, 1964), p. 325.

8. *New York Times*, July 14, 1929, sec. 9, p. 4.

9. Huff, *Charlie Chaplin*, p. 223.

10. Chaplin, *My Autobiography*, p. 326.

11. Charles J. Maland, *Chaplin and American Culture* (Princeton, N.J., 1989), pp. 114–15; Chaplin, *My Autobiography*, p. 326; Huff, *Charlie Chaplin*, pp. 220, 223; Robinson, *Chaplin: His Life and Art*, pp. 399–400.

12. Mason Wiley and Damien Bona, *Inside Oscar* (New York, 1986), pp. 6, 8.

13. Huff, *Charlie Chaplin*, pp. 221–23; Robinson, *Chaplin: His Life and Art*, pp. 399, 402, 404, 405–407.

14. Huff, *Charlie Chaplin*, pp. 222–23; Robinson, *Chaplin: His Life and Art*, pp. 406–407.

15. George Orwell, "The Lion and the Unicorn," in *The Collected Essays, Journalism and Letters of George Orwell*, eds. Sonia Orwell and Ian Angus, vol. 2 (New York, 1968), p. 75.

16. Robinson, *Chaplin: His Life and Art*, p. 437.

17. Bruce Kellner, *The Last Dandy: Ralph Barton, American Artist, 1891–1931* (Columbia, Mo., 1991), pp. 130–214, *passim*.

18. Chaplin, *My Autobiography*, p. 332; James Agee, "Comedy's Greatest Era," *Life*, September 5, 1949, p. 73.

19. Luis Buñuel, *My Last Sigh*, tr. by Abigail Israel (New York, 1983), pp. 127–28.

20. *Ibid.*, p. 129.

21. *Ibid.*, p. 49.

22. Ivor Montagu, *With Eisenstein in Hollywood* (New York, 1969), p. 87; Herbert Marshall, Preface to Sergei M. Eisenstein, *Immoral Memories*, tr. by Herbert Marshall (Boston, 1983), pp. x, xviii.

23. Montagu, *With Eisenstein in Hollywood*, pp. 74–75.

24. *Ibid.*, p. 95.

25. *Ibid.*, pp. 96–97.

26. Leon Harris, *Upton Sinclair: American Rebel* (New York, 1975), pp. 281–82; Montagu, *With Eisenstein*, p. 86.

27. Harris, *Upton Sinclair*, pp. 11, 172, 190; Chaplin, *My Autobiography*, p. 350.

28. John Willett, *Art and Politics in the Weimar Period* (New York, 1978), p. 10; Walter Laqueur, *Weimar: A Cultural History 1918–1933* (New York, 1974), p. 43; Fred Miller Robinson, *The Man in the Bowler Hat* (Chapel Hill, N.C., 1993), pp. 92, 96.

29. Arthur M. Schlesinger, Jr., *The Politics of Upheaval* (Boston, 1960), pp. 111–13.

30. Harris, *Upton Sinclair*, p. 305; Leo C. Rosten, *Hollywood: The Movie Colony, the Movie Makers* (New York, 1941), pp. 135–38.

31. Rosten, *Hollywood*, p. 137; Schlesinger, *Politics of Upheaval*, pp. 118–19.

32. Schlesinger, *Politics of Upheaval*, p. 122.

CHAPTER 11. "STRIKES AND RIOTS!"

1. Thomas Burke, *City of Encounters* (London, 1932), p. 189; Charles Chaplin, "A Comedian Sees the World," *Woman's Home Companion*, September 1933, p. 10.

2. Chaplin, "A Comedian Sees the World," pp. 86–88.

3. *Ibid.*, p. 89; Burke, *City of Encounters*, p. 170.

4. Charles Chaplin, "A Comedian Sees the World," *Woman's Home Companion*, October 1933, pp. 17, 102.

5. *Ibid.*, p. 102; Carlyle Robinson, "The Private Life of Charlie Chaplin," *Liberty*, Winter 1972, p. 45.

6. Chaplin, "A Comedian Sees the World"; Robinson, "Private Life," p. 46.

7. The text of the Freud letter is quoted in Crocker, unpublished biography of Chaplin, Margaret Herrick Library, Center for Motion Picture Studies, Beverly Hills, California.

8. Charles Chaplin, "A Comedian Sees the World," *Woman's Home Companion*, October 1933, p. 104, and November 1933, p. 15; Robinson, "Private Life," p. 46.

9. Chaplin, "A Comedian Sees the World," *Woman's Home Companion*, October 1933, p. 100; Charles Chaplin, *My Autobiography* (New York, 1964), p. 357.

10. Robinson, "Private Life," pp. 46–48; David Robinson, *Chaplin: His Life and Art* (New York, 1985), pp. 433–35.

11. Chaplin, *My Autobiography*, p. 362.

12. *Ibid.*, pp. 342, 344.

13. *Ibid.*, pp. 366–67.

14. Al Hirschfeld, *The World of Hirschfeld*, introduction by Lloyd Goodrich (New York, 1970), pp. 19–21.

15. Chaplin, *My Autobiography*, p. 372.

16. *Ibid.*, pp. 372–73.

17. *Ibid.*, pp. 373–74; Hugh Byas, *Government by Assassination* (New York, 1942), pp. 22, 26, 30.

18. Byas, *Government*, pp. 30–31; Chaplin, *My Autobiography*, pp. 372–75.

19. Byas, *Government*, pp. 31, 35.

20. Chaplin, *My Autobiography*, p. 381; Julie Gilbert, *Opposite Attraction: The Lives of Erich Maria Remarque and Paulette Goddard* (New York, 1995), pp. 50, 53; Joe Morella and Edward Z. Epstein, *Paulette: The Adventurous Life of Paulette Goddard* (New York, 1985), p. 19.

21. Chaplin, *My Autobiography*, p. 381; Robinson, *Chaplin: His Life and Art*, p. 454; author interview with Sydney Chaplin, February 6, 1995.

22. Gilbert, *Opposite Attraction*, pp. 39, 49.

23. Morella and Epstein, *Paulette*, pp. 3–5.

24. Gilbert, *Opposite Attraction*, pp. 46–50; Morella and Eptein, *Paulette*, pp. 7–8, 9–10.

25. Morella and Epstein, *Paulette*, pp. 22, 24, 27, 29; Edith Head and Paddy Calistro, *Edith Head's Hollywood* (New York, 1983), pp. 46–47.

26. Charles Chaplin, Jr., *My Father, Charlie Chaplin* (New York, 1960), pp. 98–99, 101.

27. *Ibid.*, p. 119; Chaplin, *My Autobiography*, p. 383.

28. Harry Alan Potamkin, *The Compound Cinema: The Film Writings of Harry Alan Potamkin*, ed. Lewis Jacobs (New York, 1977), pp. 49, 228.

29. Lorenzo Turrent Rozas, "Charlie Chaplin's Decline," *Living Age*, June 1934, pp. 319–23.

30. Charles J. Maland, *Chaplin and American Culture* (Princeton, N.J., 1989), pp. 145–46; Boris Shumiatsky, "Charlie Chaplin's New Picture," *New Masses*, September 24, 1935, pp. 29–30. See also Terry Ramsaye, "Chaplin Ridicules Reds' Claim Film Aids 'Cause,'" *Motion Picture Herald*, December 7, 1935, p. 1.

31. Will Hays, *The Memoirs of Will H. Hays* (Garden City, N.Y., 1955), p. 439;

Gregory D. Black, *Hollywood Censored: Morality Codes, Catholics, and the Movies* (New York, 1994), pp. 37–43, 302. My entire discussion of censorship in this section is heavily indebted to Professor Black's book, and to Stephen Vaughn, "Morality and Entertainment: The Origins of the Motion Picture Production Code," *Journal of American History*, June 1990, especially pp. 50–63.

32. Vaughn, "Morality and Entertainment," pp. 60–61.

33. *Ibid.*, pp. 62–63.

34. Black, *Hollywood Censored*, pp. 157–59.

35. *Ibid.*, pp. 2, 149, 157–63, 164, 168; Vaughn, "Morality and Entertainment," p. 64.

36. Black, *Hollywood Censored*, pp. 1, 245–46.

37. *Ibid.*, pp. 247–51, 253.

38. Statement by David Raksin; PCA file on *Modern Times*, Margaret Herrick Library.

39. Quoted in Robinson, *Chaplin: His Life and Art*, p. 463.

40. Ramsaye, "Chaplin Ridicules," pp. 1–2; Maland, *Chaplin and American Culture*, pp. 145–46.

41. PCA file on *Modern Times*, Margaret Herrick Library.

42. *Ibid.*

43. Maland, *Chaplin and American Culture*, pp. 157–58.

44. Chaplin, *My Autobiography*, p. 383.

45. Charles Chaplin, *My Life in Pictures* (New York, 1975), p. 259.

46. Henri Bergson, "Laughter" (1900), in *Comedy*, ed. Wylie Sypher (Garden City, N.Y., 1956), p. 79.

47. Jean Cocteau, *My Contemporaries*, ed. Margaret Crosland (Philadelphia, 1968), p. 86.

48. Maland, *Chaplin and American Culture*, pp. 153–54.

49. E. H. Gombrich, *The Sense of Order: A Study in the Psychology of Decorative Art* (Ithaca, N.Y., 1979), pp. 97–98.

50. Diana Trilling, *The Beginning of the Journey* (New York, 1993), p. 340.

51. Sources for section 11 of this chapter are as follows: David Raksin, "Life with Charlie," *Wonderful Inventions*, ed. Iris Newsom, with an Introduction by Erik Barnouw (Washington, D.C., 1985), pp. 159, 161, 162, 163, 170.

52. Morella and Epstein, *Paulette*, pp. 41, 56, 59; Chaplin, *My Autobiography*, p. 385; Charles Schwartz, *Gershwin. His Life and Music*, Indianapolis, 1973, *passim*.

CHAPTER 12. "WHEREVER YOU ARE, LOOK UP, HANNAH!"

1. David Robinson, *Chaplin: His Life and Art* (New York, 1985), pp. 474–75.

2. *Ibid.*, pp. 482, 483.

3. David Thomson, *Showman: The Life of David O. Selznick* (New York, 1992), pp. 269, 270.

4. *Ibid.*, pp. 279, 281.

5. *Ibid.*, pp. 282, 283.

6. Joe Morella and Edward Z. Epstein, *Paulette: The Adventurous Life of Paulette Goddard* (New York, 1985), pp. 75–76.

7. Charles Chaplin, Jr., *My Father, Charlie Chaplin* (New York, 1960), p. 181.

8. Charles Chaplin, *My Autobiography* (New York, 1964), p. 388.

9. *Ibid.*

10. Charles Chaplin, Jr., *My Father, Charlie Chaplin*, pp. 182, 184–85.

11. Quoted in Robinson, *Chaplin: His Life and Art*, p. 489.

12. Harvey Klehr, John Earl Haynes, and Fridrikh Igorevich Firsov, *The Secret World of American Communism* (New Haven, 1995), p. 104n.

13. Charles Chaplin FBI file, Washington, D.C.

14. Ivor Montagu, *With Eisenstein in Hollywood* (New York, 1969), p. 94; Charles J. Maland, *Chaplin and American Culture* (Princeton, N.J., 1989), p. 395; Chaplin, *My Autobiography*, p. 391; Louis Nizer, *My Life in Court* (New York, 1961), pp. 9–10; Joyce Milton, *Tramp* (New York, 1996), pp. 367–72, 465–66.

15. Gregory D. Black, *Hollywood Censored: Morality Codes, Catholics and the Movies* (New York, 1994), pp. 264–67; Peter Bogdanovich, *Fritz Lang in America* (New York, 1969), p. 32; Michael Shelden, *Graham Greene: The Enemy Within* (New York, 1994), p. 176.

16. Larry Ceplair and Steven Englund, *The Inquisition in Hollywood: Politics and the Film Community* (New York, 1980), pp. 95–96, 100; Erika and Klaus Mann, *Escape to Life* (Boston, 1939), p. 199; John Russell Taylor, *Strangers in Paradise: The Hollywood Émigrés* (New York, 1983), p. 27; Maland, *Chaplin and American Culture*, p. 161.

17. Ceplair and Englund, *Inquisition*, pp. 104–105, 105n., 106, 106n.

18. *Ibid.*, p. 107.

19. *Ibid.*, p. 84.

20. Chaplin, *My Autobiography*, p. 393.

21. Ceplair and Englund, *Inquisition*, p. 147.

22. Melvyn Douglas papers, State Historical Society of Wisconsin, Madison, Wisconsin.

23. Dan James's words are quoted in Robinson, *Chaplin: His Life and Art*, p. 489; Genrikh Borovik, *The Philby Files: The Secret Life of Master Spy Kim Philby*, ed. and with an introduction by Philip Knightly (Boston, 1994), pp. 142, 145, 146.

24. James's words are quoted in Robinson, *Chaplin: His Life and Art*.

25. Kenneth S. Davis, *FDR: Into the Storm 1937–1940—A History* (New York, 1993), pp. 598, 620–21.

26. Robinson, *Chaplin: His Life and Art*, pp. 494–504 *passim*.

27. *Ibid.*, pp. 494–95.

28. Chaplin, *My Autobiography*, p. 32; Morella and Epstein, *Paulette*, pp. 79–85.

29. Robinson, *Chaplin: His Life and Art*, p. 502.

30. Jack Oakie, *Jack Oakie's Double Takes* (San Francisco, 1980), p. 67.

31. *Ibid.*, pp. 79–80.

32. Letter from Dr. Georg Gyssling to Joseph I. Breen, October 31, 1938, PCA file on *The Great Dictator*, Margaret Herrick Library.

33. Cable from J. Brooke Wilkinson to Joseph I. Breen, March 2, 1939, PCA file on *The Great Dictator*, Margaret Herrick Library.

34. Letter from Joseph I. Breen to Alf Reeves, September 6, 1940, PCA file on *The Great Dictator*, Margaret Herrick Library.

35. *New York Times*, March 22, 1942, sec. 6, pp. 12–13; Maland, *Chaplin and American Culture*, pp. 178–79.

36. Anthony Heilbut, *Exiled in Paradise: German Refugee Artists and Intellectuals in America, from the 1930s to the Present* (New York, 1983), p. 296. The *New York Herald-Tribune* review is quoted in Maland, *Chaplin and American Culture*, p. 180.

37. Reinhold Niebuhr, *Moral Man and Immoral Society: A Study in Ethics and Politics* (New York, 1932), p. xx.

38. Robinson, *Chaplin: His Life and Art*, p. 508.

39. Morella and Epstein, *Paulette*, pp. 103–105; Jean Negulesco, *Things I Did and Things I Think I Did* (New York, 1984), pp. 186–87; Julie Gilbert, *Opposite Attraction: The Lives of Erich Maria Remarque and Paulette Goddard* (New York, 1995), pp. 270, 272.

40. Robinson, *Chaplin: His Life and Art*, p. 510; Charles Chaplin FBI file.

41. Chaplin, *My Autobiography*, pp. 404–405; Charles Chaplin, Jr., *My Father, Charlie Chaplin*, p. 245.

42. Charles Chaplin, Jr., *My Father, Charlie Chaplin*, p. 250.

43. Interview with Lionel Krisel, January 30, 1995; interview with Sydney Chaplin, February 6, 1995.

44. Charles Chaplin, Jr., *My Father, Charlie Chaplin*, pp. 252–55; Roy Moseley, *Rex Harrison: A Biography* (New York, 1987), p. 98.

45. Charles Chaplin, Jr., *My Father, Charlie Chaplin*, pp. 252–55.

46. Chaplin, *My Autobiography*, pp. 413–14; FBI report, Los Angeles office to Washington, D.C., November 11, 1943; FBI report, Los Angeles office to Washington, D.C., February 25, 1944.

47. FBI report, Los Angeles office to Washington, D.C., November 9, 1943.

48. Robert Lenzner, *The Great Getty: The Life and Loves of J. Paul Getty— Richest Man in the World* (New York, 1985), pp. 65–66, 71–72.

49. *Ibid.*, p. 72.

50. Chaplin, *My Autobiography*, p. 414.

51. *Ibid.*; Mark Schorer, *Sinclair Lewis. An American Life* (New York, 1961), pp. 655–57, 661–62.

52. Chaplin, *My Autobiography*, pp. 414–15.

53. The quoted material in section 11 of this chapter is from FBI interviews with Joan Barry, January 7, 10, and 11, 1944, and an FBI report on Joan Barry, February 25, 1944.

54. Ralph Levering, *American Opinion and the Russian Alliance, 1939–1945* (Chapel Hill, N.C., 1976), pp. 70–84.

55. Chaplin, *My Autobiography*, pp. 404–405.

56. *Ibid.*, pp. 408–409, 410; Maland, *Chaplin and American Culture*, p. 190; Donald Ogden Stewart, *By a Stroke of Luck! An Autobiography of Donald Ogden Stewart* (New York, 1975), p. 274.

57. *New York Times*, October 17, 1942, p. 16; *New York Herald-Tribune*, October 17, 1942, p. 4.

58. *Chicago Tribune*, November 26, 1942, p. 23.

59. *New York Times*, December 4, 1942, p. 15; FBI file on Charles Chaplin, Washington, D.C.

60. Richard Gid Powers, *Not Without Honor: The History of American Anticommunism* (New York, 1995), p. 169.

61. For calling my attention to the Pegler column, I am indebted to Maland, *Chaplin and American Culture*, p. 194.

62. FBI report on Joan Barry, February 25, 1944; Chaplin, *My Autobiography*, p. 415.

63. Chaplin, *My Autobiography*, p. 416.

64. Lenzner, *The Great Getty*, p. 84.

65. Orson Welles and Peter Bogdanovich, *This Is Orson Welles* (New York, 1992), p. 135.

66. Chaplin, *My Autobiography*, pp. 419, 420; Carol Matthau, *Among the Porcupines* (New York, 1992), p. 41.

CHAPTER 13. TWO DISTINCT PERSONALITIES

1. Charles Chaplin, *My Autobiography* (New York, 1964), pp. 419–20, FBI interviews with Joan Barry, January 7, 10, and 11, 1944; FBI report on Joan Barry, February 25, 1944; Charles Chaplin, Jr., *My Father, Charlie Chaplin* (New York, 1960), pp. 265–66; Jerry Giesler, *The Jerry Giesler Story* (New York, 1960), pp. 184, 187; "Just a Peter Pan," *New York Herald-Tribune*, December 21, 1944, p. 16.

2. FBI interviews with Joan Barry, January 7, 10, and 11, 1944; FBI report, February 25, 1944; FBI report, September 2, 1943.

3. Charles Chaplin, Jr., *My Father, Charlie Chaplin*, p. 272.

4. Letter from Evelyn J. Halpert, head of the Brearley School, to the author, April 21, 1995; interviews with Joan Ridder Challinor, Nuala O'Donnell Pell, and Harry Cushing, spring 1995; interview with Mary Stewart Doyle, February 1996; interview with Kitty Hamilton Hobbs and Whitman Hobbs, February 1996.

5. Interview with Nuala O'Donnell Pell, *op. cit*; Carol Matthau, *Among the Porcupines* (New York, 1992), pp. 6–7, 253; Arthur and Barbara Gelb, *O'Neill* (New York, 1960), pp. 850–52; Louis Sheaffer, *O'Neill: Son and Artist* (Boston, 1973), pp. 537–38.

6. FBI memo, R. B. Hood, Los Angeles, to J. Edgar Hoover, June 24, 1943.

7. FBI report on Joan Barry, February 25, 1944; Charles J. Maland, *Chaplin and American Culture* (Princeton, N.J., 1989), p. 201.

8. FBI interviews with Joan Barry, January 7, 10, and 11, 1944.

9. *Ibid.*; FBI report, February 25, 1944.

10. *New York Daily News*, June 2, 1943, p. 4; *Chicago Tribune*, June 3, 1943, p. 22; Maland, *Chaplin and American Culture*, pp. 209, 210.

11. Chaplin, *My Autobiography*, p. 421.

12. FBI memo from R. B. Hood to J. Edgar Hoover, June 24, 1943; Maland, *Chaplin and American Culture*, pp. 201–202.

13. Chaplin, *My Autobiography*, p. 421.

14. FBI file on Charles Chaplin, Washington, D.C.

15. *Ibid.*

16. Maland, *Chaplin and American Culture*, pp. 203–204; FBI memos, Los Angeles to Washington, August 14, 17, 24, 25, 1943; FBI telegram, J. Edgar Hoover to Special Agent in charge, Los Angeles, August 20, 1943; FBI memos, Los Angeles to Washington, December 22, 1943, and February 14, 1944.

17. Maland, *Chaplin and American Culture*, pp. 204–205.

18. *Ibid.*, p. 205; Giesler, *The Jerry Giesler Story*, pp. 187–88; *Chicago Tribune*, April 5, 1944, p. 1.

19. FBI memo, Los Angeles to Washington, May 11, 1944.

20. David Robinson, *Chaplin: His Life and Art* (New York, 1985), pp. 524–25.

21. *Chicago Tribune*, January 5, 1945, p. 6; *New York Times*, April 14, 1945, p. 13; *New York Times*, April 18, 1945, p. 25; *New York Times*, April 19, 1945, p. 29.

22. Chaplin, *My Autobiography*, p. 434.

23. Anthony Heilbut, *Exiled in Paradise: German Refugee Artists and Intellectuals in America, from the 1930s to the Present* (New York, 1983), p. 185; Manfred Grabs, ed., *Hanns Eisler: A Rebel in Music* (Berlin, 1978), p. 11.

24. Heilbut, *Exiled in Paradise*, pp. 370, 371.

25. Grabs, ed., *Hanns Eisler*, pp. 14, 102, 195; James K. Lyon, *Bertolt Brecht in America* (Princeton, N.J., 1980), p. 84.

26. All the quotations in section 7 of this chapter are taken from correspondence in the PCA files in the Margaret Herrick Library, Center for Motion Picture Studies, Beverly Hills, California.

27. Brian Taves, "Charlie Dearest," *Film Comment*, March-April 1988, p. 64.

28. Brian Taves, "Robert Florey: Hollywood Director and Historian" (privately printed, 1990), p. 10.

29. Brian Taves, *Robert Florey: The French Expressionist* (Metuchen, N.J., 1987), pp. 88, 125, 127; Taves, "Charlie Dearest," p. 64.

30. Robert Florey, "The Forgotten Friends," reprinted in Peter Haining, ed., *Charlie Chaplin: A Centenary Celebration* (London, 1989), p. 128.

31. *Ibid.;* Taves, "Charlie Dearest," p. 68.

32. Taves, "Charlie Dearest," p. 64.

33. *Ibid.*, pp. 64–65; Robert Florey, *Hollywood d'Hier et d'Aujourdhui* (Paris, 1948), p. 341.

34. Taves, "Charlie Dearest," pp. 63–64.

35. *Ibid.*, p. 65.

36. *Ibid.*, p. 69.

37. *Ibid.;* Florey, "The Forgotten Friends," pp. 128–29.

38. Taves, "Charlie Dearest," p. 68.

39. *Ibid.*, p. 69.

40. *Ibid.*, p. 66.

41. Robert Warshow, *The Immediate Experience* (New York, 1962), p. 215.

42. James Agee, *Agee on Film*, vol. 1 (Boston, 1964), pp. 252–62 *passim;* Max Lerner, "Chaplin—Art and Politics," *PM*, April 17, 1947, p. 2; Arnaud d'Usseau, "Chaplin's *Monsieur Verdoux*," *Mainstream*, Summer 1947, pp. 308–17 *passim*.

43. *New York Herald-Tribune*, April 12, 1947, p. 8; *New Yorker*, April 19, 1947, p. 42; *Christian Science Monitor*, April 19, 1947, as quoted in Maland, *Chaplin and American Culture*, p. 241.

44. Tina Balio, *United Artists: The Company Built by Stars* (Madison, Wis., 1976), p. 214; Maland, *Chaplin and American Culture*, pp. 244–45, 250–51.

45. Stephen E. Ambrose, *Nixon: The Education of a Politician, 1913–1962* (New York, 1987), pp. 145–47; Joseph R. Starobin, *American Communism in Crisis* (Cambridge, Mass., 1972), pp. 304–305.

46. Larry Ceplair and Steven Englund, *The Inquisition in Hollywood: Politics and the Film Community* (New York, 1980), p. 380n.; David Caute, *The Great Fear* (New York, 1978), p. 503; Grabs, ed., *Hanns Eisler*, p. 152; Heilbut, *Exiled in Paradise*, p. 374; Georges Sadoul, *Vie de Charlot* (Paris, 1978), p. 149.

47. *Congressional Record*, 80th Congress, 1st session, March 7, 1947, p. 1792; Balio, *United Artists*, pp. 211–13; Chaplin, *My Autobiography*, pp. 447–49.

48. *New York Herald-Tribune*, April 12, 1947, p. 8; Red Kann, "Insider's Outlook," *Motion Picture Daily*, April 11, 1947, p. 21.

49. "Charlie Chaplin's Monsieur Verdoux Press Conference," *Film Comment*, Winter 1969, pp. 34–43.

50. Scott Eyman, *Mary Pickford: America's Sweetheart* (New York, 1990), pp. 261–63.

51. Balio, *United Artists*, pp. 219–29.

52. Timothy J. Lyons, "The United States v. Charlie Chaplin," *American Film*, September 1984, pp. 29–34; Charles Chaplin FBI file, Washington, D.C.

53. FBI letter, Los Angeles to Hoover, October 7, 1949; Department of Justice letter, Assistant Attorney General Alexander M. Campbell to Hoover, November 10, 1949; FBI telegram, Hoover to Los Angeles, December 22, 1949; FBI tele-

gram, Los Angeles to Hoover, December 27, 1949; FBI letter, Hoover to Assistant Attorney General Peyton Ford, December 29, 1949; FBI letter, New York to Hoover, July 14, 1950; FBI report, Los Angeles to Hoover, April 5, 1951.

54. Edward A. Shils, *The Torment of Secrecy: The Background and Consequences of American Security Policy* (Chicago, 1956), pp. 14, 70, 71.

CHAPTER 14. A KING, CONDEMNED TO EXILE

1. Richard Lauterbach, "The Whys of Chaplin's Appeal," *New York Times Magazine*, May 21, 1950, pp. 24, 26.

2. Claire Bloom, *Limelight and After* (New York, 1982), p. 86.

3. *Ibid.*, pp. 100, 132–33.

4. *Ibid.*, pp. 76–78.

5. *Ibid.*, p. 86.

6. *Ibid.*, pp. 89–90.

7. David Robinson, *Chaplin: His Life and Art* (New York, 1985), p. 561.

8. Bloom, *Limelight*, pp. 92, 99, 101; Robinson, *Chaplin: His Life and Art*, pp. 561–62.

9. Bloom, *Limelight and After*, p. 88.

10. *Ibid.*, p. 108.

11. Quoted in Robinson, *Chaplin: His Life and Art*, p. 93.

12. Bloom, *Limelight and After*, pp. 111–12.

13. Sidney Skolsky, *Variety*, August 4, 1952, as quoted in Robinson, *Chaplin: His Life and Art*, p. 570.

14. Harry Crocker, unpublished biography of Chaplin, Margaret Herrick Library, Center for Motion Picture Studies, Beverly Hills, California.

15. FBI memo, September 16, 1952; FBI summary report to McGranery, September 18, 1952.

16. Alonzo L. Hamby, *Man of the People: A Life of Harry S. Truman* (New York, 1995), p. 592; interview with Regina McGranery and James P. McGranery, Jr., June 2, 1994.

17. Allen Weinstein, *Perjury: The Hiss-Chambers Case* (New York, 1978), pp. 282–83. Hamby, *Man of the People*, pp. 588–92.

18. Interview with Regina McGranery and James P. McGranery, Jr., June 2, 1994; "Papers from '40s Prove Rosenbergs Were Spies," *Washington Times*, July 12, 1995, pp. A1, A16.

19. "Rosenbergs Were Spies," p. A16; Ronald Radosh and Joyce Milton, *The Rosenberg File: A Search for the Truth* (New York, 1983), p. 156.

20. Interview with Regina McGranery and James P. McGranery, Jr.; "The Papers of James Patrick and Regina Clark McGranery," Library of Congress Manuscript Division, p. 2; *New York Times*, October 3, 1952, p. 1.

21. FBI memo, September 30, 1952; Charles J. Maland, *Chaplin and American Culture* (Princeton, N.J., 1989), pp. 283–84; Alistair Cooke, *Six Men* (New York, 1977), p. 43; note from Alistair Cooke to the author, August 1994.

22. *Daily Worker*, September 19, 1952, p. 6; September 23, 1952, p. 3; September 24, 1952, p. 5; September 25, 1952, p. 7; and October 1, 1952, p. 7; *New York Times*, September 21, 1952, sec. 4, p. 10; Dorothy Thompson, "Chaplin's Art Proclaims Him Anti-Communist," *New York Herald-Tribune*, as quoted in Maland, *Chaplin and American Culture*, pp. 304–305.

23. *Chicago Tribune*, September 20, 1952, pp. 1, 9, and sec. 2, p. 2; *New York Journal-American*, September 21, 1952, p. 4. For these quotations I am indebted to Maland, *Chaplin and American Culture*, pp. 300–301.

24. William Murray, "*Limelight:* Chaplin and His Censors," *The Nation*, March 21, 1952, p. 247; Maland, *Chaplin and American Culture*, pp. 309, 310, 311–12.

25. Chaplin, *My Autobiography*, p. 470; James P. O'Donnell, "Charlie Chaplin's Stormy Exile," *Saturday Evening Post*, March 8, 1958, p. 98.

26. Chaplin, *My Autobiography*, pp. 470 *et seq.*; Robinson, *Chaplin: His Life and Art*, pp. 576–77.

27. Bloom, *Limelight and After*, p. 131; Chaplin, *My Autobiography*, p. 468.

28. *Newsweek*, April 27, 1953, p. 37.

29. Michael Chaplin, *I Couldn't Smoke the Grass on My Father's Lawn* (London, 1966), p. 10; Patrice Chaplin, *Hidden Star: Oona O'Neill Chaplin. A Memoir* (London, 1995), pp. 49, 172.

30. James P. O'Donnell, "Charlie Chaplin's Stormy Exile," *Saturday Evening Post*, March 15, 1958, pp. 44–45, 100.

31. *Ibid.*, p. 101.

32. *Ibid.*, p. 104.

33. *Ibid.*

34. James P. O'Donnell, "Charlie Chaplin's Stormy Exile," *Saturday Evening Post*, March 22, 1958, pp. 107–108.

35. O'Donnell, "Charlie Chaplin's Stormy Exile," March 8, 1958, p. 98; Robinson, *Chaplin: His Life and Art*, p. 593.

36. Quoted in O'Donnell, "Charlie Chaplin's Stormy Exile," March 22, 1958, p. 108.

37. *Ibid.*, p. 110.

38. *Newsweek*, June 14, 1954, p. 48; *New York Times*, June 5, 1954, p. 16.

39. Chaplin, *My Autobiography*, p. 482.

40. Robinson, *Chaplin: His Life and Art*, p. 588.

41. Michael Chaplin, *I Couldn't Smoke the Grass on My Father's Lawn*, p. 2; Patrice Chaplin, *Hidden Star*, pp. 48, 104; Linda Bird Francke, "Life with Charlie," *Interview*, September 1989, pp. 83, 84.

42. Francke, "Life with Charlie," p. 84; Patrice Chaplin, *Hidden Star*, p. 151.

43. Francke, "Life with Charlie," pp. 84 *et seq.*; Patrice Chaplin, *Hidden Star*, p. 170.

44. Patrice Chaplin, *Hidden Star*, pp. 165, 166; Francke, "Life with Charlie," pp. 84–86.

45. Francke; "Life with Charlie," p. 85; Patrice Chaplin, *Hidden Star*, pp. 103, 144; Mary Ellin Barrett, *Irving Berlin: A Daughter's Memoir* (New York, 1994), p. 236; author's interview with Vivian Crespi, March 5, 1995.

46. Francke, "Life with Charlie," p. 85.

47. Ella Winter, "But It's Sad, Says Chaplin, It's Me," *The Observer*, September 15, 1957, p. 4; Dilys Powell, "Chaplin Satirizes McCarthyism," *Times* (London), September 11, 1957, p. 3; Kenneth Tynan, "Look Back in Anger," *The Observer*, September 15, 1957, p. 13; *Time*, September 23, 1947, p. 48.

48. Carol Matthau, *Among the Porcupines* (New York, 1992), pp. 121, 176–77.

49. Bosley Crowther, "The Modern—and Mellower—Times of Mr. Chaplin," *New York Times Magazine*, November 6, 1960, pp. 52–60.

50. *New York Times*, July 2, 1962, p. 28.

51. *Ibid.*

52. Maland, *Chaplin and American Culture*, pp. 329–30; *New York Herald-Tribune*, July 26, 1964, p. 26; *New York Times*, July 4, 1964, p. 8; *New York Times*, July 12, 1964, sec. 2, p. 1.

53. Maland, *Chaplin and American Culture*, p. 330; *Newsweek*, July 27, 1964.

54. Christopher Lyon, ed., *The International Dictionary of Films and Filmmakers*, vol. 1 (New York, 1984), pp. 386–87.

55. Paul Johnson, *Modern Times: The World from the Twenties to the Eighties* (New York, 1983), pp. 643–44.

56. *Publishers Weekly*, October 5, 1964, p. 132; *Publishers Weekly*, October 26, 1964, p. 74; *Publishers Weekly*, November 23, 1964, p. 223; *Publishers Weekly*, December 14, 1964, p. 106; *Publishers Weekly*, March 15, 1965, p. 98.

57. Harold Clurman, "Oona, Oxford, America and the Book," *Esquire*, November 1962, p. 182.

58. *Time*, October 2, 1964, p. 133; *National Review*, December 1, 1964, p. 1071.

59. Edward Weeks, *Atlantic Monthly*, October 1964, p. 140; Brooks Atkinson, *New York Times*, October 16, 1964, p. 36; *Newsweek*, October 5, 1964, p. 112; John Houseman, "Charlie Chaplin," *Nation*, October 12, 1964, p. 224; Robert Hatch, *Harper's*, October 1964, p. 131.

60. Harry Feldman, review, *Film Comment*, Fall 1966, pp. 86–87.

CHAPTER 15. "STAY WARM, GROUCHO, YOU'RE NEXT"

1. Gerald D. McDonald, Michael Conway, and Mark Ricci, *The Complete Films of Charlie Chaplin* (Secaucus, N.J., 1988), p. 225.

2. Kevin Brownlow, "Watching Chaplin Direct *The Countess from Hong Kong*," *Film Culture*, Spring 1966, pp. 2–3.

3. Marlon Brando, with Robert Lindsey, *Songs My Mother Never Taught Me* (New York, 1994), pp. 316–19.

4. Patrice Chaplin, *Hidden Star: Oona O'Neill Chaplin. A Memoir* (London, 1995), pp. 14, 47, 48, 49, 50.

5. *Ibid.*, p. 52; interview by the author with Harry Cushing, March 8, 1995.

6. Patrice Chaplin, *Hidden Star*, p. 50; David Robinson, *Chaplin: His Life and Art* (New York, 1985), p. 615; *New York Times*, January 7, 1967, p. 22, *National Review*, May 30, 1967, pp. 599–600; *Variety*, January 3, 1968, p. 25.

7. Patrice Chaplin, *Hidden Star*, p. 106.

8. *Ibid.*

9. Interview with Joan Ridder Challinor, February 21, 1995; Rachel Ford's words are quoted in Patrice Chaplin, *Hidden Star*, p. 127.

10. Interview with Taki Theodoracopulos, June 1, 1995.

11. Robinson, *Chaplin: His Life and Art*, p. 620.

12. Interview with Moses Rothman, April 24, 1995.

13. Robinson, *Chaplin: His Life and Art*, pp. 620–21; interview with Moses Rothman, April 24, 1995.

14. Candice Bergen, *Knock Wood* (New York, 1984), p. 245.

15. David Thomson, *A Biographical Dictionary of Film* (New York, 1981), pp. 547–48; Bo Burlingham, "Politics Under the Palms," in James Monaco, ed., *Media Culture* (New York, 1978), pp. 63–64.

16. Bergen, *Knock Wood*, pp. 233–42 *passim*; Monaco, *Media Culture*, pp. 63–64.

17. Daniel Taradash, "How Charlie Chaplin Returned to the U.S.," *1933 Magnet*, Harvard 50th Reunion of the Class of 1933, April 1983; interview with Daniel Taradash, February 7, 1995.

18. *Ibid.*

19. *New York Times*, February 8, 1972, p. 24.

20. Taradash, "How Charlie Chaplin Returned to the U.S."; letter from Daniel Taradash to Charles Chaplin, January 7, 1972.

21. *New York Times*, February 9, 1972, p. 44.

22. Interview with Bert Schneider, April 4, 1995.

23. Candice Bergen, " 'I Thought They Might Hiss,' " *Life*, April 21, 1972, p. 90; Bergen, *Knock Wood*, pp. 246–47; interview with Schneider, April 4, 1995.

24. *New York Times*, January 14, 1972, p. 18; *New York Times*, April 19, 1972, sec. C, in Gene Brown, ed., *The New York Times Encyclopedia of Film* (New York, 1984), n.p.

25. *Time*, April 17, 1972, p. 71; Bergen, " 'I Thought They Might Hiss,' " p. 90.

26. *Time*, April 17, 1972, p. 71.

27. *Ibid.*

28. *Ibid.*

29. *Ibid.*

30. *Ibid.*

31. *Ibid.*

32. Richard Meryman, " 'If Only My Children Were Here,' " *Life*, April 21, 1972, p. 89.

33. *Ibid.*

34. *Ibid.*

35. Taradash, "How Charlie Chaplin Returned to the U. S."

36. Sam Kashner and Nancy Schoenberger, *A Talent for Genius: The Life and Times of Oscar Levant* (New York, 1994), pp. 420–22.

37. Taradash, "How Charlie Chaplin Returned to the U. S."; Mason Wiley, *et al.*, *Inside Oscar* (New York, 1986), pp. 465–66.

38. Beth Pinsker, "An Offer He Could Refuse," *Entertainment Weekly*, March 24, 1995, p. 78; interview with Academy executive Bruce Davis, January 26, 1995; Brando, *Songs My Mother Never Taught Me*, p. 404.

39. Monaco, *Media Culture*, p. 63.

40. Robinson, *Chaplin: His Life and Art*, pp. 626–27.

41. *Variety*, March 12, 1975.

EPILOGUE

1. David Robinson, *Chaplin: His Life and Art* (New York, 1985), pp. 630–31; Patrice Chaplin, *Hidden Star: Oona O'Neill Chaplin. A Memoir* (London, 1995), p. 64.

2. Patrice Chaplin, *Hidden Star*, pp. 26–27.

3. Patrick Marnham, *The Man Who Wasn't Maigret: A Portrait of Georges Simenon* (New York, 1994), pp. xvi, xvii, 145, 282, 283, 293, 297; Patrice Chaplin, *Hidden Star*, pp. 34–35.

4. Patrice Chaplin, *Hidden Star*, pp. 186, 194 and *passim*.

5. *Ibid.*, p. 172.

6. *Ibid.*, pp. 196–97.

7. Gillian Anderson, "The Music of *The Circus*," *Library of Congress Information Bulletin*, September 20, 1993, p. 342.

8. *Ibid.*, p. 343.

9. *Ibid.*, pp. 344, 345, 346, 347, 348.

10. Sergei Eisenstein, "Chaplin's Vision," in *The Legend of Charlie Chaplin*, ed. Peter Haining (Secaucus, N.J., 1982), p. 151.

11. "Simply the Best," *The Guardian*, March 10, 1995, n.p.

ACKNOWLEDGMENTS

-ℯ

The obligations I have incurred in this undertaking are manifold. My main study base for a period of years was the Library of Congress's Motion Picture, Broadcasting and Recorded Sound Division. Staff members throughout the division were helpful to me, but I particularly wish to salute the movie knowledge of Madeline Matz, Patrick Sheehan, Rosemary Hanes, and Patrick Loughney, and their resourceful responses to problems I posed. And I am grateful to the division's distinguished director, David Francis, for enlightening conversations about Chaplin and for allowing me to examine his fine private collection of Chaplin photographs.

I also am conscious of how much I owe to the Margaret Herrick Library of the Academy of Motion Picture Arts and Sciences, the State Historical Society of Wisconsin, the Billy Rose Theater Collection in the New York Public Library for the Performing Arts at Lincoln Center, the Lambeth Archives Department of the Minet Library, the Columbia University Oral History Project, the Federal Bureau of Investigation, the Museum of Modern Art in New York, and the Milton S. Eisenhower Library at The Johns Hopkins University.

In London, Clare McMillan provided research assistance; Kevin Brownlow, David Gill, and Moses Rothman answered my questions; and the Chaplin scholar David Robinson was kind enough to supply me with valuable data about the early schooling of Chaplin's older half-brother, Sydney. I am indebted, too, to the courtesy of the publisher Richard Cohen.

In southern California, I benefited from the good offices and wide acquaintance of Muriel Pfaelzer Bodek. Staying as a guest in the home of Zachary Wyatt was another pleasure. And I am further indebted to Mrs. Bodek and Mr. Wyatt for undertaking certain research tasks on my behalf.

For counsel on specific points or for fruitful suggestions, I thank Alonzo Hamby, Carl Kaysen, Heather Kiernan, H. Roderick Nordell, the late Marcus Cunliffe, Gertrude Himmelfarb, Jim Deutsch, Thomas Riggio, Louis Galambos, Cynthia Grenier, Anthony Hecht, Helen Hecht, Sylvia Jukes Morris, Edmund Morris, Anthony Slide, Pierre-Marie Cordier, Stephen Vaughn, James Baughman, and above all, Jacob Stein, whose original commentaries on Chaplin and on many other popular entertainers repeatedly inspired me.

The people whom I interviewed or corresponded with who deserve mention are the late Lita Grey Chaplin, Sydney Chaplin (the younger), Wyn Evans, Yvette Eastman, Robert Hoover, Bruce Davis, Regina Clark McGranery, James P. McGranery, Jr., Charles J. Maland, the Countess Vivian Crespi, Nuala O'Donnell Pell, Joan Ridder Challinor, Evelyn J. Halpert, Mary Stewart Doyle, Ann Brewer Knox, Kitty Hamilton Hobbs, Whitman Hobbs, Taki Theodoracopulos, Bert Schneider, Alistair Cooke, Daniel Taradash, Lionel Krisel, Harry Cushing, Morton Cooper, Don Preston, Jackie Farber, and Nicola Smith.

Eric Rayman and Xavier James supplied advice on various legal questions. Lois Wallace and Wilfred McClay read the manuscript in its entirety and improved it with their criticisms, while parts of it were read to my benefit by David Spring, Andrew Lynn, Elisabeth Lynn, Sophia Lynn, and Timothy Foote.

Special thanks go to my editors at Simon & Schuster. In passage after passage, the attentiveness and critical force of Burton Beals saved me from stylistic and interpretive excesses, while the many contributions of Frederic Hills began with his fine sense of my narrative's architectural requirements. Ten years ago, I considered Mr. Hills and Mr. Beals the best editors I had ever encountered, and that is still my opinion. I also wish to thank Mr. Hills's assistant editor, Hilary Black, Ann Keene, who copyedited the manuscript, and Natalie Goldstein for her photo-sleuthing.

My greatest debt is to Valerie R. Lynn. In addition to sensitive judgments of my assessments of Chaplin and unfailing encouragement, she provided sage observations on occasions ranging from exploratory walks in South London to interviews in Los Angeles.

INDEX

Page numbers in *italics* refer to illustrations.

PHOTO CREDITS

⤴

All photos not specifically credited are from the author's collection.

ABOUT THE AUTHOR

Kenneth S. Lynn is the Arthur O. Lovejoy Professor Emeritus of History at The Johns Hopkins University. Previously he had been a professor of English and chairman of the American Civilization Program at Harvard University, where he obtained his A.B., M.A., and Ph.D. degrees. His books include *Mark Twain and Southwestern Humor*, *William Dean Howells: An American Life*, and *Hemingway*, which won the Los Angeles Times Book Award for biography in 1987 and has since been translated into several foreign languages. He lives with his wife in Washington, D.C., and is the father of three children and the grandfather of three.